AF662616

ALGEBRA

for

JEE

MAIN & ADVANCED

Rejaul Makshud

M.Sc. Calcutta University

UNICORN BOOKS

Publisher
UNICORN BOOKS

F-2/16, Ansari Road, Daryaganj, New Delhi-110002
E-mail: info@unicornbooks.in • Website: www.unicornbooks.in
☎ 011-23275434, 23262683

Branch : Mumbai
23-25, Zaoba Wadi Thakurdwar, Mumbai-401002
☎ 022-22010941, 022-22053387
E-mail: rapidex@bom5.vsnl.net.in

Showroom :
➤ **PM Publications, New Delhi**
- 10-B, Netaji Subhash Marg, Daryaganj, New Delhi-110002
- 6686, Khari Baoli, Delhi-110006

ISBN 978-81-7806-338-6

Edition: 2013

Printed at : *Param Offsetters, Okhla, New Delhi-110020*

Preface

It gives me great pleasure and satisfaction to express myself before the students through a comprehensive text book on Algebra after having taught for many years at a national level institute.

Algebra is a vital topic under mathematics and constitutes nearly 20 to 25% of all questions asked in the IIT-JEE and other engineering entrance exams. After having taught for so many years I realized that it was necessary to design a book in a systematic way, using which a reader could build their base, improve their level and also enjoy the subject.

This book has been designed after considering the new pattern of questions in JEE Main and Advanced exams. It contains seven chapters and each of them contains theory, followed by a large number of worked out problems and exercise based problems, namely

- Level – I : Questions based on Fundamentals
- Level – II : Objective type questions
- Level – III : Subjective type questions for JEE Advanced

Further included are **Linked Comprehension type, Match Matrix type, Assertion and Reason type questions** along with previous years questions from Roorkee and IIT-JEE.

Friends, no problem in mathematics is difficult. Once you understand the concept, every problem becomes easy. So do not jump directly to the exercise without going through the theory, the worked-out problems and the objective type questions. The exercise problems are so arranged that they gradually require more thinking.

I hope this book will help the students in enjoying the subject and improve their confidence when they try to solve any type of questions.

My special thanks go to Mr Rakesh Singh (IISc, Bangalore), Mr Ravi Bhushan (ITT, Delhi), Mr Manoj Kumar (IIT, Delhi), Mr Vivek Bhatt (BIET) who have helped, inspired and motivated me to accomplish this task and finally my sincere thanks to the publisher Dr. Ashok Gupta of Unicorn Books for publishing this book.

I owe a special debt of gratitude to my early teachers Mr Swapan Halder, Mr Mahadev Roy and Mr Dilip Bhattacharya for showing me, what clear and engaging mathematical teaching is all about.

I have tried my best to keep errors out of this book. I shall be grateful to the readers who point out any inadvertent errors and make constructive suggestions.

Rejaul Makshud

Contents

CHAPTER 1

SEQUENCE AND SERIES

1.1 Sequence

It is a function whose domain is the set of natural numbers. It can also be defined as, sequence is a function whose range is the set of real nos.

FOR EXAMPLES,

1. $\{1,2,3,4,..............\}$ is a sequence of natural numbers .
2. $\{2,4,6..............\}$ is a sequence of even natural numbers.
3. $\{1,3,5..............\}$ is a sequence of odd natural numbers.

1.2. Series

If a squence is connected by either +ve sign or -ve sign or both, then it is called a series.

FOR EXAMPLES,

1. $1+2+3+4+...........$ is a series.
2. $2+4-6+8-10+...........$ is a series.
3. $-1-2-3-4-6...........$ is a series.

1.3 Finite and Infinite Sequences

A sequence is said to be finite and infinite according as the number of elements is finite and infinite.

FOR EXAMPLE,

1. $\{1,3,5,7,............,99\}$ is a finite sequence.
2. $\{1,4,7,..................\}$ is an infinite sequence.

1.4 Progression

It is a sequence, where each term is followed by a certain pattern.

There are four types of progression, namely, A.P., G.P, H.P and A.G..P

1.5 Arithmetic Progression

The algebraic difference between any two consecutive terms are same throughout the sequence. i.e. $t_{n+1}-t_n$=constant = d, which is know as common diffrence.

1.6. *n*th Term of An A.P Sequence:

Let the first term is a and the common difference is d.

Then the sequence is $\{a, a+d, a+2d, a+3d,......, a+(n-1)d\}$

Thus, $t_n = a+(n-1)d$, where a is first term and d = common difference.

1.7. *n*th Term from the end of An A.P Sequence

Let the first term is a, common difference is d and the number of terms = m

Then the sequence

is $\{a, a+d, a+2d,........, l-2d, l-d, l\}$,

where $l = a+(m-1)d$

Thus, $T_n = l-nd = a+(m-n)d$, where a = first term, m = no. of terms and n = required term which we want to find out.

1.8. nth Term is a Linear Expresion of *n*

Let the first term is a and the common difference is d.

Then $t_n = a+(n-1)d = (a-d)+dn = A+Bn$,

where $A = a-d$ and $B = d$. Which is a linear expression of n.

1.9 The sum of *n*-Terms of an A.P Sequence

Let first term = a and common difference is = d.

Then the sequence is $\{a, a+d, a+2d,............, a+(n-1)d\}$

Let $S_n = a+(a+d)+(a+2d)+..........+(l-2d)+(l-d)+l$

Also $S_n = l+(l-d)+(l-2d)+.....+(a+2d)+(a+d)+a$.

By adding, we get, $2S_n = (a+l)+(a+l)+(a+l)+....+(a+l)$

$$\Rightarrow \quad S_n = \frac{n}{2}(a+l)$$

$$\Rightarrow \quad S_n = \frac{n}{2}(2a+(n-1)d).$$

NOTE

The nth term of an A.P sequence is also defined as

$$t_n = S_n - S_{n-1}$$

1.10 The sum of *n*-terms of an A.P sequence is a quadratic expression of *n*.

Let first term = a and the common difference is = d

Then
$$S_n = \frac{n}{2}(2a+(n-1)d)$$
$$= \left(na+(n^2-n)\frac{d}{2}\right)$$
$$= \left(a-\frac{d}{2}\right)n+\frac{d}{2}n^2$$
$$= An+Bn^2, \text{ where}$$
$$A = \left(a-\frac{d}{2}\right) \quad B = \frac{d}{2}$$

Which is a quadratic expression of n.

1.11 Some Solved examples.

Ex.1: If the sum of n-terms of an $A.P$ sequence is $2n^2+3n$, then find the common difference.

SOL. : The sum of n terms of an $A.P$ is $S_n = An^2+Bn$, where $A = \left(a - \frac{d}{2}\right)$ and $B = \frac{d}{2}$

Thus, the common difference is $d = 2B = 4$.

Ex.2: If $\frac{a+b}{1-ab}, b, \frac{b+c}{1-bc}$ are in $A.P$, then prove that $\frac{1}{a}, b, \frac{1}{c}$ are in $A.P$

Sol.: Since $\frac{a+b}{1-ab}, b, \frac{b+c}{1-bc}$ are in $A.P$, so we can write

$$2b = \frac{a+b}{1-ab} + \frac{b+c}{1-bc}$$

$$\Rightarrow \quad 2ab^2c + 2abc = a + c + ab^2 + b^2c$$

$$\Rightarrow \quad 2abc\,(1 + b^2) = (a + c)(1 + b^2)$$

$$\Rightarrow \quad 2abc = (a + c)$$

$$\Rightarrow \quad 2b = \left(\frac{a+c}{ac}\right) = \frac{1}{a} + \frac{1}{c}$$

$$\Rightarrow \quad \frac{1}{a}, b, \frac{1}{c} \text{ are in } A.P.$$

Ex. 3: If a,b,c,d are distinct integers in A.P such that $d = a^2 + b^2 + c^2$, then find the value of $a + b + c + d + 2011$.

Sol.: Let the common difference of the given A.P be k.

Then $b = a + k$,

$c = a + 2k$

and $d = a + 3k$.

We have, given relation is

$$d = a^2 + b^2 + c^2$$

$$\Rightarrow \quad a + 3k = a^2 + (a + k)^2 + (a + 2k)^2$$

$$\Rightarrow \quad a + 3k = 3a^2 + 5k^2 + 6ak$$

$$\Rightarrow \quad 5k^2 + 3(2a-1)k + (3a^2 - a) = 0$$

since k is real, so $D \geq 0$

$$\Rightarrow \quad 9(2a-1)^2 - 20(3a^2 - a) \geq 0$$

$$\Rightarrow \quad 24a^2 + 16a - 9 \leq 0$$

$$\Rightarrow \quad -\frac{1}{3} - \frac{\sqrt{70}}{12} \leq a \leq -\frac{1}{3} + \frac{\sqrt{70}}{12}$$

$\Rightarrow \quad a = -1, 0,$ since k is an integer.

When $a = 0$, $k = 0$ and $3/5$ (since k must be a +ive intejer, so both the values of k are rejected).

When $a = -1$, $k = 1$ and $4/5$

Thus $k = 1$.

Hence the value of $a + b + c + d + 2011$

$$= -1 + 0 + 1 + 2 + 2011 = 2013.$$

Ex. 4: If $\log 2$, $\log(2^x - 1)$, $\log(2^x + 3)$ are in A.P, then find the value of x.

Sol.: Since $\log 2$, $\log(2^x - 1)$, $\log(2^x + 3)$ are in A.P, then we can write $2\log(2^x - 1) = \log 2 + \log(2^x + 3)$

$$\Rightarrow \quad \log(2^x - 1)^2 = \log(2(2^x + 3))$$

$$\Rightarrow \quad (2^x - 1)^2 = 2.2^x + 6$$

$$\Rightarrow \quad 2^{2x} - 2.2^x + 1 = 2.2^x + 6$$

$$\Rightarrow \quad (2^x)^2 - 4.2^x - 5 = 0$$

$$\Rightarrow \quad (a)^2 - 4a - 5 = 0, \text{ where } a = 2x$$

$$\Rightarrow \quad (a - 5)(a + 1) = 0$$

$$\Rightarrow \quad a = 5, -1$$

$$\Rightarrow \quad a = 5$$

$$\Rightarrow \quad 2^x = 5$$

$$\Rightarrow \quad x = \log_2 5$$

Ex. 5: In an $A.P$, if $a_1 + a_4 + a_7 + \ldots\ldots + a_{16} = 147$, then find the value of $a_1 + a_6 + a_{11} + a_{16}$.

Sol. : We have $a_1 + a_4 + a_7 + \ldots\ldots + a_{16} = 147$

$$\Rightarrow \quad (a_1 + a_{16}) + (a_4 + a_{13}) + (a_7 + a_{10}) = 147$$

$$\Rightarrow \quad (a_1 + a_{16}) + (a_1 + a_{16}) + (a_1 + a_{16}) = 147$$

$$\Rightarrow \quad 3(a_1 + a_{16}) = 147$$

$$\Rightarrow \quad (a_1 + a_{16}) = 49$$

Now, $a_1 + a_6 + a_{11} + a_{16} = (a_1 + a_{16}) + (a_6 + a_{11})$

$$= (a_1 + a_{16}) + (a_1 + a_{16})$$

$$= 2(a_1 + a_{16})$$

$$= 2 \times 49$$

$$= 98.$$

1.12 Properties of A.P sequences:

P • 1: Let $a_1, a_2, a_3, \ldots\ldots\ldots, a_n$, are in $A.P$ and k be a non zero real number. Then

i. $a_1 + k, a_2 + k, a_3 + k, \ldots\ldots, a_n + k$ are in $A.P$

ii. $a_1 - k, a_2 - k, a_3 - k, \ldots\ldots, a_n - k$ are in $A.P$

iii. $a_1.k, a_2.k, a_3.k, \ldots\ldots, a_n k$ are in $A.P$

iv. $\frac{a_1}{k}, \frac{a_2}{k}, \frac{a_3}{k}, \ldots\ldots, \frac{a_n}{k}$ are also in $A.P$.

P • 2: If $a_1, a_2, a_3 \ldots\ldots, a_n$ and $b_1, b_2, b_3 \ldots\ldots, b_n$ are two $A.P$'s. then

i. $a_1 + b_1, a_2 + b_2, a_3 + b_3, \ldots\ldots, a_n + b_n$ are also in $A.P$

ii. $a_1 - b_1, a_2 - b_2, a_3 - b_3, \ldots\ldots, a_n - b_n$ are also in $A.P$

iii. $a_1 \times b_1, a_2 \times b_2, a_3 \times b_3, \ldots\ldots, a_n \times b_n$ are not in $A.P$

iv. $a_1 / b_1, a_2 / b_2, a_3 / b_3, \ldots, a_n / b_n$ are not in A.P.

P • 3: The sum of the terms of an $A.P$ is equidistant from the beginning and end is constant and is equal to sum of the first and the last terms. *i.e.* if $a_1, a_2, a_3, \ldots\ldots, a_n$ are in $A.P$ then $a_1 + a_n = a_2 + a_{n-1} = a_3 + a_{n-2} = \ldots\ldots$

P • 4: Any term of an $A.P$ (other than the first term) is equal to half the sum of terms which are equidistant from it. *i.e.* if $a_1, a_2, a_3, \ldots\ldots, a_n$ are in $A.P$ then $a_r = \frac{a_{r-k} + a_{r+k}}{2}$, where $0 \leq k \leq n - r$.

P • 5: If a, b, c are in A.P, then $b = \frac{a+c}{2}$

P • 6: i. Three numbers of an $A.P$ can be taken as $a - d, a, a + d$.

ii. Four numbers of an $A.P$ can be taken as $a - 3d, a - d, a + d, a - 3d$

iii. Five numbers of an $A.P$ can be taken as $a - 2d, a - d, a, a + d, a + 2d$.

iv. Six numbers of an $A.P$ can be taken as $a - 5d, a - 3d, a - d, a + d, a + 3d, a + 5d$.

P • 7: If $\log a$, $\log b$, $\log c$ are in $A.P$ then a,b,c are in $G.P$.

1.13 Some Solved Examples

Ex.1: If a,b,c and d are four distinct +ve numbers are in $A.P$, then prove that $a + d = b + c$.

Sol. : As we know that, terms of an $A.P$ sequence are equidistant from the beginning and end and their sum is equal to the sum of the first and the last term.

Thus $a + d = b + c$

Ex. 2: If a,b,c,d, e and f are in $A.P$, then find the value of $(e-c)$.

Sol.: Let A be the first term and D be the common difference.

Thus, $a=A-5D$, $b=A-3D$,
$c=A-D$, $d=A+D$,
$e=A+3D$, $f=A+5D$.

Therefore, $(e-c)=A+3D-A+D=4D$
$=(A+D)-(A-3D)=(d-b)$.

Ex.3: Find the coefficient of x^{99} of the expression $(x-1)(x-2)(x-3)..............(x-100)$

Sol.: We have $(x-1)(x-2)(x-3).........(x-100)$
$=x^{100}-(1+2+3+.....+100)x^{99}+(.....)x^{98}+(.....)x^{97}+.......$

Thus, the co-efficient of x^{99} is $=-(1+2+3+..........+100)$
$$=-\frac{100\times 101}{2}=-5050.$$

Ex. 4: The $6th$ term of an $A.P$ is 2 and if the product of $a_1a_4a_5$ is least, then find the value of the common difference of the given A.P.

Sol.: Given $t_6=2$

$\Rightarrow$ $a_1+5d=2$

Let $P=a_1a_4a_5$

$\Rightarrow$ $P=a_1(a_1+3d)(a_1+4d)$

$\Rightarrow$ $P=(2-5d)(2-2d)(2-d)$

$\Rightarrow$ $P=2\left(4-16d+17d^2-5d^3\right)$

$\Rightarrow$ $\frac{dp}{dd}=2\left(-16+34d-15d^2\right)$

For maxima and minima, $\frac{dp}{dd}=0$, we get, $d=2/3$ and $8/5$

Now, $\frac{d^2P}{dd^2}=2(34-30d)$

Since P is least, so $\frac{d^2P}{dd^2}$ is +ve at $d=2/3$

Thus, $d=2/3$

Ex. 5: Solve for x: $\log_{\sqrt{3}}x+\log_{\sqrt[4]{3}}x+\log_{\sqrt[6]{3}}x+\log_{\sqrt[8]{3}}x+.......+\log_{\sqrt[16]{3}}x=36$

Sol.: We have, $\log_{\sqrt{3}}x+\log_{\sqrt[4]{3}}x+\log_{\sqrt[6]{3}}x+\log_{\sqrt[8]{3}}x+.......+\log_{\sqrt[16]{3}}x=36$

$\Rightarrow$ $\log_3 x(2+4+6+.......+16)=36$

$\Rightarrow$ $2\times\frac{8\times 9}{2}\times\log_3 x=36$

$\Rightarrow$ $\log_3 x=\frac{36}{72}=\frac{1}{2}$

$\Rightarrow$ $x=(3)^{\frac{1}{2}}=\sqrt{3}$

Hence the value of x is $\sqrt{3}$.

2.1 G.P Sequence

The algebraic ratio between any two consecutive terms are same throughout the sequence $i.e.$ $\frac{t_{r+1}}{t_r}=\text{constant}=r$, where r is known as common ratio.

Note :

1. No term of $G.P$ sequence can be zero.
2. All terms of $G.P$ sequence can never be negative.
3. $\sqrt{ab}=\sqrt{a}\times\sqrt{b}$ is holds good only when either a or b is non – negative.

2.2 nth Term of a G.P sequence

Let first term $=a$ and the common ratio is $=r$.

Then the sequence is $\left\{a,ar,ar^2,ar^3,..........ar^{n-1}\right\}$

Thus $t_n=ar^{n-1}$

Which is also known as general term of G.P.

2.3 nth term of a G.P sequence from the End.

Let first term $=a$

and the common ratio $=r$

and the numbers of terms $=m$

Then the sequence is $\left\{a,ar,ar^2,.........,\frac{l}{r^2},\frac{l}{r},l\right\}$.

Thus $T_n=\frac{l}{r^{n-1}}=\frac{ar^{m-1}}{r^{n-1}}=ar^{m-n}$, where a is the first term, m is the number of terms and n is the required term, which one we want to find out.

2.4 Sum of *n* terms of G.P

Let first term $=a$ and the common ratio $=r$.

Then the sequence is $\left\{a,ar,ar^2,ar^3,..........ar^{n-1}\right\}$.

Let $S_n=a+ar+ar^2+ar^3+..........+ar^{n-1}$

Then $rS_n=ar+ar^2+ar^3+........+ar^{n-1}+ar^n$.

By subtracting, we get, $(1-r)S_n=a-ar^n$

$$\Rightarrow\quad S_n=\begin{cases}\left(\frac{1-r^n}{1-r}\right), r<1\\ \left(\frac{r^n-1}{r-1}\right), r>1\end{cases}$$

$$\text{Thus,}\quad S_n=\begin{cases}\left(\frac{1-r^n}{1-r}\right), r<1\\ \left(\frac{r^n-1}{r-1}\right), r>1\\ n, \quad r=1\end{cases}$$

Note :

If $r=1$, then the sum is $S_n=n$

2.5 Basic concepts of infinity:

1. $\lim_{n\to\infty}x^n=\infty$ when $x>1$
2. $\lim_{n\to\infty}x^n=0$ when $0<x<1$
3. The value of $2^\infty=\infty, 3^\infty=\infty, 4^\infty=\infty, 5^\infty=\infty$
4. The value of $\left(\frac{1}{2}\right)^\infty=0, \left(\frac{1}{3}\right)^\infty=0, \left(\frac{2}{3}\right)^\infty=0, \left(\frac{3}{4}\right)^\infty=0$.

2.6 Some solved examples:

Ex.1: If a,b,c and d are in G.P, then find the value of $(a-c)^2+(b-c)^2+(b-d)^2-(a-d)^2$

Sol.: Since a, b, c, d are in G.P, so we can write, $\frac{b}{a}=\frac{c}{b}=\frac{d}{c}$

$\Rightarrow$ $b^2=ac$, $c^2=bd$, $ad=bc$

Now, we have, $(a-c)^2+(b-c)^2+(b-d)^2-(a-d)^2$
$=2(b^2+c^2-ac-bc-bd+ad)$

$= 2(ac + bd - ac - bc - bd + bc)$
$= 0$

Ex.2: If a,b,c are non zero real numbers such that $3(a^2 + b^2 + c^2 + 1) = 2(a + b + c + ad + bc + ca)$, then prove that a,b,c are in A.P as well as in G.P.

Sol.: We have, $3(a^2 + b^2 + c^2 + 1) - 2(a + b + c + ad + bc + ca) = 0$

$\Rightarrow [(a-b)^2 + (b-c)^2 + (c-a)^2] + [(a-1)^2 + (b-1)^2 + (c-1)^2] = 0$

$\Rightarrow a - b = 0 = b - c = c - a \ \& \ a - 1 = 0 = b - 1 = c - 1$

$\Rightarrow a = b = c = 1$

Hence, a, b, c are in A.P as well as in G.P

Ex.3: If x,y,z are in G.P and $\tan^{-1}x, \tan^{-1}y, \tan^{-1}z$ are in A.P, then prove that x, y, z are in A.P

Sol.: Since x, y, z are in G.P, so $y^2 = xz$

Also, $\tan^{-1}x, \tan^{-1}y, \tan^{-1}z$ are in A.P, so

$\Rightarrow \quad 2\tan^{-1}y = \tan^{-1}x + \tan^{-1}z$

$\Rightarrow \quad \tan^{-1}\left(\frac{2y}{1-y^2}\right) = \tan^{-1}\left(\frac{x+z}{1-xz}\right)$

$\Rightarrow \quad \left(\frac{2y}{1-y^2}\right) = \left(\frac{x+z}{1-xz}\right) = \left(\frac{x+z}{1-y^2}\right)$

$\Rightarrow \quad 2y = x + z$

$\Rightarrow \quad x, y, z$ are in A.P.

Ex.4: If $(1+x)(1+x^2)(1+x^4)(1+x^8)..........(1+x^{128}) = \sum_{r=0}^{n}(x^r)$, then find the value of n.

Sol.: We have, $(1+x)(1+x^2)(1+x^4)(1+x^8).....(1+x^{128}) = \sum_{r=0}^{n}(x^r)$

$\Rightarrow \quad \left(\frac{1-x^{256}}{1-x}\right) = \left(1 + x + x^2 + x^3 + ... + x^n\right)$

$\Rightarrow \quad \left(\frac{1-x^{256}}{1-x}\right) = \left(\frac{1-x^{n+1}}{1-x}\right)$

$\Rightarrow \quad n + 1 = 256$

$\Rightarrow \quad n = 255$

Ex.5: In a G.P sequence, if $\frac{a_4}{a_6} = \frac{1}{4}$ and $a_2 + a_5 = 216$, then find the value of a_1.

Sol.: We have, $\frac{a_4}{a_6} = \frac{1}{4}$

$\Rightarrow \quad \frac{a_1r^3}{a_1r^5} = \frac{1}{4}$

$\Rightarrow \quad \frac{1}{r^2} = \frac{1}{4}$

$\Rightarrow \quad r = \pm 2$

Also, $a_2 - a_5 = 216$

$\Rightarrow a_1r + a_1r^4 = 216$

$\Rightarrow 2a_1 + 16a_1 = 216$

$\Rightarrow \quad a_1 = \frac{216}{18} = 12$

Ex.6: If $S = 5 + 55 + 555 + ...$to n terms, then find S.

Sol.: We have $S = 5 + 55 + 555 + ...$ to n terms.

$\Rightarrow \quad S = 5(1 + 11 + 111 + ...\text{to } n\text{-terms})$

$= \frac{5}{9}(9 + 99 + 999 + ...)$

$= \frac{5}{9}((10-1) + (100-1) + (1000-1) + ...)$

$= \frac{5}{9}\left((10-1) + (10^2-1) + (10^3-1) + ... + (10^n-1)\right)$

$= \frac{5}{9}\left(\left(10 + 10^2 + 10^3 + ... + 10^n\right) - n\right)$

$= \frac{5}{9}\left(\left(\frac{10(10^n-1)}{10-1}\right) - n\right)$

$= \frac{5}{9}\left(\left(\frac{(10^{n+1}-10)}{9}\right) - n\right)$

Ex.7: If $S = (222.......2)^2 + (444...........4)$ (n-terms), then find the value of S.

Sol.: We have, $S = (222.......2)^2 + (444...........4)$ (n-terms)

$\Rightarrow \quad S = \left(2(1 + 10 + 10^2 + ... + 10^{n-1})\right)^2 + 4\left((1 + 10 + 10^2 + ... + 10^{n-1})\right)$

$= \left(2\left(\frac{10^n-1}{10-1}\right)\right)^2 + 4\left(\frac{10^n-1}{10-1}\right)$

$= \frac{4}{81}\left(10^n-1\right)^2 + \frac{4}{9}\left(10^n-1\right)$

$= \frac{4}{9}\left(10^n-1\right)\left(\frac{10^n-1}{9} + 1\right)$

$= \frac{4}{81}\left(10^n-1\right)\left(10^n+8\right)$

Ex.8: If $S = \frac{3}{2} + \frac{8}{9} + \frac{26}{27} + \frac{80}{81} + ...$, to n– terms, then find the value of S.

Sol.: We have $S = \frac{3}{2} + \frac{8}{9} + \frac{26}{27} + \frac{80}{81} + ...$, to n– terms

$\Rightarrow \quad S = \left(1-\frac{1}{3}\right) + \left(1-\frac{1}{9}\right) + \left(1-\frac{1}{27}\right) + \left(1-\frac{1}{81}\right) + ...$to n– terms

$\Rightarrow \quad S = n - \left(\frac{1}{3} + \frac{1}{3^2} + \frac{1}{3^3} + ... + \frac{1}{3^n}\right)$

$\Rightarrow \quad S = n - \frac{1}{3}\left(1 + \frac{1}{3} + \frac{1}{3^2} + \frac{1}{3^3} + ... + \frac{1}{3^{n-1}}\right)$

$\Rightarrow \quad S = n - \frac{1}{3}\left(\frac{1-\left(\frac{1}{3}\right)^n}{1-\frac{1}{3}}\right) = n - \frac{1}{2}\left(\frac{3^n-1}{3^n}\right).$

Ex. 9: If x is the first term of G.P with infinite number of terms and $S_\infty = 5$, then find the value of x.

SOL.: We have $S_\infty = 5$

$\Rightarrow \frac{x}{1-r} = 5$, where r is the common ratio. In case of infinite G.P, $|r|<1$

$\Rightarrow -1 < r < 1$

$\Rightarrow -1 < 1 - \frac{x}{5} < 1$

$\Rightarrow 0 < -\frac{x}{5} < 2$

$\Rightarrow -2 < \frac{x}{5} < 0$

$\Rightarrow -10 < x < 0$

Ex.10: Consider an infinite geometric series with first term 'a' and common ratio 'r'. If its sum is 4 and the second term is 3/4, then find the value of a and r.

SOL.: We have $S = 4$ & $ar = \frac{3}{4}$

$\Rightarrow \frac{a}{1-r} = 4$ & $ar = \frac{3}{4}$

$\Rightarrow a = 4 - 4r$

$\Rightarrow ar = 4r - 4r^2$

$\Rightarrow \frac{3}{4} = 4r - 4r^2$

$\Rightarrow 3 = 12r - 12r^2$

$\Rightarrow 12r^2 - 12r + 3 = 0$

$\Rightarrow 12r^2 - 6r - 6r + 3 = 0$

$\Rightarrow 6r(2r-1) - 3(2r-1) = 0$

$\Rightarrow (2r-1)(6r-3) = 0$

$\Rightarrow r = \frac{1}{2}$ & $\frac{a}{2} = \frac{3}{4}$

$\Rightarrow r = \frac{1}{2}$ & $a = \frac{3}{2}$.

2.7 Sum of infinite terms of G.P.

As we know that $S_n = a\left(\frac{1-r^n}{1-r}\right)$, where a = first term, r = common ratio.

When $n \to \infty$, $r^n \to 0$

Thus $S_\infty = \frac{a}{1-r}$.

2.8 Properties of G. P Sequence.

P • 1: If $a_1, a_2, a_3, \ldots\ldots, a_n$ are in G.P and k be a non zero real number, then

i. $a_1 k, a_2 k, a_3 k, \ldots\ldots, a_n k$ are in G.P

ii. $a_1/k, a_2/k, a_3/k, \ldots\ldots, a_n/k$ are also in G. P

iii. $a_1+k, a_2+k, a_3+k, \ldots\ldots, a_n+k$ are not in G.P

iv. $a_1-k, a_2-k, a_3-k, \ldots\ldots, a_n-k$ are not in G.P.

P • 2: If $a_1, a_2, a_3, \ldots, a_n$ and $b_1, b_2, b_3, \ldots, b_n$ are two G.P's, then

i. $a_1b_1, a_2b_2, a_3b_3, \ldots\ldots, a_nb_n$ are also in G.P

ii. $a_1/b_1, a_2/b_2, a_3/b_3, \ldots\ldots, a_n/b_n$ are also in G.P

iii. $a_1+b_1, a_2+b_2, a_3+b_3, \ldots\ldots, a_n+b_n$ are not in G.P.

iv. $a_1-b_1, a_2-b_2, a_3-b_3, \ldots\ldots, a_n-b_n$ are not in G.P

P • 3: If $a_1, a_2, a_3, \ldots\ldots, a_n$ are in G.P, then

i. $a_1^r, a_2^r, a_3^r, \ldots\ldots, a_n^r$ are also in G.P

ii $\frac{1}{a_1}, \frac{1}{a_2}, \frac{1}{a_3}, \ldots\ldots, \frac{1}{a_n}$ are also in G.P

P • 4: If $a_1, a_2, a_3, \ldots\ldots, a_n$ are in G.P, then $\log a_1$, $\log a_2$, $\log a_3$ ……………$\log a_n$ are in A.P and vice-versa.

P • 5: If $a_1, a_2, a_3, \ldots\ldots, a_n$ are in G.P, then $a_1a_n = a_2a_{n-1} = a_3a_{n-2} = \ldots\ldots$

P • 6: If $a_1, a_2, a_3, \ldots\ldots, a_n$ are in G.P, then $a_r = \sqrt{a_{r-k} \times a_{r+k}}$ where $0 \le k \le n-r$.

P • 7: If a, b, c are in G.P, then $b^2 = ac$

P • 8: If $a_1, a_2, a_3, \ldots\ldots, a_n$ are in G.P, then $a_2^2 = a_1a_3$, $a_3^2 = a_2a_4$, $a_4^2 = a_3a_5$ and so on.

P • 9: i. Three numbers of G.P can be considered as $\frac{a}{r}, a, ar$

ii. Four numbers of G.P can be considered as $\frac{a}{r^3}, \frac{a}{r}, ar, ar^3$

iii. Five numbers of G.P can be considered as $\frac{a}{r^2}, \frac{a}{r}, a, ar, ar^2$

iv. Six numbers of G.P can be considered as $\frac{a}{r^5}, \frac{a}{r^3}, \frac{a}{r}, ar, ar^3, ar^5$

2.9 Some solved examples.

Ex.1: If $a, b, 3c$ are in A.P and $a, b, 4c$ are in G.P, find the value of a/b.

SOL.: We have $a, b, 3c$ are in A.P and $a, b, 4c$ are in G.P

$\Rightarrow 2b = a + 3c$ & $b^2 = 4ac$

$\Rightarrow 4b^2 = a^2 + 9c^2 + 6ac$

$\Rightarrow 16ac = a^2 + 9c^2 + 6ac$

$\Rightarrow a^2 + 9c^2 - 10ac = 0$

$\Rightarrow a^2 - 10ac + 9c^2 = 0$

$\Rightarrow (a-c)(a-9c) = 0$

$\Rightarrow a = c, 9c$.

when $a = c$, $b = \left(\frac{a+3c}{2}\right) = \left(\frac{c+3c}{2}\right) = 2c$,

Thus, the value of $\frac{a}{b} = \frac{c}{2c} = \frac{1}{2}$

When $a = 9c$, $b = \left(\frac{a+3c}{2}\right) = \left(\frac{9c+3c}{2}\right) = 6c$

$\Rightarrow \frac{a}{b} = \frac{9c}{6c} = \frac{3}{2}$.

Ex. 2: If $x > 1, y > 1$ and $z > 1$ are in G.P, then prove that $\frac{1}{1+\ln x}, \frac{1}{1+\ln y}, \frac{1}{1+\ln z}$ are in H.P

SOL.: Since x, y and z are in G.P

$\Rightarrow y^2 = xz$

$\Rightarrow \log(y^2) = \log(xz)$

$\Rightarrow 2\log(y) = \log(x) + \log(z)$

$\Rightarrow \log(x), \log(y), \log(z)$ are in A.P

$\Rightarrow 1 + \log(x), 1 + \log(y), 1 + \log(z)$ A.P

$$\Rightarrow \quad \frac{1}{1+\log(x)}, \frac{1}{1+\log(y)}, \frac{1}{1+\log(z)} \in H.P$$

Ex. 3: If a, b, c, d and p are distinct real numbers such that $(a^2+b^2+c^2)p^2-2(ab+bc+cd)+p(b^2+c^2+d^2) \le 0$, then prove that a, b, c, d are in G.P

Sol.: We have $(a^2+b^2+c^2)p^2-2(ab+bc+cd)+p(b^2+c^2+d^2) \le 0$

$$\Rightarrow \quad (a^2p^2-2abp+b^2)+(b^2p^2-2bcp+c^2)+(c^2p^2-2cdp+d^2) \le 0$$

$$\Rightarrow \quad (ap-b)^2+(bp-c)^2+(cp-d)^2 \le 0$$

$$\Rightarrow \quad (ap-b)^2+(bp-c)^2+(cp-d)^2 = 0$$

$$\Rightarrow \quad (ap-b)=(bp-c)=(cp-d)=0$$

$$\Rightarrow \quad \frac{b}{a}=\frac{1}{p}=\frac{c}{b}=\frac{d}{c}$$

$$\Rightarrow \quad \frac{b}{a}=\frac{c}{b}=\frac{d}{c}$$

$\Rightarrow$ a, b, c, d are in G.P

Ex. 4: If three distinct real numbers x, y, z are in G.P such that $x+y+z=ax$, then find the value of 'a'.

Sol.: Since x, y, z are in G.P, so $y=xr$, $z=xr^2$

We have, $x+y+z=ax$

$$\Rightarrow \quad x+xr+xr^2=ax$$

$$\Rightarrow \quad r^2+r+(1-a)=0$$

since r is real, so $D \ge 0$

$$\Rightarrow \quad 1-4(1-a) \ge 0$$

$$\Rightarrow \quad 1-4+4a \ge 0$$

$$\Rightarrow \quad 4a \ge 3$$

$$\Rightarrow \quad a \ge \frac{3}{4}$$

Hence, the value of a is $\left[\frac{3}{4}, \infty\right)$.

Ex.5.: Suppose a, b, c are in A.P and a^2, b^2, c^2 are in G.P. If $a<b<c$ and $a+b+c=\frac{3}{2}$, then find the value of 'a'.

Sol.: Since a, b, c are in A.P, so $2b=a+c$ and a^2, b^2, c^2 are in G.P, so $b^4=a^2c^2$

Now $\quad a+b+c=\frac{3}{2}$

$$\Rightarrow \quad (a+c)+b=\frac{3}{2}$$

$$\Rightarrow \quad 2b+b=\frac{3}{2} \qquad \Rightarrow b=\frac{1}{2}$$

Thus $a+c=1$

Now, $b^4=a^2c^2$

$$\Rightarrow \left(\frac{1}{2}\right)^4 = a^2(1-a)^2$$

$$\Rightarrow \pm\left(\frac{1}{2}\right)^2 = a(1-a) \Rightarrow \left(\frac{1}{2}\right)^2 = a-a^2$$

$$\text{or } -\left(\frac{1}{2}\right)^2 = a-a^2$$

$$\Rightarrow 4a^2-4a+1=0 \text{ or } 4a^2-4a-1=0$$

$$\Rightarrow \quad (2a-1)^2=0 \text{ or } a=\frac{4\pm\sqrt{16+16}}{8}$$

$$\Rightarrow a=\frac{1}{2} \text{ or } a=\frac{1}{2}\pm\frac{1}{\sqrt{2}}.$$

3.1 Harmonic Progression

A sequence is said to be in H.P if the reciprocals of each terms are in A.P.

If the sequence $a_1, a_2, a_3, \ldots\ldots\ldots, a_n$ are in H.P, then $\frac{1}{a_1}, \frac{1}{a_2}, \frac{1}{a_3}, \ldots\ldots\ldots \frac{1}{a_n}$ are in A.P.

Note :

1. No term of H.P can be zero.
2. The genral term of an H.P is $t_n = \frac{1}{a+(n-1)d}$
3. There is no general formula to find out the sum of n-terms of H.P
4. Questions of H.P are generally solved by inverting the terms and making use of the properties of the corresponding A.P.

3.2 Some solved examples.

Ex.1: If a_1, a_2, a_3 are in A.P; a_2, a_3, a_4 are in G.P and a_3, a_4, a_5 are in H.P, then prove that a_1, a_3, a_5 are in G.P.

Sol.: Since, a_1, a_2, a_3 are in A.P, so $2a_2=(a_1+a_3)$ ....(i)

Also, a_2, a_3, a_4 are in G.P , so $a_3^2=a_2a_4$ ....(ii)

Again, a_3, a_4, a_5 are in H.P, so $a_4=\frac{2a_3a_5}{a_3+a_5}$ ....(iii)

From (i), (ii) and (iii), we get, $a_3^2=\left(\frac{a_1+a_3}{2}\right)\times\left(\frac{2a_3a_5}{a_3+a_5}\right)$

$$\Rightarrow a_3^3+a_3^2a_5 = a_1a_3a_5+a_3^2a_5$$

$$\Rightarrow a_3^3 = a_1a_3a_5$$

$$\Rightarrow a_3^2 = a_1a_5$$

$\Rightarrow a_1, a_3, a_5$ are in G.P.

Ex.2: If a, x, b are in A.P, a, y, b are in G.P and a, z, b are in H.P such that $x = 9z$, where $a, b > 0$, then prove that $y=3|z|$ and $x=3|y|$

Sol.: Since, a, x, b are in A.P, so $2x=a+b$ ....(i)

Also, a, y, b are in G.P, so $y^2=ab$ ....(ii)

Again, a, z, b are in H.P, so $z=\frac{2ab}{a+b}$ ....(iii)

From (i), (ii) and (iii), we get, $z=\frac{2y^2}{2x} \Rightarrow y^2=xz$

$$\Rightarrow y^2=9z.\ z=9z^2$$

$$\Rightarrow y=3|z|$$

Also, from the relation, $y^2 = xz$, we can write,

$y^2 = \frac{xx}{9} = \frac{x^2}{9}$

$\Rightarrow x^2 = 9y^2$

$\Rightarrow x = 3|y|$

Hence, the result.

Ex. 3: If a, b, c, d, e are five real numbers such that first three are in A.P, the last three are in H.P and the numbers in the middle are in G.P , then prove that a, c, e are in G.P

SOL.: Since a, b, c are in A.P, so $2b = a + c$ ....(i)

Also, c, d, e are in H.P , so $d = \frac{2ce}{c+e}$ ....(ii)

Again, b, c, d are in G.P , so $c^2 = bd$ ....(iii)

From (i), (ii) and (iii) , we get, $c^2 = \left(\frac{a+c}{2}\right)\times\left(\frac{2ce}{c+e}\right)$

$\Rightarrow \quad c = \frac{(a+c)e}{c+e}$

$\Rightarrow \quad c^2 + ce = ae + ce$

$\Rightarrow \quad c^2 = ae$

$\Rightarrow \quad a, c, e$ are in G.P.

Ex.4: Let $a_1, a_2, a_3, \ldots\ldots, a_{10}$ are in A.P and $h_1, h_2, h_3, \ldots\ldots, h_{10}$ are in H.P. If $a_1 = 2 = h_1$ and $a_{10} = 3 = h_{10}$, then find the value of $a_4h_7 + 2007$.

SOL.: Given $a_1, a_2, a_3, \ldots\ldots, a_{10}$ are in A.P

Now, $a_{10} = a_1 + 9d \Rightarrow 3 = 2 + 9d \Rightarrow d = \frac{1}{9}$

Thus, $a_4 = a_1 + 3d = 2 + \frac{3}{9} = 2 + \frac{1}{3} = \frac{7}{3}$

Also, $h_1, h_2, h_3, \ldots\ldots, h_{10}$ are in H.P

$\frac{1}{h_1}, \frac{1}{h_2}, \frac{1}{h_3}, \ldots\ldots, \frac{1}{h_{10}}$ are in A.P

Now, $\frac{1}{h_{10}} = \frac{1}{h_1} + 9D \Rightarrow \quad 9D = \frac{1}{3} - \frac{1}{2} = \frac{1}{6} \Rightarrow \quad D = -\frac{1}{54}$

Thus, $\frac{1}{h_7} = \frac{1}{h_1} + 6D \Rightarrow \frac{1}{h_7} = \frac{1}{2} - \frac{1}{9} = \frac{7}{18} \Rightarrow h_7 = \frac{18}{7}$

Therefore, $a_4h_7 + 2007 = \frac{7}{3} \times \frac{18}{7} + 2007 = 2013$.

Ex.5: If $4a^2 + 9b^2 + 16c^2 = 2(3ab + 6bc + 4ac)$, where a,b,c are non zero real numbers, then prove that a,b, c are in H.P

SOL.: We have, $4a^2 + 9b^2 + 16c^2 = 2(3ab + 6bc + 4ac)$

$\Rightarrow (2a)^2 + (3b)^2 + (4c)^2 = (2a.3b + 3b.4c + 2a.4c)$

$\Rightarrow (2a)^2 + (3b)^2 + (4c)^2 - (2a.3b) - (3b.4c) - (2a.4c) = 0$

$\Rightarrow \frac{1}{2}\left[(2a - 3b)^2 + (3b - 4c)^2 + (4c - 2a)^2\right] = 0$

$\Rightarrow (2a - 3b) = 0 = (3b - 4c) = (4c - 2a)$

$\Rightarrow 2a = 3b = 4c$

$\Rightarrow \frac{a}{6} = \frac{b}{4} = \frac{c}{3}$

$\Rightarrow a,b,c$ are in H.P

Ex. 6: If a,b,c are in H.P then find value of

$$\left(\frac{1}{b}+\frac{1}{c}-\frac{1}{a}\right)\left(\frac{1}{c}+\frac{1}{a}-\frac{1}{b}\right).$$

SOL.: We have a,b,c are in H.P, so we can write , $\frac{1}{a}, \frac{1}{b}, \frac{1}{c}$ are in A.P

Thus, $\frac{2}{b} = \frac{1}{a} + \frac{1}{c}$

Now , $\left(\frac{1}{b}+\frac{1}{c}-\frac{1}{a}\right)\left(\frac{1}{c}+\frac{1}{a}-\frac{1}{b}\right)$

$= \left(\frac{3}{b}-\frac{1}{a}\right)\left(\frac{2}{b}-\frac{1}{b}\right) = \frac{1}{b}\left(\frac{3}{b}-\frac{1}{a}\right) = \frac{3}{b^2} - \frac{1}{ab}$.

Ex.7: If a,b,c are in H.P, such that $\left(\frac{a+b}{2a-b}\right)+\left(\frac{c+b}{2c-b}\right) \geq \lambda$, then find the value of λ.

SOL.: Since a,b,c are in H.P, so we can write, $\frac{1}{a}, \frac{1}{b}, \frac{1}{c}$ are in A.P

Thus, $\frac{2}{b} = \frac{1}{a} + \frac{1}{c}$.

Now, $\left(\frac{a+b}{2a-b}\right)+\left(\frac{c+b}{2c-b}\right)$

$$= \left(\frac{a+\frac{2ac}{a+c}}{2a-\frac{2ac}{a+c}}\right)+\left(\frac{c+\frac{2ac}{a+c}}{2c-\frac{2ac}{a+c}}\right)$$

$$= \left(\frac{1+\frac{2c}{a+c}}{2-\frac{2c}{a+c}}\right)+\left(\frac{1+\frac{2a}{a+c}}{2-\frac{2a}{a+c}}\right)$$

$$= \left(\frac{a+3c}{2a+2c-2c}\right)+\left(\frac{3a+c}{2a+2c-2a}\right)$$

$$= \left(\frac{a+3c}{2a}\right)+\left(\frac{3a+c}{2c}\right) = \frac{1}{2}+\frac{3}{2}\left(\frac{c}{a}+\frac{a}{c}\right)+\frac{1}{2}$$

$$= 1+\frac{3}{2}\left(\frac{c}{a}+\frac{a}{c}\right) > 4$$

Hence , the value of λ is 4.

Ex.8: If a,b,c,d are in H.P, then prove that $ab + bc + cd = 3ad$

SOL.: Given a,b,c,d are in H.P

$\Rightarrow \frac{1}{a}, \frac{1}{b}, \frac{1}{c}, \frac{1}{d}$ are in A.P

Let D be the common difference.

Thus, $\frac{1}{b} - \frac{1}{a} = D \Rightarrow ab = \frac{1}{D}(a-b)$

Similarly, $bc=\frac{1}{D}(b-c)$ and $cd=\frac{1}{D}(c-d)$

Now, $ab+bc+cd=\frac{1}{D}(a-b)+\frac{1}{D}(b-c)+\frac{1}{D}(c-d)$

$$=\frac{1}{D}(a-b+b-c+c-d)$$

$$=\frac{1}{D}(a-d)$$

$$=\left(\frac{3ad}{a-d}\right)\times(a-d)=3\text{ ad.}$$

Ex. 9: If $a^x=b^y=c^z=d^w$ and a,b,c,d are in G.P, then prove that x, y, z, w are in H.P

SOL.: Let $a^x=b^y=c^z=d^w=k$

$\Rightarrow \quad a=k^{1/x}, b=k^{1/y}, c=k^{1/z}, d=k^{1/w}$

Also, a, b, c, d are in G.P

$\Rightarrow \quad \frac{b}{a}=\frac{c}{b}=\frac{d}{c}$

$\Rightarrow \quad \frac{k^{1/y}}{k^{1/x}}=\frac{k^{1/z}}{k^{1/y}}=\frac{k^{1/w}}{k^{1/z}}$

$\Rightarrow \quad k^{\frac{1}{y}-\frac{1}{x}}=k^{\frac{1}{z}-\frac{1}{y}}=k^{\frac{1}{w}-\frac{1}{z}}$

$\Rightarrow \quad \frac{1}{y}-\frac{1}{x}=\frac{1}{z}-\frac{1}{y}=\frac{1}{w}-\frac{1}{z}$

$\Rightarrow \quad \frac{1}{x},\frac{1}{y},\frac{1}{z},\frac{1}{w}$ are in A.P

$\Rightarrow \quad x, y, z, w$ are in H.P

Ex.10: If a,b,c are in A.P ;x,y,z are in H.P ;ax,by,cz are in G.P, then prove that $\frac{x}{z}+\frac{z}{x}=\frac{a}{c}+\frac{c}{a}$.

SOL.: Since a,b,c are in A.P, $2b=a+c$..................................(i)

Also, x,y,z are in H.P , $y=\frac{2xz}{x+z}$ ....(ii)

Again, ax, by, cz are in G.P, $b^2y^2=axcz$ ....(iii)

$\Rightarrow \quad \left(\frac{a+c}{2}\right)^2\times\frac{4x^2z^2}{(x+z)^2}=acxz$

$\Rightarrow \quad \frac{(a+c)^2}{a\;c}=\frac{(x+z)^2}{x\;z}$

$\Rightarrow \quad \frac{a^2+c^2+2ac}{ac}=\frac{x^2+z^2+2xz}{xz}$

$\Rightarrow \quad \frac{a}{c}+\frac{c}{a}+2=\frac{x}{z}+\frac{z}{x}+2$

$\Rightarrow \quad \frac{a}{c}+\frac{c}{a}=\frac{x}{z}+\frac{z}{x}$

Hence, the result.

Ex.11: If $\frac{a-x}{px}=\frac{a-y}{qy}=\frac{a-z}{rz}$ and p,q,r are in A.P, then prove that x,y,z are in H.P

SOL.: We have, $\frac{a-x}{px}=\frac{a-y}{qy}=\frac{a-z}{rz}$

$\Rightarrow \quad \frac{\frac{a}{x}-1}{p}=\frac{\frac{a}{y}-1}{q}=\frac{\frac{a}{z}-1}{r}$

Since, p,q,r are in A.P, so we can write, $2q=p+r$

$\Rightarrow \quad 2\left(\frac{a}{y}-1\right)=\left(\frac{a}{x}-1\right)+\left(\frac{a}{z}-1\right)$

$\Rightarrow \quad \frac{2a}{y}-2=\frac{a}{x}+\frac{a}{z}-2$

$\Rightarrow \quad \frac{2a}{y}=\frac{a}{x}+\frac{a}{z}$

$\Rightarrow \quad \frac{a}{x},\frac{a}{y},\frac{a}{z}$ are in A.P

$\Rightarrow \quad x,y,z$ are in H.P

Ex.12: If $x_1, x_2, x_3,\ldots, x_n$ are in H.P, then prove that $x_1x_2+x_2x_3+\ldots\ldots\ldots\ldots+x_{n-1}x_n=(n-1)x_1x_n$

SOL: Since, $x_1,x_2,x_3,\ldots\ldots\ldots\ldots,x_n$ are in H.P, so we can write,

$\frac{1}{x_1},\frac{1}{x_2},\frac{1}{x_3},\ldots\ldots,\frac{1}{x_{n-1}},\frac{1}{x_n}$ are in A.P

$\Rightarrow \quad \frac{1}{x_2}-\frac{1}{x_1}=\frac{1}{x_3}-\frac{1}{x_2}=\ldots\ldots\ldots=\frac{1}{x_n}-\frac{1}{x_{n-1}}$

Now, $x_1x_2+x_2x_3+\ldots\ldots\ldots\ldots+x_{n-1}x_n$

$$=\frac{1}{d}(x_1-x_2)+\frac{1}{d}(x_2-x_3)+\ldots\ldots\ldots\ldots+\frac{1}{d}(x_{n-1}-x_n)$$

$$=\frac{1}{d}(x_1-x_2+x_2-x_3+\ldots\ldots\ldots+x_{n-1}-x_n)$$

$$=\frac{1}{d}(x_1-x_n)$$

$$=\frac{(x_1-x_n)}{\left(\frac{\frac{1}{x_n}-\frac{1}{x_1}}{(n-1)}\right)}$$

$$=(n-1)x_1x_n.$$

4.1 Recognisation of A.P, G.P and H.P

Let a,b,c be three non zero real numbers. Then

i. a,b,c are in A.P if and only if $\frac{a-b}{b-c}=\frac{a}{a}$ or $b=\frac{a+c}{2}$

ii. a,b,c are in G. P if and only if $\frac{a-b}{b-c}=\frac{a}{b}$ or $b^2=ac$

iii. a,b,c are in H.P if and onli if $\frac{a-b}{b-c}=\frac{a}{c}$ or $b=\frac{2ac}{a+c}$.

4.2 Means: (Arithmetic, Geometric and Harmonic Means)

A.: **Arithmetic Mean :** When three quantities are in A.P , then the middle-one is said to be $A.M$ of the other two.

Thus if a,b,c are in A.P , then b is A.M between a and c.

i. If $a,b \in R^+$ then A.M $= A = \left(\frac{a+b}{2}\right)$

ii. If $a,b,c \in R^+$, then A.M. $= A = \left(\frac{a+b+c}{3}\right)$

iii. If $a_1, a_2, a_3, \ldots\ldots, a_n \in R^+$, then A.M

$$A = \left(\frac{a_1 + a_2 + a_3 + \ldots\ldots + a_n}{n}\right)$$

A.1: Insertion of n-arithmetic means between two +ve real numbers: Let two +ve real numbers are *a* and *b* respectively.

Take $A_1, A_2, \ldots\ldots, A_n$ are n arithmetic means inserted between two numbers a and b.

Then $a, A_1, A_2, \ldots\ldots, A_n, b$ are in A.P.

Let common difference be d.

Thus $t_{n+2} = b \Rightarrow a + (n+1)d = b \Rightarrow d = \frac{(b-a)}{n+1}$.

Hence, $A_1 = a + d = a + \left(\frac{b-a}{n+1}\right)$.

$A_2 = a + 2d = a + 2\left(\frac{b-a}{n+1}\right)$.

....

....

$A_n = a + nd = a + n\left(\frac{b-a}{n+1}\right)$

A.2: If *n* arithmetic means inserted between two +ve real numbers, say *a* and *b*, then sum of the *n*- arithmetic means is equal to *n*-times the single arithmetic mean between two +ve real numbers. i.e. $A_1 + A_2 + A_3 + \ldots\ldots + A_n = n \times \left(\frac{a+b}{2}\right)$.

SOL: Let d be the common diference.

Then the sequence $a, A_1, A_2, A_3, \ldots\ldots, A_n$, b are in A.P.

Now, $A_1 + A_2 + A_3 + \ldots\ldots + A_n$

$$= \frac{n}{2}(A_1 + A_n)$$

$$= \frac{n}{2}(a + d + b - d)$$

$$= n \times \left(\frac{a+b}{2}\right)$$

Hence, the result.

A.3: Some solved examples:

Ex.1: If n arithmetic means are inserted between two numbers 20 and 80 such that the ratio of the first mean to the last mean is 1:3, then find n.

SOL.: Let n arithemetic means are $A_1, A_2, \ldots\ldots, A_n$.

Then $20, A_1, A_2, \ldots\ldots, A_n, 80$ are in A.P

Given $\frac{A_1}{A_n} = \frac{1}{3}$

$\Rightarrow \frac{20+d}{80-d} = \frac{1}{3}$

$\Rightarrow 60 + 3d = 80 - d$

$\Rightarrow 4d = 80 - 60$

$\Rightarrow d = 5$.

Clearly, $t_{n+2} = 80$

$\Rightarrow 20 + (n+1)d = 80$

$\Rightarrow 5(n+1) = 80 - 20 = 60$

$\Rightarrow (n+1) = 12$

$\Rightarrow n = 11$.

Ex.2: If a,b,c,d,e,f are the A.M's inserted between two +ve numbers 2 and 12 , then find the value of

$a + b + c + d + e + f + 10$.

SOL.: Clearly, 2, a, b, c, d, e, f, 12 are in A.P

$\Rightarrow a + b + c + d + e + f = \frac{8}{2}(2 + 12) = 4 \times 14 = 56$

B.: Geometric Mean: When three quantities are in G.P , then the middle one is called the geometric mean between the other two. If a, b, c are in G.P, then b is the geometric mean between a and c.

i. If $a,b \in R^+$ then $G.M = G = \sqrt{ab}$

ii. If $a,b,c \in R^+$, then $G.M. = G = \sqrt[3]{abc}$

iii. If $a_1, a_2, \ldots\ldots, a_n \in R^+$, then $G.M. = G = \sqrt[n]{a_1 a_2 \ldots\ldots a_n}$.

B.1: Insertion of *n* geometric means between two positive numbers, say, *a* and *b* respectively.

Let $G_1, G_2, \ldots\ldots, G_n$ are n geometric means inserted between two +ve numbers .

Then $a, G_1, G_2, \ldots\ldots, G_n, b$ are in G.P.

Thus, $t_{n+2} = b \Rightarrow ar^{n+1} = b \Rightarrow r = \left(\frac{b}{a}\right)^{\frac{1}{n+1}}$.

So, $G_1 = ar = a\left(\frac{b}{a}\right)^{\frac{1}{n+1}}$,

$G_2 = ar^2 = a\left(\frac{b}{a}\right)^{\frac{2}{n+1}}$, ...,

$G_n = ar^n = a\left(\frac{b}{a}\right)^{\frac{n}{n+1}}$ ...

B.2: The product of *n* geometric means, inserted between two +ve numbers, say, *a* and *b*, is equal to the nth power of the single geometric mean between two +ve numbers.

SOL: Let $G_1, G_2, \ldots\ldots, G_n$ are n geometric means inserted between two +ve numbers.

Then $a, G_1, G_2, \ldots\ldots, G_n, b$ are in G.P.

Thus, $t_{n+2} = b \Rightarrow ar^{n+1} = b \Rightarrow r = \left(\frac{b}{a}\right)^{\frac{1}{n+1}}$

Now, $G_1.G_2.G_3 \ldots\ldots G_n = (ar)(ar^2)\ldots\ldots(ar^n)$

$= a^n \times r^{1+2+3+\ldots\ldots+n}$

$$= a^n \times (r)^{\frac{n(n+1)}{2}}$$

$$= a^n \times \left(\left(\frac{b}{a}\right)^{\frac{1}{n+1}}\right)^{\frac{n(n+1)}{2}}$$

$$= a^n \times \left(\frac{b}{a}\right)^{\frac{n}{2}}$$

$$= (ab)^{\frac{n}{2}}$$

$$= \left(\sqrt{ab}\right)^n.$$

Hence, the result.

B. 3 Some solved examples.

Ex.1: If the $A.M$ and $G.M$ between numbers be 5 and 3 respectively, find the numbers.

Sol.: Let two numbers be a and b.

Given $\frac{a+b}{2} = 5 \;\&\; \sqrt{ab} = 3$

$\Rightarrow a+b = 10 \;\&\; ab = 9$

$\Rightarrow (a+b)^2 = 100 \;\&\; ab = 9$

Also $(a-b)^2 = (a+b)^2 - 4ab = 100 - 36 = 64$

Now, $\left(\frac{a-b}{a+b}\right)^2 = \frac{64}{100} \Rightarrow \left(\frac{a-b}{a+b}\right) = \frac{8}{10} \Rightarrow a = 9b$

Therefore, $9b.b = 9 \Rightarrow b^2 = 1 \Rightarrow b = 1$

Hence, $a = 9$ and $b = 1$.

Ex.2: If x be the $A.M$ and y, z be two geometric means between a and b, then prove that $\frac{y^3+z^3}{xyz} = 2$.

Sol.: Given $x = \frac{a+b}{2}$ and a, y, z, b are in G.P

Let r be the common ratio.

Now $t_4 = b \Rightarrow ar^3 = b \Rightarrow r^3 = \left(\frac{b}{a}\right) \Rightarrow r = \left(\frac{b}{a}\right)^{\frac{1}{3}}$

Thus, $y = ar = a \times \left(\frac{b}{a}\right)^{\frac{1}{3}} = a^{\frac{2}{3}} b^{\frac{1}{3}} \Rightarrow y^3 = a^2 b$

and $z = ar^2 = a \times \left(\frac{b}{a}\right)^{\frac{2}{3}} = a^{\frac{1}{3}} b^{\frac{2}{3}} \Rightarrow z^3 = ab^2$

Now $\frac{y^3+z^3}{xyz} = \frac{a^2b + b^2a}{\left(\frac{a+b}{2}\right)ab} = \frac{2ab(a+b)}{ab(a+b)} = 2$

Ex.3: If a,b,c be in G.P and x,y be the A.M's between a,b and b,c, then prove that $\frac{a}{x} + \frac{c}{y} = 2$

Sol.: Given a,b,c be in G.P $\Rightarrow b^2 = ac$

Also, $x = \frac{a+b}{2}$ & $y = \frac{b+c}{2}$

Now, $\frac{a}{x} + \frac{c}{y} = \frac{a}{\left(\frac{a+b}{2}\right)} + \frac{c}{\left(\frac{b+c}{2}\right)} = \frac{2a}{a+b} + \frac{2c}{b+c}$

$$= \frac{2(ab+ac+ac+bc)}{(a+b)(b+c)}$$

$$= \frac{2(ab+2ac+bc)}{(ab+ac+b^2+bc)}$$

$$= \frac{2(ab+2b^2+bc)}{(ab+b^2+b^2+bc)}$$

$$= \frac{2b(a+2b+c)}{b(a+2b+c)} = 2$$

C. : Harmonic Mean: When three non zero quantities are in H.P , then middle one is called the harmonic mean between the other two.

If a,b,c are in H.P, then b is called the harmonic mean between a and c.

i. If $a, b \in R^+$, then $H.M = H = \frac{2}{\frac{1}{a}+\frac{1}{b}}$

ii. If $a,b,c \in R^+$, then $H.M. = H = \frac{3}{\frac{1}{a}+\frac{1}{b}+\frac{1}{c}}$

iii. If $a_1, a_2, a_3, \ldots\ldots. a_n \in R^+$, then

$$H.M = H = \frac{n}{\frac{1}{a_1}+\frac{1}{a_2}+\frac{1}{a_3}+\ldots\ldots.+\frac{1}{a_n}}$$

C.1: Insertion of *n* harmonic means between two +ve real numbers, say, *a* and *b* respectively.

Let $H_1, H_2, \ldots\ldots\ldots\ldots, H_n$ are n harmonic means inserted between two +ve real numbers a and b.

Then $a, H_1, H_2, \ldots\ldots\ldots\ldots, H_n, b$ are in H. P.

Thus, $\frac{1}{a}, \frac{1}{H_1}, \frac{1}{H_2}, \ldots\ldots\ldots, \frac{1}{H_n}, \frac{1}{b}$ are in A.P.

Now $\frac{1}{b} = \frac{1}{a} + (n+1)d$

$\Rightarrow \frac{1}{b} - \frac{1}{a} = (n+1)d$

$\Rightarrow d = \frac{a-b}{(n+1)ab}$

Therefore, $\frac{1}{H_1} = \frac{1}{a} + d = \frac{1}{a} + \left(\frac{a-b}{(n+1)ab}\right)$

$$\frac{1}{H_2}=\frac{1}{a}+d=\frac{1}{a}+2\left(\frac{a-b}{(n+1)ab}\right)$$

$$\frac{1}{H_3}=\frac{1}{a}+d=\frac{1}{a}+3\left(\frac{a-b}{(n+1)ab}\right)$$

....

....

....

$$\frac{1}{H_n}=\frac{1}{a}+d=\frac{1}{a}+n\left(\frac{a-b}{(n+1)ab}\right)$$

Hence, the result.

C.2: The sum of the reciprocal of n harmonic mean is equal to n times the single harmonic mean between two+ve real numbers.

SOL: Let $H_1, H_2, \ldots\ldots, H_n$ are n harmonic means inserted between two +ve real numbers a and b.

Then $a, H_1, H_2, \ldots\ldots\ldots\ldots, H_n, b$ are in $H.P.$

Thus, $\frac{1}{a}, \frac{1}{H_1}, \frac{1}{H_2}, \ldots\ldots\ldots\ldots, \frac{1}{H_n}, \frac{1}{b}$ are in $A.P.$

Therefore ,

$$\frac{1}{H_1}+\frac{1}{H_2}+\ldots\ldots+\frac{1}{H_n}=n\times\left(\frac{\frac{1}{a}+\frac{1}{b}}{2}\right)=n\times\frac{1}{\left(\frac{2}{\frac{1}{a}+\frac{1}{b}}\right)}$$

Hence the result.

C.3: Relation amongst the A.M, G.M and H.M.

Let $a, b \in R^+$

Then $A.M = A = \left(\frac{a+b}{2}\right)$, $G.M = G = \sqrt{ab}$ and

$H.M = H = \left(\frac{2ab}{a+b}\right)$.

Now, $A.H = \left(\frac{a+b}{2}\right)\times\left(\frac{2ab}{a+b}\right)=ab=G^2$

Thus, A, G, H are in $G.P.$

$$\Rightarrow \quad G^2 = AH \Rightarrow \frac{A}{G}=\frac{G}{H} \quad \ldots\ldots\ldots\ldots\text{(i)}$$

Also, $A-G=\frac{a+b}{2}-\sqrt{ab}=\frac{1}{2}\left(\sqrt{a}-\sqrt{b}\right)^2 \geq 0$

$$\Rightarrow \quad A \geq G \Rightarrow \frac{A}{G} \geq 1 \quad \ldots\ldots\ldots\ldots\ldots\text{(ii)}$$

From (i) and (ii) we get , $\frac{G}{H}=\frac{A}{G}\geq 1$

$\Rightarrow \quad G \geq H$

Hence, $A \geq G \geq H$

$\Rightarrow \quad A.M \geq G.M \geq H.M$.

NOTE :

i. If $\frac{a^{n+1}+b^{n+1}}{a^n+b^n}$ is the A.M between two numbers a and b, then $n=0$

ii. If $\frac{a^{n+1}+b^{n+1}}{a^n+b^n}$ is G.M between two +ve numbers a and b, then $n=-1/2$

iii. If $\frac{a^{n+1}+b^{n+1}}{a^n+b^n}$ is the H.M between two +ve numbers a and b, then $n=-1$.

C.4: Some solved examples:

Ex..1: If A_1 & A_2 be two arithmetic means, G_1 & G_2 be two geometric means and H_1 & H_2 be two harmonic means between any two positive numbers, then prove that

$$\frac{A_1+A_2}{H_1+H_2}=\frac{G_1G_2}{H_1H_2}.$$

SOL.: Let two positive numbers be a and b respectively. Given

a, A_1, A_2, b are in A.P $\Rightarrow A_1+A_2=2\times\left(\frac{a+b}{2}\right)=a+b$

Also, a, G_1, G_2, b are in G.P$\Rightarrow$ $G_1G_2=(ab)^{\frac{2}{2}}=(ab)$

Again, a, H_1, H_2, b are in H.P

$$\Rightarrow \frac{1}{H_1}+\frac{1}{H_2}=2\times\left(\frac{\frac{1}{a}+\frac{1}{b}}{2}\right)=\frac{1}{a}+\frac{1}{b}=\frac{a+b}{ab}=\frac{A_1+A_2}{G_1G_2}$$

$$\Rightarrow \frac{H_1+H_2}{A_1+A_2}=\frac{H_1H_2}{G_1G_2}$$

$$\Rightarrow \frac{A_1+A_2}{H_1+H_2}=\frac{G_1G_2}{H_1H_2}.$$

Ex.2: Let $x+y+x=15$ if a, x, y, z, b are in A.P and $\frac{1}{x}+\frac{1}{y}+\frac{1}{z}=\frac{5}{3}$ if a, x, y, z, b are in H.P . Then find the value of a and b .

SOL.: Given a, x, y, z, b are in A.P

$$\Rightarrow \quad x+y+z=3\times\left(\frac{a+b}{2}\right)$$

$$\Rightarrow \quad 3\times\left(\frac{a+b}{2}\right)=15$$

$$\Rightarrow \quad a+b=10 \quad \ldots\ldots\ldots\ldots\ldots\ldots\text{(i)}$$

Also, a, x, y, z, b are in H.P

$\Rightarrow \quad \frac{1}{a}, \frac{1}{x}, \frac{1}{y}, \frac{1}{z}, \frac{1}{b}$ are in A.P

$$\frac{1}{x}+\frac{1}{y}+\frac{1}{z}=3\times\left(\frac{\frac{1}{a}+\frac{1}{b}}{2}\right)=\frac{3}{2}\left(\frac{a+b}{ab}\right)=\frac{3}{2}\left(\frac{10}{ab}\right)=\frac{15}{ab}$$

$\Rightarrow \quad \frac{5}{3}=\frac{15}{ab}$

$\Rightarrow \quad ab = 9$ ....(ii)

From (i) and (ii), we get, $a=1, b=9$ or $a=9, b=1$.

Ex.3: If $\cos(x-y), \cos x, \cos(x+y)$ are in H.P, then find the value of $\cos x.\sec\left(\frac{y}{2}\right)$.

Sol.: Since $\cos(x-y), \cos x, \cos(x+y)$ are in H.P, so we can write, $\cos x = \frac{2\cos(x-y).\cos(x+y)}{\cos(x-y)+\cos(x+y)}$

$\Rightarrow \quad \cos x = \frac{2\left(\cos^2 x - \sin^2 y\right)}{2\cos x \cos y}$

$\Rightarrow \quad \cos^2 x \cos y = \cos^2 x - \sin^2 y$

$\Rightarrow \quad \cos^2 x(1-\cos y) = \sin^2 y$

$\Rightarrow \quad \cos^2 x \times 2\sin^2\left(\frac{y}{2}\right) = 4\sin^2\left(\frac{y}{2}\right)\cos^2\left(\frac{y}{2}\right)$

$\Rightarrow \quad \cos^2 x \times \sec^2\left(\frac{y}{2}\right) = 2$

$\Rightarrow \quad \cos x \times \sec\left(\frac{y}{2}\right) = \pm\sqrt{2}$.

5. *m*th Powers Theorem

If $a_1, a_2, \ldots\ldots, a_n$ be a set of positive numbers and all a's are not equal, then

$$\frac{\sum_{i=1}^{n} a_i^m}{n} > \left(\frac{\sum_{i=1}^{n} a_i}{n}\right)^m, \text{ when } 0<m<1 \text{ and}$$

$$\frac{\sum_{i=1}^{n} a_i^m}{n} < \left(\frac{\sum_{i=1}^{n} a_i}{n}\right)^m \text{ when } m \in R-(0,1).$$

6. Cauchy-Schwartz Inequality

If a,b,c and x,y,z are any real numbers (positive, negative or zero), then

$$\left(a^2+b^2+c^2\right)\left(x^2+y^2+z^2\right) \geq (ax+by+cz)^2$$

7. Maximum & minimum values of positive real numbers:

Let us suppose that $x, y, z, \ldots\ldots\ldots\ldots, w$ and n are positive variables and c is constant.

i. **Maximum Value:**

Let $x+y+z+\ldots\ldots\ldots\ldots+w=c$

As we know that, $A.M \geq G.M$

Thus, $\left(\frac{x+y+z+\ldots\ldots+w}{n}\right) \geq \sqrt[n]{x.y.z\ldots\ldots w}$

Hence, the greatest value of $\sqrt[n]{x.y.z\ldots\ldots\ldots w}$ is $\left(\frac{c}{n}\right)^{1/n}$

ii. **Minimum value:**

Let $x.y.z\ldots\ldots\ldots\ldots w=c$.

As we know that, $A.M \geq G.M$

Thus, $\left(\frac{x+y+z+\ldots\ldots+w}{n}\right) \geq \sqrt[n]{x.y.z\ldots\ldots w}$

Hence, the least value of $x+y+z+\ldots\ldots+w$ is $n(c)^{1/n}$.

8. Some solved examples

Ex.1: Find the minimum value of $\left(1+a^2\right)\left(1+b^2\right)\left(1+c^2\right) \div abc$.

Sol.: As we know that $A.M \geq G.M$.

Thus $\left(\frac{1+a^2}{2}\right) \geq \sqrt{a^2} = a$.

Similarly, $\left(\frac{1+b^2}{2}\right) \geq \sqrt{b^2} = b$, $\left(\frac{1+c^2}{2}\right) \geq \sqrt{c^2} = c$

Thus, $\left(1+a^2\right)\left(1+b^2\right)\left(1+c^2\right) \geq 8abc$

Hence, the minimum value is 8.

Ex.2: Find the minimum value of $\sqrt{x^2+x} + \frac{\tan^2\alpha}{\sqrt{x^2+x}}, x>0$, $\alpha \in \left(0, \frac{\pi}{2}\right)$

Sol.: As we know that $A.M \geq G.M$.

Thus $\left(\frac{\sqrt{x^2+x}+\frac{\tan^2\alpha}{\sqrt{x^2+x}}}{2}\right) \geq \sqrt{\left(\sqrt{x^2+x}\right)\times\left(\frac{\tan^2\alpha}{\sqrt{x^2+x}}\right)}$

$= \sqrt{\tan^2\alpha} = \tan\alpha$

Hence, the minimum value is 2 $\tan\alpha$.

Ex.3: If $a,b,c > 0$, then find the minimum value of $(a+b+c)\left(\frac{1}{a}+\frac{1}{b}+\frac{1}{c}\right)$

Sol.: As we know that, $A.M \geq H.M$.

Thus, $\left(\frac{a+b+c}{3}\right) \geq \left(\frac{3}{\frac{1}{a}+\frac{1}{b}+\frac{1}{c}}\right)$

Hence, $(a+b+c)\left(\frac{1}{a}+\frac{1}{b}+\frac{1}{c}\right) \geq 9$

Thus the minimum value is 9.

Ex. 4: If $x,y,z > 0$ such that $\left(1+x+x^2\right)\left(1+y+y^2\right)\left(1+z+z^2\right) \geq kxyz$, then find the value of k.

SOL.: As we know that, $A.M. \geq G.M$

Thus, $\left(\frac{1+x+x^2}{3}\right) \geq \sqrt[3]{1.x.x^2} = x$.

$\Rightarrow (1+x+x^2) \geq 3x$

Similarly, $(1+y+y^2) \geq 3y$ & $(1+z+z^2) \geq 3z$

Thus, $(1+x+x^2)(1+y+y^2)(1+z+z^2) \geq 27xyz$

Hence, $k = 27$

Ex.5: If $a+b+c=1$ such that $(1-a)(1-b)(1-c) \geq kabc$, then find the value of k.

SOL.: As we know that, $A.M. \geq G.M$

Now, $1-a = a+b+c-a = b+c$

Similarly, $1-b = c+a$, $1-c = a+b$.

Thus $\left(\frac{b+c}{2}\right)\left(\frac{c+a}{2}\right)\left(\frac{a+b}{2}\right) \geq abc$

Hence, the value of k is 8.

Ex.6: If a,b,c are real numbers such that $a+2b+c=4$, then find the max. value of $ab+bc+ca$.

SOL.: As we know that A.M $\geq$ G.M,

where $a+2b+c = a+b+b+c$

Thus, $\left(\frac{(a+b)+(b+c)}{2}\right) \geq \sqrt{(a+b)(b+c)}$

$\Rightarrow (a+b)(b+c) \leq \left(\frac{4}{2}\right)^2 = 4$

$\Rightarrow (ab+bc+ca+b^2) \leq 4$

$\Rightarrow (ab+bc+ca) \leq 4-b^2$

Hence, the maximum value of $(ab+bc+ca)$ is 4.

Ex. 7: If a,b,c,d are positive real numbers such that $a+b+c+d=2$, then find the max. value $(a+b)(c+d)$.

SOL.: As we know that $A.M \geq G.M$

Thus, $\left(\frac{a+b+c+d}{2}\right) \geq \sqrt{(a+b)(c+d)}$.

Hence, $(a+b)(c+d) \leq \left(\frac{2}{2}\right) = 1$

Thus, the maximum value of $(a+b)(c+d)$ is 1.

Ex. 8: If $a+b+c=1$, then find the minimum value of

$$\left(\frac{1}{a}-1\right)\left(\frac{1}{b}-1\right)\left(\frac{1}{c}-1\right)$$

SOL.: We have, $\left(\frac{1}{a}-1\right) = \left(\frac{1-a}{a}\right) = \left(\frac{a+b+c-a}{a}\right) = \left(\frac{b+c}{a}\right)$

Thus $\left(\frac{b+c}{a}\right)\left(\frac{c+a}{b}\right)\left(\frac{a+b}{c}\right) \geq \left(\frac{8abc}{abc}\right) = 8$

Hence, the minimum value is 8.

Ex. 9: If a,b,c are all +ve, then prove that

$$\frac{a}{b+c}+\frac{b}{c+a}+\frac{c}{a+b} \geq \frac{3}{2}.$$

SOL.: As we know that $A.M \geq H.M$. Thus,

$$\left(\frac{(b+c)+(c+a)+(a+b)}{3}\right) \geq \left(\frac{3}{\frac{1}{(b+c)}+\frac{1}{(c+a)}+\frac{1}{(a+b)}}\right)$$

$$\Rightarrow \frac{2}{3}(a+b+c)\left(\frac{1}{b+c}+\frac{1}{c+a}+\frac{1}{a+b}\right) \geq 3$$

$$\Rightarrow (a+b+c)\left(\frac{1}{b+c}+\frac{1}{c+a}+\frac{1}{a+b}\right) \geq \frac{9}{2}$$

$$\Rightarrow \left(\frac{a+b+c}{b+c}+\frac{a+b+c}{c+a}+\frac{a+b+c}{a+b}\right) \geq \frac{9}{2}$$

$$\Rightarrow \left(\frac{a}{b+c}+1+\frac{b}{c+a}+1+\frac{c}{a+b}+1\right) \geq \frac{9}{2}$$

$$\Rightarrow \left(\frac{a}{b+c}+\frac{b}{c+a}+\frac{c}{a+b}\right) \geq \frac{9}{2}-3 = \frac{3}{2}.$$

Ex.10: If x,y,z,w are all greater than 1, then prove that

$$(1+x)(1+y)(1+z)(1+w) < 4(xy+1)(zw+1)$$

SOL.: Now $(1+x)(1+y)-2(xy+1) = 1+x+y+xy-2xy-2$
$= -1+x+y-xy = -(x-1)(y-1) = -$ve, since $x>1, y>1$

Thus, $(1+x)(1+y) < 2(xy+1)$

Similarly, $(1+z)(1+w) < 2(zw+1)$

Therefore, $(1+x)(1+y)(1+z)(1+w) < 4(xy+1)(zw+1)$.

Ex.11 : If x,y,z and w are all greater than 1, then prove that

$$(1+x)(1+y)(1+z)(1+w) < 8(xyzw+1).$$

SOL.: It can be easily prove that

$$(1+x)(1+y)(1+z)(1+w) < 4(xy+1)(zw+1)$$

Obviously, $(1+xy)(1+zw) < 2(xyzw+1)$

Hence, $(1+x)(1+y)(1+z)(1+w) < 8(xyzw+1)$

Arithmetico Geometric Progression

The combine form of A.P and G.P will form an A. GP.

Let first term of A.P = a, d is the common difference and r be the common ratio of G.P

Then A.P Sequence is $\{a, a+d, a+2d, ..., a+(n-1)d\}$

and G.P sequence is $\{1, r, r^2, ..., r^{n-1}\}$

Thus the sequence A.G. P is

$$\{a, (a+d)r, (a+2d)r^2, ..., (a+(n-1)d)r^{n-1}\}$$

9.1 *n*th term of A.G.P Sequence:

The nth term of A.G.P sequence is $t_n = (a+(n-1)d)r^{n-1}$,

where a = first term, $d = c.d$, $r = c.r$.

9.2 Sum of *n*-terms of AG.P :

Let first term = a, common difference = d and the common ratio = r

Then the $A.G.P$ sequence is

$\{a, (a+d)r, (a+2d)r^2, ..., (a+(n-1)d)r^{n-1}\}$

Let $S_n = a + (a+d)r + (a+2d)r^2 + ... + (a+(n-1)d)r^{n-1}$

$\Rightarrow rS_n = ar + (a+d)r^2 + (a+2d)r^3 + ...+(a+(n-2)d)r^{n-1} + (a+(n-1)d)r^n$

$\Rightarrow (1-r)S_n = a + (dr + dr^2 + dr^3 + ... + dr^{n-1}) + (a+(n-1)d)r^n$

$\Rightarrow (1-r)S_n = a + (1 + r + r^2 + ... + r^{n-2}) + dr(a+(n-1)d)r^n$

$$\Rightarrow S_n = \left(\frac{a}{1-r}\right) + \left(\frac{1+r+r^2+...+r^{n-2}}{1-r}\right)dr + \left(\frac{(a+(n-1)d)r^n}{r-1}\right)$$

$$\Rightarrow S_n = \left(\frac{a}{1-r}\right) + \left(\frac{1-r^{n-1}}{(1-r)^2}\right)dr + \left(\frac{(a+(n-1)d)r^n}{r-1}\right)$$

9.3 Sum of infinite terms of A.G. P

When n is infinite and $-1 < r < 1$, then $r^n, r^{n-1} \to 0$.

$$\text{Thus } S_\infty = \left(\frac{a}{1-r}\right) + \left(\frac{dr}{(1-r)^2}\right)$$

10. Summation of Series

i. Sum of first n natural numbers $= 1 + 2 + 3 + ...+ n = \dfrac{n(n+1)}{2}$

ii. Sum of first $2n$ even natural numbers $= 2 + 4 + 6 + ... + 2n = n(n+1)$

iii. Sum of first $2n-1$ odd natural numbers $= 1 + 3 + 5 + ... + (2n-1) = n^2$

iv. Sum of the squares of first n natural numbers $= 1^2 + 2^2 + ...+ n^2 = \dfrac{n(n+1)(2n+1)}{6}$

v. Sum of the cubes of first n - natural numbers $= 1^3 + 2^3 + ...+ n^3 = \left(\dfrac{n(n+1)}{2}\right)^2$

vi. Sum of the fourth power of first n-natural numbers $= 1^4 + 2^4 + ... + n^4 = \dfrac{n(n+1)(2n+1)(3n^2+3n-1)}{30}$.

vii. $a + a + a + a + ... + a(n-\text{times}) = n\,a$.

11. Method of difference

i. Consider the series $3 + 7 + 14 + 24 + 37 + ...$

Here, the differences between the successive terms are 4, 7, 10, 13, ..., which are in A.P.

Whenever the successive differences are in A.P, thenwe consider its nth term is $t_n = an^2 + bn + c$.

In order to find the value of a, b, c, we put $n = 1,2,3$. Thus, $t_1 = 3 = a + b + c$, $t_2 = 7 = 4a + 2b + c$ and $t_3 = 14 = 9a + 3b + c$.

On solving, we get, $a = \dfrac{3}{2}, b = -\dfrac{1}{2}, c = 2$.

Thus, $t_n = \dfrac{1}{2}(3n^2 - n + 4)$.

Hence, $S_n = \dfrac{1}{2}\left[3\sum n^2 - \sum n + \sum 4\right]$

$= \dfrac{1}{2}\left[3.\dfrac{n(n+1)(2n+1)}{6} - \dfrac{n(n+1)}{2} + 4n\right]$

$= \dfrac{n}{2}(n^2 + n + 4)$.

ii. Consider the series $1 + 3 + 7 + 15 + 31 + ...$

Here, the differences between the successive terms are 2,4,8,16,......, which are in G.P.

Whenever the successive differences are in G.P, then we consider its nth term is $t_n = ar^n + br^{n-1} + c$.

In order to find the value of a, b, c we put $n = 1, 2, 3$.

Thus $t_1 = 1 = a + b + c$, $t_2 = 3 = ar^2 + br + c$, $t_3 = 7 = ar^3 + br^2 + c$,

On solving we get, $r = 2, a = 0, b = 1, c = -1$.

Therefore, $t_n = 2^n - 1$

Hence, $S_n = \sum 2^n - \sum 1$

$= \left(\dfrac{2^n - 1}{2-1}\right) - n = 2^n - n - 1$.

Level- I QUESTIONS BASED ON FUNDAMENTALS

nTH TERM OF AN A.P.

1. Prove that the nth term of an A.P sequence is a linear expression of n.
2. In an A.P if $t_n = 3n + 4$, then find the common difference.
3. In a sequence, if its nth term is $5n + 6$, then the sequnce is in ....
4. If the pth term of an A.P. is q and the qth term is p, prove that its nth term is $(p + q - n)$.
5. If the mth term of an A.P. be $\dfrac{1}{n}$ and nth term be $\dfrac{1}{m}$, then show that its (mn)th term is 1.
6. If $(m+1)$th term of an A.P. is twice the $(n+1)$th term, prove that $(3m+1)$th term is twice the $(m+n+1)$th term.
7. In an A.P , if $T_p = q$, $T_{p+q} = 0$, then find T_q
8. If pth, qth and rth terms of *an A.P.* are a,b,c respectively, then show that :

   i. $a(q-r) + b(r-p) + c(p-q) = 0$

   ii. $(a-b)r + (b-c)p + (c-a)q = 0$.
9. If $< a_n >$ is an A.P. such that $\dfrac{a_4}{a_7} = \dfrac{2}{3}$, find $\dfrac{a_6}{a_8}$.

SELECTIONS OF TERMS IN AN A.P.

10. If a, b, c, d, e are in A.P., then find the value of $a - 4b + 6c - 4d + e$.
11. In an A.P, $t_7 = 15$, then find the value of common difference d that would make $t_2\, t_7\, t_{12}$ greatest.
12. The angles of a quadrilateral are in A.P. whose common difference is 10°. Find the angles.
13. If the roots of the equation $x^3 - 12x^2 + 39x - 28 = 0$ are in A.P, then find the common difference.
14. If the non zero numbers a,b,c are in A.P and $\tan^{-1}a$, $\tan^{-1}b$, $\tan^{-1}c$ are also in A.P, then prove that

    i. $b^2 = ac$

    ii. $a = b = c$.

SUM TO n-terms OF AN A.P.

15. Find the sum of the series : $5 + 13 + 21 + ... + 181$.

16. Find the sum of all three digit natural numbers, which are divisible by 7.

17. Find the sum of all natural numbers between 250 and 1000 which are exactly divisible by 3.

18. Find the sum of first 24 terms of the A.P. $a_1, a_2, a_3, ...$, if it is known that $a_1 + a_5 + a_{10} + a_{15} + a_{20} + a_{24} = 225$.

19. In an A.P, if $S_n = 3n^2 + 4n$, then find its 10th term

20. In an A.P if $S_n = 2n^2 + 5n$, then find its common difference.

21. In a sequence if the sum of n terms is $4n^2 + 7n$, then the sequence is ....

22. If the mth term of an A.P. is $\frac{1}{n}$ and the nth term is $\frac{1}{m}$, show that the sum of mn terms is $\frac{1}{2}(mn + 1)$.

23. Solve for $x : 1 + 6 + 11 + 16 + ... + x = 148$.

24. The sum of the first p, q, r terms of an A.P. are a, b, c respectively. Show that $\frac{a}{p}(q - r) + \frac{b}{q}(r - p) + \frac{c}{r}(p - q) = 0$

25. The sum of $n, 2n, 3n$ terms of an A.P. are S_1, S_2, S_3 respectively. Prove that: $S_3 = 3(S_2 - S_1)$.

26. The pth term of an A.P. is a and qth term is b. Prove that the sum of its $(p + q)$ terms is

$$\frac{p+q}{2}\left\{a+b+\frac{a-b}{p-q}\right\}.$$

27. If in an A.P. the sum of m terms is equal to n and the sum of n terms is equal to m, then prove that the sum of $(m+n)$ terms is $-(m+n)$.

28. The ratio of the sum of n terms of two A.P.'s is $(7n + 1)$: $(4n + 27)$. Find the ratio of their 11th terms.

29. The ratio of the sums of m and n terms of an A.P. is $m^2:n^2$. Show that ratio of the mth and nth terms is $(2m - 1)$: $(2n - 1)$.

30. The interior angles of a polygon are in A.P. The smallest angle is 120° and the common difference is 5°. Find the number os sides of the polygon.

31. If $S_1, S_2, S_3, ...S_m$ are the sums of n terms of m A.P.'s whose first terms are $1, 2, 3, ...m$ and common differences are $1, 3, 5, ...,$ $(2m - 1)$ respectively. Show that $S_1 + S_2 + .. + S_m$ $= \frac{mn}{2}(mn + 1)$

32. If $S_n = n^2 p$ and $S_m = m^2 p$, $m \neq n$, in an A.P., prove that $S_p = p^3$.

33. If S_1 be the sum of $(2n + 1)$ terms of an A.P. and S_2 be the sum of its odd terms, then prove that: $S_1 : S_2 = (2n + 1) : (n + 1)$

34. If the sum of n terms of an A.P. is $n P + \frac{1}{2} n(n - 1)Q$, where P and Q are constants, find the common diffference.

PROPERTIES OF A.P.

35. If a, b, c are in A.P, prove that the following are also in A.P.

i. $b + c, c + a, a + b$

ii. $a^2(b + c), b^2(c + a), c^2(a + b)$

iii. $\frac{1}{\sqrt{b}+\sqrt{c}}, \frac{1}{\sqrt{c}+\sqrt{a}}, \frac{1}{\sqrt{a}+\sqrt{b}}$

iv. $\frac{1}{bc}, \frac{1}{ca}, \frac{1}{ab}$

v. $a\left(\frac{1}{b}+\frac{1}{c}\right), b\left(\frac{1}{c}+\frac{1}{a}\right), c\left(\frac{1}{a}+\frac{1}{b}\right)$

vi. $[(b + c)^2 - a^2], [(c + a)^2 - b^2], [(a + b)^2 - c^2]$

36. If a^2, b^2, c^2 are in A.P, then prove that following are also in A.P.

i. $\frac{1}{b+c}, \frac{1}{c+a}, \frac{1}{a+b}$

ii. $\frac{a}{b+c}, \frac{b}{c+a}, \frac{c}{a+b}$

37. If a, b, c are in A.P., then show that:

i. $a^2(b + c), b^2(c + a), c^2(a + b)$

ii. $b + c - a, c + a - b, a + b - c$ are in A.P.

iii. $bc - a^2, ca - b^2, ab - c^2$ are in A.P.

38. If $\frac{b+c-a}{a}, \frac{c+a-b}{b}, \frac{a+b-c}{c}$ are in A.P. prove that $\frac{1}{a}, \frac{1}{b}, \frac{1}{c}$ are also in A.P.

INSERTION OF A.M.

39. Insert three arithmetic means between 3 and 19.

40. For what value of n, $\frac{a^{n+1}+b^{n+1}}{a^n+b^n}$ is the arithmetic means of a and b ?

41. If n arithmetic means are inserted between 20 and 80 such that the ratio of first mean to the last mean is 1:3, then find the value of n.

42. Prove that the sum of n arithmetic means between two numbers is n times the single $A.M.$ between them.

43. If the A.M between pth and qth terms of an A.P. be equal to the A.M. between rth and sth terms of the A.P., then show that $p + q = r + s$.

44. There are n A.M.s between 3 and 17. The ratio of the last mean to the first mean is 3:1. Find the value of n.

45. If x, y, z are in A.P. and A_1 is the A.M. of x and y and A_2 is the $A.M.$ of y and z, then prove that the A.M. of A_1 and A_2 is y.

ABC OF GEOMETRIC PROGRESSION

46. Find the 10th term of G.P. $\sqrt{2}, \frac{1}{\sqrt{2}}, \frac{1}{2\sqrt{2}}, ...$

47. Find the nth term of G.P. $\sqrt{3}, \frac{1}{\sqrt{3}}, \frac{1}{3\sqrt{3}} ...$

48. Which term of the G.P. $\sqrt{2}, \frac{1}{\sqrt{2}}, \frac{1}{2\sqrt{2}}, \frac{1}{4\sqrt{2}}, ...$is $\frac{1}{512\sqrt{2}}$

49. Which term of G.P. $2, 1, \frac{1}{2}, \frac{1}{4}, ...$ is $\frac{1}{128}$?

nTH TERM OF G.P.

50. If the first and the nth terms of a G.P. are a and b respectively and if P is product of the first n terms, prove that $P^2 = (ab)^n$.

51. The $(m+n)th$ and $(m-n)th$ terms of a G.P. are p and q respectively. Show that the mth and nth terms are

$$\sqrt{pq} \text{ and } p\left(\frac{q}{p}\right)^{m/2n} \text{ respectively.}$$

52. If a,b,c,d and p are different real numbers such that: $(a^2+b^2+c^2)p^2 - 2(ab+bc+cd)p + (b^2+c^2+d^2) = 0$, then show that a,b,c and d are in G.P.

53 If a,b,c are respectively the pth, qth and rth terms of a G.P., show that $(q-r)\log a + (r-p)\log b + (p-q)\log c = 0$

54. If $a^2+9b^2+25c^2 = abc\left(\frac{15}{a}+\frac{5}{b}+\frac{3}{c}\right)$, then a,b,c are in..............

55. If $(1-k)(1+2x+4x^2+8x^3+16x^4+32x^5) = 1-k^6$, where $k \neq 1$, then find the value of $\frac{k}{x}$.

56. If α,β be the roots of $x^3-3^x+a=0$ and γ,δ be the roots of $x^2-12x+b=0$ and numbers $\alpha,\beta,\gamma,\delta$(in order) form an increasing G.P, then Prove that the value of $a=2$, $b=32$.

57. Three real numbers a,b,c are in G.P such that $a+b+c = xb$, then prove that $x<-1$ or $x>3$.

SUM OF n-TERMS OF G.P.

58. Find the sum of the geometric series: $(x+y)+(x^2+xy+y^2)+(x^3+x^2y+xy^2+y^3)+ \ldots$ to n terms.

59. Find the sum of the geometric series:

$$\frac{a}{1+i}+\frac{a}{(1+i)^2}+\frac{a}{(1+i)^3}+\ldots+\frac{a}{(1+i)^n}$$

60. Evaluate the following sums :

i. $\sum_{n=1}^{n}\left(2^{n-1}+3^n\right)$

ii. $\sum_{k=1}^{n}(4^{k-1}+5^{k+1})$

iii. $\sum_{n=1}^{n}\left(\left(\frac{1}{3}\right)^{n-1}+\left(\frac{1}{5}\right)^{n+1}\right)$

61. Find the sum of the following series :

i. $5+55+555+\ldots$ to n terms

ii. $7+77+777+\ldots$ to n terms

iii. $9+99+999+\ldots$ to n terms

iv. $(6666....6)^2+(8888...8)^2$ (Upto - n-digits).

62. Find the sum of $\sum_{n=1}^{10}\left[\left(\frac{1}{2}\right)^{n-1}+\left(\frac{1}{5}\right)^{n+1}\right]$

63. Prove that the sum to n terms of the series

$11+103+1005+\ldots$ is $\frac{10}{9}(10^n-1)+n^2$.

64. Find the least value of n for which the sum $1+3+3^2+\ldots$ to n terms is greater than 7000.

65. Find the sum of n -terms of the series

$$\frac{1}{3}+\frac{5}{9}+\frac{19}{27}+\frac{65}{81}+ \ldots \ldots\ldots\ldots\ldots \text{to } n\text{–terms}$$

66. If $S=\frac{2}{3}+\frac{8}{9}+\frac{26}{27}+\frac{30}{81}+\ldots$to n–terms, then find value of S.

67. If S be the sum, P the product and R the sum of the reciprocals of n terms of a G.P., prove that $\left(\frac{S}{R}\right)^n = P^2$

68. If f is a function satisfying $f(x+y)=f(x)f(y)$ for all $x,y\in N$ such that $f(1)=3$ and $\sum_{x=1}^{n} f(x) = 120$, find the value of n.

69. Let a_n be the nth term of the G.P. of positive numbers. Let $\sum_{n=1}^{100} a_{2n} = \alpha$ and $\sum_{n=1}^{100} a_{2n-1} = \beta$, such that $\alpha \neq \beta$. Prove that the common ratio of the G.P. is $\frac{\alpha}{\beta}$.

SUM OF INFINITE G.P.

70. Sum of the following geometric series to infinity :

i. $(\sqrt{2}+1)+1+(\sqrt{2}-1)+\ldots\infty$

ii. $\frac{1}{2}+\frac{1}{3^2}+\frac{1}{2^3}+\frac{1}{3^4}+\frac{1}{2^5}+\frac{1}{3^6}+\ldots\infty$

71. If $b = a+a^2+a^3+\ldots\ldots\infty$, prove that $a=\frac{b}{1+b}$.

72. If $x = a+\frac{a}{r}+\frac{a}{r^2}+\ldots\ldots\infty$, $y = b-\frac{b}{r}+\frac{b}{r^2}-\ldots\infty$ and, $z = c+\frac{c}{r^2}+\frac{c}{r^4}+\ldots\infty$, prove that $\frac{xy}{z}=\frac{ab}{c}$

73. If $x = 1+a+a^2+\ldots\infty$, where $|a|<1$ and $y = 1+b+b^2+\ldots\infty$, where $|b|<1$. Prove that : $1+ab+a^2b^2+\ldots\infty = \frac{xy}{x+y-1}$.

74. If $A = 1+r^a+r^{2a}+\ldots$ to ∞ and $B = 1+r^b+r^{2b}+\ldots\infty$, prove that

$$r=\left(\frac{A-1}{A}\right)^{1/a}=\left(\frac{B-1}{B}\right)^{1/b}$$

75. If $x=\sum_{n=0}^{\infty}\cos^{2n}\theta$, $y=\sum_{n=0}^{\infty}\cos^{2n}\phi$, $z=\sum_{n=0}^{\infty}\cos^{2n}\theta\sin^{2n}\phi$, where $0<\theta,\phi<\pi/2$ then prove that $xz+yz-z=xy$.

76. If $|x|<1$ and $|y|<1$, find the sum to infinityof the series $(x+y)+(x^2+xy+y^2)+(x^3+x^2y+xy^2+y^3)+\ldots$

77. If S_p denotes the sum of the series $1+r^p+r^{2p}+\ldots$ to ∞ and s_p the sum of the series $1-r^p+r^{2p}-\ldots\infty$, prove that $S_p+s_p = 2.\,S_{2p}$.

78. Let $S\subset(-\pi,\pi)$ denote the set of values of x satisfying the equation $8^{1+|\cos x|+|\cos x|^2+|\cos x|^3+\ldots\ldots\text{to}\,\infty} = 4^3$, then prove that $S=\left(-\frac{\pi}{3},-\frac{2\pi}{3}\right)$.

79. If $\exp\left\{\left(\sin^2 x+\sin^4 x+\sin^6 x+.........\text{inf}\right)\log_e 2\right\}$ satisfies the equation $x^2-9x+8=0$, then prove that the value of $\frac{\cos x}{\cos x+\sin x}=\frac{1}{2}(\sqrt{3}-1)$.

80. Find the value of $(0.2)^{\log_{\sqrt{5}}\left(\frac{1}{4}+\frac{1}{8}+\frac{1}{16}+.............\text{inf}\right)}$.

PROPERTIES OF G.P.

81. If p,q,r are in A.P., show that the pth, qth and rth terms of any G.P. are in G.P.

82. If a,b,c are in A.P. and x,y,z are in G.P., then show that $x^{b-c}\, y^{c-a}\, z^{a-b}=1$.

83. If a,b,c are in G.P., then prove that $\log a^n$, $\log b^n$, $\log c^n$ are in A.P.

84. If a,b,c are in G.P. and x,y are the arithmetic means of a,b, and b,c respectively then prove that $\frac{a}{x}+\frac{c}{y}=2$ and $\frac{1}{x}+\frac{1}{y}=\frac{2}{b}$

85. If a,b,c are in G.P. prove that $\frac{1}{\log_a m}, \frac{1}{\log_b m}, \frac{1}{\log_c m}$ are in A.P.

86. If $x^a=x^{b/2}\, z^{b/2}=z^c$, then prove that $\frac{1}{a}, \frac{1}{b}, \frac{1}{c}$ are in A.p.

87. If a,b,c are three distinct real numbers in G.P and $a+b+c=xb$, then prove that $x<-1$ or $x>3$.

88. If a,b,c in G.P., prove that

i. $a(b^2+c^2)=c(a^2+b^2)$

ii. $a^2b^2c^2\left(\frac{1}{a^3}+\frac{1}{b^3}+\frac{1}{c^3}\right)=a^3+b^3+c^3$

iii. $\frac{(a+b+c)^2}{a^2+b^2+c^2}=\frac{a+b+c}{a-b+c}$

iv. $\frac{1}{a^2-b^2}+\frac{1}{b^2}=\frac{1}{b^2-c^2}$

v. $(a+2b+2c)(a-2b+2c)=a^2+4c^2$

89. If a,b,c are in G.P., then prove that: $\frac{a^2+ab+b^2}{bc+ca+ab}=\frac{b+a}{c+b}$

INSERTION OF G.M

90. Find the value of n so that $\frac{a^{n+1}+b^{n+1}}{a^n+b^n}$ may be the geometric mean between a and b.

91. Find two positive numbers whose difference is 12 and whose A.M. exceeds the G.M. by 2.

92. Let x be the arithmetic mean and y,z be two geometric means between any two positive numbers. Then, prove that

$$\frac{y^3+z^3}{xyz}=2.$$

93. If a is the A.M. of b and c and the two geometric means are G_1 and G_2, then prove that $G_1^3+G_2^3=2abc$.

94. If one geometric mean G and two arithmetic means A_1 and A_2 be inserted between two given quantities, prove that $G^2=(2A_1-A_2)(2A_2-A_1)$.

95. If a,b,c are in G.P. and the equations $ax^2+2bx+c=0$ and $dx^2+2ex+f=0$ have a common root, then show that $\frac{d}{a}, \frac{e}{b}, \frac{f}{c}$ are in $A.P.$

96. The sum of two numbers s 6 times their geometric means, show that the numbers are in the ratio $(3+2\sqrt{2}):(3-2\sqrt{2})$.

HARMONIC PROGRESSION

97. If mth term of a H.P is n and nth term is m, then prove that (mn) th term is 1.

98. If mth term of a H.P is n and nth term is m, then prove that $(m+n)$th term is $\frac{mn}{m+n}$.

99. If pth term of a H.P is $1/q$ and q th term is $1/p$, then prove that nth term is $\frac{1}{p+q-n}$.

100. If pth, qth and rth terms of a H.P are a,b,c respectively, then prove that $bc(q-r)+ca(r-p)+ab(p-q)=0$

101. If $x>1, y>1, z>1$ are in G.P, then prove that $\log_a x$, $\log_a y$, $\log_a z$ are in H.P.

102. If $a>1$, $b>1$, $c>1$ are in G.P, then prove that $\frac{1}{1+\log_x a}, \frac{1}{1+\log_x b}, \frac{1}{1+\log_x c}$ are in H.P.

103. If pth, qth and rth terms of a H.P are a,b,c respectively, then prove that $\frac{q-r}{a}+\frac{r-p}{b}+\frac{p-q}{c}=0$.

104. If $a_1, a_2, a_3, a_4, ..., a_n$ are in H.P, then prove that $a_1a_2+a_2a_3+a_3a_4+..........+a_{n-1}a_n=(n-1)a_1a_n$.

105. Let a,b,c be three distinct real numbers in A.P. such that $|a|<1, |b|<1, |c|<1$, if $x=\sum_{n=0}^{\infty} a^n, y=\sum_{n=0}^{\infty} b^n, z=\sum_{n=0}^{\infty} c^n$, then prove that x, y, z are in H.P.

106. Let $a_1, a_2, ..., a_{10}$ be in A.P and $b_1, b_2, ..., b_{10}$ be in H.P. If $a_1=b_1=2$ and $a_{10}=b_{10}=3$, then prove that the value of a_4b_7 is 6.

HARMONIC MEANS

107. For what value of n, $\frac{a^{n+1}+b^{n+1}}{a^n+b^n}$ is the harmonic mean of a and b?

108. Find harmonic mean of roots of the equation $(5+\sqrt{2})x^2-(4+\sqrt{5})x+(8+2\sqrt{5})=0$.

109. If a,b,c are in G.P and $a^x=b^y=c^z$, then prove that x,y and z are in H.P.

110. If $A_1,A_2; G_1,G_2; H_1,H_2$ are arithmetic, geometric and harmonic means respectively between two quantities a and b, then prove that

i. $\frac{G_1G_2}{H_1H_2}=\frac{A_1+A_2}{H_1+H_2}$ ii. $A_1H_2=A_2H_1=G_1G_2=ab$.

111. If $H_1, H_2, H_3, \ldots\ldots, H_n$ be n harmonic means between a and b, then prove that $\frac{H_1+a}{H_1-a}+\frac{H_1+b}{H_1-b}=2a$.

112. If H is the harmonic mean between a and b, then prove that $\frac{1}{H-a}+\frac{1}{H-b}=\frac{1}{a}+\frac{1}{b}$

113. If H is the harmonic mean between a and b, then prove that $\frac{H}{a}+\frac{H}{b}=2$.

114. If a,b,c are in H.P, prove that $\frac{a+b}{2a-b}+\frac{c+b}{2c-b}>4$.

115. If a,b,c are three positive real numbers, prove that $\frac{a}{b}+\frac{b}{c}+\frac{c}{a}\geq 3$

ARITHMETICO GEOMETRIC PROGRESSION

116. Find the nth term of the following arithmetico Geometric series:

i. $1+5x+9x^2+13x^3+\ldots\ldots$ ii. $1-3x+5x^2-7x^3+\ldots\ldots$

iii. $1+\frac{2}{3}+\frac{3}{3^2}+\frac{4}{3^3}+\ldots\ldots$

117. Find the sum of n terms of the following series :

i. $1+2x+3x^2+4x^3+\ldots.$ ii $1+4x+7x^2+10x^3+\ldots.$

iii. $1+\frac{3}{2}+\frac{5}{4}+\frac{7}{8}+\ldots\ldots$

118. Find the sum to infinity of the following series :

i. $1+2x+3x^2+4x^3+\ldots\ldots$, when $|x|<1$

ii $1+3x+5x^2+7x^3+\ldots\ldots$, when $|x|<1$

iii. $1+4x+7x^2+10x^3+\ldots\ldots$, when $|x|<1$

119. Find the sum to n terms of series $1+\frac{3}{2}+\frac{5}{4}+\frac{7}{8}+\frac{9}{16}+\ldots\ldots$

120. Find the sum to n terms of the series $\frac{1}{2}+\frac{3}{4}+\frac{7}{8}+\frac{15}{16}+\ldots\ldots$

121. Find the sum to n-terms of the series $\frac{2}{3}+\frac{8}{9}+\frac{26}{27}+\frac{80}{81}+\ldots\ldots$

122. Find the sum to n-terms of the series $2+\frac{7}{4}+\frac{5}{4}+\frac{13}{16}+\frac{1}{2}+\ldots.$

123. If the sum to infinity of series $3+(3+d)\frac{1}{4}+(3+2d)\frac{1}{4^2}+$ ....to ∞ is $\frac{44}{9}$, find d

124. If the sum to infinity of the series $1+2r+3r^2+4r^3+\ldots\ldots$ is 9/4, then find r.

SOME SPECIAL SERIES

125. Find the sum to n terms of the series

i. $1.2+2.3+3.4+5.6+\ldots\ldots$

ii. $1.4+3.7.+5.10+7.13+\ldots\ldots$

iii. $1.2.3+2.3.4+3.4.5+\ldots\ldots$

iv. $1.3.5+2.5.7+3.7.9+\ldots\ldots$

v. $1+(1+2)+(1+2+3)+(1+2+3+4)+\ldots\ldots$

vi. $1+(1+3)+(1+3+5)+(1+3+5+7)+\ldots\ldots$

vii. $1^2+(1^2+2^2)+(1^2+2^2+3^2)+(1^2+2^2+3^2+4^2)+\ldots$

viii. $\frac{1^2}{1}+\left(\frac{1^2+2^2}{1+2}\right)+\left(\frac{1^2+2^2+3^2}{1+2+3}\right)+\left(\frac{1^2+2^2+3^2+4^2}{1+2+3+4}\right)+\ldots$

ix. $\frac{1^2}{1}+\left(\frac{1^3+2^3}{1^2+2^2}\right)+\left(\frac{1^3+2^3+3^3}{1^2+2^2+3^2}\right)+\left(\frac{1^3+2^3+3^3+4^3}{1^2+2^2+3^2+4^2}\right)+\ldots$

x.. $\frac{1}{1.2}+\frac{1}{2.3}+\frac{1}{3.4}+\frac{1}{4.5}+\ldots\ldots$

xi. $\frac{1}{1.3}+\frac{1}{4.5}+\frac{1}{7.7}+\frac{1}{10.9}+\ldots\ldots$

xi. $\frac{1}{1.2.3}+\frac{1}{2.3.4}+\frac{1}{3.4.5}+\ldots\ldots$

xii. $\frac{1}{1.3.5}+\frac{1}{3.5.7}+\frac{1}{5.7.9}+\ldots\ldots$

xiii. $\frac{1}{1.4.7}+\frac{1}{4.7.10}+\frac{1}{7.10.13}+\ldots\ldots$

xiv. $\frac{1}{1.5.9.13}+\frac{1}{5.9.13.17}+\frac{1}{9.13.17.21}+\ldots\ldots$.

126. Find the sum of the series

$$\frac{1}{\log_2 4}+\frac{1}{\log_{2^2} 4}+\frac{1}{\log_{2^3} 4}+\ldots\ldots+\frac{1}{\log_{2^n} 4}.$$

127. Prove that the value of the expression

$$\left(1+\frac{1}{\omega}\right)\left(1+\frac{1}{\omega^2}\right)+\left(2+\frac{1}{\omega}\right)\left(2+\frac{1}{\omega^2}\right)+\left(3+\frac{1}{\omega}\right)\left(3+\frac{1}{\omega^2}\right)$$

$$+\ldots\ldots+\left(n+\frac{1}{\omega}\right)\left(n+\frac{1}{\omega^2}\right)=\frac{n\left(n^2+2\right)}{3}$$

128. Prove that the value of the expression $1.(2-\omega)(2-\omega^2)+2.(3-\omega)(2-\omega^2)+\ldots\ldots+(n-1).(n-\omega)(2-\omega^2)=\frac{1}{4}n^2(n+1)^2-n$.

129. Prove that sum of series

$$n.1+(n-1).2+(n-2).3+\ldots\ldots+1.n=\frac{1}{6}n(n+1)(n+2)$$

130. Prove that the sum of the series $1+3+7+15+31+\ldots\ldots$ to $n=2^{n+1}-n-2$.

131. Let the numbers $a,b,10,c,d$ are in A.P., then find the value of $a+b+c+d$.

132. If $x,y,z>0$ and $x+y+z=1$, then find the value of $\frac{xyz}{(1-x)(1-y)(1-z)}$

133. If p and q are positive real numbers such that $p+q=1$, then prove that $\left(p+\frac{1}{p}\right)^2+\left(q+\frac{1}{q}\right)^2\geq\frac{25}{2}$.

134. If a,b,c are positive numbers, then prove that $(a+b)(b+c)(c+a)>8abc$.

135. If a,b,c,d are +ve real numbers, then prove that

$$(a+b+c+d)\left(\frac{1}{a}+\frac{1}{b}+\frac{1}{c}+\frac{1}{d}\right)\geq\frac{1}{16}$$

136. If a,b,c are positive real numbers, then prove that

$(a+b+c)\ (ab+bc+ca)\geq 9$

137. If $(1+x)(1+x^2)(1+x^4).....(1+x^{128})=\sum_{r=0}^{n}x^r$, then find the value of n.

138. Let x be arithmetic mean and y, z be two geometric means between any two positive numbers, then find the value of $\frac{y^3+z^3}{xyz}$.

139. The sides of a right angled triangle form a G.P. The shortest side has length 2. The length of the hypotenuse is of the form $a+\sqrt{b}$, where $a,b\in N$, then find the value of a^2+b^2+10.

140. If a,b,c are the sides of a triangle, then prove that

$$\frac{1}{2}<\frac{ab+bc+ca}{a^2+b^2+c^2}<1.$$

141. If a,b,c,d are four +ve real numbers such that $abcd=1$, then prove that $(1+a)(1+b)(1+c)(1+d)\geq 16$.

142. If $a>1, b>1, c>1$ and $d>1$, then prove that $(1+a)(1+b)(1+c)<8\ (abcd+1)$.

143. If $x+y+z=1$, then prove that $(1-x)(1-y)(1-z)<\frac{8}{27}$.

144. If a,b,c are +ve real numbers such that $a+b+c=1$, then prove that $\frac{1}{ab}+\frac{1}{bc}+\frac{1}{ca}\geq 27$

145. If $a^2+b^2=1$ and $x^2+y^2=1$, then prove that $(ax+by)<1$.

146. If p,q,x,y are positive, then prove that $(px+qy)(pq+xy)\geq 4pqxy$

147. If $\log_2 x+\log_2 y\geq 6$, then prove that the least value of $x+y$ is 16.

148. If $a>1, b>1$, then prove that $\log_b a+\log_a b\geq 2$

149. If $x>1$, find the least value of $2\log_{10}x-\log_x(.01)$

150. If $a^2+b^2=1$, then prove that $\left(a^2-\frac{1}{a^2}\right)^2+\left(b^2-\frac{1}{b^2}\right)^2\geq\frac{9}{2}$

151. Let $a,b,c,d>0$ and $a\neq b\neq c\neq d$ such that $m=a+b+c+d$, then prove that $(m-a)\ (m-b)(m-c)(m-d)>81abcd$

152. If $a+b=1$, then find the least value of $\left(a+\frac{1}{a}\right)^2+\left(b+\frac{1}{b}\right)^2$.

153. If $x^2+y^2=2$ and $a^2+b^2=8$, then find least value of $ax+by$

154. If $a>0, b>0, c>0$ and $a+b+c=1$, then find least value of

$$\left(a+\frac{1}{a}\right)^2+\left(b+\frac{1}{b}\right)^2+\left(c+\frac{1}{c}\right)^2.$$

155. If $a+2b+3c=12$ and $a>0, b>0, c>0$, then find the greatest value of ab^2c^3.

156. If $4a+3b+2c=45$ and $a>0, b>0, c>0$, then find the greatest value of $a^2b^3c^4$.

157. If $2x+3y=10$, then find the maximum value of x^2y^3.

158. If $x+5y=18$, then find the greatest value of xy^5.

159. If three +ve real numbers a,b,c are in A.P with $abc=64$, then find the minimum value of b.

160. Find the min value of $f(x)=x^2+2+\frac{1}{x^2+1}, x>0$.

161. Find the min value of $f(x)=x^{10}+\frac{10}{x}, x>0$.

162. Find min value of $f(x)=x^{2012}+\frac{2012}{x}, x>0$

163. Find minimum value of

$f(a)=a^9+a^7+a^5+a^3+1+a-3+a-7+a-9, a>0$

164. Find the minimum value of

$$f(x)=2^{x^2+2x+2}+2^{2-2x-x^2}, x>0.$$

165. Find the minimum value of

$f(x)=2^x+3^x+4^x+5^x+2^{-x}+3^{-x}+4^{-x}+5^{-x}+10$

166. Let a,b,c,d are all positive real numbers such that $a+2b+3c+4d=10$. If M is the min. value of $(a+2b)\ (3c+4d)$ and N is the min value of $(a+c+2d)\ (b+c+d)$, then find the value of $M^2+N^2+2^2$.

167. Let $a+b+c=1$ such that $a>0, b>0, c>0$, then find the min. value of $\frac{1}{a^2}+\frac{1}{b^2}+\frac{1}{c^2}$.

168. Let $x+y+z=1$ such that $x>0, y>0, z>0$, then find the least value of $(x^3+y^3+z^3)\ (x^6+y^6+z^6)$

169. If $a>0, b>0, c>0$ and $abc=8$, then find the minimum value of $(1+a+a^2)(1+b+b^2)(1+c+c^2)$.

170. Let $x>0, y>0, z>0$ with $xyz=2$, then find the minimum value of $(1+x^3)(1+y^3)(1+z^3)$.

171. If a,b are +ve real numbers, then prove that $((1+a)(1+b))^3>3^3.a^2b^2$.

172. If a,b,c are +ve real numbers, then prove that $((1+a)(1+b)(1+c))^7>7^7.a^4b^4c^4$.

173. If a,b,c are +ve real numbers such that $a+b+c=1$, then find the minimum value of $\frac{1}{ab}+\frac{1}{bc}+\frac{1}{ca}$

174. If a,b,c,d are +ve real numbers such that $a+b+c+d+e=8$ and $a^2+b^2+c^2+d^2+e^2=16$ Then find the range of e.

175. Let a,b,c are +ve real numbers with $ab+bc+ca=8$. Then find the max. value of abc.

176. Let $\alpha,\beta,\gamma,\delta$ are four positive roots of $ax^4+bx^3+cx^2+dx+6=0$, then find the min value of pr.

ANSWER

2. 3 **3.** *A.P* **7.** *p* **10.** 0 **15.** 2139
16. 70336 **18.** 900 **19.** 61 **20.** 10 **21.** A.P
23. 36. **28.** (148/111) **30.** 9 **34.** *Q.* **40.** $n=0$
41. $n=11$ **44.** $n=6$ **46.** $\left(\frac{1}{\sqrt{2}}\right)^{17}$ **47.** $\sqrt{3}\times\left(\frac{1}{3}\right)^{n-1}$ **48.** 11th
49. 9th term. **54.** H.P **55.** 2 **58.** $\frac{1}{x-y}\left[x^2\left(\frac{x^n-1}{x-1}\right)-y^2\left(\frac{y^n-1}{y-1}\right)\right]$
59. $-ai\{1-(1+i)^{-n}\}$ **61.** (i) $\frac{5}{81}[10^{n+1}-9n-10]$, (ii) $\frac{7}{81}[10^{n+1}-9x-10]$, (iii) $\frac{1}{91}[10^{n+1}-9n-10]$, (iv) $\frac{4}{3}\left(10^n-1\right)^2$
62. $\frac{2^{10}-1}{2^9}+\frac{5^{10}-1}{4\times5^{11}}$ **64.** 9 **65.** $n+2\left(1-\left(\frac{2}{3}\right)^n\right)$ **66.** $n+\frac{\left(1-\left(\frac{1}{3}\right)^n\right)}{2}$ **68.** $n=4$.
70. (i) $\left(\frac{3+2\sqrt{2}}{\sqrt{2}}\right)$, (ii) $\left(\frac{19}{24}\right)$ **80.** 4 **90.** $-1/2$ **107.** $n=-1$ **108.** 4
126. $\log_4\left(2^{n+1}-2\right)$ **132.** $\le\left(\frac{1}{8}\right)$ **137.** $n=255$ **138.** 2 **140.** $\frac{1}{2}<\frac{ab+bc+ca}{a^2+b^2+c^2}<1$.
149. 4 **152.** 21/2 **153.** 4 **154.** 118/9 **155.** 64
156. 5^9 **157.** 32 **158.** 729 **159.** 4 **160.** 3
161. 11 **162.** 2013 **163.** 9 **164.** 8 **165.** 18
166. 3141/4 **167.** 9 **168.** $(1/3)^9$ **169.** 8 **170.** 27
173. 27 **174.** $\left[0,\frac{16}{5}\right]$. **175.** 8. **176.** 96.

Level – II FOR JEE MAIN AND ADVANCED EXAMS ONLY

1. If a,b,c are in G.P., then the equations $ax^2+2bx+c-0$ and $dx^2+2ex+f=0$ have a common root if $\frac{d}{a},\frac{e}{b},\frac{f}{c}$ are in :

   a. A.P. b. G.P.
   c. H.P. d. None of these

2. Sum of the first n terms of the series $\frac{1}{2}+\frac{3}{4}+\frac{7}{8}+\frac{15}{16}+...$ is equal to

   a. 2^n-n-1 b. $1-2^{-n}$
   c. $n+2^{-n}-1$ d. 2^n-1

3. For $0<\phi<\pi/2$ if $x=\sum_{n=0}^{\infty}\cos^{2n}\phi$, $y=\sum_{n=0}^{\infty}\sin^{2n}\phi$; $z=\sum_{n=0}^{\infty}\cos^{2n}\phi\,\sin^{2n}\phi$, then

   a. $xyz=xz+y$ b. $xyz=xy+z$
   c. $xyz=x+y+z$ d. $xyz=yz+x$.

4. If in a triangle PQR, $\sin P$, $\sin Q$, $\sin R$ are in *A.P.*, then

   a. the altitudes are in A.P. b. the altitudes are in H.P.
   c. the medians are in G.P. d. the medians are in A.P.

5. Let T_r be the rth term of an A.P., for $r=1,2,3,...$ if for some positive integers m,n we have $T_m=1/n$ and $T_n=1/m$, then T_{mn} equals

   a. 1/mn b. $1/m+1/n$
   c. 1 d. 0

6. If $x>1, y>1, z>1$ are in G.P., then $\frac{1}{1+\ln x},\frac{1}{1+\ln y},\frac{1}{1+\ln z}$ are in

   a. A.P. b. H.P.
   c. G.P. d. None of these

7. Let $a_1,a_2,....a_{10}$ be in A.P. and $h_1,h_2,...h_{10}$ be in H.P. If $a_1=h_1=2$ and $a_{10}=h_{10}=3$, then a_4h_7 is

   a. 12 b. 3
   c. 5 d. 6

8. If the sum of the first $2n$ terms of the A.P. 2,5,8,..., is equal to the sum of the first n terms of the *A.P.*57, 59, 61,... , then n equals

   a. 10 b. 12
   c. 11 d. 13

9. Let the positive numbers a,b,c,d be in A.P. Then abc, abd, acd, bcd are

   a. Not in A.P./G.P./H.P. b. in A.P.
   c. in G.P. d. in H.P.

10. If $a_1, a_2, ... a_n$ are positive real numbers whose product is a fixed number c, then the minimum value of $a_1 + a_2 + ... a_{n-1} + 2a_n$ is

a. $n(2c)^{1/n}$ b. $(n+1)c^{1/n}$
c. $2nc^{1/n}$ d. $(n+1)(2c)^{1/n}$

11. Suppose a,b,c are in A.P. and a^2, b^2, c^2 are in G.P. If $a<b<c$ and $a+b+c=\frac{3}{2}$, then the value of a is

a. $\frac{1}{2\sqrt{2}}$ b. $\frac{1}{2\sqrt{3}}$
c. $\frac{1}{2}-\frac{1}{\sqrt{3}}$ d. $\frac{1}{2}-\frac{1}{\sqrt{2}}$

12. If x,y,z are real numbers satisfying expressions $25(9x^2+y^2)+9z^2-15(5xy+zy+3zx)=0$. then x,y and z are in

a. A.P b. G.P
c. H. P d. None.

13. Let a_n be nth term of an A.P . If $\sum_{r=1}^{100} a_{2r}=\alpha$ and $\sum_{r=1}^{100} a_{2r-1}=\beta$, then the common ratio is

a. $\frac{\alpha}{\beta}$ b. $\frac{\beta}{\alpha}$
c. $\frac{\beta^2}{\alpha^2}$ d. $\frac{\alpha^2}{\beta^2}$

14. Let a_n be nth term of an A.P. If $\sum_{r=1}^{100} a_{2r}=\alpha$ and $\sum_{r=1}^{100} a_{2r-1}=\beta$, then the common difference is

a. $\alpha-\beta$ b. $\beta-\alpha$
c. $2(\beta-\alpha)$ d. $(\alpha-\beta)/100$

15. If $(r)_n = \left(\begin{matrix} r.r.r.......r \\ (n\text{–times}) \end{matrix}\right)$ such that $a=(6)_n$, $b=(8)_n$ and $c=(4)_{2n}$ then

a. $a^2+b+c=0$ b. $a^2+b-c=0$
c. $a^2+b-2c=0$ d. $a^2+b-ac=0$.

16. The sum of $1+\frac{1}{5}+\frac{3}{5^2}+\frac{5}{5^3}+\frac{7}{5^4}+$ .... to ∞ is

a. 3/8 b. 8/3
c. 11/8 d. None.

17. The co-efficient of x^n in the expansion of $\left(1+x+2x^2+3x^3+ ....+nx^n\right)^2$ where $-1<x<1$, is

a. $\frac{n(n+1)}{2}$ b. $\frac{n(n+1)(2n+1)}{6}$
c. $\frac{n(n^2+11)}{6}$ d. None.

18. If a,b,c are in G. P, x and y be the A. M 's between a,b and b,c respectively, then the value of $\left(\frac{a}{x}+\frac{c}{y}\right)\left(\frac{b}{x}+\frac{c}{y}\right)$ is

a. 2 b. -4
c. -2 d. 4.

19. If $0<x<\frac{\pi}{4}$, then minimum value of $(\sin x+\cos x+\operatorname{cosec} 2x)^3$ is

a. 27 b. 13.5
c. 6.75 d. 40.5

20. If x,y,z are positive, then minimum value of $\left(a^{\log y-\log z}+a^{\log z-\log x}+a^{\log x-\log y}\right)$ is

a. 3 b. 1
c. 9 d. 16.

21. The sum of all the product of the first n positive integers taken two at a time is

a. $\frac{1}{24}\times n(n-1)(n+1)(3n+2)$

b. $\frac{1}{48}\times n^2(n-1)(n-2)$ c. $\frac{1}{6}\times n(n+1)(n+2)(n+5)$

d. None.

22. Let $t_n = 2^{\frac{n}{2}}+2^{-\frac{n}{2}}$, then $\sum_{n=1}^{15} t_n^2$ is

a. $\frac{2^{21}-1}{2^{10}}+20$ b. $\frac{2^{21}-1}{2^{10}}+19$
c. $\frac{2^{21}-1}{2^{10}}+1$ d. None.

23. If $u_n = \sum_{n=0}^{n}\left(\frac{1}{2^n}\right)$, then the sum of $\sum_{n=1}^{n} u_n$ is

a. $2^{-n}+2n-1$ b. 2^n+2n-1
c. $2^{-n}-2n-1$ d. None.

24. If a,b,c are in A.P and a^2,b^2,c^2 are in H. P , then

a. $a=b=c$ b. a,b,c in G. P
c. $-a/2$, b, c in G.P d. $a^2=b^2=\frac{c^2}{2}$.

25. If $\sum_{k=1}^{n}\left(\sum_{m=1}^{n} m^2\right)=an^4+bn^3+cn^2+dn+e$, then

a. $a=\frac{1}{12}$ b. $b=\frac{1}{6}$
c. $d=\frac{1}{6}$ d. $e=0$

26. The real roots of $2x^3-19x^2+57x+k=0$ are in G.P, then the value of k is

a. 216 b. -108
c. -54 d. 27

27. If the roots of $x^3+px^2+qx-1=0$ form an increasing G.P, where p and q are real, then

a. $p+q=0$ b. $p-q=0$
c. $2p+3q=0$ d. $2p-3q=0$

28. Let α, β, γ, be the roots of $x^3 + px^2 + qx - q = 0$, where p and q are non zero real, then the minimum value of $\frac{1}{\alpha^2}+\frac{1}{\beta^2}+\frac{1}{\gamma^2}$ is

a. 1/3 b. 1
c. 4/3 d. 3..

29. The sum of infinite series $1+\frac{3}{4}+\frac{7}{16}+\frac{15}{64}+\frac{31}{256}+$........... is

a. 3/8 b. 8/3
c. 3/16 d. 16/3.

30. The equation $x^{x\sqrt{x}} = \left(x\sqrt{x}\right)^x$ has two solutions in+ve real numbers x. If one solution is $x = 1$, then the other one is $x =$

a. 4/9 b. 16/25
c. 9/4 d. 81/16.

31. If $x^2 + y^2 + z^2 = 9$, then the least value of $\frac{1}{x^2}+\frac{1}{y^2}+\frac{1}{z^2}$ is

a. 4 b. 9
c. 16 d. 1.

32. If $a + b + c + d = 8$ such that a,b,c,d are all +ve real numbers, then the maximum value of $(a+b)(c+d)$ is

a. 9 b. 4
c. 16 d. 25.

33. If a,b,c are all +ve real numbers such that $a+b+c = 1$, then find the minimum value of $\frac{1}{ab}+\frac{1}{bc}+\frac{1}{ca}$ is

a. 9 b. 27
c. 81 d. 243.

34. Let the sum of 3+7+13+21+........................ is of the form $\frac{n}{a}\left(bn^2 + cn + d\right), n \in N$, then the value of $(a + b + c + d)$ is

a. 10 b. 11
c. 12 d. 13.

35. Let the sum of the series $1 + 4 + 10 + 22 +$ ....is of the form $a.2^n + b.n + c, n \in N$, then the value of $(a + b + c + 10)$ is

a. 2 b. 4
c. 6 d. 8.

36. If x^3, y^3, z^3 are in A.P , then $\log_x y$, $\log_z x$, $\log_y z$, are in

a. A.P b. G.P
c. H.P d. AGP

37. The third term of a geometric progression is 4,the product of the first 5 terms is

a. 4^3 b. 4^5
c. 4^4 d. None.

38. If a,b,c are in G.P, then the equation $ax^2+2bx + c = 0$, $dx^2 + 2ex + f = 0$ have a common root if $\frac{d}{a}, \frac{e}{b}, \frac{f}{c}$ are in

a. A.P b. G.P
c. H.P d. None.

39. If a,b,c,d and p are distinct real numbers such that $(a^2 + b^2 + c^2)p^2 - 2(ab + bc + cd)p + (b^2 + c^2 + d^2) \le 0$, then a,b,c,d are in

a. $A.P$ b. GP
c. $H.P$ d. $ab = cd$.

40. Sum of the first n-terms of the series $\frac{1}{2}+\frac{3}{4}+\frac{7}{8}+\frac{15}{16}+$.............. is equal to

a. $2^n - n - 1$ b $1 - 2^{-n}$
c. $n - 1 + 2^{-n}$ d. $2^n + 1$

41. If the first and $(2n-1)$th term of an A.P, a G.P and an $H.P$ are equal and their nth terms are a,b,c respectively, then

a. $a = b = c$ b. $a \ge b \ge c$
c. $a + c = b$ d. $ac - b^2 = 0$.

42. For $0 < \phi < \frac{\pi}{2}$, if $x = \sum_{n=0}^{\infty} \cos^{2n}\phi$, $y = \sum_{n=0}^{\infty} \sin^{2n}\varphi$ and $z = \sum_{n=0}^{\infty} \cos^{2n}\varphi \sin^{2n}\varphi$, then

a. $xyz = xz + y$ b. $xyz = xy + z$
c. $xyz = x + y + z$ d. $xyz = yz + x$.

43. If In $(a + c)$, In $(a - c)$, In $(a - 2b + c)$ are in A.P, then

a. a,b,c are in A.P b. a^2,b^2,c^2 are in A.P
c. a,b,c are in G.P d. a,b,c are in H.P

44. Let T_r be the rth term of an $A.P$ for $r = 1,2,3,$ .....If for some positive integers m,n we have $T_m = 1/n$ and $T_n = 1/m$, then T_{mn} equals

a. 1/ mn b. 1/ m + 1/n
c. 1 d. 0.

45. If $x > 1, y > 1$ and $z > 1$ are in $G.P$, then $\frac{1}{1+\ln x}, \frac{1}{1+\ln y}, \frac{1}{1+\ln z}$ are in

a. A.P b. G.P
c. H.P d. None.

46. Let $a_1, a_2,$............, a_{10} be in A.P and $h_1, h_2, h_3,$................h_{10} be in H.P . If $a_1 = h_1 = 2$ and $a_{10} = h_{10} = 3$, then the value of a_4h_7 is

a. 2 b. 3
c. 5 d. 6

47. The harmonic mean of roots of equation $(5+\sqrt{2})x^2 - (4+\sqrt{5})\, x + 8 + 2\sqrt{5} = 0$ is

a. 2 b. 4
c. 6 d. 8

48. Consider an infinite series with first term a and common ratio r. If its sum is 4 and the second term is 3/4 , then

a. $a = 4/7$, $r = 3/7$ b. $a = 2$, $r = 3/8$
c. $a = 3/2$, $r = ½$ d. $a = 3$, $r = ¼$.

49. Let T_n denote the number of triangles which can be formed using the vertices of a regular polygon of n – sides. If $T_{n+1} - T_n = 21$, then n equals

a. 5 b. 7
c. 6 d. 4.

50. Let the positive numbers a,b,c,d be in $A.P$, then abc, abd, acd, bcd are

a. not in A.P/G.P/ H.P b. in A.P
c. in G.P d. in H.P

51. If the sum of the first $2n$ terms of the $A.P=\{2,5,8..........\}$ is equal to the sum of the first n terms of the $A.P.=\{57,59,61,...........\}$, then n equals

a. 100 b. 12
c. 11 d. 13.

52. If $a_1,a_2,........,a_n$ are positive real numbers whose product is a fixed number c, then the minimum value of $a_1+a_2+.........+a_{n-1}+2a_n$ is

a. $n(2c)^{1/n}$ b. $(n+1)c^{1/n}$
c $2n\,c^{1/n}$ d. $(n+1)(2c)^{1/n}$

53. Suppose a,b,c are in $A.P$ and a^2,b^2,c^2 are in $G.P$. If $a<b<c$ and $a+b+c=3/2$, then the value of a is

a. $\frac{1}{2\sqrt{2}}$ b. $\frac{1}{2\sqrt{3}}$
c. $\frac{1}{2}+\frac{1}{\sqrt{2}}$ d. $\frac{1}{2}-\frac{1}{\sqrt{2}}$

54. An infinite G.P has first term 'x' and sum '5' then

a. $x<-10$ b. $-10<x<0$
c. $0<x<10$ d. $x>10$.

55. If α,β are the roots of $ax^2+bx+c=0$ and $\alpha+\beta$, $\alpha^2+\beta^2$, $\alpha^3+\beta^3$ are in $G.P$ and $D=b^2-4ac$, then

a. $c\Delta=0b$ b. $cb\neq 0$
c. $b\Delta=0$ d. $\Delta\neq 0$.

56. If $a>0, b>0, c>0$ and $s=a+b+c$, then

$$\left[\left(\frac{1}{s-a}+\frac{1}{s-b}+\frac{1}{s-c}\right)-\frac{9}{2s}\right] \text{ is}$$

a. <0 b. $=0$
c. >0 d. ≤ 0.

57. If $I_n=\int_0^{\pi/2}\left(\frac{\sin^2 nx}{\sin^2 x}\right)dx$, then $I_1, I_2, I_3,..........$ are in

a. $A.P$ b. $G.P$
c. $H.P$ d. $A.G.P$

58. If $U_n=\sum_{n=0}^{n}\left(\frac{1}{2^n}\right)$, then $\sum_{n=1}^{n}U_n$ is

a. $2^{-n}+2n-1$ b. 2^n-2n-1
c. $2^{-n}-2n+1$ d. $2^{-n}-2n+2$

59. If $\frac{1}{a}+\frac{1}{c}+\frac{1}{a-b}+\frac{1}{c-b}=0$, then $a,\frac{b}{2},c$ are in

a. $A.P$ b. $G.P$
c. $H.P$ d. $A.G.P.$

60. The sum of n terms of the series

$$1+5\left(\frac{4n+1}{4n-3}\right)+9\left(\frac{4n+1}{4n-3}\right)^2+13\left(\frac{4n+1}{4n-3}\right)^3+........ \text{ is}$$

a. $4n^2-3n$ b. $4n^2+3n$
c. n^2+2d d. n^2+3n

61. The sum of all the product of the first n +ve integers taken two at a time is

a. $\frac{1}{24}n(n-1)(n+1)(3n+2)$

b. $\frac{1}{48}n^2(n-1)(n-2)$

c. $\frac{1}{6}n(n+1)(n+2)(n+5)$

d. $\frac{1}{12}n(n-1)(n+2)$

62. The nth term of the series $2+5+12+31+86+$ ....is

a. $n+3^{n-1}$ b. $(n-1)+3^{n-2}$
c. $(n+1)+3^n$ d. $(n-2)+3^n$

63. The sum to n-terms of the series $2+5+14+41+$................is

a. $\frac{1}{4}(3^n-1)$ b. $\frac{1}{4}(3^{n+1}-3)+\frac{n}{2}$
c. $\frac{1}{4}(3^{n+1}-2)+\frac{n}{3}$ d. $\frac{1}{4}(3^{n+1}-2)+\frac{n}{4}$

64. If the numbers a,b,c,d,e are in A.P, then the value of $a-4b+6c-4d+e$ is

a. 1 b. 2
c. 0 d. -2

65. If $a^3+b^3+6abc=8c^3$ and ω is a cube root of unity, then

a. a,c,b are in $A.P$ b. a,c,b are in G.P
c. $a+b\omega-2c\omega^2=0$ d. $a+b\omega-2c\omega=0$

Level – III For JEE-Advance Exam Only

1. In a triangle ABC, if $\cot A$, $\cot B$, $\cot C$ are in $A.P.$, then Prove that a^2, b^2, c^2 are in A. P.

2. The sum of the sequence of three distinct real numbers, which are in G.P. is S^2. If their sum is αS, show that $\alpha^2\in\left(\frac{1}{3},1\right)\cup(1,3)$

3. The sum of n terms of two arithmetic progressions are in the ratio $(7n+1):(4n+17)$. Find the ratio of their nth terms.

4. Solve the following equations for x and y, $\log_{10}x+\log_{10}x^{1/2}+\log_{10}x^{1/4}+...=y$ and $\frac{1+3+5+...+(2y-1)}{4+7+10+...+(3y+1)}=\frac{20}{7\log_{10}x}$

5. If $\log_3 2, \log_3(2^x-5)$ and $\log_3\left(2^x-\frac{7}{2}\right)$ are in arithmetic progression, determine the value of x.

6. Obtain the sum of $\frac{1}{x+1}+\frac{2}{x^2+1}+\frac{4}{x^4+1}+...+\frac{2^n}{(x^{2n}+1)}$

7. If $S_1, S_2, S_3, ... S_n$ are the sums of infinite geometric series whose first terms are 1,2,3, ... n and whose common ratios are $\frac{1}{2},\frac{1}{3},\frac{1}{4},...\frac{1}{n+1}$ respectively, then find the values of $S_1^2+S_2^2+S_3^2+...S_{2n-1}^2$.

8. If exp $(\sin^2 x + \sin^4 x + \sin^6 x + ... \text{inf}) \ln 2$ satisfies the equation $x^2 - 9x + 8 = 0$ find the value of $\dfrac{\cos x}{\cos x + \sin x}, 0 < x < \dfrac{\pi}{2}$.

9. Find the sum of following infinite series $1 + \dfrac{\sqrt{2}-1}{2\sqrt{2}} + \dfrac{3-2\sqrt{2}}{12} + \dfrac{5\sqrt{2}-7}{24\sqrt{2}} + \dfrac{17-12\sqrt{2}}{80} + ...$

10. Find the natural number a for which $\sum_{k=1}^{n} f(a+k) = 16(2^n - 1)$. Where the function f satisfies the relation $f(x+y) = f(x).f(y)$ $\forall$ natural numbers x, y and further $f(1) = 2$.

11. The real numbers x_1, x_2, x_3 satisfying the equation $x^3 - x^2 + bx + g = 0$ are in A.P. find the intervals in which b and g lie.

12. Let $x = 1 + 3a + 6a^2 + 10a^3 + ..., |a| < 1, y = 1 + 4b + 10b^2 + 20b^3 + ..., |b| < 1$. find $S = 1 + 3(ab) + 5(ab)^2 + ...$ in terms of x and y.

13. Let $(1+x^2)^2(1+x)^n = \sum_{k=0}^{n+4} a_k x^k$ If a_1, a_2 and a_3 are in arithmetic progression, find n.

14. If $\cos(x-y)$, $\cos x$ and $\cos(x+y)$ are in H.P., then $\cos x \sec(y/2) = ...,$

15. Let x be the arithmetic mean and y, z be the two geometric means between any two positive numbers, then $\dfrac{y^3 + z^3}{xyz} = ...$

16. a, b, c are the first three terms of a geometric series. If the harmonic mean of a and b is 12 and that of b and c is 36, find the first five terms of the series.

17. Given that α, γ are roots of the equation $Ax^2 - 4x + 1 = 0$, and $\beta\delta$ the roots of the equation $Bx^2 - 6x + 1 = 0$, find values of A and B such that α, β, γ, and δ an in H.P.

18. The sum of three number in $G.P.$ is 42. If the first two number are increased by 2 and third is decreasedby 4, the resulting form an $A.P$ find the numbers of G.P.

19. If a, b and c are in $A.P.$ and a^2, b^2 and c^2 are in H.P., then prove that either $a = b = c$ or a, b and $-\dfrac{c}{2}$ are in G.P..

20. If p and q are positive real numbers such that $p + q = 1$, prove that, $\left(p + \dfrac{1}{p}\right)^2 + \left(q + \dfrac{1}{q}\right)^2 \geq \dfrac{25}{2}$

21. If a, b, c are positive real numbers such that $a + b + c = 1$, prove that, $\left(a + \dfrac{1}{a}\right)\left(b + \dfrac{1}{b}\right)\left(c + \dfrac{1}{c}\right) \geq 64$

22. Find the co-efficients of x^{99} in $(x-1)(x-2)(x-3)..............(x-100)$

23. Find the co-efficients of x^{99} in $(2x-1)(2x-3)(2x-5)..........(2x-199)$

24. If the sum of first n-terms of an A.P is cn^2, then find the sum of squares of these n-terms.

25. If a, b, c are +ve real numbers such that $\{(1+a)(1+b)(1+c)\}^7 > k^m(a^4b^4c^4)$, then find the value of $k + m$.

26. If $a_n = \dfrac{3}{4} - \left(\dfrac{3}{4}\right)^2 + \left(\dfrac{3}{4}\right)^3 - .... + (-1)^{n-1}\left(\dfrac{3}{4}\right)^n$ and $b_n = 1 - a_n$, then find least natural number n_0 such that $b_n > a_n, \forall n \geq n_0$.

27. A cricket plays n (>1) matches and scores $k\left(2^{n-k+1}\right)$ runs in his k th match $(1 \leq k \leq n)$. If the total runs scored by him in the n matches is $\dfrac{1}{4}(n+1)\left(2^{n+1} - n - 2\right)$, then find the value of n.

28. If $t_r = 1, t_r - t_{r-1} = 2^{r-1}, r \geq 2$, then find the sum of $\sum_{r=1}^{n} t_r$.

29. Find the +ve real numbers x such that x, $[x]$ and $x - [x]$ are in G.P, where [,] = G. I. F.

30. One of the root of equation $2000x^6 + 100x^5 + 10cx^3 + x - 2 = 0$ is of the form $\dfrac{m + \sqrt{n}}{r}$, where m is non zero integer and n and r are relatively prime natural numbers. Find the value of $m + n + r$.

ANSWER

1. Arithmetic

3. $\dfrac{14n-6}{8n+23}$

4. $x = 10^5,\ y = 10$

5. $x = 3$

6. $\dfrac{2^{n+1}}{1-x^{2n+1}} - \dfrac{-1}{1-x}$

7. $\left[\dfrac{(n+1)(n+2)(2n+3)}{6} - 1\right] + S^2_{n+1} + S^2_{n+2} + ... + S^2_{2n-1}$

8. $\dfrac{\sqrt{3}-1}{2}$

9. $\dfrac{2\sqrt{3}}{2\sqrt{3} - \sqrt{2} + 1}$

10. $a = 3$

11. $\beta \in (-\alpha, \dfrac{1}{3}]$ and $r \in [-\dfrac{1}{27}, \alpha)$

12. $\dfrac{(2x^{1/3}y^{1/4} - x^{1/3} - y^{1/4} + 1)x^{1/3}y^{1/4}}{(x^{1/3} + y^{1/4} - 1)^2}$

13. $n = 2,3,4$

14. $\pm\sqrt{2}$

15. 2

16. 8, 24, 72, 216, 648

17. $A = 3, B = 8$

18. 24, 12, 6

22.

23.

24. $\dfrac{n\left(4n^2 - 1\right)c^2}{3}$

25. 14.

26. 6

27. 7.

28. $2^{n+1} - n - 2$

29. $\dfrac{\sqrt{5}-1}{2}$.

30. 200.

COMPREHENSIVE LINK PASSAGE : FOR JEE-MAIN AND ADVANCED EXAMS ONLY

PASSAGE–I

Let α,β,γ be the roots of $\frac{x-a}{b}+\frac{x-b}{a}=\frac{a}{x-b}+\frac{b}{x-a}$, where $a,b>0$ and $\alpha>\beta>\gamma$

1. Then β is

a. $a+b$ b. $\frac{a^2+b^2}{a+b}$

c. 0 d. $\frac{a+b}{a^2+b^2}$

2. If $\alpha = 2\beta$, then the maximum value of the area of triangle, whose perimeter 3α, is

a. a^2 b. $\frac{3}{4}a^2$

c. $a^2\sqrt{3}$ d. $2\sqrt{3}a^2$

3. If $\alpha-\beta-\gamma=c$, then

a. a,b,c are in A.P b. a,c,b are in A.P

c. a,b,c are in H.P d. a,c,b are in H.P

PASSAGE–II

Suppose $A_1,A_2,\ldots,A_n$ be A.M's; $G_1,G_2,\ldots,G_n$ be G.M's; $H_1,H_2,\ldots,H_n$ be H.M's between two +ve real numbers a and b.

1. Then A_n, G_n, H_n are in

a. A.P b. G.P

c. H.P d. A.G..P

2. Then H_1 is

a. $\frac{a+(2n-1)b}{2n}$ b. $\frac{a(2n+1)+b}{2n}$

c. $\frac{a(2n+1)-b}{2n}$ d. $\frac{2nab}{a+(2n-1)b}$

3. Then $\frac{H_1+a}{H_1-a}+\frac{H_{2n-1}+b}{H_{2n-1}-b}$ is

a. $2(n-1)$ b. $4n$

c. $4n-2$ d. $4n+2$.

PASSAGE – III

Suppose a,b,c are the sides of a triangle, which are in G.P

1. If the common ratio of the triangle is less than unity, then r is

a. $\left(n,\frac{1}{\sqrt{2}+1}\right)$ b. $\left(0,\frac{\sqrt{5}-1}{2}\right)$

c. $\left(0,\frac{\sqrt{5}+1}{4}\right)$ d*. $\left(\frac{\sqrt{5}-1}{2},1\right)$

2. If $\log a-\log 2b$, $\log 2b-\log 3c$, $\log 3c-\log a$ are in A.P, then the least side of the triangle is

a. a b. b

c. c d. $a=b=c$

3. The greatest angle of the triangle is

a. 135° b. 90°

c. 120° d. $\pi-\cos^{-1}\left(\frac{1}{3}\right)$

PASSAGE–IV

Let α,β,γ are the real roots of $ax^3+3bx^2+3cx+d=0$ such that $\alpha<\beta<\gamma$

1. If roots are in A.P, then the value of $2a^3$ is

a. $3abc+2a^2c$ b. $3abc-ac^2$

c. $3abc+ac^2$ d. $3abc-a^2c$

2. If roots are in G.P, then the value of $\frac{a}{c}$ is

a. $\left(\frac{a}{b}\right)^3$ b. $\left(\frac{b}{d}\right)^3$

c. $\left(\frac{d}{b}\right)$ d. $\left(\frac{b}{d}\right)$

3. If roots are in H.P and $a=b=c=1$, then the value of 'd' is

a. 1, 2 b. 1

c. 2 d. -2.

PASSAGE – V

Let $x_1,x_2,x_3,\ldots,x_n$ are distinct real numbers in H.P. Then

1. Which of the following is true ?

a. $x_1x_4>x_2x_3$ b. $x_1x_4<x_2x_3$

c. $x_1x_2>x_3x_4$ d. $x_1x_2<x_3x_4$

2. Which of the following is true ?

a. $x_5+x_8>x_6+x_7$ b. $x_5+x_8<x_6+x_7$

c. $x_5+x_6>x_8+x_7$ d. $x_5+x_6<x_8+x_7$

3. $x_1x_2+x_2x_3+x_3x_4+x_1x_5$ is

a. $4x_1x_5$ b. $2x_1x_5$

c $3x_1x_5$ d. $5x_1x_5$

PASSAGE – VI

Suppose $s_1,s_2,\ldots,s_n$ are the sum of n geometric series of infinte terms, whose first terms are $1,2,3,\ldots,n$ and the common ratios are $\frac{1}{2},\frac{1}{3},\ldots,\frac{1}{n+1}$ respectively .

1. If $s_1+s_2+\ldots+s_n=7$, then the value of n is

a. 12 b. 13

c. 11 d. 14

2. The value of $s_1^2+s_2^2+\ldots+s_{2n-1}^2$ is

a. $n(2n+1)(4n+1)-1$ b. $\frac{1}{3}n(2n+1)(4n+1)-1$

c. $\frac{1}{3}n(2n+1)(4n+1)$ d. $\frac{1}{3}n(2n+1)(4n+1)-2$

3. If $s_1^3+s_2^3+\ldots+s_{2k-1}^3=1800$, then the value of k is

a. 15 b. 16

c. 5 d. 6.

PASSAGE – VII

Let A_1, A_2, A_3,............,An be arithmetic means between –2 and 1027 and G_1, G_2, G_3,...................G_n be geometric means between 1 and 1024. Product of geometric means is 2^{45} and sum of the arithmetic means is 1025×1717

On the basis of above information, answer the following questions:

1. The value of n is

a. 7 b. 9

c. 11 d. None

2. The value of m is

a. 340 b. 342

c. 344 d. 346.

3. The value of $G_1 + G_2 + G_3 + ...+ G_n$ is

a. 1022 b. 2044

c. 512 d. None

4. The common difference of progression A_1, A_3, A_5,........,Am–1 is

a. 6 b. 3

c. 2 d. 1

5. The numbers $2A_{171}, (G_5)^2 + 1, 2A_{172}$ are in

a. A.P. b. G.P

c. H.P d. A.G.P

PASSAGE – VIII

There are two sets A and B each of which consists of three numbers in $A.P$, whose sum is 15 where D and d are the common differences such that $D - d = 1$. If $\frac{p}{q} = \frac{7}{8}$, where p and q are the product of the numbers respectively and $d > 0$, in two sets.

On the basis of the above information, answer the following questions:

1. Value of p is

a. 100 b. 120

c. 105 d. 110.

2. Value of q is

a. 100 b. 120

c. 105 d. 110.

3. Value of $D + d$ is

a. 1 b. 2

c. 3 d. 4.

PASSAGE – IX

Four different integers form an increasing **A.P.**.One of these numbers is equal to the sum of the squares of the other three numbers. Then

1. The smallest number is

a. –2 b. 0

c. –1 d. 2

2. The common difference of the four numbers is

a. 2 b. 1

c. 3 d. 4

3. The sum of the four numbers is

a. 10 b. 8

c. 2 d. 6

ANSWER

PASSAGE 1

1. b **2.** c **3.** d

PASSEGE II

1. b **2.** a, **3.** c

PASSEGE 1II

1. d, **2.** a , **3.** c;

PASSEGE 1V

1. d, **2.** b, **3.** c;

PASSEGE V

1. a, **2.** a, **3.** d;

PASSEGE VI

1. b, **2.** b, **3.** c;

PASSEGE VII

1. a, **2.** b, **3.** a; **4.**a, **5.**a;

PASSEGE VIII

1. c, **2.** b, **3.** c;

PASSEGE IX

1. c, **2.** b, **3.** c;

MATCHING ORDER

(FOR JEE - MAIN AND ADVANCED EXAMS ONLY)

1. Match the following columns :

I	II
A. If a^2, b^2, c^2 are in A.P, then $\frac{b+c}{a}, \frac{c+a}{b}, \frac{a+b}{c}$ are in	P A.P
B. If a, b, c are in H.P, then $\frac{a}{b+c}, \frac{b}{c+a}, \frac{c}{a+b}$ are in	Q G.P
C. If a, b, c are in A.P as well as in G.P, then a^2, b^2, c^2 are in	R H.P
D. If $b+c$, $c+a$, $a+b$ are in H.P, then $\frac{a}{b+c}, \frac{b}{c+a}, \frac{c}{a+b}$ are in	S A.G..P

2. Match the following columns :

I	II
A. If $2, A_1, A_2, A_3, A_4, 8$ are in A.P then the value of $A_1 + A_2 + A_3 + A_4$ is	P 2
B. If $2, G_1, G_2, G_3, G_4, G_5, 16$ are in G.P then the value of $G_1 \cdot G_2 \cdot G_3 \cdot G_4 \cdot G_5$ is	Q 5/2
C. If $2, H_1, H_2, H_3, H_4, H_5, H_6, 3$ are in H.P„ the value of $\frac{1}{H_1} + \frac{1}{H_2} + \frac{1}{H_3} + \frac{1}{H_4} + \frac{1}{H_5} + \frac{1}{H_6}$ is	R 20

3. Match the following columns :

I	II
A. If $x_1, x_2, x_3, \ldots x_{10}$ are in H.P then $\frac{x_1x_2 + x_2x_3 + x_3x_4 + \ldots\ldots + x_1x_{10}}{x_1x_{10}}$ is	P 60
B. If $2, x_1, x_2, \ldots, x_{10}, 10$ are in A.P then $x_1 + x_2 + \ldots\ldots + x_{10}$ is	Q 1
C. If a,b,c are in A.P and x,y,z are in $G.P$ then $x^{b-c}.y^{c-a}.z^{a-b}$ is	R 9
D. If $a^x = b^y = c^z$ and a,b,c are in $G.P$ then $y\left(\frac{1}{x}+\frac{1}{z}\right)$ is	S 2

4. Match the following columns :

I	II
A. The sum of n-terms of an A.P is $5n^2 + 4n$, then the common difference is	P 4
B. The sum of n-terms of a G.P is $\left(\frac{A^n - B}{2}\right)$, then the value of A+ B is	Q 10
C. The sum of n terms of an A.P is $4n^2 + 3n$, then t_{10} is	R 3
D. The sum of $\frac{1}{2}+\frac{3}{4}+\frac{7}{8}+\frac{15}{16}+\ldots$ to 100 terms is $100 + \left(1-\left(\frac{A}{B}\right)^{100}\right)$, then A+ B is	S 79

5. Match the following columns :

I	II
A. Suppose that $F(n+1) = \frac{2F(n)+1}{2}$ for $n = 1,2,3, \ldots$ and $F(1) = 2$, Then $F(101)$ is	P 42
B. If $a_1, a_2, a_3, \ldots, a_{21}$ are in A.P and $a_1 + a_5 + a_{11} + a_{17} + a_{19} = 10$, then the value of $\sum_{i=1}^{21} a_i$ is	Q 1620
C. 10 th term of the sequence $S = 1 + 5 + 13 + 29 + \ldots\ldots$ is	R 52
D. The sum of all two digit numbers which are not divisible by 2 or 3 is	S 2045.

6. Match the following columns :

I	II
A The arithmetic mean of two numbers is 6 and their geometric mean G and harmonic H satisfy the relation $G^2 + 3H = 48$. The two numbers are	P $\frac{240}{77}$
B. The sum of the series $\frac{5}{1^2.4^2}+\frac{11}{4^2.7^2}+\frac{17}{7^2.10^2}+\ldots$ is	Q 4, 8
C. If the first two terms of a harmonic progress ion be 1/2 and R1/3 , then harmonic mean of first four terms is	R $\frac{1}{3}$
	S 1/2

7. Match the following columns :

I	II
A. The co-efficient of x^{49} in $(x-1)(x-2)(x-3)\ldots\ldots(x-49)$ is	P 5050
B. The co-efficient of x^{99} in $(x+1)(x+2)(x+3)\ldots\ldots(x+100)$ is	Q 2500
C. The co-efficient of x^{99} in $(x-1)(x-3)(x-5)\ldots\ldots(x-99)$ is	R –2550
D. The co-efficient of x^{49} in $(x-2)(x-4)\ldots\ldots(x-100)$ is	S –1225

8. Match the following columns :

I	II
A. If $a + 2b + 3c = 12$, then the max value of ab^2c^3 is	P 1024
B. If $x + 4y + 5z = 20$, then the max value of xy^4z^5 is	Q 16
C. If $a + b + c + d = 8$, then the min value of $(a + b)(c + d)$ is	R 32
D If $abc = 4$, then the least value of $(1 + a)(1 + b)(1+ c)$ is	S 64

ANSWERS

1. **A.** → R; **B.** → P; **C.** → P, Q, R, **D.** → P.

2. **A.** → R; **B.** → P; **C.** → Q

3. **A.** → R; **B.** → P; **C.** → Q; **D.** → S

4. **A.** → Q; **B.** → P, **C.** → S; **D.** → R

5. **A.** → R; **B.** → P, **C.** → S, **D.** → Q

6. **A.** → Q, **B.** → R, **C.** → P

7. **A.** → S, **B.** → P, **C.** → Q; **D.** → R

8. **A.** → R, **B.** → P, **C.** → Q **D.** → Q

Questions asked on Roorkee Exams

1. If between any two quantities there be inserted two arithmetic means A_1, A_2, two geometric means G_1, G_2 and two harmonic means H_1, H_2, prove that $G_1G_2 : H_1H_2 = (A_1 + A_2) : (H_1 + H_2)$

—[Roorkee –1983]

2. Given that $a^x = b^y = c^z = d^u$ and a,b,c,d are in geometric progression, show that x,y,z,u are in Harmonic Progression.

– [Roorkee – 1984]

3. Balls are arranged in rows to form an equilateral triangle. The first row consists of one ball, the second of 2 balls, and so on. If 669 more balls are added, then all the balls can be arranged in the shape of a square, and each of its sides then contains 8 balls less than each side of the triangle did. Determine the initial number of balls. [Roorkee – 1985]

4. The sum of n terms of two arithmetic series are in the ratio of $(7n + 1)$: $(4n + 27)$. Find the ratio of their nth terms.

5. Solve for x and y: $\log_{10} x + \log_{10} x^{1/2} + \log_{10} x^{1/4} + \ldots\ldots\ldots = y$

$$\frac{1+3+5\ldots\ldots\ldots+(2y-1)}{4+7+10+\ldots\ldots+(3y+1)} = \frac{20}{7\log_{10}}$$

[Roorkee – 1987]

6. The sum of the fist ten terms of an $A.P$ is 155 and the sum of the first two terms of G.P is 9. Find these progressions if the first term of $A.P$ equals the common ratio of the $G.P$ and the first term of $G.P$ equals the c.d of $A.P.$

[Roorkee – 1987]

7. No questions asked in **1988.**

8. The sum of an infinite geometric progression is 2 and the sum of the geometric progression made from the cubes of the terms of this infinite series is 24. Then find the series. [Roorkee – 1989]

9. No questions asked in **1990, 1991.**

10. Find the sum S_n of the cubes of the first n terms of an A.P and show that the sum of the first n –terms of the $A.P$ is a factor of S_n. —[Roorkee – 1992]

11. The sum of first ten terms of an A.P is 155 and the sum of first two terms of a $G.P$ is 9, the first term of $A.P$ is equal to the common ratio of the $G.P$ and the first term of G.P is equal to the common difference of the $A.P$. Find the two progressions. — [Roorkee – 1993]

12. If the $(m + 1)$th, $(n + 1)$th and $(r + 1)$th terms of an $A.P$ are in $G.P$ and m,n are in $H.P$, then find the ratio of the first term of the $A.P.$ to its common difference in terms of n. [Roorkee – 1994]

13. No questions asked in **1995.**

14. Let $x = 1 + 3a + 6a^2 + 10a^3 + ..., |a| < 1$, $y = 1 + 4b + 10b^2 + 20b^3 + ..., |b| < 1$ Find $S = 1 + 3(ab) + 5(ab)^2 + ...$ in terms of x and y. [Roorkee – 1996]

15. Observing that $1^3 = 1, 2^3 = 3 + 5, 3^3 = 7 + 9 + 11, 4^3 = 13 + 15 + 17 + 19$. Find a general formula for cube of natural number n. —[Roorkee – 1997]

16. a,b,c are the first three terms of a geometric series. If the harmonic mean of a and b is 12 and that of b and c is 36, find the first five terms of the series. [Roorkee – 1998]

17. The sum of the infinite series is 162 and the sum of the first n terms is 160. If the inverse of its common ratio is an integer, find all possible values of the common ratio, n and the first term of the series. —[Roorkee – 1999]

18. No questions asked in **2000.**

20. The sum of three numbers in $G.P$ is 42. If the first two numbers are increased by 2 and third is decreased by 4, the resulting numbers form an $A.P$. Find the numbers of $G.P$. **[Roorkee – 2001]**

ANSWER

3. 1540

4. $(14n - 6) : (8n + 23)$

5. $x = 10^5, y = 10$ and $x = 10^{5/7}, y = -10/7$

6. $A.P$: 25/2, 79/6, 83/6, $G.P$: 2/3, 25/3, 625/6

8. {3,–3/2,3/4,...}, {6,–12,24......}

11. $A.P = \left\{\frac{25}{2}, \frac{79}{6}, \frac{83}{6}, ...\right\}$, G.P. $= \left\{\frac{2}{3}, \frac{25}{3}, \frac{625}{6}, ...\right\}$

12. $-n/2$

15. $n^3 = (n^2 - n + 1) + (n^2 - n + 3) + (n^2 - n + 5) + ... + (n^2 + n - 1)$

16. G.P = 8, 24, 72, 216, 648

17. $r = 1/3, n = 4, a = 108$; $r = 1/9, n = 2, a = 144$; $r = 1/81, n = 1, a = 160$

20. 6, 12, 24 or 24, 12, 6

(Questions asked on IIT-JEE Exams)

1. i. The value of $x + y + z$ is 15. If a,x,y,z, b are in $A.P$ while the value of $\frac{1}{x} + \frac{1}{y} + \frac{1}{z}$ is $\frac{5}{3}$. If a, x, y, z, b are in $H.P$, then find a and b.

   ii. If x,y,z are in $H.P$, then show that $\log(x + z) + \log(x + z - 2y) = 2\log(x - z)$. [IIT-JEE – 1978]

2. If the mth, nth and pth terms of an $A.P$ and $G.P$ are equal and x,y,z, then prove that $x^{y-z}.y^{x-y}.z^{x-y} = 1$. —[ITT-JEE–1 979]

3. The interior angles of a polygon are in A.P, the smallest angle is 120° and the common difference is 5°. Find the number of sides of the polygon. [IIT-JEE – 1980]

4. Let the angles of a triangle ABC be in $A.P$ and let $b : c = \sqrt{3} : \sqrt{2}$. Find the angle A. [IIT-JEE – 1981]

5. If $a_1, a_2, a_3, ...a_n$ are in $A.P$ where $a_i > 0$ for all I, show that

$$\frac{1}{\sqrt{a_1} + \sqrt{a_2}} + \frac{1}{\sqrt{a_2} + \sqrt{a_3}} + ... + \frac{1}{\sqrt{a_{n-1}} + \sqrt{a_n}} = \frac{n-1}{\sqrt{a_1} + \sqrt{a_n}}$$

[IIT-JEE – 1982]

6. Does there exist a $G.P$ containing 27, 8 and 12 as three of its terms? If it exists, how many such progressions are possible? [IIT–JEE– 1982]

7. The third term of a geometric progression is 4, the product of the first 5 terms is

   a. 4^3 b. 4^5

   c. 4^4 d. None. [IIT-JEE -1982].

8. Find three numbers a,b,c between 2 and 18 such that

   i. their sum is 25.

   ii. 2, a,b are consecutive terms of an $A.P$

   iii. the numbers b,c, 18 are consecutive terms of a $G.P$. [IIT-JEE – 1983]

9. The rational number, which equals the number $2.\overline{357}$ with recurring decimal is

   a. $\frac{2355}{1001}$ b. $\frac{2379}{997}$

   c. $\frac{2355}{999}$ d. None. [IIT-JEE – 1983]

10. If n is a natural number such that $n = p_1^{\alpha_1}.p_2^{\alpha_2}.p_3^{\alpha_3}....p_k^{a_k}$ and $p_1, p_2,.........p_k$ are distinct primes, then show that $\log n \geq k \log 2$ [IIT-JEE – 1984]

11. The sum of the integers from 1 to 100 that are divisible by 2 or 5 is .... [IIT-JEE – 1984]

12. In a triangle ABC if $\cot A$, $\cot B$, $\cot C$ are in $A.P$, then a,b,c are in ....progression. [IIT-JEE – 1985]

13. If three complex numbers are in A.P, then they lie on a circle in the complex plane. [IIT-JEE – 1985]

14. If a,b,c are in $G.P$, then the equation $ax^2 + 2bx + c = 0$, $dx^2 + 2ex + f = 0$ have a common root if $\frac{d}{a},\frac{e}{b},\frac{f}{c}$ are in

*a. $A.P$ b. $G.P$

c. $H.P$ d. None. [IIT-JEE – 1985]

15. The sum of the squares of three distinct real numbers, which are in G.P is s^2. If their sum is αS, show that $\alpha^2 \in \left(\frac{1}{3},1\right) \cup (1,3)$.

[IIT-JEE – 1986]

16. If a,b,c,d and p are distinct real numbers such that $(a^2+b^2+c^2)p^2 - 2(ab + bc + cd)p + (b^2 + c^2 + d^2) \leq 0$, then a,b,c,d are in

a. $A.P$ *b. $G.P$

c. $H.P$ d. $ab = cd$. [IIT-JEE – 1987]

17. The sides of a triangle inscribed in a given circle subtend angles α,β and γ at center. The minimum value of the arithmetic mean of $\cos\left(\alpha + \frac{\pi}{2}\right)$, $\cos\left(\beta + \frac{\pi}{2}\right)$ and $\cos\left(\gamma + \frac{\pi}{2}\right)$ is.........

[IIT-JEE – 1987]

18. Sum of first n-terms of series $\frac{1}{2}+\frac{3}{4}+\frac{7}{8}+\frac{15}{16}+$..... is equal to

a. $2^n - n - 1$ b. $1-2^{-n}$

c. $n - 1 + 2^{-n}$ d. $2^n + 1$ [IIT-JEE – 1988]

19. The sum of the first n terms of the series $1^2 + 2.2^2 + 3^2 + 2.4^2 + 5^2 + 2.6^2 +$... .... is $\frac{n^2(n+1)}{2}$, where n is even . Then , when n is odd, the sum is ......

[IIT-JEE – 1988]

20. If the first and $(2n-1)$th term of an $A.P$, a $G.P$ and an $H.P$ are equal and their nth terms are a,b,c respectively, then

a. $a = b = c$ b. $a \geq b \geq c$

c. $a + c = b$ d. $ac - b^2 = 0$. [IIT-JEE – 1988]

21. No questions asked in **1989.**

22. If $\log_3 2$, $\log_3 (2^x - 5)$ and $\log\left(2^x - \frac{7}{2}\right)$ are in $A.P$, determine the value of x. [IIT-JEE – 1990]

23. Let 'p' be the first of the n arithmetic means between two numbers and 'q' the first of n harmonic means between the same numbers. Show that 'q' does not lie between p and $\left(\frac{n+1}{n-1}\right)^2 p$ [IIT-JEE- 1991]

24. If $S_1,S_2,S_3,..............,S_n$ are the sums of infinite geometric series whose first terms are $\{1,2,3,.......,n\}$ and whose common ratios are $\left\{\frac{1}{2},\frac{1}{3},\frac{1}{4},..............,\frac{1}{n+1}\right\}$ respectively, then find value of $S_1^2 + S_2^2 +..............S_{2n-1}^2$.

[IIT-JEE – 1991]

25. Let the harmonic mean and geometric mean of two positive numbers be in the ratio 4:5 . Then the two numbers in the ratio .... [IIT-JEE – 1992]

26. For $0 < \phi < \frac{\pi}{2}$, if $x = \sum_{n=0}^{\infty} \cos^{2n}\phi$, $y = \sum_{n=0}^{\infty} \sin^{2n}\varphi$ and $z = \sum_{n=0}^{\infty} \cos^{2n}\varphi \sin^{2n}\varphi$, then

a. $xyz = xz + y$ *b. $xyz = xy + z$

c. $xyz = x + y + z$ d. $xyz = yz + x$. [IIT-JEE – 1993]

27. If ln $(a + c)$, ln $(a - c)$, ln $(a - 2b + c)$ are in A.P, then

a. a,b,c are in $A.P$ b. a^2,b^2,c^2 are in $A.P$

c. a,b,c are in $G.P$ *d. a,b,c are in $H.P$

[IIT-JEE – 1994]

28. No questions asked in **1995.**

29. The real number x_1,x_2,x_3 satisfying equation $x^3 - x^2 + \beta x + \gamma = 0$ are in $A.P$. Find the intervals in which β and γ lie.

[IIT-JEE – 1996]

30. For any odd integer $n \geq 1$ $n^3 - (n-1)^3 +.........+ (-1)^{n-1}.1^3 =$............. [IIT-JEE - 1996]

31. Let p and q be roots of the equation $x^2 - 2x + A = 0$ and let r and s be the roots of $x^2 - 18x + B = 0$. If $p < q < r < s$ are in arithmetic progression, then $A =$.........and $B =$..................

[IIT-JEE – 1997]

32. Let x be the arithmetic mean and y,z be the two geometric means between any two positive numbers .

Then $\frac{y^3 + z^3}{xyz} =$ ...... [IIT-JEE – 1997]

33. Let T_r be the rth term of an $A.P$ for $r = 1, 2, 3,$...... If for some positive integers m,n we have $T_m = 1/n$ and $T_n = 1/m$, then T_{mn} equals

a. $1/mn$ b. $1/m + 1/n$

c. 1 d. 0. [IIT-JEE – 1998]

34. If $x > 1, y > 1$ and $z > 1$ are in G.P , then $\frac{1}{1+Inx},\frac{1}{1+Iny},\frac{1}{1+Inz}$ are in

a. $A.P$ b. $G.P$

c. $H.P$ d. None. [IIT-JEE – 1998]

35. Let $a_1,a_2,............,a_{10}$ be in $A.P$ and $h_1,h_2,h_3,..............,h_{10}$ be in $H.P$. If $a_1 = h_1 = 2$ and $a_{10} = h_{10} = 3$, then value of a_4h_7 is

a. 2 b. 3

c. 5 d. 6 [IIT-JEE – 1999]

36. The harmonic mean of the roots of the equation $(5+\sqrt{2})x^2-(4+\sqrt{5})x+8+2\sqrt{5}=0$ is

a. 2 b. 4

c. 6 d. 8. [IIT-JEE – 1999]

37. Consider an infinite series with first term a and common ratio r. If its sum is 4 and the second term is 3/4, then

a. $a=4/7, r=3/7$ b. $a=2, r=3/8$

c. $a=3/2, r=1/2$ d. $a=3, r=1/4$. [IIT-JEE -2000]

38. The fourth power of the common difference of an A.P with integer entries in added to the product of any four consecutive terms of it, prove that the resulting sum is square of an integer. [IIT-JEE – 2000]

39. Let T_n denote the number of triangles which can be formed using the vertices of a regular polygon of n – sides. If $T_{n+1}-T_n=21$, then n equals

a. 5 b. 7

c. 6 d. 4. [IIT-JEE – 2001]

40. Let the positive numbers a,b,c,d be in A.P, then abc, abd, acd, bcd are

a. not in A.P/G.P/H.P b. in A.P

c. in G.P d. in H.P [IIT-JEE – 2001]

41. If the sum of the first $2n$ terms of the A.P = {2,5,8........}is equal to the sum of the first n terms of the A.P. = {57,59,61.....}, then n equals

a. 100 b. 12

c. 11 d. 13. [IIT-JEE – 2001]

42. Let $a_1,a_2,a_3,.........,a_n$ be positive real number in G.P for each a, let A_n, G_n, H_n be respectively, the arithmetic mean, geometric mean, harmonic mean of. Find an expression for the geometric mean $G_1, G_2, G_3,..........G_n$ in terms of $A_1, A_2, A_3,.........A_n$, $H_1, H_2,...........H_n$.

[IIT-JEE–2001]

43. If $a_1, a_2,.............,a_n$ are positive real numbers whose product is a fixed number c, then the minimum value of $a_1+a_2+.........+a_{n-1}+2a_n$ is

a. $n(2c)^{1/n}$ b. $(n+1)c^{1/n}$

c. $2n\,c^{1/n}$ d. $(n+1)(2c)^{1/n}$. [IIT-JEE–2002]

44. Suppose a,b,c are in A.P and a^2,b^2,c^2 are in G.P. If $a<b<c$ and $a+b+c=3/2$, then the value of a is

a. $\frac{1}{2\sqrt{2}}$ b. $\frac{1}{2\sqrt{3}}$

c. $\frac{1}{2}+\frac{1}{\sqrt{2}}$ d. $\frac{1}{2}-\frac{1}{\sqrt{2}}$. [IIT-JEE – 2002]

45. Let a and b are positive real numbers. If a, A_1, A_2, b are in A.P and a, G_1, G_2, b are in G.P and a, H_1, H_2, b are in H.P. Show that $\frac{G_1G_2}{H_1H_2}=\frac{A_1+A_2}{H_1+H_2}=\frac{(2a+b)(a+2b)}{9ab}$ [IIT-JEE – 2002]

46. If a,b and c are in A.P and a^2,b^2,c^2 are in H.P, then prove that either $a=b=c$ or a,b and $-c/2$ are in G.P [IIT-JEE – 2003]

47. An infinite G.P has first term 'x' and sum '5' then

a. $x<-10$ b. $-10<x<0$

c. $0<x<10$ d. $x>10$. [IIT-JEE – 2004]

48. If a,b,c are positive numbers, then prove that $(1+a)^7(1+b)^7(1+c)^7>7^7a^4b^4c^4$. [IIT-JEE – 2004]

49. If α,β are the roots of $ax^2+bx+c=0$ and $\alpha+\beta, \alpha^2\beta^2, \alpha^3+\beta^3$ are in G.P and $\Delta=b^2-4ac$, then [IIT-JEE – 2005]

a. $c\,\Delta=0$ b. $cb\neq 0$

c. $b\,\Delta=0$ d. $\Delta\neq 0$.

50. If total number of runs scored in n matches is $\left(\frac{n+1}{4}\right)(2^{n+1}-n-2)$ where $n>1$ and the runs scored in the kth match are given by $k.2^{n+1-k}$, where $1\le k\le n$, find n.

[IIT-JEE- 2005]

51. If $a_n=\frac{3}{4}-\left(\frac{3}{4}\right)^2+\left(\frac{1}{2k^2}\right)-..........................+(-1)^{n-1}\left(\frac{3}{4}\right)^n$ and $b_n=1-a_n$, then find least natural number n_0 such that $b_n>a_n$ for every $n\ge n_0$. [IIT-JEE– 2006]

52. If $\theta=\sum_{k=1}^{\infty}\tan^{-1}\left(\frac{1}{2k^2}\right)$, then find tan θ

[IIT-JEE-2006]

53. Suppose 4 distinct +ve numbers a_1,a_2,a_3,a_4 are in G.P. Let $b_1=a_1, b_2=b_1+a_2, b_3=b_2+a_3, b_4=b_3+a_4$

Statement - I : The numbers b_1,b_2,b_3,b_4 are neither in A.P nor in G.P

Statement - II : The numbers b_1,b_2,b_3,b_4 are in H.P

[IIT-JEE - 2008]

54. If the sum of first n-terms of an A.P is cn^2, then the sum of the squares of these n terms is

a. $\frac{n(4n^2-1)c^2}{6}$ b. $\frac{n(4n^2+1)c^2}{3}$

c. $\frac{n(4n^2-1)c^2}{3}$ d. $\frac{n(4n^2+1)c^2}{6}$ [IIT-JEE-2009]

55. Let $a_1,a_2.....................,a_{11}$ be real numbers satisfying $a_1=15$, $27-a_2>0$ and $ak=2a_{k-1}-ak-2$ for $k=3,4,5,.................,11$.

If $\dfrac{a_1^2+a_2^2+....+a_{11}^2}{11}=90$, then find value of

$\dfrac{a_1+a_2+.......+a_{11}}{11}$. [IIT-JEE-2010]

56. Let $a_1,a_2,......................a_{100}$ be an A.P with $a_1=3$ and $S_P=\sum_{I=1}^{P}(a_i),1\le p\le 100$. For any integer n with $1\le n\le 20$, let $m=5n$. If $\dfrac{S_m}{S_n}$ does not depend on n, then find a_2

[IIT-JEE-2011]

57. Let $a_1,a_2,.........$ be in H.P with $a_1=5$ and $a_{20}=25$. The least +ve integer n for which $a_n<0$ is

a. 22 b. 23
c. 24 d. 25. [IIT-JEE-2012]

ANSWER

1. (i) 1, 9 or 9 **3.** 9
4. 75° **6.** infinite
8. 5, 8, 12 **11.** 3050
12. A.P **13.** False
17. $-\sqrt{3}/2$ **19.** $\dfrac{n^2(n+1)}{2}$
22. $x=3$ **24.** $\dfrac{1}{3}\times[n(2n+1)(4n+1)-3]$
25. 1:4 or 4 : 1 **29.** $\beta\in\left[-\infty,\dfrac{1}{3}\right)$ and $\gamma\in\left(-\dfrac{1}{27},\infty\right]$
30. $\dfrac{1}{4}(n+1)^2(2n-1)$ **31.** $A=-3, B=77$ **32.** 2
33. (c) **34.** (b)
35. (d) **36.** (b)
37. (d) **39.** (b)
40. (d) **41.** (c)
42. $(A_1A_2.......A_n\, H_1H_2...........H_n)^{1/2n}$
43. (a) **44.** (c)
47. (c) **49.** (a)
50. $n=7$ **51.** 6
52. $\tan\theta=1$
53. Statement I is true and statement- II is false
54. (c) **55.** 0
56. 3 or 9

Self Assesment Test

TIME : 1 HOUR. **CHAPTER : SEQUENCE AND SERIES** MAX. MARKS: 100

Give answer the following questions :

1. If $\log 2,\log\left(2^x-1\right),\log\left(2^x+3\right)$ are in $A.P$, then the value of x is

a. 5/2 b. $\log_2 5$
c. $\log_3 2$ d. 3/2

2. If a,b,c,d are in G.P., then $\left(a^2+b^2+c^2\right)\left(b^2+c^2+d^2\right)$ equals to

a. $(ab+bc+cd)$ b. $(ab+bc+cd)^2$
c. $(ab+bc+cd)^4$ d. None.

3. If a_1,a_2,a_3,a_4,a_5 are in H. P, then $a_1a_2+a_2a_3+a_3a_4+a_4a_5$ is equal to

a. $2a_1a_5$ b. $3a_1a_5$
c $4a_1a_5$ d. -4.

4. If a,b,c,d are four positive real numbers such that $abcd=1$, then the minimum value of $(1+a)(1+b)(1+c)(1+d)$ is

a. 4 b. 1
c. 16 d. 18.

5. If x,y and z are in $A.P$ and $(x+2y-z)(2y+z-x)(z+x-y)=kxyz$, then k is

a. 4 b. 2
c. 1 d. None.

6. $\sum_{r=1}^{n}\dfrac{1}{\log_{3^r}a}$ is equal to

a. $\dfrac{n(n+1)}{2}\times\log_3 a$ b. $\dfrac{n(n+1)}{2}\times\log_a 3$

c. $\dfrac{n^2(n+1)^2}{4}\times\log_3 a$ d. None.

7. If a,b,c are in G.P, then prove that $a+b, 2b, c+b$ are in $H.P.$

8. The first of an A.P $a_1,a_2,a_3,..........,a_n$ is unity. For what value of the common difference is $a_1a_3+a_2a_3$ minimum?

□□□

CHAPTER 2

QUADRATIC EQUATIONS AND EXPRESSIONS

CONCEPT BOOSTER

1.1. Algebraic Expression

It is a collection of symbols + and–.

$x+2y+3z-4u, p+q-r, 2a+3b-4c$ are algebraic expressions.

1.2. Polynomial

It is an algebraic expression in which the exponent of the variable contain whole number.

Such as $2x+4, 3x^2+4x+5, 4x^3+3x^2+10x+50$, etc are polynomials.

1.3. Equation

It is an equality, which satisfies for some values of the unknown quantity. Such as $3x+6=0, x^2-3x+2=0, x^3-6x^2+11x-6=0$ etc. are equations.

1.4. Identity

The full form of identity is identical equation. It is true for every values of the unknown quantities.

Such as $a^2-b^2=(a+b)(a-b)$ is an algebraic identity, $\sin^2\theta + \cos^2\theta = 1$ is a trigonometrical identity. Those are true for every values of the variable.

1.5. Types of equations

There are four types of equations. Such as

1. Linear Equation : $ax+b=0, a\neq 0$
2. Quadratic Equation : $ax^2+bx+c=0, a\neq 0$
3. Cubic Equation : $ax^3+bx^2+cx+d=0, a\neq 0$
4. Quartic Equation : $ax^4+bx^3+cx^2+dx+e=0, a\neq 0$

1.6. Difference between an equation and identity

An identity in x is saitisfied all permissble values of x, where as equation is satisfied by some particular values of x.

FOR EXAMPLE:

$(x+1)^2 = x^2+2x+1$ is identity in x, is satisfied for all values of x. where as a quadratic equation is satisfies two values of x only.

NOTE :

1. If a linear equation is satisfied more than one root, then it is an identity.
   So $ax+b=0$ is an identity in x only if $a=0, b=0$.
2. If a quadratic equation is satisfied more than two roots, then it is also an identity. So $ax^2+bx+c=0$ is an identity in x only when $a=0$, $b=0$ and $c=0$.

FOR EXAMPLES:

1. The equation $\frac{x-a}{b-a}+\frac{x-b}{a-b}=1$ is identity in x. So number of real solutions is infinite.
2. The equation $\frac{(x-a)(x-b)}{(b-c)(c-a)}+\frac{(x-b)(x-c)}{(c-a)(a-b)}+\frac{(x-c)(x-a)}{(a-b)(b-c)}=1$ is an identity in x. So number of solutions is infinite.
3. Find the value a, if $(a^2-3a+2)x+(a^2-5a+4)=0$ is an identity in x. **ANS:** $a=1$
4. Find value of b, $(b^2-6b+8)x^2+(|b|-2)x+(b^3-6b-20)=0$ is identity in x. **ANS:** $b=2$.

1.7. The Quadratic Formula

The solution of the quadratic equation $ax^2+bx+c=0$ is given by

$$x=\frac{-b\pm\sqrt{b^2-4ac}}{2a}.$$

Wchich is known as *Shiddarth Achariya Formula* and also *D-formula.*

PROOF: We have $ax^2+bx+c=0, a\neq 0$

$$\Rightarrow \quad x^2+\left(\frac{b}{a}\right)x+\frac{c}{a}=0.$$

$$\Rightarrow \quad \left(x+\frac{b}{2a}\right)^2=\frac{b^2-4ac}{4a^2}$$

$$\Rightarrow \quad \left(x+\frac{b}{2a}\right)=\pm\frac{\sqrt{b^2-4ac}}{2a}$$

$$\Rightarrow \quad x=\frac{-b\pm\sqrt{b^2-4ac}}{2a}$$

NOTE :

i. The expression under the radical b^2-4ac is called the descriminant. It is denoted as D and defined as $D=b^2-4ac$. The value of D determines whether the quadratic equation has two real solutions, one real solution and no real solution according as D is +ve, zero and -ve.

1.8. Nature of the roots

Let $ax^2+bx+c=0, a\neq 0$, where as $D=b^2-4ac$. The nature of the roots depends on D.

i. If $D>0$, then roots are real and distinct.
ii. If $D=0$, then roots are real and equal.
iii. If $D<0$, then roots are imaginary and distinct.
iv. If $D>0$ and a perfect square, then roots are rational.

v. If $D > 0$ and not a perfect square, then roots are irrational.

vi. If $a,b,c, \in R$ and one root is imaginary, say, $\alpha + i\beta$, then its other root will be its conjugate $(\alpha + i\beta)$.

vii. If $a,b,c, \in Q$ and one root is irrational, say, $p + \sqrt{q}$, then its other root will be its conjugate $(p - \sqrt{q})$

viii. If $a = 1, b, c \in Q$ and $D = b^2 - 4ac$ is a perfect square, then both roots are integers.

ix. If $a + b + c = 0$ (i.e. the sum of the co-efficients is zero), then 1 is a root.and the other one is $\frac{c}{a}$

x. If $a - b + c = 0$, then -1 is a root and the otherone is $-\frac{c}{a}$.

xi. If the equation $ax^2 + bx + c = 0$ has real roots α and β, then we write $ax^2 + bx + c = a(x - \alpha)(x - \beta)$.

1.9 Some solved examples

Ex. 1: Prove that the equation $x^2 - 3x + 2 = 0$ has two distinct real roots

Sol.: We have $D = 9 - 8 = 1 > 0$

So, roots are real and distinct.

Ex. 2: Prove that the equation $x^2 + 3x + 5 = 0$ has imajinary roots.

Sol.: We have $D = 9 - 20 = -11 < 0$

Thus, roots are imaginary.

Ex. 3: Prove that the equation $x^2 - 6x + 9 = 0$ has equal roots.

Sol.: We have , $D = 36 - 36 = 0$.

Thus, roots are real and equal.

Ex.4 : If the roots of $x^2 + bx + 1 = 0$ are equal , then find the value of 'b'.

Sol.: Since roots are equal, so $D = 0$.

Thus, $b^2 - 4 = 0 \Rightarrow = \pm 2$

Ex.5 : If the roots of $(a - b)x^2 + (b - c)x + (c - a) = 0$ are equal, then prove that b, a, c are in A.P.

Sol.: Since the sum of co-efficients $= a - b + b - c + c - a = 0$, so 1 is a root.

Also two roots are equal.

Hence roots are 1,1.

Thus, the product of the roots = 1.1 = 1

$\Rightarrow \frac{c - a}{a - b} = 1$

$\Rightarrow c - a = a - b$

$\Rightarrow 2a = b + c$

$\Rightarrow$ b,a,c, are in A.P.

Ex.6: If $(a - b)x^2 + (a - c)x + 2(b + c - 2a) = 0$, then find the roots.

Sol.: As we know that , if $4a + 2b + c = 0$, then $x = 2$ is a root of $ax^2 + bx + c = 0$.

Therefore, $4(a - b) + 2(b - c) + 2(b + c - 2a) = 0$ implies that, 2 is a root of the given equation.

Let the other root be α.

Thus, the product of the roots $= \frac{2(b+c-2a)}{(a-b)}$

$\Rightarrow \alpha.1 = \frac{2(b+c-2a)}{(a-b)}$

$\Rightarrow \alpha = \frac{2(b+c-2a)}{(a-b)}$

$\Rightarrow \alpha = \frac{2(b+c-2a)}{(a-b)}$

Hence the roots are 1, $\frac{2(b+c-2a)}{(a-b)}$.

Ex.7: Find the integral value of 'a' for which both the roots of $ax^2 + (3a + 1)x - 5 = 0$ are integers.

Sol.: The given equation can be written as

$$x^2 + \left(\frac{(3a+1)}{a}\right) + x - \frac{5}{a} = 0$$

$$\Rightarrow x^2 + \left(3 + \frac{1}{a}\right)x - \frac{5}{a} = 0$$

Now, $3 + \frac{1}{a} \in I$, when $a = \pm 1$.

Also, $\frac{5}{a} \in I$, when $a = \pm 5, \pm 1$.

Now, we should check D is a perfect square or not. When $a = 1$, $D = 16 + 20 = 36 = a$ perfect square. Hence, the integral value of a is 1.

Ex. 8: Find the value of 'b', if the equation $bx^2 - 4x + 8 = 0$ has integral roots .

Sol.: The given equation is $bx^2 - 4x + 8 = 0$.

The given equation can be written as $x^2 - 4ax + 8a = 0$, when $b = 1/a$.

The given equation can be written as $x^2 - 4ax + 8a = 0$, when $b = 1/a$.

Now, $D = 16a^2 - 32a = 16(a^2 - 2a) = 16\{(a - 1)^2 - 1\}$ = perfect square when $a = 2$

Also, $-4a$ and $8a$ will be integers when $a = 2$.

Hence, the value of b is 1/2.

Ex.9: If the roots of equation $a(b - c)x^2 + b(c - a)x + c(a - b) = 0$ be equal prove that a,b,c are in H.P.

Sol.: Since the sum of co-efficients$= (b - c) + b(c - a) + c(a - b) = 0$.

So, 1 is a root.

Since both roots are equal, its other root will also be 1

$\therefore$ product of roots $= \frac{c(a-b)}{a(b-c)} = 1$

$\Rightarrow ca - cb = ab - ac$

$\Rightarrow 2ac = b(a+c)$

$\Rightarrow b = \frac{2ac}{a+c}$

$\Rightarrow a, b, .c$ are in H.P..

1.10 Sum and product of the roots

i. If α and β be the roots of $ax^2 + bx + c = 0$, then

a. $\alpha+\beta=-\dfrac{b}{a}$

b. $\alpha\beta=\dfrac{c}{a}$.

ii. If α,β,γ are the roots of $ax^3+bx^2+cx+d=0$, then

a. $\alpha+\beta+\gamma=-\dfrac{b}{a}$

b. $\alpha\beta+\beta\gamma+\gamma\alpha=\dfrac{c}{a}$

c. $\alpha\beta\gamma=-\dfrac{d}{a}$

iii. If α, β, γ, δ are the roots of $ax^4+bx^3+cx^2+dx+e=0$, then

a. $\alpha+\beta+\gamma+\delta=-\dfrac{b}{a}$

b. $\alpha\beta+\alpha\gamma+\alpha\delta+\beta\gamma+\beta\delta+\gamma\delta=\dfrac{c}{a}$

c. $\alpha\beta\gamma+\alpha\beta\delta+\alpha\gamma\delta+\beta\gamma\delta=-\dfrac{d}{a}$

d. $\alpha\beta\gamma\delta=-\dfrac{e}{a}$.

1.11 Symmetic Functions of the roots

In order to find the value of the symmetric function of the roots α and β, we should express the given function in terms of $\alpha+\beta$ and $\alpha\beta$.

i. $(\alpha-\beta)=\sqrt{(\alpha+\beta)^2-4\alpha\beta}$

ii. $\alpha^2+\beta^2=(\alpha+\beta)^2-2\alpha\beta$

iii. $\alpha^3+\beta^3=(\alpha+\beta)^3-3\alpha\beta(\alpha+\beta)$

iv. $\alpha^4+\beta^4=(\alpha^2+\beta^2)^2-2(\alpha\beta)^2=\{(\alpha+\beta)^2-2\alpha\beta\}^2-2(\alpha\beta)^2$

v. $\alpha^5+\beta^5=(\alpha^3+\beta^3)(\alpha^2+\beta^2)-\alpha^2\beta^2(\alpha+\beta)$

vi. $\alpha^7+\beta^7=(\alpha^4+\beta^4)(\alpha^3+\beta^3)-\alpha^3\beta^3(\alpha+\beta)$

1.12 Some solved examples:

Ex.1: If a and b are the roots of $x^2-2x-5=0$, then find value of

i. $\alpha-\beta$

ii. $\alpha^2+\alpha\beta+\beta^2$

iii. $\left(\alpha^3+\dfrac{1}{\alpha}\right)+\left(\beta^3+\dfrac{1}{\beta}\right)+2$

iv. $(\alpha^5+\beta^5+\alpha\beta^3+\beta\alpha^3)$

v. $\left(\alpha^5+\dfrac{1}{\alpha^2}+\beta^5+\dfrac{1}{\beta^2}\right)$

vi. $\left(\alpha^7+\dfrac{1}{\alpha^2\beta}+\beta^7+\dfrac{1}{\beta^2\dot{\alpha}}\right)$.

Sol.: We have $\alpha+\beta=2$ & $\alpha\beta=-5$

i. $\alpha-\beta=\sqrt{(\alpha+\beta)^2-4\alpha\beta}=\sqrt{4+20}=\sqrt{24}=2\sqrt{6}$.

ii. $\alpha^2+\alpha\beta+\beta^2=\alpha^2\beta^2+\alpha\beta=(\alpha+\beta)^2-\alpha\beta=4+5=9$

iii. $\left(\alpha^3+\dfrac{1}{\alpha}\right)+\left(\beta^3+\dfrac{1}{\beta}\right)+2=(\alpha^3+\beta^3)+\left(\dfrac{1}{\alpha}+\dfrac{1}{\beta}\right)$

$=(\alpha+\beta)^3-3\alpha\beta(\alpha+\beta)+\left(\dfrac{\alpha+\beta}{\alpha\beta}\right)$

$=8+30-\dfrac{2}{5}=38-\dfrac{2}{5}$

$=\dfrac{190-2}{5}=\dfrac{188}{5}$

iv. $(\alpha^5+\beta^5+\alpha\beta^3+\beta\alpha^3)=(\alpha^2+\beta^2)(\alpha^3+\beta^3)-\alpha^2\beta^2(\alpha+\beta)+\alpha\beta(\alpha^2+\beta^2)$

$=\{(\alpha+\beta^2)-2\alpha\beta\}\times\{(\alpha+\beta^3)-3\alpha\beta(\alpha+\beta)\}-\alpha^2\beta^2(\alpha+\beta)+\alpha\beta\{(\alpha+\beta)^2-2\alpha\beta\}$

$=14\times38+20-70=532+50=582.$

Ex.2: If the difference of the roots of $2x^2-(a+1)x+a-1=0$ is equal to their product, then prove that, the value of a is 2.

Sol.: Let α & β be the roots.

Given $\alpha-\beta=\alpha\beta$

$\Rightarrow (\alpha-\beta)^2=\alpha^2\beta^2$

$\Rightarrow (\alpha+\beta)^2-4\alpha\beta=\alpha^2\beta^2$

$\Rightarrow \left(\dfrac{a+1}{2}\right)^2-4\left(\dfrac{a-1}{2}\right)=\left(\dfrac{a-1}{2}\right)^2$

$\Rightarrow (a+1)^2-8(a-1)=(a-1)^2$

$\Rightarrow (a+1)^2-(a-1)^2=8(a-1)$

$\Rightarrow 4a=8a-8$

$\Rightarrow -4a=-8$

$\Rightarrow a=2.$

Ex.3: Find $b\in I$ for the equation $5x^2+bx-28=0$, if the roots of a and b satisfy $5\alpha+2\beta=1$.

Sol.: We have, $\alpha+\beta=\dfrac{b}{5}$ and $\alpha\beta=-\dfrac{28}{5}$

Also $5\alpha+2\beta=1$

$\Rightarrow 3\alpha+2(\alpha+\beta)=1$

$\Rightarrow 3\alpha-\dfrac{2b}{5}=1$

$\Rightarrow 3\alpha=\dfrac{2b}{5}+1$

$\Rightarrow \alpha=\dfrac{2b+5}{15}+1$

Again, $\alpha+\beta=-\dfrac{b}{5}$

$\Rightarrow \beta=-\alpha-\dfrac{b}{5}$

$\Rightarrow \beta=-\dfrac{2b+5}{15}-\dfrac{b}{5}$

$=-\dfrac{2b+5+3b}{15}$

$=-\dfrac{5b+5}{15}$

$=-\dfrac{b+1}{3}$

Now, $\alpha\beta = -\frac{28}{5}$

$\Rightarrow \frac{2b+5}{15} \times \frac{b+1}{3} = -\frac{28}{5}$

$\Rightarrow 2b^2 + 7b + 5 = 252$

$\Rightarrow 2b^2 + 7b - 247 = 0$

$\Rightarrow 2b(b+13) - 19(b+13) = 0$

$\Rightarrow (b+13)(2b-19) = 0$

$\Rightarrow b = -13$

Ex.4: Let a and b be the roots of $(x-2)(x-3) + (x-3)(x-1) + (x+1)(x-2) = 0$, then find the value of

$$\frac{1}{(\alpha+1)(\beta+1)} + \frac{1}{(\alpha-2)(\beta-2)} + \frac{1}{(\alpha-3)(\beta-3)}.$$

Sol.: We have $(x-2)(x-3) + (x-3)(x-1) + (x+1)(x-2) = 0$

$\Rightarrow 3x^2 - 10x + 7 = 0$

$\Rightarrow x = 1, \frac{7}{3}$

Now, $\frac{1}{(\alpha+1)(\beta+1)} + \frac{1}{(\alpha-2)(\beta-2)} + \frac{1}{(\alpha-3)(\beta-3)}$

$= \frac{3}{20} - 3 + \frac{3}{4} = \frac{18}{20} - 3 = \frac{9}{10} - 3$

$= \frac{9-30}{10} = -\frac{21}{10}$

Ex. 5: If α and β are the roots of $x^2 - 3x + 1 = 0$, then find the value of $(\alpha^5 + \beta^5)(\alpha^4 + \beta^4)$.

Sol.: We have, $\alpha + \beta = 3$ and $\alpha\beta = 1$.

Now, $(\alpha^5 + \beta^5)(\alpha^4 + \beta^4) = \{(\alpha^2+\beta^2)(\alpha^3+\beta^3) - \alpha^2\beta^2(\alpha+\beta)\}$

$\times \left\{\left\{(\alpha+\beta)^2 - 2\alpha\beta\right\}^2 - 2\alpha^2\beta^2\right\}$

$= \left\{\left\{(\alpha+\beta)^2 - 2\alpha\beta\right\}\left\{(\alpha+\beta)^3 - 3\alpha\beta(\alpha+\beta)\right\} - \alpha^2\beta^2(\alpha+\beta)\right\}$

$\times \left\{\left\{(\alpha+\beta)^2 - 2\alpha\beta\right\}^2 - 2\alpha^2\beta^2\right\} = 5781$

Ex.6: If α is a root of $4x^2 + 2x - 1 = 0$, then prove that $4\alpha^3 - 3\alpha$ is the other root.

Sol.: Since a is a root of $4x^2 + 2x - 1 = 0$.

Then $4\alpha^2 + 2\alpha - 1 = 0$.

$\Rightarrow \alpha = \frac{-1 \pm \sqrt{5}}{4} = \frac{\sqrt{5}-1}{4}, \frac{-\sqrt{5}-1}{4}$

$\Rightarrow \alpha = \sin 18°, -\sin 18°$

Now, $4\alpha^3 - 3\alpha = 4\sin^3 18° - 3\sin 18°$

$= -\sin 54° = -\cos 36° = -\frac{\sqrt{5}+1}{4}$

Hence, $4\alpha^3 - 3\alpha$ is the other root.

1.13 Formation of an Equation

i. If α and β are the roots of $ax^2 + bx + c = 0$, then

$$x^2 - \left(-\frac{b}{a}\right)x + \frac{c}{a} = 0$$

$\Rightarrow x^2 - (\alpha+\beta)x + \alpha\beta = 0$

ii. If α, β and γ are the roots of $ax^3 + bx^2 + cx + d = 0$, then

$$x^3 - \left(-\frac{b}{a}\right)x^2 + \frac{c}{a}x - \frac{d}{a} = 0$$

$\Rightarrow x^3 - (\alpha+\beta+\gamma)x^2 + (\alpha\beta+\beta\gamma+\gamma\alpha)x - \alpha\beta\gamma = 0.$

iii. If $\alpha, \beta, \gamma, \delta$ are the roots of $ax^4 + bx^3 + cx^2 + dx + e = 0$, then

$$x^4 - \left(-\frac{b}{a}\right)x^3 + \left(\frac{c}{a}\right)x^2 - \left(-\frac{d}{a}\right)x + \frac{e}{a} = 0.$$

$\Rightarrow x^4 - (\alpha+\beta+\gamma+\delta)x^3 + (\alpha\beta+\alpha\gamma+\alpha\delta+\beta\gamma+\beta\delta+\gamma\delta)x^2 - (\alpha\beta\gamma+\alpha\beta\delta+\alpha\gamma\delta+\beta\gamma\delta)x + \alpha\beta\gamma\delta = 0$

Ex.1: .If α and β are the roots of $x^2 - 2x + 3 = 0$, then find an equation whose roots are $\alpha + 2, \beta + 2$.

Sol.: Sum of the roots $= \alpha + \beta = 2$ and product of roots $= \alpha\beta = 3$

Now $(\alpha+2) + (\beta+2) = \alpha + \beta + 4 = 2 + 4 = 6$

and $(\alpha+2).(\beta+2) = \alpha\beta + 2(\alpha+\beta) + 4 = 3 + 4 + 4 = 11.$

Hence the required equation is $x^2 - 6x + 11 = 0$

Ex.2: If $\tan\alpha$, $\tan\beta$ are the roots of $x^2 - 3x + 1 = 0$, then find an equation whose roots are $\cot a$, $\cot b$.

Sol.: We have $\tan\alpha + \tan\beta = 3$, $\tan\alpha, \tan\beta = 1$

Now, $\cot\alpha + \cot\beta = \frac{1}{\tan\alpha} + \frac{1}{\tan\beta} = \frac{\tan\beta + \tan\alpha}{\tan\alpha\tan\beta} = \frac{3}{1} = 3$

and $\cot\alpha.\cot\beta = \frac{1}{\tan\alpha}.\frac{1}{\tan\beta} = \frac{1}{\tan\alpha\tan\beta} = 1$

Hence, the required equation is also $x^2 - 3x + 1 = 0$.

Ex.3: If α and β are the roots of $2x^2 - 5x - 4 = 0$, then find an equation whose roots are $\alpha + \frac{1}{\alpha}$, $\beta + \frac{1}{\beta}$.

Sol.: We have, $\alpha + \beta = \frac{5}{2}$ and $\alpha.\beta = -\frac{4}{2} = -2$

Now, $\left(\alpha + \frac{1}{\alpha}\right) + \left(\beta + \frac{1}{\beta}\right) = \alpha + \beta + \frac{1}{\alpha} + \frac{1}{\beta} = \alpha + \beta + \frac{\alpha+\beta}{\alpha\beta}$

$= \frac{5}{2} + \frac{\frac{5}{2}}{-2} = \frac{10}{4} - \frac{5}{4} = \frac{5}{4}$

And $\left(\alpha + \frac{1}{\alpha}\right).\left(\beta + \frac{1}{\beta}\right) = \alpha\beta + \frac{1}{\alpha\beta} + \frac{\alpha}{\beta} + \frac{\beta}{\alpha}$

$= \alpha\beta + \frac{1}{\alpha\beta} + \frac{\alpha^2+\beta^2}{\alpha\beta}$

$= \alpha\beta + \frac{1}{\alpha\beta} + \frac{(\alpha+\beta)^2 - 2\alpha\beta}{\alpha\beta}$

$= -2 - \frac{1}{2} + \frac{\frac{25}{4} + 4}{-2} = -\frac{5}{2} - \frac{41}{8}$

$= -\frac{20}{8} - \frac{41}{8} = -\frac{61}{8}$

Hence the required equation is $x^2 - \frac{5}{4}x - \frac{61}{8} = 0$

$\Rightarrow \quad 8x^2 - 10x - 61 = 0$

Ex.4: If α, β, γ are the roots of $x^3 + 3x^2 + 4x + 2 = 0$, then find an equation whose roots are $\frac{1}{\alpha}, \frac{1}{\beta}, \frac{1}{\gamma}$.

Sol.: We have $\alpha + \beta + \gamma = -3$, $\alpha\beta + \alpha\gamma + \beta\gamma = 4$ and $\alpha\beta\gamma = -2$

Now, $\frac{1}{\alpha}, \frac{1}{\beta}, \frac{1}{\gamma} = \frac{\beta\gamma + \gamma\alpha + \alpha\beta}{\alpha\beta\gamma} = \frac{4}{-2} = -2$

$\frac{1}{\alpha}\frac{1}{\beta} + \frac{1}{\beta}\frac{1}{\gamma} + \frac{1}{\gamma}\frac{1}{\alpha} = \frac{\alpha + \beta + \gamma}{\alpha\beta\gamma} = \frac{-3}{-2} = \frac{3}{2}$

and $\frac{1}{\alpha}.\frac{1}{\beta}.\frac{1}{\gamma} = \frac{1}{\alpha\beta\gamma} = \frac{1}{-2} = -\frac{1}{2}$

Hence the required equation is

$x^3 + 2x^2 + \frac{3}{2}x - \frac{1}{2} = 0$

$\Rightarrow \quad 2x^3 + 4x^2 + 3x - 1 = 0$

Ex. 5: If α,β,γ are the roots of $x^3 - 3x + 2$, then find an equation whose roots are $\alpha^2 + 2$, $\beta^2 + 2$, $\gamma^2 + 2$

Sol.: We have $\alpha + \beta + \gamma = 0$, $\alpha\beta + \beta\gamma + \gamma\alpha = 3$ and $\alpha\beta\gamma = -2$

On solving we get, $\alpha = 1, \beta = 1, \gamma = 2$

Therefore, $\alpha^2 + 2 + \beta^2 + 2 + \gamma^2 + 2 = 1 + 2 + 1 + 2 + 4 + 2 = 12$

$(\alpha^2 + 2)(\beta^2 + 2) + (\alpha^2 + 2)(\gamma^2 + 2) + (\gamma^2 + 2)(\beta^2 + 2)$

$= 3.3 + 3.6 + 6.3 = 45$

and $(\alpha^2 + 2)(\beta^2 + 2)(\gamma^2 + 2) = 3.3.6 = 54$

Hence the required equation is $x^3 - 12x^2 + 45x - 64 = 0$

1.14 Common Roots of Quadratic Equations

Let $a_1x^2 + b_1x + c_1 = 0$ and $a_2x^2 + b_2x + c_2 = 0$ be two quadratic equations.

i. **When one root is common:**

Let α be a common root between two equations. Then $a_1\alpha^2 + b_1\alpha + c_1 = 0$ and $a_2\alpha^2 + b_2\alpha + c_2 = 0$. On solving by cross multiplication method, we get,

$$\frac{\alpha^2}{b_1c_2 - b_2c_1} = \frac{\alpha}{c_1a_2 - c_2a_1} = \frac{1}{a_1b_2 - a_2b_1}$$

We have, $\alpha^2 = (\alpha)^2$

$\Rightarrow \quad \left(\frac{c_1a_2 - c_2a_1}{a_1b_2 - a_2b_1}\right)^2 = \left(\frac{b_1c_2 - b_2c_1}{a_1b_2 - a_2b_1}\right)$

$\Rightarrow \quad (c_1a_2 - c_2a_1)^2 = (b_1c_2 - b_2c_1)(a_1b_2 - a_2b_1)$

Which is the required condition ..

ii. **When two roots are common:**

In this case two equations are identical.

So the co-efficients of x^2, x and constant terms are proportional.

i.e. $\frac{a_1}{a_2} = \frac{b_1}{b_2} = \frac{c_1}{c_2}$

iii. When a_i's, b_i's, c_i's are in real and one root is common, then both roots are common.

i.e. $\frac{a_1}{a_2} = \frac{b_1}{b_2} = \frac{c_1}{c_2}$

iv When a_i's, b_i's, c_i's are in rational and one root is common, then both roots are common.

i.e. $\frac{a_1}{a_2} = \frac{b_1}{b_2} = \frac{c_1}{c_2}$

Note :

1. To find common root between equations $a_1x^2 + b_1x + c_1 = 0$ and $a_2x^2 + b_2x + c_2 = 0$ make the co-efficient of x^2 be same by multiplying the equations by a_2 and a_1 respectively and subtract the resulting equations.
2. If $f(x) = 0$ and $g(x) = 0$ are two polynomial equations having some common roots, then those common root (*s*) is/are also the roots of $h(x) = af(x) + bg(x) = 0$ but not all roots of $h(x)$ are necessarily common roots.

Ex.1: If a,b,c in R and equations $ax^2 + bx + c = 0$ and $x^2 + 2x + 5 = 0$ have a common root, then prove that $a : b : c = 1 : 2 : 5$.

Sol.: The roots of $x^2 + 2x + 5 = 0 \neq$ are imaginary. Sonce one imaginary root is common, so we conclude that both roots are common.

Thus, $\frac{a}{1} = \frac{b}{2} = \frac{c}{5}$

Ex.2: If the equations $ax^2 + bx + c = 0$ and $x^2 + 6x + 7 = 0$ have a common root, then prove that $\frac{a}{1} = \frac{b}{5} = \frac{c}{7}$

Sol.: Here the roots of $x^2 + 6x + 7 = 0$ are irrational. As we know that, if one irrational root is common, then both rotts are common.Thus, the equations have proportional co-efficients. Therefore, $\frac{a}{1} = \frac{b}{5} = \frac{c}{7}$

Ex.3: If the equations $3x^2 + px + 1 = 0$ and $2x^2 + qx + 1 = 0$ have a common root, then prove that $2p^2 + 3q^2 - 5pq + 1 = 0$.

Sol.: The given equations are

$3x^2 + px + 1 = 0$ ...i

and $2x^2 + qx + 1 = 0$ ...ii

Multiplying (i) by 2 and (ii) by 3 and subtracting,we get,

$2px + 2 - 3qx - 3 = 0$

Thus, $(2p - 3q) = 1$

$\Rightarrow \quad x = \frac{1}{2p - 3q}$

Put value of x, in (i), we get,

$3\left(\frac{1}{2p - 3q}\right)^2 + p\left(\frac{1}{2p - 3q}\right) + 1 = 0$

$\Rightarrow \quad 3 + p(2p - 3p) + (2p - 3p)^2 = 0$

$\Rightarrow \quad 3 + (2p^2 - 3pq) + (4p^2 - 9q^2 - 12pq) = 0$

$\Rightarrow \quad (6p^2 + 9q^2 - 15pq + 3) = 0$

$\Rightarrow \quad (2p^2 + 3p^2 - 5pq + 1) = 0$

1.15 Graph of a Quadratic Polynomial.

Let $y = ax^2 + bx + c,\ a \neq 0$

$= a\left(x^2 + \frac{b}{a}x + \frac{c}{a}\right) = a\left(x + \frac{b}{2a}\right)^2 - \frac{b^2}{4a} + c$

$$= a\left(x+\frac{b}{2a}\right)^2 - \frac{b^2-4ac}{4a} = a\left(x+\frac{b}{2a}\right)^2 - \frac{D}{4a}$$

$$\Rightarrow\ y+\frac{D}{4a} = a\left(x+\frac{b}{2a}\right)^2$$

$$\Rightarrow\ Y = aX^2,\ X = \left(x+\frac{b}{2a}\right),\ Y = y+\frac{D}{4a}$$

$$\Rightarrow\ Y = aX^2,\ X = \left(x+\frac{b}{2a}\right),\ Y = y+\frac{D}{4a}$$

Which represents a parabola.with vertices $\left(-\frac{b}{2a}, -\frac{D}{4a}\right)$.

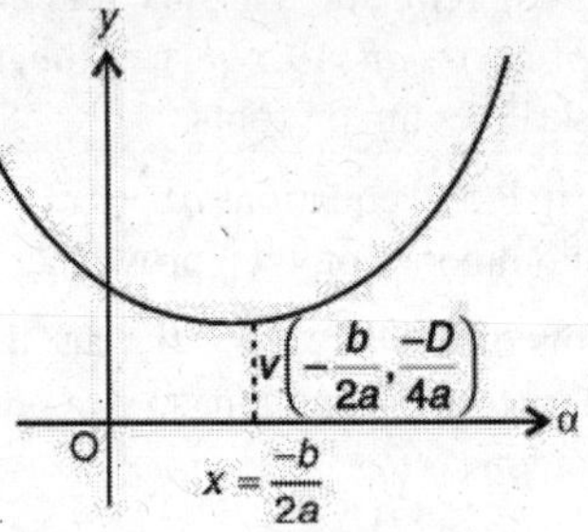

CASE 1. When $a > 0$

In this case we get, an upward parabola. This quadratic polynomial will provide us a minimum value. and the minimum value is $-\frac{D}{4a}$, where the point of minima is $x = -\frac{b}{2a}$

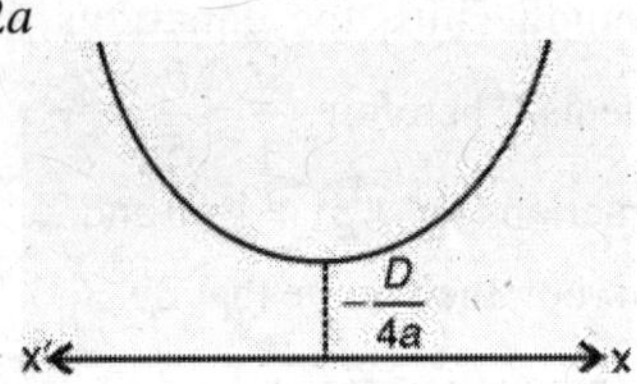

CASE 2. When $a > 0$

In this case, we get a downward parabola. So, the quadratic polynomial will provide us a maximum value and the maximum value is also $-\frac{D}{4a}$, where the point of maxima is $x = -\frac{b}{2a}$

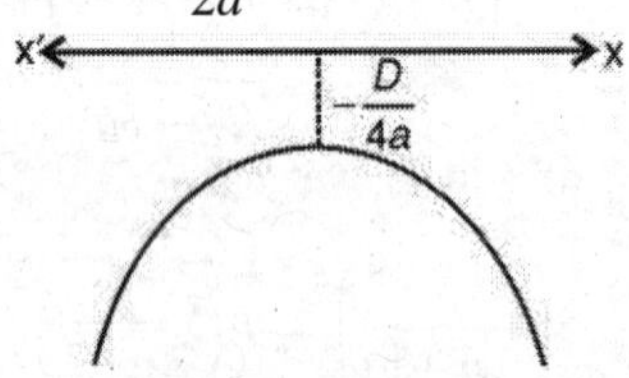

Ex.1: Find the minimum value of $f(x) = x^2 + x + 1$

SOL.: Here $a = 1 > 0$ and $D = 1 - 4 = -3 < 0$. Thus the expression $f(x)$ will provide us the minimum value and the min value is

$$= -\frac{D}{4a} = -\frac{1-3}{41} = \frac{3}{4}$$

Ex.2: Find the maximum value of $f(x) = -x^2 + 2x - 10$

SOL.: Here $a = -1 < 0$ and $D = 4 - 40 = -36$.

Thus the expression $f(x)$ will provide us the maximum value and the maximum value is $= -\frac{D}{4a} = -\frac{-36}{4(-1)} = -9$.

NOTE :

1. Let $f(x) = ax^2 + bx + c$.
   If $a > 0$, then range of the quadratic polynomial is [min Value, ∞). If $a < 0$, then range of the quadratic polynomial is $(-\infty$, max value]

CASE 3. If $a > 0, D < 0 \Leftrightarrow f(x) > 0$

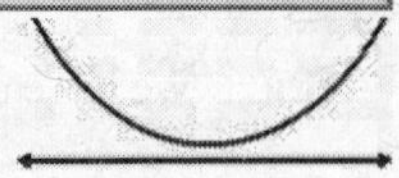

Ex.1: Let $f(x) = x^2 + 2x + 4$

Here $a = 1 > 0$ and $D = 4 - 16 = -12 < 0$

Thus $f(x) > 0$ for every x in R.

CASE 4. If $a < 0, D > 0 \Leftrightarrow f(x) < 0$

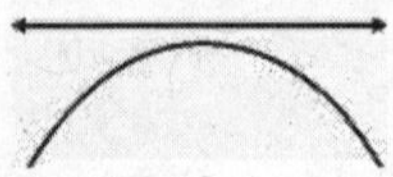

Ex.2: Let $f(x) = -x^2 + 3x - 8$

Here, $a = -1 < 0$, $D = 9 - 32 = -23 < 0$

Thus, $f(x) < 0$ for every x in R

Ex.3: Find the value of 'b' for which $x^2 + bx + 1 > 0$.

SOL.: Since $a = 1 > 0$ and $f(x) > 0$, then $D < 0$

Thus, $b^2 - 4 < 0$

$\Rightarrow\quad (b+2)(b-2) < 0$

$\Rightarrow\quad -2 > b > 2$

$\Rightarrow\quad b \in (-2, 2)$

CASE 5. Range in restricted domain.

Consider $f(x) = ax^2 + bx + c\ \forall \in [d, e]$.

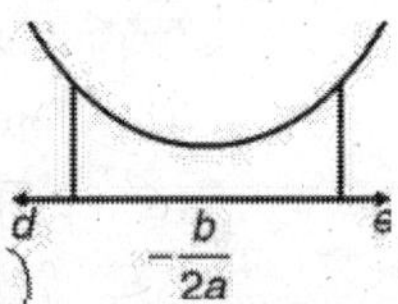

First we find the values of $f(d)$, $f(e)$, $f\left(-\frac{b}{2a}\right)$

$$\text{Max Value} = M = \max\left\{f(d), f(e), f\left(-\frac{b}{2a}\right)\right\}$$

$$\text{Min Value} = m = \min\left\{f(d), f(e), f\left(-\frac{b}{2a}\right)\right\}.$$

Ex.1: Find the range of $f(x) = 2x^2 - 3x + 2$ in [0,2].

SOL.: We have $f\left(-\frac{b}{2a}\right) = f\left(\frac{3}{4}\right) = 2\left(\frac{3}{4}\right)^2 - 3\left(\frac{3}{4}\right) + 2$

$$= \frac{9}{8} - \frac{9}{4} + 2 = 2 - \frac{9}{8} = \frac{7}{8}$$

$f(0) = 2$ and $f(2) = .(2)^2 - 3.2 + 2 = 8 - 6 + 2 = 4$.

Thus, the max value = 4 and the min value = $\frac{7}{8}$.

Hence, $R_f = \left[\frac{7}{8}, 4\right]$.

Ex.2: Find the range of $f(x) = 3x^2 - x + 5$ in [1,2]

SOL. We have, $f\left(\frac{1}{3}\right) = 3\left(\frac{1}{3}\right)^2 - \frac{1}{3} + 5 = 3.\frac{1}{9} - \frac{1}{3} + 5 = 5$

$f(1) = 3 - 1 + 5 = 7$ and $f(2) = 3.(2)^2 - 2 + 5 = 12 - 2 + 5 = 15$.

Thus, the max value = 15 and min value = 5.

Hence, $R_f = [5, 15]$.

CASE 6. Maximum and Minimum values of a Rational Function:

Let $y = \dfrac{ax^2+bx+c}{px^2+qx+r}$

To find the max and min values of y we should remember the following points.

i. First we make it a quadratic equation of x.

ii. Since x, y in R, then $D \ge 0$

iii. and then solve the quadratic inequation of y.

iv. If $y \in [A,B]$, then max value $= A$ and Min Value $= B$

v. If $y \in (-\infty, A] \cup [B, \infty)$, then the maximum and minimum values are not defined.

vi. If $y \in (-\infty, \infty)$, then the maximum and minimum values are also not defined.

Ex.1: If x be a real, then find the max and min values of

$$f(x) = \frac{x^2-x+1}{x^2+x+1}$$

SOL.: Let $\quad y = \dfrac{x^2-x+1}{x^2+x+1}$

$\Rightarrow \quad y(x^2+x+1) = x^2-x+1$

$\Rightarrow \quad (y-1)x^2+(y+1)x+(y-1)=0$

Since x is real, so $D \ge 0$

$\Rightarrow \quad (y+1)x^2-4(y-1)^2 \ge 0$

$\Rightarrow \quad (y+1)^2-(2y-2)^2 \ge 0$

$\Rightarrow \quad (y+1+2y-2)(y+1-2y+2) \ge 0$

$\Rightarrow \quad (3y-1)(-y+3) \ge 0$

$\Rightarrow \quad (3y-1)(y-3) \le 0$

$\Rightarrow \quad \dfrac{1}{3} \le y \le 3$

Hence, the Max. Value = 3 and the Min value = 1/3.

Ex.2: Find the max and min values of $f(x) = \dfrac{x}{x^2+x+1}$.

We have $f(x) = \dfrac{x}{x^2+x+1} = \dfrac{1}{x+\frac{1}{x}+1}$

Let $g(x) = x+\dfrac{1}{x}+1$. Then $g'(x) = 1-\dfrac{1}{x^2}$

For max or min, $g'(x)=0$ gives $1-\dfrac{1}{x^2}=0 \Rightarrow x=\pm 1$

Hence the max Value $= -1$ at $x = -1$ and the min value $= \dfrac{1}{3}$ at $x = 1$.

Ex.3: Find the max or min values of $f(x) \dfrac{3^{2x}-3^x+1}{3^{2x}+3^x+1}$.

SOL.: Let $t = 3^x$, then given expression reduces to

$$f(t) = \frac{t^2-t+1}{t^2+t+1}$$

Thus the max value = 3 and the min value $= \dfrac{1}{3}$.

Ex.4: If $\dfrac{mx^2+3x+4}{x^2+3x+4} < 5$ for all x in R, then find the possible values of m.

SOL. We have $\dfrac{mx^2+3x+4}{x^2+3x+4} < 5$

$\Rightarrow mx^2+3x+4 < 5(x^2+3x+4)$

$\Rightarrow (m-5)x^2+3x-15x+4-20<0$

$\Rightarrow (m-5)x^2-12-16<0$

Thus $(m-5)<0$ and $144+64(m-5)<0$

$\Rightarrow m<5, 9+4(m-5)<0$

$\Rightarrow m<5,\ 4m-11<0$

$\Rightarrow m<5, m<\dfrac{11}{4}$

Hence the values of $m \in \left(\infty, \dfrac{11}{4}\right)$.

15. Resolution of a second degree expression in x and y

Let $f(x,y) = ax^2+2hxy+by^2+2gx+2fy+c$

Now, $f(x,y)=0$ gives $ax^2+2(hy+g)x+(by^2+2fy+c)=0$

$$\Rightarrow \quad x = \frac{-2(hy+g)\pm 2\sqrt{(hy+g)^2-a(by^2+2fy+c)}}{2a}$$

$$= \frac{-(hy+g)\pm\sqrt{(hy+g)^2-a(by^2+2fy+c)}}{a}$$

$$\Rightarrow ax+hy+g = \pm\sqrt{(h^2-ab)y^2+2(hg-af)y+(g^2-ac)}$$

Now in order that $f(x,y)$ may be the product of two linear factors of the form $px+qy+r$, the quantity under the radical sign must be a perfect square, hence under the radical sign must be a perfect square, hence

$(hg-af)^2 = (h^2-ab)(g^2-bc)$

$\Rightarrow \quad (h^2g^2+a^2f^2-2afgh) = (g^2h^2-g^2ab-h^2bc+a^2bc)$

$\Rightarrow \quad abc+2fgh-af^2-bg^2-ch^2=0$

$$\Rightarrow \quad \begin{vmatrix} a & h & g \\ h & b & f \\ g & f & c \end{vmatrix} = 0$$

Ex.1: Find the values of m for which expression $12x^2-10xy+2y^2+11x-5y+m$ as a product of linear factors.

SOL.: We have $a=12$, $h=-5$, $b=2$, $g=11/2$, $f=-5/2$ and $c=m$

Since the given expression as a product of two linear factors, so we can write

$$\Rightarrow \quad \begin{vmatrix} a & h & g \\ h & b & f \\ g & f & c \end{vmatrix} = 0$$

$$\Rightarrow \quad \begin{vmatrix} 12 & -5 & 11/2 \\ -5 & 2 & -5/2 \\ 11/2 & -5/2 & m \end{vmatrix} = 0$$

On solving we get, $m = 2$

Ex.2: If x is real and $4y + 4xy + x + 6 = 0$, then find the set of values of x for which y is real.

Sol.: We have $4y + 4xy + x + 6 = 0$

$\Rightarrow \quad 4y^2 + 4x\,y + x + 6 = 0$

Since $y \in R$, $D \geq 0$

$\Rightarrow \quad 16x^2 - 16(x+6) \geq 0$

$\Rightarrow \quad x^2 - x - 6 \geq 0$

$\Rightarrow \quad (x-3)(x+2) \geq 0$

$\Rightarrow \quad x \in (-\infty, -2] \cup [3, \infty)$

16. Location of Roots

Let $f(x) = ax^2 + bx + c$ where $a \neq 0$ and α, β be the roots of $f(x) = 0$.

For simplicity, we can assume that $\alpha \leq \beta$ where $\alpha = \dfrac{-b-\sqrt{D}}{2a}$ and $\beta = \dfrac{-b+\sqrt{D}}{2a}$, $D = b^2 - 4ac$

1. When both roots are +ve
   i. Sum of the roots > 0
   ii. Product of the roots > 0
   iii. For real roots, $D \geq 0$

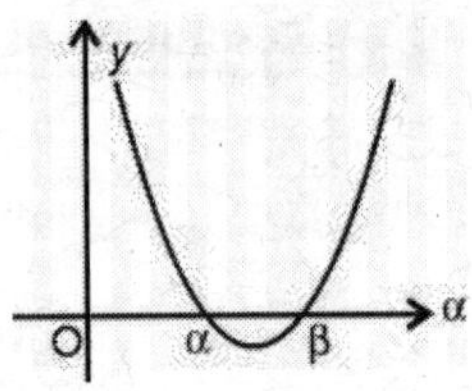

2. When both roots are –ve
   i. Sum of the roots < 0
   ii. Product of the roots > 0
   iii. For real roots, $D \geq 0$

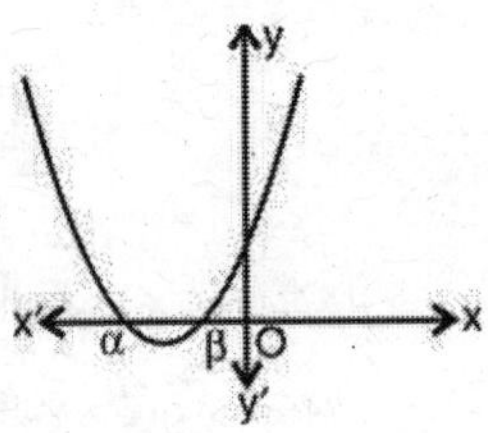

3. When roots are of opposite signs
   i. Product of the roots < 0

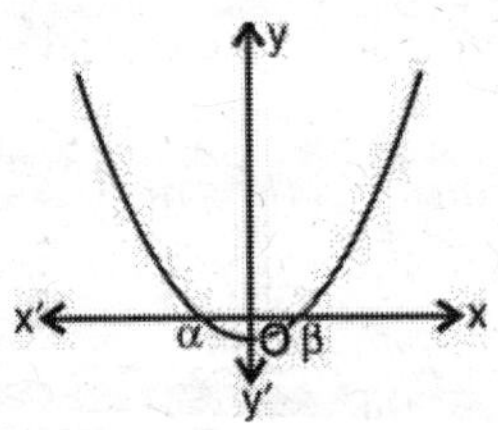

4. When boths roots are greater than k.
   i. $D \geq 0$ ii. $af(k) > 0$ iii. $\alpha + \beta < 2k$

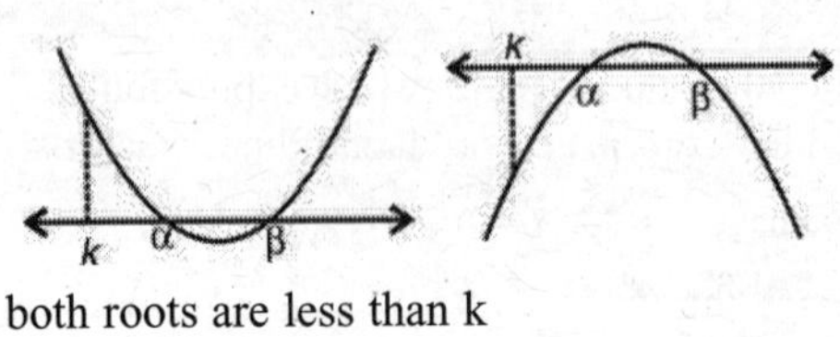

5. When both roots are less than k
   i. D 0 ii. $af(k) > 0$ iii. $\alpha + \beta < 2k$

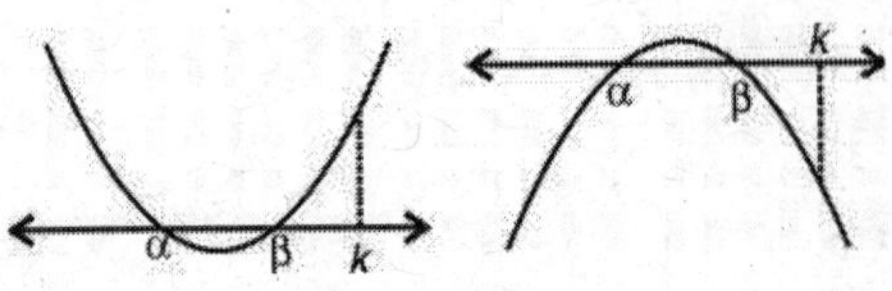

6. When k lies between the roots
   i $D > 0$ ii. $af(k) < 0$

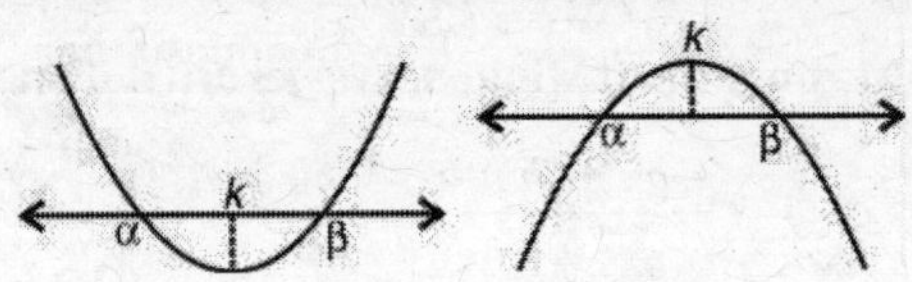

7. When both roots are confined by k_1 and k_2 such that $k_1 < k_2$
   i. $D \geq 0$ ii. $af(k_1) > 0$
   iii. $af(k_2) > 0$ iv. $k_1 < \dfrac{\alpha+\beta}{2} < k_2$

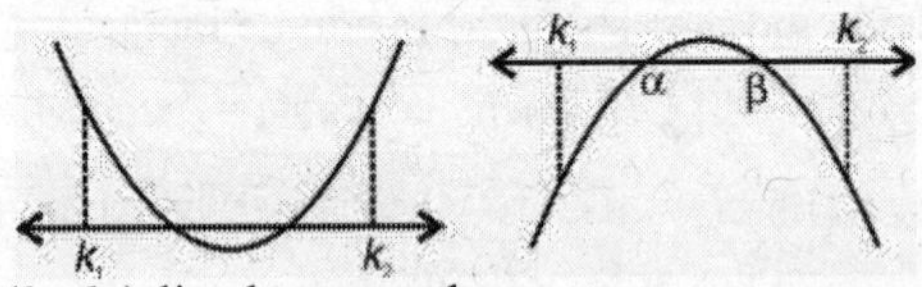

8. When (k_1, k_2) lies between the roots.
   i. $D > 0$ ii. $af(k_1) > 0$ iii. $af(k_2) > 0$

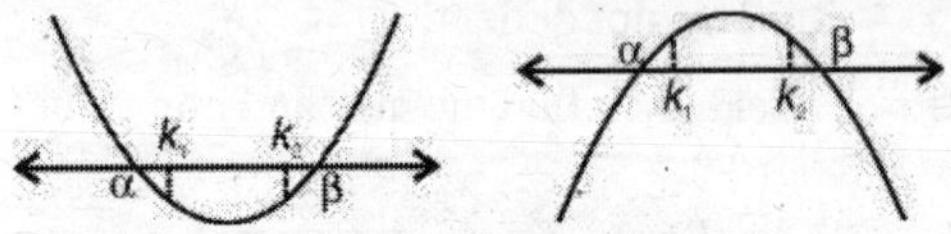

9. When exactly one root lies in (k_1, k_2).
   i. $D > 0$ ii. $f(k_1)f(k_2) < 0$

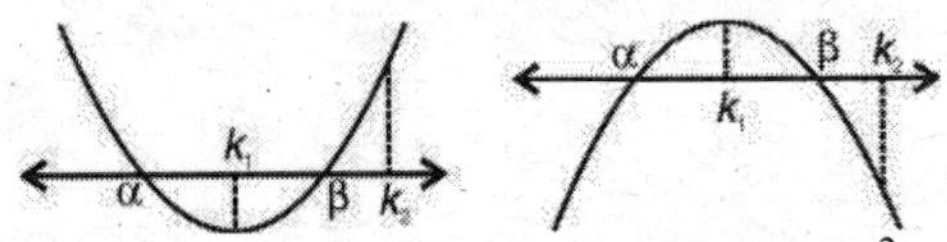

Ex.1: Find values of 'm' for which both roots of $x^2 + mx + 1 = 0$ are greater than unity.

Sol.: We have,

i. $D \geq 0$ ii. $af(1) > 0$ iii. $\alpha + \beta > 2$

Now from (i), $m^2 - 4 \geq 0$

$\Rightarrow (m+2)(m-2) \geq 0$

$\Rightarrow m \in (-\infty, -2) \cup (2, \infty)$ ...(A)

Now from (ii), $af(1) > 0$

$\Rightarrow 1.(1 + m + 1) > 0$

$\Rightarrow m + 2 > 0$

$\Rightarrow m > -2$ .... (B)

From (iii), we get , $-m > 2 \quad m < -2 \Rightarrow$ ...(C)

From (A), (B) and (C), we get, $m \in (-8, -2)$.

Ex.2: Find the values of m for which both roots of $x^2 - (m-3)x + m = 0$ are less than 2.

Sol.: We have,

i. $D \geq 0$ ii. $af(2) > 0$ iii. $\alpha + \beta > 4$

Now from (i), we get, $(m-3)^2 - 4m \geq 0$

$\Rightarrow (m-1)(m-9) \geq 0$

$\Rightarrow m \in (-\infty, 1] \cup [9, \infty)$ ...(A)

Also from (ii), we get, $1.(1 - m + 3 + m) > 0$

$\Rightarrow 4 > 0$

$\Rightarrow m \in R$ ...(B)

Again, from (iii), we get, $m - 3 < 4$

$\Rightarrow m > 7$ ....(C)

Thus, from (A), (B) and (C), we get, $m \in (-\infty, 1) \cup (1, 7)$.

Ex.3: If roots of $ax^2+bx+c=0$ are of opposite sign lying in the interval $(-2, 2)$, then prove that $1+\frac{c}{4a}-\left|\frac{b}{2a}\right|>0$

Sol.: Since roots are of opposite sign, so $af(-2)>0$ & $af(2)>0$

$\Rightarrow a(4a-2b+c)>0$ and $a(4a+2b+c)>0$

$\Rightarrow \left(a-\frac{b}{2}+\frac{c}{4}\right)>0$ and $\left(a+\frac{b}{2}+\frac{c}{4}\right)>0$

$\Rightarrow \left(1-\frac{b}{2a}+\frac{c}{4a}\right)$ and $\left(1+\frac{b}{2a}+\frac{c}{4a}\right)$

$\Rightarrow \left(1+\frac{c}{4a}-\left|\frac{b}{2a}\right|\right)$

Hence, the result.

Ex.4: Find value of m, if both roots of $(m-2)x^2-2x+(m-3)=0$ are of opposite sign.

Sol.: Since the roots are of opposite sign, so product of their roots is negative.

Therefore, $(m-2)(m-3)<0$

$\Rightarrow 2<m<3$

Level – I Questions Based on Fundamentals

ABC of Quadratic Equation

1. Find the roots of the equation :

i. $x^2-2x-8=0$

ii. $x^2-4x+1=0$

iii. $x^2+14x+45=0$

iv. $8x^2+12x+3=0$

v. $\sqrt{\frac{x}{1-x}}+\sqrt{\frac{1-x}{x}}=\frac{13}{6}$

vi. $\sqrt{x}+\sqrt{x-\sqrt{1-x}}=1$.

vii If $x=\sqrt{2+\sqrt{2+\sqrt{2....\text{to }\infty}}}$, then find x.

viii. If $x=2+2^{2/3}+2^{1/3}$, then find the value of x^3-6x^2+6x.

ix. If $xy=2(x+y)$; $x\le y$ and $x, y\in N$, then find the number of solution of the equation.

x. If $p(x)=ax^2+bx$ and $q(x)=lx^2+mx+n$ with $p(1)=q(1)$; $p(2)-q(2)=1$ and $p(3)-q(3)=4$, then find $p(4)-q(4)$.

xi. If a, b, c are three real numbers, then find the roots of the equation $\frac{(x-b)(x-c)}{(a-b)(a-c)}a^2+\frac{(x-a)(x-c)}{(b-a)(b-c)}b^2+\frac{(x-b)(x-a)}{(c-b)(c-a)}c^2-x^2=0$

xii. Find number of real solutions of $x-\frac{1}{x^2-4}=2-\frac{1}{x^2-4}$.

xiii. Find the number of real roots of equation $(x-1)^2+(x-2)^2+(x-3)^2=0$

xiv. Find the roots of x, if $\frac{x-ab}{a+b}+\frac{x-ac}{a+c}+\frac{x-bc}{b+c}=a+b+c$

xv. Find the roots of x, if $\frac{x-a}{b+c}+\frac{x-b}{c+a}+\frac{x-c}{a+b}=3$.

xvi. Find the number of roots of x, if $\frac{x-b}{a-b}+\frac{x-a}{b-a}=1$.

xvii. Find values of a, if $(a^2-3a+2)x^2+(|a|-1)x+(a^2-5a+4)$ gives more than two roots.

xviii. If x and y are integers and $(x-8)(x-10)=2^y$, then prove that the number of solution of the pair (x,y) is only 1.

Nature of Roots

2. i. Prove that roots of equation $x^2-2(a+b)x+2(a^2+b^2)=0$ are imaginary and distinct.

ii. If roots of equation $(c^2-ab)x^2-2(a^2-bc)x+(b^2-ac)=0$ be equal, then prove that either $a=0$ or $a^3+b^3+c^3=3abc$

iii. For what values of m, the roots of equation $x^2-2(1+3m)x+7(3+2m)=0$ will be equal?

iv. The product of roots of equation $x^2-3\lambda x+2.e^{2\log\lambda}-1=0$ is 7. If the roots be real, then prove that $\lambda=2$

v. If the roots of equation $(b-c)x^2+(c-a)x+(a-b)=0$ be equal, then prove that a, b, c are in A.P.

vi. If roots of equation $a(b-c)x^2+b(c-a)x+c(a-b)=0$ has equal roots, prove that a,b, c are in H.P.

vii. If a,b,c are positive and are in A.P, prove that roots of the quadratic equation $ax^2+bx+c=0$ are real for $\left|\frac{c}{a}-7\right|\ge 4\sqrt{3}$.

viii. Discuss the nature of roots of equation $4ax^2+3bx+2c=0$, where $a, b, c\in R$ and are connected by relation $a+b+c=0$.

ix. If the roots of equation $x^2-2cx+ab=0$ be real and unequal, then prove that roots of $x^2-2(a+b)x+(a^2+b^2+2c^2)=0$.

x. If roots of equation $(a-1)(x^2+x+1)^2=(a+1)(x^4+x^2+1)$ are real and distinct, then prove that $a^2-4>0$.

Sum and Product of Roots

3. i. If a and b are the roots of equation $x^2-5x+6=0$, then find the value of $\alpha^2+\beta^2, \alpha^3+\beta^3., \alpha-\beta, \alpha^5+\beta^5, \alpha^7+\beta^7$.

ii. If the product of roots of equation $mx^2-2x+(2m-1)=0$ is 3, then find the value of m.

iii. If the equation $(k-2)x^2-(k-4)x-2=0$ has difference of roots as 3, then find the value of k.

iv. If α, β and the roots of the equation $ax^2+bx+c=0$, then find the value of $\frac{1}{(a\alpha+b)}+\frac{1}{(a\beta+b)}$.

v. If r be the ratio of the roots of equation $ax^2+bx+c=0$, then prove that $\frac{(r+1)^2}{r}=\frac{b^2}{ac}$

vi. If the roots of equation $\frac{1}{x+p}+\frac{1}{x+q}=\frac{1}{r}$ are equal in magnitude but in opposite sign, then prove that $p+q=2r$, and the product of the roots is $-\frac{1}{2}\left(p^2+q^2\right)$.

vii. For the equation $3x^2+px+3=0$, $p>0$, if one of roots is square of the other, then find p.

viii. If one root of equation $ax^2+bx+c=0$ be the square of the other, then prove that $b^3+ac^2+a^2c=3abc$

ix. If the roots of equation $3x^2+2(k^2+1)x+(k^2-3k+2)=0$ be of opposite signs, then prove that $1<k<2$.

x. In a triangle PQR, $\angle R=\pi/2$. If $\tan\left(\frac{P}{2}\right)$ and $\tan\left(\frac{Q}{2}\right)$ are the roots of equation $ax^2+bx+c=0$, $a\neq 0$, then prove that $a+b=c$.

xi. Let p and q be the roots of the equation $x^2-2x+A=0$ and let r and s be the roots of the equation $x^2-18x+B=0$. If $p<q<r<s$ are in A.P., then Find A and B.

xii. If the roots of equation $ax^2+cx+c=0$ are in the ratio $p:q$, then prove that $\sqrt{\frac{p}{q}}+\sqrt{\frac{q}{p}}+\sqrt{\frac{c}{a}}=0$.

4. i. If α,β are the roots of equation $x^2+px+q=0$ and γ,δ are roots of $x^2+px-r=0$, then find value of $(\alpha-\gamma)(\alpha-\delta)$.

ii. If α,β are the roots of equation $x^2+px+1=0$ and γ,δ are the roots of the equation $x^2+qx+1=0$, then find value of $(\alpha-\gamma)(\beta-\gamma)(\alpha+\delta)(\beta+\delta)$.

iii. If α,β are the roots of $x^2+px-q=0$ and γ,δ are roots of $x^2+px+r=0$, prove that $(\alpha-\gamma)(\alpha-\delta)=(\beta-\gamma)(\beta-\delta)$ $=q+r$

iv. If α,β are the roots of $x^2-x+p=0$ and γ,δ are the roots of $x^2-4x+q=0$. If $\alpha,\beta,\gamma,\delta$ are in G.P, then find the intgral values of p and q.

v. If one root of the equation $x^2-px+q=0$ be twice the other, show that $2p^2=9q$.

vi. If the difference of the roots of $x^2-px+q=0$ is unity, then prove that

a. $p^2-4q=1$ b. $p^2+4q^2=(1+2q)^2$

vii. If α,β are the roots of the equation $x^2-x-1=0$, then find the value of $\sum\left(\frac{1-\alpha}{1+\alpha}\right)$.

viii. If α,β,γ are the roots of $x^3+px^2+qx+r=0$, then prove that $\left(\alpha-\frac{1}{\beta\gamma}\right)\left(\beta-\frac{1}{\gamma\alpha}\right)\left(\gamma-\frac{1}{\alpha\beta}\right)=-\frac{(1+r)^3}{r^2}$.

ix. If α,β are roots of $6x^2-6x+1=0$, then prove that $\frac{1}{2}(p+q\alpha+r\alpha^2+s\alpha^3)+\frac{1}{2}(p+q\beta+r\beta^2+s\beta^3)$ is $\frac{p}{1}+\frac{q}{2}+\frac{r}{3}+\frac{s}{4}$.

x. If α,β are the roots of $ax^2+2bx+c=0$ and $\alpha+\delta,\beta+\delta$ are the roots of $Ax^2+2Bx+C=0$, then prove that

$$\frac{b^2-ac}{B^2-AC}=\left(\frac{a}{A}\right)^2.$$

xi. Let a,b,c,d be real numbers in G.P. If u,v,w satisfy the system of equations $u+2v+3w=6$, $4u+5v+6w=12$, $6u+9v=4$, then prove that the roots of the equation $\left(\frac{1}{u}+\frac{1}{v}+\frac{1}{w}\right)x^2+[(b-c)^2(c-a)^2+(a-b)^2]x+u+v+w=0$ and $20x^2+10(a-d)^2x-9=0$ are reciprocals to each other.

Formation of Quadratic Equation with Given Roots

5. i. Find the quadratic equation whose one root is $2-i\sqrt{3}$.

ii. If α,β are the roots of a quadratic equation $x^2-3x+5=0$, then find the equation whose roots are $(\alpha^2-3\alpha+7)$ and $(\beta^2-3\beta+7)$.

iii. If α,β are roots of the equation $x^2-5x+6=0$ then find the equation whose roots are $\alpha+3$ and $\beta+3$.

iv. If α,β,γ are the roots of the equation $9x^3-7x+6=0$, then find the equation whose roots are $3\alpha+2, 3\beta+2, 3\gamma+2$.

v. If α and β are the roots of $2x^2-3x-6=0$ then find the equation whose roots are α^2+2 and β^2+2.

vi. If $\alpha\neq\beta$ and $\alpha^2=5\alpha-3$, $\beta^2=5\beta-3$, form the quadratic equation whose roots are $\frac{\alpha}{\beta}$ and $\frac{\beta}{\alpha}$.

vii. If the roots of the equation $(x-a)(x-b)-k=0$ be c and d, then prove that the roots of equation $(x-c)(x-d)+k=0$ are a and b.

viii. If α,β are the roots of the equation $(x-a)(x-b)+c=0$, then find the roots of the equation $(x-\alpha)(x-\beta)=c$

ix. α,β are the roots of equation $\lambda(x^2-x)+x+5=0$. If λ_1 and λ_2 be the two values of λ, determined from the equation $\frac{\alpha}{\beta}+\frac{\beta}{\alpha}=\frac{4}{5}$, then prove that the value of $\frac{\lambda_1}{\lambda_2}+\frac{\lambda_2}{\lambda_1}=254$.

6. If α,β are the roots of $x^2-(x+1)p-c=0$ then find the value of $\frac{\alpha^2+2\alpha+1}{\alpha^2+2\alpha+c}+\frac{\beta^2+2\beta+1}{\beta^2+2\beta+c}$

Common Roots of Two Quadratic Equations

7. i. If the equation $x^2+2x+3\lambda=0$, $2x^2+3x+5\lambda=0$ have a non zero common root, then find λ.

ii. If the equations $ax^2+bx+c=0$ and $cx^2+bx+a=0$, $a\neq c$ have a negative common root, then find the values of $a-b+c$.

iii. If the equation $x^2+ax+b=0$ and $x^2+bx+a=0$ have a common root, then find the value of $a+b$.

iv. If equations $ax^2+2cx+b=0$ and $ax^2+2bx+c=0$ $(b\neq c)$ have a common root, then prove that $a+4b+4c=0$.

v. If $x^2+mx+1=0$ and $(a-b)x^2+(b-c)x+(c-a)=0$ have both roots common, then prove that

a. $m=-2$ b. b, a, c are in A.P.

c. $2a-b-c=0$.

vi. If the equations $ax^2+bx+c=0$ and $x^2+2x+3=0$ have common root, then prove that $a:b:c=1:2:3$.

vii. If the equations $ax^2+bx+c=0$ and $x^3+3x^2+3x+2=0$ have two common roots then prove that $a=b=c$.

viii. Find the value of a for which the equation $x^3+ax+1=0$ and $ax^4+ax^2+1=0$ have a common root.

SIGN OF QUADRATIC EXPRESSION

8. i. Sove for x:

a. $x^2-2x-3<0$ b. $x^2-3x+2>0$

ii. For what values of k is inequality $x^2-(k-3)x-k+6>0$ valid for all real x? **ANS.:** $-3<k<5$

iii. For what values of k, inequality $(k-2)x^2+8x+k+4<0$ satisfies for all real values of x? **ANS.:** $-6<k<4$

iv For what values of m, equation $mx^2-(m+1)x+2m-1=0$ does not possesses any real g roots. **ANS.:** $m>1$ & $m<-\frac{1}{7}$

v. For what values of p curves $y=2px+1$ and $y=(p-6)x^2-2$ do not intersect? **ANS.:** $-3<p<6$.

vi. For what values of k, curve $y=x^2+kx+4$ touches the x-axis.? **ANS.:** $k=\pm 4$

vii. Find integral values of k for which equation $(k-12)x^2+2(k-12)x+2=0$ possess no real roots. **ANS.:** $12<k<14$.

viii. Find the value of 'b' $x^2+bx+1>0$. **ANS.:** $-2<b<2$

ix. Find a, if $x^2+2ax+10-3a>0, \forall x \in R$. **ANS.:** $-5<a<2$

x. Find λ, if $x^2-2(4\lambda-1)x+(15\lambda^2-2\lambda-7)>0 \; \forall x \in R$. **ANS.:** $2<\lambda<4$.

RANGE OF A QUADRATIC POLYNOMIAL

9. i. Find the maximum and minimum values of

a. $f(x)=x^2+2x+4$

b. $f(x)=x^2+4x+4$

c. $f(x)=x^2-5x+4$

d. $f(x)=-x^2+x-4$

e. $f(x)=-x^2+6x-9$

f. $f(x)=-x^2+6x-4$

ii. Find the ranges of

a. $f(x)=x^2+x+1$

b. $f(x)=x^2+3x+2$

c. $f(x)=-x^2+3x-10$

iii. Let $p(x)=ax^2+bx+8$ is a quadratic polynomial. If the minimum value of $p(x)$ is 6 at $x=2$ then find the value of a and b.

iv. Find the range of $f(x)=2x^2-3x+2$ in $[0,2]$

v. Find the range of $f(x)=-x^2+6x-1$ in $[0,4]$

MAXIMUM AND MINIMUM VALUES OF A RATIONAL FUNCTION

10. i. If $x \in R$, find the least and greatest value of the expression $\frac{x^2-6x+1}{x^2+6x+1}$.

ii. If $y=\frac{x^2-2x+4}{x^2+2x+4}, \forall x \in R$, then find max and min value of y.

iii. If $y=\frac{x^2-x+1}{x^2+x+1}$, " $x \in R$, then prove that $\frac{1}{3} \le y \le 3$.

iv. Find the greatest and least value of $y=\frac{x^2+x+1}{x^2-x+1}$.

v. If x is real, prove that maximum value of $\frac{3x^2+9x+17}{3x^2+9x+7}$ is 41.

vi. If $x \in R$, then prove that, $\frac{x^2+2x+a}{x^2+4x+3a}$ can take all real values if $a \in [0,1]$.

vii. If $y=\tan x \cot 3x$, $\forall x \in R$, then find y.

viii. Find the range of expression $f(\theta)=\frac{\tan^2\theta-2\tan\theta-8}{\tan^2\theta-4\tan\theta-5}$.

ix. Find the range of expression

$$f(\theta)=\frac{(\cot^2\theta+5)(\cot^2\theta+10)}{(\cot^2\theta+1)}$$

x Find range of values a, such that $f(x)$

$$=\frac{ax^2+2(a+1)x+9a-4}{x^2-8x+32}$$ is always negative.

xi. Show that the function $z=2x^2+2xy+y^2-2x+2y+2$ is not smaller that -3.

xii. Find the minimum value of

$$f(x)=\frac{\left(x+\frac{1}{x}\right)^6-\left(x^6+\frac{1}{x^6}\right)-2}{\left(x+\frac{1}{x}\right)^3+\left(x^3+\frac{1}{x^3}\right)}$$ for $x>0$

xiii. Let x be a positive real. Find the maximum possible value of the expression $y=\frac{x^2+2-\sqrt{x^4+4}}{x}$

RESOLUTION INTO TWO LINEAR FACTORS

11. i. Find the values of m for which the expression $2x^2+mxy+3y^2-5y-2$ may be resolve into two linear factors.

ii. Find value of k for which expression $x^2+2xy+ky^2+2x+k=0$ may resolve into two linear factors.

iii. If the expression $ax^2+by^2+cz^2+2ayz+2bzx+2cxy$ be resolved into two rational factors, then prove that, $a^3+b^3+c^3=3abc$.

iv. If x, y and z are real and distinct, then prove that $f(x,y)=x^2+4y^2+9z^2-6yz-3zx-2xy$ is always non negative.

v. If x is real and $4y^2+4xy+x+6=0$, then find the complete set of values of x for which y is real.

vi. Find the greatest and least values of x and y satisfying relation $x^2+y^2=6x-8y$

Location of Roots

12. i. Find values of m for which both roots of equation $x^2-mx+1=0$ are less than unity.

ii. For what real values of m both roots of equation $x^2-6mx+9m^2-2m+2=0$ exceed 3 ?

iii. Find all values of p so that 6 lies between roots of the equation $x^2+2(p-3)x+9=0$

iv. Find the values of m for which exactly one root of the equation $x^2-2mx+m^2-1=0$ lies in the interval $(-2, 4)$.

v. Find all values of a for which the equation $4x^2-2x+a=0$ has two roots lie in the interval $(-1, 1)$

vi. Find the values of a for which one root of equation $(a-5)x^2-2ax+a-4=0$ is smaller than 1 and other greater than 2.

vii. If the roots of equation $x^2-2ax+a^2+a-3=0$ are real and less than 3 then prove that $a<2$.

viii. If both the roots of the equation $x^2-12kx+k^2+k-5=0$ are less than 5, then prove that $k\in(-2, 4)$

ix. If both the roots of equation $x^2-6ax+2-2a+9a^2=0$ exceed 3, then prove that $a>\frac{11}{9}$.

x. If the equation $ax^2+bx+c=0$ $(a>0)$ has two roots α and β such that $\alpha<-2$ and $\beta>2$ then

a. $b^2-4ac>0$

b. $4a+2|b|+c<0$

c. $a+|b|+c=0$

d. $c<0$

xi. Find the value of 'λ' for which $2x^2-2(2\lambda+1)x+\lambda(\lambda+1)=10$ may have one root less than l and other root greater than l.

xii. Find the value of 'a' for which equation $2x^2-2(2a+1)x+a(a-1)=0$ has roots α and β such that $\alpha<a<\beta$.

Location of Roots in Inequalities

13. i. Find all values of m for which inequality $mx^2-4x+3m+1>0$ is satisfied for all +ve values of x.

ii. Find all values of b for which $x^2-x+b-3<0$ for atleast one -ve x.

iii. Find all values of k for which the inequality $k.4^x+(k-1).2^{x+2}+(k-1)>1$ is satisfied for all x in R.

iv. Find all possible parameters 'a' for which $f(x)=(a^2+a-2)x^2-(a+5)x-2$ is non +ve for every xÎ $[0,1]$

1.18 Some Special types of Quadratic Equations

i. An equation is of the form $(x-a)(x-b)(x-c)(x-d)=k$, where $a<b<c<d$, $b-a=d-c$.

Put $y=\frac{(x-a)+(x-b)+(x-c)+(x-d)}{4}$

$=x-\frac{(a+b+c+d)}{4}$

ii. An equation is of the form $(x-a)(x-b)(x-c)(x-d)=kx^2$, where $ab=cd$.

put $y=x+\frac{ab}{x}$.

iii. An equation is of the form $(x-a)^4+(x-b)^4=k$

put $y=\frac{(x-a)+(x-b)}{2}$.

iv. An equation is of the form $ax^4+bx^3+cx^2+bx+a=0$, where $a,b,c\in R-\{0\}$

1. Divide by x^2 of both the sides.

2. Put $x+\frac{1}{x}=y$.

v. An equation is of the form $ax^5+bx^4+cx^3-cx^2-bx-a=0$

$x-1$ is factor of the given equation.

vi. An equation is of the form $ax^{2n}+bx^n+c=0$, $a\neq 0$, $n\in N$

Put $x^n=y$.

Exercise-I

1. $x^4-5x+4=0$ **2.** $2x^4-x^2-3=0$ **3.** $(x-1)^4+(x-5)^4=82$

4. $2x^4-x^3-11x^2-x+2=0$ **5.** $(x-1)(x-2)(x-3)(x-4)=8$. **6.** $x^2+\frac{x^2}{(x+1)^2}=3$

1.19 Transformation of Polynomial Equation

Let $\alpha, \beta, \gamma, ...$ be the roots of $f(x)=0$, then

1. The equation whose roots are $-\alpha, -\beta, -\gamma$ is $f(-x)=0$.

2. The equation whose roots are $\frac{1}{\alpha}, \frac{1}{\beta}, \frac{1}{\gamma}$ is $f\left(\frac{1}{x}\right)=0$

3. The equation whose roots are $k\alpha, k\beta, k\gamma$ is $f(xk)=0$.

4. The equation whose roots are $\alpha - h, \beta - h, \gamma - h$ is $f(x+h) = 0$.

5. The equation whose roots are $\sqrt{\alpha}, \sqrt{\beta}, \sqrt{\gamma}$ is $f(x^2) = 0$.

6. The equation whose roots are $\alpha^2, \beta^2, \gamma^2$ is $f\left(\sqrt{x}\right) = 0$.

7. The equation whose roots are $\alpha^3, \beta^3, \gamma^3$ is $f\left(\sqrt[3]{x}\right) = 0$.

8. The equation whose roots are $\frac{1}{\alpha\beta}, \frac{1}{\beta\gamma}, \frac{1}{\gamma\alpha}$ is $f(\alpha\beta\gamma \times x) = 0$.

9. Equation whose roots are $\frac{\alpha+1}{\alpha-1}, \frac{\beta+1}{\beta-1}, \frac{\gamma+1}{\gamma-1}$ is $f\left(\frac{x+1}{x-1}\right) = 0$.

Exercise-II

1. Solve: $3x^3 - 22x^2 + 48x - 72 = 0$ when the roots are in H.P.
2. Solve: $6x^3 - 11x^2 + 6x - 1 = 0$, when the roots are in H.P.
3. If α, β, γ be the roots of $x^3 + px^2 + qx + r = 0$, then find a cubic equation whose roots are $\alpha(\beta + \gamma), \beta(\gamma + \alpha), \gamma(\alpha + \beta)$.
4. If α, β, γ be the roots of $x^3 - px^2 + r = 0$, then find a cubic equation whose roots are $\frac{\beta+\gamma}{\alpha}, \frac{\gamma+\alpha}{\beta}, \frac{\alpha+\beta}{\gamma}$.
5. If α, β, γ be the roots of $x^3 + x^2 - 4x + 7 = 0$, then find a cubic equation whose roots are $\beta + \gamma, \gamma + \alpha, \alpha + \beta$.
6. If α, β, γ be the roots of $x^3 + x + 2 = 0$, then find a cubic equation whose roots are $(\alpha - \beta)^2, (\beta - \gamma)^2, (\gamma - \alpha)^2$.

1.20 Intermediate Value Theorem

Let $f(x)$ be a polynomial function and $a, b, \in R$ such that $a < b$.

If $f(a)$ and $f(b)$ are of opposite signs, then there is aleast one root between a and b.

If $f(a)$ and $f(b)$ are off the same sign, then either no root or even number of roots lie between α and β.

Note

Let $f(x) = a_0x^n + a_1x^{n-1} + a_2x^{n-2} + ... + a_n$.

1. Every equation of an odd degree has atleast one real root whose sign is opposite to that of its last term, provided the leading co-efficients is positive.

   In this function, we shall substitute in place of x are $-\infty, 0, +\infty$ respectively.

   Thus, $f(-\infty) = -\infty$, $f(0) = a_n$, $f(\infty) = \infty$.

   If a_n is positive, then $f(x) = 0$ has a root luing between $-\infty$ and 0 and if a_n is negative then $f(x)$ has a root lying between 0 and ∞.

2. Every equation, which is of an even degree and has its last term-ve, has at-least two real roots, one +ve and one negative, providing the leading co-efficents is +ve.

   In this function, we shall substitute in place of x are $-\infty, 0, +\infty$ respectively.

   Thus, $f(-\infty) = -\infty$, $f(0) = a_n$, $f(\infty) = \infty$.

   Since a_n is negative, $f(x) = 0$ has a root lying between $-\infty$ and 0 and a root lying between 0 and ∞.

3. **To determine the nature of roots we should remember the following rules:**

   a. If the co-efficients are all +ve, equation has no positive root. Thus, equation $x^5 + 4x^3 + 2x + 1 = 0$ has no positive root.

   b. If the co-efficients of the even powers of x are all of one sign and the co-efficients of the odd powers of x are all off opposite sign, then the equation has no negative root.

      Thus, the equation $x^7 + x^5 - 3x^4 + x^3 - 3x^2 + 2x - 5 = 0$ has no negative root.

   c. If the equation contains only even powers of x and the co-efficients are all of the same sign, the equation has no real root. Thus the equation.

   d. If the equation contains only odd powers of x, and the co-efficients arr all of the same sign, the equation has no real roots other than $x = 0$.

      Thus, the equation $x^9 + 4x^5 + 5x^3 + 3x = 0$ has no real root other than $x = 0$.

1.21 Descartes Rule of Signs

Consider a polynomial equation

$f(x) = a_0x^n + a_1x^{n-1} + a_2x^{n-2} + ... + a_n$ with real coefficients and $a_n \neq 0, n \in W$.

We have $f(-x) = a_0(-x)^n + a_1(-x)^{n-1} + a_2(-x)^{n-2} + ... + a_n$

By observing sign variation, in the co-efficients of $f(x)$ and $f(-x)$, we can predict the following things about nature of roots.

i. The maximum number of positive roots of $f(x)$ is equal to the number of sign changes in the co-efficients of $f(x)$. Let this number be p.

ii. The maximum number of -ve roots of $f(x)$ is equal to the number of sign changes in co-efficients of $f(-x)$. Let this number be q.

iii. The maximum number of imaginary roots of $f(x) = n - (p + q)$.

EXERCISE-III

1. Find the number of +ve and -ve roots of $x^5 - x^4 + x^3 + 8x^2 + 2x - 2 = 0$
2. Find the number and position of real roots of $x^4 - 41x^2 + 40x + 126 = 0$
3. Find the number and position of the real roots of $x^4 - 14x^2 + 16x + 9 = 0$.
4. Find the nature of the roots of $3x^4 + 12x^2 + 5x - 4 = 0$.
5. Find the least possible number of imaginary roots of $x^9 - x^5 + x^4 + x^2 + 1 = 0$.
6. Show that $x^7 - 3x^4 + 2x^3 - 1 = 0$ has atleast four imaginary roots.

ANSWERS

1. (i) $x = -2, 4$ (ii) $x = 2 \pm \sqrt{3}$ (iii) $x = -9, -5$

(iv) $x = \dfrac{-3 \pm \sqrt{3}}{4}$ (v) $x = 9/13, 4/13$ (vi) $x = 16/25$

(vii) $x = 2$ (viii) $x = 2$ (ix) 2

(xi) infinite (xii) 0 (xiii) 0

(xiv) $x = ab + bc + ca$ (xv) $x = a + b + c$

(xvi) infinite (xvii) $a = 1$

2. (iii) $m = 2, -10/9$

3. (i) 13, 35, -1, 275, 2315. (ii) $m = -1$

(iii) $k = 3, 3/2$ (iv) b / ac (v) $p = 3$

(vi) $A = -3, B = 77$

4. (i) $-(q+r)$ (ii) $q^2 - p^2$ (iv) $p = -2, q = -32$

(vii) -1

5. (i) $x^2 - 4x + 1 = 0$ (ii) $x^2 - 4x + 4 = 0$

(iii) $x^2 - 11x + 30 = 0$

(iv) $x^3 - 6x^2 + 5x + 24 = 0$ (v) $4x^2 - 49x + 48 = 0$

(vi) $3x^2 - 19x + 3 = 0$ (viii) $x = a, b$

6. 1

7. (i) -1 (ii) 0 (iii) -1

8. (i) (a) (-1, 3) (b) $(-\infty, 1) \cup (2, \infty)$

(ii) $-3 < k < 5$

(iii) $-6 < k < 4$ (iv) $m > 1$ and $m < -1/7$

(v) $-3 < p < 6$ (vi) $k = \pm 4$ (vii) $12 < k < 14$

(viii) $-2 < b < 2$ (ix) $-5 < a < 2$ (x) $2 < \lambda < 4$

9. (i) (a) Min Val = 3, (b) Min Val = 0 (c) Min Val = -9/4

(d) Max Val = -15/4 (e) Max Val = 0 (f) Max Val = 5

(ii) (a) $\left[\dfrac{3}{4}, \infty\right)$ (b) $\left[-\dfrac{1}{4}, \infty\right)$ (c) $\left(-\infty, -\dfrac{31}{4}\right]$

(iii) $a = 3/2, b = -6$ (iv) $R_f = \left[\dfrac{7}{8}, 4\right]$ (v) [-1, 10]

10. (i) G.V = -1/2, L.V = -2 (ii) Max V. = 3 and Min Val = 1/3

(iii) G.V = 3 and L.V = 1/3 (vii) $y \ge 3, y \le \dfrac{1}{3}$

(viii) R (ix) $[25, \infty)$

(x) $\left(-\infty, -\dfrac{1}{2}\right)$ (xii) 20 (xiii) $2(\sqrt{2} - 1)$, when $x = \sqrt{2}$

11. (i) $m = 7, -7$ (ii) $x = 0, 2$ (iii) $k \in (-\infty, -2] \cup [3, \infty)$

(iv) $-2 \le x \le 8, -9 \le y \le 1$

12. (i) $m \in (-\infty, -2]$ (ii) $m \in \left(\dfrac{11}{9}, \infty\right)$ (iii) $p \in \left(-\infty, -\dfrac{3}{4}\right)$

(iv) $m \in (-3, -1) \cup (3, 5)$ (v) $a \in \left(-2, \dfrac{1}{4}\right)$

(vi) $a \in (5, 24)$ (x) (a, b)

ANSWERS

Exercise-I

1. $x = \pm 1, \pm 2i$
2. $x = \pm\sqrt{\frac{3}{2}}, \pm i$
3. $x = 4, 2, 3 \pm 5i$
4. $x = -2, \frac{1}{2}, \frac{3 \pm \sqrt{5}}{2}$
5. $x = \frac{5 \pm \sqrt{17}}{2}, \frac{5 \pm i\sqrt{7}}{2}$
6. $x = \frac{1 \pm \sqrt{5}}{2}$

Exercise : II

1. 4, 2, 4/3
2. 1, 1/2, 1/3
3. $(x-q)^3 + 3(x-q)^2 + p(x-q)r + r^2 = 0$
4. $(x+1)^3 - p^3 x = 0$
5. $(x+1)^3 - (x+1)^2 + 4(x+1) - 1 = 0$
6. $x^3 - 6x^2 + 27x - 54 = 0.$

Exercise-III

1. +ve root = 1, -ve root = 2.
2. + ve root = 2, which lie between 2 and 3 and another one between 5 and 6. -ve root = 2 , which lie between –1 and –2 and another one between – 6 and –7.
3. +ve root = 2, which lie between 2 and 3, $f(2) > 0, f\left(2\frac{1}{4}\right) < 0$, $f(3) > 0$. -ve root = 2, which lie between 0 and –1 and between – 4 and – 5.

INEQUATION

1.22 Concept of solving Algebraic Inequation

Solving an algebraic in-equation $f(x) > 0$, where $f(x)$ is a product (or quotient or both) of distinct linear factors. We proceed methodically

i. Make sure that coefficients of x in all the linear factors are positive.

ii. Equate all factors to zero to get the critical points (the points where these factor change their sign) $c_1, c_2, c_3, \ldots$ where $c_1 < c_2 < c_3 < \ldots\ldots$

iii. Write + and –sign alternately on the number line starting from the extreme right.

iv. If $f(x) > 0$, then we shall use open interval with critical points

v. If $f(x) \geq 0$ or ≤ 0, then we shall use the closed interval with critical points.

vi. If $f(x)$ contains an even power factors, say, $x^2, (x-2)^2, (x-3)^{10}, (x-4)^{100}$, then we shall not represent them on the number line we neglect them.

vii. If $f(x)$ contain an irreducible quadratic factor $(ax^2 + bx + c)$, where $a > 0$ and $d < 0$, then we discard it .

EXCERCISES

TYPE 1: ABC of Inequation

1. $x^2 - 3x + 2 > 0$
2. $x^2 - 5x + 4 \leq 0$
3. $x^2 - 7x + 12 \leq 0$
4. $x^2 - 8x + 12 < 0$
5. $x^3 - 6x^2 + 11x - 6 < 0$
6. $x^3 - 4x \leq 0$
7. $x^3 - 6x^2 + 12x - 8 \geq 0$

TYPE 2: Co-efficient of the highest Power of x is always + ve

1. $-x^2 + 3x - 2 > 0$
2. $-x^2 + 5x - 6 < 0$
3. $-x^2 + 10x - 21 \leq 0$
4. $-x^3 + x \leq 0$
5. $-x^2 + 4x \geq 0$
6. $(x-2)(1-x^2) \geq 0$
7. $-x^3 + x^2 - 2x \geq 0$

TYPE 3: Transpose is allowed but cross multiplication is not allowed)

1. $\frac{1}{x} > 1$
2. $\frac{2}{x} \geq 1$
3. $\frac{1}{x} > \frac{1}{x-1}$
4. $\frac{1}{x+2} \leq \frac{1}{x-3}$
5. $\frac{1}{x} - 1 \geq 0$
6. $\frac{(x-1)(x-2)}{(x-3)(x-4)} \geq 0$
7. $\frac{(x-1)(x-2)}{(x-2)(x-4)} \leq 0$
8. $\frac{1}{x+1} - 1 \geq 2 - \frac{1}{x-2}$

TYPE - 4: If $f(x)$ contains an even power factors, then we shall not represent them on the number line, we neglect them.

1. $x^2(x-1)>0$
2. $x^2(x-1)^{10}(x+2)^{11}>0$
3. $\dfrac{(x-1)^4(x-2)^{12}}{(x-3)^{17}(x-5)^{2012}}>0$
4. $\dfrac{(x+1)^{201}(x-4)^{2012}}{(x+3)^{2012}(x-2)^{2013}}>0$
5. $\dfrac{1}{x^2}-1\geq 0$

6 $x^3-3x+2>0$

7 $x^3+7x^2-36\geq 0$

TYPE 5: If $f(x)=ax^2+bx+c$, where $a>0$ and $D<0$, then we discard it

1. $(x-2)(x^2+x+2)>0$
2. $(x-3)(-x^2+x+1)>0$
3. $x^3+4x\geq 0$
4. $x^4-9\geq 0$
5. $x^3-5x+4\geq 0$
6. $x^3-3x^2+3x-9\geq 0$
7. $x^3-6x^2+12x-9\geq 0$

TYPE 6: Common values of x in $f(x)\geq 0$ and $g(x)\geq 0$ or $f(x)\geq 0$ and $g(x)\leq 0$

1. $x^2-4x+3\geq 0$, $x^2-4\leq 0$
2. $x^2-9\geq 0$, $x^2-4\leq 0$
3. $x^2-6x+8\geq 0$, $x^2-3x+2\geq 0$
4. $x^2-5x+6\geq 0$, $x^2-10x+24\leq 0$
5. $x^2-x\geq 0$, $x^2-12x+27\leq 0$
6. $x^3+x\geq 0$, $x^2-9\leq 0$
7. $x^3-9x\geq 0$, $x^3+4x\leq 0$

EXERCISE (MIXED PROBLEMS)

1. .... x:

i. $\dfrac{(x-1)}{(x-2)}>0$

ii. $\dfrac{x}{(x+3)}>0$

iii. $\dfrac{1}{(x-1)}>\dfrac{2}{(x-2)}$

iv. $\dfrac{(x-1)(x-2)}{(x-3)(x-4)}>0$

v. $\dfrac{(x-1)(x+2)}{(x+3)(x-4)}>0$

vi. $\dfrac{x^2}{(x-1)}>0$

vii. $\dfrac{x^2(x-2)^{10}}{(x-1)}>0$

viii. $\dfrac{(x-1)^5(x+10)^{100}(x+4)}{(2x-1)(3x-5)}<0$

ix. $\dfrac{1}{x}-1\geq 0$

x. $1-\dfrac{2}{(x+1)}\leq 0$

2. Solve for x:

i. $(x^3-1)(x^4-1)\leq 0$

ii. $(x-1)(x^2-3x-8)\leq 0$

iii. $\dfrac{1}{(x+1)}-\dfrac{1}{x}\leq\dfrac{1}{(x-1)}-\dfrac{1}{(x-2)}$

iv. $\dfrac{2x}{(2x^2+5x+2)}>\dfrac{1}{(x+1)}$

v. $\dfrac{1}{(x^2-5x+6)}\geq\dfrac{1}{2}$

vi. $\dfrac{4}{1+x}+\dfrac{2}{1-x}<1$

viii. $\dfrac{x^2+2x-3}{x^2+1}<0$

ix. Find the smallest integer x such that $\dfrac{x-5}{x^2+5x-14}>0$

x. Find the greatest and least values of x for which $x^2-5|x|+6\leq 0$ holds.

xi. If $x^2+6x-27>0$ and $x^2-3x-4<0$ then prove that $3<x<4$.

xii. Find the greatest negative integer satisfying $x^2-4x-77<0$ and $x^2>4$

xiii. Find the set of all real values of a such that a^2+2a, $2a+3$ and a^2+3a+8 are the sides of a triangle.

xiv. $(x+3)^4+(x-1)^4\geq 82$.

xv If $6+10x-2x^2\leq k$, a constant, for all $x\in R$, then prove that the minimum value of k is $\dfrac{37}{2}$.

ANSWERS

vi $x\in(-\infty,-1)\cup(1,\infty)$

vii. $\dfrac{(x-1)(x-2)}{(x+5)}>1$

(ix) $x=-6$

(x) $x=3,-3$

(xiii) $a>5$

(xiv) $x\in(-\infty,-2]\cup[0,\infty)$

1.23 Equation Containing Absolute Values

Definition: Let for every x in R, then the magnitude of x is called its modulus and absolute value. It is denoted by $|x|$.

Thus, $f(x) = |x| = \begin{cases} x, & x \geq 0 \\ -x, & x < 0 \end{cases}$.

1.24 Properties of Modulus

i. $||x|| = |-x| = |x|$

ii. $|x| = \max(-x, x)$

iii. $-|x| = \min(-x, x)$

iv. $\sqrt{x^2} = |x|$

v. $|x+y| \leq |x| + |y|$, when x and y are opposite sign $\Rightarrow xy \leq 0$

vi. $|x+y| = |x| + |y|$, when x and y are same sign $\Rightarrow xy \geq 0$

vii. $|xy| = |x|\,|y|$.

viii. $\left|\frac{x}{y}\right| = \frac{|x|}{|y|}$, $y \neq 0$.

ix. Geometrically, modulus of x means, it is the distance between x and 0.

x. $|x| = 1 \Rightarrow x = \pm 1$

xi. $|x| = -2 \Rightarrow x = \phi$

xii. $|x| < 1 \Rightarrow -1 < x < 1$

xiii. $|x| > 1 \Rightarrow x > 1$ and $x < -1$

Solve Following Equations

1. $x^2 + 5|x| + 6 = 0$
2. $x^2 - 3|x| + 2 = 0$
3. $|x-1| + |x-3| = 5$
4. $|x| + |x-2| = 4$
5. $|x| + |x-2| + |x-4| = 6$
6. Solve for x: $|x+1| + |x| + |x-1| = 3$
7. Solve for x: $\left|\frac{x}{x-1}\right| + |x| = \frac{x^2}{|x-1|}$
8. Solve for x: $|x^2-1| + |x^2-4| = 3$
9. Solve for x: $|x^2-3x+2| + |x^2-9| = |3x-11|$
10. Solve for x: $2^{|x+1|} - 2^x = |2^x - 1| + 1$
11. Solve for x: $2^{|x+2|} - |2^{x+1} - 1| = 2^{x+1} + 1$
12. Solve for x: $2^{|y|} + |2^y - 1| = 2^{y-1} + 1$
13. Solve for x: $|x|^{x^2-x-2} = 1$

Answers

4.	$x = -1, 3$	5.	$x = 0, 4$	10.	$x \in [0, \infty)$	11.	$x \in [-1, \infty)$
6.	$x = -1, 1$	7.	$x \in (1, \infty)$	12.	$y \geq 1, y = -1$	**13.**	$x = -1, 1, 2$
8.	$x \in [-2, -1] \cup [1, 2]$	9.	$x \in (1, \infty)$				

Inequalities with Absolute Value

Solve for x:

1. $|x-1| < 2$
2. $\frac{1}{|x|-3} < \frac{1}{2}$
3. $|1-2x| > 3-x$
4. $|x+8| + 1 \leq 3x$
5. $|x-2| > |x-3|$
6. $|x+2| + |5x-2| > |3x+4|$
7. $|x-1| + 2|x+1| + |x-2| \leq 8$
8. $\left|\frac{x-3}{x^2-4}\right| \leq 1$
9. $|x^2-3x-15| < 2x^2 - x$
10. $|2x^2+x+1| > x^2 - 5x + 6$

Answers

1. $x \in (-1, 3)$
2. $x \in (-8, -2) \cup \left(\frac{1}{3}, \infty\right)$.
3. $x \in (-\infty, -5) \cup (-3, 3) \cup (5, \infty)$.
4. $x \in (4.5, \infty)$
5. $x \in (2.5, \infty)$
6. $x \in (-\infty, 0) \cup \left(\frac{1}{3}, \infty\right)$
7. $x \in \left[-\frac{7}{4}, \frac{9}{4}\right]$
9. $x \in \left(-\infty, -\frac{5}{3}\right) \cup (3, \infty)$
10. $x \in (-\infty, -5) \cup (-1, -\infty)$.

1.25 Irrational Equations

Solve the following irrational equations:

1. $\sqrt{(2x+7)}+\sqrt{(x+4)}=0$
2. $\sqrt{(x-4)}=-5$
3. $\sqrt{(x-6)}-\sqrt{(8-x)}=2$
4. $\sqrt{(-2-x)}=\sqrt[5]{(x-7)}$
5. $\sqrt{x}+\sqrt{(x+16)}=3$
6. $7\sqrt{x}+8\sqrt{-x}+\frac{15}{x^3}=98.$
7. $\sqrt{x-2}+\sqrt{4-x}=\sqrt{6-x}$
8. $\sqrt{2x^2+5x-2}-\sqrt{2x^2+5x-9}=1$
9. $\sqrt{5x^2-6x+8}-\sqrt{5x^2-6x-7}=1\cdot$
10. $\sqrt{x+3-4\times\sqrt{x-1}}+\sqrt{x+8-6\times\sqrt{x-1}}=1\cdot$
11. $\sqrt{x}+\sqrt{x-\sqrt{1-x}}=1$
12. $\sqrt[3]{(2x-1)}+\sqrt[3]{(x-1)}=1.$

ANSWERS :

1. $x=\phi$ 2. $x=\phi$ 3. $x=\phi$ 4. $x=\phi$ 5. $x=\phi$

6. $x=\phi$ 7. $x=2$ 8. $x=2,-9/29.$ $x=-3, 21/5$

10. $5\le x\le 10$ 12. $x=1.$

IRRATIONAL INEQUATIONS

TYPE I: An inequation is of form $\sqrt[2n+1]{f(x)}<\sqrt[2n+1]{g(x)}$, $n\in N$

$\Rightarrow\ f(x)<g(x)$

1. Solve for x: $\sqrt[5]{\left[\frac{3}{x+1}+\frac{7}{x+2}\right]}<\sqrt[5]{\frac{6}{x-1}}$

2. Solve for x : $\sqrt[3]{\frac{x-2}{x-1}}<\sqrt[3]{\frac{1}{x-1}}$

ANSWERS : 1. $x\in(\infty,\ 2)\cup\cup(1,5)$

TYPE II: An inequation is of form $\sqrt[2n]{f(x)}<\sqrt[2n]{g(x)}$, $n\in N$

$$\Rightarrow \begin{cases} f(x)\ge 0 \\ g(x)>f(x) \end{cases}$$

1. Solve for x: $\sqrt{3x-2}<\sqrt{x+4}$

2. Solve for x: $\sqrt{4x-3}<\sqrt{2x+5}$

ANSWERS : $x\in\left[\frac{2}{3},3\right)$

TYPE III: An inequation is of form $\sqrt[2n+1]{f(x)}<g(x)$, $n\in N$

$\Rightarrow\ f(x)<g^{2n+1}(x)$

1. Solve for x: $\sqrt[3]{(3x-5)}<(x-1)$

2. Solve for x: $\sqrt[3]{3x-2}<x$

ANSWERS : 1. $(-1,\infty)$

TYPE IV: An inequation is of form $\sqrt[2n]{f(x)}<g(x)$, $n\in N$

1. Solve for x: $\sqrt{(x+14)}<(x+2)$

2. Solve for x: $\sqrt{2x-2}<x-1$

ANSWERS : 1. $x\in(2,\infty)$ 2. $x\in(3,\infty)$

TYPE V: An inequation is of form $\sqrt[2n+1]{f(x)}>g(x)$, $n\in N$

$\Rightarrow\ f(x)>g^{2n+1}(x)$

1. Solve for x: $\sqrt[3]{5x-4}>x$

2. Solve for x: $\sqrt[3]{x^3-7x^2}>(-36)^{1/3}$

ANSWERS :

1. $x\in\left(-\infty,-\frac{\sqrt{17}+1}{2}\right)\cup\left(1,\frac{\sqrt{17}-1}{2}\right)$
2. $x\in(-2, 3)\cup(6,\infty)$

TYPE VI : An inequation is of form $\sqrt[2n]{f(x)}>g(x)$, $n\in N.$

$$\Rightarrow \begin{cases} g(x)\ge 0 \\ f(x)>g^{2n}(x) \end{cases} \text{ AND } \begin{cases} g(x)<0 \\ f(x)\ge 0 \end{cases}$$

Solve for x:

1. $\sqrt{-x^2+4x-3}>(6-2x)$
2. $\sqrt{-x^2+3x-2}>4-2x$
3. $\sqrt{-x^2+9x-18}>x-6$

ANSWERS :

1. $x\in\left(\frac{13}{5},3\right)$ 2. $x\in\left(\frac{9}{5},2\right]$ 3. $x\in\left(\frac{9}{2},6\right]$

1.26 Exponential Equations

TYPE I: An equation is of form $a^{f(x)}=1$, $a>0$, $a\ne 1$

$\Rightarrow\ f(x)=0$

1. Solve for x: $5^{x^2+3x+2}=1$

2. Solve for x: $3^{x^2+5|x|+6}=1$

ANSWERS : 1. $x=-1,-2$ 2. $x=\phi$

TYPE II: An equation is of form $f(a^x)=0\Rightarrow f(t)=0$, where $t=a^x$. If $t_1,t_2,t_3,\ldots\ldots..t_n$ are the roots of $f(t)=0$, then $a^x=t_1,\ldots\ldots\ldots\ldots\ldots a^x=t_n.$

3. Solve for x: $5^{2x}-24.5^x-25=0$

ANSWERS : 3. $x=2$

TYPE III: An equation is of form $\alpha.a^{f(x)}+\beta.b^{f(x)}+\gamma.c^{f(x)}=0$, where $\alpha,\beta,\gamma,\in R$ and $\alpha,\beta,\gamma\ne 0$ and the bases satisfy the condition $b^2=ac.$

$\Rightarrow \quad \alpha.t^2+\beta.t+\gamma=0$, where $t=\left(\frac{a}{b}\right)^{f(x)}$

4. Solve for x: $64.9^x-84.12^x+27.16^x=0$

ANSWERS : 4. $x=1,2$.

TYPE IV: An equation is of form $\alpha.a^{f(x)}+\beta.b^{f(x)}+c=0$, where $\alpha,\beta,c\in R$, $\alpha,\beta,c\neq 0$ and $ab=1$ (where a and b are inverse +ve numbers).

$\Rightarrow \quad \alpha.t^2+c.t+\beta=0$, where $t=a^{f(x)}$.

5. Solve for x: $15.2^{x+1}+15.2^{2-x}=135$

Answers : 5. $x=-1, 2$.

TYPE V: An equation is of the form $a^{f(x)}+b^{f(x)}=c$, where a, b,c$\in R$ and $a^2+b^2=c$. Then the solution of the given equation is $f(x)=2$.

6. Solve for x: $3^{x-4}+5^{x-4}=34$.

7. Solve for x: $3^x+4^x=5^x$.

8. Solve for x: $1+3^{x/2}=2^x$

9. Solve for x: $(\sin a)^x+(\cos a)^x=1$

10. Solve for x: $3^{x^2}+4^{x^2}=5^{x^2}$

11. Solve for x: $\left(\frac{3}{5}\right)^x+\frac{7}{5}=2^x$

ANSWERS : 6. $x=6$ 7. $x=2$ 8. $x=2$ 9. $x=2$ 10. $x=\pm\sqrt{2}$ 11. $x=1$

TYPE VI: An equation is of form $a^{f(x)}+b^{f(x)}+c^{f(x)}=d$, where $a,b,c,d\in R$ and $a^3+b^3+c^3=d$.

Then reqd solution is $f(x)=3$.

12. Solve for x: i. $3^x+4^x+5^x=6^x$

ii. $1^x+6^x+8^x=9^x$

ANSWERS : (i) $x=3$ (ii) $x=3$.

TYPE VII: An equation is of form $a^{f(x)}+a^{g(x)}=c$,

where $f(x)+g(x)=1$, a, c $(\neq 0)$.

Then we shall put $a^{f(x)}=t$

13. Solve for x :

i. $16^{\sin^2 x}+16^{\cos^2 x}=10$.

ii. $9^{\sin^2 x}+9^{\cos^2 x}=10$

ANSWERS :

(i) $x=n\pi\pm\frac{\pi}{4},\ n\pi\pm\frac{\pi}{3}, n\in I$

(ii) $x=n\pi\pm\frac{\pi}{2},\ n\pi, n\in I$

TYPE VIII: An equation is of form

$a^{f(x)}+a^{f(x)-1}+a^{f(x)-2}=b^{f(x)}+b^{f(x)-1}+b^{f(x)-2}$

Then reqd solution is $f(x)-2=\log_{a/b}\left(\frac{b^2+b+1}{a^2+a+1}\right)$.

14. Solve for x :

i. $2^x+2^{x-1}+2^{x-2}=5^x+5^{x-1}+5^{x-2}$

ii. $3^x+3^{x-1}+3^{x-2}=7^x+7^{x-1}+7^{x-2}$

ANSWERS : (i) $x=\log_{(2/5)}\left(\frac{124}{175}\right)$ (ii) $x=\log_{(3/7)}\left(\frac{513}{617}\right)$

TYPE - IX: An equation is of the form

$\left(a+\sqrt{b}\right)^{L(x),Q(x)}+\left(a-\sqrt{b}\right)^{L(x),Q(x)}=c,$

where $a^2-b=1$.

Then we shall put $\left(a+\sqrt{b}\right)^{L(x),Q(x)}=t$

15. Solve for x : $\left(5+2\sqrt{6}\right)^{x^2-3}+\left(5-2\sqrt{6}\right)^{x^2-3}=10$.

16. Solve for x : $\left(15+4\sqrt{14}\right)^x+\left(15-4\sqrt{14}\right)^x=30$

17. Solve for x : $\left(7-4\sqrt{3}\right)^{x^2-4x+3}+\left(7+4\sqrt{3}\right)^{x^2-4x+3}=14$

18. Solve for x : $\left(\sqrt{3}+\sqrt{2}\right)^x+\left(\sqrt{3}-\sqrt{2}\right)^x=10$

19. Solve for x : $\left(5+2\sqrt{6}\right)^{x/2}+\left(5-2\sqrt{6}\right)^{x/2}=10$.

ANSWERS : 15. $x=\pm 2, \pm\sqrt{2}$ 16. $x=\pm 1$ 17. $x=2, 2\pm\sqrt{2}$

18. $x=2, -2$ 19. $x=2, -2$.

TYPE X: Different types of equation on L.H.S = R.H.S. Then we shall use the graphical method or somewhere we can also be used the concept of A.M $\geq$ GM. Find the number of solutions of

20. $|x-1|=e^x$

21. $\sin x=x^2+x+1$.

22. $\left(\frac{3}{2}\right)^x=-x^2+2x-3$.

23. $\sin(2^x)\cos(2^x)=\frac{1}{4}\left(2^x+2^{-x}\right)$

24. $\sin(e^x)=(5^x+5^{-x})$

25. $(5^x+5^{-x})=\log_{10}25, x\in R$

26. $n^{-|x|}|m-|x||=1$, where $m,n>1$ and $n>m$.

27. For every real x, $p^x+p^{-x}=\log_q q^2-1$, where $p,q\in R$.

28. $\log_{0.5}x=|x|$

29. $\sin x+\cos x=x^2-2x+\sqrt{16}$.

30. $2^x+x^2=1$.

31. $e^{\sin x}-e^{-\sin x}-4=0$.

32. $\sin^2 x=\log_a b+\log_b a$

33. $\sin x=|\cos x|, x\in[-\pi,\pi]$

34. $\cos x=|\sin x|, x\in[-\pi,\pi]$

35. $2^{\sin x} = \sin x,\ x \in [0, 2\pi]$

36. $2^{\sin x} = |\sin x|,\ x \in [0, 2\pi]$

37. $2^{\cos x} = |\sin x|,\ x \in [0, 2\pi]$

ANSWERS :

20. 1	**21.** 0	**22.** 0	**23.** infinite	**24.** 0
25. 0	**26.** 2	**27.** 0	**28.** 1	**29.** 0
30. 1	**31.** 0	**32.** 0	**33.** 4	**34.** 2
35. 0	**36.** 2	**37.** 4		

EXPONENTIAL INEQUATIONS

RULES :

Inequalities	Solution set for the inequality	Solution set for the inequality.
1. $a^{f(x)} > b$	1. $\begin{cases} a>1 \\ f(x) > \log_a b \end{cases}$	1. $\begin{cases} 0<a<1 \\ f(x) < \log_a b \end{cases}$
2. $a^{f(x)} > b$	2. $\begin{cases} a>1 \\ f(x) < \log_a b \end{cases}$	2. $\begin{cases} 0<a<1 \\ f(x) > \log_a b \end{cases}$
3. $f(x)^{g(x)} > f(x)^{h(x)}$	3. $\begin{cases} f(x) > 1 \\ g(x) > h(x) \end{cases}$	3. $\begin{cases} 0< f(x) < 1 \\ g(x) < h(x) \end{cases}$
4. $f(x)^{g(x)} < f(x)^{h(x)}$	4. $\begin{cases} f(x) > 1 \\ g(x) < h(x) \end{cases}$	4. $\begin{cases} 0< f(x) < 1 \\ g(x) > h(x) \end{cases}$

Solve for x:

1. $2^x + 2^{-x+1} - 3 < 0.$
2. $2^{2x+1} - 21\left(\frac{1}{2}\right)^{2x+3} + 2 \geq 0$
3. $4^x - 2^{2(x-1)} + 8^{\frac{2(x-2)}{3}} \geq 52.$
4. $x^{\log_2 x} - 3\log x + 1 > 1000.$
5. $|x|^{x^2-x-2} < 1.$

ANSWERS :

1. (0, 1) 2. $(3, \infty)$ 3. $\left[\frac{1}{2}\log_2 3 - 2, \infty\right)$ 4. $(10^3, \infty)$ 5. (1,2)

LOGARITHM

BASIC FORMULAE ON LOGARITHM

STEP • 1

1. If $a^x = n$, then $x = \log_a n$, where $n > 0$, $a > 0$ and $a \neq 1$.
2. Exponential function is always positive.
3. $\log_a a = 1$
4. $\log_{\text{any base}} 1 = 0$
5. $\log_a 0 = \pm\infty$
6. $\log_a \infty = \infty$

STEP • 2

1. $\log_a m + \log_a n = \log_a mm$
2. $\log_a m - \log_a n = \log_a\left(\frac{m}{n}\right)$
3. $\log_a n^m = m \log_a n$
4. $a^{\log_a n} = n.$

STEP • 3

1. $\log_{a^\alpha} n = \frac{1}{\alpha}\log_a n$
2. $\log_{a^\alpha} n^\beta = \frac{\beta}{\alpha}\log_a n.$
3. $a^{\log_n b} = b^{\log_n a}$
4. $\log_a b = \frac{\log_m b}{\log_n a}$

STEP • 4

1. $\log_a b = \frac{1}{\log_b a}$
2. $\log_a b \times \log_b a = 1$
3. $\log_a b \times \log_b c \times \log_c d \times \log_d a = 1$
4. $\log_a b \times \log_b c \times \log_c d \times .... \times \log_z a = 1$

STEP • 5

1. If $x > y \Rightarrow \log_a x > \log_a y$, when $a > 1$
2. If $x > y \Rightarrow \log_a x < \log_a y$, when $0 < a < 1$.

ABC OF LOGARITHM

1. Find the value of

   i. $\log_2 32$ ii. $\log_3\left(\frac{1}{243}\right)$

   iii. $\log_{5\sqrt{5}} 5$ iv. $\log_{100}(0.1)$

   v. $10^{\log_{10} m + \log_{10} n}$ vi. $\log_3 \log_5 \log_3 (243)$

2. Find the value of

   i. $\log_2 \log_3 \log_4 (64)$ ii. $3^{\frac{1}{3}\log_3 7}$

   iii. $2^{2-\log_2 5}$ iv. $2^{\log_3 5} - 5^{\log_3 2}$

   v. $\log_9 27 - \log_{27} 9$ vi. 0

3. Find the value of

   i. $\log_{10}\tan 40° + \log_{10}\tan 41° + \log_{10}\tan 42° + ... + \log_{10}\tan 50°$

   ii. $\log_{10}\tan 1° + \log_{10}\tan 2° + \log_{10}\tan 3° + ... + \log_{10}\tan 89°$

   iii. $\log_3 4.\log_4 5.\log_5 6.\log_6 7.\log_7 8.\log_8 9.$

4. i. If $\log_5 a.\log_a x = 2$, then find the value of x.

ii. If $\log_k x.\log_5 k = \log_x 5$, where $k \neq 1, k > 0$, then find x.

iii. If $A = \log_2 \log_2 \log_4 256$ and $B = 2\log_{\sqrt{2}} 2$, then find the value of A + B + 10.

iv. If $a = \log_{\sqrt{3}} 5$, $b = \log_{\sqrt{3}} 2$, then find value of $\log_{\sqrt{3}} 300$.

5. Find the minimum value of

i. $\log_b a + \log_a b$

ii. $\log_b a + \log_c b + \log_a c$.

6. Prove that

$$\frac{1}{\log_2 n}+\frac{1}{\log_3 n}+\frac{1}{\log_4 n}+.....+\frac{1}{\log_{43} n}=\frac{1}{\log_{43!} n}.$$

7. If $n = 1983!$, then prove that

$$\frac{1}{\log_2 n}+\frac{1}{\log_3 n}+\frac{1}{\log_4 n}+.....+\frac{1}{\log_{1983} n}=1.$$

8. Determine b satisfying

i. $\log_{\sqrt{8}} b = 3\frac{1}{3}$

ii. $\log_{\sqrt{8}} b = 3^{\frac{1}{3}}$

iii. $\log_a 2.\log_b 625 = \log_{10} 16.\log_a 10$.

iv. $\log_3 \log_2 \log_{\sqrt{5}} (625) = b$

9. If $\log_a ab = x$, then find the value of $\log_b ab$.

10. If $\log_{10} 2 = x$, then find the value of $\log_{10} 5$

11. If $a = \log_4 5$ and $b = \log_5 6$, then find $\log_3 2$.

12. Find the value of $\log_{12} 54$, where $b = \log_{12} 24$.

13. Find the value of $\frac{1}{\log_2 36}+\frac{1}{\log_3 36}$

14. Prove that $\frac{1}{\log_3 \pi}+\frac{1}{\log_4 \pi} > 2$.

15. Simplify: $7.\log\frac{16}{15}+5.\log\frac{25}{24}+3.\log\frac{81}{80}$

16. If $a^2+b^2=7ab$, then prove that $\log\frac{1}{3}(a+b)=\frac{1}{2}(\log a+\log b)$

17. If $a^2+b^2=11ab$, then prove that $\log\left(\frac{a-b}{3}\right)=\frac{1}{2}(\log a+\log b)$.

18. Prove that $\frac{\log_a n}{\log_{ab} n}=1+\log_a b$.

19. If log 225 = a and log 225 = b, then prove that

$$\log\left(\left(\frac{1}{9}\right)^2\right)+\log\left(\frac{1}{2250}\right)=2a-3b-1$$

20. If a, b, c are in G.P, then prove that, $\log_a n$, $\log_b n$, $\log_c n$ are in H.P.

21. If $\log_3 2, \log_3(2^x-5), \log_3\left(2^x-\frac{7}{2}\right)$ are in A.P., then find the value of x.

22. If $y = a^{\frac{1}{1-\log_a x}}$, $z = a^{\frac{1}{1-\log_a y}}$, then prove that, $x = a^{\frac{1}{1-\log_a z}}$.

23. If $x = \log_c b + \log_b c$, $y = \log_a c + \log_c a$ and $z = \log_b a + \log_a b$, then find the minimum value of $x^2+y^2+z^2-xyz$.

24. If $\frac{\log a}{b-c}=\frac{\log b}{c-a}=\frac{\log c}{a-b}$, then prove that $a^a b^b c^c = 1$.

25. Find the value of $81^{\frac{1}{\log_5 3}}+27^{\log_9 36}+3^{\frac{4}{\log_7 9}}$

26. Prove that $\frac{1}{1+\log_b a+\log_b c}+\frac{1}{1+\log_c a+\log_c b}+$

$$\frac{1}{1+\log_a b+\log_a c}=1$$

27. Find x, if $\log_2 x+\log_4 x+\log_8 x=11$

28. Find x, if $\log_2 x+\log_4 x+\log_8 x+\log_{16}$

29. If $\log_a x = \alpha, \log_b x = \beta, \log_c x = \gamma$ and $\log_d x = \delta$, then find the value of $\log_{abcd} x$.

30. If $x = \log_a bc$, $y = \log_b ca$ and $z = \log_c ab$ then find the value of $\frac{1}{1+x}+\frac{1}{1+y}+\frac{1}{1+z}$.

31. If $y = 2^{\frac{1}{\log_x 4}}$, then find x.

32. If $N = 6^{\log_{10} 40}.5^{\log_{10} 36}$, then find the value of $N+10$.

33. Find the value of $(0.5)^{\log_{\frac{1}{2^2}}\left(\frac{1}{4}+\frac{1}{8}+\frac{1}{16}+.........to\ \infty\right)}$.

34. If $x = 2^{\log_{10} 3}$ and $y = 3^{\log_{10} 2}$, then find a relation between x and y.

35. Find the value of

$$2^{\log_{10} 3-\log_{10} 5}\times 3^{\log_{10} 5-\log_{10} 2}\times 5^{\log_{10} 2-\log_{10} 3}.$$

36. If $a = \log_{30} 3$ and $b = \log_{30} 5$, then find the value of $\log_{10} 8$.

37. If $a = \log_{12} 18$ and $b = \log_{24} 54$, then prove that $ab+5(a-b)=1$.

38. If $a = \log_7 12$ and $b = \log_{12} 24$, then find value of $\log_{54} 168$.

39. If $a = \log_6 30$, $b = \log_{15} 24$, then prove that

$$\log_{12} 60 = \left(\frac{2ab+2a-1}{ab+b+1}\right).$$

40. Find x, if $\log_7 \log_5\left(\sqrt{x+5}+\sqrt{x}\right)=0$

41. If $\log_2 x+\log_2 y \geq 6$, then find least value of $x+y$. **Ans.:** 16.

42. Solve for x and y: $4^{\log x} = 3^{\log y}$, $(3x)^{\log 3} = (4y)^{\log 4}$.

43. If $x^{18} = y^{21} = z^{28} = k$, then prove that, 3, 3 $\log_y x$, 7 $\log_x z$ are in A.P.

44. If $\frac{1}{\log_3 \pi}+\frac{1}{\log_4 \pi}>x$, then find the value of x.

45. If $\log_{0.3}(x-1) < \log_{0.09}(x-1)$, then x lies in the interval

a. $(2,\infty)$ b. $(-2,-1)$

c. $(1,2)$ d. None.

46. If $\log_e \log_5\left(\sqrt{2x-2}+3\right)=0$, then find the value of x.

47. Find least value of $2.\log_{10} x-\log_x(0.01)$ for $x>1$.

48. Find x, if $4^{\log_9 3}+9^{\log_2 4}=10^{\log_x 83}$

49. Find x, if $3^{4\log_9(x+1)}=2^{2\log_2 x}+3$

50. If $a=\log_{24}12$, $b=\log_{36}24$ and $c=\log_{48}36$ then prove that $\left(\frac{abc+1}{bc}\right)=2$

51. If $\log_{10}\left(\sin\left(x+\frac{\pi}{4}\right)\right)=\frac{1}{2}(\log_{10}6-1)$, then find value of $\log_{10}\sin x+\log_{10}\cos x$.

52. If a,b,c are in G.P, then prove that $\frac{1}{1+\log a},\frac{1}{1+\log b},\frac{1}{1+\log c}$ are in H.P.

53. find x, if $5^{\log_{10} x}=50-x^{\log_{10} 5}$

54. Find x, if $\log_5\left[2+\log(3+x)\right]=0$.

55. Find the number of real solutions of

i. $\log_4(x-1)=\log_2(x-1)$

ii. $\log_4(x-2)=\log_2(x-2)$

iii $\log_9(x-1)=\log_3(x-1)$

iv. $\log_2 x+\log_2(x+3)=1/4$

v. $\log_4\left(x^2+x\right)-\log_4(x+1)=2$

vi. $1+2\log_{(x+2)}5=\log_5(x+2)$

vii. $\log_2 x+\log_4(x+2)=2$

viii. $\log_{10}(x-1)^3-3\log_{10}(x-3)=\log_{10}8$

56. Solve for x:

i. $\log_5\left(x^2-3x+3\right)>0$

ii. $\log_7\log_5\left(x^2-7x+15\right)>0$

iii. $\log_{(1/2)}\log_5\left(x^2-7x+17\right)>0$

iv. $\log_{(1/2)}\log_5\log_2\left(x^2-6x+40\right)>0$

v. $\log_3\log_5\log_2\left(x^2-9x+50\right)>0$

vi. $\log_6\left(\frac{x-2}{6-x}\right)>0$

vii. $\log_{(1/2)}x>\log_{(1/3)}x$

viii. $\log_{0.5}\left(x^2-5x+6\right)>-1$

ix. $\log_8\left(x^2-4x+3\right)<1$

x. $\log_{(1/4)}\left(\frac{35-x^2}{x}\right)\geq-\frac{1}{2}$.

ANSWER

1. (*i*) 5, (*ii*) –5, (*iii*) $\frac{2}{3}$, (*iv*) $-\frac{1}{2}$, (*v*) $m+n$, (*vi*) 0

3. (*i*) 0, (*ii*) 0, (*iii*) 2

4. (*i*) 25, (*ii*) 25, (*iii*) 12

5. (*i*) 2, (*ii*) 3

8. (*i*) 32, (*ii*) 2, (*iii*) 24, (*iv*) 21

9. $\frac{x}{\lambda-1}$ **10.** $1-x$ **11.** $\frac{1}{2ab-1}$

13. $\frac{1}{2}$ **15.** log 2. **21.** $x=3$

25. 216. **27.** 64 **28.** $\frac{25}{4}$

29. $\frac{1}{\alpha^{-1}+\beta^{-1}+r^{-1}+\delta^{-1}}$ **30.** 1

31. $x=y^2$ **32.** 226 **33.** 4

34. $x=y$ **40.** $x=4$ **44.** $x=2$

45. (*a*) **46.** $x=3$ **47.** 4

48. $x=\ln n$ **49.** $x=1$ **51.** –1

53. $x=100$ **54.** $x=1$

55. (i) 1, (ii) 1, (iii) 1; (iv) 2, (v) 1 (vi) 1, (vii) 1

56. (i) $x\in(-\infty,1)\cup(2,\infty)$ (ii) $x\in(-\infty,2)\cup(5,\infty)$ (iii) $x\in(3,4)$, (iv) $x\in(2,4)$, (v) $x\in(-\infty,3)\cup(6,\infty)$ (vi) $x\in(4,6)$, (viii) $x\in(1,4)$, (ix) $x\in(-1,5)$ (x) $x\in(-1,0)\cup(5,\infty)$

LOGARITHMIC EQUATION

TYPE I : A logarithmic equation is of the form $\log_{g(x)} f(x) = b$

$\Rightarrow \quad f(x) = g(x)^b\,,\ g(x) > 0,\ g(x) \neq 1$

1. Solve for x: $\log_x \left(3x^2 + 10x\right) = 3$

2. Solve for x: $\log_{x+1}\left(x^2 - 3x + 5\right) = 2$.

ANSWERS : 1. $x = 5$, 2. $x = 4/5$

TYPE II: A logarithmic equation is of the form

$$\log_{f_1(x)} \left\{\log_{f_2(x)} f(x)\right\} = 0$$

$$\Rightarrow \quad f_2(x) = f(x),\ \begin{matrix} f_1(x) > 0,\ f_1(x) \neq 1 \\ f_2(x) > 0,\ f_2(x) \neq 1 \end{matrix}$$

1. Solve for x: $\log_{x^2+6x+6}\left\{\log_{2x^2+2x+3}\left(x^2 - 2x\right)\right\} = 0$

2. Solve for x : $\log_{x^2+x+1}\left\{\log_{2x^2+3x+5}\left(x^2 + 3\right)\right\} = 0$

ANSWERS : 1. x = -1, -3 2. x = -1 , -2

TYPE III: A logarithmic equation is of the form

$$\log_a f_1(x) = \log_a f_2(x),\ a > 0,\ a \neq 1.$$

$$\Rightarrow \quad f_1(x) = f_2(x),\ f_1(x) > 0 \text{ or } f_2(x) > 0$$

1. Solve for x: $\log_5\left(x^2 - 4x + 3\right) = \log_5(3x + 21)$

2. Solve for x: $\log_{1/3}\left(2\left(\frac{1}{2}\right)^x - 1\right) = \log_{1/3}\left(\left(\frac{1}{4}\right)^x - 4\right)$

ANSWERS : 1. $x = -2, 9$ 2. $x = -\log_2 3$

TYPE IV: A logarithmic equation is of the form

$$\log_{f_1(x)} A = \log_{f_2(x)} A$$

$$\Rightarrow \quad f_1(x) = f_2(x),\ \begin{matrix} f_1(x) > 0,\ f_1(x) \neq 1 \\ or \\ f_2(x) > 0,\ f_2(x) \neq 1 \end{matrix}$$

1. Solve for x: $\log_{\frac{x+5}{3}} 3 = \log_{\frac{-1}{x+1}} 3$

2. Solve for x: $\log_{\frac{x+2}{3}} 5 = \log_{\frac{4}{x-3}} 5$

ANSWERS : 1. $x = -4$ 2. $x = \phi$

TYPE V: A logarithmic equation is of the form

$$\log_{f(x)} g_1(x) = \log_{f(x)} g_2(x)$$

$$\Rightarrow \quad g_1(x) = g_2(x),\ \begin{matrix} g_1(x) > 0,\ f(x) > 0,\ \neq 1 \\ or \\ g_1(x) > 0,\ f(x) > 0,\ \neq 1 \end{matrix}$$

1. Solve for x: $\log_{x^2-1}\left(x^3 + 6\right) = \log_{x^2-1}\left(4x^2 - x\right)$

2. Solve for x: $\log_{\left(x^2-1\right)}\left(x^3 + 6\right) = \log_{\left(x^2-1\right)}\left(2x^2 + 5x\right)$.

ANSWERS : 1. $x = 3$, 2. $x = 3$

TYPE VI: A logarithmic equation is of the form

$$\log_{g_1(x)} f(x) = \log_{g_2(x)} f(x),$$

$$\Rightarrow \quad g(x) = g(x),\ \begin{matrix} g_1(x) > 0,\ \neq 1,\ f(x) > 0 \\ or \\ g_1(x) > 0,\ \neq 1,\ f(x) > 0 \end{matrix}$$

1. Solve for x: $\log_{x^3+x}\left(x^2 - 4\right) = \log_{4x^2-6}\left(x^2 - 4\right)$

2. Solve for x: $\log_{\left(x^3+6\right)}\left(x^2 - 1\right) = \log_{\left(2x^2+5x\right)}\left(x^2 - 1\right)$

ANSWERS : 1. $x = 3$, 2. $x = 3$.

TYPE VII: A logarithmic equation is of the form

$$2n \log_a f_1(x) = \log_a f_2(x),\ a > 0,\ a \neq 1,\ n \in N.$$

$$\Rightarrow \quad f_1^{2n}(x) = f_2(x),\ f_1(x) > 0$$

1. Solve for x: $2\log_3 2x = 2\log_3(4x + 15)$

2. Solve for x: $2\log_5 2x = \log_5\left(7x - 2 - 2x^2\right)$

ANSWERS: 1. $x = 3/2$, 2. $x = 1/2, 2/3$

TYPE VIII: A logarithmic equation

$$(2n+1)\log_a f_1(x) = \log_a f_2(x),\ a > 0,\ a \neq 1,\ n \in N$$

$$\Rightarrow \quad f_1^{(2n+1)}(x) = f_2(x),\ f_1(x) > 0$$

1. Solve for x: $\log\left(8 - 10x - 12x^2\right) = 3\log(2x - 1)$.

2. Solve for x: $\log\left(3x^2 + x - 3\right) = 3\log(3x - 2)$

ANSWERS : 1. $x = \phi$ 2. $x = \frac{5 - \sqrt{10}}{9}$.

TYPE IX: A logarithmic equation is of the form

$$\log_a f(x) + \log_a g(x) = \log_a m(x),\ a > 0,\ a \neq 1$$

$$\Rightarrow \quad \begin{cases} f(x) > 0 \\ g(x) > 0 \\ f(x)g(x) = m(x) \end{cases}$$

1. Solve for x: $2\log_3 x + \log_3\left(x^2 - 3\right) = \log_3(0.5) + \log_3 8$

ANSWERS : 1. $x = 2$

TYPE X: A logarithmic equation is of the form

$$\log_a f(x) - \log_a g(x) = \log_a h(x) - \log_a t(x),$$

where $a > 0,\ a \neq 1$

$$\Rightarrow \log_a f(x) + \log_a t(x) = \log_a g(x) + \log_a h(x)$$

$$\Rightarrow \begin{cases} f(x) > 0, t(x) > 0, g(x) > 0, h(x) > 0 \\ f(x)\,t(x) = g(x).h(x) \end{cases}$$

1. Solve for x :

$$\log_2(3 - x) - \log_2\left(\frac{\sin(3\pi/4)}{5 - x}\right) = \frac{1}{2} + \log_2(x + 7).$$

ANSWERS : $x = 1$

1.32 Logarithmic Inequation

TYPE I: A logarithmic inequation is of the form

$$\begin{cases}\log_a f(x)>\log_a g(x)\\ a>1\end{cases} \Rightarrow \begin{cases} g(x)>0\\ a>1\\ f(x)>g(x)\end{cases}$$

1. Solve for x: $\log_{(2x+3)} x^2 < \log_{(2x+3)}(2x+3), x>-1$

ANSWERS : $x\in(-1,3)$.

TYPE II: A logarithmic inequation is of the form

$$\begin{cases}\log_a f(x)>\log_a g(x)\\ 0<a<1\end{cases} \Rightarrow \begin{cases} f(x)>0\\ 0<a<1\\ f(x)<g(x)\end{cases}.$$

1. Solve for x : $\log_{0.3}(x-1)<\log_{0.09}(x-1)$

ANSWERS : 1. $x > 2$.

TYPE III: A logarithmic inequation is of the form

1. $\begin{cases}\log_a x>0\\ a>1\end{cases} \Rightarrow \begin{cases}x>0\\ a>1\end{cases}$

2. $\begin{cases}\log_a x>0\\ 0<a<1\end{cases} \Rightarrow \begin{cases}0<x<1\\ 0<a<1\end{cases}$

3. $\begin{cases}\log_a x<0\\ a>1\end{cases} \Rightarrow \begin{cases}0<x<1\\ a>1\end{cases}$

4. $\begin{cases}\log_a x<0\\ 0<a<1\end{cases} \Rightarrow \begin{cases}x>1\\ 0<a<1\end{cases}$

1. Solve for x: $\log_{1/2}(2x+3)>0$

2. Solve for x: $\log_2^2 x-\log_2 x-\log 15>0$

ANSWERS : 1. $x\in\left(-\frac{3}{2},-1\right)$ 2. $x\in\left(0,2^{-6}\right)\cup\left(2^{10},\infty\right)$

EXERCISES

(Solve the inequality, wherever base is not given, take it as 10)

1. $(\log_2 x)^4-\left(\log_{\frac{1}{2}}\frac{x^5}{4}\right)^2-20\log_2 x+148<0$

2. $(\log 100x)^2+(\log 10x)^2+\log x\le 14$.

3. $\log_{1/2}(x+1)>\log_2(2-x)$

4. $\log_{1/5}\left(2x^2+5x+1\right)<0$

5. $\log_{1/2}x+\log_3 x>1$

6. $\log_x\left(\frac{4x+5}{6-5x}\right)<-1$ (where base is 2)

ANSWER

1. $x\in\left(\frac{1}{16},\frac{1}{8}\right)\cup(8,16)$ 2. $x\in\left[\frac{1}{\sqrt{10}},10\right]$

3. $-1<x<\frac{1-\sqrt{5}}{2}$ or $\frac{1+\sqrt{5}}{2}<x<2$.

4. $x\in(-\infty,-2.5)\cup(0,\infty)$. 5. $0<x<3^{\frac{1}{1-\log 3}}$

6. $1/2<x<1$.

A TRIGONOMETRIC INEQUATIONS

RULES

Suppose we have to solve $f(x)>k$ and $f(x)<k$.

When solving the inequation , often we use the graphs of the functions $y=f(x)$ and $y=k$.

Then the solution of the inequality $f(x)>k$ is the value of x for each of which the point $(x,f(x))$ of the graph $y=f(x)$ lies above the staight line $y=k$.

Then the solution of the inequality $f(x)<k$ is the value of x for each of which the point $(x,f(x))$ of the graph $y=f(x)$ lies below the staight line $y=k$.

Solution of elementary trigonometric inequalities:

Inequalities	Solution set of inequality, $n\in Z$
1. $\sin x>k\ (\lvert k\rvert<1)$	1. $x\in\left(2n\pi+\sin^{-1}k,\ 2n\pi+\pi-\sin^{-1}k\right)$
2. $\sin x<k\ (\lvert k\rvert<1)$	2. $x\in\left(2n\pi-\pi-\sin^{-1}k,\ 2n\pi+\sin^{-1}k\right)$.
3. $\cos x>k\ (\lvert k\rvert<1)$	3. $x\in\left(2n\pi-\cos^{-1}k,\ 2n\pi+\cos^{-1}k\right)$.
4. $\cos x<k\ (\lvert k\rvert<1)$	4. $x\in\left(2n\pi+\cos^{-1}k,\ 2n\pi+2\pi-\cos^{-1}k\right)$
5. $\tan x>k$	5. $x\in\left(n\pi+\tan^{-1}k,\ n\pi+\frac{\pi}{2}\right)$
6. $\tan x<k$	6. $x\in\left(n\pi-\frac{\pi}{2},\ n\pi+\tan^{-1}k\right)$.

1. Solve for x: $\sin x > -\frac{1}{2}$
2. Solve for x: $\tan x < 2$
3. Solve for x: $\sin\left(\frac{3}{2}x + \frac{\pi}{12}\right) < \frac{1}{\sqrt{2}}$
4. Solve for x: $2\sin^2 x - 7\sin x + 3 > 0$
5. Solve for x: $2\cos^2 x > \frac{3}{2}$
6. Solve for x: $\cos 2x + 3\sin x > -1$

ANSWER

1. $x \in \bigcup_{n \in I}\left(2n\pi - \frac{\pi}{6},\ 2n\pi + \pi + \frac{\pi}{6}\right)$
2. $x \in \bigcup_{n \in I}\left(n\pi - \frac{\pi}{2},\ n\pi + \tan^{-1}2\right)$
3. $x \in \bigcup_{n \in I}\left(\frac{4}{3}n\pi + \frac{4}{9}\pi,\ \frac{4}{3}n\pi + \frac{13}{9}\pi\right)$
4. $x \in \bigcup_{n \in I}\left(2n\pi - \frac{7\pi}{6},\ 2n\pi + \frac{\pi}{6}\right)$
5. $x \in \bigcup_{n \in I}\left(n\pi - \frac{\pi}{6},\ n\pi + \frac{\pi}{6}\right)$
6. $x \in \bigcup_{n \in I}\left(n\pi - \frac{\pi}{6},\ n\pi + \frac{7\pi}{6}\right)$

1.34 Greatest Integer

$[x]$ denotes the greatest integer less than or equal to x. *i.e.* $[x] \le x$. It is known as floor of x.

If n is an integer and x is any real number between n and $(n+1)$ *i.e.* if $n \le x < n+1$ then $[x] = n$

1.35 Properties of Greatest Integer

i. $[-x] = -[x], x \in I$

ii. $[-x] = -[x] - 1, x \notin I$

iii. $[x+n] = n + [x], n \in I$

iv. $x = [x] + \{x\}$, $\{\ \}$ denote the fractional part of x.

v. $[x] - [-x] = 2n$ if $x < n, n \in I$

vi. $[x] - [-x] = 2n + 1$ if $x = n + \{x\}, n \in Z$

vii. $[x] \ge n \Rightarrow x \ge n, n \in I$

viii. $[x] > n \Rightarrow x \ge n+1, n \in I$

ix. $[x] \le n \Rightarrow x < n+1, n \in I$

x. $[x] < n \Rightarrow x < n, n \in I$

xi. $[x+y] = \begin{cases} x+y, & x, y \in I \\ [x]+[y], & 0 \le f_x + f_y < 1 \\ [x]+[y]+1, & 1 \le f_x + f_y < 2 \end{cases}$

xii. $\left[\frac{n+1}{2}\right] + \left[\frac{n+2}{4}\right] + \left[\frac{n+4}{8}\right] + \left[\frac{n+8}{16}\right] + \ldots\ldots\ldots \textit{to}\ \infty$

xiii. $[x] + \left[x + \frac{1}{n}\right] + \left[x + \frac{2}{n}\right] + \ldots + \left[x + \frac{n-1}{n}\right] = [nx].$

LEAST INTEGER

(x) denotes the least integer greater than or equal to x,

i.e., $(x) \le [x] + 1$.

It is known as **ceiling** of x.

PROPERTIES OF LEAST INTEGER

i. $(x) = [x]$, if $x \in I$ and $(x) = [x] + 1$, if $x \notin I$

ii. $(x+n) = n + (x), n \in I$

iii. $(-x) = -(x), x \in I$

iv. $(-x) = -(x) + 1, x \notin I$

EXCERCISES

1. If $[x]$ denotes the integral part of x, then find the value of

$$\left[\frac{1}{4}\right] + \left[\frac{1}{4} + \frac{1}{200}\right] + \left[\frac{1}{4} + \frac{2}{200}\right] + \left[\frac{1}{4} + \frac{3}{200}\right] + \ldots + \left[\frac{1}{4} + \frac{199}{200}\right]$$

2. Find the value of

$$\left[\frac{2013}{2}\right] + \left[\frac{2014}{4}\right] + \left[\frac{2016}{8}\right] + \left[\frac{2020}{16}\right] + \ldots\ldots\ldots\ldots \textit{to}\ \infty$$

3. If x is positive real number, then prove that

$$\left[\frac{x}{2}\right] + \left[\frac{x+1}{2}\right] = [x].$$

4. If $[x]^2 = [x+2]$, where $[,]$ = G.I.F, then find x.

5. Let $f(x)$ be a function is defined by $f(x) = x - [x], x \in R\ (\neq 0)$, where $[,]$ = G.I.F. Then find the number of solutions of $F(x) + F\left(\frac{1}{x}\right) = 1$.

6. Solve for x: $4\{x\} = x + [x]$, $[,]$ = G.I.F, $\{,\}$ = F.P.F

7. If $5\{x\} = x + [x]$ and $[x] - \{x\} = 1/2$, then find x.

8. Find the solution set of $(x)^2 + (x+1)^2 = 25$

9. If the roots of $x^3 - 3x + 1 = 0$ has roots α, β, γ, then find the value of $[\alpha] + [\beta] + [\gamma]$.

10. Solve for x:

i. $[x]^2 - 3[x] + 2 = 0$

ii. $[x]^2 - 7[x] + 10 = 0$

iii. $[x]^2 - [x] = 0$.

ANSWER

1. 50	2. 2012	4. $x \in [-1,0) \cup (2,3)$	5. Infinite.	6. {0, 5/3}
7. $x = 3/2$.	8. $(-5,-4] \cup (2,3]$	9. –1	10. (i) $x \in [1, 3)$, (ii) $x \in [2, 3) \cup [5, 6)$, (iii) $x \in [0, 2)$	

Level – II For JEE – Main and Advanced xams only

1. The roots of the quadratic equation $(a+b-2c)x^2-(2a-b-c)x+(a-2b+c)=0$ are

a. $a+b+c, a-b+c$ b. $\frac{1}{2}, a-2b+c$

c. $a-2b+c, \frac{1}{a+b-c}$ d. None of these

2. If the equation $x^2+ax+b=0$ and $x^2+bx+a=0$ have a common root, then the numberical value of $a+b$ is

a. 1 b. 0

c. –1 d. None of these

3. If $(1-p)$ is a root of quadratic equation $x^2+px+(1-p)=0$, then its roots are :

a. 0, 1 b. –1, 1

c. 0, –1 d. –1, 2

4. The set of values of p for which root sof equation $3x^2+2x+p(p-1)=0$ are of opposite sign is :

a. $(-\infty, 0)$ b. $(0, 1)$

c. $1, \infty$ d. $(0, \infty)$

5. The value of p for which both the roots of the equation $4x^2-20px+(25p^2+15p-66)=0$ are less than 2, lies in

a. $\left(\frac{4}{5}, 2\right)$ b. $(2, \infty)$

c. $\left(-1, \frac{-4}{5}\right)$ c. $(-\infty, -1)$

6. The number of values of k for which the equation $x^2-3x+k=0$ has two distinct roots lying in the interval (0,1) is :

a. three b. two

c. infinitely many d. no value of k satisfies the requirement

7. If $\alpha\beta$ be the roots of $(x-a)(x-b)+c=0, c\neq 0$, then, the roots of $(\alpha\beta-c)x^2+(\alpha+\beta)x+1=0$ are

a. $\frac{1}{a}, \frac{1}{b}$ b. $-\frac{1}{a}, \frac{1}{b}$

c. $\frac{1}{a}, -\frac{1}{b}$ d. $-\frac{1}{a}, -\frac{1}{b}$

8. The quadratic equation with real coefficients one of whose complex roots has the real part 12 and modulus 13 is

a. $x^2-12x+13=0$ b. $x^2-24x+13=0$

c. $x^2-24x+169=0$ d. $x^2-24x-169=0$

9. The root of the equation $x=\sqrt{6+\sqrt{6+\sqrt{6+\ldots\infty}}}$ is

a. 3 b. 2

c. –3 d. 2

10. If $x^2+mx+1=0$ and $(a-b)x^2+(b-c)x+(c-a)=0$ have both roots common then which of the following is true ?

a. $m=-1$ b. $m=2$

c. $m=-2$ d. a, b, c are in AP

11. If quadratic equation $p(q-r)x^2+q(r-p)x+r(p-q)=0$ has equal roots, then $\frac{2}{q}=$

a. $\frac{1}{p}+\frac{1}{r}$ b. $p+r$

c. $\frac{1}{p}+r$ d. $p+\frac{1}{r}$

12. If x, y, z are real and unequal then expression $x^2+4y^2+9z^2-6yz-3zx-2xy$ is always

a. non-negative b. non-positive

c. zero d. none of these

13. Both the roots of the equation: $(x-1)(x-2)+(x-2)(x-3)+(x-3)(x-1)=0$ are :

a. complex numbers b. always real

c. integers d. rational numbers

14. The number of real roots of the equation $(x-3)^2+(x-5)^2+(x-7)^2=0$ is

a. 2 b. 0

c. 4 d. infinitely many

15. The equation $x^2+5|x|+4=0$ has

a. 4 real roots b. 2 real roots

c. no real root d. 6 real roots

16. The roots of $x^2-8|x|+12=0$

a. do not form a progression

b. form an AP with 0 sum

c. form an AP with non-zero sum

d. form a GP

17. If $\alpha, \beta, \gamma, \delta$ be the roots of $16x^4+4x^2+1=0$, then the value of $\alpha^4+\beta^4+\gamma^4+\delta^4$ is

a. $-\frac{1}{8}$ b. 0

c. $\frac{1}{8}$ d. 1

18. If α, β,γ , δ be the roots of $x^4 + x^2 + 1 = 0$, then value of $(\alpha+\beta)(\alpha+\gamma)(\alpha+\delta)(\beta+\gamma)(\beta+\delta)(\gamma+\delta) =$

a. -1 b. 0

c. 1 d. None of these

19. The value of a for which the equation $(a^2 + 4a + 3)x^2 + (a^2 - a - 2)x + (a + 1) = 0$ in x has more than two roots

a. 1 b. -1

c. 2 d. no value of a

20. The number of values of the triplet (a, b, c) for which $a\cos 2x + b\sin^2 x + c = 0$ is satisfied by all real x is

a. 2 b. 4

c. 6 d. infinite

21. If the roots of $ax^2 + bx + c = 0$ are the reciprocals of those of $lx^2 + mx + n = 0$, where all the coefficients are non-zero real numbers, then

a. $\frac{a}{l} = \frac{b}{m} = \frac{c}{n}$ b. $\frac{a}{n} = \frac{b}{m} = \frac{c}{l}$

c. $al = bm = cn$ d. none of these

22. If the equations $x^2 + ax + 12 = 0; x^2 + bx + 15 = 0; x^2 + (a + b)x + 36 = 0$ have a common positive root, then the values of a and b respectively, are

a. $-7, -8$ b. $-8, -7$

c. $-5, -3$ d. no value of a exist

23. If x is any real number, then the value of the expression

$$f(x) = \frac{x^2 - 5x + 4}{x^2 + 5x + 4}$$

a. lies between -9 and $-\frac{1}{9}$

b. do not lies between -9 and $-\frac{1}{9}$

c. may be any real number

d. is always positive

24. The greatest and least values of $\frac{x^2 - x + 1}{x^2 + x + 1}$ for real values of x are:

a. 4 and $\frac{1}{4}$ b. 2 and $\frac{1}{2}$

c. 3 and $\frac{1}{3}$ d. $-\frac{1}{3}$ and -3

25. Given that for all real x, the expression $\frac{x - 2x + 4}{x + 2x + 4}$ lies between $\frac{1}{3}$ and 3. The values between which the expression $\frac{9.3 + 6.3 + 4}{9.3 - 6.3 + 4}$ lies are :

a. $\frac{1}{3}$ and 3 b. -2 and 0

c. -1 and 1 d 0 and 2

26. If α, β, γ are the roots of the equation $x^3 + 4x + 1 = 0$, then $(\alpha+\beta)^{-1} + (\beta+\gamma)^{-1} + (\gamma+\alpha)^{-1} =$

a. 2 b. 3

c. 4 d. 5

27. If a,b,c are sides of a triangle ABC such that $x^2 - 2(a + b + c)x + 3\lambda(ab + bc + ca) = 0$ has real roots, then :

a. $\lambda < \frac{4}{3}$ b. $\lambda > \frac{5}{3}$

c. $\lambda \in \left(\frac{4}{3}, \frac{5}{3}\right)$ d. $\lambda \in \left(\frac{1}{3}, \frac{5}{3}\right)$

28. If $a^2 + b^2 = 2$ and a, b are real then $a + b$ lies in the interval

a. $[-1, 1]$ b. $[-2, 1]$

c. $[1, 2]$ d. $[-2, 2]$

29. If a, b, c are real numbers and $a^2 + b^2 + c^2 = 3$, then the value of $ab + bc + ca$ lies in the interval

a. $\left[-\frac{3}{2}, 1\right]$ b. $\left[-\frac{3}{2}, 3\right]$

c. $\left[-\frac{1}{2}, 1\right]$ d. $[-1, 2]$

30. The number of real solution of the equation $(5 + 2\sqrt{6})^{x^2-3} + (5 - 2\sqrt{6})^{x^2-3} = 10$ is

a. 2 b. 4

c. 6 d. None of these

31. The number of real solution of the equation $(2 + \sqrt{3})^{x^2-2x+1} + (2 - \sqrt{3})^{x^2-2x-1} = \frac{2}{2 - \sqrt{3}}$ is

a. 0 b. 2

c. 4 d. 6

32. The number of real solutions of equation $\left(\frac{9}{10}\right) = -3 + x - x^2$, is $(K \in R)$

a. 0 b. 1

c. 2 d. more than 2

33. The coefficient of x^9 in the polynomial given by $(x + 1)(x + 2)\ldots(x + 10) + (x + 2)(x + 3)\ldots(x + 11) + \ldots + (x + 11)(x + 12)\ldots(x + 20)$ is

a. 1155 b. 1515

c. 5151 d. 5511

34. How many roots does the following equation $3^{|x|}\,|2 - |x|| = 1$ possess?

a. 1 b. 2

c. 3 d. 4

35. The coefficiet of x^6 in $(x-1)(x-2)(x-3)....(x-8)$ is

a. 236 b. 216
c. 546 d. 36

36. The number of real roots of equation $x^8 - x^5 + x^2 - x + 1 = 0$ is equal to

a. 0 b. 2
c. d.

37. Missing

a. b.
c. d.

38. Missing

a. b.
c. d.

39. The number of values of x satisfying $3^x + 4^x = 5^x$ is

a. 0 b. 1
c. 2 d. 3

40. The largest interval in which x lies satisfying $x^{12} - x^9 + x^4 - x + 1 > 0$ is

a. $[0, \infty)$ b. $(-\infty, 0]$
c. $(-\infty, \infty)$ d. None

41. The number of real solutions of 2 $= x + 1$ is

a. 1 b. 2
c. 0 d. 4

42. The number of real solutions $\sqrt{x-2} + \sqrt{6-x} = 2$ is

a. 1 b. 0
c. 2 d. None.

43. The number of real solutions of $|x| + |x-2| = 2$ is

a. 1 b. 2
c. 0 d. infinite.

44. The number of real solutions $x - \dfrac{1}{x-2} = 2 - \dfrac{1}{x-2}$ is

a. 1 b. 2
c. 3 d. 0

45. The number of real solutions $3^x + 4^x + 5^x = 6^x$ is

a. 1 b. 2
c. 4 d. more than 4.

46. If $a, b, c > 0$, $a^2 = bc$ and $a + b + c = abc$, then the least value of $a^4 + a^2 + 7$ is

a. 18 b. 19
c. 20 d. 21

47. If $\alpha\beta$ are the roots of $x^2 - 8x + A = 0$ and γ, δ are the roots of $x^2 - 72x + B = 0$. If $\alpha < \beta < \gamma < \delta$ are in G.P, then the value of $A + B$ is

a. 980 b. 982
c. 984 d. 986

48. Given that for all x in R, the expression $\dfrac{x^2-2x+4}{x^2+2x+4}$ lies between 1/3 and 3, the value between which the expression $\dfrac{9.3^{2x}+6.3^x+4}{9.3^{2x}-6.3^x+4}$ lies in

a. 1/3 and 3 b. 1/2 and 2
c. –1 and 1 d. 0 and 2

49. The total number of solutions of $\sin \pi x = |\ln|x||$ is

a. 2 b. 4
c. 6 d. 8

50. The minimum value of $y = \dfrac{x^3+x+2}{x}, x > 0$ is

a. 3 b. 4
c. 5 d. 2

51. If $P(x) = ax^2 + bx + c$ and $Q(x) = -ax^2 + dx + c$, where $ac \neq 0$, then $P(x).Q(x) = 0$ has

a. Exactly one root b. atleast two real root
c. exactly three real roots d. all four are real roots.

52. Let $a > 0, b > 0$ and $c > 0$. Then both the roots of the equation $ax^2 + bx + c = 0$

a. are real & negative b. have negative real parts
c. are rational numbers d. None.

53. The real values of 'a' for which quadratic equation $2x^2 - (a^3 + 8a - 1)x - a^2 - 4a = 0$ possesses roots of opposite signs is given by

a. $a > 5$ b. $0 < a < 4$
c. $a > 0$ d. $a > 7$

54. Suppose a, b and c are positive numbers such that $a + b + c = 1$. Then the maximum value of $ab + bc + ca$ is

a. 1/3 b. 1/4
c. 1/2 d. 2/3

55. The roots of $(x-1)(x-3) + k(x-2)(x-4) = 0$, $k > 0$ are

a. real b. real and equal
c. imaginary d. one real & other Im.

56. Largest Integral value of m for which the quadratic expression $y = x^2 - (2m+6)x + 4m + 12$ is always positive, for every x in R, is

a. –1 b. –2
c. 0 d. 2.

57. Let $r1$, $r2$ and $r3$ be the solutions of the equation $x^3 - 2x^2 + 4x + 5074 = 0$, then the value of $(r_1+2)(r_2+2)(r_3+2)$ is

a. 5050 b. 5066
c. –5050 d. – 5066

58. The equation whose roots are $\sec^2\alpha$ and $\mathrm{cosec}^2\alpha$ can be

a. $2x^2 - x - 1 = 0$ b. $x^2 - 3x + 3 = 0$
c. $x^2 - 9x + 9 = 0$ d. None.

59. Let a,b,c be the three roots of the equation $x^3 + x^2 - 333x - 1002 = 0$, then the value of $a^3 + b^3 + c^3$ is

a. 2006 b. 2005
c. 2003 d. 2002.

60. The absolute term in the quadratic expression $\sum_{k=1}^{n}\left(x-\frac{1}{k+1}\right)\left(x-\frac{1}{k}\right)$ as $n \to \infty$, is

a. 1 b. –1

c. 0 d. 1/2

61. Number of values of the parameter $\alpha \in [0,2\pi]$ for which the quadratic function $\sin\alpha . x^2 + 2x.\cos\alpha + \frac{1}{2}(\cos\alpha + \sin\alpha)$ is the square of a linear function , is

a. 2 b. 3

c. 4 d. 1.

62. The set of values of a for which the inequality $(x - 3a)(x - a - 3) < 0$ is satisfied for all $x \in [1,3]$ is

a. (1/3, 3) b. (0, 1/3)

c. (–2, 0) d. (–2, 3).

63. If α, β and γ are the roots of the equation, $x^3 - x - 1 = 0$, then the value of $\frac{1+\alpha}{1-\alpha}+\frac{1+\beta}{1-\beta}+\frac{1+\gamma}{1-\gamma}$ is

a. 0 b. –1

c. –7 d. 1

64. For every x in R, the polynomial $x^8 - x^5 + x^2 - x + 1$ is

a. +ve b. never positive

c. +ve and –ve d. –ve

65. If the roots of the cubic, $x^3 + ax^2 + bx + c = 0$ are three consecutive positive integers. Then the value of $\frac{a^2}{b+1}$ is

a. 3 b. 2

c. 1 d. 1/3

66. If both roots of $(3a+1)x^2 - (2a+3b)x + 3 = 0$ are infinite, then

a. $a = \infty,\ b = 0$ b. $a = 0,\ b = \infty$

c. $a = 1/3, b = 2/9$ d. $a = \infty,\ b = \infty$

67. If $\tan\alpha, \tan\beta$ and $\tan\gamma$ are the roots of equation $x^3 - (a+1)x^2 + (b-a)x - b = 0, (b - a \neq 1)$,where $\alpha+\beta+\gamma$ lies between 0 and π, then the value of $(\alpha+\beta+\gamma)$ is

a. $\pi/4$ b. $\pi/2$

c. $3\pi/4$ d. None.

68. Three roots of the equation $x^4 - px^3 + qx^2 - rx + s = 0$ are $\tan A$, $\tan B$ and $\tan C$, where A,B,C are the angles of a triangle. The fourth root of the biquadratic is

a. $\frac{q-r}{1-q+s}$ b. $\frac{p-r}{1+q-s}$

c. $\frac{p+r}{1-q+s}$ d. $\frac{p+r}{1+q-s}$

69. The number of rea.051 roots of $(x+3)^4 + (x+5)^4 = 16$ is

a. 0 b. 2

c. 4 d. None.

70. Let α, β be the roots of .05.05equation $x^2 - ax + b = 0$ and $A_n = \alpha_n + \beta_n$. Then $A_{n+1} - aA_n + bA_{n-1}$ is equal to

a. $-a$ b. b

c. 0 d. $a - b$

71. If α,β,γ are such that $\alpha+\beta+\gamma = 2\alpha^2 + \beta^2 + \gamma^2 = 6, \alpha^3 + \beta^3 + \gamma^3 = 8$, then the value of $\alpha^4 + \beta^4 + \gamma^4$ is

a. 5 b. 18

c. 12 d. 36.

72. Number of irrational solutions of equation $\sqrt{x^2+\sqrt{x^2+11}} + \sqrt{x^2-\sqrt{x^2+11}} = 4$ is

a. 0 b. 2

c. 4 d. 11

73. The number of solution of $10^{2x} + 25^{1/x} = \left(\frac{65}{8}\right) \times 50^{1/x}$ is

a. 0 b. 2

c. 4 d. infinite.

74. The equation $(2.4)^x = (2.6)^x - 1$ has

a. no solution b. exactly one sol

c. at-least 2 sol d. infinite sol.

75. If $n \in N$, then number of real roots of $1 + x + \frac{x^2}{2!} + ... \frac{x^{2n}}{(2n)!} = 0$ is

a. n b. 2

c. 0 d. None.

76. The number of real roots of equation $2^x + 2^{x-1} + 2^{x-2} = 7^x + 7^{x-1} + 7^{x-2}$ is

a. 4 b. 2

c 1 d. 0

77. The number of real solutions of $x - \frac{1}{x^2-4} = 2 - \frac{1}{x^2-4}$ is

a. 0 b. 1

c. 2 d. infinite

78. The number of real solutions of equation $2^{x/2} + \left(\sqrt{2}+1\right)^x = \left(5+2\sqrt{2}\right)^{x/2}$ is

a. infinite b. 6

c. 4 d. 1

79. The number of values of 'a' for which $\left(a^2-3a+2\right)x^2 + \left(a^2-5a+6\right)x + a^2 - 4 = 0$ is an identity in x is

a. 0 b. 1

c. 2 d. 3

80. If $y = 2[x] + 3 = 3[x-2] + 5$, then value of $[x+y]$ is, where [,] = G. I. F

a. 10 b. 12

c. 15 d. None.

81. If $0<x<1000$ and $\left[\frac{x}{2}\right]+\left[\frac{x}{3}\right]+\left[\frac{x}{5}\right]=\frac{31}{30}x$, here [,] = G.I.F, then the possible values of x is

a. 34 b. 33
c. 32 d. None.

82. Let $|x|+|x-2|=2$. Then the value of x lies in

a. $(-\infty,0]$ b. $(1,2]$
c. $[0,2]$ d. $[2,\infty)$.

83. If $|x|+|x+2|+|x-2|=k$, then the equation has only one solution if k is

a. 2 b. 4
c. 6 d. 8

84. Let $y=\frac{x}{x^2+x+4}$. Then the minimum value of y is

a. 1/3 b. 1/5
c. 1/4 d. 1/8.

85. The number of real solutions of $|x|+|x^2-1|=\frac{7}{6}$ is

a. 6 b. 4
c. 5 d. 8

86. Real values of x of $\sqrt{x+3-4\sqrt{x-1}}+\sqrt{x+8-6\sqrt{x-1}}=1$ lies in

a. (4.5) b. [5,10]
c. [4,10] d. [4,5]

87. The real values of x of $|x^2-1|+|x^2-4|=3$ lies in

a. $[-1,1]\cup[-2,2]$ b. $[-2,1]\cup[-1,2]$
c. $[-4,1]\cup[1,4]$ d. None.

88. If $a=\log_{24}12$, $b=\log_{36}24$, and $c=\log_{48}36$, then the value of $abc+1$is

a. $2ac$ b. $2bc$
c. $2ca$ d. None.

89. If $x=1+\log_a bc$, $y=1+\log_b ac$ and $z=1+\log_c ab$, then the value of $\frac{xyz}{xy+yz+xz}$ is

a. 0 b. –1
c. 2 d. 1.

90. If $[x]^2-5[x]+6=0$, where [,] = G.I.F, the value of x lies in

a*. [3,4) b. [2,3)
c. [4,5) d. None.

91. If $P(x)=ax^2+bx+c$ and $Q(x)=-ax^2+dx+c$, where ac ¹ 0, then $P(x).Q(x)=0$ has

a. Exactly one root b. atleast two real root
c. exactly three real roots d. all four are real roots.

92. Let $a>0, b>0$ and $c>0$. Then both the roots of the equation $ax^2+bx+c=0$

a. are real & negative b. have negative real parts
c. are rational numbers d. None.

93. The real values of 'a' for which the quadratic equation $2x^2-(a^3+8a-1)x-a^2-4a=0$ possesses roots of opposite signs is given by

a. $a>5$ b. $0<a<4$
c. $a>0$ d. $a>7$

94. Suppose a, b and c are positive numbers such that $a+b+c=1$. Then the maximum value of $ab+bc+ca$ is

a. 1/3 b. 1/4
c. 1/2 d. 2/3

95. The roots of $(x-1)(x-3)+k(x-2)(x-4)=0$, $k>0$ are

a. real b. real and equal
c. imaginary d. one real & other Im.

96. Largest Integral value of m for which the quadratic expression $y=x^2-(2m+6)x+4m+12$ is always positive, for every x in R, is

a. –1 b. –2
c. 0 d. 2.

97. Let $r1$, $r2$ and $r3$ be the solutions of the equation $x^3-2x^2+4x+5074=0$, then the value of $(r_1+2)(r_2+2)(r_3+2)$ is

a. 5050 b. 5066
c. – 5050 d. – 5066

98. The equation whose roots are $\sec^2$ a and cos ec^2 a can be

a. $2x^2-x-1=0$ b. $x^2-3x+3=0$
c. $x^2-9x+9=0$ d. None.

99. Let a, b, c be the three roots of the equation $x^3+x^2-333x-1002=0$, then the value of $a^3+b^3+c^3$ is

a. 2006 b. 2005
c. 2003 d. 2002.

100. The absolute term in quadratic expression $\sum_{k=1}^{n}\left(x-\frac{1}{k+1}\right)\left(x-\frac{1}{k}\right)$ as $n\to\infty$, is

a. 1 b. –1
c. 0 d. 1/2

101. Number of values of the parameter $\alpha\in[0,2\pi]$ for which the quadratic function $\sin\alpha\, x^2+2x.\cos\alpha+\frac{1}{2}(\cos\alpha+\sin\alpha)$ is the square of a linear function, is

a. 2 b. 3
c. 4 d. 1.

102. The set of values of a for which the inequality $(x-3a)(x-a-3)<0$ is satisfied for all $x\in[1,3]$ is

a. (1/3, 3) b. (0, 1/3)
c. (–2, 0) d. (–2, 3).

103. If $\alpha\beta$ and γ are the roots of the equation, $x^3-x-1=0$, then the value of $\frac{1+\alpha}{1-\alpha}+\frac{1+\beta}{1-\beta}+\frac{1+\gamma}{1-\gamma}$ is

a. 0 b. –1
c. –7 d. 1

104. For every x in R, the polynomial $x^8 - x^5 + x^2 - x + 1$ is

a. +ve b. never positive
c. +ve and –ve d. –ve

105. If the roots of cubic, $x^3 + ax^2 + bx + c = 0$ are three consecutive positive integers. Then the value of $\frac{a^2}{b+1}$ is

a. 3 b. 2
c. 1 d. 1/3

106. If both roots of $(3a+1)x^2 - (2a+3b)x + 3 = 0$ are infinite, then

a. $a = \infty, b = 0$ b. $a = 0, b = \infty$
c. $a = 1/3, b = 2/9$ d. $a = \infty, b = \infty$.

107. If $\tan\alpha$, $\tan\beta$ and $\tan\gamma$ are the roots of equation $x^3 - (a+1)x^2 + (b-a)x - b = 0$, $(b - a \neq 1)$, where $\alpha + \beta + \gamma$ lies between 0 and π, then the value of $(\alpha + \beta + \gamma)$ is

a. $\pi/4$ b. $\pi/2$
c. $3\pi/4$ d. None.

108. Three roots of the equation $x^4 - px^3 + qx^2 - rx + s = 0$ are $\tan A$, $\tan B$ and $\tan C$, where A, B, C are the angles of a triangle. The fourth root of the biquadratic is

a. $\frac{q-r}{1-q+s}$ b. $\frac{p-r}{1+q-s}$
c. $\frac{p+r}{1-q+s}$ d. $\frac{p+r}{1+q-s}$

109. The number of real roots of $(x+3)^4 + (x+5)^4 = 16$ is

a. 0 b. 2
c. 4 d. None.

110. Let α, β be the roots of equation $x^2 - ax + b = 0$ and $A_n = \alpha^n + \beta^n$. Then $A_{n+1} - aA_n + bA_{n-1}$ is equal to

a. $-a$ b. b
c. 0 d. $a - b$

111. If α, β, γ are such that $\alpha + \beta + \gamma = 2$, $\alpha^2 + \beta^2 + \gamma^2 = 6$, $\alpha^3 + \beta^3 + \gamma^3 = 8$, then the value of $\alpha^4 + \beta^4 + \gamma^4$ is

a. 5 b. 18
c. 12 d. 36.

112. Number of irrational solutions of equation $\sqrt{x^2 + \sqrt{x^2 + 11}} + \sqrt{x^2 - \sqrt{x^2 + 11}} = 4$ is

a. 0 b. 2
c. 4 d. 11

113. The number of solution of $10^{2x} + 25^{1/x} = \left(\frac{65}{8}\right) \times 50^{1/x}$ is

a. 0 b. 2
c. 4 d. infinite.

114. The equation $(2.4)^x = (2.6)^x - 1$ has

a. no solution b. exactly one sol
c. at-least 2 sol d. infinite sol.

115. If $n \in N$, then number of real roots of $1 + x + \frac{x^2}{2!} + \ldots\ldots\ldots\ldots + \frac{x^{2n}}{(2n)!} = 0$ is

a. n b. 2
c. 0 d. None.

116. The number of real roots of equation $2^x + 2^{x-1} + 2^{x-2} = 7^x + 7^{x-1} + 7^{x-2}$ is

a. 4 b. 2
c. 1 d. 0

117. The number of real solutions of $x - \frac{1}{x^2-4} = 2 - \frac{1}{x^2-4}$ is

a. 0 b. 1
c. 2 d. infinite

118. The number of real solutions of equation $2^{x/2} + (\sqrt{2}+1)^x = (5 + 2\sqrt{2})^{x/2}$ is

a. infinite b. 6
c. 4 d. 1

119. The number of the values of 'a' for which $(a^2 - 3a + 2)x^2 + (a^2 - 5a + 6)x + a^2 - 4 = 0$ is an identity in x is

a. 0 b. 1
c. 2 d. 3

120. If $y = 2[x] + 3 = 3[x-2] + 5$, then the value of $[x+y]$ is, where $[.] =$ G. I. F

a. 10 b. 12
c. 15 d. None.

121. If $0 < x < 1000$ and $\left[\frac{x}{2}\right] + \left[\frac{x}{3}\right] + \left[\frac{x}{5}\right] = \frac{31}{30}x$, where $[.]$ = G. I. F, then the possible values of x is

a. 34 b. 33
c. 32 d. None.

122. If $a, b, c > 0$, $a^2 = bc$ and $a + b + c = abc$, then the least value of $a^4 + a^2 + 7$ is

a. 18 b. 19
c. 20 d. 21

123. If α, β are the roots of $x^2 - 8x + A = 0$ and γ, δ are roots of $x^2 - 72x + B = 0$. If $\alpha < \beta < \gamma < \delta$ are in G.P, then the value of $A + B$ is

a. 980 b. 982
c. 984 d. 986

124. Given that for all x in R, the expression $\frac{x^2 - 2x + 4}{x^2 + 2x + 4}$ lies between 1/3 and 3, value between which the expression $\frac{9.3^{2x} + 6.3^x + 4}{9.3^{2x} - 6.3^x + 4}$ lies in

a. *1/3 and 3 b. 1/2 and 2
c. –1 and 1 d. 0 and 2

125. The total number of solutions of $\sin \pi x = \left|\ln|x|\right|$ is

a. 2 b. 4
c. 6 d. 8

Answers

1. d	2. c	3. c	4. b	5. d	6. d	7. d	8. b
9. a	10. c	11. a	12. a	13. b	14. b	15. c	16. b
17. a	18. b	19. b	20. d	21. b	22. a	23. b	24. c
25. a	26. c	27. a	28. d	29. b	30. b	31. b	32. a
33. a	34. d	35. c	36. a	37. c	38. a	39. b	40. c
41. b	42. c	43. d	44. d	45. a	46. b	47. c	48. a
49. c	50. b	51. b	52. b	53. b	54. a	55. a	56. c
57. c	58. c	59. a	60. a	61. a	62. b	63. c	64. a
65. a	66. c	67. a	68. a	69. b	70. c	71. b	72. c
73. b	74. c	75. c	76. c	77. a	78. d	79. b	80. c
81. b	82. c	83. b	84. b	85. a	86. b	87. b	88. b
89. d	90. b	91. b	92. b	93. b	94. a	95. a	96. c
97. c	98. c	99. a	100. a	101. a	102. b	103. c	104. a
105. a	106. c	107. a	108. a	109. b	110. c	111. b	112. c
113. b	114. b	115. c	116. c	117. a	118. d	119. b	120. c
121. b	122. b	123. c	124. a	125. c			

Level–III For JEE- Main and Advanced Exams Only

1. Find the range of the expression $y=\dfrac{\tan^2\theta-2\tan\theta-8}{\tan^2\theta-4\tan\theta-5}$

2. Find the range of expression $y=\dfrac{(\cot^2\theta+5)(\cot^2\theta+10)}{(\cot^2\theta+1)}$

3. If x is real, then find max or min value of $y=\dfrac{2x^2-3x+2}{2x^2+3x+2}$

4. Find the value of k for which expression $12x^2-10xy+2y^2+11x-5y+k$ is the product of two linear factors.

5. Find the greatest and the least values of x and y satisfying the relation $x^2+y^2=6x-8y$

6. If a,b,c,d are in G.P then prove that ax^3+bx^2+cx+d is divisible by (ax^2+c)

7. Prove that ax^3+bx+c is divisible by x^2+px+1 if $a^2-c^2=ab$

8. Prove that x^3+px^2+qx+r will be a perfect cube if $p^2=27r$ and $3pr=q^2$.

9. Find the integral roots of $x^4-x^3-19x^2+49x-30=0$.

10. Solve for x: $(6-x)^4+(8-x)^4=16$

11. Let α & β be the roots of $x^3+ax^2+bx+c=0$ satisfying the relations $\alpha\beta+1=0$. Then prove that $c^2+ac+b+1=0$

12. If α,β,γ be the roots of $x^3+x+2=0$, then find an equation whose roots are $(\alpha-\beta)^2,(\beta-\gamma)^2,(\gamma-\alpha)^2$

13. If α,β,γ be the roots of $x^3+qx+r=0$, then prove that $\left(\dfrac{\alpha^5+\beta^5+\gamma^5}{5}\right)=\left(\dfrac{\alpha^2+\beta^2+\gamma^2}{2}\right)\times\left(\dfrac{\alpha^3+\beta^3+\gamma^3}{3}\right)$.

14. Solve for x : $x^3-27x+27=0$

15. Solve for x : $8x^3-4x^2-4x+1=0$

16. Let a and b be the roots of the equation $x^2-10cx-11d=0$ and those of $x^2-10ax-11b=0$ are c,d then find the value of $a+b+c+d$ when $a\neq b\neq c\neq d$.

17. Let p and q be real numbers such that $p\neq 0, p^3=-q$. If α and β are non zero complex numbers satisfying $\alpha+\beta=-p$, $\alpha^3+\beta^3=q$, then find a quadratic equation having roots $\dfrac{\alpha}{\beta}$ and $\dfrac{\beta}{\alpha}$.

18. Let $\alpha(a)$ and $\beta(a)$ be roots of $\left(\sqrt[3]{a+1}-1\right)x^2+\left(\sqrt{1+a}-1\right)x+\left(\sqrt[6]{a+1}-1\right)=0$, where $a>-1$. such that $L=\lim\limits_{\alpha\to a^+}\alpha(a)$ and $M=\lim\limits_{\alpha\to a^+}\beta(a)$, then find the value of $L+M+3$.

19. Find the smallest integral value of k for which both the roots of $x^2-8kx+16(k^2-k+1)=0$ are real and distinct and have value at-least 4.

20. If α,β,γ are the roots of $x^3+qx+r=0$, then prove that the equation whose roots are $\dfrac{\alpha}{\beta}+\dfrac{\beta}{\alpha},\dfrac{\beta}{\gamma}+\dfrac{\gamma}{\beta},\dfrac{\gamma}{\alpha}+\dfrac{\alpha}{\gamma}$ is $r^2(x+1)^3+q^3(x+1)+q^3=0$

ANSWERS

1. R
2. $[25, \infty)$
3. Max Value = 7, Min value = 1/7.
4. Ans. $k = 2$.
5. $-2 \le x \le 8$ and $-9 \le y \le 1$
9. 1,2,3 & –5
10. 6, 8
12. $x^3 + 6x^2 + 9x + 12 = 0$
14. $6\cos\left(\frac{2\pi}{9}\right), 6\cos\left(\frac{4\pi}{9}\right), 6\cos\left(\frac{8\pi}{9}\right)$
15. $\cos\left(\frac{\pi}{7}\right), \cos\left(\frac{3\pi}{7}\right), \cos\left(\frac{5\pi}{7}\right)$
16. 1210
17. $(p^3 + q)x^2 - (p^3 - 2q)x + (p^3 + q) = 0$
18. (3/2).
19. 2

PASSAGE–I

Let the quadratic equation be $ax^2 + bx + c = 0$, where a,b,c are all real and α, β be its roots .

Also if, a_1, a_2, a_3,........ are in A.P, then $a_2 - a_1 = a_3 - a_2 = a_4 - a_3 =$......... and if b_1, b_2, b_3............ are in G.P, then $\frac{b_2}{b_1} = \frac{b_3}{b_2} = \frac{b_4}{b_3} =$ ....

and also, if, c_1, c_2, c_3,................. are in H.P then $\frac{1}{c_2} - \frac{1}{c_1} = \frac{1}{c_3} - \frac{1}{c_2} = \frac{1}{c_4} - \frac{1}{c_3} =$ ...., where $a_1 \ne 0, b_1 \ne 0, c_1 \ne 0, i = 1,2,3,....$

On the basis of the above information , answer the following questions .

1. Let p and q be the roots of $x^2 - 2x + A = 0$ and r, s be the roots of $x^2 + 18x + B = 0$. If $p < q < r < s$ are in A.P. Then the values of A and B are
   a. –5, 67 b. –3, 77
   c. 67, –5 d. 77, –3
2. Let α, β be the roots of $x^2 - x + p = 0$ and γ, δ be the roots of $x^2 - 4x + q = 0$. If $\alpha, \beta, \gamma, \delta$ are in G.P, then the integral values of p and q are
   a. –2, –32 b. –2, 3
   c. –6, 3 d. –6, –32.
3. Let α, β be the roots of $Ax^2 - 4x + 1 = 0$ and γ, δ be the roots of $Bx^2 - 6x + 1 = 0$. If $\alpha, \beta, \gamma, \delta$ are in H.P , then the integral values of A and B are
   a. –3, 8 b. –3, 16
   c. 3, 8 d. 3, 16.

PASSAGE–II

Consider a quadratic equation $(1 + m)x^2 - 2(1 + 3m)x + (1 + 8m) = 0$, where $m \in R - \{-1\}$

On the basis of above information, answer the following questions:

1. The number of integral values of m such that given quadratic equation has imaginary roots are
   a. 0 b. 1
   c. 2 d. 3
2. The set of values of m such that the given quadratic equation has at least one roots is negative is
   a. $m \in (-\infty, -1)$ b. $m \in \left(-\frac{1}{8}, \infty\right)$
   c. $m \in \left(-1, -\frac{1}{8}\right)$ d. $m \in R$
3. The set of values of m such that the given quadratic equation has both roots are positive is
   a. $m \in R$ b. $m \in (-1,3)$
   c. $m \in [3, \infty)$ d. $m \in (-\infty, -1) \cup [3, \infty)$
4. The set of value of m such that the given equation has at least one roots is positive is
   a. $m \in (-\infty, -1) \cup \left(-1, -\frac{1}{8}\right) \cup \left(-\frac{1}{3}, \infty\right)$
   b. $m \in (-\infty, -1) \cup \left(-\frac{1}{3}, -\frac{1}{8}\right) \cup [3, \infty)$
   c. $m \in \left(-\frac{1}{3}, -\frac{1}{8}\right)$
   d. $m \in (-\infty, -1) \cup \left(-1, -\frac{1}{8}\right) \cup [3, \infty)$

PASSAGE–III

Let $(a + \sqrt{b})^{Q(x)} + (a - \sqrt{b})^{Q(x) - 2\lambda} = A$, where $\lambda \in N$, $A \in R$ and $a^2 - b = 1 \Rightarrow (a + \sqrt{b})(a - \sqrt{b}) = 1 \Rightarrow (a + \sqrt{b})(a - \sqrt{b})^{-1}$ and $\Rightarrow (a - \sqrt{b})(a + \sqrt{b})^{-1}$ i.e $(a \pm \sqrt{b}) = (a + \sqrt{b})^{\pm}$ or $(a - \sqrt{b})^{\pm 1}$

On the basis of above information, answers the following uestions:

1. If $(4 + \sqrt{15})^{[x]} + (4 - \sqrt{15})^{[x]} = 62$, where [.] = G. I. F, then
   a. $x \in [-3, -2) \cup [1,2)$ b. $x \in [-3, -2)$
   c. $x \in [-2, -1) \cup [2,3)$ d. $x \in [-2, 3)$
2. The solutions of $(2 + \sqrt{3})^{x^2 - 2x + 1} + (2 - \sqrt{3})^{x^2 - 2x - 1} = \frac{4}{2 - \sqrt{3}}$
   a. $1 \pm \sqrt{3}, 1$ b. $1 \pm \sqrt{2}, 1$
   c. $1 \pm \sqrt{3}, 2$ d. $1 \pm \sqrt{2}, 2$

3. The number of real solutions of the equation $(15+4\sqrt{14})^t + (15-4\sqrt{14})^t = 30$ are, where $t = x^2 - 2|x|$

a. 0 b. 2
c. 4 d. 6

4. If α, β are the roots of equation $1! + 2! + 3! + ...+ (x-1)! + x! = k^2$ and $k \in I$ where $\alpha < \beta$ and if $\alpha_1, \alpha_2, a_3, \alpha_4$, are the roots of the equation $(a+\sqrt{b})^{x^2-[1+2\alpha+3\alpha^2+4\alpha^3+5\alpha^4]} + (a-\sqrt{b})^{x^2+[-5\beta]} = 2a$, where $a^2 - b = 1$ and [,] = G.I.F , then the value of $|\alpha_1 + \alpha_2 + \alpha_3 + \alpha_4 - \alpha_1\alpha_2\alpha_3\alpha_4|\, a$ is

a. 216 b. 221
c. 224 d. 209

PASSAGE–IV

Consider the cubic equation $f(x) = ax^3 + bx^2 + cx + d = 0$, where a, b, c, d are real numbers.

On the basis of the above information , answer the following questions.

1. If two roots are equal in magnitude but opposite in sign, then

a. $bc + ad = 0$ b. $bc - ad = 0$
c. $ab = cd$ d. $ab + cd = 0$.

2. If the equation has one and only one +ve real roots , then

a. $b^2 < 3ac, ad > 0$ b. $b^2 > 3ac, ad > 0$
c. $b^2 < 3ac, ad < 0$ d. $b^2 > 3ac, ad < 0$

3. If $a = 1$ and one root of the given equation is unity, then the value of $b + c + d$ is

a. 36 b. 0
c. – 1 d. 1

PASSAGE–V

Let α, β be the roots of $x^2 + px + q = 0$ and $\gamma\delta$ are the roots of $x^2 + rx + s = 0$

On the basis of the above information, answer the following questions.

1. If $\alpha, \beta, \gamma, \delta$ are in G.P, then

a. $q^2r^2 = p^2s^2$ b. $q^2r^2 = p^2s^2 = 0$
c. $qr^2 = ps^2 = 0$ d. $qr^2 = ps^2$

2. If $\alpha, \beta, \gamma, \delta$ are in A.P, then

a. $p^2 + r^2 = 4(s+q)$ b. $p^2 - r^2 = 4(s-q)$
c. $p^2 - r^2 = 2(s-q)$ d. $p^2 + r^2 = 2(s+q)$

3. The value of $(\alpha-\gamma)(\alpha-\delta)(\beta-\gamma)(\beta-\delta)$ is

a. $q^2s^2 - pr(q+s) + s(p^2-2q) + qr^2$

b. $q^2 - s^2 - pr(q+s) + s(p^2-2q) + qr^2$

c. $q^2 + s^2 - pr(q+s) + s(p^2-2q) + qr^2$

d. $q^2 + s^2 - pr(q-s) + s(p^2 - 2q + qr^2)$

ANSWERS

PASSEGE 1

1. b **2.** c **3.** a

PASSEGE 2

1. c **2.** c **3.** c **4.** d

PASSEGE 3

1. c **2.** b **3.** c **4.** c

PASSEGE 4

1. b **2.** c **3.** c

PASSEGE 5

1. d **2.** b **3.** c

MATCH MATRIX

(FOR JEE - MAIN AND ADVANCED EXAMS ONLY)

1. Observe the following Columns :

I	II
A. The number of solutions of the system of equations $x + 2y = 6$ and $|x-3| = y$ is m, then	P m is the A.M of n and p.
B. If x and y are integers and $(x-8)(x-10) = 2^y$, the Number of solutions is n, then	Q n is the G.M of m and p
C. The number of integral solutions for the equation $x + 2y = 2xy$ is p, then	R p is the H.M of m and n
	S $n = \dfrac{m^p + p^m}{mp}$
	T $m = \sqrt{n\sqrt{p\sqrt{n\sqrt{p\sqrt{n............\infty}}}}}$

2. Observe the following Columns :

I	II
A. If $a + b + 2c = 0$, $c \neq 0$, then the equation $ax^2 + bx + c = 0$ has	P at least one root in (-2, 0)
	Q at – least one root in (-1, 0)
B. Let $a,b,c \in R$ such that $2a + 3b + 6c = 0$, then The equation $ax^2 + bx + c = 0$ has	R at least one root in (-1, 1)
	S at least one root in (0, 1)
C. Let a, b, c be non zero real numbers such that $\int_0^1 (1+\cos^8 x)(ax^2bx+c)\,dx = \int_0^2 (1+\cos^8 x)(ax^2bx+c)\,dx$, then equation $ax^2 + bx + c = 0$ has	T at least one root in (0, 2)

3. Observe the following Columns :

I	II	
A. If N be the number of solutions and S be the sum of all Roots of the equation $\|x-\|4-x\|-2x=4$, then	P	S = 0
	Q	N = 1
B. If N be the number of solutions and S be the sum of all Roots of the equation $\|x^2-x-6\| = x+2$, then	R	N = 2
	S	N = 3
C. If N be the number of solutions and S be the sum of all Roots of the equation $\|x^2-3\|x\|-4=0$, then	T	S = 4

4. Observe the following Columns :

I		II
A. If a, b, c, d are four non zero real numbers such that $(d+a-b)+(d+b-c)^2=0$ and roots of the equation $a(b-c)x^2+b(c-a)x+c(a-b)=0$ are real and unequal, Then	P	$a+b+c\neq 0$
	Q	a, b, c are in A.P
B. If a,b,c are three non zero real numbers such that Equation $(b-c)x^2+(c-a)x+(a-b)=0$ are real and equal, then	R	a,b,c are in G.P
	S	a, b, c are in H.P
C. If the three equations $x^2+px+12=0$, $x^2+qx+15=0$ and $x^2+(p+q)x+36=0$ have a common positive root and a,b,c be their other roots, then	T	$a=b=c$

ANSWER

1. A → (P, T); B → (Q, S); C → (R)
2. A → R, S T; B → P, Q, R; C → R, S, T
3. A → (P, Q); B → (S, T); C → (P, R)
4. A → P, Q, R, S, T; B → P, Q; C → R

ASSERTION AND REASON

(A) Both A and R are true and R is the correct explananation of A.

(B) Both A and R are true and R is not the correct explanation of A.

(C) A is true and R is false

(D) A is false and R is true.

1. Assertion (A): If the equations $ax\ 2+bx+c=0$, where a,b,c are real numbers, and $x^2+2x+3=0$ have a common root, then $a:b:c=1:2:3$

Reason (R) : Roots of $x^2+2x+3=0$ are imaginary .

2. Assertion (A) : The number of real solutions of the equation

$$\sin\left(2^x\right)\cos\left(2^x\right)=\frac{1}{4}\left(2^x+2^{-x}\right) \text{ is } 2$$

Reason (R) : A.M $\geq$ G.M

3. Aseertion (A): If a,b,c are rationals and $2^{1/3}$ satisfies $a+bx+cx^2=0$ then $a=0=b=c$.

Reason (R) : A polynomial equation with rational co efficients have irrational roots.

4. Assertion (A): If x, y, z are reals and $2x^2+y^2+z^2=2x-4y+2xz-5$ then the maximum possible value of $x-y+z$ is 4.

Reason (R) : The above equation re-arranges as such of three squareds equated to zero.

5. Assertion (A): If $(a-b)x^2+(b-c)x+(c-a)=0$, then $x=1$ is a root.

Reason (R) : If sum of the co-efficients of $ax^2+bx+c=0$ is zero, then 1 is a root.

6. Assertion (A): If $a+b+c>0$ and $a<0<b<c$, then both the roots of $a(x-b)(x-c)+b(x-a)(x-b)+c(x-a)(x-b)=0$ are negative

Reason (R) : If both roots are negative, then the sum of the roots is -ve as well as product of the roots.

7. Assertion (A) : The co-efficient of x^{49} in $(x-1)(x-2)$.........

Reason (R) : If a, b, c, d are in G.P, then $\frac{a}{b}=\frac{b}{c}=\frac{c}{d}$.

8. Assertion (A) : If $(a^2+b^2+c^2)p^2-2(ab+bc+cd)p+(b^2+c^2+d^2)\leq 0$, then a, b, c, d are in G.P

Reason (R) : The number of real solution of $\sin x=x^2+x+1$ is zero.

9. Assertion (A) : If $\left|\frac{x}{x-1}\right|+|x|=\frac{x^2}{|x-1|}$, then $x\in(1,\infty)$

Reason (R) : If $f(x)+g(x)=f(x)g(x)$, then $f(x)g(x)\geq 0$

10. Assertion (A) : If the number of real solutions of $2^x+2^{x-1}+2^{x-2}=7^x+7^{x-1}+7^{x-2}$ is 1

Reason (R) : If $a^x+a^{x-1}+a^{x-2}=b^x+b^{x-1}+b^{x-2}$, then

$$x=2+\log_{(a/b)}\left(\frac{b^2+b+1}{a^2+a+1}\right)$$

ANSWERS

1. b 2. d 3. c 4. b 5. a 6. d 7. b 8. b 9. a 10. b

Questions asked in Roorkee Exams

1. Find out the range in which value of function $\frac{x^2+34x-71}{x^2+2x-7}$ lies for all real values of x, Justify your answer.

[Roorkee – 1983]

2. No questions asked in **1984.**

3. Solve for x ; $\sqrt{5x^2-6x+8}-\sqrt{5x^2-6x+7}=1$

[Roorkee – 1985]

4. Solve for x ; $\frac{2\sqrt{x+1}}{3-\sqrt{x}}=\frac{11-3\sqrt{x}}{5\sqrt{x-9}}$

[Roorkee – 1985]

5. Solve for x: $(x^2+2)^2+8x^2=5x(x^2+2)$

[Roorkee – 1986]

6. What is wrong with the following calculations?

$1=\sqrt{1}=\sqrt{(-1)\times(-1)}=\times\sqrt{(-1)}=i\times i=-1$

—[Roorkee– 1987]

7. Solve for x; $3x^3=\lfloor x^2+x\sqrt{18}+\sqrt{32}\rfloor\lfloor x^2-x\sqrt{18}-\sqrt{32}\rfloor-4x$

[Roorkee – 1988]

8. Solve for x; $2^{|x+1|}-2^x=|2^x-1|+1$

[Roorkee – 1989]

9. Let there be a quotient of two natural numbers in which the denominator is one less than the square of the numerator. If we add 2 to both numerator and denominator, the quotient will exceed 1/3 , and if subtract 3 from numerator, the quotient will lie between 0 and 1/10. Determine the quotient.

[Roorkee –1990]

10. Solve for x: $(15+4\sqrt{14})+(15-4\sqrt{14})=30$, where $t=x^2-2|x|$

[Roorkee – 1991]

11. Find the positive solutions of system of equations $x^{x+y}=y^n$, $y^{x+y}=x^{2n}y^n$, where $n>0$.

[Roorkee – 1992]

12. Obtain real solutions of simultaneous equations $xy+3y^2-x+4y-7=0$; $2xy+y^2-2x-2y+1=0$

[Roorkee – 1993]

13. If α and β are the roots of the equation $x^2-px+q=0$, then find the quadratic equation the roots of which are $(\alpha^2-\beta^2)(\alpha^3-\beta^3)$ and $\alpha^3\beta^2+\alpha^2\beta^3$

[Roorkee –1994]

14. If the roots of $10x^3-cx^2-54x-27=0$ are in H.P, then find the value of c and all the roots.

[Roorkee – 1995].

15. No questions asked in **1996, 1997, 1998.**

16. Let $a+i\beta$; $\alpha\beta\in R$ be a root of the equation $x^3+qx+r=0$; $q,r,\in R$. Find a real cubic equation, independent of α and β, whose one roots is 2α.

[Roorkee–1999]

17. If α,β are the roots of the equation $(x-a)(x-b)+c=0$, then find the roots of the equation $(x-\alpha)(x-\beta)-c=0$

[Roorkee–2000]

18. Given that $\alpha,\gamma,$ are the roots of $Ax^2-4x+1=0$ and β,δ and are the roots of $Bx^2-6x+1=0$, then find the values of A and B such that α,β,γ, and δ are in H.P.

[Roorkee – 2000]

19. The sum of the roots of the equation $ax^2+bx+c=0$ is equal to the sum of squares of their reciprocals. Find whether bc^2, ca^2 and ab^2 are in A.P., G.P. or H.P ?

[Roorkee – 2001]

ANSWER

1. $(-\infty,5]\cup[9,\infty)$ **2.** $x=4$ or $-14/5$ **4.** The data in the question is incorrect **5.** $x=(2\pm\sqrt{2});1\pm i$

7. $x=3\pm\sqrt{17},\ \frac{-3\pm i\sqrt{7}}{2}$ **8.** $x=0,-2$ **9.** 4/15 **10.** $x=1,-1$

11. $x=\frac{3\sqrt{n-1}}{2},y=\frac{4n-3\sqrt{n+1}}{2}$ **12.** $x=0,y=1$ and $x=-2,y=-3$

13. $x^2-p(p^4-5p^2q+5q^2)x+p^2q^2(p^4-5p^2q+4q^2)=0$ **14.** $c=9$; $-3/2,-3/5,3$

16. $x^3+qx-r=0$ **17.** a,b **18.** $A=3,B=8$ **19.** A.P.

Questions asked in IIT-JEE Exams

1. Show that the square of $\frac{\sqrt{26-15\sqrt{3}}}{5\sqrt{2}-\sqrt{38+5\sqrt{3}}}$ is a rational number. [IIT-JEE – 1978]
2. If α, β are the roots of the equation $x^2+px+1=0$ and γ, δ are the roots of $x^2 + qx + 1 = 0$, then find the value of $(\alpha - \gamma)(\beta - \gamma)(\alpha + \delta)(\beta + \delta)$ [IIT-JEE –1978]
3. If α and β are the roots of $x^2+px+q=0$ and γ, δ are the roots of $x^2+rx+s=0$, then find the value of $(\alpha-\gamma)(\beta-\gamma)(\alpha-\delta)(\beta-\delta)$ in terms of p, q, r and s. [IIT-JEE – 1979]
4. Show that for any triangle with sides a,b,c; $3(ab+bc+ca) \leq (a+b+c)^2 \leq 4(ab+bc+ca)$ [IIT-JEE – 1979]
5. Find the integral solutions of the following systems of inequalities

   i. $5x-1<(x+1)^2<7x-3$ ii. $\frac{x}{2x+1!} \geq \frac{1}{4}; \frac{6x}{4x-1} < \frac{1}{2}$

   [IIT-JEE – 1979]
6. If x, y, z are all real and distinct then $U = x^2+4y^2+9z^2-6yz-3zx-2xy$ is always

   a. non negative b. non positive
   c. zero d. None. [IIT-JEE–1979]
7. Let $a>0, b>0$ and $c>0$. Then both the roots of the equation $ax^2+bx+c=0$

   a. are real and negative b. have negative real parts
   c. have positive real parts d. None. [IIT-JEE–1979]
8. For what values of 'm' does the system of equations $3x+my=m$, $2x-5y=20$ has solution satisfying the condition $x>0$, $y>0$. [IIT-JEE-1980]
9. Show that the equation $e^{\sin x}-e^{-\sin x}-4=0$ has no real solution [IIT-JEE – 1980]
10. Both roots of the equation $(x-b)(x-c)+(x-c)(x-a)+(x-a)(x-b)$ are always [IIT-JEE – 1980]

    a. positive b. negative
    c. real d. None
11. No questions asked in **1981.**
12. The number of real solutions of equation $|x|^2-3|x|+2=0$ is

    a. 4 b. 1
    c. 3 d. 2 [IIT-JEE –1982]
13. mn squares of equal size are arranged to form a rectangle of dimension m by n, where m and n are natural numbers. Two squares will be called neighbours if they have exactly one common side. A natural number is written in each square such that the number written in any square is the arithmetic mean of the numbers written in its neighbouring squares. Show that this is possible only if all the numbers used are equal. [IIT-JEE – 1982]
14. If $x_1, x_2, \ldots, x_n$ are any real numbers and n is any positive integer, then

    a. $n\sum_{i=1}^{n} x_i^2 < \left(n\sum_{i=1}^{n} x_i\right)^2$ b. $\sum_{i=1}^{n} x_i^2 \geq \left(\sum_{i=1}^{n} x_i\right)^2$
    c. $\sum_{i=1}^{n} x_i^2 \geq n\left(\sum_{i=1}^{n} x_i\right)^2$ d. None. [IIT-JEE – 1982]
15. The largest interval for which $x^{12}-x^9+x^4-x+1>0$ is

    a. $-4<x\leq 0$ b. $0<x<1$
    c. $-100<x<100$ d. R. [IIT-JEE – 1982]
16. Two towns A and B are 60 km apart. A school is to be built to serve 150 students in town A and 5o students in town B. If the total distance to be travelled by all 200 students is to be as small as possible, then the school should be built at

    a. Town B b. 45 km from town A
    c. town A d. 45 km from town B.
    [IIT-JEE – 1982]
17. If p, q, r are any real numbers, then

    a. max $(p,q)<$ max (p,q,r) b. max $(p,q) = \frac{1}{2}(p+q-|p-q|)$
    c. max $(p,q)<$ min (p,q,r) d. None. [IIT-JEE - 1982]
18. If $a+b+c=0$, then quadratic equation $3ax^2+2bx+c=0$ has

    a. at least one root in $(0,1)$
    b. one root in $(2, 3)$ and the other in $(-2, -1)$.
    c. Imaginary roots
    d. None [IIT-JEE-1983]
19. If one root of the equation $ax^2+bx+c=0$ is equal to the nth power of other, then show that $(ac^n)^{\frac{1}{n+1}}+(a^nc)^{\frac{1}{n+1}}+b=0$

    [IIT-JEE–1983]
20. Find all real values of x which satisfy $x^2-3x+2>0$ and $x^2-3x-4\leq 0$ [IIT-JEE–1983]
21. If $a,b,c>0$, then prove that $(a+b+c)\left(\frac{1}{a}+\frac{1}{b}+\frac{1}{c}\right)\geq 9$.

    [IIT-JEE–1983]
22. If $2+i\sqrt{3}$ is a root of the equation $x^2+px+q=0$, where p and q are real, then $(p,q) =$ ....

    [IIT-JEE–1982]
23. The equation $2x^2+3x+1=0$ has an irrational root? Is it true/false ? [IIT-JEE – 1983]
24. If $a<b<c<d$, then the roots of equation $(x-a)(x-c)+2(x-b)(x-d)=0$ are real and distinct. Is it true or false ? [IIT-JEE – 1984]
25. The equation $x-\frac{2}{x-1}=1-\frac{2}{x-1}$ has

    a. no root b. one root
    c. two equal root d. infinitely many roots.
    [IIT-JEE – 1984]
26. If $a^2+b^2+c^2=1$, then $ab+bc+ca$ lies in the interval

    a. $\left[\frac{1}{2}, 2\right]$ b. $[-1,2]$
    c. $\left[-\frac{1}{2}, 2\right]$ d. $\left[-1, \frac{1}{2}\right]$ [IIT-JEE – 1984]

27. For real x, the function $\frac{(x-a)(x-b)}{(x-c)}$ will assume all real values provided

a. $a>b>c$ b. $a<b<c$

c. $a>c>b$ d. $a<c<b$. [IIT-JEE–1984]

28. If the product of the roots of equation $x^2-3kx+2e^{\sin x}-1=0$ is 7, then the roots are real for $k=$...................... [IIT-JEE–1984]

29. Solve for x; $(5+2\sqrt{6})^{x^2-3}+(5-2\sqrt{6})^{x^2-3}=10$ [IIT-JEE – 1984]

30. If $p(x)=ax^2+bx+c$ and $Q(x)=-ax^2+dx+c$ where $ac\neq 0$, then $p(x)$, $Q(x)$ has at least two real roots. [IIT-JEE –1985]

31. The solution of the equation $\log_7\left(\log_5\left(\sqrt{x+5}+\sqrt{x}\right)\right)=0$ is..........................

32. If the quadratic equations $x^2+ax+b=0$ and $x^2+bx+a=0$ $(a\neq b)$ have a common root, then the numerical value of '$a+b$' is .... [IIT-JEE – 1986]

33. If a, b and c are distinct positive numbers, then the expression $(b+c-a)(c+a-b)(a+b-c)-abc$ is

a. positive b. negative

c. non-positive d. None. [IIT-JEE–1986]

34. If S is set of all real x, such that $\left(\frac{2x-1}{2x^3+3x^2+x}\right)$ is positive, then S contains

a. $\left(-\infty,-\frac{3}{2}\right)$ b. $\left(-3,-\frac{1}{4}\right)$

c. $\left(-\frac{1}{4},\frac{1}{2}\right)$ d. $\left(-\frac{1}{2},3\right)$ [IIT-JEE–1986]

35. For $a\leq 0$, determine all real roots of equation $x^2-2a|x-a|-3a^2=0$. [IIT-JEE–1986]

36. Find the set of all x for which $\frac{2x}{2x2+5x+2}>\frac{1}{x+1}$ [IIT-JEE – 1987]

37. Let $\alpha_1,\alpha_2,\beta_1,\beta_2$ be the roots os $ax^2+bx+c=0$ and $px^2+qx+r=0$ respectively. If system of equations $\alpha_1 y+a_2 z=0$ and $\beta_1 y+\beta_2 z=a$ and has non trivial solution, then prove that $\frac{b^2}{q^2}=\frac{ac}{pr}$. [IIT-JEE–1987]

38. Solve for x: $\log_{(2x+3)}(6x^2+23x+21)=4-\log_{(3x+7)}(4x^2+12x+9)$ [IIT-JEE – 1987]

39. Solve for x: $|x^2+4x+3|+2x+5=0$ [IIT-JEE– 1988]

40. The equation $x^{3/4}\log_2 x\left(2+\log_2 x-\frac{5}{4}\right)=\sqrt{2}$ has

a. at least one real solution

b. exactly three real solutions.

c. exactly one irrational solution

d. Complex roots. [IIT-JEE – 1988]

41. If x and y are positive real numbers and m and n are any positive integers, then $\frac{x^n y^m}{(1+x^{2n})(1+x^{2m})}>\frac{1}{4}$. Is it true or false? [IIT-JEE – 1989]

42. There are exactly two distinct linear function .... and .... which maps $(-1, 1)$ into $(0, 2)$. [IIT-JEE – 1989]

43. If α and β are the roots of $x^2+px+q=0$ and α^4,β^4 are the roots of $x^2-rx+s=0$, then the equation $x^2-4qx+2q^2-r=0$ has always [IIT-JEE – 1989]

a. two real roots

b. two positive roots

c. two negative roots

d. one positive and one negative root.

44. Let a,b,c be real numbers, $a\neq 0$. If α is a root of $a^2x^2+bx+c=0$, β is the root of $a^2x^2-bx-2c=0$ and $0<\alpha<\beta$, then the

a. $\gamma=\frac{\alpha+\beta}{2}$ b. $\gamma=\alpha+\frac{\beta}{2}$

c. $\gamma=\alpha$ d. $\alpha<\gamma<\beta$

45. If $x<0, y<0$, $x+y+\frac{x}{y}=\frac{1}{2}$ and $(x+y)\frac{x}{y}=-\frac{1}{2}$, then $x=$ .... and $y=$ .... [IIT-JEE – 1990]

46. No questions asked in **1991**.

47. Let α,β be the roots of equation $(x-a)(x-b)=c, c\neq 0$. Then the roots of the equation $(x-\alpha)(x-\beta)+c=0$ are

a. a, c b. b, c

c. a, b d. $a+c, b+c$ [IIT-JEE – 1992]

48. The expression $\left(x+\left(x^3-1\right)^{1/2}\right)^5+\left(x-\left(x^3-1\right)^{1/2}\right)^5$ is a polynomial of degree

a. 5 b. 6

c. 7 d. 8. [IIT-JEE –1992]

49. No questions in **1993.**

50. The number of points of intersection of two curves $y=2\sin x$ and $y=5x^2+2x+3$ is

a. 0 b. 1

c. 2 d. infinite. [IIT-JEE – 1994]

51. If p,q,r are positive and are in A.P, the roots of quadratic equation $px^2+qx+r=0$ are all real for

a. $\left|\frac{r}{p}-7\right|\geq 4\sqrt{3}$ b. $\left|\frac{p}{r}-7\right|\geq 4\sqrt{3}$

c. all p and r d. no p and r. [IIT-JEE –1994]

52. Let $p,q \in \{1,2,3,4\}$. The number of equations of the form $px^2+qx+r=0$ having real roots is
a. 15 b. 9
c. 7 d. 8. [IIT-JEE – 1994]

53. Let $a, b, c \in R$ and α,β be the roots of $ax^2+bx+c=0$ such that $\alpha<-1$ and $\beta>1$, then show that $1+\frac{c}{a}+\left|\frac{b}{a}\right|=0$.
[IIT-JEE – 1995]

54. No questions in **1996.**

55. The equation $\sqrt{x+1}-\sqrt{x-1}=\sqrt{4x-1}$ has
a. no solution b. one solution
c. two solutions d. more than two soln.
[IIT-JEE – 1997]

56. Find the set of all solutions of the equation $2^{|y|}-|2^{y-1}-1|=2^{y-1}+1$

57. The sum of all the real roots of equation $|x-2|^2+|x-2|-2=0$ is .... [IIT-JEE – 1997]

58. No questions in **1998.**

59. Let a, b, c, d be real numbers in G.P. If u, v, w satisfy the system of equations $U+2v+3w=6$, $4u+5v+6w=12,6$ $u+9v=4$, then show that roots of the equation $\left(\frac{1}{u}+\frac{1}{v}+\frac{1}{w}\right)$ $x^2+[(b-c)^2+(c-a)^2+(a-b)^2]x+u+v+w=0$ and $20x^2+10(a-d)^2x-9=0$ are reciprocal to each other.
IIT-JEE- 1999]

60. The roots of the equation $x^2-2ax+a^2+a-3=0$ are real less than 3, then
a. $a<2$ b. $2\le a\le 3$
c. $3\le a\le 4$ d. $a>4$. [IIT-JEE – 1999]

61. If α and β $(\alpha<\beta)$ are the roots of equation $x^2+bx+c=0$, where $c<0<b$, then
a. $0<\alpha<\beta$ b. $\alpha<0<\beta<|\alpha|$
c. $\alpha<\beta<0$ d. $\alpha<0\,(\alpha)<\beta$
[IIT-JEE – 2000]

62. The domain of definition of the function $y(x)$ is given by the equation $2^x+2^y=2$ is
a. $0<x\le 1$ b. $0\le x\le 1$
c. $-\infty<x\le 0$ d. $-\infty<x<1$
[IIT-JEE – 2000]

63. If a,b,c,d are positive real numbers such that $a+b+c+d=2$, then $M=(a+b)(c+d)$ satisfies the relation
a. $0\le M\le 1$ b. $1\le M\le 2$
c. $2\le M\le 3$ d. $3\le M\le 4$
[IIT-JEE – 2000]

64. If $b>a$, then the equation $(x-a)(x-b)-1=0$ has
a. both roots in $[a, b]$ b. both roots in $(-\infty, a)$
c. both roots in (b, ∞) d. one roots in and other in .

65. For the equation $3x^2+px+3=0, p>0$, if one of the roots is square of the other, then p is
a. 1/3 b. 1
c. 3 d. 2/3. [IIT-JEE – 2000]

66. For all $x \in (0,1)$, then
a. $e^x<1+x$ b. $\log_e(1+x)<x(c)$
c. $\sin x>x$ d. $\log_e x>x$ [IIT-JEE – 2000]

67. If α,β are roots of $ax^2+bx+c=0$, $(a\ne 0)$ and $\alpha+\delta, \beta+\delta$ are the roots of $Ax^2+Bx+C=0, (A\ne 0)$ for some constant δ, then prove that $\frac{b^2-4ac}{a^2}=\frac{B^2-4AC}{A^2}$. [IIT-JEE – 2000]

68. Suppose $p(x)=a_0+a_1x+a_2x^2+a_3x^3+.......................+a_nx_n$. If $|p(x)|\le|e^x-1|$ for all $x\ge 0$, prove that $|a_1+2a_2+3a_3+.......+na_n|\le 1$. [IIT-JEE – 2000]

69. For every integer n, prove that $\sqrt{(4n+1)}<\left(\sqrt{n}+\sqrt{n+1}\right)<\sqrt{(4n+2)}$. Hence or otherwise, prove that $\left\lfloor\sqrt{n}+\sqrt{(n+1)}\right\rfloor=\left\lfloor\sqrt{(4n+1)}\right\rfloor$, where [x] denotes greatest integer not exceeding x. [IIT-JEE –2000]

70. Let a,b,c be real numbers with $a\ne 0$ and let α,β be the roots of the equation $ax^2+bx+c=0$. Express the roots of $a^2x^2+abcx+c^2=0$ in terms of α,β [IIT-JEE - 2001]

71. Let α,β be the roots of $x^2-x+p=0$ and γ,δ be the roots of $4x^2-4x+q=0$. If $\alpha,\beta,\gamma,\delta$ are in G.P, then the integral values of p and q respectively, are
a. –2, –32 b. –2, 3
c –6, 3 d. –6, –32 . [IIT-JEE-2001]

72. Let $f(x)=(1+b^2)x^2+2bx+1$ and let $m(b)$ be the minimum value of $f(x)$. As b varies, the range of $m(b)$ in
a. (0, 1] b. [0, 1/2]
c. [1/2, 1] d. [0, 1] [IIT-JEE- 2001]

73. The number of solutions of $\log_4(x-1)=\log_2(x-3)$ is
a. 3 b. 1
c. 2 d. 0 [IIT-JEE – 2001]

74. The number of values of k, for which the system of equations $(k+1)x+8y=4k$, $kx+(k+3)y=3k-1$ has infinitely many solution is
a. 0 b. 1
c. 2 d. infinite. [IIT-JEE -2002]

75. If $a_1, a_2, ..., a_n$ are positive real number whose product is a fixed number c, then the minimum value of $a_1+a_2+a_3+..........a_{n-1}+2a_n$ is
a. $n(2c)^{1/n}$ b. $(n+1)c^{1/n}$
c. $2n\,c^{1/n}$ d. $(n+1)(2c)^{1/n}$
[IIT-JEE -2002]

76. The set of all real numbers x for which $x^2-|x+2|+x>0$ is
a. $(-\infty,-2)\cup(2,\infty)$ b. $(-\infty,-\sqrt{2})\cup(\sqrt{2},\infty)$
c. $(-\infty,-1)\cup(1,\infty)$ d. $(\sqrt{2},\infty)$ [IIT-JEE- 2002]

77. If $a\in\left(0,\frac{\pi}{2}\right)$, then $\sqrt{x^2+x}+\frac{\tan^2\alpha}{\sqrt{x^2+x}}$ is always greater than or equal to
a. $2\tan\alpha$ b. 1

c. 2 d. $\sec^2\alpha$ [IIT-JEE–2003]

78. If $x^2 + (a - b)x + (1 - a - b) = 0$, where $a, b \in R$, then find the values of 'a' for which the equation has unequal real roots for all values of 'b'. [IIT-JEE – 2003]

79. If $f(x) = x^3 + bx^2 + cx + d$ and $0 < b^2 < c$, then in $(-\infty, \infty)$
a. $f(x)$ is strictly increasing function
b. $f(x)$ has a local maxima
c. $f(x)$ is a strictly decreasing function
d. $f(x)$ is bounded. [IIT-JEE – 2004]

80. For all 'x', $x^2 + 2ax + 10 - 3a > 0$, then the interval in which 'a' lies is
a. $a < -3$ b. $-5 < a < 2$
c. $a > 5$ d. $2 < a < 5$. [IIT-JEE – 2004]

81. If one root is square of other root of equation $x^2 + px + q = 0$, then the relation b/w p and q is
a. $p^3 - q(3p - 1) + q^2 = 0$ b. $p^3 - q(3p + 1) + q^2 = 0$
c. $p^3 + q(3p - 1) + q^2 = 0$ d. $p^3 + q(3p + 1) + q^2 = 0$
[IIT-JEE–2004]

82. The second degree polynomial $f(x)$, satisfying $f(0) = 0$, $f(1) = 1$, $f'(x) > 0$ for all $x \in (0,1)$
a. $ax + (1 - a)x^2, a \in R$ b. $ax + (1 - a)x^2, a \in (0, \infty)$
c. no polynomial d. $ax + (1 - a)x^2, a \in (0, 2)$
[IIT-JEE – 2005]

83. Let a,b,c be the sides of a triangle where $a \neq c$ and $\lambda \in R$. If the roots of the equation $x^2 + 2(a + b + c)x + 3\lambda(ab + bc + ca) = 0$ are real, then

a. $\lambda < \frac{4}{3}$ b $\lambda < \frac{5}{3}$

c. $\lambda \in \left(\frac{1}{3}, \frac{5}{3}\right)$ d. $\lambda \in \left(\frac{4}{3}, \frac{5}{3}\right)$.

[IIT-JEE– 2006].

84. Let a and b be the roots of the equation $x^2 - 10cx - 11d = 0$ and those of $x^2 - 10ax - 11b = 0$ are c, d then find the value of $a + b + c + d$ when $a \neq b \neq c \neq d$. [IIT-JEE – 2006]

85. The number of solutions of the pair of equations $2\sin^2\theta - \cos 2\theta 0$, $2\cos 2\theta - 3\sin\theta = 0$ in the interval $[0, 2\pi]$ is
[IIT-JEE–2007]
a. 0 b. 1
c. 2 d. 4.

86. Let α, β be the roots of equation $x^2 - px + r = 0$ and $\frac{\alpha}{2}, 2\beta$ be the roots of the equation $x^2 - qx + r = 0$. Then the value of 'r' is

a. $\frac{2}{9}(p-q)(2q-p)$ b. $\frac{2}{9}(q-p)(2p-q)$

c. $\frac{2}{9}(q-2p)(2q-p)$ d. $\frac{2}{9}(2p-q)(2q-p)$

[IIT-JEE – 2007]

87. Let $f(x) = \frac{x^2 - 6x + 5}{x^2 - 5x + 6}$.

Column– I	Column – II
i. If $-1 < x < 1$, then $f(x)$ satisfies	A $0 < f(x) < 1$
ii. If $1 < x < 2$, then $f(x)$ satisfies	B $f(x) < 0$
iii. If $3 < x < 5$, then $f(x)$ satisfies	C $f(x) > 0$
iv. If $x > 5$, then $f(x)$ satisfies	D $f(x) < 1$.

[IIT-JEE – 2007].

88. Let a, b, c, p, q be real numbers. Suppose α, β are the roots of the equation $x^2 + 2px + q = 0$ and $\alpha, \frac{1}{\beta}$ are the roots of the equation $ax^2 + 2bx + c = 0$, where $\beta^2 \in \{-1, 0, 1\}$.
Statement 1 : $(p^2 - q)(b^2 - ac) \geq 0$
Statement 2 : $b \neq pa$ or $c \neq qa$ [IIT-JEE – 2008]

89. The smallest integral value of k for which both the roots of $x^2 - 8kx + 16(k^2 - k + 1) = 0$ are real and distinct and have valueat-least 4, is [i009] [IIT-JEE-2009]

90. Let p and q be real numbers such that $p \neq 0, p^3 = -q$. If α and β are non zero complex numbers satisfying $\alpha + \beta - p$, $\alpha^3 + \beta^3 = q$, then a quadratic equation having roots $\frac{\alpha}{\beta}$ and $\frac{\beta}{\alpha}$ is
a. $(p^3 + q)x^2 - (p^3 + 2q)x + (p^3 + q) = 0$
b. $(p^3 + q)x^2 - (p^3 - 2q)x + (p^3 + q) = 0$
c. $(p^3 - q)x^2 - (5p^3 - 2q)x + (p^3 - q) = 0$
d. $(p^3 - q)x^2 - (5p^3 + 2q)x + (p^3 - q) = 0$ [IIT - JEE- 2010]

91. Let α and β be roots of $x^2 - 6x - 2 = 0$ with $\alpha > \beta$. If $a_n = \alpha^n - \beta^n$ for $n \geq 1$, then the value of $\frac{a_{10} - 2a_8}{2a_9}$ is
a. 1 b. 2
c. 3 d. 4 [IIT-JEE-2011]

92. A value of b for which the equations $x^2 + bx - 1 = 0$ and $x^2 + x + b = 0$ have one root in common is
a. $-\sqrt{2}$ b. $-i\sqrt{3}$
c. $-i\sqrt{5}$ d. $\sqrt{2}$ [IIT-JEE-2011]

93. The value of

$$6 + \log_{3/2}\left(\frac{1}{3\sqrt{2}}\sqrt{4 - \frac{1}{3\sqrt{2}}\sqrt{4 - \frac{1}{3\sqrt{2}}\sqrt{4 - \frac{1}{3\sqrt{2}}\cdots\cdots}}}\right)$$ is

[IIT-JEE-2012]

94. Let $\alpha(a)$ and $\beta(a)$ be roots of $\left(\sqrt[3]{a+1} - 1\right)x^2 + \left(\sqrt{1+a} - 1\right)x + \left(\sqrt[6]{a+1} - 1\right) = 0$, where $a > -1$. Then $\lim_{\alpha \to a^+} \alpha(a)$ and $\lim_{\alpha \to a^+} \beta(a)$ are
a. $-5/2, 1$ b. $-1/2, -1$
c. $-7/2, 2$ d. $-9/2, 3$. [IIT-JEE-2012]

ANSWER

2. q^2-p^2 **3.** $(q-s)^2-2pqr+sp^2+rq^2-2qs$ **5.** (i) x = 3 ; (ii) No integral solution.

6. (a) **7.** (b) **8.** $x\in\left(-\infty,-\frac{15}{2}\right)\cup(30,\infty)$

10. (a) **12.** (a) **14.** (d) **15.** (d) **17.** (b)

18. (a) **20.** $[-1,1]\cup[2,4]$ **22.** (4, –7) **23.** False **24.** True

25. (a) **26.** (c) **27.** (c) **28.** $k=2,-2$ **29.** $x=2,-2\sqrt{2},-\sqrt{2}$

30. True **31.** $x=4$ **32.** $x=-1$ **33.** (b) **34.** (d)

35. $x\in\lfloor a\pm a\sqrt{2},-a\pm a\sqrt{6}\rfloor$ **36.** $-2<x<-1$ or $-2/3<x<-1/2$ **38.** $x=-¼$.

39. $x=-1-\sqrt{3}$ **40.** (a), (b), (c) **41.** True **42.** $y=x+1, y=-x+1$

43. (a) **44.** (d) **45.** $x=-¼, y=-¼$ **47.** (c) **48.** (c)

50. (a) **51.** (b) **52.** (c) **55.** (a) **56.** $[1,\infty)\cup\{-1\}$

57. 4 **60.** (a) **61.** (b) **62.** (d) **63.** (a)

64. (d) **65.** (c) **66.** (b) **71.** (a) **72.** (a)

73. (b) **74.** (b) **75.** (a) **76.** (a) **77.** (b)

78. $a>1$ **79.** (a) **80.** (b) **81.** (a) **82.** (d)

83. (a) **85.** (c) **86.** (d) **87.** **i.** A,C,D; **ii.** B,D; **iii.** B,D; **iv.** A,C,D

89. 2 **90.** (b) **91.** (c) **92.** (b) **93.** 4

94. (b) **95.** 1. a, 2. b, 3. c, 4. d, 5. a, 6. b, 7. c, 8. d, 9. a, 10. b, 11. b, 12. b, 13. b, 14. c, 15. c

Self Assesment Test

TIME : 2 HOUR. **CHAPTER : QUADRATIC EQUATIONS AND EXPRESSIONS** MAX. MARKS: 50

1. If $\alpha,\beta,\gamma,\delta$ be the roots of $16x^4+4x^2+1=0$, then the value of $\alpha^4+\beta^4+\gamma^4+\delta^4$ is
   a. $-\frac{1}{8}$ b. 0
   c. $\frac{1}{8}$ d. 1

2. If $\alpha,\beta,\gamma,\delta$ be the roots of $x^4+x^2+1=0$, then the value of $(\alpha+\beta)(\alpha+\gamma)(\alpha+\delta)(\beta+\gamma)(\beta+\delta)(\gamma+\delta)=$
   a. –1 b. 0
   c. 1 d. 2.

3. The number of solutions of $\sqrt{x+1}-\sqrt{x-1}=\sqrt{4x-1}$ is
   a. 2 b. 1
   c. 0 d. infinity.

4. The largest interval for which $x^{12}-x^9+x^4-x+1>0$ is
   a. $-4<x<0$ b. $0<x<1$
   c. $100<x<100$ d. R.

5. If $x^2-10ax-11b=0$ have roots c and d, $x^2-10cx-11d=0$ have roots a and b, then the value of $a+b+c+d$ is
   a. 1210 b. 1205
   c. 1010 d. 1110.

6. If $\alpha\beta$ be the roots of $x^2+px-q=0$ and $\gamma\delta$ be the roots of $x^2+px+r=0$, then the value of $\frac{(\alpha-\gamma)(\alpha-\delta)}{(\beta-\gamma)(\beta-\delta)}$ is
   a. 2 b. 1
   c. 3 d. –1

7. The sum of all the real values of x satisfying $[x]^2-5[x]+5-2\cos x=0$, where [,] = G. I. F and $0<x<\pi$.
   a. $8\pi/3$ b. $7\pi/3$
   c. π d. 2π.

8. If both the roots of $x^2-2ax+a^2-1=0$ lie between –3 and 4, then $[a]$ can not be where [,] = G. I .F.
   a. 0 b. –1
   1 d. 4.

9. Suppose a, b and c are positive numbers such that $a+b+c=1$. Then the maximum value of $ab+bc+ca$ is
   a. 1/3 b. 1/4
   c. 1/2 d. 2/3

10. If x is real, then maximum value of $\frac{3x^2+9x+17}{3x^2+9x+7}$ is
    a. 43 b. 41
    c. 42 d. None.

11. The number of solutions of $n^{-|x|}\left|m-|x|\right|=1$, where $m,n>1$ and $n>m$. is
    a. 1 b. 2
    c. 3 d. 4

12. If $\left|\frac{x}{x-1}\right|+|x|=\frac{x^2}{|x-1|}$, then the values of x lies in
    a. (2, 3) b. $(1,\infty)$
    c. $(-\infty,\infty)$ d. $(0,\infty)$

13. The least value of $2\log_{10} x - \log_x(0.01)$ is

a. 2 b. 4

c. −2 d. -4

14. If $\log_{0.3}(x-1) < \log_{0.09}(x-1)$, then x lies in the interval

a. $(2, \infty)$ b. $(-2, -1)$

c. $(1, 2)$ d. $(2, 3)$.

TIME : 2 HOUR. **CHAPTER : QUADRATIC EQUATIONS AND EXPRESSIONS** MAX. MARKS: 50

1. If $\alpha, \beta, \gamma, \delta$ be the roots of $16x^4 + 4x^2 + 1 = 0$, then the value of $\alpha^4 + \beta^4 + \gamma^4 + \delta^4$ is

a. $-\frac{1}{8}$ b. 0

c. $\frac{1}{8}$ d. 1

2. If $\alpha, \beta, \gamma, \delta$ be the roots of $x^4 + x^2 + 1 = 0$, then the value of $(\alpha+\beta)(\alpha+\gamma)(\alpha+\delta)(\beta+\gamma)(\beta+\delta)(\gamma+\delta) =$

a. −1 b. 0

c. 1 d. 2.

3. The number of solutions of $\sqrt{x+1} - \sqrt{x-1} = \sqrt{4x-1}$ is

a. 2 b. 1

c. 0 d. infinity.

4. The largest interval for which $x^{12} - x^9 + x^4 - x + 1 > 0$ is

a. $-4 < x < 0$ b. $0 < x < 1$

c. $100 < x < 100$ d. R.

5. If $x^2 - 10ax - 11b = 0$ have roots c and d, $x^2 - 10cx - 11d = 0$ have roots a and b, then the value of $a + b + c + d$ is

a. 1210 b. 1205

c. 1010 d. 1110.

6. If α, β be the roots of $x^2 + px - q = 0$ and γ, δ be the roots of $x^2 + px + r = 0$, then the value of $\frac{(\alpha-\gamma)(\alpha-\delta)}{(\beta-\gamma)(\beta-\delta)}$ is

a. 2 b. 1

c. 3 d. −1

7. The sum of all the real values of x satisfying $[x]^2 - 5[x] + 5 - 2\cos x = 0$, where [,] = G. I. F and $0 < x < \pi$.

a. $8\pi/3$ b. $7\pi/3$

c. π d. 2π.

8. If both the roots of $x^2 - 2ax + a^2 - 1 = 0$ lie between −3 and 4, then $[a]$ can not be where [,] = G. I .F.

a. 0 b. −1

1 d. 4.

9. Suppose a, b and c are positive numbers such that $a + b + c = 1$. Then the maximum value of $ab + bc + ca$ is

a. 1/3 b. 1/4

c. 1/2 d. 2/3

10. If x is real, then maximum value of $\frac{3x^2 + 9x + 17}{3x^2 + 9x + 7}$ is

a. 43 b. 41

c. 42 d. None.

11. The number of solutions of $n^{-|x|}\left|m - |x|\right| = 1$, where $m, n > 1$ and $n > m$. is

a. 1 b. 2

c. 3 d. 4

12. If $\left|\frac{x}{x-1}\right| + |x| = \frac{x^2}{|x-1|}$, then the values of x lies in

a. $(2, 3)$ b. $(1, \infty)$

c. $(-\infty, \infty)$ d. $(0, \infty)$

13. The least value of $2\log_{10} x - \log_x(0.01)$ is

a. 2 b. 4

c. −2 d. -4

14. If $\log_{0.3}(x-1) < \log_{0.09}(x-1)$, then x lies in the interval

a. $(2, \infty)$ b. $(-2, -1)$

c. $(1, 2)$ d. $(2, 3)$.

□□□

CHAPTER 3

COMPLEX NUMBER

CONCEPT BOOSTER

3.0 The Complex Number System.

There is no real number x which satisfies the polynomial equation $x^2+1=0$. To permit solutions of this and similar equations, the set of complex number is introduced.

We can consider a complex number as having the form $a+ib$ where a and b are real number and i, which is called the imaginary unit, has the property $i^2=-1$.

It is denoted by z .i.e $z=a+ib$, 'a' is called as real part of z which is denoted by $Re(z)$ and 'b' is called as an imaginary part of z, which is denoted by $\text{Im}(z)$.

Any complex number $z = a + i b$ is

i. Purely real, if $b = 0$
ii. Purely imaginary, if $a = 0$
iii. Imaginary, if $b \neq 0$

NOTE:

a. The set R of real numbers is a proper subset of the complex numbers.
Hence complete number system is $N \subset W \subset I \subset Q \subset R \subset C$.
b. Zero is the only real number, which is purely real as well as purely imaginary, but not imaginary.
c. $i=\sqrt{-1}$, is called the imaginary unit. Also, $i^2=-1$, $i^3=-1$, $i^4=-1$ etc.
d. The period of iota is 4.
e. $i^{4n}=1, i^{4n+1}=i, i^{4n+2}=-1, i^{4n+3}=-i$.
f. The sum of the first four ith consecutive powers is zero. *i.e.* $i+i^2+i^3+i^4=0$
g. $\sqrt{a}\sqrt{b}=\sqrt{ab}$ holds only, if at least one of a or b is non-negative.

3.1 Some Solved Examples

Ex.1: Find the value of $i^n+i^{n+1}+i^{n+2}+i^{n+3}, n\in I$

SOL.: We have $=i^n+i^{n+1}+i^{n+2}+i^{n+3}=i^n\left(1+i+i^2+i^3\right)=i\times 0=0$

Ex. 2: Find the value of $i^{2010}+i^{2011}+i^{2012}+i^{2013}$

SOL.: We have $i^{2010}+i^{2011}+i^{2012}+i^{2013}$

$$= i^{2010}\left(1+i+i^2+i^3\right)=i^{2010}\times 0=0$$

Ex. 3: Find the smallest integer n for which $\left(\frac{1+i}{1-i}\right)^n=1$

SOL.: We have $\left(\frac{1+i}{1-i}\right)^n=1 \Rightarrow \left(\frac{1+i}{1-i}\times\frac{1+i}{1+i}\right)^n=1$

$$\Rightarrow \left(\frac{(1+i)^2}{2}\right)^n=1 \quad \Rightarrow \quad (i)^n=1 \Rightarrow n=4k, k\in I$$

Therefore, infinite number of values of n is satisfied the given relation.

Thus n is not clearly defined.

Ex.4: Find the sum of $\sum_{n=1}^{2013}\left(i^n+i^{n+1}\right)$

SOL.: We have, $\sum_{n=1}^{2013}\left(i^n+i^{n+1}\right)$

$$=(i+i^2+i^3+i^4+.......+i^{2013})+(i^2+i^3+i^4......+i^{2014})$$

$$=i+i^2=i-1$$

Ex.5: Find the value of $a^6+a^4+a^2+1$, if $a=\frac{1+i}{\sqrt{2}}$

SOL.: We have $a=\frac{1+i}{\sqrt{2}} \Rightarrow a^2=\frac{1+i^2+2i}{2}=\frac{1-1+2i}{2}=i$

Now, $a^6+a^4+a^2+1=i^3+i^2+i+1=0$

Ex.6: Find the value of $x^4+4x^3+6x+4x+10$, if $x=-1+2i$

SOL.: We have $x=-1+2i$

$\Rightarrow (x+1)=2i$

$\Rightarrow (x+1)^4=(2i)^4$

$\Rightarrow x^4+4x^3+6x^2+4x+1=2^4i^4=16$

$\Rightarrow x^4+4x^3+6x^2+4x+10=16+9=25$

Ex.7: Find the value of $i^P+i^Q+i^R+i^S$, where P,Q,R,S are consecutive integers.

SOL.: We have $i^P+i^Q+i^R+i^S=i^P(1+i+i^2+i^3)=i^P\times 0=0$

Ex. 8: Find the value of $(1+i^6)+(1-i)^{6n}$, where n is odd integers.

SOL.: We have, $(1+i^6)+(1-i)^{6n}$

Put $n=1$, we get, $(1+i^6)+(1-i)^{6n}$

$$=2(1+{}^6C_2\,i^2+{}^6C_4\,i^4+{}^6C_6\,i^6)=2(1-15+15-1)=0.$$

Put $n=3$, we get, $(1+i^6)+(1-i)^{6n}$

$$=2(1+{}^{18}C_2i^2+{}^{18}C_4i^4+{}^{18}C_6i^6+{}^{18}C_8i^8+{}^{18}C_{10}i^{10}+{}^{18}C_{12}i^{12}+{}^{18}C_{14}i^{14}+{}^{18}C_{16}i^{16}+{}^{18}C_{18}i^{18})$$

$$=2(1-{}^{18}C_2+{}^{18}C_4+{}^{18}C_6+{}^{18}C_8+{}^{18}C_{10}+{}^{18}C_{12}-{}^{18}C_{14}+{}^{18}C_{16}-{}^{18}C_{18})$$

$$=2\times 0$$

$$=0$$

3.2 Algebra of Complex Numbers

Fundamental operations with complex numbers we can proceed as in the algebra of real numbers replacing i^2 by -1 when it occurs.

i. Addition : $(a+ib)+(c+id)=(a+c)+i(b+d)$

ii. Subtraction : $(a+ib)-(c+id)=(a-c)+i(b-d)$.

iii. Multiplication : $(a+ib)\ (c+id)=(ac-bd)+i(ad+bc)$.

iv. Division : $\dfrac{a+ib}{c+id}=\dfrac{ac+bd}{c^2+d^2}+i\dfrac{bc-ad}{c^2+d^2}$

Inequalities in complex numbers are not defined. There is no validity if we say that complex number is positive or negative.

> **NOTE:**
> 1. $z>0$ or $4+2i>2+4i$ are meaningless.
> 2. In real numbers, if, $a^2+b^2=0$, then $a=0=b$, however in complex numbers $z_1^2+z_1^2=0$ does not imply that $z_1=z_2=0$.

3.3 Equality of Complex Numbers

Two complex numbers $z_1=a+ib$ and $z_2=c+id$ are said to be equal if and only if their real and imaginary parts are separately equal respectively.

i.e $z_1=z_2 \Rightarrow$ $\text{Re}(z_1)=\text{Re}(z_2)$ and $\text{Im}(z_1)=\text{Im}(z_2)$.

i.e. $a=c$ and $b=d$.

Some Solved Examples

Ex.1: If $a+ib>c+id$, then find the value of $b+d+2013$.

Sol.: The given relation $a+ib>c+id$ holds only when $b=0$ and $d=0$

Thus, $b+d+2013=2013$.

Ex. 2: Find the least +ve integer n for which

$$\left(\frac{1+i}{1-i}\right)^n=\frac{2}{\pi}\left(\sin^{-1}x+\sec^{-1}\left(\frac{1}{x}\right)\right)$$

Sol.: We have, $\left(\dfrac{1+i}{1-i}\right)^n=\dfrac{2}{\pi}\left(\sin^{-1}x+\sec^{-1}\left(\dfrac{1}{x}\right)\right)$

$$\Rightarrow \left(\frac{1+i}{1-i}\right)^n=\frac{2}{\pi}\left(\sin^{-1}x+\cos^{-1}x\right)=\frac{2}{\pi}\times\frac{\pi}{2}=1$$

$$\Rightarrow n=4$$

Ex. 4: If $(x+iy)^{\frac{1}{3}}=a+ib$, then prove that $\dfrac{x}{a}+\dfrac{y}{b}=4\left(a^2-b^2\right)$.

Sol.: We have, $(x+iy)^{1/3}=a+ib$

$\Rightarrow (x+iy)=(x+ib)^3=a^3+i3a^2b-3ab^2-ib^3$

$=(a^3-3ab^2)+i(3a^2b-b^3)$

$\Rightarrow (x+iy)=(a^3-3ab^2)+i(3a^2b-b^3)$

$\Rightarrow x=(x^3-3ab^2),\ y=(3a^2-b-b^3)$

$\Rightarrow \dfrac{x}{a}=\left(a^2-3b^2\right),\dfrac{y}{b}=\left(3a^2-b^2\right)$.

$\Rightarrow \dfrac{x}{a}+\dfrac{y}{b}=4\left(a^2-b^2\right)$

Ex. 4: If $a+ib=\dfrac{3}{2+\cos\theta+i\sin\theta}$ and $a^2+b^2=Ma+N$, then find the value of $M+N+10$.

Sol.: We have

$$a+ib=\frac{3}{2+\cos\theta+i\sin\theta}$$

$$=\frac{3((2+\cos\theta)-i\sin\theta)}{((2+\cos\theta)+i\sin\theta)((2+\cos\theta)-i\sin\theta)}$$

$$\Rightarrow a+ib=\frac{3((2+\cos\theta)-i\sin\theta)}{\left((2+\cos\theta)^2+\sin^2\theta\right)}$$

$$\Rightarrow a+ib=\frac{3((2+\cos\theta)-i\sin\theta)}{5+2\cos?}$$

$$\Rightarrow a=\frac{3(2+\cos?)}{5+2\cos?},\ b=\frac{-3\sin?}{5+2\cos?}$$

$$\Rightarrow a^2+b^2=\left(\frac{3(2+\cos\theta)}{5+2\cos\theta}\right)^2+\left(\frac{-3\sin\theta}{5+2\cos\theta}\right)^2$$

$$\Rightarrow a^2+b^2=\frac{9(5+4\cos\theta)}{(5+2\cos\theta)^2}$$

$$\Rightarrow a^2+b^2+3=\frac{9(5+4\cos\theta)}{(5+2\cos\theta)^2}+3$$

$$=\frac{9(5+4\cos?)+3(25+20\cos?+4\cos^2?)}{(5+2\cos?)^2}$$

$$=\frac{(45+75)+96\cos\theta+12\cos^2\theta}{(5+2\cos\theta)^2}$$

$$=\frac{12\left(\cos^2\theta+8\cos\theta+10\right)}{(5+2\cos\theta)^2}$$

$$=\frac{12(2+\cos\theta)(5+2\cos\theta)}{(5+2\cos\theta)^2}$$

$$=4\times\frac{3(2+\cos\theta)}{(5+2\cos\theta)}=4a$$

$\Rightarrow a^2+b^2=4a-3$

$\Rightarrow M=4,\ N=-3$

Hence, the value of $M+N+10=4-3+10=11$.

3.4 Conjugate of a Complex Number

The conjugate of a complex number $z=a+ib$ is denoted by $\overline{z}$ and is defined as $\overline{z}=a-ib$.

In a complex number, if we replace i by $-i$, we get, the conjugate of the complex number.

Geometrically, $\overline{z}$ is the mirror image of z with respect to real axis on the Argand Plane.

3.4.1 Properties of Conjugates

Let z, z_1, z_2 be three complex numbers. Then

i. $\overline{z}$ is the mirror image of z along the real axis.

ii. $\overline{\overline{z}}=z$

iii. $z=\overline{z} \Rightarrow$ z is purely real.

iv. $z=-\overline{z} \Rightarrow$ z is purely imaginary.

v. $Re(z)=Re(\overline{z})=\dfrac{z+\overline{z}}{2}$

vi. $Im(z)=\dfrac{z+\overline{z}}{2i}$

vii. $\overline{z_1+z_2}=\overline{z_1}+\overline{z_2}$

viii. $\overline{z_1-z_2}=\overline{z_1}-\overline{z_2}$

ix. $\overline{z_1z_2}=\overline{z_1}\ \overline{z_2}$

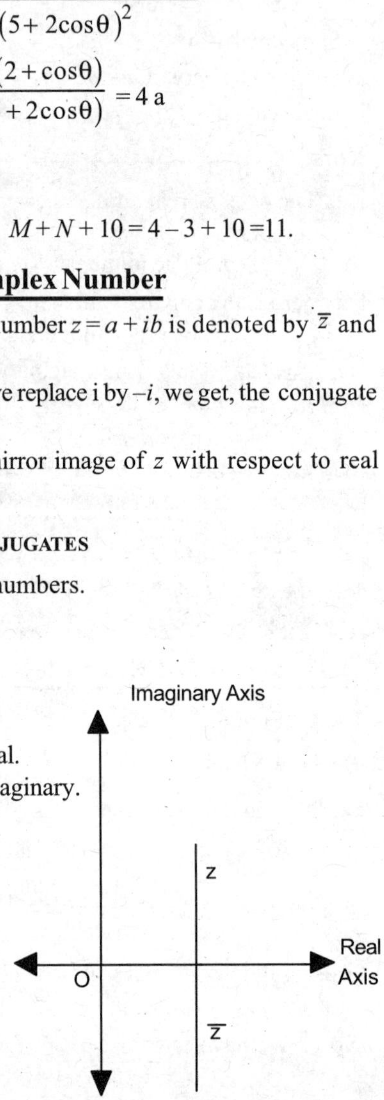

x. $\left(\overline{\frac{z_1}{z_2}}\right) = \left(\frac{\overline{z_1}}{\overline{z_2}}\right)$

xi. $z_1.\overline{z_2} + z_2.\overline{z_1} = 2\text{Re}(z_1\overline{z_2}) = 2\text{Re}(\overline{z_1}z_2)$

xii. $\overline{z^n} = (\overline{z})^n$

xiii. If $z = f(z_1)$, then $\overline{z} = f(\overline{z_1})$

3.5 Modulus of A Complex Number

Let $z = a + ib$ be a complex number. The modulus of a complex number z is denoted by $|z|$ and is defined as $|z| = |a + bi| = \sqrt{a^2 + b^2}$

Geometrically, $|z|$ is distance of the point z from the origin.

3.5.1 Properties of Modulus

i. $\text{Re}(z) \le |z|$, $\text{Im}(z) \le |z|$,

ii. $\text{Re}(z) \ge -|z|$, $\text{Im}(z) \ge -|z|$,

iii. $|z| = |\overline{z}| = |-z| = |-\overline{z}|$.

iv. $z.\overline{z} = |z|^2$.

v. $|z|^2 = |z^2|$.

vi. $|z_1.z_2| = |z_1|.|z_2|$. In general, $|z_1.z_2.........z_n| = |z_1|.|z_2|.........|z_n|$.

vii. $\left|\frac{z_1}{z_2}\right| = \frac{|z_1|}{|z_2|}$

viii. $|z_1 \pm z_2|^2 = |z_1|^2 + |z_2|^2 \pm 2\text{Re}(z_1\overline{z_2})$.

PROOF: $|z_1 \pm z_2|^2 = (z_1 + z_2).\overline{(z_1 + z_2)}$

$= (z_1 + z_2).(\overline{z_1} + \overline{z_2})$

$= (z_1.\overline{z_1} + z_1\overline{z_2} + z_2.\overline{z_1} + z_2.\overline{z_2})$

$= |z_1|^2 + |z_2|^2 + (z_1.\overline{z_2} + z_2.\overline{z_1})$

$= |z_1|^2 + |z_2|^2 + (z_1.\overline{z_2} + \overline{z_1.\overline{z_2}})$

$= |z_1|^2 + |z_2|^2 + 2\text{Re}(z_1.\overline{z_2})$ $(\because z + \overline{z} = 2\text{Re}(z))$

Hence, the result.

ix. $|z_1 + z_2|^2 + |z_1 - z_2|^2 = 2(|z_1|^2 + |z_2|^2)$

3.6 Some solved examples

Ex.1: If $a + ib = (1+i)(1+2i)(1+3i)............(1+in)$, then find the value of $a^2 + b^2$

SOL.: We have $a + ib = (1+i)(1+2i)(1+3i)........(1+in)$ ....(i)
Replace i by $-i$ in (i), we get, $a - ib = (1-i)(1-2i)(1-3i)$ ......$(1-in)$ .....(ii)

Multiplying (i) and (ii), we get $(a^2 + b^2) = 2.5.10.......(1+n^2)$

Ex.2: If α, β are complex numbers, then find the maximum value of $\frac{\alpha\overline{\beta} + \beta\overline{\alpha}}{|\alpha\beta|}$

SOL.: We have $\left|\frac{\alpha\overline{\beta} + \beta\overline{\alpha}}{\alpha\beta}\right| = \frac{|\alpha\overline{\beta} + \beta\overline{\alpha}|}{|\alpha\beta|} \le \frac{|\alpha\overline{\beta}| + |\beta\overline{\alpha}|}{|\alpha\beta|}$

$= \frac{|\alpha||\overline{\beta}| + |\beta||\overline{\alpha}|}{|\alpha||\beta|} = 2$

Hence the maximum value is 2.

Ex.3: If $|z_1| = |z_2| = |z_3| = \left|\frac{1}{z_1} + \frac{1}{z_2} + \frac{1}{z_3}\right| = 1$, then find the value of $|z_1 + z_2 + z_3|$.

SOL.: Given $|z_1| = 1 \Rightarrow |z_1|^2 = 1 \Rightarrow z_1.\overline{z_1} \Rightarrow \overline{z_1} = \frac{1}{z_1}$

Similarly, $\overline{z_2} = \frac{1}{z_2}$ & $\overline{z_3} = \frac{1}{z_3}$

Now, $\left|\frac{1}{z_1} + \frac{1}{z_2} + \frac{1}{z_3}\right| = 1$

$\Rightarrow |\overline{z_1} + \overline{z_2} + \overline{z_3}| = 1$

$\Rightarrow |\overline{z_1 + z_2 + z_3}| = 1$

$\Rightarrow |z_1 + z_2 + z_3| = 1$

Ex. 4: If α & β are different complex numbers with, $|\beta| = 1$, then find the value of $\left|\frac{\beta - \alpha}{1 - \overline{\alpha}\beta}\right|$

SOL.: Given $|\beta| = 1 \Rightarrow |\beta|^2 = 1 \Rightarrow \beta.\overline{\beta} = 1 \Rightarrow \overline{\beta} = \frac{1}{\beta}$

Now $\left|\frac{\beta - \alpha}{1 - \overline{\alpha}\beta}\right| = \left|\frac{\beta - \alpha}{1 - \overline{\alpha}\frac{1}{\overline{\beta}}}\right| = \left|\frac{\overline{\beta}(\beta - \alpha)}{\overline{\beta} - \overline{\alpha}}\right| = \frac{|\overline{\beta}||\beta - \alpha|}{|\overline{\beta - \alpha}|}$

$= \frac{|\overline{\beta}||\beta - \alpha|}{|\beta - \alpha|} = |\overline{\beta}| = 1$

Ex.5: Find the complex number z, if $|z + 1| = z + 2(1 + i)$

SOL.: We have $|z + 1| = z + 2(1 + i)$.

$\Rightarrow \sqrt{(x+1)^2 + y^2} = (x+2)^2, y = -2$

$\Rightarrow (x+1)^2 + y^2 = (x+2)^2, y = -2$

$\Rightarrow x = \frac{1}{2}, y = -2$

Thus, $z = x + iy = \frac{1}{2} - 2i$

3.7.3 Argument of a Complex Number

The argument or amplitude of a complex number $z = a + ib$ is the value of θ which satisfies the equation $\theta = \tan^{-1}\left(\frac{y}{x}\right)$. It is denoted by arg($z$) or amp($z$).

Argument of a complex number is not unique, since if θ be a value of the argument, so also $2n\pi + \theta$, where $n \in I$.

The value of θ which satisfies the inequality $-\pi < \theta \le \pi$ is called the principal value of the argument.

NOTE:

Thus, argument of a complex number $z = a + ib = r(\cos\theta + i\sin\theta)$ is the value of θ satisfying $r\cos\theta = a$ and $r\sin\theta = b$

3.8 Principal Value of Argument of A Complex Number Z.

If $z = a + ib$, where $a, b \in R$, then arg $(z) = \tan^{-1}\left(\frac{b}{a}\right)$ always gives us the principal value. It depends on the quadrant in which where the point (a, b) lies.

i. If (a,b) lies in the first quadrant, $a > 0$, $b > 0$.

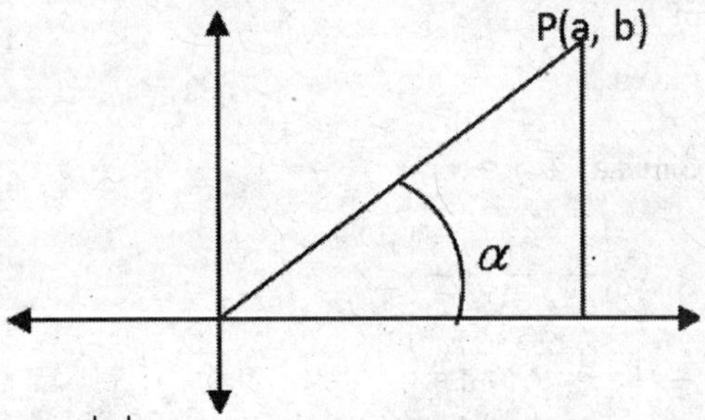

$\alpha = \tan^{-1}\left|\frac{b}{a}\right|$

Then $\arg(z) = \theta = \alpha$.

ii. If (a,b) lies in second quadrant, $a < 0$, $b > 0$.

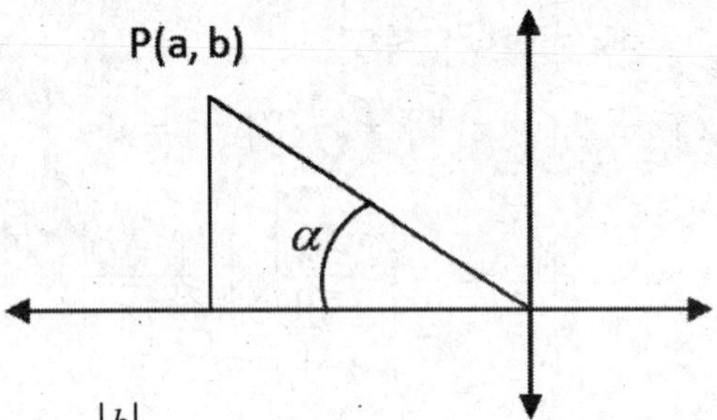

$\alpha = \tan^{-1}\left|\frac{b}{a}\right|$

Then $\arg(z) = \theta = \pi - \alpha$.

iii. If (a,b) lies in the third quadrant, $a < 0$, $b < 0$.

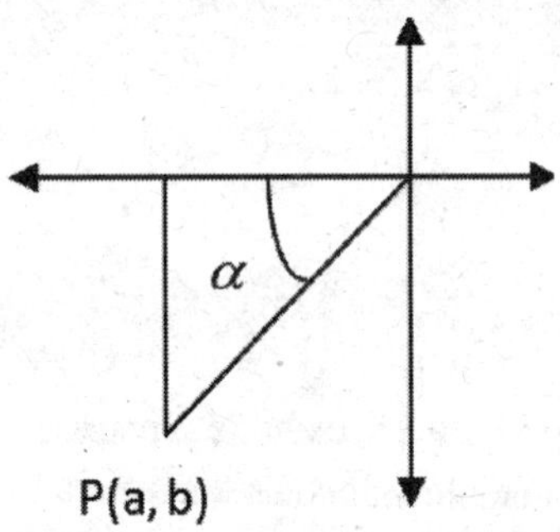

$\alpha = \tan^{-1}\left|\frac{b}{a}\right|$

Then the $\arg(z) = \theta = -(\pi - \alpha)$.

iv. If (a,b) lies in fourth quadrant, $a > 0$, $b < 0$.

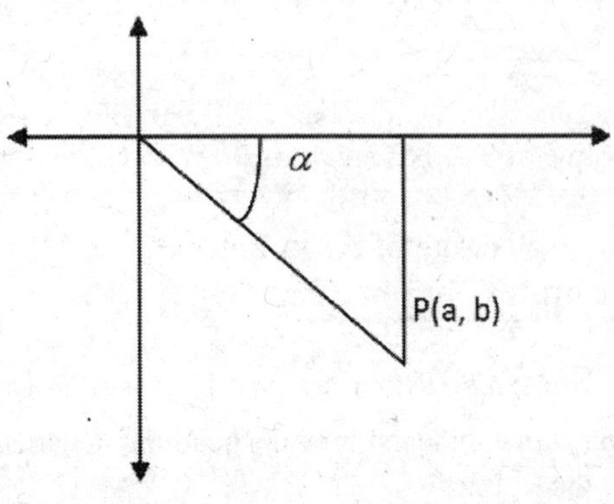

$\alpha = \tan^{-1}\left|\frac{b}{a}\right|$

Then the $\arg(z) = \theta = -\alpha$

Q.1: Find the arguments of

i. $1+i$ ii. $1-i$ iii. $-1+I$ iv. $-1-i$
v. 0 vi. 2013 vii. -2013 viii. $2i$
ix $-2i$ x.. $1/(1+i)$.

Sol.: i. Let $z = 1 + i = (1,1)$

We have $\alpha = \tan^{-1}\left|\frac{1}{1}\right| = \tan^{-1}(1) = \frac{\pi}{4}$

Since the given complex number lies in the first quadrant, so $\arg(z) = \theta = \alpha = \frac{\pi}{4}$

ii. Let $z = 1 - i = (1, -1)$

We have, $\alpha = \tan^{-1}\left|\frac{-1}{1}\right| = \tan^{-1}(1) = \frac{\pi}{4}$

Since the complex number z lies in the 4th quadrant, so $\arg(z) = \theta = -\alpha = \frac{\pi}{4}$

iii Let $z = -1 + I = (-1, 1)$

We have $\alpha = \tan^{-1}\left|\frac{-1}{1}\right| = \tan^{-1}(1) = \frac{\pi}{4}$

Since the complex number z lies in 2nd quadrant, so $\arg(z) = \theta = \pi - \alpha = \pi - \frac{\pi}{4} = \frac{3\pi}{4}$

iv. Let $z = -1 - i = (-1, -1)$

We have, $\alpha = \tan^{-1}\left|\frac{-1}{-1}\right| = \tan^{-1}(1) = \frac{\pi}{4}$

Since the complex number z lies in the 3rd quadrant, so $\arg(z) = \theta = -(\pi - \alpha) = \left(\pi - \frac{\pi}{4}\right) = \frac{3\pi}{4}$

Similarly, you can solve the other parts.

3.9 Representation of A Complex Numbers

a. *Cartesian Form (Geometrical Representation):* Every complex number $z = x + iy$ can be represented by a point on the Cartesian plane, known as complex plane or argand plane or z-plane and the diagram is called Argand diagram., by the ordered pair (x,y).

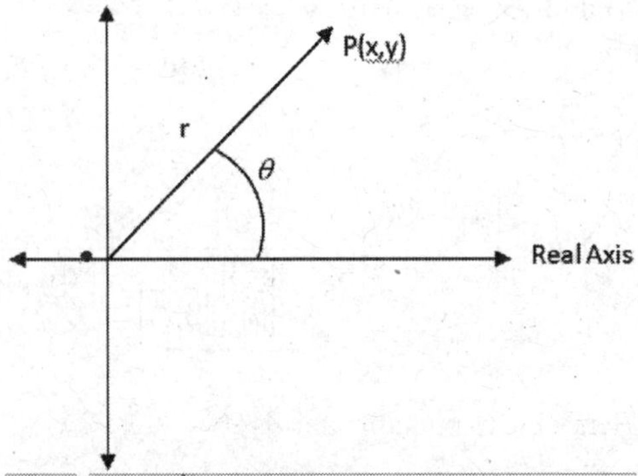

Length OP is called the modulus of the complex number, which is denoted by $|z|$ and θ is called the argument or amplitude of a complex number $z = x + iy$.

Here, $|z| = \sqrt{x^2 + y^2}$ and $\theta \tan^{-1}\left(\frac{y}{x}\right)$ (angle made by OP with positive x-axis).

NOTE :

i. Argument of a complex number is a many valued function. If θ is the argument of a complex number, then $2n\pi + \theta, n \in I$ will also be the argument of that complex number. Any two arguments of a complex number is differ by $2np$.

ii. The unique value of θ such that $-\pi < \theta \pi \leq$ is called the principal value of the argument. Unless otherwise stated, amp z implies principal value of the argument.

iii. By specifying the modulus and argument of a complex number is defined completely. For the complex number $0 = 0 + i0$, the argument is not defined and this is the only complex number which is only given by its modulus.

b. *Trigonometric / Polar Representation:* $Z = r(\cos\theta\ i\sin\theta)$ where $|z| = r$, $\arg z = \theta$, $z = r(\cos\theta - i\sin\theta)$

NOTE:

$\cos\theta + i\sin\theta$ is also known as cis θ or $e^{i\theta}$.

Also, $\cos\theta = \dfrac{e^{i\theta} + e^{-i\theta}}{2}$ and $\sin\theta = \dfrac{e^{i\theta} - e^{-i\theta}}{2}$ are also known as Euler's Identities.

c. *Euler's Representation:*
$z = re^{i\theta}, |z| = r, \arg z = \theta$ and $\bar{z} = re^{-i\theta}$

d. *Vectorial Representation:* Every complex number can be expressed as the position vector of a point. If the point P represents complex number z such that $\overrightarrow{OP} = z$ and $|\overrightarrow{OP}| = |z|$.

3.10 Some solved examples

Ex.1: If $z = \frac{\sqrt{3}}{2} + i\frac{1}{2}$, then find the Arg $(-z)$.

SOL.: Now $-z = -\frac{\sqrt{3}}{2} - i\frac{1}{2} = \left(-\frac{\sqrt{3}}{2}, -\frac{1}{2}\right)$

We have $a = \tan^{-1}\left|\frac{-1/2}{\sqrt{3}/2}\right| = \tan^{-1}\left(\frac{1}{\sqrt{3}}\right) = \frac{\pi}{6}$

Since the complex number $-z$ lies in the 3rd quadrant, so.

$$\arg(-z) = \theta = -(\pi - \alpha) = -\left(\pi - \frac{\pi}{6}\right) = -\frac{5\pi}{6}$$

Q.2: If $z < 0$, then find the value of Arg(z) – Arg$(-z)$.

SOL.: Since z is –ve, so z lies either in 3rd or 4th quadrant.
Let z lies in the 3rd quadrant, so $(-z)$ lies in the first quadrant.
Thus, $\arg(z) - \arg(-z) = -(\pi - \theta) - \theta = -\pi$

Ex.3: If $z = x + iy$ such that $|z+1| = |z-1|$ and $Amp\left(\frac{z-1}{z+1}\right) = \frac{\pi}{4}$, then find z.

SOL.: Given $|z - 1| = |z + 1|$

$$\Rightarrow \sqrt{(x-1)^2 + y^2} = \sqrt{(x+1)^2 + y^2}$$

$$\Rightarrow x = 0$$

Also $Amp\left(\frac{z-1}{z+1}\right) = \frac{\pi}{4}$

$$\Rightarrow \text{Amp}(z-1) - \text{Amp}(z+1) = \frac{\pi}{4}$$

$$\Rightarrow \tan^{-1}\left(\frac{y}{x-1}\right) - \tan^{-1}\left(\frac{y}{x+1}\right) = \frac{\pi}{4}$$

$$\Rightarrow \tan^{-1}\left(\frac{\frac{y}{x-1} - \frac{y}{x+1}}{1 + \frac{y}{x-1} \times \frac{y}{x+1}}\right) = \frac{\pi}{4}$$

$$\Rightarrow \tan^{-1}\left(\frac{xy + y - xy + y}{x^2 + y^2 - 1}\right) = \frac{\pi}{4}$$

$$\Rightarrow \left(\frac{y+y}{x^2 + y^2 - 1}\right) = \tan\left(\frac{\pi}{4}\right) = 1$$

$$\Rightarrow 2y = x^2 + y^2 - 1$$

$$\Rightarrow 2y = y^2 - 1$$

$$\Rightarrow y^2 - 2y - 1 = 0$$

$$\Rightarrow y = \frac{2 \pm \sqrt{8}}{2} = 1 \pm \sqrt{2}$$

Hence, the complex number $z = x + iy = i\left(1 \pm \sqrt{2}\right)$.

Ex. 4: If z_1 and z_2 are two non zero complex number such that, $|z_1 + z_2| = |z_1 - z_2|$ then Find the value of amp (z_1/z_2).

SOL.: Given $|z_1 + z_2| = |z_1 - z_2| \Rightarrow |z_1 + z_2|^2 = |z_1 - z_2|^2$

$$\Rightarrow |z_1|^2 + |z_2|^2 + 2Re\left(z_1\overline{z_2}\right) = |z_1|^2 + |z_2|^2 - 2Re\left(z_1\overline{z_2}\right)$$

$$\Rightarrow 4Re\left(z_1\overline{z_2}\right) = 0 \qquad \Rightarrow Re\left(e^{i\theta_1} \times e^{-i\theta_2}\right) = 0$$

$$\Rightarrow Re\left(e^{i(\theta_1 - \theta_2)}\right) = 0$$

$$\Rightarrow Re\left(\cos(\theta_1 - \theta_2) + i\sin(\theta_1 - \theta_2)\right) = 0$$

$$\Rightarrow \cos(\theta_1 - \theta_2) = 0$$

$$\Rightarrow (\theta_1 - \theta_2) = \frac{\pi}{2}$$

Thus, $Amp\left(\frac{z_1}{z_2}\right) = (\theta_1 - \theta_2) = \frac{\pi}{2}$

Ex.5: Let $z = \left(\frac{\cos\theta + i\sin\theta}{\cos\theta - i\sin\theta}\right), \frac{\pi}{4} < \theta < \frac{\pi}{2}$, then find Arg$(z)$.

SOL.: We have, $z = \left(\frac{\cos\theta + i\sin\theta}{\cos\theta - i\sin\theta}\right) = \cos 2\theta + i\sin 2\theta$

Also, it is given that $\frac{\pi}{4} < \theta < \frac{\pi}{2} \Rightarrow \frac{\pi}{2} < 2\theta < \pi$,

Thus the $\arg(z) = \pi - 2\theta$

3.11 Properties of Arguments

i. Argument of a complex number`0` is not defined.

ii. If $\arg(z) = \frac{\pi}{2}$ or $-\frac{\pi}{2}$, then z is purely imaginary.

iii. If $\arg(z) = 0$ or π, then z is purely real .

iv. $\arg(z_1 . z_2) = \arg(z_1) + \arg(z_2) + 2m\pi$, for some integer m.

v. $\arg(z_1/z_2) = \arg(z_1) - \arg(z_2) + 2m\pi$, for some integer m.

vi. $\arg(z^n) = n\arg(z) + 2m\pi$, for some integer m.

vii. If $\arg\left(\frac{z_2}{z_1}\right) = \theta$, then $\arg\left(\frac{z_1}{z_2}\right) = 2k\pi - \theta,\ k \in I$.

viii. $\arg(z_2 - z_1)$ = angle of the line segment $P'Q'$!!PQ where P' lies on real axis, with the real axis.

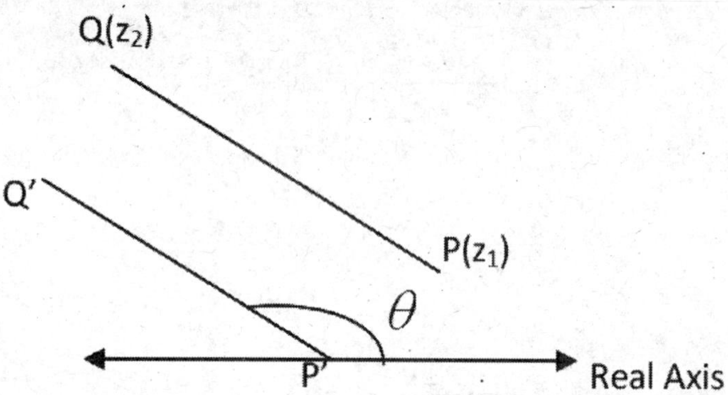

Advance Properties of Modulus and Argument of Complex Numbers

$$|z_1 + z_2| \le |z_1| + |z_2|$$

Proof: $|z_1 + z_2|^2 = |z_1|^2 + |z_2|^2 + 2|z_1||z_2|\cos(\theta_1 - \theta_2)$

$\le |z_1|^2 + |z_2|^2 + 2|z_1||z_2|$, $(\because \cos(\theta_1 - \theta_2) \le 1)$

$= \left(|z_1|^2 + |z_2|^2\right)$

$\Rightarrow |z_1 + z_2| \le |z_1| + |z_2|$

Aliter Proof:

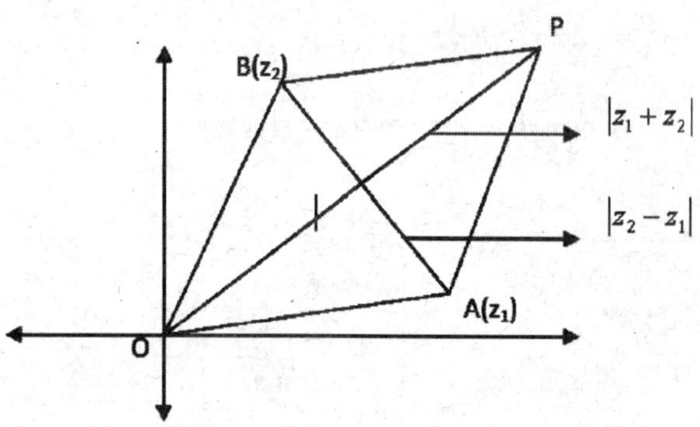

In a triangle OAP, OA + AP OP

$\Rightarrow \quad |z_1| + |z_2| \ge |z_1 + z_2|$

$\Rightarrow \quad |z_1 + z_2| \le |z_1| + |z_2|$

xi. $|z_1 - z_2| \ge \big||z_1| - |z_2|\big|$

Proof: $|z_1| = |z_1 - z_2 + z_2| \le |z_1 - z_2| + |z_2|$

$\Rightarrow \quad |z_1| - |z_2| \le |z_1 - z_2|$

Replacing z_1 by z_2, we get, $\Rightarrow |z_2| - |z_1| \le |z_2 - z_1|$

Thus, $|z_1 - z_2| \ge \big||z_1| - |z_2|\big|$

Aliter Proof: From the above figure, $|OA - OB| \le AB$

$\Rightarrow \big||z_1| - |z_2|\big| \le |z_1 - z_2|$

Hence , the result.

xi. $|z_1 + z_2| = |z_1 - z_2| \Leftrightarrow arg(z_1) - arg(z_2) = \frac{\pi}{2}$

Proof : Given, $|z_1 + z_2| = |z_1 - z_2|$

$\Rightarrow |z_1 + z_2|^2 = |z_1 - z_2|^2$

$\Rightarrow |z_1|^2 + |z_2|^2 + 2|z_1||z_2|\cos(\theta_1 - \theta_2)$

$= |z_1|^2 + |z_2|^2 - 2|z_1||z_2|\cos(\theta_1 - \theta_2)$

$\Rightarrow 4|z_1||z_2|\cos(\theta_1 - \theta_2) = 0$

$\Rightarrow \theta 1 - \theta_2 = \frac{\pi}{2}$

$\Rightarrow \arg(z_1) - \arg(z_2) = \frac{\pi}{2}$

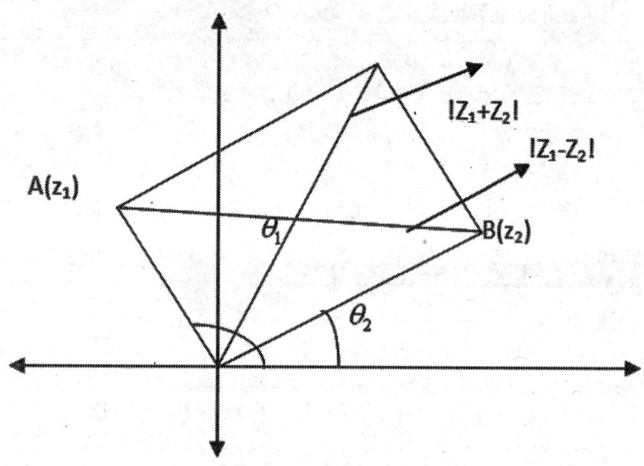

Aliter Proof: Given $|z_1 + z_2| = |z_1 - z_2|$

$\Rightarrow$ diagonal OP = diagonal AB

$\Rightarrow$ $OABP$ is a rectangle.

$\Rightarrow$ $OA \perp OB$

$\Rightarrow$ $Arg(z_1) = Arg(z_2)$.

Hence, the result.

xii. $|z_1 + z_2| = |z_1| + |z_2| \Rightarrow arg(z_1) = arg(z_2)$

Proof: Given $|z_1 + z_2| = |z_1| + |z_2|$

$\Rightarrow |z_1 + z_2|^2 = (|z_1| + |z_2|)^2$

$\Rightarrow |z_1|^2 + |z_2|^2 + 2|z_1||z_2|\cos(\theta_1 - \theta_2) = |z_1|^2 + |z_2|^2 + 2|z_1||z_2|$

$\Rightarrow \cos(\theta_1 - \theta_2) = 1$

$\Rightarrow (\theta_1 - \theta_2) = 0$

$\Rightarrow Arg(z_1) = Arg(z_2)$

xiii. If $|z_1 + iz_2| = |z_1| + |z_2| \Leftrightarrow arg(z_1) - arg(z_2) = \frac{\pi}{2}$

PROOF : Given relation is possible only if 0, z_1 and $i z_2$ are on the same side of a straight line.

Thus arg (z_1) = arg (iz_2)

$\Rightarrow arg\ (z_1) = arg(i) + arg(z_2)$

$\Rightarrow arg\ (z_1) - arg(z_2) = \frac{\pi}{2}$

xiv. If $|z_1 - z_2| = |z_1| + |z_2| \Rightarrow z_1 + kz_2 = 0, k \in I^+$

PROOF: Given$|z_1 - z_2| = |z_1 + z_2|$

$\Rightarrow (|z_1 - z_2|)^2 = (|z_1| + |z_2|)^2$

$\Rightarrow |z_1|^2 + |z_2|^2 - 2|z_1||z_2|\cos(\theta_1 - \theta_2) = |z_1|^2 + |z_2|^2 + 2|z_1||z_2|$

$\Rightarrow \cos(\theta_1 - \theta_2) = -1 = \cos(\pi)$

$\Rightarrow arg\ (z_1) - arg\ (z_2) = \pi$

$\Rightarrow arg\left(\frac{z_1}{z_2}\right) = \pi$

$\Rightarrow \left(\frac{z_1}{z_2}\right) = -k,\ k \in I^+$

$\Rightarrow z_1 + kz_2 = 0.$

xv. $|z_1 + z_2|^2 = |z_1|^2 + |z_2|^2 \Leftrightarrow \frac{z_1}{z_2}$ is purely imaginary number.

PROOF: Given $|z_1 + z_2|^2 = |z_1|^2 + |z_2|^2$

$\Rightarrow |z_1|^2 + |z_2|^2 + 2|z_1||z_2|\cos(\theta_1 - \theta_2) = |z_1|^2 + |z_2|^2$

$\Rightarrow \cos(\theta_1 - \theta_2) = 0$

$\Rightarrow (\theta_1 - \theta_2) = \frac{\pi}{2}$

Now, $\frac{z_1}{z_2} = \frac{|z_1|}{|z_2|}(\cos(\theta_1 - \theta_1) + i\sin(\theta_1 - \theta_2)) = i\frac{|z_1|}{|z_2|}$

$\Rightarrow \frac{z_1}{z_2}$ is purely imaginary number.

xvi. If $|z_1| \le 1, |z_2| \le 1$, then

a. $|z_1 - z_2|^2 \le (|z_1| - |z_2|)^2 + (arg\ z_1 - arg\ z_2)^2$

b. $|z_1 + z_2|^2 \le (|z_1| - |z_2|)^2 - (arg\ z_1 - arg z_2)^2$

PROOF: $|z_1 + z_2|^2 = r_1^2 + r_2^2 - 2r_1r_2\cos(\theta_1 - \theta_2)$

$= r_1^2 + r_2^2 - 2r_1r_2 + 2r_1r_2 - 2r_1r_2\cos(\theta_1 - \theta_2)$

$= (r_1 - r_2)^2 + 2r_1r_2(1 - \cos(\theta_1 - \theta_2))$

$= (r_1 - r_2)^2 + 4.2r_1r_2\sin^2\left(\frac{\theta_1 - \theta_2}{2}\right)$

$\le (r_1 - r_2)^2 + 4.\left(\frac{\theta_1 - \theta_2}{2}\right)^2$

$= (r_1 - r_2)^2 + .(\theta_1 - \theta_2)^2$

$\Rightarrow |z_1 - z_2|^2 \le (r_1 - r_2)^2 + .(Arg(z_1) - Arg(z_2))^2$

Hence, the result.

3.13 Square Root of A Complex Number

Let $z = a + ib$ be a complex number.

Then $\sqrt{z} = \sqrt{a+ib} = \begin{cases} \pm\left\{\sqrt{\frac{|z|+a}{2}} + i\sqrt{\frac{|z|-a}{2}}\right\} : \ for\ b > 0 \\ \pm\left\{\sqrt{\frac{|z|+a}{2}} - i\sqrt{\frac{|z|-a}{2}}\right\} : \ for\ b < 0 \end{cases}$

NOTE:

1. The square root of i are $\pm\left(\frac{1+i}{\sqrt{2}}\right)$
2. The square root of $-i$ are $\pm\left(\frac{1-i}{\sqrt{2}}\right)$
3. The value of $\sqrt{i} + \sqrt{-i} = \pm\sqrt{2}$
4. The value of $\sqrt{i} - \sqrt{-i} = \pm i\sqrt{2}$.
5. The square root of ω are $\pm\omega^2$
6. The square root of ω^2 are $\pm\omega$.

Q.1: Find the square root of

i. $3 + 4i$ ii. $5 + 12i$ iii. $8 - 6I$ iv. $3i$

SOL.: i. $3 + 4i = 3 + 2.\ 2.\ i = (2)^2 + i^2 + 2.2.i = (2 + i)^2$

Thus, $\sqrt{3+4i} = \pm(4 + i)$.

ii. $5 + 12i = 5 + 2.3.2i = (3)^2 + (2i)^2 + 2.3.2i = (3 + 2i)^2$

Thus, $\sqrt{5+12i} = \pm(3 + 2i)$

iii. $8 - 6i = 8 - 2.3.i = (3)^2 + i^2 - 2.3.i = (3 - i)^2$

Thus, $\sqrt{8-6i} = \pm(3 - i)$

iv. $3i = 3(i) = \frac{3}{2}(2i) = \frac{3}{2}(2i.1) = \frac{3}{2}(i^2 + 1^2 + 2i.1) = \frac{3}{2}(1+i)^2$

Thus, $\sqrt{3i} = \pm\sqrt{\frac{3}{2}}(1+i)$

3.14 Cube Roots of Unity

Let $x = \sqrt[3]{1}$

$\Rightarrow x^3 - 1 = 0$

$\Rightarrow (x-1)(x^2 + x + 1) = 0$

$\Rightarrow x = 1, \frac{-1 \pm i\sqrt{3}}{2}$

$\Rightarrow x = 1, \frac{-1 + i\sqrt{3}}{2}, \frac{-1 - i\sqrt{3}}{2}$

$\Rightarrow x = 1, \omega, \omega^2$

Thus, the cube roots of unity are 1, ω, ω^2

3.14.1 PROPERTIES OF CUBE ROOTS OF UNITY

i. $1 + \omega + \omega^2 = 0$

ii. $\omega^3 = 1, \omega^{3n} = 1, \omega^{3n+1} = \omega, \omega^{3n+2} = \omega^2$

iii. $\overline{\omega} = \omega^2, \overline{\omega^2} = \omega$

iv. A complex number $a+ib$ for which $|a : b| = 1 : \sqrt{3}$ or $\sqrt{3} : 1$ can always be expressed in terms of i, ω, ω^2

FOR EXAMPLES:

a. $\left(1+i\sqrt{3}\right)=-\left(-1-i\sqrt{3}\right)=-2\left(-\frac{1}{2}-\frac{i\sqrt{3}}{2}\right)=-2w^2$.

b. $\sqrt{3}+i=\frac{i(\sqrt{3}+i)}{i}=\frac{-1+i\sqrt{3}}{i}=\frac{2}{i}\left(-\frac{1}{2}+i\frac{\sqrt{3}}{2}\right)=\frac{2}{i}\times\omega$

v. The cube roots of unity when represent on complex plane lie on the vertices of an equilateral triangle inscribed in a unit circle, having centre is origin . One vertex lying on positive real axis.

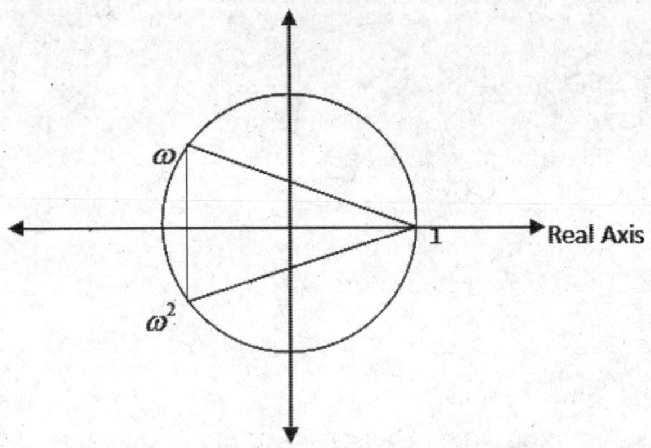

vi. $a+b\omega+c\omega^2=0 \Rightarrow a=b=c$ if a,b,c are real.

vii. The following factorization should be remembered:

a. $x^2+x+1=(x-\omega)(x-\omega^2)$

b. $x^2-x+1=(x+\omega)(x+\omega^2)$

c. $x^2+xy+y^2=(x-y\omega)(xy-\omega^2)$

d. $x^2-xy+y^2=(x+y\omega)(xy+\omega^2)$

e. $x^3+y^3=(x+y)(x+y\omega)(x+y\omega^2)$

f. $x^3-y^3=(x-y)(x-y\omega)(x-y\omega^2)$

g. $x^2+y^2+z^2-xy-yz-xz=(x+y\omega+z\omega^2)(x+y\omega^2+z\omega)$

h. $x^3+y^3+z^3-3xyz=(x+y+z)(x+y\omega+z\omega^2)(x+y\omega^2+z\omega)$

SOME SOLVED EXAMPLES:

Ex.1: If ω is the complex cube roots of unity, then find the value of $(2+3\omega+3\omega^2)^{2013}$

SOL.: We have, $(2+3\omega+3\omega^2)^{2013}=(2+3(\omega+\omega^2))^{2013}$
$=(2-3)^{2013}=-1$

Ex. 2: If ω is the complex cube root of unity, then find the value of $(3+4\omega+5\omega^2)^{10}$

SOL.: We have, $\left(3+4\omega+5\omega^2\right)^{10}=\left(3\left(1+\omega+\omega^2\right)+\omega+2\omega^2\right)^{10}$

$=\left(\omega+2\omega^2\right)^{10}=\left(-\frac{1}{2}+i\frac{\sqrt{3}}{2}+2\left(-\frac{1}{2}-i\frac{\sqrt{3}}{2}\right)\right)^{10}$

$=3^5\times\left(\frac{\sqrt{3}}{2}+\frac{i}{2}\right)^{10}$

Ex.3: If ω is the non real cube root of unity, then find the sum of

$\omega+\omega^{\left(\frac{1}{2}+\frac{3}{8}+\frac{9}{32}+\frac{27}{128}+\dots\dots\right)}$

SOL.: Let $S=\frac{1}{2}+\frac{3}{8}+\frac{9}{32}+\frac{27}{128}+\dots\dots$

$\Rightarrow \quad S=\frac{1}{2}\left(1+\frac{3}{4}+\left(\frac{3}{4}\right)^2+\left(\frac{3}{4}\right)^3+\dots\dots\right)$

$=\frac{1}{2}\times\frac{1}{1-\frac{3}{4}}=\frac{1}{2}\times\frac{4}{4-3}=2$

Thus, $\omega+\omega^S=\omega+\omega^2=-1$

Ex. 4: Find the common roots of the equation $z^3+2z^2+2z+1=0$ and $z^{2013}+z^{2014}+z^{2015}=0$

SOL.: We have $z^3+2z^2+2z+1=0$

$\Rightarrow \quad z^2(z+1)+z(z+1)+(z+1)=0$

$\Rightarrow \quad (z+1)(z^2+z+1)=0.$

$\Rightarrow \quad (z+1)=0$ and $(z^2+z+1)=0.$

$\Rightarrow \quad z=-1,\omega,\omega^2.$

When $z=-1$, then $z^{2013}+z^{2014}+z^{2015}=-1+1-1=-1\neq 0$

When $z=\omega$, then $z^{2013}+z^{2014}+z^{2015}=1+\omega+\omega^2=0$

When $z=\omega^2$, then $z^{2013}+z^{2014}+z^{2015}=1+\omega^2+\omega=0$

Hence , the common roots are ω,ω^2.

Ex. 5: If α,β,γ are cube roots of (–2013), then for any x, y, and z, find the value of $\frac{x\alpha+y\beta+z\gamma}{x\beta+y\gamma+z\alpha}$

SOL.: Let $p=-2013$.

Then, $\sqrt[3]{p}=\sqrt[3]{p}$, $\sqrt[3]{p}\omega$, $\sqrt[3]{p}\omega^2$

So a = $\sqrt[3]{p}$, ß = $\sqrt[3]{p}$? , ? = $\sqrt[3]{p}$?^{2}

Thus, $\frac{x\alpha+y\beta+z\gamma}{x\beta+y\gamma+z\alpha}$

$=\frac{x\sqrt[3]{p}+y\sqrt[3]{p}\,\omega+z\sqrt[3]{p}\,\omega^2}{x\sqrt[3]{p}\,\omega+y\sqrt[3]{p}\,\omega^2+z\sqrt[3]{p}}$

$=\frac{x+y\omega+z\omega^2}{x\omega+y\omega^2+z}$

$=\frac{x+y\omega+z\omega^2}{\omega\left(x+y\omega+z\omega^2\right)}=\frac{1}{\omega}=\omega^2$

3.15 Demoivre's Theorem

CASE **1.** *Statement:*

i. If n is any integer, then
$(\cos\theta+i\sin\theta)^n=\cos n\theta+i\sin n\theta$

ii. $(\cos\theta_1+i\sin\theta_1)(\cos\theta_2+i\sin\theta_2)(\cos\theta_3+i\sin\theta_3)$ ....$(\cos\theta_n+i\sin\theta_n)$
$=\cos(\theta_1+\theta_2+\theta_3+\dots\dots+\theta_n)+\sin(\theta_1+\theta_2+\theta_3+\dots\dots+\theta_n)$

CASE **2.** *Statement:* If $p, q \in$ Z and $q\neq 0$, then

$(\cos\theta+i\sin\theta)^{p/q}=\cos\left(\frac{2k\pi+p\theta}{q}\right)+i\sin\left(\frac{2k\pi+p\theta}{q}\right)$

Where $k=0, 1, 2, 3, \dots\dots\dots\dots, q-1$.

SOME SOLVED EXAMPLES :

Ex.1: If x satisfies the equation, $\left(x^2 - 2x\cos\theta + 1\right) = 0$, then find the value of $\left(x^n + \frac{1}{x^n}\right)$

SOL.: We have, $x^2 - 2x\cos\theta + 1 = 0$

$$\Rightarrow x = \frac{2\cos\theta \pm \sqrt{4\cos^2\theta - 4}}{2} = \frac{2\cos\theta \pm i\,2\sin\theta}{2}$$

$$= \frac{2(\cos\theta \pm i\sin\theta)}{2} = \cos\theta \pm i\sin\theta$$

When $x = \cos\theta + i\sin\theta$

$\Rightarrow$ $x^n = (\cos\theta + i\sin\theta)^n = \cos(n\theta) + i\sin(n\theta)$

And $\frac{1}{x^n} = x^{-n} = \cos(n\theta) - i\sin(n\theta)$

Thus, $x^n + \frac{1}{x^n} = \cos(n\theta) + i\sin(n\theta) + \cos(n\theta) - i\sin(n\theta)$
$= 2\cos(n\theta)$

Similarly, when $x = \cos\theta - i\sin\theta$, $x^n + \frac{1}{x^n} = 2\cos(n\theta)$

Ex.2: If $z_r = \cos\left(\frac{2r\pi}{5}\right) + i\sin\left(\frac{2r\pi}{5}\right)$, $r = 1,2,3,4,5$ then find the value of $z_1.z_2.z_3.z_4.z_5$.

SOL.: We have, $z_r = \cos\left(\frac{2r\pi}{5}\right) + i\sin\left(\frac{2r\pi}{5}\right) = e^{i\left(\frac{2r\pi}{5}\right)}$

Thus, $z_1.z_2.z_3.z_4.z_5 = e^{i\frac{2\pi}{5}(1+2+3+4+5)} = e^{i\frac{2\pi}{5}\times\frac{5\times6}{2}} = e^{i6\pi}$
$= \cos(6\pi) + i\sin(6\pi) = 1$

Ex.3: If $\sin\alpha + \sin\beta + \sin\gamma = 0 = \cos\alpha + \cos\beta + \cos\gamma$, then find the value of

i. $\sin 3\alpha + \sin 3\beta + \sin 3\gamma$
ii. $\cos 3\alpha + \cos 3\beta + \cos 3\gamma$

SOL.: Let $x = \cos\alpha + i\sin\alpha, y = \cos\beta + i\sin\beta, z = \cos\gamma + i\sin\gamma$
Now, $x + y + z = (\cos\alpha + i\sin\alpha) + (\cos\beta + i\sin\beta) + (\cos\gamma + i\sin\gamma) = (\cos\alpha + \cos\beta + \cos\gamma) + i(\sin\alpha + \sin\beta + \sin\gamma) = 0$

$\Rightarrow x^3 + y^3 + z^3 = 3xyz$

$\Rightarrow (\cos\alpha + i\sin\alpha)^3 + (\cos\beta + i\sin\beta)^3 + (\cos\gamma + i\sin\gamma)^3 = 3(\cos(\alpha+\beta+\gamma) + i\sin(\alpha+\beta+\gamma))$

$\Rightarrow (\cos 3\alpha + i\sin 3\alpha) + (\cos 3\beta + i\sin 3\beta) + (\cos 3\gamma + i\sin 3\gamma) = 3(\cos(\alpha+\beta+\gamma) + i\sin(\alpha+\beta+\gamma))$

$\Rightarrow (\cos 3\alpha + \cos 3\beta + \cos 3\gamma) = 3\cos(\alpha+\beta+\gamma)$
and $(\sin 3\alpha + \sin 3\beta + \sin 3\gamma) = 3\sin(\alpha+\beta+\gamma)$.

Ex.4: If, $z_r = \cos\left(\frac{\pi}{2^r}\right) + i\sin\left(\frac{\pi}{2^r}\right)$, then find value of $z_1.z_2.z_3$ .... to ∞

SOL.: We have $z_r = \cos\left(\frac{\pi}{2^r}\right) + i\sin\left(\frac{\pi}{2^r}\right) = e^{i\left(\frac{\pi}{2^r}\right)}$

$z_1.z_2.z_3$ ...... to ∞ $= e^{i\frac{\pi}{2}\left(1+\frac{1}{2}+\frac{1}{4}+......\right)} = e^{\frac{i\pi}{2}\times\frac{1}{1-\frac{1}{2}}} = e^{i\pi}$
$= \cos\pi + i\sin\pi = -1$

3.16 The *n*th roots of unity

Let $x = \sqrt[n]{1}$
$\Rightarrow$ $x^n - 1 = 0$
$\Rightarrow$ $x^n = 1 = \cos 0 + i\sin 0 = \cos 2k\pi + i\sin 2k\pi$
$\Rightarrow$ $x = (\cos 2k\pi + i\sin 2k\pi)^{1/n}$
$\Rightarrow$ $x = \cos\left(\frac{2k\pi}{n}\right) + i\sin\left(\frac{2k\pi}{n}\right)$, where $k = 0, 1, 2, 3, ..., n-1$.

Let $\alpha = \cos\left(\frac{2\pi}{n}\right) + i\sin\left(\frac{2\pi}{n}\right)$

Then the nth rotts of unity are α^t, where $t = 0, 1, 2, 3, ..., n-1$. *i.e.* the nth roots of unity are $1, \alpha, \alpha^2, \alpha^3, \alpha^4, ..., \alpha^{n-1}$

i. Sum of the *n*th roots of unity is zero.

PROOF: $1 + \alpha + \alpha^2 + \alpha^3 + \alpha^4 + ... + a^{n-1}$

$$= \frac{1-\alpha^n}{1-\alpha}$$

$$= \frac{1-\left(\cos\left(\frac{2\pi}{n}\right) + i\sin\left(\frac{2\pi}{n}\right)\right)^n}{1-\alpha}$$

$$= \frac{1-(\cos(2\pi) + i\sin(2\pi))^n}{1-\alpha}$$

$$= \frac{1-1}{1-\alpha} = 0.$$

Hence, the result.

ii. Product of the *n*th roots of unity is $(-1)^{n-1}$.

PROOF: $P = 1.a.a^2.a^3............a^{n-1}$
$= \alpha^{1+2+3+............a^{n-1}}$
$= \alpha^{\frac{n(n-1)}{2}}$
$= \left(\alpha^{\frac{n}{2}}\right)^{n-1}$
$= \left(\left(\cos\left(\frac{2\pi}{n}\right) + i\sin\left(\frac{2\pi}{n}\right)\right)^{\frac{n}{2}}\right)^{n-1}$
$= (\cos\pi + i\sin\pi)^{n-1}$
$= (-1)^{n-1}$.

iii. Prove that the sum of the *p*th powers of the *n*th roots of unity is zero.

PROOF: $S = 1 + \alpha^p + \alpha^{2p} + \alpha^{3p} + ... + \alpha^{(n-1)p}$

$$= \frac{1-(\alpha^n)^p}{1-\alpha^p}$$

$$= \frac{1-1}{1-\alpha} = 0.$$

NOTE:

If $p = kn$, when $\alpha^p = \alpha^{kn} = (\alpha^n) = 1$.

Thus, $S = 1 + \alpha^p + \alpha^{2p} + \alpha^{3p} + ...\alpha^{(n-1)p}$
$= 1 + 1 + 1 + 1 + ...+1$ (n-times)
$= n$.

vi. Prove that $(1-a)(1-a^2)(1-a^3)..........(1-a^{n-1}) = n$.

PROOF: As we know that,

$$(x^n - 1) = (x-1)(x-\alpha)(x-\alpha^2)(x-\alpha^3)....\ ....(x-\alpha^{n-1})$$

$$\Rightarrow (x-\alpha)(x-\alpha^2)(x-\alpha^3)..........(x-\alpha^{n-1}) = \left(\frac{(x^n-1)}{(x-1)}\right)$$

$$\Rightarrow (x-\alpha)(x-\alpha^2)(x-\alpha^3).........(x-\alpha^{n-1}) = (1+x+x^2+x^3+x^4+ .... + x^{n-1})$$

Put $x = 1$, we get,

$$\Rightarrow (1-\alpha)(1-\alpha^2)(1-\alpha^3)...........(1-\alpha^{n-1}) = 1+1+1+...........+1(n - \text{times}) = n.$$

Hence, the result.

v. Prove that $(1+a)(1+a^2)(1+a^3)$ .... $(1+a^{n-1})$

$$= \begin{cases} 0: \text{when } n \text{ iseven} \\ 1: \text{when } n \text{ is odd} \end{cases}$$

PROOF: As we know that,

$$(x^n - 1) = (x-1)(x-a)(x-a^2)(x-\alpha^3)...........(x-\alpha^{n-1})$$

$$\Rightarrow (x-a)(x-a^2)(x-a^3).........(x-a^{n-1}) = \left(\frac{(x^n-1)}{(x-1)}\right)$$

Put $x = -1$, we get

$$\Rightarrow (-1)^{n-1}(1+\alpha)(1+\alpha^2)(1+\alpha^3).....(1+a^{n-1}) = \frac{(-1)^n - 1}{-2}$$

$$\Rightarrow (1+\alpha)(1+\alpha^2)(1+\alpha^3)........(1+\alpha^{n-1}) = \frac{(-1)^n - 1}{-2(-1)^{n-1}}$$

$$\Rightarrow (1+\alpha)(1+\alpha^2)(1+\alpha^3).....(1+\alpha^{n-1}) = \begin{cases} 0: \text{when } n \text{ iseven} \\ 1: \text{when } n \text{ isodd} \end{cases}$$

Hence, the result.

vi. nth roots of unity are in G.P with common ratio $e^{i\left(\frac{2\pi}{n}\right)}$.

The sum of the following series should be remembered.

i. $\cos\theta + \cos 2\theta + \cos 3\theta + \cos 4\theta + ...$ $..............+ \cos n\theta$

$$= \frac{\sin\left(\frac{n\theta}{2}\right)}{\sin\left(\frac{\theta}{2}\right)} \times \cos\left(\frac{n+1}{2}\right)\theta$$

ii. $\sin\theta + \sin 2\theta + \sin 3\theta + \sin 4\theta + ...$ $.......................+ \sin n\theta$

$$= \frac{\sin\left(\frac{n\theta}{2}\right)}{\sin\left(\frac{\theta}{2}\right)} \times \sin\left(\frac{n+1}{2}\right)\theta$$

3.17 Some Solved Examples

Ex.1: If $z = \frac{\sqrt{3}-i}{2}$, then find the value of $\left(z^{101} + z^{103}\right)^{106}$

SOL.: We have $z = \frac{\sqrt{3}-i}{2} = i\left(-\frac{1}{2} - i\frac{\sqrt{3}}{2}\right) = i\omega^2$

Now, $z^{101} + z^{103} = i^{101}.\omega^{202} + i^{103}.\omega^{206}$

$$= i\omega + i^3\omega^2 = i\omega - i\omega^2 = i(\omega - \omega^2)$$

$$= i\left(-\frac{1}{2} + i\frac{\sqrt{3}}{2} + \frac{1}{2} + i\frac{\sqrt{3}}{2}\right)$$

$$= i(i\sqrt{3}) = -\sqrt{3}.$$

Thus, $\left(z^{101} + z^{103}\right)^{106} = \left(-\sqrt{3}\right)^{106} = 3^{53}$.

Ex.2: Find the 5th roots of unity.

SOL.: Let $x = \sqrt[5]{1}$

$$\Rightarrow x = \left(\cos\left(\frac{2r\pi}{5}\right) + i\sin\left(\frac{2r\pi}{5}\right)\right), r = 0,1,2,3,4.$$

$$\Rightarrow x = 1, \cos\left(\frac{2\pi}{5}\right) + i\sin\left(\frac{2\pi}{5}\right), \cos\left(\frac{4\pi}{5}\right) + i\sin\left(\frac{4\pi}{5}\right),$$
$$\cos\left(\frac{6\pi}{5}\right) + i\sin\left(\frac{6\pi}{5}\right), \cos\left(\frac{8\pi}{5}\right) + i\sin\left(\frac{8\pi}{5}\right)$$

Ex.3: Let $z = x + iy$ be a complex number, where x and y are integers. Find the area of the rectangle whose vertices are the roots of $\bar{z}.z^3 + z\bar{z}^3 = 350$.

SOL.: We have $\bar{z}.z^3 + z\bar{z}^3 = 350$.

$$\Rightarrow |z|^2 z^2 + |z|^2 \bar{z}^2 = 350$$

$$\Rightarrow |z|^2\left(z^2 + \bar{z}^2\right) = 350$$

$$\Rightarrow 2\left(x^2+y^2\right)\left(x^2-y^2\right) = 350$$

$$\Rightarrow \left(x^2+y^2\right)\left(x^2-y^2\right) = 175$$

$$\Rightarrow \left(x^2+y^2\right)\left(x^2-y^2\right) = 25 \times 7$$

$$\Rightarrow \left(x^2+y^2\right) = 25 \ \&\ \left(x^2-y^2\right) = 7$$

$\Rightarrow x = 4$ and $y = 3$

Hence, the area of rectangle $= 2x \times 2y = 4 \times 4 \times 3 = 48$ Sq. units.

Ex. 4: Let $z = \cos\theta + i\sin\theta$, then find value of $\sum_{m=1}^{15} Im\left(z^{2m-1}\right)$ at $\theta = 2°$

SOL.: We have $\sum_{m=1}^{15}\left(z^{2m-1}\right) = Im(z + z^3 + z^5 + z^7 + ...+ z^{29})$

$$= \sin\theta + \sin 3\theta + \sin 5\theta + ...+ \sin 29\theta$$

$$= \frac{\sin(15\theta)}{\sin\theta} \times \sin(\theta + 14\theta)$$

$$= \frac{\sin^2(15?)}{\sin ?}$$

$$= \frac{\sin^2(30°)}{\sin(2°)}$$

$$= \frac{1}{4\sin(2^\circ)}$$

Ex.5: Let a complex number α, $\alpha \neq 1$, be a root of the equation $z^{p+q} - z^p - z^q + 1 = 0$, where p and q are distinct primes. Show that either $1 + \alpha + \alpha^2 + \ldots + \alpha^{p-1} = 0$ or $1 + \alpha + \alpha^2 + \ldots + a^{q-1} = 0$ but not both.

SOL.: We have $z^{p+q} - z^p - z^q + 1 = 0$

$\Rightarrow z^p(z^q - 1) - 1(z^q - 1) = 0$

$\Rightarrow (z^p - 1)(z^q - 1) = 0$

$\Rightarrow$ either $(z^p - 1) = 0$ or $(z^q - 1) = 0$

$\Rightarrow$ either $(z-1)(1 + z + z^2 + z^3 + \ldots + z^{p-1}) = 0$ or $(z-1)(1 + z + z^2 + z^3 + \ldots + z^{p-1}) = 0$

$\Rightarrow$ either $(1 + z + z^2 + z^3 + \ldots + z^{p-1}) = 0$ or $(1 + z + z^2 + z^3 + \ldots + z^{q-1}) = 0$, $(\because z \neq 1)$

Henc,e the result.

Ex. 6: Solve for x: $x^6 - 9x^3 + 8 = 0$

SOL.: We have $x^6 - 9x^3 + 8 = 0$

$\Rightarrow (x^3 - 1)(x^3 - 8) = 0$

$\Rightarrow (x^3 - 1) = 0$ & $(x^3 - 8) = 0$

$\Rightarrow x^3 = 1, \omega, \omega^2$ & $x = 2, 2\omega, 2\omega^2$.

$\Rightarrow x = 1, 2, \omega, 2\omega, \omega^2, 2\omega^2$;

Ex.7: Find the real factors of $x^6 + 1$.

SOL.: We have $x^6 + 1 = (x^2 + 1)(x^4 - x^2 + 1)$

$$= (x^2+1) \times \left\{(x^2+1)^2 - 3x^2\right\}$$

$$= (x^2+1) \times (x^2 + x\sqrt{3} + 1)(x^2 - x\sqrt{3} + 1)$$

Ex. 8: Solve for x: $x^{12} - x^{11} + x^{10} - x^9 + \ldots + 1 = 0$

SOL.: We have $x^{12} - x^{11} + x^{10} - x^9 + \ldots + 1 = 0$

$\Rightarrow (x^{13} + 1) = 0$

$\Rightarrow x^{13} = -1$

$$\Rightarrow x = \left(\cos\left(\frac{2r+1}{13}\right)\pi + i\sin\left(\frac{2r+1}{13}\right)\pi\right),$$

$r = 0, \pm 1, \pm 2, \pm 3, \pm 4, \pm 5, \pm 6$

$$\Rightarrow x = \left(\cos\left(\frac{2r+1}{13}\right)\pi \pm i\sin\left(\frac{2r+1}{13}\right)\pi\right) r = 0, 1, 2, 3, 4, 5, 6$$

Hence, roots are $x = \left(\cos\left(\frac{2r+1}{13}\right)p \pm i\sin\left(\frac{2r+1}{13}\right)p\right)$,

$r = 0, 1, 2, 3, 4, 5, 6$

Ex.9: Find the value of $\sum_{k=1}^{10}\left(\sin\left(\frac{2k\pi}{11}\right) - i\cos\left(\frac{2k\pi}{11}\right)\right)$

SOL.: Let $z = \sin\left(\frac{2k\pi}{11}\right) - i\cos\left(\frac{2k\pi}{11}\right)$

$$\Rightarrow z = -i\left(\cos\left(\frac{2k\pi}{11}\right) + i\sin\left(\frac{2k\pi}{11}\right)\right) = -i\, e^{i\frac{2k\pi}{11}}$$

Now, $\sum_{k=1}^{10}\left(-ie^{i\frac{2k\pi}{11}}\right)$

$$= -i\left(e^{i\frac{2\pi}{11}} + e^{i\frac{4\pi}{11}} + e^{i\frac{6\pi}{11}} + \ldots + e^{i\frac{20\pi}{11}}\right)$$

$$= -ie^{i\frac{2\pi}{11}}\left(1 + e^{i\frac{2\pi}{11}} + e^{i\frac{4\pi}{11}} + e^{i\frac{6\pi}{11}} + \ldots + e^{i\frac{18\pi}{11}}\right)$$

$$= -ie^{i\frac{2\pi}{11}}\left(\frac{1 - e^{i\frac{20\pi}{11}}}{1 - e^{i\frac{2\pi}{11}}}\right) = -i\left(\frac{e^{i\frac{2\pi}{11}} - e^{i\frac{22\pi}{11}}}{1 - e^{i\frac{2\pi}{11}}}\right)$$

$$= -i\left(\frac{e^{i\frac{2\pi}{11}} - 1}{1 - e^{i\frac{2\pi}{11}}}\right) = i$$

Ex.10: Solve for z: $z^8 + 1 = 0$

SOL.: We have $z^8 + 1 = 0$

$\Rightarrow \quad z^8 = -1$

$$\Rightarrow z = \cos\left(\frac{(2r+1)\pi}{8}\right) + i\sin\left(\frac{(2r+1)\pi}{8}\right),$$

$r = 0, \pm 1, \pm 2, \ldots, \pm 7.$

$$\Rightarrow \quad z = \cos\left(\frac{(2r+1)\pi}{8}\right) \pm i\sin\left(\frac{(2r+1)\pi}{8}\right)$$

$r = 0, 1, 2, \ldots, 7.$

$$\Rightarrow z = \cos\left(\frac{\pi}{8}\right) \pm i\sin\left(\frac{\pi}{8}\right), \cos\left(\frac{3\pi}{8}\right) \pm i\sin\left(\frac{3\pi}{8}\right),$$

$$\cos\left(\frac{5\pi}{8}\right) \pm i\sin\left(\frac{5\pi}{8}\right), \cos\left(\frac{7\pi}{8}\right) \pm i\sin\left(\frac{7\pi}{8}\right)$$

Ex.11: Solve for z: $z^7 - 1 = 0$ and deduce that.

$$\cos\left(\frac{\pi}{7}\right).\cos\left(\frac{2\pi}{7}\right).\cos\left(\frac{4\pi}{7}\right) = \frac{1}{8}$$

SOL.: We have, $z^7 - 1 = 0 \Rightarrow z^7 = 1$

$$\Rightarrow z = \cos\left(\frac{2r\pi}{7}\right) + i\sin\left(\frac{2r\pi}{7}\right), \ r = 0, 1, 2, \ldots, 6$$

$$\Rightarrow z = 1, \cos\left(\frac{2\pi}{7}\right) \pm i\sin\left(\frac{2\pi}{7}\right), \cos\left(\frac{4\pi}{7}\right) + i\sin\left(\frac{4\pi}{7}\right),$$

$$\cos\left(\frac{6\pi}{7}\right) \pm i\sin\left(\frac{6\pi}{7}\right)$$

$$\Rightarrow \quad z^7 - 1 = (z-1)\left(z^2 - 2\cos\left(\frac{2\pi}{7}\right)z + 1\right)$$

$$\left(z^2 - 2\cos\left(\frac{4\pi}{7}\right)z + 1\right)$$

$$\left(z^2 - 2\cos\left(\frac{6\pi}{7}\right)z + 1\right)$$

Put $z = i$, then

$-(i+1) = (i-1) \quad \left(-2\cos\left(\frac{2\pi}{7}\right)i\right)$

$$\left(-2\cos\left(\frac{4\pi}{7}\right)i\right)\left(-2\cos\left(\frac{6\pi}{7}\right)i\right)$$

$$\Rightarrow -(i+1) = -i^3(i-1)\left(2\cos\left(\frac{2\pi}{7}\right)\times 2\cos\left(\frac{4\pi}{7}\right)\right.$$

$$\left.\times\, 2\cos\left(\frac{6\pi}{7}\right)\right)$$

$$\Rightarrow \left(2\cos\left(\frac{2\pi}{7}\right)\times 2\cos\left(\frac{4\pi}{7}\right)\times 2\cos\left(\frac{6\pi}{7}\right)\right) = \frac{(i+1)}{i(i-1)}$$

$$= \frac{(i+1)}{(-i-1)} = -1$$

$$\Rightarrow \cos\left(\frac{2\pi}{7}\right)\cos\left(\frac{4\pi}{7}\right)\cos\left(\frac{6\pi}{7}\right) = -\frac{1}{8}$$

Ex.12: Solve for $z : z^5+1=0$ and deduce that $4\sin\left(\frac{\pi}{10}\right).\cos\left(\frac{\pi}{5}\right)=1$

Sol.: We have $z^5+1=10 \Rightarrow z=\cos\left(\frac{(2r+1)\pi}{5}\right)+i\sin\left(\frac{(2r+1)\pi}{5}\right)$,

$r = 0, 1, 2, 3, 4$

$$\Rightarrow z = -1, \cos\left(\frac{p}{5}\right)\pm\sin\left(\frac{p}{5}\right), \cos\left(\frac{2p}{5}\right)\pm\sin\left(\frac{2p}{5}\right)$$

Also, $z^5+1=(z+1)\left(z^2-2\cos\left(\frac{\pi}{5}\right)z+1\right)$

$$\left(z^2-2\cos\left(\frac{2\pi}{5}\right)z+1\right)$$

Put $z=i$, then $(i+1)=(i+1)\left(-2\cos\left(\frac{\pi}{5}\right)\right)\left(-2\cos\left(\frac{2\pi}{5}\right)\right)$

$$\Rightarrow \left(-2\cos\left(\frac{\pi}{5}\right)\right)\left(-2\cos\left(\frac{2\pi}{5}\right)\right)=1$$

$$\Rightarrow 4\cos\left(\frac{p}{5}\right)\cos\left(\frac{2p}{5}\right)=1$$

$$\Rightarrow 4\cos\left(\frac{p}{5}\right)\sin\left(\frac{\pi}{2}-\frac{2p}{5}\right)=1$$

$$\Rightarrow 4\cos\left(\frac{p}{5}\right)\sin\left(\frac{\pi}{10}\right)=1$$

Ex.13: Solve for $x : x^{10}+x^5+1=0$

Sol.: We have $x^{10}+x^5+1=0$

$\Rightarrow \quad (x^5)^2+x^5+1=0$

$\Rightarrow \quad x^5=\omega, \omega^2$

When $x^5=\omega$

$$\Rightarrow x^5 = -\frac{1}{2}+i\frac{\sqrt{3}}{2}=\cos\left(\frac{2\pi}{3}\right)+i\sin\left(\frac{2\pi}{3}\right)$$

$$\Rightarrow x=\cos\left(\frac{6r\pi+2\pi}{15}\right)+i\sin\left(\frac{6r\pi+2\pi}{15}\right), r=0,1,2,3,4$$

$$\Rightarrow x=\cos\left(\frac{2p}{15}\right)+i\sin\left(\frac{2p}{15}\right), \cos\left(\frac{8p}{15}\right)+i\sin\left(\frac{8p}{15}\right)$$

$$\cos\left(\frac{14p}{15}\right)+i\sin\left(\frac{14p}{15}\right), \cos\left(\frac{20p}{15}\right)+i\sin\left(\frac{20p}{15}\right),$$

$$\cos\left(\frac{26p}{15}\right)+i\sin\left(\frac{26p}{15}\right)$$

$$\Rightarrow x=\cos\left(\frac{2p}{3}\right)-i\sin\left(\frac{2p}{3}\right), \cos\left(\frac{2p}{15}\right)+i\sin\left(\frac{2p}{15}\right)$$

$$\cos\left(\frac{4p}{15}\right)-i\sin\left(\frac{4p}{15}\right), \cos\left(\frac{16p}{15}\right)-i\sin\left(\frac{16p}{15}\right),$$

$$\cos\left(\frac{26p}{15}\right)+i\sin\left(\frac{26p}{15}\right)$$

Similarly, we can easily find the other roots.

Ex.14: If ω is an imaginary 5th root of 2 and, $x=\omega+\omega^2$, then find the value of x^5-10x^2-10x

Sol.: We have $\omega^5=2$.

Now, $x=\omega+\omega^2$

$\Rightarrow \quad x^5=(\omega+\omega^2)^5=\omega^5+5\omega^6+10\omega^7+18\omega^8+5\omega^9+\omega^{10}$

$\Rightarrow \quad x^5=2+10\omega+20\omega^2+20\omega^3+20\omega^3+4$

$\Rightarrow \quad x^5=6+10(\omega^2+2\omega^3+\omega^4)+10(\omega^3+\omega)$

$\Rightarrow \quad x^5=6+10(\omega+\omega^2)^2+10(\omega^2+\omega)$

$\Rightarrow \quad x^5=6+10x^2+10x$

$\Rightarrow \quad x^5-10x^2-10x=6.$

3.18 Rotation

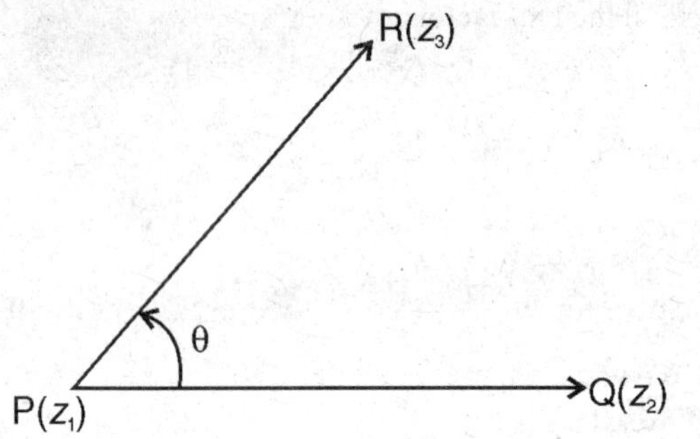

After plotting the points, mark the arrow in anticlockwise direction.

$$\theta = arg\left(\frac{z_3-z_1}{z_2-z_1}\right)$$

Here, $z_3-z_1=\overrightarrow{PR}$, where $\overrightarrow{PR}$ is vector on which arrow goes.

$z_2-z_1=\overrightarrow{PQ}$, where $\overrightarrow{PQ}$ is vector from which arrow starts. θ will be positive or negative according as it is measured in anti- clockwise or clock-wise direction.

Coni Method

If z_1, z_2, z_3 be affixes of the vertices of a ΔABC, described in anti-clockwise sense, then $\frac{z_3-z_1}{z_2-z_1}=\frac{CA}{BA}\times e^{i\theta}$

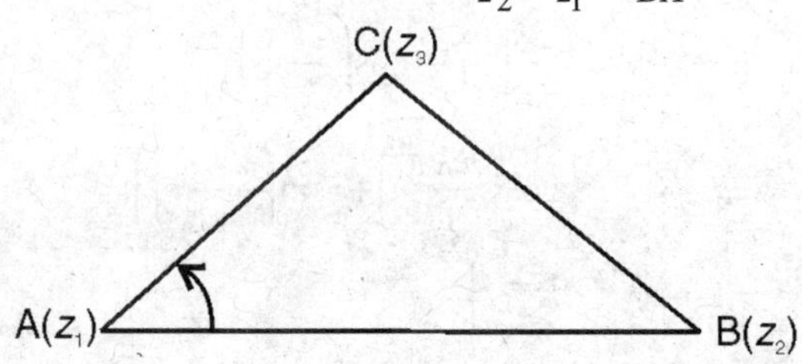

NOTE:

If θ is measured in clockwise sense, then

$$\frac{z_3 - z_1}{z_2 - z_1} = \frac{CA}{BA} \times e^{-i\theta}$$

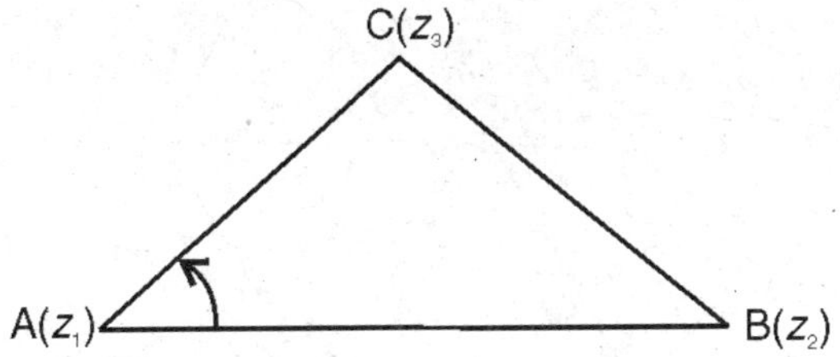

CONDITION OF AN EQUILATERAL TRIANGLE

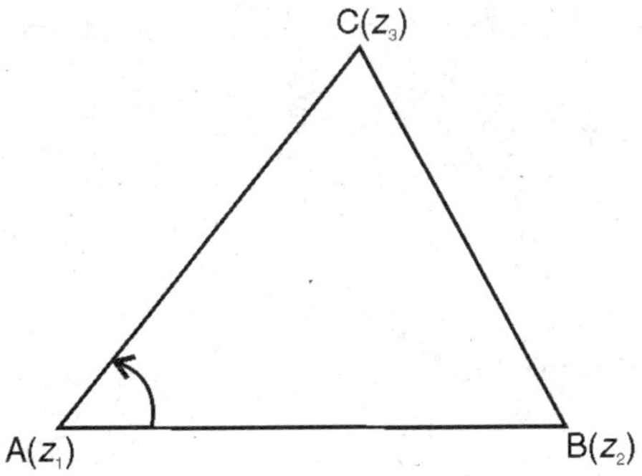

From Coni method, $arg\left(\frac{z_1 - z_2}{z_3 - z_2}\right) = \frac{\pi}{3}$

$$\Rightarrow \frac{z_1 - z_2}{z_3 - z_2} = \frac{AB}{AC} \times e^{i\frac{\pi}{3}} = \frac{1}{2} + i\frac{\sqrt{3}}{2}$$

$$\Rightarrow \left(\frac{z_1 - z_2}{z_3 - z_2} - \frac{1}{2}\right) = i\frac{\sqrt{3}}{2}$$

$$\Rightarrow \left(\frac{2z_1 - 2z_2 - z_3 + z_2}{2(z_3 - z_2)}\right) = i\frac{\sqrt{3}}{2}$$

$$\Rightarrow (2z_1 - z_2 - z_3)^2 = -3(z_3 - z_2)^2$$

$$\Rightarrow 4z_1^2 + z_2^2 + z_3^2 - 4z_1z_2 - 4z_1z_3 + 2z_2z_3 = -3(z_3^2 + z_2^2 - 2z_2z_3)$$

$$\Rightarrow 4z_1^2 + 4z_2^2 + 4z_3^2 - 4z_1z_2 - 4z_1z_3 - 4z_2z_3 = 0$$

$$\Rightarrow \boxed{z_1^2 + z_2^2 + z_3^2 - z_1z_2 - z_1z_3 - z_2z_3 = 0}$$

Also, $(z_1 - z_2)(z_2 - z_3) + (z_2 - z_3)(z_3 - z_1) + (z_3 - z_1)(z_1 - z_2) = 0$

Dividing both the sides by '$(z_1 - z_2)(z_2 - z_3)(z_3 - z_1)$', we get,

$$\Rightarrow \frac{1}{z_3 - z_1} + \frac{1}{z_1 - z_2} + \frac{1}{z_2 - z_3} = 0$$

$$\Rightarrow \boxed{\frac{1}{z_1 - z_2} + \frac{1}{z_2 - z_3} + \frac{1}{z_3 - z_1} = 0}$$

This is the one more condition for an equilateral triangle.

3.19.3 CONDITION OF AN ISOSCELES RIGHT ANGLED TRIANGLE

Let z_1, z_2, z_3 are the vertices A,B and C respectively of an isosceles right angle triangle with right angle at C.

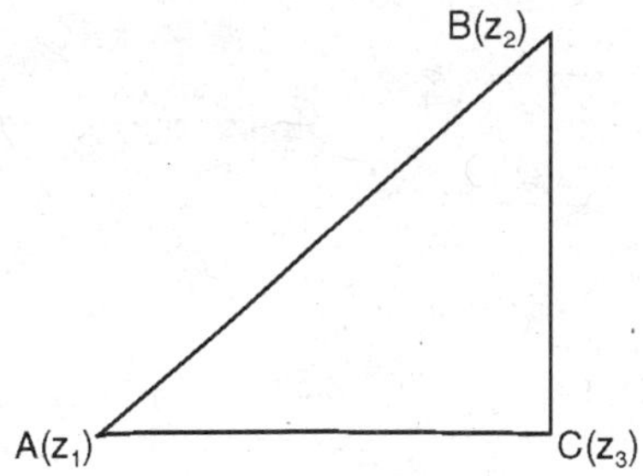

By Coni method, $\frac{z_2 - z_3}{z_1 - z_3} = \frac{BC}{AC} . e^{i\frac{\pi}{2}}$

$$\Rightarrow \frac{z_2 - z_3}{z_1 - z_3} = i$$

$$\Rightarrow (z_2 - z_3)^2 = -(z_1 - z_3)^2$$

$$\Rightarrow z_2^2 + z_3^2 - 2z_2z_3 = -z_1^2 - z_3^2 + 2z_1z_3$$

$$\Rightarrow z_1^2 + z_2^2 - 2z_1z_2 = 2z_1z_3 + 2z_2z_3 - 2z_1z_2 - 2z_3^2$$

$$\Rightarrow \boxed{(z_1 - z_2)^2 = 2(z_1 - z_3)(z_3 - z_2)}$$

3.19.4 CONDITION OF CIRCUMCENTRE WITH RESPECT TO AN EQUILATERAL TRIANGLE

In an equilateral triangle, the circumcentre and centroid are the same point.

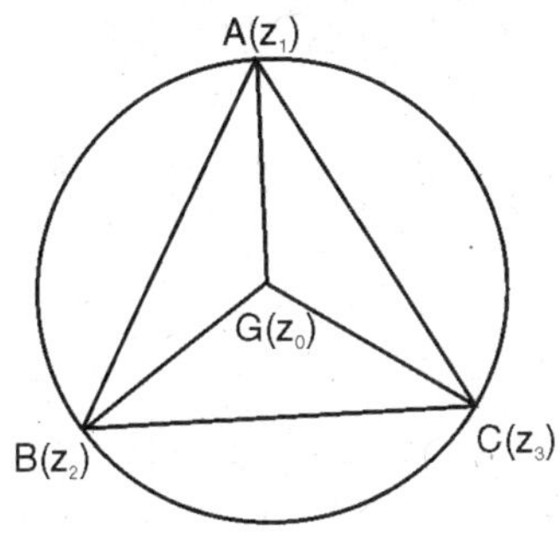

Therefore, $z_0 = \frac{z_1 + z_2 + z_3}{3}$

$$\Rightarrow (z_1 + z_2 + z_3)^2 = 9z_0^2$$

$$\Rightarrow z_1^2 + z_2^2 + z_3^2 + 2z_1z_2 + 2z_2z_3 + 2z_3z_1 = 0$$

$$\Rightarrow (z_1z_2 + z_2z_3 + z_3z_1) = \frac{9z_0^2 - z_1^2 - z_2^2 - z_3^2}{2}$$

Since z_1, z_2, z_3 are the vertices of an equilateral triangle, then

$$z_1^2 + z_2^2 + z_3^2 = z_1z_2 + z_2z_3 + z_3z_1$$

Thus, $z_1^2 + z_2^2 + z_3^2 = \frac{9z_0^2 - z_1^2 - z_2^2 - z_3^2}{2}$

$$\Rightarrow 3(z_1^2 + z_2^2 + z_3^2) = 9z_0^2$$

$$\Rightarrow \boxed{(z_1^2 + z_2^2 + z_3^2) = 3z_0^2}$$

This is the required condition.

3.19.5 Condition of Parallelism /Coincidence / Perpendicularity:

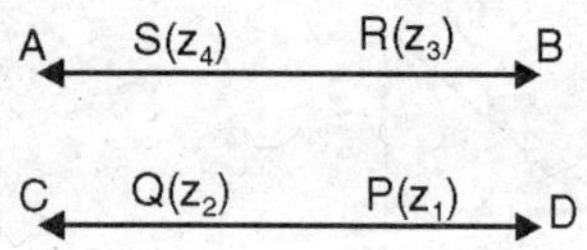

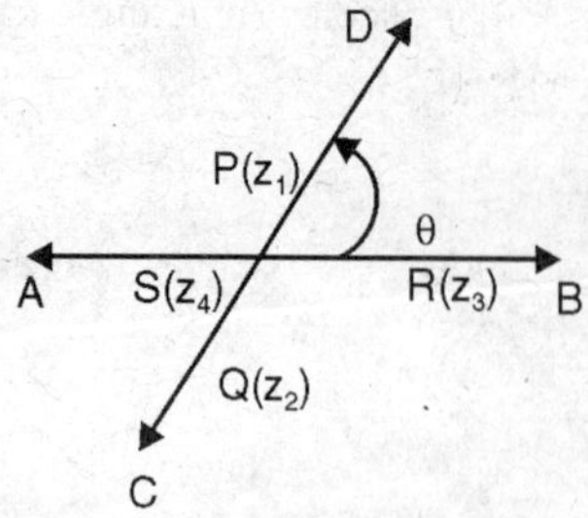

Let $arg\left(\dfrac{z_1 - z_2}{z_3 - z_4}\right) = \theta$.

If AB || CD, then $\theta = 0$ or $\pm\pi$

$$\Rightarrow arg\left(\frac{z_1 - z_2}{z_3 - z_4}\right) = 0 \text{ or } \pm\pi$$

$$\Rightarrow \frac{z_1 - z_2}{z_3 - z_4} \text{ is real.}$$

A,B,C,D are collinear.

3.19.6 Condition of Perpendicularity

If $AB \perp CD$, then $\theta = \pm\dfrac{\pi}{2}$

$$\Rightarrow arg\left(\frac{z_1 - z_2}{z_3 - z_4}\right) = \pm\frac{\pi}{2}$$

$$\Rightarrow \left(\frac{z_1 - z_2}{z_3 - z_4}\right) \text{ is purely imaginary.}$$

$\Rightarrow z_1 - z_2 = \pm k(z_3 - z_4)$, where *k* is purely imaginary number.

$\Rightarrow$ AB and CD are perpendicular to each other.

3.19.6 Condition of a Parallelogram

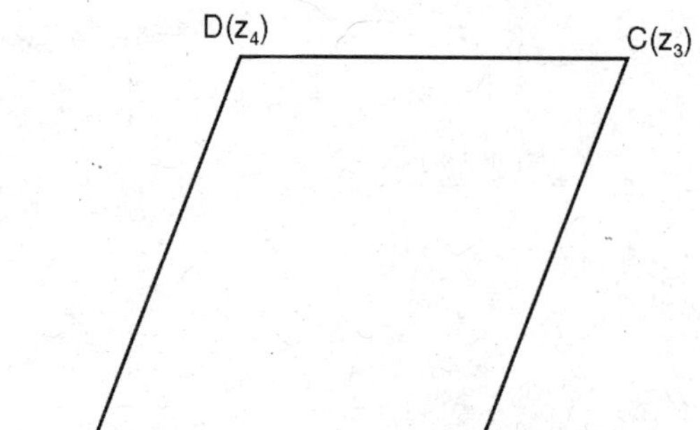

Diagonals of a parallelogram bisect each other.

$\Rightarrow$ Mid point of *AC* = Mid point of *BD*

$$\Rightarrow \frac{z_1 + z_3}{2} = \frac{z_2 + z_4}{2}$$

$$\Rightarrow z_1 + z_3 = z_2 + z_4$$

3.19.7 Regular Polygon of *n* – Sides

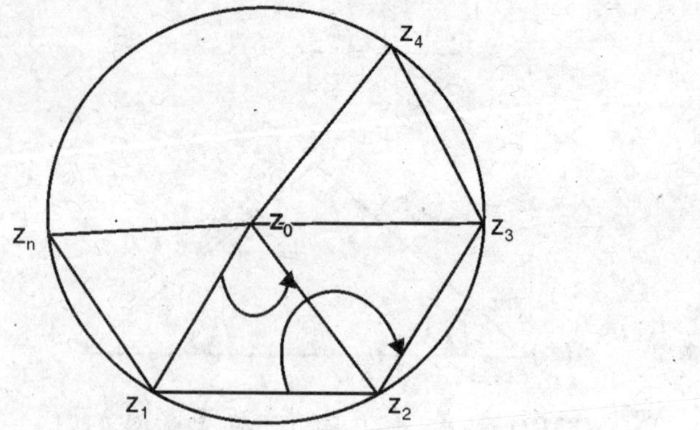

Centre at z_0 is = $2\pi/n$

i. Given z_1 and z_0, then find z_2 and z_3 in terms of z_1 and z_0.

$$\frac{z_2 - z_0}{z_1 - z_0} = \frac{|z_2 - z_0|}{|z_1 - z_0|} e^{i\frac{2\pi}{n}} = e^{i\frac{2\pi}{n}}$$

$(\because |z_2 - z_0|$ and $|z_1 - z_0|$ are the radii of the circle$)$

$$\Rightarrow z_2 - z_0 = (z_1 - z_0)e^{i\frac{2\pi}{n}}$$

$$\Rightarrow z_2 = z_0 + (z_1 - z_0)e^{i\frac{2\pi}{n}}$$

Similarly, we can shown that, $z_3 = z_0 + (z_1 - z_0)e^{i\frac{4\pi}{n}}$

$$z_4 = z_0 + (z_1 - z_0)e^{i\frac{6\pi}{n}}$$

....

....

$$z_n = z_0 + (z_1 - z_0)e^{i\frac{2(n-1)\pi}{n}}$$

ii. Given z_1, z_2 then find z_3, z_4, z_5, and so on.

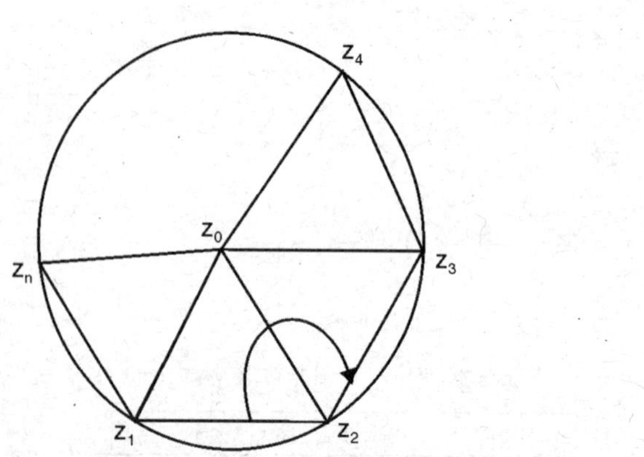

As we know that, sum of the angles of a polygon = $(n-2)\pi$.

$$\therefore \theta = \frac{(n-2)\pi}{n}$$

$$z_3 - z_2 = (z_1 - z_2) \cdot e^{-i\left(\frac{n-2}{n}\right)\pi}$$

$$\Rightarrow z_3 = z_2 + (z_1 - z_2) \cdot e^{-i\left(\frac{n-2}{n}\right)\pi}$$

Similarly, we can prove that, $z_4 = z_2 + (z_1 - z_2) . e^{-i2\left(\frac{n-2}{n}\right)\pi}$

$$z_6 = z_2 + (z_1 - z_2) . e^{-i4\left(\frac{n-2}{n}\right)\pi}$$

$$z_8 = z_2 + (z_1 - z_2) . e^{-i6\left(\frac{n-2}{n}\right)\pi}.$$

....

....

and so on.

3.19.8 Condition for Points to be Concyclic

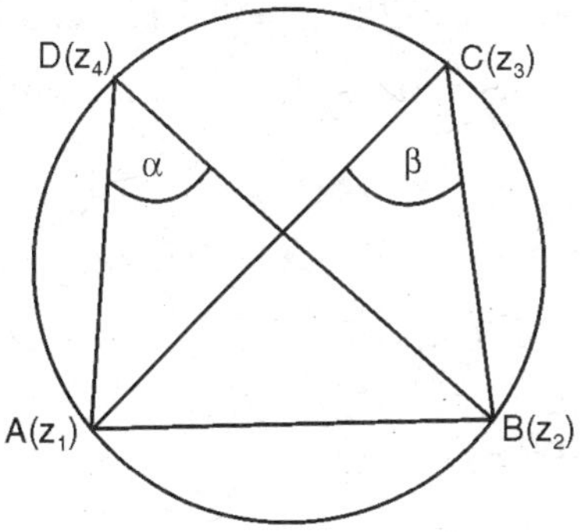

Let z_1, z_2, z_3 and z_4 are taken in order, representing the points. If z_1, z_2, z_3 and z_4 are concyclic, then (since, angles on the same segment of a circle are same.)

$$\Rightarrow \quad arg\left(\frac{z_4 - z_2}{z_4 - z_1}\right) = arg\left(\frac{z_3 - z_2}{z_3 - z_1}\right)$$

$$\Rightarrow \quad \arg\left(\left(\frac{z_4 - z_2}{z_4 - z_1}\right) / \left(\frac{z_3 - z_2}{z_3 - z_1}\right)\right) = 0$$

$$\Rightarrow \quad \arg\left(\left(\frac{z_4 - z_2}{z_4 - z_1}\right) \times \left(\frac{z_3 - z_1}{z_3 - z_2}\right)\right) = 0$$

$$\Rightarrow \quad \left(\frac{z_4 - z_2}{z_4 - z_1}\right) \times \left(\frac{z_3 - z_1}{z_3 - z_2}\right) \text{ is real.}$$

Note:

If z_1, z_2, z_3 and z_4 are not in order, then also this result is valid.

3.19.9 Some Solved Examples

Ex.1: If a point $P(3, 4)$ is rotated through an angle 90° in anti-clock-wise sense about origin, then find new position of P.

Sol.: Let $z = 3 + 4i$. If it is rotated through an angle of 90°, then it is converted to $ze^{i\frac{\pi}{2}}$

Thus, $ze^{i\frac{\pi}{2}} = iz = i(3 + 4i) = -4 + 3i = (-4, 3)$

Hence the new position of P is (–4, 3).

Ex.2: If a point $Q(2,3)$ is rotated through an angle of 180° in anti-clockwise sense about the origin, then find the new position of Q.

Sol.: Let $z = 2 + 3i$. If it is rotated through an angle of 180°, then it is converted to $z.e^{i\pi}$

Thus, $z.e^{i\pi} = z.(\cos\pi + i\sin\pi) = -z = -2 - 3i = (-2, -3)$

Hence, the new position of Q is (–2, –3).

Ex.3: If a point $P(3,4)$ is rotated through an angle of 60° in anti-clockwise sense about the point $Q(1,0)$, then find the new position of P.

Sol.: Let the new position of P be R.

Also, let P, Q, R represents the complex numbers z_1, z_2, z_3 respectively.

By Coni method, $\frac{z_3 - z_2}{z_1 - z_2} = e^{i\frac{\pi}{6}}$

$$\Rightarrow \frac{z_3 - z_2}{z_1 - z_2} = \cos\left(\frac{\pi}{6}\right) + i\sin\left(\frac{\pi}{6}\right) = \frac{\sqrt{3}}{2} + \frac{i}{2}$$

$$\Rightarrow z_3 - z_2 = 2(1 + 2i) \times \frac{1}{2}\left(\sqrt{3} + i\right) = (1 + 2i) \times \left(\sqrt{3} + i\right)$$

$$\Rightarrow z_2 = z_3 + \left(\sqrt{3} - 2\right) + i\left(1 + 2\sqrt{3}\right)$$

$$= 1 + \left(\sqrt{3} - 2\right) + i\left(1 + 2\sqrt{3}\right)$$

$$= \left(\sqrt{3} - 1\right) + i\left(1 + 2\sqrt{3}\right) = \left(\sqrt{3} - 1, 1 + 2\sqrt{3}\right)$$

Hence, the new position of P is $\left(\sqrt{3} - 1, 1 + 2\sqrt{3}\right)$.

Ex. 4: The complex number $\sqrt{3} + i$ becomes $-1 + i\sqrt{3}$ after rotating by an angle θ about the origin in anti-clock-wise direction. Then find the angle θ.

Sol.: Let $z_1 = \sqrt{3} + i = \left(\sqrt{3}, 1\right)$ and $z_2 = -1 + i\sqrt{3} = \left(-1, \sqrt{3}\right)$

Now, $z_2 = -1 + i\sqrt{3} = i\left(i + \sqrt{3}\right) = iz_1$

Also, $i = 0 + 1.i = \cos\left(\frac{\pi}{2}\right) + i\sin\left(\frac{\pi}{2}\right) = e^{i\frac{\pi}{2}}$

Thus, $\theta = \frac{p}{2}$

Ex. 5: The three vertices of a triangle are represented by the complex numbers $0, z_1, z_2$. If the triangle is equilateral, then prove that $z_1^2 + z_2^2 = z_1z_2$

Sol.: As we know that, if z_1, z_2, z_3 are the vertices of an equilateral triangle, then $z_1^2 + z_2^2 + z_3^2 - z_1z_2 - z_2z_3 - z_3z_1 = 0$

Put, $z_3 = 0$, then we get, $z_1^2 + z_2^2 - z_1z_2 = 0$

$\Rightarrow \quad z_1^2 + z_2^2 = z_1z_2.$

Ex. 6: If the origin and the roots of the equation $z^2 + az + b = 0$ form an equilateral triangle, then prove that $a^2 = 3b$.

Sol.: Let z_1 & z_2 are the roots of $z^2 + az + b = 0$.

Then $z_1 + z_2 = -a$, $z_1z_2 = b$

As we know that, if $0, z_1, z_2$ represents the vertices of an equilateral triangle, then

$$z_1^2 + z_2^2 = z_1z_2$$

$\Rightarrow (z_1 + z_2)^2 - 2z_1z_2 = z_1z_2$

$\Rightarrow (z_1 + z_2)^2 - 3z_1z_2$

$\Rightarrow a^2 = 3b$

Ex.7: If the area of the triangle on the complex plane z, iz and $z + iz$ is 50 sq. units, then prove that $|z|$ is 10.

Sol.: Clearly it is a right angle triangle.

Hence, the area of the given triangle is $= \frac{1}{2} \times |z| \times |iz|$

It is given that, $\frac{1}{2} \times |z| \times |iz| = 50$

$\Rightarrow |z| \times |iz| = 100$

$\Rightarrow |z| \times |i||z| = 100$

$\Rightarrow |z^2| = 100$

$\Rightarrow |z| = 10$

Ex. 8: Let z_1 and z_2 are the nth roots of unity which subtend a right angle at the origin. Then prove that n must be of the form is $4k$.

Sol.: Given $\frac{z_z - z_0}{z_1 - z_0} = \left|\frac{z_z - z_0}{z_1 - z_0}\right| e^{i\frac{\pi}{2}}$

$\Rightarrow \frac{z_z - z_0}{z_1 - z_0} = \frac{|z_z - z_0|}{|z_1 - z_0|} e^{i\frac{\pi}{2}}$

$\Rightarrow \frac{z_z}{z_1} = \frac{|z_z - z_0|}{|z_1 - z_0|} e^{i\frac{\pi}{2}}$

$\Rightarrow \frac{e^{i\frac{4k\pi}{n}}}{e^{i\frac{2k\pi}{n}}} = e^{i\frac{\pi}{2}}$

$\Rightarrow e^{i\frac{4k\pi}{n} - i\frac{2k\pi}{n}} = e^{i\frac{\pi}{2}}$

$\Rightarrow e^{i\frac{2k\pi}{n}} = e^{i\frac{\pi}{2}}$

$\Rightarrow \frac{2k\pi}{n} = \frac{\pi}{2}$

$\Rightarrow n = 4k$

Ex.9: Suppose z_1, z_2, z_3 are the vertices of an equilateral triangle inscribed in the circle $|z| = 2$. If $z_1 = 1 + i\sqrt{3}$, then prove that, $z_2 = -2$ and $z_3 = 1 - i\sqrt{3}$.

Sol.: We have, $\frac{z_2 - z_0}{z_1 - z_0} = \left|\frac{z_2 - z_0}{z_1 - z_0}\right| e^{i\frac{\pi}{3}}$

$\Rightarrow \frac{z_2 - z_0}{z_1 - z_0} = \frac{|z_2 - z_0|}{|z_1 - z_0|} \times e^{i\frac{\pi}{3}}$

$\Rightarrow \frac{z_2 - z_0}{z_1 - z_0} = e^{i\frac{\pi}{3}}$

$\Rightarrow \frac{z_2}{z_1} = e^{i\frac{\pi}{3}}$

$\Rightarrow z_2 = z_1 e^{i\frac{2\pi}{3}} = (1 + i\sqrt{3}) \times \left(-\frac{1}{2} + i\frac{\sqrt{3}}{2}\right)$

$= -\frac{1}{2}(1+3) = -2$

Also, $\frac{z_3 - z_0}{z_2 - z_0} = \left|\frac{z_3 - z_0}{z_2 - z_0}\right| e^{i\frac{2\pi}{3}}$

$\Rightarrow \frac{z_3}{z_2} = e^{i\frac{2\pi}{3}}$

$\Rightarrow z_3 = z_2 e^{i\frac{2\pi}{3}} = -2\left(-\frac{1}{2} + i\frac{\sqrt{3}}{2}\right) = (1 - i\sqrt{3})$

Ex.10: If a and b are real numbers between 0 and 1 such that the points $z_1 = a + i$, $z_2 = 1 + bi$ and $z_3 = 0$ is form an equilateral triangle, then prove that $a = 2 - \sqrt{3} = b$.

Sol.: As we know that, if $z_1, z_2, 0$ represents the vertices of an equilateral triangle, then $z_1^2 + z_2^2 = z_1 z_2$

$\Rightarrow (a + i)^2 + (1 + bi)^2 = (a + i)(1 + bi)$

$\Rightarrow a^2 - b^2 = a - b,\ ab + 1 = 2a + 2b$

$\Rightarrow a = b,\ ab + 1 = 2a + 2b$

$\Rightarrow a^2 - 4a + 1 = 0$

$\Rightarrow (a-2)^2 = (\sqrt{3})^2$

$\Rightarrow (a-2) = \pm\sqrt{3}$

$\Rightarrow a = 2 \pm \sqrt{3}$

$\Rightarrow a = 2 - \sqrt{3} = b$ $\quad (\because 0 < a, b < 1)$.

Ex.11: The adjacent vertices of a regular polygon of n – sides are the point's z and it's conjugate $\bar{z}$. If $\frac{Im(z)}{Re(z)} = \sqrt{2} - 1$, then prove that the value of n is 8.

Sol.: Let $z = \cos\theta + i\sin\theta$. Then $\bar{z} = \cos\theta - i\sin\theta$.

We have $\frac{z - z_0}{\bar{z} - z_0} = \left|\frac{z - z_0}{\bar{z} - z_0}\right| \times e^{i\frac{\pi}{n}}$

$\Rightarrow \frac{z - z_0}{\bar{z} - z_0} = \frac{|z - z_0|}{|\bar{z} - z_0|} \times e^{i\frac{\pi}{n}}$

$\Rightarrow \frac{z}{\bar{z}} = e^{i\frac{\pi}{n}}$

$\Rightarrow e^{i2\theta} = e^{i\frac{\pi}{n}}$

$\Rightarrow 2\theta = \frac{2\pi}{n}$

$\Rightarrow \theta = \frac{\pi}{n}$ ....(i)

Also $\frac{Im(z)}{Re(z)} = \sqrt{2} - 1$

$\Rightarrow \tan\theta = \sqrt{2} - 1$

$\Rightarrow \tan\theta = \tan\left(\frac{\pi}{8}\right)$

$\Rightarrow \theta = \frac{p}{8}$

From (*i*), we get , $\frac{\pi}{n} = \frac{\pi}{8} \Rightarrow n = 8$.

Ex.12: The vertices A and C of a square $ABCD$ are $2 + 3i$ and $3 - 2i$ respectively. Then find the vertices B and D.

Sol.: Let $A(z_1)$, $B(z_2)$, $C(z_3)$ & $D(z_4)$ represents the vertices of a square ABCD respectively.

We have, $\frac{z_3 - z_2}{z_1 - z_2} = e^{-i\frac{\pi}{2}} = -i$

$\Rightarrow z_3 - z_2 = -i(z_1 - z_2)$

$\Rightarrow z_3 + iz_1 = (1 + i)z_2$

$\Rightarrow z_2 = \left(\frac{z_3 + iz_1}{1 + i}\right) = \frac{3 - 2i - 2 + 2i}{(1+i)} = 0 = (0, 0)$.

The diagonals AC and BD bisect each other and they intersect at O, whose co-ordinates are $\left(\frac{5}{2}, \frac{1}{2}\right)$

Let $z_4 = (\alpha\beta)$

Now, $\frac{\alpha+0}{2}=\frac{5}{2} \Rightarrow \alpha = 5$ and $\frac{\beta+0}{2}=\frac{1}{2} \Rightarrow \beta = 1$

Hence, the co-ordinates of $D = (5, 1)$.

Ex.13: A, B, C are the vertices of an equilateral triangle whose centre is i. If A represents the complex number $-i$, then find the vertices of B and C. **Ans.:** $B=\left(2i-\sqrt{3}\right), C=\left(2i+\sqrt{3}\right)$

Sol.: Let $A(z_1), B(z_2), C(z_3)$ represents the vertices of an equilateral triangle and its centre is $z_0 = i$

We have, $\frac{z_2-z_0}{z_1-z_0}=\left|\frac{z_2-z_0}{z_1-z_0}\right|\times e^{i\frac{2\pi}{3}}$

$$\Rightarrow \frac{z_2-z_0}{z_1-z_0}=\frac{|z_2-z_0|}{|z_1-z_0|}\times e^{i\frac{2\pi}{3}}$$

$$\Rightarrow z_2-z_0=(z_1-z_0)\times e^{i\frac{2\pi}{3}}$$

$$\Rightarrow z_2=z_0+(z_1-z_0)\times e^{i\frac{2\pi}{3}}$$

$$\Rightarrow z_2=i+(-2i)\times\left(-\frac{1}{2}+i\frac{\sqrt{3}}{2}\right)$$

$$=i+(i)\times(1+i\sqrt{3})=i+i-\sqrt{3}=2i-\sqrt{3}$$

Similarly, we can find, $C=(2i+\sqrt{3})$.

3.20 Loci in Complex Plane

i. *Distance formula:* If z_1 and z_2 are the affixes of the two points P and Q respectively, then the distance between P and Q is $|z_1-z_2|$.

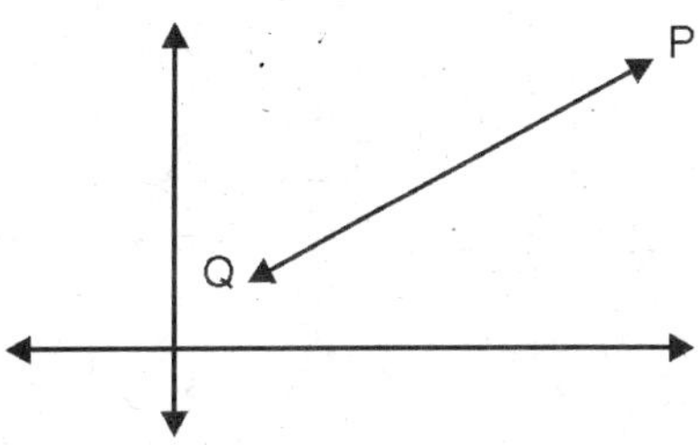

Distance between P and Q is $=PQ=|(x_1-x_2)+i(y_1-y_2)|=|z_1-z_2|$.

ii. *Section formula:* If z_1 and z_2 are the affixes of two points P and Q respectively and point C divides the line joining P and Q internally in the ratio $m{:}n$, then affix z of R is given by $z=\frac{mz_2+nz_1}{m+n}$

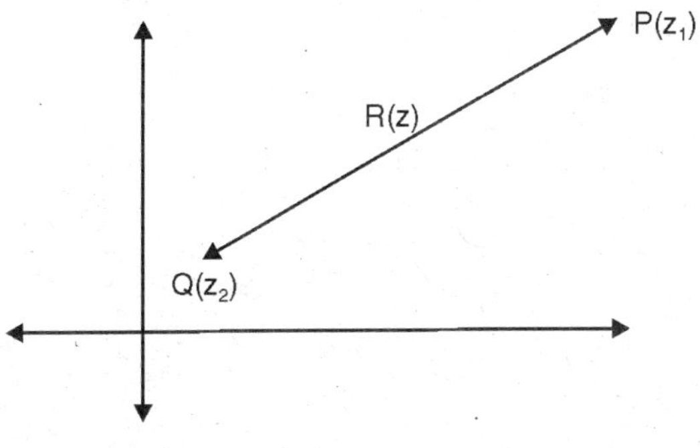

If C divides PQ in the ration $m{:}n$ externally, then $z=\frac{mz_2-nz_1}{m-n}$

iii. If a,b,c are three real numbers such that $a z_1 + b z_2 + c z_3 = 0$, where $a+b+c=0$ and a,b,c are not all simultaneously zero, then the complex number z_1, z_2 and z_3 are collinear.

iv. If the vertices A,B,C of a ABC represent the complex numbers z_1, z_2, z_3 respectively and a,b,c are the length of sides, then

a. Centroid of $\Delta ABC=\frac{z_1+z_2+z_3}{3}$

b. Orthocentre of the Δ ABC

$$=\frac{(a\sec A)z_1+(a\sec B)z_2+(a\sec C)z_3}{a\sec A+b\sec B+c\sec C}$$

or

$$=\frac{(\tan A)z_1+(\tan B)z_2+(\tan C)z_3}{a\tan A+b\tan B+c\tan C}$$

c. Incenter of the $\Delta ABC=\frac{az_1+bz_2+cz_3}{a+b+c}$

d. Circumcenter of the ΔABC

$$=\frac{(\sin 2A)z_1+(\sin 2B)z_2+(\sin 2C)z_3}{\sin 2A+\sin 2B+\sin 2C}$$

3.21 The Straight Line

i. We consider two fixed points A (z_1) and $B(z_2)$ and a variable point P moving on the straight line passing through the points A and B.

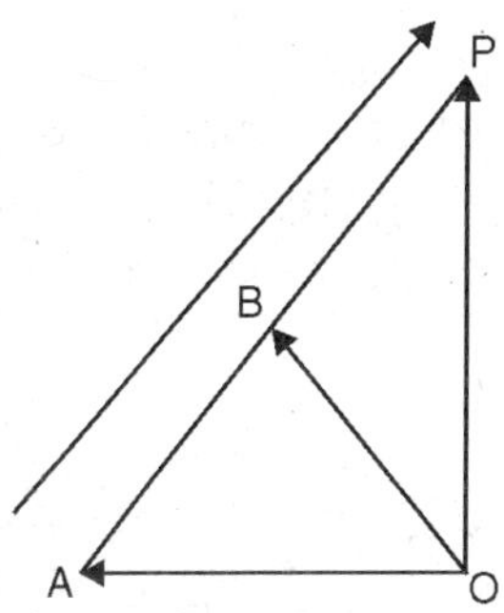

By the triangle law of vector addition $\overrightarrow{OP}=\overrightarrow{OA}+\overrightarrow{AP}$

$\Rightarrow \overrightarrow{OP}=\overrightarrow{OA}+t\overrightarrow{AB}$, (where t is some suitable real number)

Now writing corresponding complex number,

we get, $z=z_1+t\ (z_2-z_1)$ ....(1)

t is called parameter and the equation (1) is called the parametric equation of the straight line passing through the fixed points $A(z_1)$ and $B(z_2)$.

ii. Also equation (1) can be written as, $\frac{z-z_1}{z_2-z_1}=t$, where t is a real number.

$$\Rightarrow Im\left(\frac{z-z_1}{z_2-z_1}\right)=0$$

$$\Rightarrow \frac{z-z_1}{z_2-z_1}=\overline{\frac{z-z_1}{z_2-z_1}}$$

$$\Rightarrow \frac{z-z_1}{z_2-z_1}=\frac{\bar{z}-\bar{z}_1}{\bar{z}_2-\bar{z}_1}$$

$$\Rightarrow \begin{vmatrix} z & \bar{z} & 1 \\ z_1 & \bar{z_1} & 1 \\ z_2 & \bar{z_2} & 1 \end{vmatrix} = 0$$

Which represents the non parametric form of equation of a straight line passing through the points $A(z_1)$ and $B(z_2)$.

iii. $|z-z_1|+|z-z_2|=|z_1-z_2|$ is the perpendicular bisector of the line joining z_1 to z_2.

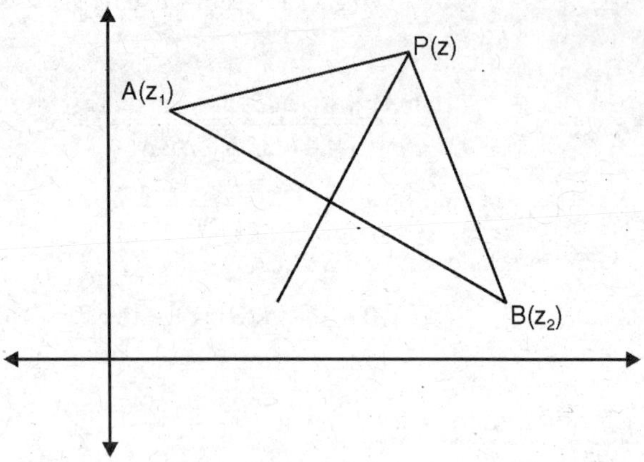

From geometry, it is follow that P lies on the perpendicular bisector of the segment AB.

iv. If $A(z_1)$ and $B(z_2)$ are two fixed points and P is a variable point moving on the line segment AB then $AP+PB=AB$

i.e., $|z-z_1| + |z-z_2| = |z_1-z_2|$

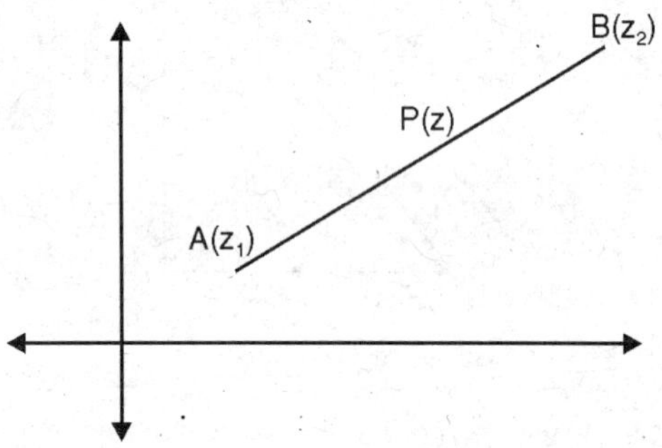

This represents the line segment AB.

v. From the above figure, we can write

$$\frac{z_1-z}{z_2-z} = \frac{PAe^{i\arg(z_1-z)}}{PBe^{i\arg(z_2-z)}} = \frac{PA}{PB}e^{i(\arg(z_1-z)-\arg(z_2-z))}$$

$$\Rightarrow \frac{z-z_1}{z-z_2} = \rho e^{i\pi}$$

$$\Rightarrow arg\left(\frac{z-z_1}{z-z_2}\right) = \pi$$

This represents the locus of a straight line.

vi. We consider two fixed points $A(z_1)$ and $B(z_2)$ and a variable point P lying on the line passing through A and B but not lying on the line segment AB.

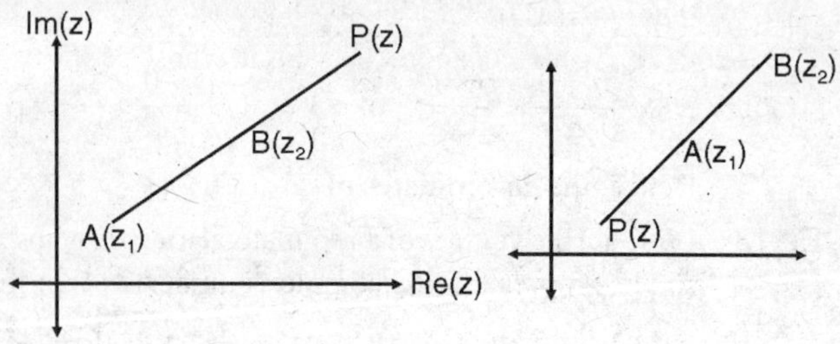

Therefore, $PA-PB=AB$

$$\Rightarrow |z-z_1|-|z-z_2|=|z_1-z_2| \quad \text{...............(1)}$$

This represents a straight line.

Also, $PA-PB=-AB$

$$|z-z_1|-|z-z_2|=-|z_1-z_2| \quad \text{.........................(2)}$$

This represents also a straight line.

Combining (1) and (2) we get, $|z-z_1|-|z-z_2|=\pm|z_1-z_2|$

Also, $\frac{z_1-z}{z_2-z}=\frac{AP}{BP}\times e^{i0}$

Thus, $arg\left(\frac{z_1-z}{z_2-z}\right)=0$

This also represents a straight line.

vii. We consider a fixed point $A(z_0)$ and a variable point P moving in such a way that PA always form an angle α with positive $Re(z)$ axis.

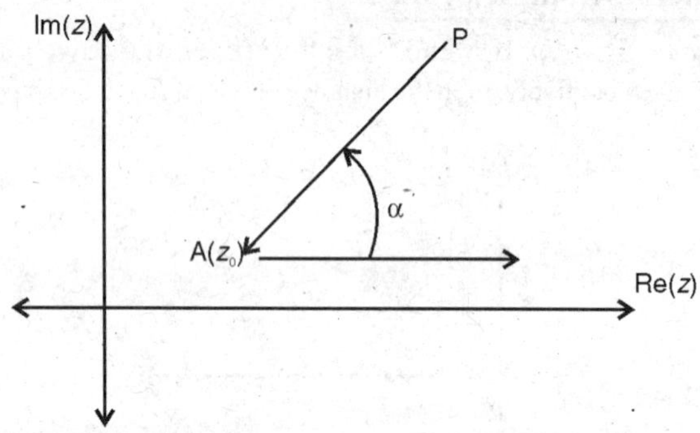

Thus, $z-z_0=PA.e^{i\alpha} \Rightarrow \arg(z-z_0)=\alpha$

This equation represents a ray originating from A (but excluding the point A) making an angle with positive $Re(z)$ axis.

NOTE:

When, $z_0=10$, then $\arg z=\alpha$, which represents a rayoriginating from origin (but excluding origin) and making an angle α with positive $Re(z)$ axis.

3.22 The Circle

i. We consider a fixed point $C(z_0)$ and a variable point $P(z)$ which is moving keeping its distance from the point C a constant 'b'.

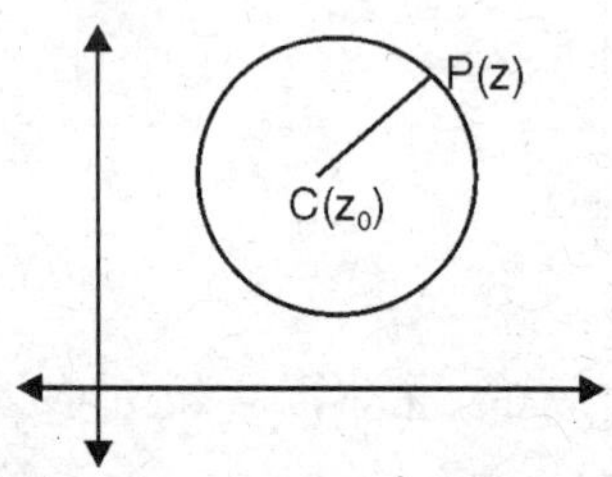

At any position, $P(z)$ satisfies the equation $|z-z_0|=b$ ....(1)
This equation represents point on a circle whose centre is z_0 and radius is b.

ii.

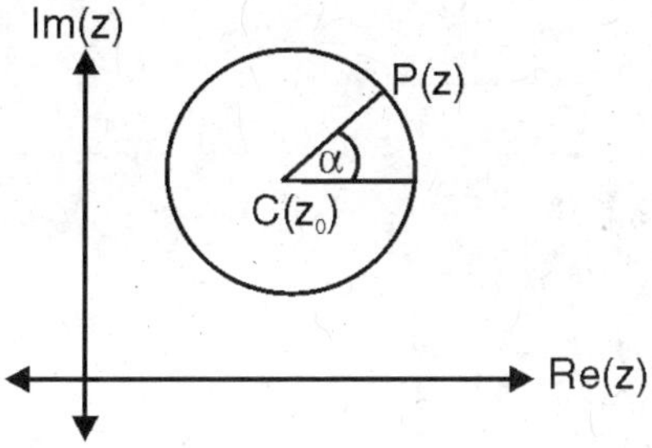

For all complex number satisfying (1) modulus of $z-z_0$ is a constant but its argument is variable.
If we define this variable argument by θ, then we can write,

$$z-z_0=be^{i0}$$

As θ changes, $P(z)$ moves on the circle.
Here, θ is called parameter and the equation is called parametric equation of the circle whose centre is z_0 and radius is b.

iii. From equation (1), we have, $|z-z_0|^2=b^2$

$\Rightarrow \quad (z-z_0)\overline{(z-z_0)}=b^2$

$\Rightarrow \quad (z-z_0)(\bar{z}-\bar{z}_0)=b^2$

$\Rightarrow \quad z\bar{z}-\bar{z}z_0-z\bar{z}_0+|z_0|^2-b^2=0$

$\Rightarrow \quad |z|^2+\bar{\omega}z+\omega\bar{z}+d=0$, where $\omega=-z_0$ and $d=|z_0|^2-b^2$ .... (2)

This represents a circle whose centre is $z_0=-\omega$ and radius is $b=\sqrt{|z_0|^2-d}=\sqrt{|z_0|^2-d}$.

iii. We consider two fixed points $A(z_1)$ and $B(z_2)$ and $P(z)$ is a variable point, moving in such way that $\dfrac{PA}{PB}$ = constant.= k ('1)

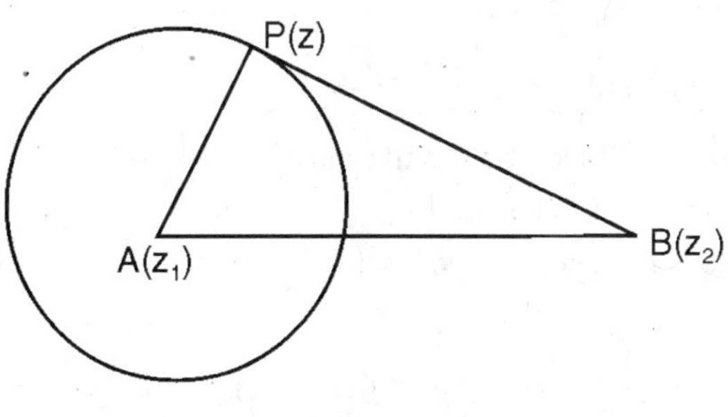

Thus, $\dfrac{|z-z_1|}{|z-z_2|}=k$

$\Rightarrow \left|\dfrac{z-z_1}{z-z_2}\right|=k$, where $k\neq 1$

v. If $A(z_1)$ and $B(z_2)$ are two fixed points and $P(z)$ is a variable point moving on the circle whose diameter is AB.

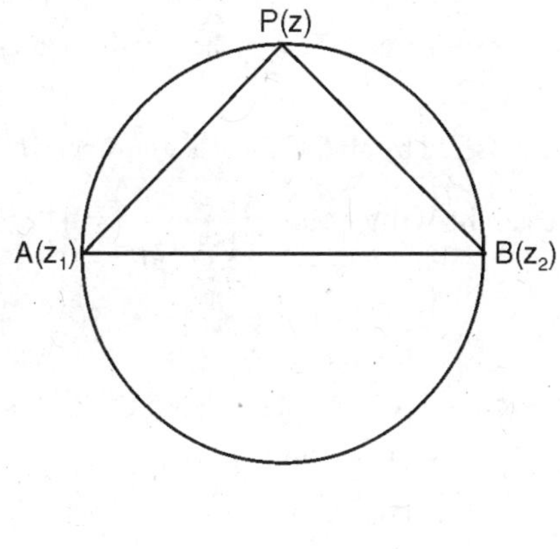

Then $PA^2+PB^2=AB^2$

$\Rightarrow |z-z_1|^2+|z-z_2|^2=|z_1-z_2|^2$ ....(3)

This equation represents a circle whose centre is $\left(\dfrac{z_1+z_2}{2}\right)$ and radius is $=\dfrac{1}{2}|z_1-z_2|$.

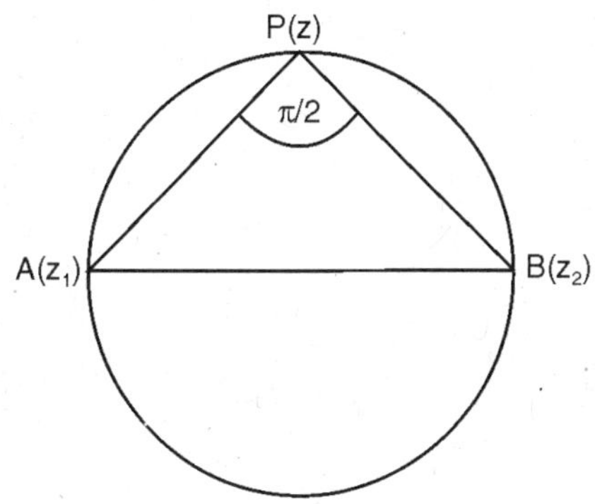

Thus, $\dfrac{z_2-z}{z_1-z}=\dfrac{PB\times e^{i\arg(z_2-z)}}{PA\times e^{i\arg(z_1-z)}}=\beta\times e^{i\arg((z_2-z)-(z_1-z))}$.

$\Rightarrow \dfrac{z_2-z}{z_1-z}=\beta\times e^{i\pi/2}$, where β is a variable whose value depends upon the position of P.
Therefore, this equation satisfied by all the complex number lying on the circle is $arg\left(\dfrac{z-z_2}{z-z_1}\right)=\dfrac{\pi}{2}$.

vii. We consider two fixed points $A(z_1)$, $B(z_2)$ and $P(z)$ is a variable point moving such that the angle subtended by segment on the moving point P is a constant (α).

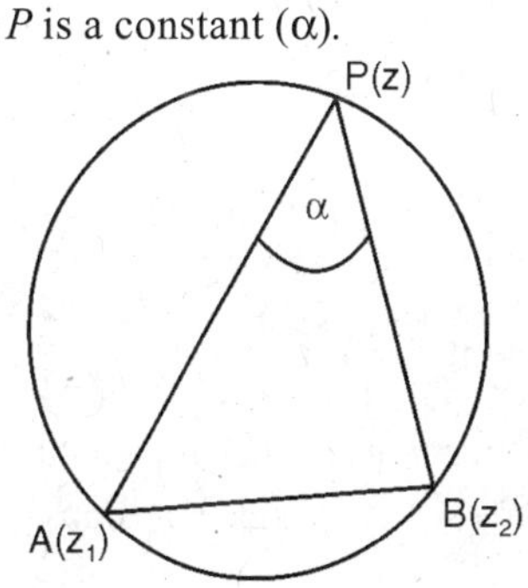

arc of a circle whose chord is AB.

$\frac{z_2 - z}{z_1 - z} = \rho \times e^{i\alpha}$, where α is a parameter, whose value depends upon the position of P.

Thus, this equation satisfied by all the complex number z lying on the arc of circle can be written as, $arg\left(\frac{z - z_2}{z - z_1}\right) = a$, where $a \neq 0\pi$

THE ELLIPSE

i. If, $|z - z_1| + |z - z_2| = 2a$ where $2a > |z_1 - z_2|$, then point z describes an ellipse having foci at z_1 and z_2 respectively z_2 and $a \in R^+$

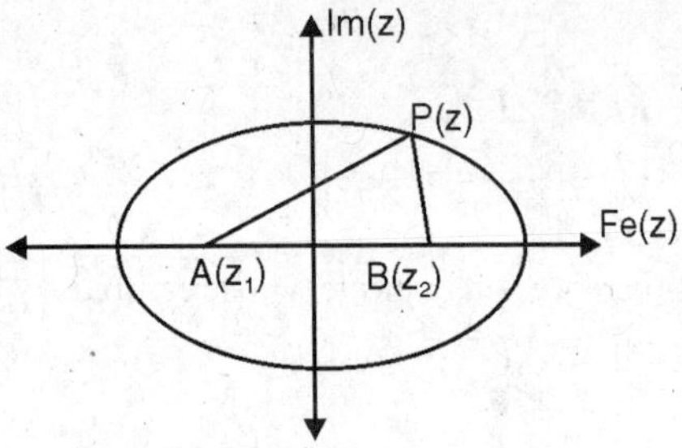

THE HYPERBOLA

i. If $\left|z - z_1\right| - \left|z - z_2\right| = 2a$ where, $2a < |z_1 - z_2|$, then point z describe a hyperbola having foci at z_1 and z_2 respectively and $a \in R^+$.

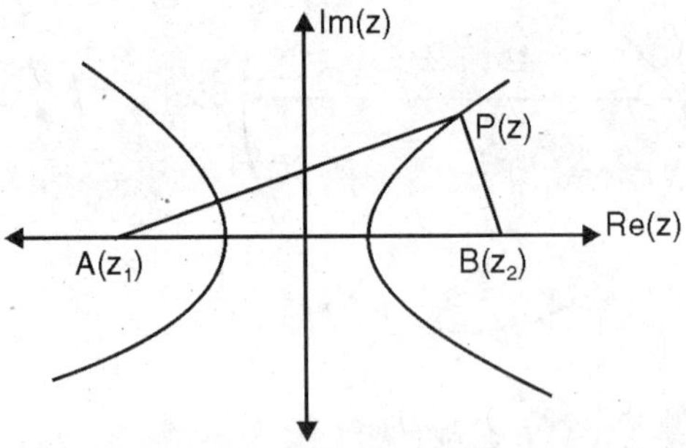

3.23 Inverse Points with Respect to A Circle

Two points P and Q are said to be inverse with respect to a circle with centre O and radius r, if

i. The points O, P, Q are collinear and on the same side of O.

ii. $OP \cdot OQ = r^2$

NOTE:

Two points z_1 and z_2 will be the inverse points with respect to the circle $z.\bar{z} + \bar{\alpha}.z + \alpha.\bar{z} + r = 0$ if and only if

$z_1.\bar{z}_2 + \bar{\alpha}.z_1 + \alpha.\bar{z}_2 + r = 0.$

3.24 Ptolemy's Theorem

It states that the product of the lengths of the diagonal of a convex quadrilateral inscribed in a circle is equal to the sum of the lengths of the two pairs of its opposite sides.

i.e. $AC.\ BD = AB.\ CD + AD.\ BC$

$\Rightarrow \quad |z_1 - z_3||z_2 - z_4| = |z_1 - z_2||z_3 - z_4| + |z_1 - z_4||z_2 - z_4|$ d

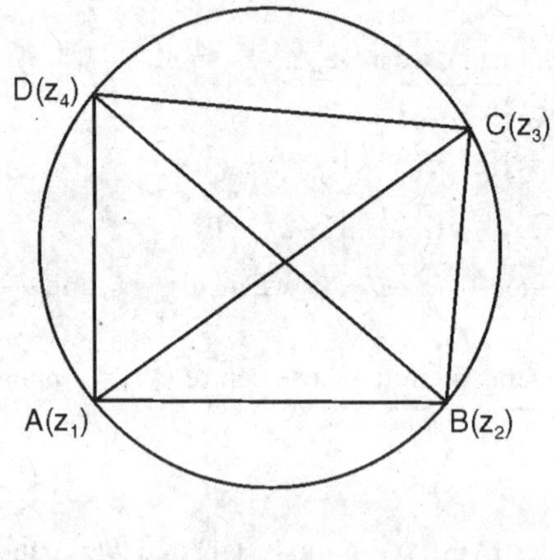

Level – I QUESTIONS BASED ON FUNDAMENTALS

ABC OF COMPLEX NUMBERS

1. Simplify and express the result in the form of $A + iB$.

i. $\frac{3+2i}{4-5i}$ ii. $\frac{3+2i}{2-5i} + \frac{3-2i}{2+5i}$ iii. $\frac{1-i}{1+i}$

iv. $\frac{1+i}{1-i}$ v. $i^{57} + \left(\frac{1}{i}\right)^{125}$ vi. $\left(\frac{2i}{1+i}\right)^2$

vii. $\left(\frac{(1+i)^2}{3-i}\right)$. viii. $\left(\frac{4i^3 - 1}{2i+1}\right)^2$

ix. $i^{2010} + i^{2009} + i^{2008} + i^{2012} + i^{2011}$.

2. Find the smallest integer n for which $\left(\frac{1+i}{1-i}\right)^n = 1$.

3. Find the smallest positive integer n for which $(1+i)^{2n} = (1-i)^{2n}$

4. Prove that $i^2 + i^4 + i^6 + \ldots\ldots\ldots\ldots (2n+1)$ terms $= -1$.

5. Find the sum of $\sum_{n=1}^{13}\left(i^{n+1} + i^n\right)$.

6. If $i = \sqrt{-1}$ and n is a positive integer, then prove that, $i^n + i^{n+1} + i^{n+2} + i^{n+3} = 0$.

7. If p, q, r and s are four consecutive integers, then find the value of $i^p + i^q + i^r + i^s$.

8. If $z = \frac{3-4i}{(4-2i)(1+i)}$, then find $Re(z)$.

9. Find all real values of θ for which $\frac{1 - i\sin\theta}{1 + i\cos\theta}$ is purely real.

10. Find all complex numbers z for which $\frac{z-2}{z+2}$ is purely imaginary.

EQUALITY OF COMPLEX NUMBERS

11. If $(x + iy)(2-3i) = 4 + i$, then find x and y.

12. $(x+iy)(p+iq) = (x^2+y^2)i$, then find x and y.

13. $\left(\frac{1+i}{1-i}\right)^3 - \left(\frac{1-i}{1+i}\right)^3 = x+iy$, then find x and y.

14. If $x+iy = \sqrt{\frac{a^2+b^2}{c^2+d^2}}$, then prove that $\left(x^2+y^2\right)^2 = \left(\frac{a^2+b^2}{c^2+d^2}\right)^2$

15. If $z = x+iy$ and $z^{1/3} = a-ib$, then prove that, $\frac{x}{a} - \frac{y}{b} = 4\left(a^2-b^2\right)$.

16. i. $\frac{x}{1+2i} + \frac{y}{3+3i} = \frac{5+6i}{8i-1}$

 ii. $x^2 - y^2 - i(2x+y) = 2i$

 iii. If $x = \sqrt{-2} - 1$, then find value of $x^4 + 4x^3 + 6x^2 + 4x + 9$

 iv. Find the value of $x^4 - x^3 + x^2 + 3x - 5$, if $x = 2+3i$

 v. Find the value of $a^6 + a^4 + a^2 + 1$, when $a = \frac{1+i}{\sqrt{2}}$.

 vi. Express $(1+a^2)(1+b^2)$ as a sum of two squares.

 vii. Find the multiplicative inverse of $3+2i$, $4-5i$.

Conjugate of Complex Numbers

17. If the complex numbers $\sin x + i\cos 2x$ and $\cos x - i\sin 2x$ are conjugate to each other, then find x.

18. If $-3 + ix^2y$ and $x^2 + y + 4i$ be conjugate complex numbers, then prove that $x = 1, -1$ and $y = 1, -4$.

19. Find the real values of x and y for which $9y^2 - 10ix - 4$ and $8y^2 - 20i$ are conjugate complex numbers to each other.

20. If $(a_1+ib_1)(a_2+ib_2)(a_3+ib_3)\ldots\ldots(a_4+ib_4) = A+iB$, then prove that $(a_1^2+b_1^2)(a_2^2+b_2^2)(a_3^2+b_3^2)\ldots\ldots(a_n^2+b_n^2) = A^2+B^2$.

21. If $x+iy = (1+i)(1+2i)(1+3i)\ldots\ldots\ldots(1+ni)$, prove that $2.5.10\ldots\ldots\ldots(1+n^2) = x^2+y^2$.

22. If $\frac{x+i}{x-i} = a+ib$, then prove that $a^2+b^2 = 1$.

Modulus of Complex Numbers

23. For any two complex numbers z_1, z_2, prove that

 $|z_1+z_2|^2 + |z_1-z_2|^2 = 2\left(|z_1|^2 + |z_2|^2\right)$.

24. For any two complex numbers z_1, z_2 and any two real numbers a, b, then prove that $|az_1 - bz_2|^2 + |bz_1 + az_2|^2 = (a^2+b^2)\left(|z_1|^2 + |z_2|^2\right)$

25. If $|z_1| = |z_2| = 1$, then prove that $|z_1+z_2| = \left|\frac{1}{z_1} + \frac{1}{z_2}\right|$

26. If $|z-2| = 2|z-1|$, where z is a complex number, show that $|z|^2 = \frac{4}{3}Re(z)$

27. Show that $\left|\frac{z-3}{z+3}\right| = 2$ represents a circle.

28. Find the locus of complex number z in Argand plane if $\left|\frac{1-iz}{z-i}\right| = 1$.

29. If $|2z-1| = |z-2|$, then prove that $|z| = 1$

30. If $\frac{z-1}{z+1}$ is purely imaginary number, then prove that $|z| = 1$.

31. If $|z+6| = |$[illegible]$+2|$, then prove that $|z| = 3$.

32. If $|z^2-1| = |z|^2+1$, then prove that the locus of z is a straight line.

33. If α and β are different complex numbers with $|\beta| = 1$, then prove that $\left|\frac{\beta-\alpha}{1-\bar{\alpha}\beta}\right| = 1$.

34. If $|z_1| = |z_2| = |z_3| = \ldots\ldots\ldots = |z_n| = 1$, then prove that, $|z_1+z_2+z_3+\ldots\ldots\ldots+z_n| = \left|\frac{1}{z_1} + \frac{1}{z_2} + \frac{1}{z_3} + \ldots\ldots\ldots + \frac{1}{z_n}\right|$

35. If z_1, z_2, z_3 are complex numbers such that $|z_1| = |z_2| = |z_3|$ $\left|\frac{1}{z_1} + \frac{1}{z_2} + \frac{1}{z_3}\right| = 1$. Then prove that $|z_1+z_2+z_3| = 1$.

36. If $iz^3 + z^2 - z + 1 = 0$, then find the value of $|z|$.

37. If $2(z-i) = |z|$, then find the complex number z.

38. If z satisfies $|z| = |z-1|$, then find the $Re(z)$.

39. If $z = x+iy$ and $|z+6| = |2z+3|$, prove that $x^2+y^2 = 9$.

40. If $|z| = 2$, then show that the points representing the complex numbers $-1+5z$ lie on a circle.

41. Find all complex number z satisfy the following equations:

 i. $\bar{z} = 2 - z$ ii. $z^2 = -\bar{z}$ iii. $z^2 + |z| = 0$

 iv. $\bar{z} = iz^2$ v. $|z| + z = 2 + i$ vi. $z^2 - (3-2i)z = (5i-5)$.

Argument of Complex Numbers

42. Find the argument of complex number

 i $1+i\sqrt{3}$ ii. $1-i\sqrt{3}$ iii. $-i$ iv. i^i.

 v. $1+\cos\left(\frac{10\pi}{9}\right) + i\sin\left(\frac{10\pi}{9}\right)$ vi. $(\tan 1 - i)^2$

43. Find the amplitude of a complex number $\frac{1+i\sqrt{3}}{\sqrt{3}+i}$

44. Find the argument of a complex number $\frac{(1+i\sqrt{3})^2}{4i(1-i\sqrt{3})}$

45. If $x = 1+i\sqrt{3}$, $y = 1-i\sqrt{3}$ and $z = 2$, then prove that $x^p + y^p = z^p$ for every prime $p > 3$.

46. If $|z| = 2$ and $arg(z) = \frac{\pi}{4}$, then find z.

47. Find the locus of z, if $arg\left(\frac{z-1}{z+1}\right) = \frac{\pi}{4}$

48. If $(a+ib)(c+id) = -\sqrt{3}+i$, then prove that $\tan^{-1}\left(\frac{a}{b}\right) + \tan^{-1}\left(\frac{c}{d}\right) = n\pi + \frac{\pi}{6}, n \in Z$

49. If $arg(z) < 0$, prove that $arg(-z) - arg(z) = \pi$.

50. Let z and w be two non zero complex numbers such that $|z| = |w|$ and $\arg z + arg\ w = \pi$, then find z.

51. If $arg(z-a) = \frac{\pi}{4}$, where $a \in R$, then prove that the locus of z is a straight line.

52. If z_1 and z_2 are two non zero complex numbers such that $|z_1+z_2| = |z_1| + |z_2|$, then prove that $arg(z_1) - arg(z_2) = 0, \pi$

53. For any two complex numbers z_1 and z_2 such that $|z_1+z_2| = |z_1-z_2|$, then prove that $arg(z_1) - arg(z_2) = \frac{\pi}{2}$.

54. If $arg\left(\frac{2-z}{2+z}\right) = \frac{\pi}{6}$, then prove that the locus of z is a circle.

55. Find the argument of $z = \sin\left(\frac{\pi}{5}\right) + i\left(1-\cos\left(\frac{\pi}{5}\right)\right)$.

56. If z and w are two non zero complex numbers such that $|zw| = 1$ and $Arg(z) - Arg(w) = \frac{\pi}{2}$, then find the complex number zw.

57. If $\arg(z) = \frac{\pi}{3}$ and $\arg(z-1) = \frac{5\pi}{6}$, then find complex number z.

58. If z is represented on Argand plane by a point on the circle $|z-1| = 1$, prove that $\frac{z-2}{z} = i\tan(\arg z)$

59. Let $z_1 = 10+6i$ and $z_2 = 4+6i$. If z is a complex number such that the argument of $\frac{z-z_1}{z-z_2}$ is $\frac{\pi}{4}$, then prove that, $|z-7-9i| = 3\sqrt{2}$.

60. Solve for z: $\arg\left(\frac{3z-6-3i}{2z-8-6i}\right) = \frac{\pi}{4}$ and $|z-3+i| = 4$.

61. If z is any non zero complex number, then prove that $\left|\frac{z}{|z|}-1\right| \geq |\arg z|$

62. If $|z| \leq 1, |w| \leq 1$, show that, $|z-w|^2 \leq (|z|-|w|)^2 + (Arg\, z - Arg\, w)^2$

63. If α, β, γ and a, b, c are complex numbers such that $\frac{\alpha}{a}+\frac{\beta}{b}+\frac{\gamma}{c} = 1+i$ and $\frac{a}{\alpha}+\frac{b}{\beta}+\frac{c}{\gamma} = 0$, then prove that value of $\frac{\alpha^2}{a^2}+\frac{\beta^2}{b^2}+\frac{\gamma^2}{c^2} = 2i$.

64. Find the number of solution of $z^2 + \bar{z} = 2$

65. Find the greatest and least value of $|z+1|$ if $|z+4| \leq 3$.

66. Find the max or min value of $|z|$ if $|z|$ if $\left|z+\frac{2}{z}\right| = 2$.

67. If $|z| \geq 3$, prove that the least value of $\left|z+\frac{1}{z}\right|$ is 8/3.

68. Find greatest and the least value of modulus of complex number z satisfying the equation $\left|z-\frac{4}{z}\right| = 2$.

69. For any complex number z, Prove that the
    i. Minimum value of $|z| + |z-1|$ is 1.
    ii. Maximum value of $|z| - |z-1|$. Is 1
    iii. Minimum value of $|z| + |z-1| + |2z-3|$ is 2.
    iv. Minimum value of $|z+1| + |z-1|$ is 2.

70. If $|z-3+2i| \leq 4$, then prove that the difference between the greatest and the least value of $|z|$ is 8.

71. If z_1 and z_2 are two complex number such that $\frac{z_1-2z_2}{2-z_1\bar{z}_2}$ is unimodular, while z_2 is not unimodular, then prove that the value of $|z_1|$ is 2.

72. If z_1, z_2, z_3 are three complex numbers and a, b, c are three positive real numbers such that $\frac{a}{|z_2-z_3|} = \frac{b}{|z_3-z_1|} = \frac{c}{|z_1-z_2|}$, then prove that $\frac{a^2}{z_2-z_3}+\frac{b^2}{z_3-z_1}+\frac{c^2}{z_1-z_2} = 0$.

73. If α and β are different complex numbers then prove that, the maximum value of $\frac{\alpha\bar{\beta}+\bar{\alpha}\beta}{|\alpha\beta|}$ is 2.

74. Let z be a complex number satisfying $|z-5i| \leq 1$ such that amplitude is minimum, then prove that $z = \frac{2\sqrt{6}}{5}+i\frac{24}{5}$.

75. Among the complex number z which satisfy equation $|z-25i| \leq 15$. Find the complex number having the least positive and the greatest positive argument.

76. Find the complex number z, the least in absolute value which satisfies the condition $|z-2+2i| = 1$.

Square Root of A Complex Number

77. Find the square roots of
    i. $-7-24I$
    ii. $8-15$ i.
    iii. $-5-12i$
    iv. $6\sqrt{-2}-7$
    v. $4ab-2(a^2-b^2)i$.
    vi. $2+3\sqrt{-5}$
    vii. $x^2+\frac{1}{x^2}+4i\left(x-\frac{1}{x}\right)-6$
    viii. $\sqrt{i}+\sqrt{-i}$.
    ix. $\frac{x^2}{y^2}+\frac{y^2}{x^2}+\frac{1}{2i}\left(\frac{x}{y}+\frac{y}{x}\right)+\frac{31}{16}$.

78. If $z^2+5 = 12\sqrt{-1}$, then find the complex number z.

Cube Roots of A Unity

79. If ω is cube root of a unity, then
    i. $(3+\omega+\omega^2)^4$
    ii. $(1+\omega-\omega^2)^7$
    iii. $(1+\omega)^3-(1+\omega^2)^3$
    iv. $\sin\left\{\left(\omega^{13}+\omega^{20}\right)\pi+\frac{\pi}{4}\right\}$.
    v. $(3+\omega+3\omega^2)^6$
    vi. $(1+\omega)(1+\omega^2)(1+\omega^4)(1+\omega^5)$
    vii. $(1-\omega+\omega^2)(1-\omega^2+\omega^4)(1-\omega^4+\omega^8)(1-\omega^8+\omega^{16})$
    viii. $\left(\frac{\sqrt{3}+i}{2}\right)^6+\left(\frac{i-\sqrt{3}}{2}\right)^6$
    ix. $2+\left(-\frac{1}{2}+i\frac{\sqrt{3}}{2}\right)^{2010}+\left(\frac{1}{2}+i\frac{\sqrt{3}}{2}\right)^{2010}+2\left(-\frac{1}{2}-i\frac{\sqrt{3}}{2}\right)^{2011}$
    x. If $a+b+c = 0$, then find the value of $(a+b\omega+c\omega^2)^3+(a+b\omega^2+c\omega)^3$

80. If $x+\frac{1}{x} = 1$, then find the value of $x^{2012}+\frac{1}{x^{2012}}$.

81. If $\alpha = -\frac{1}{2}+i\frac{\sqrt{3}}{2}$ and $\beta = -\frac{1}{2}-i\frac{\sqrt{3}}{2}$, then prove that $\frac{\alpha}{\beta}+\frac{\beta}{\alpha}+1 = 0$

82. If p, q, r are positive integers and ω be an imaginary cube root of unity and $f(x) = x^{3p}+x^{3q+1}+x^{3r+2}$, then find the value of $f(\omega)$.

83. If $x+\frac{1}{x} = 1$, then find the value of $x^{10}+x^{20}+x^{30}+\ldots\ldots+x^{100}$.

84. If $1, \omega, \omega^2$ are the cube roots of unity, then find value of $(a+b)^2+(a\omega+b\omega^2)^2+(a\omega^2+b\omega)^2$.

85. If ω be a cube root of unity and $(1+\omega^2)^n = (1+\omega^4)^n$, then prove that the least +ve value of n is 3.

86. If α and β are the complex cube root of unity, then prove that $(\alpha^4+\beta^4)+\alpha^{-1}\beta^{-1} = 0$

87. If ω is a cube root of unity and $(1+\omega)^7 = A + B\omega$, then prove that $A = B = 1$.

88. If $i=\sqrt{-1}$, then prove that the value of

$$4+5\left(-\frac{1}{2}+\frac{i\sqrt{3}}{2}\right)^{334}+5\left(-\frac{1}{2}+\frac{i\sqrt{3}}{2}\right)^{365}=-1.$$

89. If $t^2+t+1=0$, then prove that value of

$$\left(t+\frac{1}{t}\right)^2+\left(t^2+\frac{1}{t^2}\right)^2+\left(t^3+\frac{1}{t^3}\right)^2+\ldots\ldots+\left(t^{27}+\frac{1}{t^{27}}\right)^2=54.$$

90. If the cube roots of unity are $1, w, w^2$, then prove that the roots of the equation $(x-1)^3+8=0$ are $-1, 1-2w, 1-2w^2$.

91. If $x=a+b, y=aw+bw^2$ and $z=aw^2+bw$, then prove that $x^3+y^3+z^3=3(a^3+b^3)$.

92. Prove that $\dfrac{a+bw+cw^2}{c+aw+bw^2}+\dfrac{a+bw+cw^2}{b+cw+aw^2}=-1.$

93. i. If α,β,γ are the cube roots of $p<0$, then prove that for any x,y,z $\dfrac{x\alpha+y\beta+z\gamma}{x\beta+y\gamma+z\alpha}=\omega^2$.

ii. If α,β,γ are the roots of $x^3-3x^2+3x+7=0$, then prove that the value of $\dfrac{\alpha-1}{\beta-1}+\dfrac{\beta-1}{\gamma-1}+\dfrac{\gamma-1}{\alpha-1}$ is $3w^2$.

94. If ω be a complex cube root of unity satisfying the equation

$$\frac{1}{a+\omega}+\frac{1}{b+\omega}+\frac{1}{c+\omega}=2\omega^2 \text{ and } \frac{1}{a+\omega^2}+\frac{1}{b+\omega^2}+\frac{1}{c+\omega^2}$$

$=2\omega$, then prove that, $\dfrac{1}{a+1}+\dfrac{1}{b+1}+\dfrac{1}{c+1}=2$.

De, Moivre's Theorem

95. Prove that the value of $(1+i)^8+(1-i)^8$ is 32.

96. i. Prove that the solution of $\left(1+i\sqrt{3}\right)^x=2^x$ are in A.P.

ii. Prove that, the value of i^i is $e^{-\frac{\pi}{2}}$.

97. Find the integral solutions of $(1-i)^x=(1+i)^x$.

98. Find the integral solutions of $(1-i)^x=2^x$.

99. If $z_r=\cos\left(\dfrac{\pi}{2^r}\right)+i\sin\left(\dfrac{\pi}{2^r}\right)$, where $r=1,2,3,\ldots$.to infinity, then prove that the product of $z_1z_2z_3\ldots\ldots\infty$ is -1.

100. If $z_r=\cos\left(\dfrac{\pi}{3^r}\right)+i\sin\left(\dfrac{\pi}{3^r}\right)$, where $r=1,2,3,\ldots$.to infinity, then prove that the product of $z_1z_2z_3\ldots\ldots\infty$ is i.

101. Prove that the value of $\displaystyle\sum_{k=1}^{10}\left(\sin\left(\frac{2k\pi}{11}\right)+i\cos\left(\frac{2k\pi}{11}\right)\right)$ is $-i$.

102. Prove that the value of $\displaystyle\sum_{k=1}^{6}\left(\sin\left(\frac{2k\pi}{7}\right)-i\cos\left(\frac{2k\pi}{7}\right)\right)$ is i.

103. If x satisfies the equation $x^2-2x\cos\theta+1=\theta$, then prove that the value of $x^n+\dfrac{1}{x^n}$ is $2\cos n\theta$.

104. Prove that value of $1+\displaystyle\sum_{k=0}^{13}\left\{\cos\left(\frac{2k+1}{13}\right)\pi+i\sin\left(\frac{2k+1}{13}\right)\pi\right\}$ is 1.

105. If $\sin\alpha+\sin\beta+\sin\gamma=0=\cos\alpha+\cos\beta+\cos\gamma$, then prove that

i. $\sin3\alpha+\sin3\beta+\sin3\gamma=3\sin(\alpha+\beta+\gamma)$

ii. $\cos3\alpha+\cos3\beta+\cos3\gamma=3\cos(\alpha+\beta+\gamma)$

iii. $\sin2\alpha+\sin2\beta+\sin2\gamma=0$

iv. $\cos2\alpha+\cos2\beta+\cos2\gamma=0$

nth Roots of Unity

106. i. Prove that the sum of the nth roots of unity is zero.

ii. Prove that the sum of the p-th power of the nth roots of unity is zero.

iii. Prove that the product of the nth roots of unity is $(-1)^{n-1}$.

107. If $1,\omega,\omega^2,\omega^3\ldots\ldots\ldots\omega^{n-1}$ are the nth roots of unity, then prove that the value of $(1-\omega)(1-\omega^2)(1-\omega^3)\ldots\ldots\ldots(1-\omega^{n-1})$ is n.

108. If ω is the 5th root of unity, then prove that $\log2|1+\omega+\omega^2+\omega^3-\omega^{-1}|=1$.

109. If the roots of cubic equation $(z+ab)^3=a^3, a\neq0$, represents the vertices of a triangle, then prove that the length of the side is $|a|\sqrt{3}$.

110. If $1,\alpha,\alpha^2,\alpha^3,\ldots\ldots\ldots\ldots,\alpha^{n-1}$ are the nth roots of unity, then prove that the value of

i. $(3-\alpha)(3-\alpha^2)(3-\alpha^3)\ldots\ldots\ldots\ldots(3-\alpha^{n-1})=\dfrac{3^n-1}{2}$

ii. $\dfrac{1}{2-\alpha}+\dfrac{1}{2-\alpha^2}+\ldots\ldots+\dfrac{1}{2-\alpha^{n-1}}=\dfrac{(n-2)2^{n-1}+1}{2^n-1}$

iii. $(1-\alpha_1)(1-\alpha_2)(1-\alpha_3)\ldots\ldots\ldots\ldots(1-\alpha_{n-1})=n$ and deduce that $\sin\left(\dfrac{\pi}{n}\right)\sin\left(\dfrac{2\pi}{n}\right).\sin\left(\dfrac{3\pi}{n}\right)\ldots\ldots\ldots\sin\left(\dfrac{(n-1)\pi}{n}\right)=\dfrac{n}{2^{n-1}}$

111. Solve the equation $z^7-1=0$ and deduce that

i. $\cos\left(\dfrac{2\pi}{7}\right)+\cos\left(\dfrac{4\pi}{7}\right)+\cos\left(\dfrac{6\pi}{7}\right)=-\dfrac{1}{2}$

ii. $\cos\left(\dfrac{2\pi}{7}\right)\cos\left(\dfrac{4\pi}{7}\right)\cos\left(\dfrac{6\pi}{7}\right)=\dfrac{1}{8}$

112. Solve the equation $z^7+1=0$ and deduce that

i. $\cos\left(\dfrac{\pi}{7}\right)\cos\left(\dfrac{3\pi}{7}\right)\cos\left(\dfrac{5\pi}{7}\right)=-\dfrac{1}{8}$

ii. $\cos\left(\dfrac{\pi}{14}\right)\cos\left(\dfrac{3\pi}{14}\right)\cos\left(\dfrac{5\pi}{14}\right)=\dfrac{\sqrt{7}}{8}$

iii. $\sin\left(\dfrac{\pi}{14}\right)\sin\left(\dfrac{3\pi}{14}\right)\sin\left(\dfrac{5\pi}{14}\right)=\dfrac{1}{8}$

iv. $\tan^2\left(\dfrac{\pi}{14}\right)+\tan^2\left(\dfrac{3\pi}{14}\right)+\tan^2\left(\dfrac{5\pi}{14}\right)=5$

Rotation

113. i. The three vertices of a triangle are represented by the complex numbers $0, z_1, z_2$. If the triangle is equilateral, then prove that $z_1^2+z_2^2=z_1z_2$.

ii. If the origin and the roots of the equation $z^2+az+b=0$ form an equilateral triangle, then prove that $a^2=3b$.

114. Let z_1 and z_2 be the roots of the equation $z^2+pz+q=0$ where the co-efficients of p and q may be complex numbers. Let A and B represent z_1, z_2 in the complex plane. If $\angle AOB=\alpha$, $\alpha\neq0$, and $OA=OB$, where O is the origin, then prove that $p^2=4q\cos^2(\alpha/2)$

115. If the area of the triangle on the complex plane z, iz and $z+iz$ is 50 sq. units, then prove that $|z|$ is 10.

116. Let z_1 and z_2 are the nth roots of unity which subtend a right angle at origin. Then prove that n must be of the form is 4k.

117. Prove that the triangle with vertices at the points z_1, z_2 and $(1-i)z_1 + iz_2$ is the right angled isosceles.

118. Suppose z_1, z_2, z_3 are the vertices of an equilateral triangle inscribed in the circle $|z|=2$. If $z_1 = 1+i\sqrt{3}$, then prove that, $z_2 = -2$ and $z_3 = 1+i\sqrt{3}$.

119. If the complex number z_1, z_2, z_3 represent the vertices of an equilateral triangle such that $|z_1|=|z_2|=|z_3|$, then prove that, $z_1 + z_2 + z_3 = 0$.

120. If a and b are real numbers between 0 and 1 such that the points $z_1 = a+i$, $z_2 = 1+bi$ and $z_3 = 0$ is form an equilateral triangle, then prove that $a = 2-\sqrt{3} = b$.

121. The adjacent vertices of a regular polygon of n–sides are the point's z and it's conjugate $\bar{z}$. If $\dfrac{\text{Im}(z)}{\text{Re}(z)} = \sqrt{2}-1$, then prove that the value of n is 8.

122. The vertices A and C of a square $ABCD$ are $2+3i$ and $3-2i$ respectively. Then find the vertices B and D.

123. A, B, C are the vertices of an equilateral triangle whose centre is i. If A represents the complex number $-i$, then find the vertices of B and C.

124. Let A and B represent complex numbers $a+i$ and $3+bi$ and O be the origin. If triangle OAB forms an isosceles triangle with right angle at B, then find the value of a and b.

125. The complex number $\sqrt{3}+i$ becomes $-1+i\sqrt{3}$ after rotating by an angle θ about the origin in anti-clock-wise direction. Then find the angle θ.

126. $ABCD$ is a rhombus. Its diagonal AC and BD intersect at the point M and satisfy $BD = 2$ AC. If the points D and M are $1+i$ and $2-i$ respectively. Then find the possible values of A.

127. If affixes of opposite vertices of a square are a and b respectively. Find the affixes of remaining two vertices.

128. If z_1, z_2, z_3, z_4 be the affixes of a square $ABCD$ taken in the anti-clock-wise direction. Prove that $z_3 = iz_1+(i+i)z_2, z_4 = iz_2+(i-i)z_1$.

129. A man walks a distance of 3 units from the origin towards the north-east ($N\,45E$) direction. From there, he walks a distance of 4 units towards the north west ($N\,45W$) direction to reach a point P. Then find the position of P in the Argand plane.

130. A particle P starts from the point $z_0 = 1+2i$, where $i=\sqrt{-1}$. It moves horizontally away from origin by 5 units and then vertically away from origin by 3 units to reach a point z_1. From z_1 the particle moves $\sqrt{2}$ units in the direction of $i+j$ and then it moves through an angle $\pi/2$ in anti-clockwise direction on a circle with center at origin, to reach a point z_2. Find the point z_2.

Solutions of Complex Equations

131. Prove that the number of the solutions of the equation $z_2 + |z|^2 = 0$, where $z \in C$, is infinite.

132. Prove that the complex number z which satisfies the equation $z + |z+1|\sqrt{2} + i = 0$ is $-2-i$.

133. Prove that the number of solution of the system of equations is given by $|z| = 3$and $|z+1-i| = \sqrt{2}$ is zero.

134. Prove that the number of values of z which satisfy both the equations $|z-1-i| = \sqrt{2}$ and is $|z+1+i| = 2$ is 2.

135. For all complex numbers z_1, z_2 satisfying and $|z_1| = 12$ and $|z_2 - 3 - 4i| = 5$, prove that the minimum value of $|z_1 - z_2|$ is 2.

Answers

2. n is not defined **3.** $n=1$ **5.** $i-1$ **7.** 0 **8.** 13/15 **9.** $\theta = n\pi + \dfrac{\pi}{4}, n \in I$ **10.** $x^2+y^2=4$

11. $x = \dfrac{1}{2}, y=1$ **12.** $x=q=p$ **13.** $x=0, y=-2$ **16.** iii. 12 v. 0 vi. $\dfrac{1}{4}\left[\left(a^2+b^2+2\right)^2 + i\left(a^2-b^2\right)^2\right]$.

28. x-axis. **36.** $|z|=1$ **37.** $\dfrac{1}{\sqrt{3}}+i, -\dfrac{1}{\sqrt{3}}+i$ **38.** $Re(z) = \dfrac{1}{2}$ **47.** $x^2+y^2-2y-1=0$

50. $z = -\overline{w}$ **56.** $zw = -i$ **57.** $z = \dfrac{1}{2} + i\dfrac{\sqrt{3}}{2}$ **60.** $\left(4-\dfrac{4}{\sqrt{5}}\right)+i\left(1+\dfrac{2}{\sqrt{5}}\right), \left(4+\dfrac{4}{\sqrt{5}}\right)+i\left(1-\dfrac{2}{\sqrt{5}}\right)$

64. 4. **65.** $G.V=6, L.V=0$ **66.** $G.V=\sqrt{3}+1, L.V=-\sqrt{3}+1$ **68.** $G.V=\sqrt{5}+1, L.V=-\sqrt{5}+1$

75. $z = 12+i\,16$, when $\theta = \tan^{-1}\left(\dfrac{4}{3}\right)$, $z=-12+i\,16$, when $\theta = \pi - \tan^{-1}\left(\dfrac{4}{3}\right)$ **76.** $2\sqrt{2}-1$

97. $4n$, where n is Integer. **98.** 0 **122.** $B=(0,0), D=(5,1)$ **123.** $B=\left(2i-\sqrt{3}\right)$,

124. $a=7, b=4$ **125.** $\pi/2$ **126.** $A = 3-\dfrac{1}{2}i, 1-\dfrac{3}{2}i$ $C = \left(2i+\sqrt{3}\right)$. **127.** $\dfrac{a+b}{2}+i\dfrac{a-b}{2}, \dfrac{a+b}{2}-i\dfrac{a-b}{2}$

129. $(3+4i)e^{i\pi/4}$ **130.** $-6+7i$

Level – II FOR JEE – MAIN AND ADVANCED EXAMS ONLY

1. The locus of point z satisfying the condition $arg\left(\frac{z-1}{z+1}\right)=\frac{\pi}{3}$ is
   a. St. Line *b. a circle
   c. a parabola d. None.

2. The region of the z-plane for which $\left|\frac{z-a}{z+a}\right|=1$, $(Re\,(a) \neq 0)$, is
   a. x-axis *b. y-axis
   c. the st.line $|x| = a$ d. None.

3. If, $Re\left(\frac{z-8i}{z+6}\right) = 0$ then z lies on the curve
   *a. $x^2 + y^2 + 6x - 8y = 0$ b. $4x - 3y + 24 = 0$
   c. $x^2 + y^2 - 8 = 0$ d. None.

4. The locus represented by $|z-1| = |z+i|$ is
   a. a circle of radius 1
   b. an ellipse with foci (1,0) and (0,-1).
   *c. a st. line through the origin.
   d. a circle on the line joining (1,0), (0,1) as diameter.

5. If $|\bar{z}| = 25$, then the points representing the complex number $-1 + 75\bar{z}$ will lie on
   *a. circle b. parabola
   c. ellipse d. hyperbola.

6. z_1, z_2, z_3, z_4 are distinct complex numbers representing the vertices of a quadrilateral $ABCD$ taken in order. If $z_1 - z_4 = z_2 - z_3$ and, $arg\left(\frac{z_4 - z_1}{z_2 - z_1}\right) = \frac{\pi}{2}$, then the quadrilateral is
   *a. rectangle b. rhombus
   c. square d. trapezium.

7. If $\omega = \alpha + \beta$, $\beta \neq 0$ and $\frac{\omega - \bar{\omega}z}{1-z}$ is real, then z will satisfy
   a. $z.|z| \neq 1$ *b. $z.|z| = 1$
   c. $z.z \neq 1$ d. $z.z = \bar{z}$.

8. If $u = \frac{2z+5i}{z-3}$ and $|u| = 2$, then the locus z is a
   *a. st. line b. circle
   c. parabola d. none.

9. If $\omega = \frac{z}{z - \frac{1}{3}i}$ and $|\omega| = 1$, then z lies on
   *a. st. line b. parabola
   c. circle d. ellipse.

10. z_1, z_2, z_3 are the affixes of the vertices of a triangle having its circumcentre at the origin. If z is the affix of its orthocenter, then
    *a. $z_1 + z_2 + z_3 - z = 0$ b. $z_1 + z_2 - z_3 + z = 0$
    c. $z_1 - z_2 + z_3 + z = 0$ d. $-z_1 + z_2 - z_3 + z = 0$

11. Let A, B and C respectively represent the complex number z_1, z_2, z_3 on the complex plane. If the circumcentre of the triangle ABC lies at the origin, then the orthocenter is represented by the complex number
    a. $z_1 + z_2 - z_3$ b. $-z_1 + z_2 + z_3$
    c. $z_1 - z_2 + z_3$ *d. $z_1 + z_2 + z_3$

12. The complex number $z = 1 + i$ is rotated through an angle $\frac{3\pi}{2}$ in anticlockwise direction about the origin and stretched by additional $\sqrt{2}$ units, then the new complex number is.
    a. $2(1+i)$ *b. $2(1-i)$
    c. $(1-i)$ d. $-(1+i)$.

13. The vector $z = 4 + 5i$ is turned counterclockwise through an angle of 180 degree and stretched 3/2 times. The complex number corresponding to newly obtained vector is
    *a. $6 - \frac{15}{2}i$ b. $-6 + \frac{15}{2}i$
    c. $6 + \frac{15}{2}i$ d. None.

14. The number of 15th roots unity which are also the 25th roots of unity is
    a. 3 b*. 5
    c. 10 d. 13

15. The complex number z satisfies the equation $\left|z - \frac{25}{z}\right| = 24$. The maximum distance from the origin to z is
    a*. 25 b. 30
    c. 32 d. 40

16. If the area of the triangle formed by the points z, iz and $z + iz$, is 200, then $|z|$ is
    a. 5 b. 10
    c. 15 d*. 20.

17. Let z be a root of $x^5 - 1 = 0$ with $z \neq 1$. Then the value of $z^{15} + z^{16} + \ldots\ldots\ldots + z^{50}$ is
    a*. 1 b. -1
    c. 0 d. 5.

18. The set of all real x satisfying the inequality $|4i| - 1 - \log_2 x| \geq 5$ is
    a. $\left(0, \frac{1}{16}\right]$ b*. $\left(0, \frac{1}{16}\right] \cup [4, \infty)$
    c. $[4, \infty)$ d. $\left(\frac{1}{16}, 4\right]$

19. The number of roots of the equation, $\left(\frac{x+1}{x-1}\right)^n = 1$, where $n \in N$ and $x \in R$, is
    a. n b. 1
    c*. $n-1$ d. $n-2$.

20. If ω is an imaginary fifth root of 2 and $x = \omega + \omega^2$, then the value of $x^5 - 10x^2 - 10x$ is
    a. 4 b*. 6
    c. 20 d. 12

21. Suppose A is a complex number and $n \in N$ such that $A^n = (A+1)^n = 1$ then the least Value of n is
    a. 3 b. 6
    c. 9 d*. 12

22. If $z^3 - iz^2 - 2iz - 2 = 0$, then z can be
    a. $1 - I$ b*. I
    c*. $1 + I$ d. $-1 - i$.

23. If $\left(\sqrt{3} + i\right)^{100} = 2^{99}\,(a + ib)$, then the value of $a^2 + b^2$ is
    a. 1 b. 2
    c. 3 d*. 4

24. The points of intersection of the two curves and in an Argand plane are

a. $\frac{1}{2}\left(7 \pm i\sqrt{3}\right)$ b*. $\frac{1}{2}\left(3 \pm i\sqrt{3}\right)$

c. $\left(\frac{3}{2} \pm i\sqrt{\frac{7}{2}}\right)$ d. $\left(\frac{7}{2} \pm i\sqrt{\frac{3}{2}}\right)$

25. Let α&β be the roots of $x^2+x+1=0$. Then the equation whose roots are α^{19}, β^7 is

a. $x^2-x-1=0$ b. $x^2-x+1=0$

c. $x^2+x-1=0$ d*. $x^2+x+1=0$

26. If a,b,c,p,q,r are complex numbers such that $\frac{p}{a}+\frac{q}{b}+\frac{r}{c}=1+i$ and $\frac{a}{p}+\frac{b}{q}+\frac{c}{r}=0$, then. The value of $\frac{p^2}{a^2}+\frac{q^2}{b^2}+\frac{r^2}{c^2}$ is

a. 0 b. –1

c*. $2i$ d. $-2i$

27. Let $|z_1|=|z_2|=c$, then the value of $|z_1+z_2|^2+|z_1+z_2|^2$ is

a. c^2 b*. $2c^2$

c. $-c^2$ d. $c^2/2$.

28. The adjacent vertices of a regular polygon of n– sides are the point's z and it's conjugate $\bar{z}$. If, $\frac{\text{Im}(z)}{\text{Re}(z)}=\sqrt{2}-1$, then the value of n is

a. 4 b*. 8

c. 6 d. 10

29. The vertices A and C of a square $ABCD$ are $2+3i$ and $3-2i$ respectively. Then the vertices B and D are

a*. $B=(0,0), D=(5,1)$ b. $B=(0,-1), D=(-5,1)$

c. $B=(1,0), D=(-5,-1)$ d. $B=(1,1), D=(5,-1)$

30. A,B,C are the vertices of an equilateral triangle whose centre is i. If A represents the complex number $-i$, then the vertices of B and C are .

a*. $B=\left(2i-\sqrt{3}\right), C=\left(2i+\sqrt{3}\right)$ b. $B=\left(2i+\sqrt{3}\right), C=\left(2i+\sqrt{3}\right)$

c. $B=\left(2i-\sqrt{3}\right), C=\left(2i-\sqrt{3}\right)$ d. $B=\left(2i-\sqrt{3}\right), C=-\left(2i+\sqrt{3}\right)$

31. Let A and B represent complex numbers $a+i$ and $3+bi$ and O be the origin. If triangle OAB forms an isosceles triangle with right angle at B, then the value of a and b are

a*. $a=7, b=4$. b. $a=4, b=4$

c. $a=4, b=7$ d. $a=7, b=7$

32. The complex number $\sqrt{3}+i$ becomes $-1+i\sqrt{3}$ after rotating by an angle about the origin in anti-clock-wise direction. Then the angle θ is

a. $\pi/2$ b. $\pi/4$

c. $-\pi/4$ d. $\pi/6$

33. $ABCD$ is a rhombus. Its diagonal AC and BD intersect at the point M and satisfy $BD=2AC$. If the points D and M are $1+i$ and $2-i$ respectively. Then the possible values of A is

a*. $A=3-\frac{1}{2}i, 1-\frac{3}{2}i$. b. $A=3-\frac{1}{2}i, 3-\frac{3}{2}i$

c. $A=1-\frac{3}{2}i, 1-\frac{3}{2}i$. d. $A=1-\frac{1}{2}i, 1-\frac{3}{2}i$.

Answers

1. b	2. b	3. a	4. c	5. d	6. a	7. b	8. a	9. a	10. a
11. d	12. b	13. a	14. b	15. a	16. d	17. a	18. b	19. c	20. b
21. d	22. c	23. d	24. b	25. d	26. c	27. b	28. b	29. a	30. a
31. a	32. a	33. a							

Level –III For JEE Advanced Exams Only

1. If z_1, z_2, z_3 be three uni-modular complex numbers,then prove that $E=|z_1-z_2|^2+|z_2-z_3|^2+|z_3-z_1|^2$ cannot exceed 9.

2. Find the area of the triangle on the Argand Plane formed by the complex numbers $-z, iz, z-iz$.

3. If a complex number z lies on a circle of radius ½ , then prove that the complex number $(-1+4z)$ lies on a circle of radius of radius 2.

4. If $|z_1|=1, |z_2|=2, |z_3|=3$ and $|9z_1z_2+4z_1z_3+z_2z_3|=12$ then find the value of $|z_1+z_2+z_3|$.

5. If z_1, z_2, z_3 are complex numbers representing the points A,B,C such that, $\frac{2}{z_1}=\frac{1}{z_2}+\frac{1}{z_3}$, then prove that a circle through A,B,C passes through origin.

6. Let a,b,c be distinct complex numbers such that $\frac{a}{1-a}=\frac{b}{1-b}=\frac{c}{1-c}=k$. Find the value of k

7. If a and b are positive integers such that $N=(a+ib)^3-107i$ is a positive integer. Find N.

8. Find the set of points on the Argand plane for which the real part of the complex number $(1+i)z^2$ is positive, where $z=x+iy$ $x,y \in R$, and $i=\sqrt{-1}$.

9. C is the complex number and $f: C \to R$ is defined by $f(z)=|z^3-z+2|$. What is the maximum value of f on the unit circle $|z|=1$.

10. Let $z=x+iy$ be a complex number, where x and y are real numbers. Let A and B be sets defined by $A=\{z:|z|\le 2\}$ and $B=\{z:(1-i)z+(1+i)\bar{z}\le 4\}$. Find the area of the region $A \cap B$.

11. Show that product, $\left[1+\left(\frac{1+i}{2}\right)\right]\left[1+\left(\frac{1+i}{2}\right)^2\right]\left[1+\left(\frac{1+i}{2}\right)^{2^2}\right]$ .... $\left[1+\left(\frac{1+i}{2}\right)^{2^n}\right]=\left(1-\frac{1}{2^{2^n}}\right)(1+i)$ where $n \ge 2$

12. Show that the locus formed by z in the equation $z^3+iz=1$ never crosses the co-ordinate axes in the Argand's Plane. Further, show that $|z|=\sqrt{\frac{-\text{Im}(z)}{2\text{Re}(z)\text{Im}(z)+1}}$.

13. For all real numbers x, let the function $f(x) = \frac{1}{x-1}$, where $i=\sqrt{-1}$. If there exist real number a,b,c and d for which $f(a)$, $f(b)$, $f(c)$ and $f(d)$ form a square on the complex plane. Find the area of the square.

14. If $\alpha = e^{\frac{i2\pi}{n}}$ and $f(x) = A_0 + \sum_{k=1}^{20} A_k x^k$, then find the value of, $f(x)+f(\alpha x)+f(\alpha^2 x)+ \ldots\ldots\ldots\ldots + f(\alpha^6 x)$, which is independent of α.

15. Solve the equation $z^7-1=0$ and deduce that

i. $\cos\left(\frac{2\pi}{7}\right)+\cos\left(\frac{4\pi}{7}\right)+\cos\left(\frac{6\pi}{7}\right)=-\frac{1}{2}$

ii. $\cos\left(\frac{2\pi}{7}\right)\cos\left(\frac{4\pi}{7}\right)\cos\left(\frac{6\pi}{7}\right)=\frac{1}{8}$

16. Solve the equation $z^7+1=0$ and deduce that

i. $\cos\left(\frac{\pi}{7}\right)\cos\left(\frac{3\pi}{7}\right)\cos\left(\frac{5\pi}{7}\right)=-\frac{1}{8}$

ii. $\cos\left(\frac{\pi}{14}\right)\cos\left(\frac{3\pi}{14}\right)\cos\left(\frac{5\pi}{14}\right)=\frac{\sqrt{7}}{8}$

iii. $\sin\left(\frac{\pi}{14}\right)\sin\left(\frac{3\pi}{14}\right)\sin\left(\frac{5\pi}{14}\right)=\frac{1}{8}$

iv. $\tan^2\left(\frac{\pi}{14}\right)+\tan^2\left(\frac{3\pi}{14}\right)+\tan^2\left(\frac{5\pi}{14}\right)=5$

17. If ω is the nth root of unity z_1 and z_2 and are any two complex numbers, then prove that $\sum_{k=0}^{n-1}\left|z_1+\omega^k z_2\right|^2 = n\left(|z_1|^2+|z_2|^2\right)$

18. Given that $|z-1|=1$, where z is a point on the Argand plane. Show that $\frac{z-2}{z} = i\tan(\arg(z))$.

19. Given $z=\cos\left(\frac{2\pi}{2n+1}\right)+i\sin\left(\frac{2\pi}{2n+1}\right)$, where n is a positive integer, then find the equation whose roots are $\alpha = z+z^3+\ldots\ldots+z^{2n-1}$ and $b = z^2+z^4+\ldots\ldots+z^{2n}$

20. If α and β are the roots of $z+\frac{1}{z}=2(\cos\theta+i\sin\theta)$, where, $0<\theta<\pi$, then show that $|\alpha-i| \stackrel{Z}{=} |\beta-i|$

21. If a complex number z lies on the curve $|2-(-1+i)|=1$, then find the locus of the complex number $\omega=\frac{z+i}{1-i}$, $i=\sqrt{-1}$

22. Consider a triangle formed by the points $A\left(\frac{2}{\sqrt{3}}e^{i\frac{\pi}{2}}\right)$, $B\left(\frac{2}{\sqrt{3}}e^{-i\frac{\pi}{6}}\right)$, $C\left(\frac{2}{\sqrt{3}}e^{-i\frac{5\pi}{6}}\right)$. Let $P(z)$ be any point on its circle, then prove that $AP^2+BP^2+CP^2=5$.

23. Find the common tangents of the curve $Re(z)=|z=2a|$ and $|z-4a|=3a$.

24. Show that the complex numbers whose real and imaginary parts are integers and satisfy the equation $z\bar{z}^3+\bar{z}z^3=350$ form a rectangle in the Argand plane with the length of the diagonal having an integral number of units.

25. If $\beta \neq 1$ be any nth root of unity, then prove that the value of $1+3\beta+5\beta^2+\ldots\ldots\ldots n$–tems is $\frac{2n}{\beta-1}$.

26. The equation $x^3=-9+i46$, where $i=\sqrt{-1}$ has a solution of the form $a+ib$, where a and b are integers. Find the value of (a^3+b^3).

27. If ω is the fifth root of 2 and $x=\omega+\omega^2$, then prove that $x^5=10x^2+10x+6$

28. Let Z is a complex number satisfying the equation $z^2-(3+i)z+m+2i=0$, where $m\in R$. Suppose the equation has a real root, then find the value of m.

29. a,b,c are real numbers in the polynomial, $P(Z)=2Z^4+aZ^3+bz^2+cZ+3$. If two roots of the equation $P(Z)=0$ are 2 and i(iota), then find the value of a.

30. Resolve z^5+1 into linear and quadratic factors with real coefficients. Deduce that $4\sin\left(\frac{\pi}{10}\right)\cos\left(\frac{\pi}{5}\right)=1$.

31. If the equation $(z+1)^7+z^7=0$ has roots $z_1, z_2, \ldots\ldots\ldots, z_7$, then find the value of

i. $\sum_{r=1}^{7} Re(Z_r)$ ii. $\sum_{r=1}^{7} \operatorname{Im}(Z_r)$

32. Find all real values of the parameter 'a' for which the equation $(a-1)z^4-4z^2-a+2=0$ has only pure imaginary roots.

33. If the bi-quadratic x4+ax3+bx2+cx+d=0 $(a,b,c,d\in R)$ has 4 non real roots, two with sum $3+4i$ and the other two with product $13+1i$. Find the value of b.

34. If $Z_r, r=1,2,3,\ldots\ldots\ldots\ldots, 2m, m\in N$ are the roots of the equation $Z^{2m}+Z^{2m-1}+Z^{2m-2}+\ldots\ldots\ldots\ldots+Z+1=0$, then prove that $\sum_{r=1}^{2m}\left(\frac{1}{Z_r-1}\right)=-m$.

ANSWERS

2. $\frac{3}{2}|z|^2$ **4.** 2 **6.** $k=-\omega$ or $-\omega^2$ **7.** 198

8. Required set is constituted by the angles without their boundaries, whose sides are straight lines $y=(\sqrt{2}-1)x$ and $y=-(\sqrt{2}+1)x$ containing the x-axis.

9. $|f(z)|$ is maximum when $z=\omega$, where ω is the cube root of unity and $|f(z)|=\sqrt{13}$.

10. $\pi-2$ **13.** 51 **14.** 14 **19.** $4x^2+4x+\sec^2\left(\frac{\pi}{2n+1}\right)=0$

21. The locus of ω is a circle, whose center is $\left(-\frac{3}{2},\frac{1}{2}\right)$ and radius is $\frac{1}{\sqrt{2}}$

23. $x=a, y=\frac{1}{\sqrt{3}}x+\frac{2a}{\sqrt{3}}$ and $y=-\frac{1}{\sqrt{3}}x-\frac{2a}{\sqrt{3}}$. **26.** 35. **28.** $m=2$ **29.** $-\frac{11}{2}$ **31.** i. $-\frac{7}{2}$ ii. 0

32. $[-3,-2]$ **33.** 31.

LINKED COMPREHENSION TYPE

In these questions, a paragraph has been given followed by questions based on each of the passages. You have to answer the questions based on the passage given.

PASSAGE–I

If $x^2+1=0 \Rightarrow x^2=-1 \Rightarrow x=\pm\sqrt{-1}=\pm i$ (iota) is called the imaginary unit. Also, $i^2=-1, i^3=-1$ i.e. $i^n+i^{n+1}+i^{n+2}+i^{n+3}=0, \forall\ n\in I$ and $x^3-1=0 \Rightarrow (x-1)(x^2+x+1)=0 \Rightarrow (x-1)(x-w)(x-w^2)=0$
$\Rightarrow x=1, \omega, \omega^2$ are the cube roots of unity.
i.e. $\omega^n+\omega^{n+1}+\omega^{n+2}=0, \forall\ n\in I$

Now let $z=a+ib$, if $|a:b|=\sqrt{3}:1$ or $1:\sqrt{3}$. Then convert z in terms of ω or ω^2.

Also, $|1-\omega|=|1-\omega^2|=\sqrt{3}$

On the basis of above information, answer the following questions.

1. The value of the sum, $\sum_{n=1}^{16}\left(i^n+i^{n+1}\right)$, where $i=\sqrt{-1}$, is
   a. I b. $i-1$
   c. $-i$ d. 0
2. For positive integers n_1, n_2 the value of the expression $(1+i)^{n_1}+\left(1+i^3\right)^{n_1}+\left(1+i^5\right)^{n_2}+\left(1+i^7\right)^{n_2}$ ie real if
   a. $n_1=n_2+1$ b. $n_1=n_2-1$
   c. $n_1=n_2$ d. $n_1>0, n_2>0$
3. If ($\omega\neq 1$) is a cube root of unity and $i=\sqrt{-1}$,
   then $\begin{vmatrix}1 & 1+i+\omega^2 & \omega^2\\ 1-i & -1 & \omega^2-1\\ -i & -i+\omega-1 & -1\end{vmatrix}$ is
   a. 0 b. 1
   c. i d. ω
4. Let, $\omega=-\frac{1}{2}+i\frac{\sqrt{3}}{2}$, where $i=\sqrt{-1}$, then the value of the determinant $\begin{vmatrix}1 & 1 & 1\\ 1 & -1-\omega^2 & \omega^2\\ 1 & \omega^2 & \omega^4\end{vmatrix}$ is
   a. 3ω b. $3\omega(\omega-1)$
   c. $3\omega^2$ d. $3\omega(1-\omega)$
5. If $i=\sqrt{-1}$, then value of $4+5\left(-\frac{1}{2}+i\frac{\sqrt{3}}{2}\right)^{334}+3\left(-\frac{1}{2}+i\frac{\sqrt{3}}{2}\right)^{365}$ is
   a. $1-i\sqrt{3}$ b. $-1+i\sqrt{3}$
   c. $i\sqrt{3}$ d. $-i\sqrt{3}$
6. The complex numbers z_1, z_2 and z_3 satisfying $\frac{z_1-z_3}{z_2-z_3}=\frac{1-i\sqrt{3}}{2}$ are the vertices of a triangle which is:
   a. of area zero b. *rt* angled isosceles
   c. equilateral d. obtuse angled isosceles.
7. The value of $\sum_{r=2}^{n}(r-1)(r-\omega)\left(r-\omega^2\right)$, where ω is an imaginary cube root of unity, is
   a. $\left(\sum n\right)^2-2n$ b. $\left(\sum n\right)^2-n$
   c. $\left(\sum n\right)^2+n$ d. $\left(\sum n\right)^2+2n$
8. The smallest positive integer n, for which $\left(\frac{1+i}{1-i}\right)^n=1$, where $i=\sqrt{-1}$, is
   a. 1 b. 2
   c. 3 d. 4
9. If α,β, and γ are the roots of $x^3-3x^2+3x+7=0$, then the value of $\sum\left(\frac{\alpha-1}{\beta-1}\right)$ is
   a. 0 b. 3ω
   c. $3/\omega$ d. 4
10. If $\left(\frac{3}{2}+\frac{i\sqrt{3}}{2}\right)^{50}=3^{25}(x-y)$, where x,y are real, then the ordered pair (x,y) is given by
    a. (0, 3) b. $\left(\frac{1}{2},-\frac{\sqrt{3}}{2}\right)$
    c. (–3, 0) d. $\left(-\frac{1}{2},\frac{\sqrt{3}}{2}\right)$
11. The roots of the cubic equation $(z+\alpha\beta)^3=\alpha^3, (\alpha\neq 0)$ represent the vertices of a triangle of sides of length
    a. $\frac{1}{\sqrt{3}}|\alpha\beta|$ b. $\sqrt{3}|\alpha|$
    c. $\sqrt{3}|\beta|$ d. $\frac{1}{\sqrt{3}}|\alpha|$
12. If, $z=\frac{\sqrt{3}+i}{2}$, where $i=\sqrt{-1}$, then $(z^{101}+i^{103})^{105}$ is equal to
    a. z b. z^2
    c. z^3 d. z^4

PASSAGE–II

Let $z=a+ib=re^{i\theta}$, where $a,b,\theta\in R$ and $i=\sqrt{-1}$

Then $r=\sqrt{a^2+b^2}=|z|$ and $\theta=\tan^{-1}\left(\frac{b}{a}\right)=arg(z)$

Now $|z|^2=a^2+b^2=(a+ib)(a-ib)=z\bar{z} \Rightarrow \frac{1}{z}=\frac{\bar{z}}{|z|^2}$ and $|z_1z_2z_3 .... z_n|$

If $|f(z)| = 1|$, then $f(z)$ is called unimodular. In this case, $f(z)$ can always be expressed as $f(z) = e^{i\alpha}, \alpha \in R$

Also, $e^{i\alpha} + e^{i\beta} = e^{i\left(\frac{\alpha+\beta}{2}\right)} 2\cos\left(\frac{\alpha-\beta}{2}\right)$ and $e^{i\alpha} - e^{i\beta} = e^{i\left(\frac{\alpha+\beta}{2}\right)} 2i\sin\left(\frac{\alpha-\beta}{2}\right)$, $\alpha, \beta \in R$

On the basis of above information, answer the following questions:

1. If z_1, z_2, z_3 are complex numbers such that $|z_1| = |z_2| = |z_3| = |z_1 + z_2 + z_3| = 1$, then $\left|\frac{1}{z_1} + \frac{1}{z_2} + \frac{1}{z_3}\right|$ is
   a. 1 b. < 1
   c. > 3 d. 3
2. If $|z_1| = 1$, $|z_2| = 2$, $|z_3| = 3$ and $|z_1 + z_2 + z_3| = 1$, then $|9z_1z_2 + 4z_1z_3 + z_2z_3|$ is equal to
   a. 6 b. 36
   c. 216 d. 1296.
3. If $|z_1| = |z_2| = |z_3| = ... = |z_n| = 1$, then the value of $|z_1 + z_2 + z_3 + ... + z_n|$ is
   a. 1 b. $|z_1| + |z_2| + |z_3| + ... + |z_n|$
   c. $\left|\frac{1}{z_1} + \frac{1}{z_2} + \frac{1}{z_3} + ... + \frac{1}{z_n}\right|$ d. n
4. If $z = x + iy$ is a complex number with rational x and y and $i = \sqrt{-1}$ and $|z| = 1$, then $|z^{2n} - 1|$ is $(n \in N)$
   a. an irrational number
   b. a rational number
   c. non terminating and non recurring
   d. a positive real number
5. The value of $\tan\left(i \ln\left(\frac{a-ib}{a+ib}\right)\right)$ is
   a. $\frac{2ab}{b^2 - a^2}$ b. $\frac{2ab}{a^2 - b^2}$
   c. $\frac{a^2 + b^2}{a^2 - b^2}$ d. $\frac{a^2 - b^2}{a^2 + b^2}$
6. If $|z - 3i| = 3$, (where $i = \sqrt{-1}$) and $arg\, z \in \left(0, \frac{\pi}{2}\right)$, then $\cot(\arg z) - \frac{6}{z}$ is equal to
   a. 0 b. $-i$
   c. i d. π
7. If z_1 and z_2 are complex numbers satisfying $\left|\frac{z_1 + z_2}{z_1 - z_2}\right| = 1$ and $arg\left(\frac{z_1 - z_2}{z_1 + z_2}\right) \neq m\pi$ where $m \in I$, then $\frac{z_1}{z_2}$ is
   a. 0 b. a rational number
   c. a +ve real No d. a purely img.

PASSAGE – III

Let $z = a + ib = (a,b)$ be any complex number for every $a, b \in R$ and $i = \sqrt{-1}$. If $(a, b) \neq (0, 0)$, then $\arg(z) = \tan^{-1}\left(\frac{b}{a}\right)$, where $-\pi < \arg(z) \leq \pi$ and $\arg(z) + arg(\bar{z}) = \begin{cases} p, \text{if } \arg(z) < 0 \\ -p, \text{if } \arg(z) > 0 \end{cases}$

On the basis of above information, answer following questions:

1. If arg $(z) < 0$, then arg $(-z)$ – arg (z) is equal to
   a. π b. $-\pi$
   c. $-\pi/2$ d. $\pi/2$.
2. Let z and w be two complex numbers such that and, then z equals
   a. w b. $-w$
   c. $\bar{w}$ d. $-\bar{w}$
3. If, $\arg(2z_1) - \arg(3z_2) = \pi$, then the value of $\left|\frac{z_1}{z_2}\right|$ is equal to
   a. 0.5 b. 1
   c. 1.5 d. 2
4. If arg $(z) > 0$, then arg $(-z)$ – arg $(z) = \lambda_1$ and if arg$(z) < 0$, then arg (z) – arg $(-z) = \lambda_2$, then
   a. $\lambda_1 + \lambda_2 = 0$ b. $\lambda_2 - \lambda_2 = 0$
   c. $3\lambda_1 - 2\lambda_2 = 0$ d. $2\lambda_1 - 3\lambda_2 = 0$
5. The value of $\sqrt{\{\arg(z) + \arg(-z) - 2\pi\}\{\arg(-z) + \arg(\bar{z})\}}$ for every $z = x + iy$, where $x, y > 0$
   a. π b. $-\pi$
   c. 0 d. None.

PASSAGE – IV

The equation $x^n - 1 = 0$ has n roots, which are called the nth roots of unity. Then n, nth roots of unity are $1, \alpha, \alpha^2, \alpha^3, ... \alpha^{n-1}$ which are in G.P., where $\alpha = \cos\left(\frac{2\pi}{n}\right) + i\sin\left(\frac{2\pi}{n}\right)$, $i = \sqrt{-1}$, then we have the following results:

i. $\sum_{r=0}^{n-1} \alpha^r = 0$ or $\sum_{r=0}^{n-1} \cos\left(\frac{2\pi r}{n}\right) = 0$ and $\sum_{r=0}^{n-1} \sin\left(\frac{2\pi r}{n}\right) = 0$

ii. $z^n - 1 = \prod_{r=0}^{n-1} (z - \alpha^r)$ iii. $\prod_{r=0}^{n-1} \alpha^r = (-1)^{n-1}$

iv. $\sum_{r=0}^{n-1} \alpha^{kr} = \begin{cases} n, \text{ if } k \text{ is multiple of } n \\ 0, \text{ if } k \text{ isnotmultipleof } n \end{cases}$

On the basis of above information, answer the following questions:

1. The value of $\sum_{r=1}^{n-1} \left(\frac{1}{2 - \alpha^r}\right)$ is equal to
   a. $(n-2)2^n$ b. $\frac{(n-2)2^{n-1} + 1}{2^n - 1}$
   c. $\frac{(n-2)2^{n-1}}{2^n - 1}$ d. $\frac{(n-1)2^{n-1}}{2^n - 1}$
2. If ω be non real complex cube root of unity, then the value of $\frac{\prod_{p=1}^{4}(\omega + \alpha^p)}{\prod_{q=1}^{7}(\omega^2 - \alpha^q)}$ is equal to
   a. $\left(\frac{-1 + i\sqrt{3}}{2}\right)$ b. $\left(\frac{1 - i\sqrt{3}}{2}\right)$
   c. $\left(\frac{-1 - i\sqrt{3}}{2}\right)$ d. $\left(\frac{1 + i\sqrt{3}}{2}\right)$

3. The algebraic sum of perpendicular distances from the points $1, \alpha, \alpha^2, \ldots\ldots\ldots \alpha^{n-1}$ to the line, $a\bar{z} + \bar{a}\bar{z} + b = 0$, (where a is complex number and b is real) is equal to

a. $\frac{n}{2|a|}$

b. $\frac{n|b|}{2a}$

c. $\frac{nb}{|a|}$

d. $\frac{nb}{2|a|}$

4. If, $\alpha = \cos\left(\frac{2\pi}{7}\right) + i\sin\left(\frac{2\pi}{7}\right)$, then equation whose roots are a $+\alpha^2 + \alpha^4$ and $\alpha^3 + \alpha^5 + \alpha^6$ is

a. $z^2 - z - 2 = 0$ b. $z^2 - z + 2 = 0$
c. $z^2 + z - 2 = 0$ d. $z^2 + z + 2 = 0$

5. If $n \in N$, then the value of $\sum_{r=1}^{n-1} \sin\left(\frac{r\pi}{n}\right)$ is equal to

a. $\frac{n}{2^{n-1}}$ b. $n.2^{n-1}$

c. $\frac{n}{2^{n-1}}$ d. $n.2^{n+1}$

6. If $n \in I, n \leq 2$, then the value of $\sum_{r=1}^{n-1} (n-r)\cos\left(\frac{2r\pi}{n}\right)$ is equal to

a. $-n$ b. n
c. $-n/2$ d. $n/2$

7. The expression $\sum_{m=1}^{4n+1} \left\{\sum_{k=1}^{m-1}\left(\sin\left(\frac{2\pi k}{m}\right) - i\cos\left(\frac{2\pi k}{m}\right)\right)\right\}^m$

a. has real part equal to 1 b. purely real
c. purely imaginary d. has imaginary part equal to 2.

PASSAGE – V

If $A(\alpha)$, $B(\beta)$, $C(\gamma)$ are the vertices of a triangle where α, β, γ are unimodular complex numbers.

1. The orthocenter of the triangle ABC must be represented by the complex number

a. $\sqrt{\alpha^2 + \beta^2 + \gamma^2 - \alpha\beta - \beta\gamma - \gamma\alpha}$ b. $\sqrt{\alpha^2 + \beta^2 + \gamma^2}$

c. $\frac{\alpha^2 + \beta^2 + \gamma^2}{3}$ d*. $\alpha+\beta+\gamma$

2. The area of the triangle must be

a. $\begin{vmatrix} \alpha & \bar{\alpha} & 1 \\ \beta & \bar{\beta} & 1 \\ \gamma & \bar{\gamma} & 1 \end{vmatrix}$ b. $\frac{1}{2}\begin{vmatrix} \alpha & \bar{\alpha} & 1 \\ \beta & \bar{\beta} & 1 \\ \gamma & \bar{\gamma} & 1 \end{vmatrix}$

c*. $\frac{1}{4}\begin{vmatrix} \alpha & \bar{\alpha} & 1 \\ \beta & \bar{\beta} & 1 \\ \gamma & \bar{\gamma} & 1 \end{vmatrix}$ d. $\frac{1}{8}\begin{vmatrix} \alpha & \bar{\alpha} & 1 \\ \beta & \bar{\beta} & 1 \\ \gamma & \bar{\gamma} & 1 \end{vmatrix}$

3. If a perpendicular AD from A is dropped on BC and is produced to a point E on the circle $|z| = 1$, then E must have affix

a*. $-\frac{\beta\gamma}{\alpha}$ b. $-\frac{\alpha\beta}{\gamma}$

c. $-\frac{\alpha\gamma}{\beta}$ d. $-\frac{\beta\gamma}{\alpha}$

ANSWERS

PASSEGE I

1. d 2. d 3. a 4. b 5. c 6. c 7. b 8. d 9. c 10. b
11. b 12. c

PASSEGE II

1. a 2. a 3. c 4. b 5. b 6. c 7. d

PASSEGE III

1. a 2. d 3. c 4. b 5. (d)

PASSEGE IV

1. b 2. b 3. d 4. d 5. c 6. c 7. c

PASSEGE V

1. d 2. c 3. a

MATRIX MATCH TYPE

Given below are Matching type questions with two columns (each having some terms) each. Each term of column I has to be matched with the items of Column II, by encircling the correct matches.

NOTE

An item of Column I can be matched with more than one items of Column II . All the items of Column II have to matched.

1. Observe the following columns :

I	II
A. Locus of the point z satisfying the equation $Re\,(z^2) = Re(z + \bar{z})$	P A hyperbola with eccentricity $\sqrt{2}$
B. Locus of the point z satisfying the equation $\|z - z_1\| + \|z - z_2\| = \lambda,\ \lambda \in R^+$ and $\lambda \nless \|z - z_2\|$	Q A straight line
C. Locus of the point z satisfying the equation $\left\|\frac{2z - i}{z + 1}\right\| = m$, where $m \in R^+$	R An Ellipse
	S A rectangular Hyperbola
	T A circle.

2. Observe the following columns .

I	II
A. If z_1, z_2, z_3 are the vertices of an equilateral Triangle with z_0 as its nine point center, then $z_1^2 + z_2^2 + z_3^2$ is	P $(z_1-z_2)^2 = 2(z_1-z_3)(z_3-z_2)$
	Q $3\,z_0^2$
	R $(z_2-z_3)^2 = 3(z_3-z_1)(z_1-z_2)$
B. If z_1, z_2, z_3 are vertices A,B,C resp. of an Isosceles triangle with rt angle at C, then	S $z_1z_2 + z_2z_3 + z_3z_1$
C. If z_1, z_2, z_3 are the vertices A,B,C resp. of an Isosceles triangle and the angles B and C are each Equal to $\pi/6$, then	T $\frac{z_2 - z_3}{z_1 - z_3} = e^{i\frac{\pi}{2}}$

3. Observe the following Columns :

I	II
A. If $1, \omega, \omega^2, ..., \omega^{n-1}$ are the n, nth roots of unity, then $(2-\omega)(2-\omega^2).....(2-\omega^{n-1})$ is	P 2^n-1
	Q 0
B. If $z_1, z_2, z_3, ..., z_n$ lie on a circle $\|z\| = 2$, then Value of $\|z_1+z_2+ ....+z_n\| - \left\|\frac{1}{z_1}+\frac{1}{z_2}+....+\frac{1}{z_n}\right\|$ is	R $C_1 + C_2 + ... + C_n$
C. If p is a multiple of n, then the sum of the pth power of nth roots of unity is	S C_1
	T $\sqrt{^{2n+1}C_1 + {}^{2n+1}C_2 + ... + {}^{2n+1}C_n} - 1$

4. Observe the following columns :

I	II
A. If G be greatest and L be least value of $\|z-1\|$, if $\|z + 2 + i\| \le 1$, then	P $LG = 9$
	Q $L + G = 6$
B. If G be the greatest and L be the least value of $\|z-2i\|$, if $1 \le \|z + 2i\| \le 3$	R $\left(\sqrt{2G} - \sqrt{2L}\right)^2 = 4$
C. If G be the greatest and L be the least values of $\|z-2\|$, if $\|z + i\| \le 1$, then	S $LG = 4$
	T $G - L = 2$

5. Observe the following columns: If $1, z_1, z_2, ..., z_{10}$ are the iith roots of unity , then

I	II
A. The value of $(1- z_1)(1- z_2)........(1- z_{10})$ is	P 1
B. The value of is $z_1^{100} + z_2^{100} + ... + z_{10}^{100}$ is	Q –1
C. The value of is $(1 + z_1)(1 + z_2)...... (1 + z_{10})$ is	R 0
D. The value of is $z_1.z_2..............z_{10}$ is	S 11

6. Observe the following columns :

I	II
A. The smallest +ve integer n for which $(1 + i)^{2n} = (1 - i)^{2n}$ is	P 3
B. The value of x+y, if x and y satisfy the equation $\frac{(1+i)x - 2i}{3+i} + \frac{(2-3i)+i}{3-i} = i$ is	Q 2
C. If $z = 3 - 4$ I, then is $z^4 - 3z^3 + 3z^2 + 99z - 95$ is	R 4
D. If $z = x + $ I y, $z^{1/3} = a - ib$ and $\frac{x}{a} - \frac{y}{b} = k\left(a^2 - b^2\right)$ Then the value of k is	S 5

ANSWER

1. A→ (P,S), B→ (Q,R), C→ (Q,T)
2. A→ (Q,S), B→ (P,T), C→ (R)
3. A→ (P,R,T), B→ (P), C→ (S)
4. A→ (P,T), B→ (Q,R,S), C→ (S,T)
5. A→ (S), B→ (Q), C→ (P), D→ (P),
6. A→ (Q), B→ (Q), C→ (S), D→ (R),

Assertion and Reason

The following questions consists of two statements, one labeled as 'Assertion (A)' and the other labeled as 'Reason (R)' . You are examine these two statements carefully and decide if the Assertion (A) and the reason (R) are individually true and if so, whether the Reason (R) is the correct explanation for the given Assertion (A). Select your answer to these items using the codes given below and then select the correct option.

Codes :

A. Both A and B are individually true and R is correct explanation of A

B. Both A and R are individually true is not the correct explanation of A

C. A is true but R is false

D. A is false but R is true.

1. Assertion A : If z is a complex number $(z \neq 1)$,

then $\left|\frac{z}{|z|}-1\right| \leq |\arg(z)|$

Reason R : In a unit radius circle chord $(AP) \leq$ arc (AP)

a*. A b. B
c. C d. D

2. Assertion A : If $|z| \geq 2$, then least value of $\left|z+\frac{1}{2}\right|$ is $\frac{3}{2}$

Reason R : $|z_1+z_2| \leq |z_1|+|z_2|$

a. A b*. B
c. C d. D

3. Assertion A : $7+4i > 5+3i$, where $i=\sqrt{-1}$

Reason R : $7>5$ and $4>3$

a. A b. B
c. C d*. D

4. Assertion A : If $\frac{5z_2}{11z_1}$ is purely imaginary,

then $\left|\frac{2z_1+3z_2}{2z_1-3z_2}\right|=1$

Reason R : $|z|=|\bar{z}|$ *i.e.* $|a+ib|=|a-ib|$

a*. A b. B
c. C d. D

5. Assertion A : If $|z_1|=1, |z_2|=2, |z_3|=3$ and $|z_1+2z_2+3z_3|=6$ then value of $|z_2z_3+8z_1z_3+27z_1z_2|$ is 36

Reason R : $|z_1+z_2+z_3| \leq |z_1|+|z_2|+|z_3|$

a. A b*. B
c. C d. D

6. Assertion A : If $|z-3+2i| \leq 4$, then the sum of least and greatest value of $|z|$ is 8.

Reason R : $\left||z_1|-|z_2|\right| \leq |z_1+z_2| \leq |z_1|+|z_2|$

a*. A b. B
c. C d. D

7. Assertion A : If $\cos(1-i)=a+ib$, where $a,b \in R$ and $i=\sqrt{-1}$, then $a=\frac{1}{2}\left(e+\frac{1}{e}\right)\cos 1$ and $b=\frac{1}{2}\left(e+\frac{1}{e}\right)\sin 1$

Reason R : $e^{i\theta}=\cos\theta+i\sin\theta$

a*. A b. B
c. C d. D

8. Assertion A : If $z_1=9+5i$ and $z_2=3+5i$ and $\arg\left(\frac{z-z_1}{z-z_2}\right)=\frac{\pi}{4}$, then value of $|z-6-8i|=3\sqrt{2}$

Reason R : The three points are non collinear, thenthey must lie on a circle and angle at center by a chord is double angle on circumference by that chord .

a*. A b. B
c. C d. D

9. Assertion A : If $|z|<\sqrt{2}-1$, then $|z^2+2z\sin\alpha|<1$

Reason R : $|z_1+z_2|<|z_1|+|z_2|$ and $|\sin\alpha| \leq 1$

a*. A b. B
c. C d. D

10. Assertion A : $A(z_1)$, $B(z_2)$, $C(z_3)$ are the vertices of an equilateral triangle ABC, then

$$\arg\left(\frac{z_2+z_3-2z_1}{z_3-z_2}\right)=\frac{\pi}{4}$$

Reason R : $\angle B=\alpha$, $\arg\left(\frac{z_1-z_2}{z_3-z_2}\right)=\alpha$

a*. A b. B
c. C d. D

Questions asked in Roorkee Exams

1. Find the real values of x and y if, $(x^2+2ix)-(3x^2+iy)=(3-5i)+(3x^2+iy)$ **Ans.:** $x=2,-2$ and $y=3, 1/3$.—[Roorkee – 1984]
2. No questions asked in **1985, 1986, 1987, 1988.**
3. Let A and B be two complex numbers such that $\frac{A}{B}+\frac{B}{A}=1$. Prove that the origin and the two points represented by A and B form an vertices of an equilateral triangle. —[Roorkee–1989]
4. For every real value of $a>0$, determine the complex numbers which will satisfy equation. —[Roorkee – 1990]
5. Find the range of real number 'a' for which the equation $|z|+a|z-1|+2i=0$ has a solution. Also find the solution. —[Roorkee – 1991]
6. Find the equation in complex variable of all circles which are orthogonal to $|z|=1$ and $|z-1|=4$. —[Roorkee – 1992]
7. Find the complex number z which simultaneously satisfy the equaions, $\left|\frac{z-12}{z-8i}\right|=\frac{5}{3}, \left|\frac{z-4}{z-8}\right|=1$ —[Roorkee – 1993]
8. Use De Moivre's Theorem, to solve the equation $2\sqrt{2}\,x^4=(\sqrt{3}-1)+i(\sqrt{3}+1)$ —[Roorkee – 1994]
9. Find all complex number number z for which $\arg\left(\frac{3z-6-3i}{2z-8-6i}\right)=\frac{\pi}{4}$ and $|z-3+i|=3$. —[Roorkee – 1995]
10. Find all complex numbers satisfying the equation $2|z|^2+z^2-5+i\sqrt{3}=0$ —[Roorkee– 1996].
11. Evaluate: $\sum_{p=1}^{32}(3p+2)\left(\sum_{q=1}^{10}\left(\sin\left(\frac{2q\pi}{11}\right)-i\left(\frac{2q\pi}{11}\right)\right)\right)$ —[Roorkee – 1997].
12. Find all the roots of equation $(3z-1)^4+(z-2)^4=0$ in simplified form of $a+ib$. —[Roorkee – 1998]
13. If $\alpha=e^{2\pi i/7}$ and $f(x)=A_0+\sum_{K-1}^{20}A_k x^k$, then find the value of $f(x)+f(ax)+f(\alpha^2x)+.................+f(\alpha^k x)$ is independent of α. —[Roorkee – 1999]

14. Given, $z=\cos\left(\frac{2\pi}{2n+1}\right)+i\sin\left(\frac{2\pi}{2n+1}\right)$, n being a positive integer, find the equation whose roots are $\alpha=z+z^3+z^5+\ldots\ldots\ldots+z^{2n-1}$ and $\beta=z^2+z^4+z^4+\ldots\ldots\ldots\ldots+z^{2n}$.

— [Roorkee – 2000]

15. Find all those roots of the equation $z^{12}-56z^6-512=0$, whose imaginary part is +ve.

—[Roorkee – 2001]

Answer

1. $x=2, -2$ and $y=3, 1/3$

4. $0\le a\le 1$

5. $a\in\left[-\frac{5}{4},\frac{5}{4}\right]-(1,-1)$; $z=x-2i$

6. $\left|z-\left(-\frac{15}{2}+ik\right)\right|=\sqrt{\frac{221}{4}+k^2}$, where k is a parameter

7. $Z=6+17i$, $Z=6+8i$

8. $x=\cos\frac{1}{4}\left(2\pi k+\frac{5\pi}{12}\right)+i\sin\frac{1}{4}\left(2\pi k+\frac{5\pi}{12}\right)$, $k=0, 1, 2, 3.$

9. $\left(4-\frac{4}{\sqrt{5}}\right)+i\left(1+\frac{2}{\sqrt{5}}\right)$ and $\left(4+\frac{4}{\sqrt{5}}\right)+i\left(1-\frac{2}{\sqrt{5}}\right)$

10. $(x,y)=\left(\mp\sqrt{\frac{3}{2}},\pm\frac{1}{\sqrt{2}}\right),\left(\mp\frac{1}{\sqrt{6}},\pm\frac{3}{\sqrt{2}}\right)$

11. $48(1-i)$.

12. when $n=0, a+ib=\left(\frac{10-7\sqrt{2}}{20-6\sqrt{2}}\right)+i\left(\frac{-5\sqrt{2}}{20-6\sqrt{2}}\right)$, similarly for $n=1, 2, 3$

13. $7A_0$

14. $x^2+x+\frac{1}{4}\sec^2\left(\frac{\pi}{2n+1}\right)=0$

15. $x=\pm 2, \pm i\sqrt{2}$

Questions asked in IIT-JEE Exams

1. If $x+iy=\sqrt{\frac{a+ib}{c+id}}$ prove that $(x^2+y^2)=\frac{a^2+b^2}{c^2+d^2}$ [IIT-JEE-1978]

2. If $x=a+b, y=a\alpha+b\beta$ and $z=a\beta+b\alpha$ where α,β are complex cube roots of unity, then prove that $xyz=\alpha^3+\beta^3$.

[IIT-JEE – 1979]

3. Express $\frac{1}{(1-\cos\theta)+2i\sin\theta}$ in the form of $A+iB$.

[IIT-JEE – 1979]

4. Find the real values of x and y for which the following equation is satisfied: $\frac{(1+i)x-2i}{3+i}+\frac{(2-3i)y+i}{3-i}=i$

[IIT-JEE – 1980]

5. The smallest positive integer n for which $\left(\frac{1+i}{1-i}\right)^n=1$ is

a. 8 b. 16
c. 12 d*. None. [IIT-JEE – 1980]

6. Let the complex numbers z_1, z_2 and z_3 be the vertices of an equilateral triangle. If z_0 be the circum-center of the triangle, then prove that $z_1^2+z_2^2+z_3^2=3z_0^2$. [IIT-JEE – 1981]

7. For complex number $z_1=x_1+iy_1$ and $z_2=x_2+iy_2$, we write $z_1\cap z_2$, if $x_1\le x_2$ and $y_1\le y_2$. Then for all complex numbers z with $1\cap z$, we have $\frac{1-z}{1+z}\cap\{0\}$. Is it true? (T) [IIT-JEE – 1981]

8. The complex number $z=x+iy$ which satisfy the equation $\left|\frac{z-5i}{z+5i}\right|=1$ lie on

a*. the x-axis b. the straight line $y=5$
c. the circle passing through the origin
d. None [IIT-JEE – 1981]

9. A relation R on the set of complex numbers is defined by z_1Rz_2 if and only if $\frac{z_1-z_2}{z_1+z_2}$ is real. Show that R is an equivalence relation.

10. If $z=\left(\frac{\sqrt{3}}{2}+\frac{i}{2}\right)^5+\left(\frac{\sqrt{3}}{2}-\frac{i}{2}\right)^5$, then

a. $Re(z)=0$ b*. $Im(z)=0$
c. $Re(z)=0$, $Im(z)>0$ d. $Re(z)>0$, $Im(z)<0$.

11. The inequality $|z-4|<|z-2|$ represents the region given by

a. $Re(z)$ 0 b. $Re(z)<0$
c*. $Re(z)>0$ d. None [IIT-JEE – 1982]

12. If $z=x+iy$ and $\omega=\frac{1-iz}{z-i}$ then $|\omega|=1$ implies that in the complex plane

a. z lies on the imaginary axis.
b*. z lies on the real axis. c. z lies on the unit circle
d. None. [IIT-JEE – 1983]

13. The points z_1, z_2, z_3, z_4 in the complex plane are the vertices of a parallelogram if and only if

a. $z_1+z_2=z_2+z_3$ b*. $z_1+z_3=z_2+z_4$
c. $z_1+z_2=z_3+z_4$ d. None [IIT-JEE – 1983]

14. Prove that the complex numbers z_1,z_2 and the origin form an equilateral triangle only if $z_1^2+z_2^2-z_1z_2=0$ [IIT-JEE – 1983]

15. If $1, a_1, a_2, \ldots\ldots\ldots a_{n-1}$ are the nth roots of unity, then show that

[IIT-JEE – 1984]

16. If the complex numbers Z_1, Z_2, and Z_3 represent the vertices of an equilateral triangle such that $|Z_1|=|Z_2|=|Z_3|$ then $Z_1+Z_2+Z_3=0$. Is it true or false? (T) [IIT-JEE – 1984]

17. If three complex numbers are in A.P., then they lie on a circle in the complex plane. Is it true or false? (F) [IIT-JEE – 1985]

18. It is given that n is an odd integer greater than three, but n is not a multiple of 3. Prove that $x^3+x^2+x^3$ is a factor of $(x+1)^n-x^n-1$. [IIT-JEE – 1985]

19. If a,b,c,u,v,w are complex numbers representing the vertices of

two triangles such that $c = (1-r)a + rb$ $w = (1-r)u + r\,v$ where r is a complex number, then the two triangles

a. have the same size b*. are similar
c. are congruent d. None. [IIT-JEE- 1985]

20. If $z_1 = a + ib$ and $z_2 = c + id$ are complex numbers such that $|z_1| = |z_2| = 1$ and $Re\left(z_1\overline{z_2}\right) = 0$, then the pair of complex numbers $w_1 = u + iv$ and $w_2 = b + id$ satisfies

a*. $|w_1| = 1$ b*. $|w_2| = 1$
c*. $Re\left(\omega_1\overline{\omega_2}\right)$ d. None [IIT-JEE – 1985]

21. Shown that the area of the triangle in the Argand diagram is formed by the complex numbers z, iz and $z + iz$ is $\frac{1}{2}\times|z|^2$.
[IIT-JEE – 1986]

22. Complex numbers z_1, z_2, z_3 are the vertices A, B, C respectively of an isosceles right angled triangle with right angle at C, show that $(z_1-z_2)^2 = 2(z_1-z_2)(z_3-z_2)$. [IIT-JEE – 1986]

23. Let z_1 and z_2 be two complex numbers such that $z_1 \neq z_2$ and $|z_1| = |z_2|$. If z_1 has positive real part and z_2 has negative imaginary part, then $\frac{z_1+z_2}{z_1-z_2}$ may be

a*. zero b. real and positive
c. real and negative d*. None [IIT-JEE – 1986]

24. If the expression $\frac{\left[\sin\left(\frac{x}{2}\right)+\cos\left(\frac{x}{2}\right)+i\tan x\right]}{1+2i\sin\left(\frac{x}{2}\right)}$ is real, then the set of all possible values of x is............
[IIT-JEE – 1987]

25. If z_1 and z_2 are two non zero complex number such that, $|z_1+z_2| = |z_1| + |z_2|$, then $\text{Arg}(z_1) - \text{Arg}(z_2)$ is equal to

a. $-\pi$ b*. $-\pi/2$ c. 0
d. $\pi/2$ e. π [IIT-JEE – 1987]

26. The value of $\sum_{k=1}^{6}\left(\sin\frac{2\pi k}{7} - i\cos\frac{2\pi k}{7}\right)$ is

a. -1 b. 0 c. $-I$
d*. i e. None [IIT-JEE – 1987]

27. The cube roots of unity when represented on Argand diagram from the vertices of an equilateral triangle.
Is it true or false? (T) [IIT-JEE – 1988]

28. For any two complex numbers z_1, z_2 and any real numbers a and b, $|az_1 - bz_2|^2 + |bz_1 + az_2|^2 =$...............
[IIT-JEE – 1988]

29. The complex number $\sin x + i\cos 2x$ and $\cos x - i\sin 2x$ are conjugate to each other, for

a. $x = n\pi$ b. $x = 0$
c. $x = (2n+1)\frac{\pi}{2}$ d*. no value of x [IIT-JEE – 1988]

30. If a and b are real numbers b/w 0 and 1 such that points $z_1 = a + i$, $z_3 = 1 + ib$, $z_3 = 0$ form an equilateral triangle, then $a =$........and $b =$............... [IIT-JEE – 1989]

31. Let $z_1 = 10 + 6i$ and $z_2 = 4 + 6i$. If z is any complex number such that the argument of $\left(\frac{z-z_1}{z-z_2}\right)$ is $\frac{\pi}{4}$. Then prove that $|z-7-9i| = 3\sqrt{2}$.
[IIT-JEE- 1990]

32. $z \neq 0$ is a complex number.

I	II
i. $Re\ z = 0$	A $Re\ z^2 = 0$
ii. $Arg\ z = \frac{\pi}{4}$	B $Im\ z^2 = 0$
	C $Re\ z^2 = Im\ z^2$.

[IIT-JEE–1992]

33. $ABCD$ is a rhombus. Its diagonals AC and BD intersect at the point M and satisfy $BD = 2AC$. If the points D and M represents the complex numbers $1 + i$, $2 - i$ respectively, then A represents the complex number.................. or ....
IIT-JEE – 1993]

34. Suppose z_1, z_2, z_3 are vertices of an equilateral triangle inscribed in the circle $|z| = 2$. If $z_1 = i + i\sqrt{3}$, then =............ and =...........
[IIT-JEE – 1994]

35. If $\omega(\neq 1)$ is a cube root of unity and $(1+\omega)^7 = A + B\omega$ then A and B are respectively

a. 0, 1 b*. 1, 1
c. 1, 0 d. -1, 1 [IIT-JEE – 1995]

36. Let z and w be two non zero complex numbers such that $|z| = |\omega|$ and $\text{Arg}(z) + \text{Arg}(\omega) = \pi$, then z is

a. ω b. $-\omega$
c. $\overline{\omega}$ d*. $-\overline{\omega}$ [IIT-JEE – 1995]

37. Let z and w be two complex numbers such that $|z| \leq 1$, $|\omega| \leq 1$ and $|z + i\omega| = |z - i\overline{\omega}| = 2$, then z is

a. 1 or i b. i or $-i$
c*. 1 or -1 d. i or -1 [IIT-JEE – 1995]

38. If $iz^3 + z^2 - z + i = 0$, then show that $|z| = 1$. [IIT-JEE – 1995]

39. For positive integers n_1 and n_2, the values of the expression $(1+i)^{n_1} + (1+i^3)^{n_1} + (1+i^5)^{n_2} + (1+i^7)^{n_2}$, When $i = \sqrt{-1}$ is real if and only if [IIT-JEE – 1996]

a. $n_1 = n_2 + 1$ b. $n_1 = n_2 - 1$
c. $n_1 = n_2$ d*. $n_1 > 0, n_2 > 0$.

40. Let z and w be two complex numbers such that $|z| \leq 1$, $|\omega| \leq 1$, then show that $|z-\omega|^2 \leq (|z|-|\omega|)^2 + (\text{Arg}z - \text{Arg}\,\omega)^2$
[IIT-JEE– 1996]

41. Find all non zero complex number z satisfying $\overline{z} = iz^3$.
[IIT-JEE – 1996]

42. The value of the expression $1.(2-\omega)(2-\omega^2) + 2.(3-\omega)(3-\omega^2) + \ldots\ldots\ldots + (n-1)(n-\omega)(n-\omega^2)$, where ω is an imaginary cube root of unity, is ....
[IIT-JEE – 1996]

43. Let z_1 and z_2 be two roots of the equation $z^2 + pz + q = 0$, where the co-ordinates p and q may be complex numbers. Let A and B represents z_1 and z_2 in the complex plane. If $\angle AOB = \alpha$ and $OA = OB$, where O is the origin. Prove that $p^2 = 4q\cos^2\left(\frac{\alpha}{2}\right)$
[IIT-JEE – 1997]

44. Prove that $\sum_{k=1}^{n-1}(n-k)\cos\left(\frac{2k\pi}{n}\right) = -\frac{n}{2}$, where $n \geq 3$ is an integer.
[IIT-JEE – 1997]

45. Let $\overline{b}z$, $b\overline{z} = c$, $b \neq 0$, be a line in the complex plane, where $\overline{b}$ is

the complex conjugate of b, if a point z_1 is the deflection of a point z_2 through the line, then show that $c = b\,\overline{z_1} + z_2\,\overline{b}$

[IIT-JEE-1997]

46. If ω is an imaginary cube roots of unity, then $(1 + \omega - \omega^2)^7$ is [IIT-JEE – 1998]

a. $128\,\omega$ b. $-128\,\omega$
c. $128\,\omega^2$ d*. $-128\,\omega^2$

47. The value of sum $\sum_{n=1}^{13}\left(i^n + i^{n+1}\right)$, where is $i = \sqrt{-1}$

a. i b*. $i-1$
c. $-i$ d. 0 [IIT-JEE – 1998]

48. If $i=\sqrt{-1}$,then $4+5\left(-\frac{1}{2}+\frac{i\sqrt{3}}{2}\right)^{334}+3\left(-\frac{1}{2}+\frac{i\sqrt{3}}{2}\right)^{365}$ is equal to

a. $1-i\sqrt{3}$ b. $-1+i\sqrt{3}$
c*. $i\sqrt{3}$ d. $-i\sqrt{3}$ [IIT-JEE – 1999]

49. For complex numbers z and w, prove that $|z|^2\omega - |\omega|^2 z = z - \omega$ if and only if $z = w$ or $z\,\overline{\omega} = 1$. [IIT-JEE – 1999]

50. If $arg\ (z) < 0$, then $arg\ (-z) - arg\ (z) =$

a*. π b. $-\pi$
c. $-\pi/2$ d. $\pi/2$ [IIT-JEE – 2000]

51. If z_1, z_2, z_3 are complex numbers such that $|z_1|=|z_1|=|z_1|=$ $\left|\frac{1}{z_1}+\frac{1}{z_2}+\frac{1}{z_3}\right| = 1$, then $|z_1 + z_2 + z_3|$ is

a*. 1 b. <1
c. >3 d. $=3$ [IIT-JEE – 2000]

52. Let z_1 and z_2 be nth roots of unity which subtend a right angle at the origin, then n must be of the form

a. $4k+1$ b. $4k+2$
c. $4k+3$ d*. $4k$. [IIT-JEE – 2001]

53. The complex number z_1, z_2 and z_3 satisfying $\frac{z_1 - z_2}{z_2 - z_3} = \frac{1-i\sqrt{3}}{2}$ are the vertices of the triangle which is

a. of area zero b. rt angled isosceles
c*. quilateral d. obtuse angled

[IIT-JEE – 2001]

54. Let $\omega = -\frac{1}{2} + i\frac{\sqrt{3}}{2}$. Then the value of $\begin{vmatrix} 1 & 1 & -1 \\ 1 & -1-\omega^2 & \omega^2 \\ 1 & \omega^2 & \omega^4 \end{vmatrix}$ is

a. 3ω b*. $3\omega(\omega - 1)$
c. $3\omega^2$ d. $-3\omega(\omega-1)$ [IIT-JEE – 2002]

55. For all complex numbers z_1, z_2 satisfying $|z_1| = 12$ and $|z^2 - 3 - 4i| =$ 5, then the minimum value of $|z_1 - z_2|$ is

a. 0 b*. 2
c. 7 d. 17 [IIT-JEE – 2002]

56. If $|z| = 1$ and $\omega = \frac{z-1}{z+1}$ (where $z \neq -1$), then $Re\ (w)$ is

a*. 0 b. $-\frac{1}{|z+1|^2}$

c. $\left|\frac{z}{z+1}\right|\frac{1}{|z+1|^2}$ d. $\frac{\sqrt{2}}{|z+1|^2}$ [IIT-JEE – 2003]

57. Let a complex numbers α, $\alpha \neq 1$ be a root of the equation $z^{p+q} - z^p - z^q + 1 = 0$, when p,q are distinct primes. Show that either $1+\alpha+\alpha^2+..........+\alpha^{p-1} = 0$ or $1+\alpha+\alpha^2+.......+\alpha^{q-1} = 0$, but not both are integers. [IIT-JEE – 2002]

58. If z_1 and z_2 are two complex numbers such that $|z_1|<1, |z_2|<1$, then prove that $\left|\frac{1 - z_1\overline{z_2}}{z_1 - z_2}\right| < 1$. [IIT-JEE – 2003]

59. Prove that there exists no complex number z such that $|z| < \frac{1}{3}$ and $\sum_{r=1}^{n}\left(a_r\,z^r\right) = 1$ where $|a_r| < 2$. [IIT-JEE – 2003]

60. If $\omega(\neq 1)$ be a cube root of unity and $(1+\omega^2)^n = (1+\omega^4)^n$, then the least positive value of n is

a. 2 b*. 3
c. 5 d. 6 [IIT-JEE – 2004]

61. $|z-1| = \sqrt{2}$ is a circle inscribed in a square whose one vertex is $2 + i\sqrt{3}$. Find the remaining vertices.

[IIT-JEE – 2005]

62. PQ and PR are two infinite rays, QAR is an arc. Point lying in the shaded region excluding the boundary satisfies

a*. $|z+1| > 2 : |arg\ (z-1)| < \frac{\pi}{4}$

b. $|z+1| < 2 : |arg\ (z+1)| < \frac{\pi}{2}$

c. $|z-1| < 2 : |arg\ (z-1)| < \frac{\pi}{4}$

d. $|z-1| < 2 : |arg\ (z-1)| < \frac{\pi}{2}$

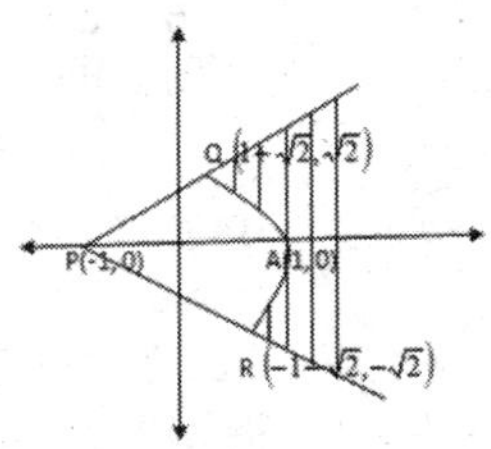

63. The minimum value of $|a + b\omega + c\omega^2|$, where a,b and c are all not equal integers and ($\omega \neq 1$) is a cube root of unity, is

a*. 1 b. 0
c. $\sqrt{3}$ d. $\frac{1}{2}$ [IIT-JEE – 2005]

64. If $\frac{\omega - \overline{\omega} z}{1 - z}$ is purely real where $\omega = \alpha + i\beta, \beta \neq 0$ and $z \neq 1$, then the set of values of z is

a. $\{z : |z| = 1\}$ b. $\{z : z = \overline{z}\}$
c. $\{z : z \neq 1\}$ d*. $\{z : |z| = 1, z \neq 1\}$

[IIT-JEE – 2006]

65. A man walks a distance of 3 units from the origin towards the north east ($N 45^\circ E$) direction . From there, he walks a distance of 4 units towards the north – west ($N 45^\circ W$) direction to reach a point P. Then the position of P in the Argand plane is

a. $3e^{i\pi/4} + 4i$. b. $(3-4i)e^{i\pi/4}$
c. $(4+3i)e^{i\pi/4}$ d*. $(3+4i)e^{i\pi/4}$ [IIT-JEE – 2007]

66. If $|z| = 1$ and $z \neq 1$, then all the values of $\omega = \frac{z}{1-z^2}$ lie on

a. a line not passing through the origin
b. $|z| = \sqrt{2}$
c. the x-axis
d. the y – axis [IIT-JEE – 2007]

67. A particle P starts from the point $z_0 = 1 + 2i$, where $i = \sqrt{-1}$. It moves first horizontally away from origin by 5 units and then vertically away from origin 3 units to reach a point z_1. From z_1 the particle moves $\sqrt{2}$ units in the direction of $i + j$ and then it moves through an angle of $\frac{\pi}{2}$ in anti-clock-wise direction on a circle with centre at origin, to reach a point z_2. The point z_2 is given by

a. $6+7i$ b. $-7+6i$
c. $7+6I$ d*. $-6+7i$ [IIT-JEE-2008]

Link Comprehension Type

68. Let A, B, C be three sets of complex numbers defined below
$A = \{z : Im(z) \geq 1\}$; $B = \{z : |z-2-i| = 3\}$; $C = \{z : Re((1-i)z) = \sqrt{2}\}$

1. The number of elements in the set $A \cap B \cap C$ is
   a. 0 b*. 1
   c. 2 d. ∞
2. Let z be any point in $A \cap B \cap C$. Then $|z+1-i|^2 + |z-5-i|^2$ lies between
   a. 25 and 29 b. 30 and 34
   c*. 35 and 39 d. 40 and 44.
3. Let z be any point in $A \cap B \cap C$ and let ω be any point satisfying $|\omega - 2 - i| < 3$. Then $|z| - |\omega| + 3$ lies between
   a. -6 and 3 b. -3 and 6
   c. -6 and 6 d*. -3 and 9. [IIT-JEE-2008]

69. Let $z = \cos\theta + i\sin\theta$. Then the value of $\sum_{m=1}^{15}\left(z^{2m-1}\right)$ at $\theta = 2^\circ$ is

a. $\frac{1}{\sin 2^\circ}$ b. $\frac{1}{3\sin 2^\circ}$

c. $\frac{1}{2\sin 2^\circ}$ d* $\frac{1}{4\sin 2^\circ}$ [IIT-JEE-2009]

70. Let $z = x + iy$ be a complex number where x and y are integers. Then the area of the rectangle whose vertices are the roots of $z\bar{z}^3 + \bar{z}z^3 = 350$ is

a*. 48 b. 32
c. 40 d. 80 [IIT-JEE-2009]

71. Let ω be the complex number $\cos\left(\frac{2\pi}{3}\right) + i\sin\left(\frac{2\pi}{3}\right)$. Then the number of distinct complex number z satisfying

$$\begin{vmatrix} z+1 & \omega & \omega^2 \\ \omega & z+\omega^2 & 1 \\ \omega^2 & 1 & z+\omega \end{vmatrix} = 0$$ is .... [IIT-JEE-2010]

72. Match the following columns :

I	II
A. The set of points of z satisfying $\left\|z - i\|z\|\right\| = \left\|z + i\|z\|\right\|$ is contained in or Equal to	P an ellipse with eccentricity 4/5
B. The set of points z satisfying $\|z+4\| + \|z-4\| = 10$ is contained in or Equal to	Q the set of points z satisfying $Im\ z = 0$
C. If $\|\omega\| = 2$, then the set of points $z = \omega - \frac{1}{\omega}$ is contained in or equal to	R the set of points z satisfying $\|Im(z)\| \leq 1$
D. If $\|\omega\| = 1$, then the set of points $z = \omega + \frac{1}{\omega}$ is contained in or equal to	S the set of points z satisfying $\|Re(z)\| \leq 2$
	T the set of points z satisfying $\|z\| \leq 3$.

[IIT-JEE-2010]

73. Let z_1 & z_2 be two distinct complex numbers and $z = (1-t)z_1 + t z_2$ for some real number t with $0 < t < 1$. If $Arg(\omega)$ denotes the principal argument of a non zero complex number ω, then

a. $|z - z_1| + |z - z_2| = |z_1 - z_2|$ b*. $Arg(z - z_1) = Arg(z - z_2)$

c*. $\begin{vmatrix} z - z_1 & \bar{z} - \bar{z}_1 \\ z_2 - z_1 & \bar{z}_2 - \bar{z}_1 \end{vmatrix} = 0$ d*. $Arg(z - z_1) = Arg(z_2 - z_1)$

[IIT-JEE-2010]

74. If z is any complex number satisfying $|z - 3 - 2i| \leq 2$. Then the minimum value of $|2z - 6 + 5i|$ is .... [IIT-JEE-2011]

75. Let $\omega = e^{i\frac{\pi}{3}}$ and a, b, c, x, y, z are non zero complex numbers such that $a + b + c = x$, $a + b\omega + c\omega^2 = y$, $a + b\omega^2 + c\omega = z$, then the value of $\frac{|x|^2 + |y|^2 + |z|^2}{|a|^2 + |b|^2 + |c|^2}$ is.... —[IIT-JEE-2011]

76. Let z be a complex number such that imaginary part of z is non zero and $a = z^2 + z + 1$ is real . Then a cannot take the value

a. -1 b. 1/3
c. 1/2 d*. 3/4 [IIT-JEE-2012]

ANSWER

4. $x = 3, y = -1$ **24.** $x = 2n\pi, 2n\pi + \frac{\pi}{4}$ **28.** $(a^2 + b^2)(|z_1|^2 + |z_2|^2)$ **30.** $a = 2 - \sqrt{3} = b$ **32.** i. $\to B$; ii. $\to A$

33. $3 - \frac{i}{2}, 1 - \frac{3}{2}i$ **34.** $z_2 = -2, z_3 = 1 - i\sqrt{3}$ **42.** $\frac{1}{2} \times n(n-1)(n^2 + 3n + 4)$ **61.** $(i + 1 - \sqrt{3}), i\sqrt{3}, (1 + \sqrt{3} - i)$

71. 1 **72.** A→Q, R ; B→P ; C→ P ; D→Q,R,S,T **74.** 5 **75.** 9

Self Assesment Test

TIME : 1 HOURS. CHAPTER : COMPLEX NUMBER MAX MARKS: 50

NOTE: Give answers of the following questions by yourself only

1. The value of the sum $\sum_{n=1}^{13}\left(i^n+i^{n+1}\right)$, where, $i=\sqrt{-1}$, is
   a. i b. $i-1$
   c. $-i$ d. 0
2. The value of $(1+i)^6$ is
   a. i b. $2(-1+5i)$
   c. $1-5i$ d. None.
3. If n_1, n_2 are positive integers, then $(1+i)^{n_1}+\left(1+i^3\right)^{n_1}+\left(1+i^5\right)^{n_2}+\left(1+i^7\right)^{n_2}$ is a real number if and only if
   a. $n_1=n_2+1$ b. $n_1+1=n_2$
   c. $n_1=n_2$ d. n_1,n_2 are any two positive integers.
4. The complex number z is purely imaginary if
   a. $z\bar{z}$ is real b. $z=\bar{z}$
   c. $z+\bar{z}=0$ d. None.
5. If $z=x+iy$ satisfies amp$(z-1)=$ amp$(z+3i)$, then the value of $(x-1):y$ is
   a. 2:1 b. 1:3
   c. $-1:3$ d. None.
6. $x^{3m}+x^{3n-1}+x^{3r-2}$, where $m,n,r\in N$, is divisible by
   a. x^2-x+1 b. x^2+x+1
   c. x^2+x-1 d. x^2-x-1
7. If $e^{i\theta}=\cos\theta+i\sin\theta$, then for the ΔABC, $e^{iA}, e^{iB} e^{iC}$ is
   a. $-i$ b. 1
   c. -1 d. None.
8. Let z be a complex number satisfying $z^4+z^3+2z^2+z+1=0$, then $|z|$ is equal to
   a. ½ b. ¾
   c. 1 d. None.
9. If $|z-i|\le 2$ and $z_0=5+3i$, then the maximum value of $|iz+z_0|$ is
   a. $\sqrt{31}+2$ b. 7
   c. $\sqrt{31}-2$ d. None.
10. The area of the triangle whose vertices are i, α,β, where $i=\sqrt{-1}$ and α,β are the non real cube roots of unity, is
    a. $\frac{3\sqrt{3}}{2}$ b. $\frac{3\sqrt{3}}{4}$
    c. 0 d. $\frac{\sqrt{3}}{4}$
11. Let $z=1-t+i\sqrt{t^2+t+2}$, where t is a real parameter. The locus of z in the Argand plane is
    a. a hyperbola b. an ellipse
    c. a straight line d. None.
12. Let $OP.OQ=1$ and let, O, P, Q be three collinear points. If O and Q represent the complex numbers 0 and z, then P represents
    a. $\frac{1}{z}$ b. $\bar{z}$
    c. $\frac{1}{\bar{z}}$ d. None.
13. The equation $|z-i|+|z+i|=k, k>0$ can represent an ellipse, if k is
    a. 1 b. 2
    c. 4 d. None.
14. If the roots of $z^3+iz^2+2i=0$ represent the vertices of a ΔABC in the Argand plane, then the area of the triangle is
    a. $\frac{3\sqrt{7}}{2}$ b. $\frac{3\sqrt{7}}{4}$
    c. 2 d. None.
15. The point of intersection of the curves are $\arg(z-3i)=\frac{3p}{4}$ and $\arg(2z+1-2i)=\frac{p}{4}$ is
    a. $\frac{1}{4}(3+9i)$ b. $\frac{1}{4}(3-9i)$
    c. $\frac{1}{2}(3+2i)$ d. None.
16. If $|z-1|+|z+3|\le 8$, then the range of value of $|z-4|$ is
    a. 0, 7 b. 1, 8
    *c. [1, 9] d. [2, 5]
17. The smallest value of $|z|^2+|z-3|^2+|z-6i|^2$, where z is a complex number occurs for $z=$
    a. 0 b. 3
    c. $6i$ d. $1+2i$
18. If the imaginary part of the expression $\frac{z-1}{e^{i\theta}}+\frac{e^{i\theta}}{z-1}$ be zero, then the locus of z
    a. a straight line parallel to x–axis
    b. a parabola
    c. a circle of radius 1
    d. None.
19. The locus represented by the complex equation $|z-2-i|=|z|\sin\left(\frac{\pi}{4}-\arg z\right)$ is the part of
    a. a pair of straight line b. a circle
    c. a parabola d. a rectangular hyperbola.
20. If $\frac{1}{a+\omega}+\frac{1}{b+\omega}+\frac{1}{c+\omega}+\frac{1}{d+\omega}=\frac{1}{\omega}$, where $a,b,c,d\in R$ and ω is a cube root of unity, then the value of $\sum\frac{1}{a^2-a+1}$ is
    a. 1 b. 2
    c. 3 d. None.

□□□

CHAPTER

4 BINOMIAL THEOREM

CONCEPT BOOSTER

4.1 Definition

An algebraic expression which contains two and only two terms is called a binomial expansion. For example, $a+b$, $x+y$, $x+\frac{2}{y}$, $\frac{3}{x}-\frac{1}{x^3}$ are called the binomial expressions.

In general, expressions containing more than two terms are known as multinomial expressions.

4.2 Binomial Theorem for Positive Integral Index

If $a, b \in R$ and $n \in N$, then $(a+x)^n = {}^nC_0 a^n x^0 + {}^nC_1 . a^{n-1} x + {}^nC_2 . a^{n-2} . x^2 + ... + nC_r a^{n-r} . x^r + ... + {}^nC_n a^{n-n} x^n$ is called a binomial theorem, where ${}^nC_0, {}^nC_1, {}^nC_2, ..., {}^nC_r, ..., {}^nC_n$ are called the binomial co-efficients.

NOTE:

i. The total number of terms in the expansion of $(a+x)^n$ is $n+1$.

ii. The sum of the powers of a and x in each term in the expansion $(a+x)^n$ is n.

iii. In any term the suffix of C is equal to the index of a and the index of $x = n -$ (suffix of C)

iv. The co-efficient of x^r in the expansion of $(1+x)^n$ is ${}^nC_r$.

v. The co-efficient of x^r in the expansion of $(1-x)^n$ is $(-1)^r . {}^nC_r$.

Ex.1: Expand of $\left(\frac{x}{5}+\frac{1}{x}\right)^5$.

SOL.: We have $\left(\frac{x}{5}+\frac{1}{x}\right)^5 = {}^5C_0\left(\frac{x}{5}\right)^5\left(\frac{1}{x}\right)^0 + {}^5C_0\left(\frac{x}{5}\right)^4\left(\frac{1}{x}\right)^1$

$+ {}^5C_0\left(\frac{x}{5}\right)^3\left(\frac{1}{x}\right)^2 + {}^5C_0\left(\frac{x}{5}\right)^2\left(\frac{1}{x}\right)^3 + {}^5C_0\left(\frac{x}{5}\right)^1\left(\frac{1}{x}\right)^4$

$+ {}^5C_5\left(\frac{x}{5}\right)^0\left(\frac{1}{x}\right)^5$.

Ex. 2: Write the expansion of $(x+1)^6$

SOL.: We have $(x+1)^6 = {}^6C_0 x^6 + {}^6C_1 x^5 + {}^6C_2 x^4 + {}^6C_3 x^3 + {}^6C_4 x^2 + {}^6C_5 x + {}^6C_6 x^0$

$= x^6 + 6x^5 + 15x^4 + 20x^3 + 15x^2 + 6x + 1$

Ex.3: Find the Number of Terms in the Expansion of

i. $(1+x)^{2013}$ ii. $(1+2x+x^2)^{1007}$

iii. $(1+3x+3x^2+x^3)^{668}$ iv. $(1+4x+6x^2+4x^3+x^4)^{503}$

v. $(1+x)(1+x^2)^{10}$ vi. $(1-x)^{11}(1+x+x^2)^{10}$

SOL.: i. The number of terms of $(1+x)^{2013}$ is 2014.

ii. The number of terms of $(1+2x+x^2)^{1007} = (1+x)^{2014}$ is 2015.

iii. The number of terms of $(1+3x+3x^2+3x^3)^{668} = (1+x)^{2004}$ is 2005.

iv. The number of terms of $(1+4x+6x^2+4x^3+x^4)^{503} = (1+x)^{2012}$ is 2013.

v. The number of terms of $(1+x)(1+x^2)$ is 12.

vi. The number of terms of $(1+x)^{11}(1+x+x^2)^{10} = (1-x)(1-x^3)^{10}$ is 12.

4.3 Number of terms in the Expansion of $(a+x)^n + (a-x)^n$.

CASE 1. When n is even

The number of terms $= \left(\frac{n}{2}+1\right)$

2. When n is odd .

The number of terms $= \left(\frac{n+1}{2}\right)$

4.4 Number of terms in the Expansions of $(a+x)^n - (a-x)^n$.

CASE 1. When n is even.

The number of terms $= \left(\frac{n}{2}\right)$

2. When n is odd .

The number of terms $= \left(\frac{n+1}{2}\right)$

Ex.1: Find the number of terms in the expansion of

i. $\left(\frac{x}{2}+\frac{3}{x^2}\right)^{50} + \left(\frac{x}{2}-\frac{3}{x^2}\right)^{50}$

ii. $(a+b)^{99} - (a-b)^{99}$

iii. $(x+y^2)^{25} + (x-y^2)^{25}$

iv. $\left(\frac{2}{x}+x^3\right)^{2014} - \left(\frac{2}{x}-x^3\right)^{2014}$

SOL.: i. The number of term of $\left(\frac{x}{2}+\frac{3}{x^2}\right)^{50} + \left(\frac{x}{2}-\frac{3}{x^2}\right)^{50}$ is $\left(\frac{50}{2}+1\right) = 26$

ii. The number of terms of $(a+b)^{99} - (a-b)^{99}$ is $\left(\frac{99+1}{2}\right) = 50$

iii. The number of terms of $(x+y^2)^{25} + (x-y^2)^{25}$ is $\left(\frac{25+1}{2}\right) = 13$

iv. The numbert of terms of $\left(\frac{2}{x}+x^3\right)^{2014}-\left(\frac{2}{x}-x^3\right)^{2014}$ is $\left(\frac{2014}{2}\right)=1007$.

Ex.2: Simplify: $\left(x+\sqrt{x^2-1}\right)^6+\left(x-\sqrt{x^2-1}\right)^6$

Sol.: Let $a=\sqrt{x^2-1}$

Thus, $(x+a)^6+(x-1)^6$

$=(x^6+{}^6C_1x^5a+{}^6C_2x^4a^2+{}^6C_3x^3a^3+{}^6C_4x^2a^4+{}^6C_5xa^5+{}^6C_6x^0a^6)+(x^6-{}^6C_1x^5a+{}^6C_2x^4a^2-{}^6C_3x^3a^3+{}^6C_4x^2a^4-{}^6C_5xa^5+{}^6C_6x^0a^6)$

$=2(x^6+{}^6C_2x^4a^2+{}^6C_4x^2a^4+{}^6C_6x^0a^6)$

$=2(x^6+{}^6C_2x^4(x^2-1)+{}^6C_4x^2(x^2-1)^2+{}^6C_6(x^2-1)^3)$

4.5 General Term in the Expansion of $(a+x)^n$

$$t_{r+1}={}^nC_r a^{n-r}x^r$$

Note:

i. Co-efficient of x^r in the expansion of $(1+x)^n={}^nC_r$

ii. The rth term from the end in the expansion of $(a+x)^n$ = $(n-r+2)$ th term from the beginning.

Ex.1: F.ind the 13th term in expansion of $\left(9x-\frac{1}{3\sqrt{x}}\right)^{18}$, $x\neq 0$ **Ans.** ${}^{18}C_{12}$.

Sol.: We have, $t_{13}=t_{12+1}={}^{18}C_{12}(9x)^{18-12}\left(-\frac{1}{3\sqrt{x}}\right)^{12}$

$={}^{18}C_{12}$

Ex.2: Find 4th term from the end in expansion of $\left(\frac{3}{x^2}-\frac{x^3}{6}\right)^7$

Sol.: 4th term from the end = $(7-4+2)$ the term from the beginning.

= 5th term from the beginning

We have, $t_5=t_{4+1}={}^7C_4\times\left(\frac{3}{x^2}\right)^{7-4}\times\left(-\frac{x^3}{6}\right)^4$

$={}^7C_4\times\left(\frac{3}{x^2}\right)^3\times\left(\frac{x^3}{6}\right)^4$

$={}^7C_4\times\left(\frac{x^6}{48}\right)=\frac{35}{48}x^6$.

Ex.3: Find the term in the independent of x in the expansion of $\left(\frac{3}{2}x^2-\frac{1}{3x}\right)^6$.

Sol.: Let t_{r+1} the term be independent of x.

Then $t_{r+1}={}^6C_r\times\left(\frac{3}{2}x^2\right)^{6-r}\times\left(-\frac{1}{3x}\right)^r$

$={}^6C_r\times\left(\frac{3}{2}\right)^{6-r}\times\left(-\frac{1}{3}\right)^r\times\left(x^{12-3r}\right)$

Since the term independent of x, $12-3r=0.\Rightarrow r=4$.

Thus, the 5th term is the independent of x.

Ex.4: Find the co-efficient of x^7in expansion of $\left(3x^2+\frac{1}{5x}\right)^{11}$

Sol.: Let $t_{r+1}={}^{11}C_r\times\left(3x^2\right)^{11-r}\times\left(\frac{1}{5x}\right)^r$

$={}^{11}C_r\times 3^{11-r}\times 5^{-r}\times(x^{22-3r})$

Given, $22-3r=7\Rightarrow 3r=15\Rightarrow r=5$.

Thus, the co-efficient of $x^7$is $={}^{11}C_4\times 3^{11-4}\times 5^{-4}$

$={}^{11}C_4\times 3^7\times 5^{-4}$

Ex.5: Find the co-efficientof x^n in the expansion of $(1-x)(1+x)^n$

Sol.: We have $(1-x)(1+x)^n=(1-x)(1+{}^nC_1\cdot x+{}^nC_1\cdot x^2+{}^nC_1\cdot x^3+\ldots\ldots+nC_{n-1}\cdot x^{n-1}+{}^nC_n\cdot x^n)$.

Thus, the co-efficient of $x^n={}^nC_n-{}^nC_{n-1}=1-n$.

Ex.6: Find the co-efficient of x^n in the expansion of $(1+x)^2(1-x)^n$

Sol.: We have $(1+x)^2(1-x)^n=(1+2x+x^2)\times(1-{}^nC_1x+{}^nC_2\cdot x^2-\ldots\ldots\ldots\ldots+(-1)^{n-2n}C_{n-2}x^{n-2}+(-1)^{n-1n}C_{n-1}x^{n-1}+(-1)^{n\,n}C_nx^n)$

Thus, the co-ef ficient of $x^n=(-1)^n\cdot{}^nC_n+2.(-1)^{n-1}\cdot{}^nC_{n-1}+(-1)^{n-2}\cdot{}^nC_{n-2}=(-1)^n\cdot({}^nC_n-2{}^nC_{n-1}+{}^nC_{n-2})$

$=(-1)^n\cdot\left(1-2n+\frac{n(n-1)}{2}\right)=\frac{(-1)^n}{2}\times(n^2-5n+2)$

Ex.7: Find co-efficient of x^4 in expansion cf $(1+x+x^2+x^3)^{11}$

Sol.: We have, $(1+x+x^2+x^3)^{11}=(1+x)^{11}\times(1+x^2)^{11}=(1+{}^{11}C_1x+{}^{11}C_2x^2+11C_3x^3+{}^{11}C_4x^4+\ldots\ldots)\times(1+{}^{11}C_1x^2+{}^{11}C_2x^4+\ldots..)$

Thus, the co-efficient of $x^4={}^{11}C_4+{}^{11}C_2+{}^{11}C_2\times C_1$

Ex.8: Find the co-efficient of x^{50} in expansion of $(1+x)^{41}\times(1-x+x^2)^{40}$

Sol.: We have $(1+x)^{41}\times(1-x+x^2)^{40}=(1+x)\times((1+x)(1-x+x^2))^{40}=(1+x)\times(1+x^3)^{40}=(1+x)\times(1+{}^{40}C_0x^3+{}^{40}C_1x^6+{}^{40}C_3x^9+\ldots\ldots+{}^{40}C_{16}x^{48}+{}^{40}C_{17}x^{51}+\ldots\ldots)$

Thus, the co-efficient of $x^{50}=0$.

Ex.9: Find the co-efficient of x^{10} in the expansion of $(1+x)^{21}+(1+x)^{22}+\ldots\ldots\ldots\ldots+(1+x)^{30}$

Sol.: We have $(1+x)^{21}+(1+x)^{22}+\ldots\ldots\ldots\ldots+(1+x)^{30}$

$=(1+x)^{21}(1+(1+x)+(1+x)^2+\ldots\ldots..+(1+x)^9)$

$=(1+x)^{21}\times\left(\frac{(1+x)^{10}-1}{(1+x)-1}\right)=\left(\frac{(1+x)^{31}-(1+x)^{21}}{x}\right)$

Thus, the co-efficient of $=x^{10}={}^{31}C_{11}-{}^{21}C_{11}$.

Ex.10: Find the co-efficient of x^r in expansion of $(x+3)^{n-1}+(x+3)^{n-2}(x+2)+(x+3)^{n-3}(x+2)^2+\ldots\ldots\ldots+(x+2)^{n-1}$

Sol.: We have, $(x+3)^{n-1}+(x+3)^{n-2}(x+2)+(x+3)^{n-3}+(x+2)^2+\ldots\ldots\ldots+(x+2)^{n-1}$

$=+(x+3)^{n-1}\left(\frac{x+2}{x+3}\right)+\left(\frac{x+2}{x+3}\right)^2+\left(\frac{x+2}{x+3}\right)^3+\ldots..+\left(\frac{x+2}{x+3}\right)^{n-1}\Big)$

$=(x+3)^{n-1}\times\frac{\left(\frac{x+2}{x+3}\right)^n-1}{\left(\frac{x+2}{x+3}\right)-1}=\left(\frac{(x+2)^n-(x+3)^n}{(x+2)-(x+3)}\right)$

$= ((x+3)^n - (x+2)^n)$

Thus, the co-efficient of $= x^r = (3^{n-r} - 2^{n-r})$.

4.6 Middle term in the expansion of : $(a+x)^n$:

In the expansion of $(a+x)^n$, the number of terms is $n+1$.
If n is even, then $(n+1)$ is an odd number.
If n is odd, then $(n+1)$ is an even number.

CASE 1. When n is an even number.

Let $n = 2m$

Number of terms $= n+1 = 2m+1$.

In this case, there will be only one middle term.

This middle term is $(m+1)$ the term.

Hence, middle term $= t_{m+1} = {}^nC_m a^{n-m} x^m$
$= {}^nC_{n/2} a^{n/2} x^{n/2}$.

2. When n is an odd number.

Let $n = 2m+1$

Number of terms $= n+1 = 2m+2$

In this case, there will be two middle terms.

These middle terms will be $(m+1)^{th}$ and $(m+2)^{th}$ terms

$$t_{m+1} = {}^nC_m a^{n-m} x^m = {}^nC_{\frac{n-1}{2}} a^{\frac{n+1}{2}} x^{\frac{n-1}{2}}.$$

Ex.1: Find the mid dle term in the expansion of $\left(\frac{2x^2}{3} - \frac{3}{2x}\right)^{12}$.

SOL.: Here n is even. So middle term is $= \left(\frac{12}{2}+1\right) =$ 7th term

Thus, $t_7 = t_{6+1} = {}^{12}C_6 \times \left(\frac{2x^2}{3}\right)^{12-6} \times \left(-\frac{3}{2x}\right)^6$

$= {}^{12}C_6 \times \left(\frac{2x^2}{3}\right)^6 \times \left(\frac{3}{2x}\right)^6$

Ex.2: Find the middle term in the expansion of $\left(3x - \frac{x^3}{6}\right)^9$.

SOL.: Here n is odd, so the middle terms are $\left(\frac{9+1}{2}\right)^{th}$ and $\left(\frac{9+3}{2}\right)^{th}$ i.e. 5th and 6th terms

Thus, $t_5 = t_{4+1} = {}^9C_4 \times (3x)^{9-4} \times \left(-\frac{x^3}{6}\right)^4$

$= {}^9C_4 \times \left(-\frac{3}{16}\right) \times \left(x^{17}\right)$

$t_6 = t_{5+1} = {}^9C_5 \times (3x)^{9-5} \times \left(-\frac{x^3}{6}\right)^5$

$= {}^9C_5 \times \left(-\frac{x^{19}}{32}\right)$

Ex.3: Prove that the middle term in expansion of $(1+x)^{2n}$ is $\frac{1.3.5......(2n-1)}{(n)!} \times 2^n x^n$.

SOL.: Here en is even, so middle term is $\left(\frac{2n}{2}+1\right)^{th} = (n+1)^{th}$

Thus, $t_{n+1} = {}^{2n}C_n \times (1)^{2n-n} \times (x)^n = {}^{2n}C_n \times (x)^n$

$= \frac{(2n)!}{n! \times n!} \times (x)^n$

$= \frac{2^n \times \{1.3.5...........(2n-1)\} \times n!}{n! \times n!} \times (x)^n$

$= \frac{2^n \times \{1.3.5...........(2n-1)\} \times (x)^n}{n!}$

Ex.4: Prove that the co-efficient of the middle term in $(1+x)^{2n}$ is equal to the sum of the co-efficients of the two middle terms in $(1+x)^{2n-1}$.

SOL.: The co-efficient of the middle term of $(1+x)^{2n}$ is ${}^{2n}C_n$

The co-efficient of the middle terms of $(1+x)^{2n-1}$ are ${}^{2n-1}C_{n-1}$ and ${}^{2n-1}C_n$

Now, ${}^{2n-1}C_{n-1} + {}^{2n-1}C_n = {}^{(2n-1)+1}C_n = {}^{2n}C_n$.

Hence, the result.

4.7 Greatest term in the expansion of $(a+x)^n$.

To determine the numerically greatest term in expansion of $(a+x)^n$, where n is a positive integer.

Consider $\left|\frac{t_{r+1}}{t_r}\right| = \left|\frac{{}^nC_r \; a^{n-r} x^r}{{}^nC_{r-1} \; a^{n-r+1} x^{r-1}}\right| = \left|\frac{{}^nC_r}{{}^nC_{r-1}}\right| \times \left|\frac{x}{a}\right|$

$= \left|\frac{n-r+1}{r}\right| \times \left|\frac{x}{a}\right| = \left|\frac{n+1}{r} - 1\right| \times \left|\frac{x}{a}\right|$

Thus, $|t_{r+1}| > |t_r|$, if $\left|\frac{n+1}{r} - 1\right| \left|\frac{x}{a}\right| > 1$

$\Rightarrow \quad \frac{n+1}{r} > 1 + \left|\frac{a}{x}\right|$

$\Rightarrow \quad r < \frac{n+1}{1+\left|\frac{a}{x}\right|}$.

From this, the value of r is determined.

If r is an integer, say m, then m th and $(m+1)$th terms are numerically greatest terms of the expansion and are equal.

But r is a fraction, and then next integer is the number of greatest term.

ALTERNATIVE METHOD

To determine the greatest term in the expansion of $(a+x)^n$ we should use the following method.

1. Calculate $m = \left|\frac{(n+1)|x|}{a+|x|}\right|$
2. If $m \in Z$, then t_m and t_{m+1} are two numerically greatest terms.
3. If $m \notin Z$, then $t_{[m]+1}$ is the numerically greatest term, where $[.] =$ G.I.F.

Ex.1: Find the greatest term in the expansion of $(2+3x)^{10}$, when $x = 3/5$.

SOL.: We have, $m = \left|\frac{(n+1)x}{a+x}\right|$

$\Rightarrow \quad m = \left|\frac{(10+1)\left(\frac{3}{2} \times \frac{3}{5}\right)}{1+\left(\frac{3}{2} \times \frac{3}{5}\right)}\right|$

$= \frac{99}{19} = 5\frac{4}{19} \neq$ not an integer.

Thus, greatest term $= t_{\left[5\frac{4}{19}\right]+1} = t_6 = 6^{th}$ term

Ex.2: Find the greatest term in expansion of $(3-5x)^{15}$, when $x = 1/5$.

Sol.: We have, $m = \left|\frac{(n+1)|x|}{a+|x|}\right|$

$$\Rightarrow \quad m = \left|\frac{(15+1)\left|\left(-\frac{5}{3}\times\frac{1}{5}\right)\right|}{\left(1+\left|\left(-\frac{5}{3}\times\frac{1}{5}\right)\right|\right)}\right|$$

$$\Rightarrow \quad m = \frac{16/3}{4/3} = 4 = \text{integer.}$$

Thus, the greatest term are t_4 and t_{4+1} i.e. 4th and 5th terms.

4.8 Greatest Binomial Co-efficient

In a binomial expansion, it can be seen that the middle terms has (have) the greatest co-efficient.

When n is even, then the greatest co-efficient is ${}^nC_{n/2}$

When n is odd, then the greatest co-efficient are ${}^nC_{n-1/2}$ and ${}^nC_{n+1/2}$.

Ex.1: Show that, if the greatest term in expansion of $(1+x)^{2n}$ has the greatest co-efficient x lies between $\frac{n}{n+1}$ and $\frac{n+1}{n}$.

Sol.: We have, $t_{n+1} = {}^{2n}C_n \times x^n = \frac{(2n)!}{n!\times n!}x^n$

$$t_{n+2} = {}^{2n}C_{n+1} \times x^{n+1} = \frac{(2n)!}{(n+1)!\times(n-1)!}x^{n+1}$$

and $$t_n = {}^{2n}C_{n-1} \times x^{n-1} = \frac{(2n)!}{(n+1)!\times(n-1)!}x^{n-1}$$

Now, $\frac{t_{n+1}}{t_{n+2}} = \left(\frac{n+1}{n}\right)\frac{1}{x} \Rightarrow \left(\frac{n+1}{n}\right)\frac{1}{x} > 1$

$$\Rightarrow x < \left(\frac{n+1}{n}\right) \quad \text{... (i)}$$

Again, $\frac{t_{n+1}}{t_n} = \left(\frac{n+1}{n}\right)x \Rightarrow \left(\frac{n+1}{n}\right)x > 1$

$$\Rightarrow x > \left(\frac{n}{n+1}\right) \quad \text{... (ii)}$$

From (i) and (ii), we get, $\frac{n}{n+1} < x < \frac{n+1}{n}$

4.9 Divisibility related problem by Binomial Theorem

Consider the expansion

$$(1+b)^n = (1 + {}^nC_1.b + {}^nC_2.b^2 + {}^nC_3.b^3 + ... + {}^nC_n.b^n)$$

$\Rightarrow \quad (1+b)^n - 1 = ({}^nC_1.b + {}^nC_2.b^2 + {}^nC_3.b^3 + ... + {}^nC_n.b^n)$

$\Rightarrow \quad (1+b)^n - 1$ is divisib le by b

Also, $(1+b)^n - n.b - 1 = ({}^nC_2.b^2 + {}^nC_3.b^3 + ... + {}^nC_n.b^n)$

$\Rightarrow \quad (1+b)^n - n.b - 1$ is divisible by b^2 and so on

Ex.1: If n is a positive integer, then prove that $4^n - 3n - 1$ is divisible by 9.

Sol.: We have $4^n - 3n - 1 = (1+3)^n - 3n - 1$
$= (1 + {}^nC_1.3 + {}^nC_2.3^2 + {}^nC_3.3^3 + {}^nC_4.3^4 + ... + {}^nC_n.3^n) - 3n - 1$
$= (1 + 3n + {}^nC_2.3^2 + {}^nC_3.3^3 + {}^nC_4.3^4 + ... + {}^nC_n.3^n) - 3n - 1$
$= 32({}^nC_2 + {}^nC_3.3 + {}^nC_4.3^2 + ... + {}^nC_n.3^{n-2})$

Thus, $4n - 3n - 1$ is divisible by 9.

Ex.2: If n is a positive integer, then prove that $3^{2n+2} - 8n - 9$ is divisible by 64.

Sol.: We have $3^{2n+2} - 8n - 9 = 9(1+8)^n - 8n - 9$
$= 9(1 + {}^nC_1.8 + {}^nC_2.8^2 + {}^nC_3.8^3 + {}^nC_4.8^4 + ... + {}^nC_n.8^n) - 8n - 9$
$= 9(1 + 8n + {}^nC_2.8^2 + {}^nC_3.8^3 + {}^nC_4.8^4 + ... + {}^nC_n.8^n) - 8n - 9$
$= (64n + {}^nC_2.8^2 + {}^nC_3.8^3 + {}^nC_4.8^4 + ... + {}^nC_n.8^n)$
$= 64(n + {}^nC_2. + {}^nC_3.8 + {}^nC_4.8^2 + ... + {}^nC_n.8^{n-2})$

Thus, $3^{2n+2} - 8n - 9$ is divisible by 64.

Ex.3: Find the remainder when 7^{98} is divided by 5.

Sol.: We have $7^{98} = (7^2)49 = (50-1)^{49}$
$= (50^{49} - {}^{49}C_1.50^{48} + {}^{49}C_2.50^{47} - {}^{49}C_3.50^{46} + ... + {}^{49}C_{48}.50 + (-1)^{49}C_{49})$
$= (50^{49} - {}^{49}C_1.50^{48} + {}^{49}C_2.50^{47} - {}^{49}C_3.50^{46} + ... + {}^{49}C^{48}.50) - 1$

Hence, the remainder is 4.

Ex.4: Prove that $11^{10} - 1$ is divisible by 100.

Sol.: We have $11^{10} - 1 = (1+10)^{10} - 1$
$= (1 + {}^{10}C_1.10 + {}^{10}C_2.10^2 + {}^{10}C_3.10^3 + ... + {}^{10}C_{10}.10^{10}) - 1$
$= (100 + {}^{10}C_2.10^2 + {}^{10}C_3.10^3 + ... + {}^{10}C_{10}.10^{10})$
$= 100(1 + {}^{10}C_2.10 + {}^{10}C_3.10^2 + ... + {}^{10}C_{10}.10^8)$

Thus, $11^{10} - 1$ is divisible by 100.

4.9.1 Divisibility of $a^n \pm b^n$ by $a \pm b$, where $a, b, n \in N$

i. When n is even $a^n - b^n$ is divisible by $a+b$ and $a-b$.

ii. When n is odd $a^n - b^n$ is divisible by $a-b$.

iii. When n is odd $a^n + b^n$ is divisible by $a+b$

Ex.1: Prove that $1^{2013} + 2^{2013} + 3^{2013} + ... + 2011^{2013} + 2012^{2013}$ is divisible by 2013.

Sol.: We have $1^{2013} + 2^{2013} + 3^{2013} + ... + 2013^{2013}$
$= (1^{2013} + 2012^{2013)} + (2^{2013} + 2011^{2013}) + (1006^{2013} + 1007^{2013})$

Therefore, each bracket is of the form $(a^{2n+1} + b^{2n+1})$ is divisible by $(a+b)$

Thus, the given expression is divisible by 2013.

Ex.2: Prove that $1992^{1998} - 1955^{1998} - 1938^{1998} + 1901^{1998}$ is divisible by 1998.

Sol.: We have $1992^{1998} - 1955^{1998} - 1938^{1998} + 1901^{1998}$
$= (1992^{1998} - 1938^{1998}) - (1938^{1998} - 1901^{1998})$

Now, $(1992^{1998} - 1938^{1998})$ is divisible by $(1992-1938) = 54$

Also, $(1938^{1998} - 1901^{1998})$ is divisible by $(1938-1901) = 37$.

Thus, given expression is divisible by $54\times37 = 1998$.

4.9.2 UNIT DIGIT OF A NATURAL NUMBER

Unit digit of a number is depends on the period of that number.

The period of 2 is 4

$2^1 = 2, 2^2 = 4, 2^3 = 8, 2^4 = 16$

$2^5 = 32$, here unit digit is repeated after the power 4.

Similarly, the period of 3 is 4, period of 7 is also 4.

FOR EXAMPLES,

1. the unit digit of $2^{2013} = 2^{(4 \times 503 + 1)}$ is 2
2. the unit digit of $3^{2014} = 3^{(4 \times 503 + 2)}$ is 9
3. the unit digit of $= (27)^{50} = (3^3)^{50} = 3^{(4 \times 37 + 2)}$ is 9
4. the unit digit of $(2013)^{2013}$ is same as of $3^{2013} = 3^{(4\times503+1)}$ is 3
5. the unit digit of 9^{9^9} is 9 (since , the period of 9 is 2)

4.10 The Important Application of Binomial Theorem

i. **To find the term free from radical terms or rational term in the expansion of $(a^{1/p} + b^{1/q})^n$, where a and b are prime integers and $n \in N$.**

1. First of all, we find the $(r + 1)$th term in the expansion of $(a^{1/p} + b^{1/q})^n$ i.e. $t_{r+1} = {}^nC_r\, a^{\frac{n-r}{p}} b^{\frac{r}{q}}$
2. Now by inspection, putting the values of $0 \le r \le n$, when indices of a, b are integers.
3. Which will give the values of r and hence $(r + 1)$th term is obtained.

Ex.1: Find the number of integral terms in the expansion of $(9^{1/4} + 8^{1/6})^{500}$.

SOL.: We have, $t_{r+1} = 500C_r \times \left(9^{\frac{1}{4}}\right)^{500-r} \times \left(8^{\frac{1}{6}}\right)^r$

$= 500C_r \times \left(9^{\frac{500-r}{4}}\right) \times \left(8^{\frac{r}{6}}\right)$

$= 500C_r \times \left(3^{\frac{500-r}{2}}\right) \times \left(2^{\frac{r}{2}}\right)$

Thus, $r = 0, 2, 4, 6, 8, \ldots\ldots, 500$.

Hence, the number of integral terms = 251.

Ex.2: Find the number of irrational terms in the expansion of $(5^{1/8} + 2^{1/6})^{100}$.

SOL.: We have, $t_{r+1} = {}^{100}C_r \times \left(5^{\frac{1}{8}}\right)^{100-r} \times \left(2^{\frac{1}{6}}\right)^r$

$= {}^{100}C_r \times \left(5^{\frac{100-r}{8}}\right) \times \left(2^{\frac{r}{6}}\right)$

Therefore, $r = 0, 24, 48, 72$.

Thus, the number of integral terms = 4

Total terms of the binomial expansion = 101

Hence, the number of irrational terms = 101 – 4 = 97.

ii. **If $\left(\sqrt{P}+Q\right)^n = I + f$ where I and $n \in N$, n being odd and $0 \le f < 1$, then show that $(I + f) f = k^n$, where $P - Q^2 = k > 0$ and $\sqrt{Q} - p < 1$.**

PROOF: Given $\sqrt{Q} - p < 1 \Rightarrow 0 < \left(\sqrt{P}-Q\right)^n < 1$

Let, $\left(\sqrt{P}-Q\right)^n = f'$, Where $0 < f' < 1$

Now, $\left(\sqrt{P}+Q\right)^n - \left(\sqrt{P}-Q\right)^n = I + f - f'$.

L.H.S contains even powers of $\sqrt{P}$ (since n is odd)

Hence L.H.S and I are integers.

Thus, $f - f'$ is an integer.

But $0 < f < 1$ and $0 < f' < 1 \Rightarrow -1 < f - f' < 1 \Rightarrow f - f' = 0$.

Thus, $(I + f) f' = \left(\sqrt{P}+Q\right)^n = \left(\sqrt{P}-Q\right)^n = (p - Q^2) = k^n$.

iii. **If $\left(\sqrt{P}+Q\right)^n = I + f$ where I and $n \in N$, n being even and $0 \le f > 1$, then show that, $(1+f)(1-f) = k^n$, where $P - Q^2 = k > 0$ and $\sqrt{Q} - p < 1$.**

PROOF: Given $\sqrt{Q} - p < 1 \Rightarrow 0 < \left(\sqrt{P}+Q\right)^n < 1$

Let $\left(\sqrt{P}+Q\right)^n = f$, where $0 < f' < 1$ $\left(\sqrt{P}+Q\right)^n + \left(\sqrt{P}-Q\right)^n$

$I + f + f'$

Hence , $f + f'$ must be a positive integer.

But $0 < f < 1$ and $0 < f' < 1 \quad \Rightarrow 0 < f + f' < 2$

$\Rightarrow f + f' = 1. f' = 1 - f.$

Hence, $(I + f)(1 - f) = (I + f) f'$

$= \left(\sqrt{P}+Q\right)^n \times \left(\sqrt{P}-Q\right)^n$

$= (P - Q^2)^n = k^n$.

Ex.1: Prove that the integral part of $\left(5\sqrt{5}+11\right)^{2n+1}$ is even when $n \in N$ and hence if $R = \left(5\sqrt{5}+11\right)^{2n+1}$ and $f = R - [R]$, where [,] = G.I.F , then prove that $Rf = 4^{2n+1}$.

SOL.: Let I and F denote the integral part and fractional part of R respectively.

Given $f = R - [R]$ = fractional part of $R = F$.

Let $R = I + F = I + f = \left(5\sqrt{5}+11\right)^{2n+1}$, $0 < f < 1$

Also, $f' = \left(5\sqrt{5}+11\right)^{2n+1}$

Now, $R - f = \left(5\sqrt{5}+11\right)^{2n+1} - \left(5\sqrt{5}-11\right)^{2n+1}$

$= 2\left({}^{2n+1}C_1\left(\sqrt{5}\right)^{2n+1} \times 11 + {}^{2n+1}C_3\left(\sqrt{5}\right)^{2n-2} \times 11^3 + {}^{2n+1}C_5\left(\sqrt{5}\right)^{2n-4} \times 11^5 + \ldots\ldots\right)$

= an even integer.

Since f is an integer, $f - f'$ is also an integer. But $0 < f < 1$ and $0 < f' < 1$

$\Rightarrow f - f = 0 \Rightarrow f - f'$

Now $Rf = \left(5\sqrt{5}+11\right)^{2n+1} = \left(5\sqrt{5}-11\right)^{2n+1}$

$= (125-121)2^{n+1} = 4^{2n+1}$.

Ex.2: If $x = \left(8+3\sqrt{7}\right)^n$, $n \in N$, Prove that integral part of x is an odd integer and show that $x - x^2 + x[x] = 1$, where [,] = G.I.F .

SOL.: Let $x = R + f = \left(8+3\sqrt{7}\right)^n$, where $0 < f < 1$ and

$f = \left(8-3\sqrt{7}\right)^n$, where $0 < f' < 1$

Now, $R + f + f' = \left(8+3\sqrt{7}\right)^n + \left(8-3\sqrt{7}\right)^n$

$= 2\left(8^n + {}^nC_2 \times 8^{n-2} \times \left(3\sqrt{7}\right)^2 + \right.$

$^nC_4 \times 8^{n-4} \times (3\sqrt{7})^4 + ...)$

$=$ Even integer.

Since $0 < f < 1$ and $0 < f' < 1$, so $0 < f + f' < 2$

$\Rightarrow \quad f + f' = 1$

Thus, $R + f + f' = 2k \quad \Rightarrow R + 1 = 2k$

$\Rightarrow R = 2k - 1 =$ odd integer.

$\Rightarrow [x] = 2k - 1 =$ odd integer.

Now, $x - x^2 + x[x] = x - x(x - [x]) = x - xf = x(1-f) = xf'$.

$= (8+3\sqrt{7})^n \cdot (8-3\sqrt{7})^n$

$= (64 - 63)^n = 1^n = 1$

Ex.3: If $(8+3\sqrt{7})^n$ $\alpha + \beta$ where n and α are positive integers and β is a positive proper fraction, then prove that $(1-\beta)(\alpha+\beta) = 1$.

Sol.: Given $\alpha + \beta = (8+3\sqrt{7})^n$, where $0 < \beta < 1$

Let $\beta' = (8-3\sqrt{7})^n$, where $0 < \beta' < 1$

Now, $\alpha + \beta + \beta' = (8+3\sqrt{7})^n + (8-3\sqrt{7})^n$

$= 2(8^n + {}^nC_2 \times 8^{n-2} \times (7\sqrt{3})^2 + {}^nC_4 \times 8^{n-4} \times (7\sqrt{3})^4 + ...)$

$=$ Even integer

Also, $0 < \beta < 1$ and $0 < \beta' < 1 \Rightarrow 0 < \beta + \beta' < 2$

$\Rightarrow \beta' = 1 - \beta$

Thus, $(1-\beta)(\alpha+\beta) = (8-3\sqrt{7})^n \cdot (8+3\sqrt{7})^n$

$= (64 - .63)^n = 1.$

Ex. 4: Find the integer just greater than the number $(3+\sqrt{5})^5$

Sol.: Let $I + f = (3+\sqrt{5})^5$, where $0 < f < 1$.

Let $f' = (3-\sqrt{5})$, where $0 < f' < 1$

Hence, the integer just greater than the number $(3+\sqrt{5})^5$ is $I + f + f'$.

Now, $I + f + f' = (3+\sqrt{5})^5 + (3-\sqrt{5})^5$

$= 2(3^5 + {}^5C_2 \times 3^3 \times (\sqrt{5})^2 + {}^5C_4 \times 3^1 \times (\sqrt{5})^4)$

$= 2(243 + 1350 + 375)$.

$= 3936$

4.11 Properties of Binomial Co-efficients:

Let ${}^nC_0, {}^nC_1, {}^nC_2, ..., {}^nC_{n-1}, {}^nC_n$ are the binomial co-efficients in the expansion of $(1-x)^n$

i. ${}^nC_0 + {}^nC_1 + {}^nC_2 + ... + {}^nC_{n-1} + {}^nC_n = 2^n$

ii. ${}^nC_1 + {}^nC_2 + {}^nC_3 + ... + {}^nC_{n-1} = 2^n - 2$

iii. ${}^nC_0 + {}^nC_2 + {}^nC_4 + {}^nC_6 + ... {}^nC_1 + {}^nC_3 + {}^nC_5 + {}^nC_7 + ... = 2^{n-1}$

Sol.: We have

$(1+x)^n = C_0 + C_1x + C_2x^2 + C_3x^3 + ... + C_nx^n$ .... (i)

i. Put $x = 1$ in (i), we get, $C_0 + C_1 + C_2 + ... + C_n = (1+1)^n = 2^n$

$\Rightarrow {}^nC_0 + {}^nC_1 + {}^nC_2 + ... + {}^nC_n = 2^n$.

Ex.1: Find the value of $20C_0 + 20C_1 + 20C_2 + ... + {}^{20}C_{20}$

Sol.: We have, $20C_0 + 20C_1 + 20C_2 + ... + {}^{20}C_{20} = 2^{20}$

Ex.2: Find the value of ${}^{2013}C_0 + {}^{2013}C_1 + {}^{2013}C_2 + ... + {}^{2013}C_{2012}$

Sol.: We have, ${}^{2013}C_0 + {}^{2013}C_1 + {}^{2013}C_2 + ... + {}^{2013}C_{2012} = 2^{2013} - {}^{2013}C_{2013} = 2^{2013} - 1$.

ii. ${}^nC_1 + {}^nC_2 + ... + {}^nC_{n-1} = 2^n - ({}^nC_0 + {}^nC_n) = 2^n - 2$

Ex.1: Find the value of ${}^{10}C_1 + {}^{10}C_2 + {}^{10}C_3 + ... + {}^{10}C_9$

Sol.: We have, ${}^{10}C_1 + {}^{10}C_2 + {}^{10}C_3 + ... + {}^{10}C_9$

$= 2^{10} - ({}^{10}C_0 + {}^{10}C_1) = 2^{10} - 2 = 1024 - 2 = 1022$

Ex.2: Find the value of ${}^{20}C_2 + {}^{20}C_3 + {}^{20}C_4 + ... + {}^{20}C_{19}$.

Sol.: We have, ${}^{20}C_2 + {}^{20}C_3 + {}^{20}C_4 + ... + {}^{20}C_{19}$

$= {}^{20}C_0 + {}^{20}C_1 + {}^{20}C_2 + {}^{20}C_3 + {}^{20}C_4 + ... + {}^{20}C_{19} + {}^{20}C_{20} - ({}^{20}C_0 + {}^{20}C_1 + {}^{20}C_{20})$

$= 220 - (1 + 20 - 1)$

$= 220 - 22$

Ex.3: Find the value of ${}^{30}C_1 + {}^{30}C_2 + {}^{30}C_3 + ... + {}^{30}C_{27}$.

Sol: We have, ${}^{30}C_1 + {}^{30}C_2 + {}^{30}C_3 + ... + {}^{30}C_{27}$.

$= {}^{30}C_0 + {}^{30}C_1 + ... + {}^{30}C_{27} + {}^{30}C_{28} + {}^{30}C_{29} + {}^{30}C_{30} - ({}^{30}C_0 + {}^{30}C_{28} + {}^{30}C_{29} + {}^{30}C_{30})$

$= 2^{30} - (1 + 435 + 30 + 1)$

$= 2^{30} - 467$.

Ex.4: Find the value of ${}^{16}C_3 + {}^{16}C_4 + ... + {}^{16}C_{15} +$

Sol.: We have, ${}^{16}C_3 + {}^{16}C_4 + ... + {}^{16}C_{15} +$

$= {}^{16}C_0 + {}^{16}C_1 + {}^{16}C_2 + {}^{16}C_3 + ... + {}^6C_{15} + {}^{16}C_{16} - ({}^{16}C_0 + {}^{16}C_1 + {}^{16}C_2 + {}^{16}C_{16})$

$= 2^{16} - (1 + 16 + 120 + 1)$

$= 2^{16} - 138$.

iii. Let ${}^nC_1 + {}^nC_3 + {}^nC_5 + ... = {}^nC_2 + {}^nC_4 + {}^nC_6 + ... = y$

As we know that, ${}^nC_0 + {}^nC_1 + {}^nC_2 + ... + {}^nC_n = 2^n$

$\Rightarrow ({}^nC_0 + {}^nC_2 + {}^nC_4 + ...) + ({}^nC_1 + {}^nC_3 + {}^nC_5 + ...) = 2^n$

$\Rightarrow y + y = 2^n$

$\Rightarrow y = \frac{2^n}{2} = 2^{n-1}$

Thus, ${}^nC_0 + {}^nC_2 + {}^nC_4 + {}^nC_6 + ... = {}^nC_1 + {}^nC_3 + {}^nC_5 + {}^nC_7 + ... = 2^{n-1}$

Ex.1: Find the value of ${}^{15}C_1 + {}^{15}C_3 + {}^{15}C_5 + ... + {}^{15}C_{15}$

Sol.: We have, ${}^{15}C_1 + {}^{15}C_3 + {}^{15}C_5 + ... + {}^{15}C_{15} = 2^{15-1} = 2^{14}$

Ex.2: Find the value of ${}^{20}C_1 + {}^{20}C_3 + {}^{20}C_5 + ... + {}^{20}C_{17}$

Sol.: We have, ${}^{20}C_1 + {}^{20}C_3 + {}^{20}C_5 + ... + {}^{20}C_{17}$

$= ({}^{20}C_1 + {}^{20}C_3 + {}^{20}C_5 + ... + {}^{20}C_{17} + {}^{20}C_{19}) - {}^{20}C_{19}$

$= 2^{20-1} - 20 = 2^{19} - 20$

Ex.3: Find the value of ${}^{30}C_2 + {}^{30}C_4 + {}^{30}C_6 + ... + {}^{30}C_{28}$

Sol:. We have, ${}^{30}C_2 + {}^{30}C_4 + {}^{30}C_6 + ... + {}^{30}C_{28}$

$= {}^{30}C_0 + {}^{30}C_2 + {}^{30}C_4 + {}^{30}C_6 + ... + {}^{30}C_{28} + {}^{30}C_{30} - ({}^{30}C_0 + {}^{30}C_{30})$.

$= 2^{30-1} - 2 = 2^{29} - 2$

Ex-4: Find the value of $^{50}C_4 + ^{50}C_6 + ^{50}C_8 + \dots\dots\dots + ^{50}C_{48}$

Sol: We have, $^{50}C_4 + ^{50}C_6 + ^{50}C_8 + \dots\dots\dots + ^{50}C_{48}$

$$= ^{50}C_0 + ^{50}C_2 + ^{50}C_4 + ^{50}C_6 + ^{50}C_8 + \dots\dots + ^{50}C_{48} + ^{50}C_{50} - (^{50}C_0 + ^{50}C_2 + ^{50}C_{50})$$

$$= 2^{50-1} - (1 + 1225 + 1) = 2^{49} - 1227.$$

iv $^nC_r = ^nC_{n-r}$

Sol.: We have $^nC_r = \dfrac{n!}{r! \times (n-r)!} = \dfrac{n!}{(n-r)! \times (n-(n-r))!} = ^nC_{n-r}$

Note:

i. $^nC_0 = ^nC_n$, $^nC_1 = ^nC_{n-1}$, $^nC_2 = ^nC_{n-2}$ and so on

ii. $^{10}C_0 = ^{10}C_{10} = 1$; $^{10}C_1 = ^{10}C_9 = 10$; $^{10}C_2 = ^{10}C_8 = 45$ and so on

Ex.1: Prove that the co-efficients of a^m and a^n in the expansion of $(1 + a)^{m+n}$ are equal.

Sol.: The co-efficient of a^m in $(1 + a)^{m+n} = ^{m+n}C_m$

The co-efficient of a^n in $(1 + a)^{m+n} = ^{m+n}C_n = ^{m+n}C_m$

Hence, the result.

v. If $^nC_x = ^nC_y \quad \Rightarrow x = y$ or $x + y = n$

Sol.: Given $^nC_x = ^nC_y \quad \Rightarrow x = y$

Also, $^nC_x = ^nC_y = ^nC_{n-y} \Rightarrow x = n - y \Rightarrow x + y = n$

Ex.1: If $^{10}C_r = ^{10}C_{r+4}$, then find the value of r.

Sol.: We have, $^{10}C_r = ^{10}C_{r+4}$

$\Rightarrow \quad r + r + 4 = 10$

$\Rightarrow \quad 2r = 10 - 4 = 16$

$\Rightarrow \quad r = \dfrac{6}{2} = 3$

vi. $^nC_r = \dfrac{n}{r} \times ^{n-1}C_{r-1} = \dfrac{n(n-1)}{r(r-1)} \times ^{n-2}C_{r-2}$ and so on

Proof: We have, $^nC_r = \dfrac{n!}{r! \times (n-r)!}$

$$= \frac{n \times (n-1)!}{r \times (r-1)! \times ((n-1)-(r-1))!} = \frac{n}{r} \times ^{n-1}C_{r-1}$$

$$= \frac{n \times (n-1) \times (n-2)!}{r \times (r-1) \times (r-2)! \times ((n-2)-(r-2))!}$$

$$= \frac{n(n-1)}{r(r-1)} \times ^{n-2}C_{r-2} \text{ and so on}$$

For Examples:

1. $^{10}C_5 = \dfrac{10}{5}\, ^9C_4 = \dfrac{10.9}{5.4} \times ^8C_3$
2. $^{22}C_{15} = \dfrac{22}{15} \times ^{21}C_{14} = \dfrac{22.21}{15.14} \times ^{20}C_{13}$

vii. $\dfrac{^nC_r}{^nC_{r-1}} = \left(\dfrac{n-r+1}{r}\right)$

Proof: We have $\dfrac{^nC_r}{^nC_{r-1}} = \dfrac{n!}{r! \times (n-r)!} \times \dfrac{(r-1)! \times (n-r+1)!}{n!}$

$$= \frac{(r-1)! \times (n-r+1)!}{(n-r)! \times r!}$$

$$= \frac{(r-1)! \times (n-r+1) \times (n-r)!}{(n-r)! \times r \times (r-1)!} = \frac{(n-r+1)}{r}$$

Ex.1: Find value of $\left(1+\dfrac{C_1}{C_0}\right)\left(1+\dfrac{C_2}{C_1}\right)\left(1+\dfrac{C_3}{C_2}\right)\dots\left(1+\dfrac{C_n}{C_{n-1}}\right)$

Sol.: We have $\left(1+\dfrac{C_1}{C_0}\right)\left(1+\dfrac{C_2}{C_1}\right)\left(1+\dfrac{C_3}{C_2}\right)\dots\left(1+\dfrac{C_n}{C_{n-1}}\right)$

$$= \left(1+\frac{n}{1}\right)\left(1+\frac{n-1}{2}\right)\left(1+\frac{n-2}{3}\right)\dots\dots\left(1+\frac{1}{n}\right)$$

$$= \left(\frac{1+n}{1}\right)\left(\frac{1+n}{2}\right)\left(\frac{1+n}{3}\right)\dots\dots\left(\frac{1+n}{n}\right)$$

$$= \frac{(n+1)^n}{n!}$$

Ex.2: Find the value of $(^nC_0 + ^nC_1)(^nC_1 + ^nC_2)(^nC_2 + ^nC_3)\dots\dots (^nC_{n-1} + ^nC_n)$, if $^nC_0 \cdot ^nC_1 \cdot ^nC_2 \dots\dots ^nC_{n-1} = (2013)!$

Sol.: We have, $(^nC_0 + ^nC_1)(^nC_1 + ^nC_2)(^nC_2 + ^nC_3)\dots(^nC_{n-1} + ^nC_n)$

$$= ^nC_0\left(1+\frac{^nC_1}{^nC_0}\right) \cdot ^nC_1\left(1+\frac{^nC_2}{^nC_1}\right) \cdot ^nC_2\left(1+\frac{^nC_3}{^nC_2}\right) \dots\dots ^nC_{n-1} \cdot \left(1+\frac{^nC_n}{^nC_{n-1}}\right)$$

$$= \left(1+\frac{^nC_1}{^nC_0}\right)\left(1+\frac{^nC_2}{^nC_1}\right)\left(1+\frac{^nC_3}{^nC_2}\right)\left(1+\frac{^nC_n}{^nC_{n-1}}\right) \, ^nC_0 \cdot ^nC_1 \cdot ^nC_2 \dots\dots ^nC_{n-1}.$$

$$= \frac{(n+1)^n}{n!} \times (2013)!$$

Ex.3: Prove that $\dfrac{C_1}{C_0} + 2.\dfrac{C_2}{C_1} + 3.\dfrac{C_3}{C_2} + \dots + n.\dfrac{C_n}{C_{n-1}} = \dfrac{n(n+1)}{2}$.

Sol.: We have $\dfrac{C_1}{C_0} + 2.\dfrac{C_2}{C_1} + 3.\dfrac{C_3}{C_2} + \dots\dots\dots + n.\dfrac{C_n}{C_{n-1}}$

$$= n + 2.\left(\frac{n-1}{2}\right) + 3.\left(\frac{n-2}{3}\right) + 4.\left(\frac{n-3}{4}\right) + \dots\dots\dots + 2 + 1$$

$$= \frac{n(n+1)}{2}$$

viii. $^nC_r + ^nC_{r-1} = ^{n+1}C_r$

Proof: We have $^nC_r + ^nC_{r-1} = \dfrac{n!}{r! \times (n-r)!} + \dfrac{n!}{(r-1)!(n-r+1)!}$

$$= \frac{n!}{(r-1)! \times (n-r)!} \times \left\{\frac{1}{r} + \frac{1}{n-r+1}\right\}$$

$$= \frac{n! \times (n+1)}{(r-1)! \times r \times (n-r)! \times (n-r+1)}$$

$$= \frac{(n+1)!}{r! \times (n-r+1)!} = ^{n+1}C_r$$

Ex.1. For $2 \le r \le n$, prove that $\dbinom{n}{r} + 2.\dbinom{n}{r-1} + \dbinom{n}{r-2} = \dbinom{n+2}{r}$

Sol.: We have, $\dbinom{n}{r} + 2.\dbinom{n}{r-1} + \dbinom{n}{r-2}$

$$= \left(\binom{n}{r}+\binom{n}{r-1}\right)+\left(\binom{n}{r-1}+\binom{n}{r-2}\right)$$

$$= \left(\binom{n+1}{r}+\binom{n+1}{r-1}\right)$$

$$= \binom{n+2}{r}$$

Ex.2: For $3\le r\le n$, $\binom{n}{r}+3.\binom{n}{r-1}+3.\binom{n}{r-2}+\binom{n}{r-3} = \binom{n+3}{r}$

Sol.: We have, $\binom{n}{r}+3.\binom{n}{r-1}+3.\binom{n}{r-2}+\binom{n}{r-3}$

$$= \left(\binom{n}{r}+\binom{n}{r-1}\right)+2\left(\binom{n}{r-1}+\binom{n}{r-2}\right)+\left(\binom{n}{r-2}+\binom{n}{r-3}\right)$$

$$= \binom{n+1}{r}+2\binom{n+1}{r-1}+\binom{n+1}{r-2}$$

$$= \left(\binom{n+1}{r}+\binom{n+1}{r-1}\right)+\left(\binom{n+1}{r-1}+\binom{n+1}{r-2}\right)$$

$$= \binom{n+2}{r}+\binom{n+2}{r-1}$$

$$= \binom{n+3}{r}$$

Ex.3: Find the sum of ${}^mC_m + {}^{m+1}C_m + {}^{m+2}C_m + \ldots\ldots\ldots + {}^nC_m$

Sol.: We have, ${}^mC_m + {}^{m+1}C_m + {}^{m+2}C_m + \ldots\ldots\ldots + {}^nC_m$

$$= \left({}^{m+1}C_{m+1} + {}^{m+1}C_m\right) + {}^{m+2}C_m + \ldots\ldots\ldots + {}^nC_m$$

$$= \left({}^{m+2}C_{m+1} + {}^{m+2}C_m\right) + {}^{m+3}C_m + \ldots\ldots\ldots + {}^nC_m$$

$$= \left({}^{m+3}C_{m+1} + {}^{m+3}C_m\right) + {}^{m+4}C_m + \ldots\ldots\ldots + {}^nC_m$$

$$= {}^{m+4}C_{m+1} + \ldots\ldots\ldots + {}^nC_m$$

$$= {}^nC_{m+1} + {}^nC_m$$

$$= {}^{n+1}C_{m+1}$$

Ex.4. Find the value of ${}^{2012}C_{50} + {}^{2013}C_{50} + {}^{2014}C_{50} + {}^{2015}C_{50} + \ldots\ldots\ldots\ldots\ldots\ldots {}^{2050}C_{50}$

Sol.: We have, ${}^{2012}C_{50}+{}^{2013}C_{50}+{}^{2014}C_{50}+{}^{2015}C_{50}+\ldots\ldots {}^{2050}C_{50}$

$$= {}^{2051}C_{51}$$

ix. ${}^nC_r + {}^{n-1}C_r + {}^{n-2}C_r + {}^{n-3}C_r + \ldots\ldots\ldots + {}^rC_r = {}^{n-1}C_{r+1}$

Sol.: We have, ${}^nC_r + {}^{n-1}C_r + {}^{n-2}C_r + {}^{n-3}C_r + \ldots\ldots\ldots\ldots + {}^rC_r$

Now, co-efficient of x^r in the expansion of

$(1+x)^n + (1+x)^{n-1} + (1+x)^{n-2} + \ldots\ldots\ldots\ldots\ldots\ldots + (1+x)^{n+1}(1+x)^r$

Let $S = (1+x)^n + (1+x)^{n-1} + (1+x)^{n-2} + \ldots\ldots\ldots\ldots\ldots + (1+x)^{r+1}(1+x)^r$

$$= (1+x)^r + (1+x)^{r+1} + (1+x)^{r+2} + \ldots\ldots + (1+x)^{n-1} + (1+x)^n$$

$$= (1+x)^r + \left(1+(1+x)+(1+x)^2+(1+x)^3+\ldots\ldots+(1+x)^{n-r}\right)$$

$$= (1+x)^r \times \left(\frac{1-(1+x)^{n-r+1}}{1-(1+x)}\right)$$

$$= (1+x)^r \times \left(\frac{(1+x)^{n-r+1}-1}{x}\right)$$

$\Rightarrow$ Co-efficient of x^r in $(1+x)^r \times \left(\frac{(1+x)^{n-r+1}-1}{x}\right)$

$\Rightarrow$ Co-efficient of x^{r+1}in $(1+x)^r \times \left((1+x)^{n-r+1}-1\right) = (1+x)^{n+1} + (1+x)^r$

$$= {}^{n+1}C_{r+1}$$

Ex.1. Find the value of

i. ${}^{2012}C_5 + {}^{2011}C_5 + {}^{2010}C_5 + \ldots\ldots\ldots\ldots\ldots\ldots\ldots + {}^5C_5$

ii. ${}^{2000}C_{10} + {}^{1999}C_{10} + {}^{1998}C_{10} + \ldots\ldots\ldots\ldots + {}^{10}C_{10}$

iii. ${}^{30}C_3 + {}^{29}C_3 + {}^{28}C_3 + \ldots\ldots\ldots\ldots\ldots\ldots\ldots + {}^3C_3$

iv. ${}^{78}C_5 + {}^{77}C_5 + {}^{76}C_5 + \ldots\ldots\ldots\ldots\ldots\ldots\ldots + {}^5C_5$

Sol.: i. ${}^{2012}C_5 + {}^{2011}C_5 + {}^{2010}C_5 + \ldots\ldots\ldots\ldots + {}^5C_5 = {}^{2013}C_6$

ii. ${}^{2000}C_{10} + {}^{1999}C_{10} + {}^{1998}C_{10} + \ldots\ldots + {}^{10}C_{10} = {}^{2001}C_{11}$

iii. ${}^{30}C_3 + {}^{29}C_3 + {}^{28}C_3 + \ldots\ldots\ldots\ldots + {}^3C_3 = {}^{31}C_4$

iv. ${}^{78}C_5 + {}^{77}C_5 + {}^{76}C_5 + \ldots\ldots\ldots\ldots + {}^5C_5 = {}^{79}C_6$

x. Summation Upto Middle Term

$${}^{2n}C_0 + {}^{2n}C_1 + {}^{2n}C_2 + {}^{2n}C_3 + \ldots\ldots + {}^{2n}C_n = 2^{2n-1} + \frac{1}{2} \times {}^{2n}C_n$$

Proof: Let $S = {}^{2n}C_0 + {}^{2n}C_1 + {}^{2n}C_2 + {}^{2n}C_3 + \ldots\ldots\ldots + {}^{2n}C_n$ ....(i)

Also, $S = {}^{2n}C_{2n} + {}^{2n}C_{2n-1} + {}^{2n}C_{2n-2} + \ldots\ldots + {}^{2n}C_n$ ....(ii)

Adding (i) and (ii), we get,

$$2S = \left({}^{2n}C_0 + {}^{2n}C_1 + {}^{2n}C_2 + \ldots + {}^{2n}C_n + {}^{2n}C_{n+1} + \ldots + {}^{2n}C_{2n}\right) + {}^{2n}C_n$$

$$= 2^{2n} + {}^{2n}C_n$$

$$\Rightarrow S = 2^{2n-1} + \frac{1}{2}\left({}^{2n}C_n\right)$$

Ex.1: Find the value of ${}^{20}C_0 + {}^{20}C_1 + {}^{20}C_2 + \ldots\ldots\ldots + {}^{20}C_{10}$

Sol.: Let $S = {}^{20}C_0 + {}^{20}C_1 + {}^{20}C_2 + \ldots\ldots\ldots + {}^{20}C_{10}$ ....(i)

$\Rightarrow S = {}^{20}C_{20} + {}^{20}C_{19} + {}^{20}C_{18} + \ldots\ldots\ldots + {}^{20}C_{10}$ ....(ii)

Adding (i) and (ii), we get,

$$2S = \left({}^{20}C_0 + {}^{2n}C_1 + {}^{20}C_2 + \ldots\ldots + {}^{2n}C_{10} + {}^{2n}C_{11} + {}^{2n}C_{12} + \ldots\ldots + {}^{20}C_{20}\right) + {}^{20}C_{10}$$

$$\Rightarrow 2S = 2^{20} + {}^{20}C_{10}$$

$$\Rightarrow S = 2^{19} + \frac{1}{2}\left({}^{20}C_{10}\right).$$

Ex.2: Find the value of ${}^{50}C_{25} + {}^{50}C_{26} + {}^{50}C_{27} + \ldots\ldots\ldots\ldots\ldots + {}^{50}C_{50}$

Sol.: Let $S = {}^{50}C_{25} + {}^{50}C_{26} + {}^{50}C_{27} + \ldots\ldots\ldots\ldots + {}^{50}C_{50}$ ....(i)

$\Rightarrow S = {}^{50}C_{25} + {}^{50}C_{24} + {}^{50}C_{23} + \ldots\ldots\ldots\ldots + {}^{50}C_0$ ....(ii)

Adding (i) and (ii), we get,

$$2S = \left({}^{50}C_0 + {}^{50}C_1 + {}^{50}C_2 + \ldots\ldots\ldots + {}^{50}C_{25} + {}^{50}C_{26} + {}^{50}C_{27} + \ldots\ldots\ldots + {}^{50}C_{50}\right) + {}^{50}C_{25}$$

$$\Rightarrow 2S = 2^{50} + {}^{50}C_{25}$$

$$\Rightarrow S = 2^{49} + \frac{1}{2}\left({}^{50}C_{25}\right).$$

xi. Summation of a Series:

$^{2n}C_m + {}^{2n-1}C_m + {}^{2n-2}C_m + ... + {}^nC_m = {}^{2n+1}C_{m+1}$

Proof: We have $^{2n}C_m + {}^{2n-1}C_m + {}^{2n-2}C_m + ... + {}^nC_m$

= Co-efficient of x^n in the expansion of

$(1+x)^{2n} + (1+x)^{2n-1} + (1+x)^{2n-2} + (1+x)^{2n-3} + ... + (1+x)^n$

= Co-efficient of x^m in the expansion of

$(1+x)^n\left(1 + (1+x) + (1+x)^2 + (1+x)^3 + ... + (1+x)^n\right)$

= Co-efficient of x^m in the expansion of

$$(1+x)^n\left(\frac{(1+x)^{n+1}-1}{(1+x)-1}\right)$$

= Co-efficient of x^{m+1} in the expansion of

$(1+x)^n\left((1+x)^{n+1}-1\right)$

= Co-efficient of x^{m+1} in the expansion of

$\left((1+x)^{2n+1} - ((1+x)^n\right)$.

$= {}^{2n+1}C_{m+1}$.

Ex.1: Find the sum of $^nC_3 + 2.{}^{n+1}C_3 + 3.{}^{n+2}C_3 + ... + n.{}^{2n-1}C_3$

Sol.: We have $^nC_3 + 2.{}^{n+1}C_3 + 3.{}^{n+2}C_3 + ... + n.{}^{2n-1}C_3$

= Co-efficient of x^3 in the expansion of

$(1+x)^n + 2.(1+x)^{n+1} + 3.(1+x)^{n+2} + ... + n(1+x)^{2n-1}$

Let $S = (1+x)^n + 2.(1+x)^{n+1} + 3.(1+x)^{n+2} + ... + n(1+x)^{2n-1}$ ....(i)

$\Rightarrow (1+x)S = (1+x)^{n+1} + 2.(1+x)^{n+2} + 3.(1+x)^{n+3} + ... + n(1+x)^{2n}$ ....(ii)

Subtracting (ii) from (i) , we get,

$-xS = (1+x)^n + (1+x)^{n+1} + ... + (1+x)^{2n-1} - n(1+x)^{2n}$

$\Rightarrow -xS = (1+x)^n\left(1 + (1+x) + (1+x)^2 + (1+x)^3 + ... + (1+x)^{n-1}\right) - n(1+x)^{2n}$

$$\Rightarrow -xS = (1+x)^n\left(\frac{(1+x)^n-1}{(1+x)-1}\right) - n(1+x)^{2n}$$

$$\Rightarrow S = \left(\frac{-(1+x)^{2n}+(1+x)^n}{x^2}\right) + \frac{n(1+x)^{2n}}{x}$$

Hence, the co-efficient of x^3 is $-{}^{2n}C_5 + {}^nC_5 + n.{}^{2n}C_4$

Ex.2: Find the sum of $^{100}C_{50} + 2.{}^{99}C_{49} + 3.{}^{98}C_{48} + ... + 51.{}^{50}C_0$

Sol. We have $^{100}C_{50} + 2.{}^{99}C_{49} + 3.{}^{98}C_{48} + ... + 51.{}^{50}C_0$.

$= {}^{100}C_{50} + 2.{}^{99}C_{50} + 3.{}^{98}C_{50} + 4.{}^{97}C_{50} + ... + 51.{}^{50}C_{50}$

= Co-efficient of x^{50} in $(1+x)^{100} + 2.(1+x)^{99} + 3.(1+x)^{98} + ... + 51.(1+x)^{50}$

Let $S = (1+x)^{100} + 2.(1+x)^{99} + 3.(1+x)^{98} + ... + 51.(1+x)^{50}$ i

$$\Rightarrow \frac{S}{(1+x)} = (1+x)^{99} + 2.(1+x)^{98} + 3.(1+x)^{97} + ... + 51(1+x)^{49}$$ ii

Subtracting (ii) from (i), we get

$$\left(1-\frac{1}{1+x}\right)S = (1+x)^{100} + (1+x)^{99} + (1+x)^{98} + ... + (1+x)^{50} - 51(1+x)^{49}$$

$$\Rightarrow \left(\frac{x}{1+x}\right)S = (1+x)^{50}\left(\frac{(1+x)^{51}-1}{(1+x)-1}\right) - 51(1+x)^{49}$$

$$\Rightarrow \left(\frac{x}{1+x}\right)S = \left(\frac{(1+x)^{101}-(1+x)^{50}}{x}\right) - 51(1+x)^{49}$$

$$\Rightarrow xS = \left(\frac{(1+x)^{102}-(1+x)^{51}}{x}\right) - 51(1+x)^{49}$$

$$\Rightarrow S = \left(\frac{(1+x)^{102}-(1+x)^{51}}{x^2}\right) - 51\frac{(1+x)^{50}}{x}$$

Hence, the co-efficient of $x50$ is $^{102}C_{52} = {}^{102}C_{50}$.

xii. Algebraical Method to Find the Sum

First we write the series converted into the form of $\sum_{r=0}^{n} f(r) \times {}^nC_r$ or $\sum_{r=0}^{n} f(r) \times {}^nC_r$.

Also use in place of $r.{}^nC_r = r.\left(\frac{n}{r}\right){}^{n-1}C_{r-1}$

and $r^2.{}^nC_r = (r(r-1)+1)$.

$${}^nC_r = \left(\frac{r(r-1)}{n(n-1)}.{}^{n-2}C_{r-2}\right) + \left(\frac{n}{r}.{}^{n-1}C_{r-1}\right)$$

Ex1. Find the sum of $C_1 + 2.C_2 + 3.C_3 + ... + n.C_r$

Sol. Let $t_r = r.C_r = r.{}^nC_r = r.\times\frac{n}{r}\times{}^{n-1}C_{r-1} = n.{}^{n-1}C_{r-1}$

Thus, $S_n = C_1 + 2.C_3 + 3.C_3 + ... + n.C_r$

$$= \sum_{r=1}^{n} t_r$$

$$= \sum_{r=1}^{n} n.{}^{n-1}C_{r-1}$$

$$= n\sum_{r=1}^{n} {}^{n-1}C_{r-1}$$

$$= n.2^{n-1}$$

Ex.2: Find the sum of $C_0 + 2.C_1 + 3.C_2 + ... + (n+1).C_n$

Sol.: Let $t_{r+1} = (r+1).C_r = (r+1).{}^nC_r$

$= r.{}^nC_r + {}^nC_r$

$= r.\left(\frac{n}{r}\right){}^{n-1}C_{r-1} + {}^nC_r$

$= n.{}^{n+1}C_{r-1} + {}^nC_r$

Thus, $S_n = n\sum_{r=0}^{n} t_{r+1} = \sum_{r=0}^{n}\left(n.{}^{n-1}C_{r-1} + {}^nC_r\right)$

$$= \sum_{r=0}^{n} n.{}^{n-1}C_{r-1} + \sum_{r=0}^{n} {}^nC_r$$

$= n.2^{n-1} + 2^n$

$= (n+2)2^{n-1}$

Ex.3. Find the sum of $C_1 + 2^2.C_2 + 3^3.C_3 + ... + n^2.C_n$

SOL.: Let $t_r = r^2.Cr = r^2.{}^nC_r$

$= \{r(r-1)+r\}.{}^nC_r$

$= \{r(r-1)\,{}^nC_r + r.{}^nC_r\}$

$= \{n(n-1)\,{}^{n-2}C_{r-2} + n.{}^{n-1}C_{r-1}\}$

Thus, $S_n = \sum_{r=1}^{n} \left(n(n-1)^{n-2}C_{r-2} + n.{}^{n-1}C_{r-1}\right)$

$= \sum_{r=1}^{n} n(n-1)^{n-2}C_{r-2} + n\sum_{r=1}^{n} {}^{n-1}C_{r-1}.$

$= \left(n(n-1)\,2^{n-2} + n\right)2^{n-1}$

$= \left(n(n-1)\,2 + n\right)2^{n-2}$

$= \left(n(n-1)\right)2^{n-2}$

EX.4 Find the sum of $C_0 + \frac{C_1}{2} + \frac{C_2}{3} + \ldots\ldots\ldots\ldots + \frac{C_n}{n+1}$

SOL.: Let $tr+1 = \frac{C_r}{r+1} = \frac{{}^nC_r}{r+1} = \frac{1}{n+1}\left(\frac{n+1}{r+1}\,{}^nC_r\right)$

$= \frac{1}{n+1} \times {}^{n+1}C_{r+1}$

Thus, $Sn = \sum_{r=0}^{n} t_{r+1} = \sum_{r=0}^{n}\left(\frac{1}{n+1} \times {}^{n+1}C_{r+1}\right)$

$= \frac{1}{n+1}\sum_{r=0}^{n}\left({}^{n+1}C_{r+1}\right)$

$= \frac{1}{n+1}\left(2^{n+1} - 1\right)$

$= \left(\frac{2^{n+1}-1}{n+1}\right)$

EX.5: Find the sum of $\frac{C_0}{1.2} + \frac{C_1}{2.3} + \frac{C_2}{3.4} + \ldots\ldots\ldots + \frac{C_n}{(n+1)(n+2)}$

SOL.: Let $tr + 1 = \frac{C_r}{(r+1)(r+2)} = \frac{{}^nC_r}{(r+1)(r+2)}$

$= \left(\frac{1}{(n+1)(n+2)}\right) \times \left(\frac{(n+1)(n+2)}{(r+1)(r+2)}\,{}^nC_r\right)$

$= \left(\frac{1}{(n+1)(n+2)}\right) \times {}^{n+2}C_{r+2}$

Thus, $S_n = \sum_{r=0}^{n} t_{r+1} = \sum_{r=0}^{n}\left(\frac{1}{(n+1)(n+2)}\right) \times {}^{n+2}C_{r+2}$

$= \frac{1}{(n+1)(n+2)}\left(2^{n+2} - {}^{n+2}C_0 - {}^{n+2}C_1\right).$

$= \frac{\left(2^{n+2} - n - 3\right)}{(n+1)(n+2)}.$

xiii. Sum of the series, when the sum of the lower suffices are same.

${}^mC_r\,{}^nC_0 + {}^mC_{r-1}.{}^nC_1 + {}^mC_{r-2}.{}^nC_2 + \ldots\ldots\ldots + {}^mC_m.{}^nC_r = {}^{m+n}C_r$

SOL.: We have, $(1+x)^m = {}^mC_0 + {}^mC_1.x + \ldots\ldots + {}^mC_r\,x^r + {}^mC_{r-1}.x^{r-1} + {}^mC_{r-2}.x^{r-2} + \ldots\ldots\ldots + {}^mC_m.x^m$ ...(i)

Also $(x+1)^n = {}^mC_0\,x^n + {}^nC_1.x^{n-1} + \ldots\ldots + {}^nC_r\,x^{n-r} + {}^nC_{r-1}.x^{n-r+1} + \ldots\ldots + {}^nC_n$ ..... (ii)

Multiplying (i) and (ii), we get,

$(1+x)^{m+n} = \left({}^mC_r.{}^nC_0 + {}^mC_{r-1}.{}^nC_1 + {}^mC_{r-2}.{}^nC_2 + \ldots\ldots + {}^mC_0.{}^nC_r\right)x^n + (\ldots\ldots)\,x^{n-1} + (\ldots\ldots)\,x^{n-2} + \ldots$

Comparing the co-efficient of x^n of both the sides, we get,

${}^mC_r.{}^nC_0 + {}^mC_{r-1}.{}^nC_1 + {}^mC_{r-2}.{}^nC_2 + \ldots\ldots\ldots + {}^mC_m.{}^nC_r = {}^{m+n}C_r$

Hence, the result.

EX.1: Find the sum of $C_0.C_n + C_1.C_{n-1} + C_2.C_{n-2} + \ldots\ldots + C_n.C_0$

SOL.: We have, $(1+x)^n = {}^nC_0 + {}^nC_0.x + {}^nC_0.x^2 + \ldots + {}^nC_r.x^r + {}^nC_{r+1}x^{r+1} + \ldots\ldots\ldots + {}^nC_nx^n$ ....(i)

Also, $(x+1)^n = {}^nC_0.x^n + {}^nC_0.x^{n-1} + {}^nC_0.x^{n-2} + \ldots\ldots + {}^nC_rx^{n-r} + {}^nC_{r+1}x^{n-r-1} + \ldots + {}^nC_n$ ....(ii)

Multiplying (i) and (ii), we get,

$(1+x)^{2n} = (C_0.C_0 + C_1.C_1 + C_2.C_2 + \ldots + C_n.C_n)\,x^n + (\ldots)\,x^{n-1} + (\ldots)\,x^{n-2} + \ldots$

Comparing the co-efficients of x^n of both sides, we get,

$(C_0.C_0 + C_1.C_1 + C_2.C_2 + \ldots\ldots\ldots + C_n.C_n) = {}^{2n}C_n$

$\Rightarrow C_0.C_n + C_1.C_{n-1} + C_2.C_{n-2} + \ldots\ldots + C_n.C_0 = {}^{2n}C_n$

xiv. Sum of the series when the difference of the lower suffices are same ${}^nC_r.{}^nC_n + {}^nC_{r-1}.{}^nC_{n-1} + {}^nC_{r-2}.{}^nC_{n-2} + \ldots\ldots\ldots\ldots + {}^nC_0.{}^nC_{n-r} = {}^{2n}C_{n-r}$

SOL.: We have, $(1+x)^n = {}^nC_0 + {}^nC_1x + {}^nC_2.x^2 + \ldots\ldots + {}^nC_{r-2}x^{r-2} + {}^nC_{r-1}x^{r-1} + {}^nC_r.x^r + \ldots\ldots + {}^nC_nx^n$ ...(i)

Also, $(x+1)^n = {}^nC_0x^n + nC_1.x^{n-1} + {}^nC_2x^{n-2} + \ldots\ldots\ldots\ldots + {}^nC_{n-2}\,x^2 + {}^nC_{n-1}x + nC_n$ ....(ii)

Multiplying (i) and (ii), we get,

$(1+x)^{2n} = ({}^nC_r.{}^nC_n + {}^nC_{r-1}.{}^nC_{r-1}.{}^nC_{r-2}.{}^nC_{n-2} + \ldots + {}^nC_0.{}^nC_{n-r})x^r + (\ldots\ldots)x^{r+1} + \ldots\ldots$

Comparing the co-efficients of x^r of both the sides, we get,

${}^nC_r.{}^nC_n + {}^nC_{r-1}.{}^nC_{n-1} + {}^nC_{r-2}.{}^nC_{n-2} + \ldots\ldots + {}^nC_0.{}^nC_{n-r} = {}^{2n}C_{n-r}$

EX.1: Find the sum of $C_0.C_1 + C_1.C_2 + C_2.C_3 + \ldots\ldots\ldots\ldots + C_{n-1}.C_n$

SOL.: We have $(1+x)^n = {}^nC_0 + {}^nC_1.x + {}^nC_2.x^2 + {}^nC_3.x^3 + \ldots\ldots\ldots + {}^nC_n.x^n$ ....(i)

Also, $(x+1)^n = {}^nC_0.x^n + C_1.x^{n-1} + {}^nC_2.x^{n-2} + {}^nC_3.x^{n-3} + \ldots\ldots\ldots + {}^nC_n$ ....(ii)

Multiplying (i) and (ii), we get,

$(1+x)^{2n} = ({}^nC_0.{}^nC_1 + {}^nC_1.{}^nC_2 + {}^nC_3 + \ldots\ldots + {}^nC_{n-1}.{}^nC_n)x^{n+1} + (\ldots\ldots)x^n + (\ldots\ldots)x^{n+2} + \ldots\ldots$

Comparing the co-efficient of x^r of both the sides, we get,

$C_0.C_1 + C_1.C_2.C_3 + \ldots\ldots\ldots + C_{n-2}.C_n.$

$= {}^{2n}C_{n+1} = \frac{(2n)!}{(n-1)! \times (n+1)!}.$

4.12 Multinomial Theorem for A Positive Integral Index

1. $(a_1 + a_2) = a_1^2 + 2a_1a^2 + a_2^2$

$= {}^2C_0a_1^2a_2^0 + {}^2C_1a_1^{2-1}a_2 + {}^2C_2a_1^{2-2}\,a_2^2$

$= \sum_{k=0}^{2} {}^2c_ka_1^{2-k}a_2^k$

$$= \sum_{k=0}^{2} \binom{2}{k} a_1^{2-k} a_2^{k}$$

$$= \sum_{k_1+k_2=2} \binom{2}{k_1, k_2} a_1^{k_1} a_2^{k_2}, k_1 + k_2 = k.$$

2. $(a_1 + a_2)^3 = {}^3C_0\, a_1^3 a_2^0 + {}^3C_1\, a_1^{3-1} a_2^1 + {}^3C_2\, a_1^{3-2} a_2^2 + {}^3C_3\, a_1^{3-3} a_2^3$

$$= \sum_{k=0}^{3} {}^3C_k a_1^{3-k} a_2^{k}$$

$$= \sum_{k=0}^{3} \binom{3}{k} a_1^{3-k} a_2^{k}$$

$$= \sum_{k_1+k_2=3} \binom{3}{k_1, k_2} a_1^{k_1} a_2^{k_2}, \; k_1+k_2 = k$$

3. $(a_1 + a_2 + a_3)^2 = (a_1 + (a_2 + a_3))^2$

$$= a_1^2 + 2.a_1.(a_2 + a_3) + (a_2 + a_3)^2$$

$$= \sum_{k=0}^{2} \binom{2}{k} \cdot a_1^{2-k} \cdot (a_1 + a_3)^k$$

$$= \sum_{k=0}^{2} \binom{2}{k_1, k_2} \cdot a_1^{k_1} \cdot (a_2 + a_3)^k$$

$$= \sum_{k_1+k_2=2} \binom{2}{k_1, k_2} .a_1^{k_1} . \sum_{r=0}^{k} \binom{k}{r} \cdot a_2^{k-r} . a_3^{r}$$

$$= \sum_{k_1+k_2+k_3=2} \binom{2}{k_1, k_2, k_3} .a_1^{k_1} .a_2^{k_2} .a_3^{k_3}$$

4. $(a_1 + a_2 + a_3)^5 = \sum_{k_1+k_2+k_3=5} \binom{5}{k_1, k_2, k_3} \cdot a_1^{k_1} .a_2^{k_2} .a_3^{k_3}$

Thus $(a_1 + a_2 + a_3 + ... + a_m)^n = \sum_{k_1+k_2+k_3+........+k_m=n} \binom{n}{k_1, k_2, k_3, ..., k_m} \cdot a_1^{k_1} .a_2^{k_2} .a_3^{k_3} .... a_m^{k_m}$

4.13 Important Results

Result 1. The co-efficient of $a_1^{k_1} .a_2^{k_2} .a_3^{k_3} .... a_m^{k_m}$ in $(a_1 + a_2 + a_3 + ... + a_m)^n$ is $\dfrac{n!}{k_1!.k_2!........k_m!}$

Ex.1: Find the coefficient of $a^5 b^4 c^2 d$ in the expansion of $(a + b + c + d)^{15}$.

Sol: The co-efficient of $a^5 b^4 c^2 d$ in the expansion of $(a + b + c + d)^{15}$ is $\dfrac{15!}{5! \times 4! \times 2! \times 1!}$

Ex.2: Find the co-efficient of $a^3 b^4 c^7$ in the expansion of $(ab + bc + ca)^8$

Sol.: We have $= a^3 b^4 c^7 = (ab)^x (bc)^y (ca)^z$

$\Rightarrow \quad x + z = 3, x + y = 4, y + z = 7$

$\Rightarrow \quad x = 0, y = 4, z = 3$

Thus, the co-efficient of $a^3 b^4 c^7$ in the expansion of $(ab + bc + ca)^8 =$ the co-efficient of $(ab)^0 (bc)^4 (ca)^3$ in the expansion of $(ab + bc + ca)^8 = \dfrac{8!}{0!4!3!} = 280.$

Result 2. The greatest co-efficient in expansion of $(a_1+a_2+a_3+..+a_m)^n$ is $\dfrac{n!}{(q!)^{m-r} \times ((q+1)!)^r}$ where q = quotient, r = remainder, when n is divided by m.

Ex.2: Find the greatest co-efficient in $(a + b + c + d + e)^{53}$

Sol.: Here $n = 53$ and $m = 5$

So quotient is 10 and the remainder is 3

Hence, the greatest co-efficient is $= \dfrac{53!}{(3!)^{5-3} \times ((3+1)!)^3}$

$$= \frac{(53)!}{(3!)^2 \times (4!)^3}$$

Result 3. The number of terms in the expansion of $(a_1+a_2+a_3+ ......+ a_m)^n$ is $n + m-1C_{m-1}$.

Ex.3: Find the number of terms of

i. $(a + b + c)^n$

ii. $(a + b + c + d)^n$

iii. $(a + b + c + d + e)^n$.

Sol.: i. The number of terms of $(a+b+c)^n$ is ${}^{n+3-1}C_{3-1} = {}^{n+2}C_2$

ii. The number of terms of $(a+b+c+d)^n$ is ${}^{n+4-1}C_{4-1} = {}^{n+3}C_3$

iii. The number of terms of $(a+b+c+d+e)^n$ is ${}^{n+5-1}C_{5-1} = {}^{n+4}C_4$

Result 4. If n is a positive integer and $a_1, a_2, ..., a_m \in C$, then the co-efficient of x^r in the expansion of $(a_1 + a_2 x + a_3 x^2 + ... + a_m x^{m-1})$ is $\sum \left(\dfrac{n!}{n_1! \times n_2! \times n_3! \times .... \times n_m!} \right) \times a_1^{n_1} a_2^{n_2} .... a_m^{n_m}$,

where $n_1, n_2, ..., n_m$ are non negative integers subject to the condition $n_1 + n_2 + ... + nm = n$ and $n_1 + 2n_2 + 3n_3 .... + (m-1)n_m = r$

Ex.1: Find the co-efficient of x^7 in the expansion of $(1+3x-2x^3)^{10}$

Sol:. The co-efficient of x^7 in the expansion of $(1+3x-2x^3)^{10}$ is $\sum \left(\dfrac{10!}{n_1! \times n_2! \times n_3!} \right) \times (1)^{n_1} (3)^{n_2} (-2)^{n_3}$, where $n_1 + n_2 + n_3 = 10$ and $n_2 + 3n_3 = 7$. The possible values of n_1, n_2, n_3 are shown here.

n_1	n_2	n_3
3	7	0
5	4	1
7	1	2

Hence, the co-efficient of x^7

$$= \frac{10!}{3!7!0!} (1)^3 (3)^7 (-2)^0 + \frac{10!}{5!4!1!} (1)^5 (3)^4 (-2)^1 + \frac{10!}{7!1!2!} (1)^7 (3)^1 (-2)^3$$

$= 262440 - 204120 + 4320 = 62640.$

4.14 Binomial Theorem for Any Index

Statement: Let n be a rational number and x be a real number such that $|x|<1$, then $(1 + x)^n = 1 + nx + \dfrac{n(n-1)}{2!} x^2 + \dfrac{n(n-1)(n-2)}{3!} x^3 + ... + \dfrac{n(n-1)(n-2)....(n-r+1)}{n!} x^r + ... \infty$

NOTE

1. The condition $|x|< 1$ is un-necessary, if n is a whole number while the same condition is essential if n is a rational number other than a whole number.
2. Note that there are infinite number of terms in the expansion of $(1+x)^n$, where n is a negative integer or a fraction.
3. If the first term is not unity and the index of the binomial is either a negative or a fraction, then the expand as follows:

$$(x+a)^n = \left\{a\left(1+\frac{x}{a}\right)\right\}^n$$

$$= a^n a^n \left\{1+n.\frac{x}{a}+\frac{n(n-1)}{2!}\left(\frac{x}{a}\right)^2+\frac{n(n-1)(n-2)}{3!}.\left(\frac{x}{a}\right)^3+.......\right\}$$

4. If n is a positive integer, then the above expansion contains $(n+1)$ terms and coincides with $(1+x)^n = {}^nC_0 + {}^nC_1.x + {}^nC_2.x^2 + {}^nC_3.x^3 + ...+ {}^nC_n.x^n$, because ${}^nC_0 = 1 = {}^nC_n$, ${}^nC_1 = n = {}^nC_{n-1}$, ${}^nC_2 = \frac{n(n-1)}{2} = {}^nC_{n-2}$ and so on.
5. General term in the expansion of $(1+x)^n$.
$$T_{r+1} = \frac{n(n-1)(n-2)......(n-r+1)}{r!} \times x^r$$
6. General term in the expansion of $(1-x)^n$
$$T_{r+1} = (-1)^r \times \frac{n(n+1)(n+2)......(n+r-1)}{r!} x^r$$
7. General term in the expansion of $(1-x)^n$
$$T_{r+1} = (-1)^r \times \frac{n(n-1)(n-2)(n-3)........(n-r+1)}{r!} \times x^r$$
8. General term in the expansion of $(1-x)^{-n}$.
$$T_{r+1} = \frac{n(n+1)(n+2)(n+3)........(n+r-1)}{r!} \times x^r$$

4.15 Difference between the Binomial theorem for positive integer exponent and for general exponent

i. If n is a positive integer, then $(1+x)^n$ contains $(n+1)$ terms i.e. a finite number of terms. When n is general exponent, then the expansions of $(1+x)^n$ contains infinite number of terms.

ii. When n is a positive integer, then the expansion of $(1+x)^n$ is valid for all values of x. If n general exponent, the expansion of $(1+x)^n$ is valid for all those values of x satisfying the condition $|x|< 1$.

iii. When n is a positive integer, the exact value of $(1+x)$ is obtained $(n+1)$ terms of the binomial expansion. If n is not a positive integer, then the actual calculation of $(1+x)^n$ through the binomial expansion can be done only a finite number of terms. The value calculated up to these finite number of terms with only be an approximate value of $(1+x)^n$, and not its exact value.

4.16 Important Expansions to Remember.

STEP. • 1

i. $(1+x)^{-1} = 1-x+x^2-x^3+x^4-x^5+........+(-1)^r.x^r+.....$ to. ∞

ii. $(1+x)^{-2} = 1-2x+3x^2-4x^3+5x^4-6x^5+..........+(-1)^r.(r+1)x^r+......$ to ∞

iii. $(1+x)^{-3} = 1-3x+6x^2-10x^3+.....+(-1)^r.\frac{(r+1)(r+2)}{2}x^r+......$ to. ∞

STEP. • 2

i. $(1-x)^{-1} = 1+x+x^2+x^3+........+x^r+..........$ to ∞

ii. $(1-x)^{-2} = 1+2x+3x^2+4x^3+.....+(r+1)x^r+....$ to ∞

iii. $(1-x)^{-3} = 1+3x+6x^2+10x^3+....+\frac{(r+1)(r+2)}{2}x^r+...$ to ∞

4.17 Some Solved Examples

Ex.1: Find the co-efficient of x^n in each of the following:

i. $\frac{1}{1+2x}$ ii. $\frac{1}{1-3x}$

iii. $\frac{1}{(1-ax)(1-bx)}$ iv. $\frac{1}{1+9x+20x}$

SOL.: i. We have $\frac{1}{1+2x} = (1+2x)^{-1} = (1-2x+4x^2-8x^3+16x^4-......+(-1)^n 2^n x^n+....)$. Thus, the co-efficient of x^n is $(-1)^n.2^n$

ii. We have $\frac{1}{1-3x} = (1-3x)^{-1} = (1+3x+3^2x^2+3^3x^3+..........+3^nx^n+.......)$ Thus, the co-efficient of is x^n is 3^n

iii. We have $\frac{1}{(1-ax)(1-bx)}$

$$= \frac{1}{(a-b)} \times \left(\frac{a}{1-ax} - \frac{b}{1-bx}\right)$$

$$= \frac{1}{(a-b)} \times \left(a(1-ax)^{-1} - b(1-bx)-1\right)$$

$$= \frac{1}{(a-b)} \times a(1-ax+a^2+x^2+a^3x^3+...........+a^nx^n+....) - b(1+bx+b^2x^2+b^3x^3+.......+b^nx^n+.....)$$

Thus, the co-efficient of x^n is $\left(\frac{a^{n+1}-b^{n+1}}{a-b}\right)$

iv. We have $\frac{1}{1+9x+20x^2}$

$$= \frac{1}{(1+4x)(1+5x)}$$

$$= \left(\frac{5}{1+5x} - \frac{4}{1+4x}\right)$$

$$= 5(1+5x)^{-1} - 4(1+4x)^{-1}$$

$$= 5(1-5x+5^2x^2-5^3x^3+.......+(-1)^n 5^n x^n+...) - 4(1-4x+4^2x^2-4^3x^3+...+(-1)^n 4^n x^n+.....).$$

Thus, the co-efficient of x^n is $(-1)^n(5^{n+1}-4^{n+1})$

Ex.2: Find the co-efficient of x^n in each of the following.

i. $(1-2x+3x^2-4x^3+...$ to $\infty)$ ii. $\left(\frac{1+x}{1-x}\right)^2$

iii. $\left(\frac{1-x}{1+x}\right)^2$ iv. $\frac{1+x-2x^2}{(1-x)^3}$

Sol. i. We have $(1-2x+3x^2-4x^3+$.................to ∞)

$= (1-2x+3x^2-4x^3+5x^4-......+(-1)^n(n+1)x^n+....)$

Thus, the co-efficient of x^n is $(-1)^n (n+1)$

ii. We have $\left(\frac{1+x}{1-x}\right)^2$

$= (1+x)^2 \times (1-x)^2$

$= (1+2x+x^2) \times (1-2x+3x^2-4x^3+....+(n-1)x^{n-2} + .n.x^{n-1} + (n+1)x^n)$

Thus, the co-efficient of x^n is $(n+1+2n+n-1) = 4n$

iii. We have $\left(\frac{1-x}{1+x}\right)^2$

$= (1-x)^2 \times (1+x)^{-2}$

$= (1-2x+x^2) \times (1-2x+3x^2-......+(-1)^{n-2}(n-1)x^{n-2} + (-1)^{n-1}.n.x^{n-1} + (-1)^n.(n+1)x^n+....)$

Thus, the co-efficient of x^n is $(-1)^n \times (n+1+2n+n-1)$

$= (-1)^n \times 4n$

iv. We have $\frac{1+x-2x^2}{(1-x)^3}$.

$= (1+x-2x^2) \times (1-x)^{-3}$

$= (1+x-2x^2) \times (1+3x+6x^2+10x^3+....+\frac{n(n-1)}{2}x^{n-2} + \frac{n(n+1)}{2}x^{n-1} + \frac{(n+1)(n+2)}{2}x^n+.....)$

Thus, the co-efficient of x^n is

$$= \frac{(n+1)(n+2)}{2} + \frac{n(n+1)}{2} - 2.\frac{n(n-1)}{2} = 2n+2$$

Ex.3: Find the co-efficient of x^n in the expansion of $(1-2x)^{-1/2}$

Sol: As we know that, general term in expansion of $(1-x)^{-n}$.

$$T_{r+1} = \frac{n(n+1)(n+2)(n+3)........(n+r-1)}{r!} \times x^r$$

Thus, the co-efficient of x^n is

$$= \frac{\frac{1}{2}\left(\frac{1}{2}+1\right)\left(\frac{1}{2}+2\right)......\left(\frac{1}{2}+n-1\right)}{n!} \times (2)^n$$

$$= \frac{1.3.5.........(2n-1)}{2^n.n!} \times 2^n$$

$$= \frac{1.3.5.........(2n-1)}{n!}$$

Ex-4: Find the co-efficient of x^n in $(1+x)^n \times (1+x)^{-2}$

Sol.: We have $(1+x)^n \times (1+x)^{-2}$

$= \left(C_0 + C_1x + C_2x^2.........+C_nx^n\right)$

$\times \left(1-2x+3x^2-4x^3+......+(-1)^n(n+1)x^n+.....\right)$

Thus, the co-efficient of x^n is

$= \left(C_n - 2C_{n-1} + 3C_{n-2} - 4C_{n-3} + ...+(-1)^n(n+1)C_0\right)$

Ex.5: Find the first negative term in expansion of $\left(1+\frac{3}{4}x\right)^{13/3}$, where $0 < x < \frac{4}{3}$

Sol.: Let T_{r+1} th term be negative.

We have $T_{r+1} = \frac{n(n-1)(n-2).....(n-(r-1))}{r!} \times \left(\frac{3}{4}x\right)^r$

$\Rightarrow T_{r+1}$ is negative when $(n-r+1) < 0$

Thus, $\frac{13}{3} - r + 1 < 0 \quad \Rightarrow r > \frac{16}{3} = 5\frac{1}{3}$

$\Rightarrow r = 6$

Thus, the first negative term is the 7th term

Ex.6: If $y = x - x^2 + x^3 - x^4 +$....... to ∞, where $|x| < 1$, then prove that $x = \frac{y}{1-y}$.

Sol.: We have $y = x - x^2 + x^3 - x^4 +$......: to ∞

$\Rightarrow \quad -y = -x + x^2 - x^3 + x^4 -$...............

$\Rightarrow \quad 1-y = 1-x+x^2-x^3+x^4-$...............

$\Rightarrow \quad 1-y = (1+x)^{-1} = \frac{1}{(1+x)}$

$\Rightarrow \quad 1+x = \frac{1}{1-y}$

$\Rightarrow \quad x = \frac{1}{1-y} - 1 = \frac{1-1+y}{1-y} = \frac{y}{1-y}$

Ex.7: If $y = 2x+3x^2+4x^3+$....to ∞, then express x in terms of y.

Sol.: We have $\quad y = 2x+3x^2+4x^3+$......... to ∞

$\Rightarrow \quad 1+y = 1+2x+3x^2+4x^3+$ ....

$\Rightarrow \quad 1+y = (1-x)^2$

$\Rightarrow \quad 1+y = \frac{1}{(1-x)^2}$

$\Rightarrow \quad (1-x)^2 = \frac{1}{1+y}$

$\Rightarrow \quad (1-x) = \sqrt{\frac{1}{1+y}}$

$\Rightarrow \quad x = 1 - \sqrt{\frac{1}{1+y}}$

Ex. 8: If x be so small that its square and higher power may be neglected, find the value of the $\frac{(1+2x)^{1/2}(16+3x)^{1/4}}{(1-x)^2}$ at $x = ½$.

Sol.: We have $\frac{(1+2x)^{1/2}(16+3x)^{1/4}}{(1-x)^2}$.

$$= \frac{(1+2x)^{\frac{1}{2}} \times 2\left(1+\frac{3}{4}x\right)^{\frac{1}{4}}}{(1-x)^2}$$

$$\frac{2\times(1+x+..)\times\left(1+\frac{3}{4}\times\frac{1}{4}x+...\right)}{(1-x)^2}$$

$$= \frac{2\times(1+x)\times\left(1+\frac{3}{16}x\right)}{(1-x)^2}$$

$$= 2\left(1+x+\frac{3}{16}x\right)\times(1-x)^{-2}$$
$$= 2\left(1+\frac{19}{16}x\right)\times(1+2x+....)$$
$$= 2\left(1+2x+\frac{19}{16}x\right)$$
$$= 2\left(1+\frac{51}{16}x\right)$$

Hence, the required value $= 2\left(1+\frac{51}{32}\right) = 2\times\frac{83}{32} = \frac{83}{16}$

$$= 5\frac{3}{16}$$

Ex. 9: If for small values of x, $\frac{(1+2x)^{1/2}+(16+3x)^{1/4}}{(1-2x)^{1/4}}$ is very nearly equal to $a+bx$, then find the values of a and b.

Sol.: We have $\frac{(1+2x)^{1/2}+(16+3x)^{1/4}}{(1-2x)^{1/4}}$

$$= \frac{(1+x+..)+2\left(1+\frac{3}{4}x\right)^{\frac{1}{4}}}{(1-2x)^{\frac{1}{4}}}$$
$$= \frac{(1+x+..)+2\left(1+\frac{3}{16}x\right)}{(1-2x)^{\frac{1}{4}}}$$
$$= \left(3+\frac{11}{8}x\right)\times(1-2x)^{-\frac{1}{4}}$$
$$= \left(3+\frac{11}{8}x\right)\times\left(1+\frac{1}{2}x\right)$$
$$= \left(3+\frac{23}{8}x\right)$$

Thus , $a = 3$ and $b = \frac{23}{8}$

Ex.10: If x be a quantity so small that x^3 may be neglected in comparison of a^3, prove that

$$\sqrt{\frac{a}{a+x}}+\sqrt{\frac{a}{a-x}} = 2+\frac{3x^2}{4a^2}$$

Sol.: We have $\sqrt{\frac{a}{a+x}}+\sqrt{\frac{a}{a-x}}$

$$= \left(1+\frac{x}{a}\right)^{-\frac{1}{2}}+\left(1-\frac{x}{a}\right)^{-\frac{1}{2}}$$
$$= \left(1-\frac{x}{2a}+\frac{3x^2}{8a^2}-..\right)+\left(1+\frac{x}{2a}+\frac{3x^2}{8a^2}+..\right)$$
$$= \left(2+\frac{3x^2}{4a^2}\right)$$

Ex.11: If p be nearly equal to q, then prove that

$$\frac{5p+4q}{4p+5q} = \left(\frac{p}{q}\right)^{1/9}$$

Sol.: Let $p = q + h$.

$$\Rightarrow \frac{p}{q} = 1+\frac{q}{h}$$

We have $\frac{5p+4q}{4p+5q}$

$$= \frac{5\left(\frac{p}{q}\right)+4}{4\left(\frac{p}{q}\right)+5} = \frac{5\left(1+\frac{q}{h}\right)+4}{4\left(1+\frac{q}{h}\right)+5} = \frac{\left(9+\frac{5q}{h}\right)}{\left(9+\frac{4q}{h}\right)}$$
$$= \left(1+\frac{5q}{9h}\right)\left(1+\frac{4q}{9h}\right)^{-1} = \left(1+\frac{5q}{9h}\right)\left(1-\frac{4q}{9h}\right)$$
$$= \left(1+\frac{5q}{9h}-\frac{4q}{9h}\right) = \left(1+\frac{q}{9h}\right)$$
$$= \left(1+\frac{q}{h}\right)^{\frac{1}{9}} = \left(\frac{p}{q}\right)^{\frac{1}{9}}$$

Ex.12: If x be nearly equal to 1, then prove that

$$\frac{mx^m - nx^n}{m-n} = x^{m+n}$$

Sol.: Let $x = 1+h$.

Then $\frac{mx^m - nx^n}{m-n} = \frac{m(1+h)^m - n(1+h)^n}{m-n}$

$$= \frac{m(1+mh+...)-n(1+nh+...)}{m-n}$$
$$= \frac{(m-n)+h(m^2-n^2)}{m-n}$$
$$= (1+(m+n)\,h)$$
$$= (1+h)^{(m+n)}$$
$$= x^{(m+n)}$$

Ex.13: Find the sum of the infinite series $1+\frac{1}{3}+\frac{1.3}{3.6}+\frac{1.3.5}{3.6.9}+....$

Sol.: As we know that $(1+x)^n = 1+nx+\frac{n(n-1)}{2}x^2+....$

On comparing, we get, $nx = \frac{1}{3}$ & $\frac{nx(nx-x)}{2} = \frac{1}{6}$

$\Rightarrow$ $x = -\frac{2}{3}$ and $n = -\frac{1}{2}$

Thus, the require sum $= \left(1-\frac{2}{3}\right)^{-\frac{1}{2}}$

$$= \left(\frac{1}{3}\right)^{-\frac{1}{2}}$$
$$= \sqrt{3}$$

Level – I Questions Based on Fundamentals

ABC of Binomial Theorem

1. Expand the following expression by binomial theorem :
   i. $(x^2+2a)^5$ ii. $(2x-3y)^4$ iii. $(a+b)^4$
   iv. $(a+b)^5$ v. $(a+b)^6$ vi. $(1+x^2)^4$
2. Find the number of terms in the expansion of
   i. $\left(x+\frac{1}{x}\right)^{10}$ ii. $\left(\frac{2}{x}+\frac{x}{2}\right)^8$
   iii. $(3x+3y)^n$ iv. $(1+2x+x^2)^{20}$
   v. $(x^3-3x^2+3x-1)^{33}$ vi. $(x^4+4x^3+6x^2+4x+1)^{50}$
   vii. $(a+b)^{50}+(a-b)^{50}$ viii. $(a+b)^{25}+(a-b)^{25}$
   ix. $(a+b)^{15}-(a-b)^{15}$
3. Find the
   i. 10th term in the expansion of $\left(2x^2+\frac{1}{x}\right)^{12}$
   ii. 6th term in the expansion of $\left(\frac{4x}{5}-\frac{5}{2x}\right)^9$
   iii. 7th term in the expansion of $\left(3x-\frac{x^3}{6}\right)^{10}$
   iv. 5th term from the end in the expansion of $\left(\frac{x^3}{2}-\frac{2}{x^2}\right)^9$
   v. 4th term from the end in the expansion of $\left(y+\frac{1}{y}\right)^{20}$
   vi. 11th term from the end in the expansion of $\left(2x-\frac{1}{x^2}\right)^{25}$

General Terms of the Binomial Expansion

4. Wrtite down the general terms in the expansion of
   i. $(x^2-y)^6$ ii. $(1-x^2)^{12}$ iii. $\left(x^2-\frac{1}{x}\right)^{10}$
   iv. $\left(\frac{x^2}{a^2}+\frac{b^2}{x^3}\right)^{20}$ v. $(1+2x+x^2)$ vi. $\left(x+\frac{1}{x}\right)^{50}$
5. Find the co-efficient of
   i. x^{10} in the expansion of $\left(2x^2-\frac{1}{x}\right)^{20}$
   ii. x^7 in the expansion of $\left(x-\frac{1}{x^2}\right)^{40}$
   iii. x^9 in the expansion of $\left(x^2-\frac{1}{3x}\right)^9$
   iv. x^m in the expansion of $\left(x+\frac{1}{x}\right)^n$
   v. x^5 in the expansion of $(1+2x)^6\ (1-x)^7$
6. Find co-efficient of x^{50} in expansion of $(1+x)^{41}(1-x+x^2)^{40}$.
7. Prove that co-efficient of x^p in expansion of $\left(x^2+\frac{1}{x}\right)^{2n}$ is $\left(\frac{(2n)!}{((4n-P)/3)!((2n+P)/3)!}\right)$.
8. In the binomial expansion of $(1+a)^{m+n}$, prove that the co-efficient of a^m and a^n are equal.
9. Prove that the co-efficient of x^n in $(1+x)^{2n}$ is twice the co-efficient of x^n is $(1+x)^{2n-1}$.
10. In the expansion of $(1+x)^n$, the co-efficients of the pth and qth terms are equal, prove that $p+q=n+2,\ p\neq q$.
11. If the co-efficient. of 2nd, and 3rd and 4th terms in expansion of $(1+x)^{2n}$ are in $A.P.$, prove that $2n^2-9n+7=0$.
12. If in the expansion of $(1-x)^{2n-1}$, co-efficient of x^r is denoted by a_r, then prove that $a_{r-1}+a_{2n-r}=0$.
13. If a_1, a_2, a_3, a_4 be the co-efficient of four consecutive terms in the expansion of $(1+x)^n$, prove that
   $$\frac{a_1}{a_1+a_2}+\frac{a_3}{a_3+a_4}=\frac{2a_2}{a_2+a_3}.$$

Middle Term in the Binomial Expansion

14. Find the middle term in the expansion of
   i. $\left(\frac{a}{x}+bx\right)^{12}$ ii. $\left(x^2-\frac{2}{x}\right)^{10}$ iii. $\left(\frac{x}{a}-\frac{a}{x}\right)^{10}$
   iv. $\left(2x^2-\frac{1}{x}\right)^7$ v. $\left(x^4-\frac{1}{x}\right)^{11}$ vi. $\left(2x-\frac{2}{x^2}\right)^{15}$
   vii. $(x+x^2)^{2013}$ viii. $(1+3x+3x^2+x^3)^{2n}$
15. Prove that the middle term in the expansion of $(1+x)^{2n}$ is $\frac{1.3.5........(2n-1)}{n!}\times 2^n\times x^n$.

Term Independent of the Variable

16. Find the term independent of variable in the expansion of
   i. $\left(3x^2-\frac{1}{2x^3}\right)^{10}$ ii. $\left(x-\frac{1}{x}\right)^{12}$
   iii. $\left(2x-\frac{1}{x}\right)^{10}$ iv. $\left(\frac{3}{2}x^2-\frac{1}{3x}\right)^6$
17. Find the absolute term in the expansion of $\left(x-\frac{1}{x}\right)^{12}$
18. Find the constant terms in the expansion of $\left(x+\frac{1}{x^4}\right)^{10}$
19. Find the term in the expansion of $\left(x^3-\frac{3}{x^2}\right)^{15}$ which does not contain x.

Co-efficient Related Problems

20. Find the coefficient of x^n in the expansion of $(1+x)(1-x)^n$
21. Find the co-efficient of x^n in the expansion of $(1-x)^2(1+x)^n$
22. If the coefficient of x and x^2 in the expansion of $(1+x)^m(1-x)^n$ are 3 and –6 respectively, then find the values of m and n.
23. If the third term in the expansion of $\left(\frac{1}{x}+x^{\log x}\right)^5$ is 1000, find n.
24. Find the co-efficient of x^4 in expansion of $(1+x+x^2+x^3)^n$
25. Find the co-efficient of x^5 in the expansion of $(1+x+x^3)^{10}$

26. Find the co-efficient of x^4 in expansion of $(1+x+x^2+x^3)^{10}$.
27. How many terms are free from radical signs in the expansion of $\left(x^{\frac{1}{5}}+y^{\frac{-1}{10}}\right)^{55}$
28. Find number of integral terms in expansion of $\left(5^{\frac{1}{2}}+7^{\frac{1}{8}}\right)^{1024}$
29. Find the sum of the rational term in $\left(2^{\frac{1}{2}}+3^{\frac{1}{5}}\right)^{10}$
30. Find the co-efficient of x^8 in $1+(1+x)+(1+x)^2+(1+x)^3+..........+(1+x)^n$
31. Find the co-efficient of x^5 in the expansion of $(1+x)^{21}+(1+x)^{22}+.......+(1+x)^{30}$.
32. Find the number of term in $(1+x)^{101}(1-x+x^2)^{100}$
33. Find the co-efficient of x^{10} in $(1+x)^{11}+(1+x)^{22}+(1+x)^{23}+.........+(1+x)^{50}$
34. Find the co-efficent of x^r in $(x+3)^{n-1}+(x+3)^{n-2}(x+2)+(x+3)^{n-3}(x+2)^2+.........+(x+2)^{n-1}$
35. Find the coefficient of t^{24} in $(1+t^2)^{12}(1+t^{12})(1+t^{24})$.

Divisibility Related Problems

36. Using Binomial Theorem
    i. Prove that $2^{3n}-7n-1$ is divisible by 49, $n\in N$
    ii. Prove that $9^{n+1}-8n-9$ is divisible by 64, $n\in N$
    iii. Prove that $6^{n+2}+7^{2n+1}$ is divisible by 43, $n\in N$
    iv. Prove that $2^{3n+3}-7n-8$ is divisible by 49, $n\in N$
    v. Prove that 4^n-3n-1 is divisible by 9, $n\in N$
    vi. Prove that $3^{4n+1}+16n-3$ is divisible by 256., $n\in N$
    vii. Prove that $11^{n+2}+12^{2n+1}$ is divisible by 133, $n\in N$
    viii. Prove that $2^{n+1}-9n^2+3n-2$ is divisible by 54 for sll n.
    ix. Suppose m, n are integers and $m=n^2-n$, then prove that m^2-2m is divisible by 24.
    x. Find the remainder when 6^n-5n is divided by 25.
    xi. Find the remainder when 7^{98} is divided by 5.
    xii. Prove that $11^{10}-1$ is divisible by 100.
    xiii. Prove that $53^{53}-33^3$ is divisible by 10.

Unit Digit/Last Two Digit of a Number

37. i. Find the unit digit of the number 27^{50}
    ii. Find the unit digit of the number 9^{9^9}
    iii. Find the unit digit of the number 2^{3^4}
    iv. Find the last two digit of the number 17^{10}
    v. Find the last two digit of the number 3^{999}
    vi. Prove that $1^{1997}+2^{1997}+3^{1997}+.....1996^{1997}$ is divisible by 1997.

Integral and Fractional Part of a Number

38. Show that integral part of $\left(5+2\sqrt{6}\right)^n$ is odd, where $n\in N$
39. Show that integral part of $\left(11+5\sqrt{5}\right)^{2n+1}$ is even, where $n\in N$.
40. If $x=\left(8+3\sqrt{7}\right)^n$, where $n\in N$, then prove that $x-x^2+x[x]=1$, where [,] = G.I.F
41. If $\left(7+4\sqrt{3}\right)^n=x+t$, where n and x are +ve integers and t is a proper fraction . Show that $(1-t)(x+t)=1$
42. Find integer just greater than number $\left(3+\sqrt{5}\right)^5$
43. Find the integer just less than or equal to $\left(\sqrt{3}+1\right)^6$

Properties of Binomial Coefficients

44. Prove that in the expansion of $(1+x)^n$
    i. $C_0+C_1+C_2+..........+C_n=2^n$
    ii $C_1+C_2+...............+C_n=2^n-1$
    iii. $C_0+C_2+C_4+..............=2^{n-1}$
    iv. $C_1+C_3+C_5+..............=2^{n-1}$
    v. ${}^nC_r={}^nC_{n-r}$
    vi. ${}^nC_x={}^nC_y\Rightarrow x=y$ or $x+y=n$
    vii. ${}^nC_r=\frac{n}{r}\times{}^{n-1}C_{r-1}=\frac{n(n-1)}{r(r-1)}\times{}^{n-2}C_{r-2}$ and so on.
    viii. $\frac{{}^nC_r}{{}^nC_{r-1}}=\frac{n-r+1}{r}$
    ix. ${}^nC_r+{}^nC_{r-1}={}^{n+1}C_r$
    x. ${}^nc_1-2.{}^nc_2+3.{}^nc_3-4.{}^nc_4+5.{}^nc_5-......-n.{}^nc_n=0$
    xi. ${}^{2n+1}c_0+{}^{2n+1}c_1+{}^{2n+1}c_2+........+{}^{2n+1}c_n=2^{2n}$
45. Find the values of each of the followings:
    i. ${}^{10}c_0+{}^{10}c_1+{}^{10}c_2+...........+{}^{10}c_{10}$
    ii. ${}^{11}c_1+{}^{11}c_2+{}^{11}c_3+.............+{}^{11}c_{10}$.
    iii. ${}^{16}c_4+{}^{16}c_5+..........+{}^{16}c_{16}$.
    iv. ${}^{20}c_{10}+{}^{20}c_{11}+............+{}^{20}c_{20}$.
    v. $\sum_{r=0}^{10}{}^{20}c_r$
    vi. ${}^{13}C_1+{}^{13}C_3+{}^{13}C_5+.............+{}^{13}C_{11}$
    vii. ${}^{20}C_2+{}^{20}C_4+{}^{20}C_6+.............+{}^{20}C_{18}$
    viii. ${}^{13}c_2+{}^{13}c_3+{}^{13}c_4+............+{}^{13}c_{13}$
    ix. If $S=\frac{1}{2}{}^{10}c_0-{}^{10}c_1+2.{}^{10}c_2-2^2.{}^{10}c_3+.....+2^9.{}^{10}c_{10}$, then find S
    x. ${}^{16}C_1-2.{}^{16}C_2+3.{}^{16}C_3-...........-16.{}^{16}C_{16}$.

46. Prove that

i. $\sum_{r=0}^{n} 3^r\,{}^nc_r = 4^n$

ii. $\sum_{r=0}^{n} 7^r\,{}^nc_r = 8^n$

iii. $\sum_{r=0}^{n} \left(\frac{1}{2}\right)^r {}^nc_r = \left(\frac{3}{2}\right)^n$

iv. $nC_1 + nC_2 + nC_3 + nC_4 + \dots nC_n$
$= 1 + 2 + 2^2 + 2^3 + \dots + 2^{n-1}$

47. Prove that

$${}^nC_r + {}^{n-1}C_r + {}^{n-2}C_r + \dots\dots + {}^rC_r = {}^{n+1}C_{r+1}$$

48. Find the value of

i. ${}^{20}C_2 + {}^{19}C_2 + {}^{18}C_2 + {}^{17}C_2 + \dots\dots + {}^2C_2$

ii. ${}^{50}C_4 + {}^{49}C_4 + {}^{48}C_4 + {}^{47}C_4 + \dots\dots + {}^4C_4$

iii. ${}^{2n+1}C_n + {}^{2n}C_n + {}^{2n-1}C_n + {}^{2n-2}C_n + \dots\dots + {}^nC_n$.

iv. ${}^{11}C_3 + {}^{10}C_3 + {}^9C_3 + {}^8C_3 + \dots\dots + {}^3C_3$

v. ${}^{2011}C_{11} + {}^{2010}C_{11} + {}^{2009}C_{11} + \dots\dots + {}^{11}C_{11}$

49. If $\left(1+x+x^2\right)^n = a_0 + a_1x + a_2x^2 + a_3x^3 + \dots\dots + a_{2n}x^{2n}$, then prove that

i. $a_0 + a_1 + a_2 + \dots\dots + a_{2n} = 3^n$

ii. $a_0 - a_1 + a_2 - \dots\dots + a_{2n} = 1$

iii. $a_0 + a_2 + a_4 + \dots\dots + a_{2n} = \frac{3^n + 1}{2}$

iv. $a_1 + a_3 + a_5 + \dots\dots + a_{2n-1} = \frac{3^n - 1}{2}$.

50. If $\frac{\left(1+x-x^2\right)^{10}}{1+x^2} = a_0 + a_1x + a_2x^2 + \dots + a_nx^n + \dots$, then prove that

i. $a_0 + a_1 + a_2 + \dots\dots = \frac{1}{2}$

ii. $a_0 - a_1 + a_2 - \dots\dots = \frac{1}{2}$

iii. $a_0 + a_2 + a_4 + \dots\dots = \frac{1}{2}$

iv. $a_1 + a_3 + a_5 + \dots\dots = 0$

51. Prove that

i. $c_0 - c_2 + c_4 - c_6 + \dots\dots = 2^{\frac{n}{2}}\cos\left(\frac{n\pi}{4}\right)$

ii. $c_1 - c_3 + c_5 - c_7 + \dots\dots = 2^{\frac{n}{2}}\sin\left(\frac{n\pi}{4}\right)$

iii. $c_0 + c_4 + c_8 + c_{12} + \dots\dots = 2^{n-2} + 2^{\frac{n}{2}}\cos\left(\frac{n\pi}{4}\right)$.

iv. $c_1 + c_5 + c_9 + c_{13} + \dots\dots = 2^{n-2} + 2^{\frac{n}{2}}\sin\left(\frac{n\pi}{4}\right)$

52. Find the co-efficient of x^{50} in the expression

$$(1+x)^{1000} + 2x(1+x)^{999} + 3x^2(1+x)^{998} + \dots + 1001x^{1000}$$

53. Given $s_n = 1 + q + q^2 + \dots + q^n$ and

$T_n = 1 + \frac{q+1}{2} + \left(\frac{q+1}{2}\right)^2 + \left(\frac{q+1}{2}\right)^3 + \dots + \left(\frac{q+1}{2}\right)^n, q \neq -1$

then prove that

$${}^{n+1}C_1 + {}^{n+!}C_2.s_1 + {}^{n+!}C_3.s_2 \rightleftarrows + \dots\dots + {}^{n+!}C_{n+1}.s_n = 2^n.T_n$$

54. If $(1+x)^n = \sum^{n} {}^nC_rx^r$, then prove the following:

i. $C_0 + 2C_1 + 3.C_2 + \dots + (n+1)C_n = (n+2).2^{n-1}$

ii. $C_1 + 2.C_2 + 3.C_3 + \dots\dots + nC_n = n.2^{n-1}$

iii. $C_0 + 3.C_1 + 5.C_2 + \dots\dots + (2n+1)\,C_n = (n+1).2^{n-1}$

iv. $C_3 + 2.C_4 + 3.C_5 + \dots + (n-2)\,C_n = (n-4)2^{n-1} + n + 2, n \geq 3$

v. $C_0 - 3.C_1 + 5.C_2 - \dots\dots + (-1)n\,(2n+1)\,C_n = 0$

vi. $C_0 - 2.C_1 + 3.C_2 - \dots\dots + (-1)^n\,(n+1)\,C_n = 0$

vii. $a - (a-1)C_1 + (a-2)C_2 - (a-3)C_3 + \dots\dots + (-1)^n$
$(a-n)\,C_n = 0$

viii. $1^2C_1 + 2^2.C_2 + 3^2.C_3 + \dots\dots + n^2.C_n = n(n+1).2^{n-2}$.

ix. $C_0 + \frac{C_1}{2} + \frac{C_2}{3} + \dots\dots + \frac{C_n}{n+1} = \frac{2^{n+1}}{n+1}$

x. $2C_0 + \frac{2^2.C_1}{2} + \frac{2^3.C_2}{3} + \dots\dots + \frac{2^{n+1}.C_n}{n+1} = \frac{3^{n+2} - 2n - 5}{(n+1)(n+2)}$

xi. $\frac{2^2}{1.2}C_0 + \frac{2^3}{2.3}C_1 + \frac{2^4}{3.4}C_2 + \dots\dots + \frac{2^{n+1}.C_n}{(n+1)(n+2)}$
$= \frac{3^{n+2} - 2n - 5}{(n+1)(n+2)}$

xii. $\frac{C_1}{C_0} + \frac{2.C_2}{C_1} + \frac{3.C_3}{C_2} + \dots\dots + \frac{n.C_n}{C_{n-1}} = \frac{1}{2} \times n(n+1)$.

xiii. $(C_0 + C_1)(C_1 + C_2)(C_2 + C_3)\dots\dots(C_{n-1} + C_n)$
$= C_1.C_2.C_3 \dots\dots C_n \frac{(n+1)^n}{(n)!}$

xiv. $C_0C_r + C_1C_{r+1} + C_2C_{r+2} + \dots\dots + C_{n-r}C_n$
$= \frac{(2n)!}{(n-r)! \times (n+r)}$.

xv. ${}^mC_r{}^mC_0 + {}^mC_{r-1}{}^nC_1 + {}^mC_{r-2}{}^nC_2 + \dots\dots + {}^mC_0{}^nC_r = {}^{m+n}C_r$.

xvi. $C_0^2 - C_1^2 + C_2^2 - C_3^2 + \dots\dots + (-1)^nC_n^2 = \begin{cases} 0, \text{if } n \text{ is odd} \\ (-1)^{n/2}\,{}^nC_{n/2}, \\ \text{if } n \text{ iseven} \end{cases}$

xvii. ${}^{2n}C_0^2 - {}^{2n}C_1^2 + {}^{2n}C_2^2 - {}^{2n}C_3^2 + \dots + (-1)^n.{}^{2n}C_{2n}^2$
$= (-1)^n.\,{}^{2n}C_n$.

xviii. $C_1^2 + 2.C_2^2 + 3.C_3^2 + \dots\dots + n.C_n^2 = \frac{(2n-1)!}{\{(n-1)!\}^2}$

55. If $a_n = \sum_{r=0}^{n}\left(\frac{1}{^nC_r}\right)$, then prove that $\sum_{r=0}^{n}\left(\frac{r}{^nC_r}\right) = \frac{na_n}{2}$.

56. If $a_1, a_2, a_3, \ldots, a_n$ are in A.P, then prove that $\sum_{k=0}^{n} {^nC_k}.a_{k+1}$ $= 2^{n-1}(a_1 + a_{n+1})$.

57. Prove that $\sum_{r=1}^{n}\left(\frac{^{2n}C_{2r-1}}{r}\right) = \frac{2}{2n+1}\left(2^{2n}-1\right)$.

58. Prove that $\sum_{r=0}^{n} {^nC_r}(2r-n)^2 = n.2^n$.

59. Prove that

i. $\frac{C_1}{C_0} + 2.\frac{C_2}{C_1} + 3.\frac{C_3}{C_2} + \ldots\ldots + n.\frac{C_{n+!}}{C_n} = \frac{n(n+1)}{2}$

ii. $(C_0 + C_1)(C_1 + C_2)\ldots\ldots(C_{n-1} + C_n)$ $= \frac{(n+1)^n}{n!} \times C_0.C_1.C_2\ldots\ldots C_{n-1}$

60. In the expansion of $(1+x)^n$, prove that

i. $c_0^2 + c_1^2 + \ldots\ldots + c_n^2 = \frac{(2n)!}{(n!)^2}$

ii. $c_0c_1 + c_1c_2 + c_2c_3 + \ldots + c_{n-1}c_n = \frac{n \times 2^n \times \{1.3.5\ldots(2n-1)\}}{(n+1)!}$

iii. $c_0c_r + c_1c_{r+1} + \ldots\ldots + c_{n-r}c_n = \frac{(2n)!}{(n-r)!(n+r)!}$.

iv. $^{14}C_0.{^{15}C_1} + {^{14}C_1}.{^{15}C_2} + {^{14}C_2}.{^{15}C_3} + \ldots + {^{14}C_{14}}.{^{15}C_{15}} = {^{29}C_{14}}$

v. $\binom{30}{0}\binom{30}{10} - \binom{30}{1}\binom{30}{11} + \binom{30}{2}\binom{30}{12} + \ldots + \binom{30}{20}\binom{30}{30} = {^{30}C_{10}}$.

vi. $^mC_r + {^mC_{r-1}}.{^mC_1} + {^mC_{r-2}}.{^mC_2} + \ldots + {^mC_1}.{^nC_{r-1}} + {^nC_r}$ $= {^{m+n}C_r}$.

Greatest Term in Expansion of $(a+x)^n$

61. Find the greatest term in the expnasion of

i. $(3+2x)^{50}$, where x = 1/5

ii. $(2-5x)^{21}$, where x = 1/3

iii. $(2+3x)^9$, where x = 3/2

Greatest Coefficients in Expansion of $(1+x)^n$

62. Find the greatest coefficient in the expansion of

i. $(1+x)^{10}$ ii. $(1+x)^{2n+2}$ iii. $(1+x)^{2n}$

Sum of Co-efficients

63. Find the sum of the co-efficients in the expansion of

i. $(x+2y+z)^{10}$

ii. $(p^2x^2-2px+1)^{51}$, when $p = 1$

iii. $(1+2x-3x^2)^{2010}$

iv. $(x^3-x-1)^{2012}$

v. $(2x+3y-4z)^{2011}$.

Multinomial Theorem (For a Positive Integral Index)

64. Find the co-efficient of $a^4b^3c^2d$ in expansion of $(a-b+c-d)^9$

65. Find the greatest co-efficient in expansion of $(a+b+c+d)^{15}$.

66. Find the co-efficient of x^7 in the expansion of $(1+3x-2x^3)^{10}$

67. Find the number of terms in expansion of $(x+y+z+w)^n$, $n \in N$.

68. Find the co-efficient of $a^3b^4c^5$ in expansion of $(bc+ca+ab)^6$

Use of Differentiation

69. If $(1+x)^n = C_0 + C_1x + C_2x^2 + \ldots\ldots + C_nx^n$, then prove that

i. $C_1 + 2.C_2 + 3.C_3 + \ldots\ldots + n.C_n = 2.2^{n-1}$

ii. $C_0 + 2.C_1 + 3.C_2 + \ldots\ldots + (n+1)C_n = (n+2)2^{n-1}$

iii. $C_0 + 3C_1 + 5C_2 + \ldots\ldots + (2n+1)C_n = (n+1)2^n$.

iv. $C_0 - 2C_1 + 3C_2 - 4C_3 + \ldots\ldots + (-1)^n(n+1)C_n = 0$

v. $C_0 - 3C_1 + 5C_2 - 7C_3 + \ldots + (-1)^n(2n+1)C_n = 0$

vi. $C_1 + 2^2C_2 + 3^2C_3 + \ldots\ldots + n^2C_n = n(n+1)2^{n-2}$

Use of Integration

70. If $C_r = {^nC_r}$, then prove that

i. $C_0 + \frac{C_1}{2} + \frac{C_2}{3} + \ldots\ldots + \frac{C_n}{n+1} = \frac{2^{n+1}-1}{n+1}$

ii. $C_0 - \frac{C_1}{2} + \frac{C_2}{3} - \ldots\ldots + (-1)^n\frac{C_n}{n+1} = \frac{1}{n+1}$.

iii. $\frac{C_0}{1} + \frac{C_2}{3} + \frac{C_4}{5} + \ldots\ldots = \frac{2^n}{n+1}$.

iv. $\frac{C_1}{2} + \frac{C_3}{4} + \frac{C_5}{6} + \ldots\ldots = \frac{2^n-1}{n+1}$.

v. $3C_0 + 3^2\frac{C_1}{2} + 3^3\frac{C_2}{3} + 3^4\frac{C_3}{4} + \ldots + 3^{n+1}\frac{C_n}{n+1} = \frac{4^{n+1}-1}{n+1}$

vi. $C_0 - \frac{C_1}{2} + \frac{C_2}{3} - \frac{C_3}{4} + \ldots\ldots + (-1)^n\frac{C_n}{n+1} = \frac{1}{n+1}$.

Binomial Theorem for Any Index

71. Write down the expansion of

i. $(1+x)^{-1}$ ii. $(1+x)^{-2}$ iii. $(1+x)^{-3}$

72. Write down the expaqnsion of

i. $(1-x)^{-1}$ ii. $(1-x)^{-2}$ iii. $(1-x)^{-3}$

73. Find the co-efficient of x^n in the expansion of

i $\frac{1}{1-3x}$ ii. $\frac{1}{1+4x}$ iii. $\frac{1}{(1-3x)(1-4x)}$

iv. $\frac{1}{(1-ax)(1-bx)}$ v. $\left(\frac{1-x}{1+x}\right)^2$ vi. $\left(\frac{1+x}{1-x}\right)^2$

74. Find the first negative term in expansion of $\left(1+\frac{3}{4}x\right)^{13/3}$, where $0<x<4/3$.

75. Find the coefficient of x^4 in the expansion of $\frac{1-x}{1+x}$, where $|x|<1$

76. Find the co-efficient of x^n in the expansion of $(1-4x)^{-1/2}$

77. Find a,b so that the co-efficient of x^n in the expansion of $\frac{a+bx}{(1-x)^2}$ may be $2n+1$ and hence find the sum of the series

$$1+3\left(\frac{1}{2}\right)+5\left(\frac{1}{2}\right)^2+\ldots\ldots$$

78. Find the co-efficient of x^{12} in expansion of $(1+x+x^2+x^3+\ldots\ldots\ldots x^n)^4$

79. Assuming that x to be so small such that x^2 and higher power of x be neglected, show that

$$\frac{\left(1+\frac{3}{4}x\right)^{-4}(16-3x)^{1/2}}{(8+x)^{2/3}}=\left(1-\frac{305}{96}x\right).$$

80. Assuming theat x is very small so that its second and higher powers may be neglected, then prove that

$$\frac{(1-2x)^{2/3}(4+5x)^{3/2}}{\sqrt{1-x}}=\left(8+\frac{25}{3}x\right)$$

81. If p is nearly equal to q and $n>1$, then show that

$$\frac{(n+1)p+(n-1)q}{(n-1)p+(n+1)q}=\left(\frac{p}{q}\right)^{1/n}$$

82. If x is nearly equal to 1, prove that $\frac{ax^b-bx^a}{x^b-x^a}=\frac{1}{1-x}$ nearly.

83. Find the sum of the series $1+\frac{1}{3}+\frac{1.3}{5.6}+\frac{1.3.5}{3.6.9}+\ldots\ldots$ to ∞

84. Find the sum of the series $1+\frac{1}{4}+\frac{1.3}{4.8}+\frac{1.3.5}{4.8.12}+\ldots\ldots$ to ∞

85. Find the sum of the series $1+\frac{2}{6}+\frac{2.5}{6.12}+\frac{2.5.8}{6.12.18}+\ldots\ldots$ to ∞

Answers Key

37. i. 9, ii. 9, iii. 2, iv 49, v. 67 **39.** 3936 **40.** 415 **74.** 7th terrm **75.** 2

76. $\frac{(2n)!}{(n!)^2}$ **77.** 6 **78.** 375. **83.** $\sqrt{3}$ **84.** 2 **85.** $4^{1/3}$

Level – II For JEE- Main and Advanced Exams

1. The first 3 terms in the expansion of $(1+ax)^n$ $(n\neq 0)$ are 1, $6x$ and $16x^2$. Then the value of a and n are respectively.

i. 2 and 9 ii. 3 and 2
iii. 2/3 and 9 iv. 3/2 and 6

2. The last term in the binomial expansion of $\left(\sqrt[3]{2}-\frac{1}{\sqrt{2}}\right)^n$ is $\left(\frac{1}{3.\sqrt[3]{9}}\right)^{\log_3 8}$ Then the 5th term from the beginning is

a. ${}^{10}C_6$ b. $2.{}^{10}C_4$
c. $\frac{1}{2}\,{}^{10}C_4$ d. None of these

3. If 6th term in the expansion of $\left(\frac{1}{x^{8/3}}+x^2\log_{10}x\right)^8$ is 5600, then $x=$

a. 8 b. 9
c. 10 d. None of these

4. In the expension of $\left(\frac{3x^2}{2}-\frac{1}{3x}\right)^9$, term independent of x is

a. ${}^9C_3\cdot\frac{1}{6^3}$ b. ${}^9C_3\left(\frac{3}{2}\right)^3$
c. ${}^9C_3$ d. None of these

5. In the expansion of $\left(x+\frac{1}{x}\right)^{2n}$ $(n\in N)$, the term independent of x is

a. $\frac{1.3.5....(2n-1)}{n!}2^n$ b. $\frac{(2n)!}{n!}$
c. $\frac{(2n)!}{n!}2^n$ d. $\frac{n!}{(2n)!}$

6. The coefficient of x^7 in the expansion of $\left(\frac{x^2}{2}-\frac{2}{x}\right)^8$ is

a. –56 b. 56
c. –14 d. 14

7. If the coefficient of $(2r+4)^{th}$ and $(r-2)^{th}$ terms in the expension of $(1+x)^{18}$ are equal, then $r=$

a. 12 b. 10
c. 8 d. 6

8. If the co-efficients of T_r, T_{r+1}, T_{r+2} terms of $(1+x)^{14}$ are in A.P., then $r=$

a. 6 b. 7
c. 8 d. 9

9. The coefficient of x^3 in $\left(\sqrt{x^5}+\frac{3}{\sqrt{x^3}}\right)^6$ is

a. 0 b. 120
c. 420 d. 540

10. In the expension of $(1+ax)^n, n \in N$, the coefficient of x and x^2 are 8 and 24 respectively. Then

a. $a=2, n=4$ b. $a=4, n=2$
c. $a=2, n=2$ d. $a=-2, n=4$

11. The number of terms in the expansion of (a+b+c)n will be

a. $n+1$ b. $n+3$
c. $\frac{(n+1)(n+2)}{2}$ d. None of these

12. The expression $[x+(x^3-1)^{1/2}]^5+[x-(x^3-1)^{1/2}]^5$ is a polynomial of degree

a. 5 b. 6
c. 7 d. 8

13. The number of terms whose values depend on x in expansion of $\left(x^2-2+\frac{1}{x^2}\right)^n$ is

a. $2n+1$ b. $2n$
c. n d. None of these

14. The number of distinct terms in the expansion of $(x+2y-3z+5w-7u)^n$ is

a. $n+1$ b. ${}^{n+4}C_4$
c. ${}^{n+4}C_n$ d. $\frac{(n+1)(n+2)(n+3)(n+4)}{24}$

15. In how many terms in the expansion of $(x^{1/5}+y^{1/10})^{55}$ do not have fractional power of the variable.

a. 6 b. 7
c. 8 d. 10

16. The middle term in the expansion of $\left(\frac{2x}{3}-\frac{3}{2x^2}\right)^{2n}$ is

a. ${}^{2n}C_n$ b. $(-1)^n\frac{(2n)!}{(n!)^2}, x^{-n}$
c. ${}^{2n}C_n \cdot \frac{1}{x^n}$ d. None

17. If the sum of the coefficients in the expansion of $(x+y)^n$ is 1024, then value of the greatest coefficient in expansion is

a, 356 b. 252
c. 210 d. 120

18. The numerically greatest term of $(2+3x)^9$ when $x=3/2$ is

a. T_6 b. T_7
c. T_8 d. None of these

19. $\binom{n}{0}+2\binom{n}{1}+2^2\binom{n}{2}+.....+2^n\binom{n}{n}=$

a. 2^n b. 0
c. 3^n d. None of these

20. $C_0C_r+C_1C_{r+1}+C_2C_{r+2}+.......+C_{n-r}C_n=$

a. $\frac{(2n)!}{(n-r)!(n+r)!}$ b. $\frac{n!}{(-r)!(n+r)!}$
c. $\frac{n!}{(n-r)!}$ d. None

21. $\frac{C_1}{C_0}+2\frac{C_2}{C_1}+3\frac{C_3}{C_2}+......+15\frac{C_{15}}{C_{14}}=$

a. 100 b. 120
c. –120 d. one of these

22. The sum of $C_0^2-C_1^2+C_2^2-......+(-1)^nC_n^2$ where n is an even integer, is

a. ${}^{2n}C_n$ b. $(-1)^n\,{}^{2n}C_n$
c. ${}^{2n}C_{n-1}$ d. None of these

23. The sum of the coefficients of all the integral powers of x in the expansion of $(1+2\sqrt{x})^{40}$ is

a. $3^{40}+1$ b. $3^{40}-1$
c. $\frac{1}{2}(3^{40}-1)$ d. $\frac{1}{2}(3^{40}+1)$

24. The sum of all the coefficients in the binomial expansion of $(x^2+x-3)^{319}$ is

a. 1 b. 2
c. –1 d. 0

25. The sum of the coefficients in expansion of $(1+x-3x^2)^{2148}$ is

a. 7 b. 8
c. –1 d. 1

26. $\frac{1}{\sqrt{5+4x}}$ can be expanded by binomial theorem, if

a. $x<1$ b. $|x|<1$
c. $|x|<\frac{5}{4}$ d. $|x|<\frac{4}{5}$

27. The coefficient of x^4 in $\frac{1+2x+3x^2}{(1-x)^2}$ is

a. 13 b. 15
c. 20 d. 22

28. If n is a positive integer and three consecutive coefficients in the expansion of $(1+x)^n$ are in the ratio 6 : 33 : 110, then $n=$

a. 4 b. 6
c. 12 d. 16

29. The coefficient of x^3 in the expansion of $(1-x+x^2)^5$ is

a. 10 b. –20
c. –50 d. –30

30. The coefficient of $a^8b^6c^4$ in the expansion of $(a+b+c)^{18}$ is

a. ${}^{18}C_{14}.{}^{14}C_8$ b. ${}^{18}C_{10}.{}^{10}C_6$
c. ${}^{18}C_6.{}^{12}C_8$ d. ${}^{18}C_4.{}^{14}C_6$

31. The coefficient of $x^3.y^4.z$ in the expansion of $(1+x+y-z)^9$ is

a. $2.{}^9C_7.{}^7C_4$ b. $-2.{}^9C_2.{}^7C_3$
c. ${}^9C_7.{}^7C_4$ d. None of these

32. The number of integral terms in expansion of $(5^{1/2}+7^{1/6})^{642}$ is

a. 106 b. 108
c. 103 d. 109

33. The sum of the rational terms in expansion of $\left(\sqrt{2}+\sqrt[5]{3}\right)^{10}$ is

a. 32 b. 9
c. 41 d. None of these

34. If $R=\left(\sqrt{2}+1\right)^{2n+1}$ and $f=R-[R]$, where [ ] denotes the greatest integer function, then $[R]$ equal

a. $f+\frac{1}{f}$ b. $f-\frac{1}{f}$
c. $\frac{1}{f}-f$ d. None of these

35. If $\left(5+2\sqrt{6}\right)^n=1+f$, where $I\in N$, and $0\le f\le 1$, then 1 equals

a. $\frac{1}{f}-f$ b. $\frac{1}{1+f}-f$
(c) $\frac{1}{1-f}-f$ (d) $\frac{1}{1-f}+f$

36. If $R=\left(7+4\sqrt{3}\right)^{2n}=1+f$, where $I\in N$ and $0<f<1$, then $R(1-f)$ equals

a. $\left(7-4\sqrt{3}\right)^{2n}$ b. $\frac{1}{\left(7+4\sqrt{3}\right)}$
c. 1 d. None of these

37. The number of non-negative integral solutions of the equation $x+y+3z=33$ is

a. 120 b. 135
c. 210 d. 520

38. The coefficient of x^6 in the expansion of $(1+x-x^3)^8$ is

a. 80 b. 84
c. 88 d. 92

39. If the second term in expansion $\left(\sqrt[13]{a}+\frac{a}{\sqrt{a^{-1}}}\right)^n$ is $14a^{5/2}$, then the value of ${}^nC_3/{}^nC_2$ is

a. 4 b. 3
c. 12 c. 6

40. The coefficient of $x^8y^6z^4$ in the expansion of $(x+y+z)^{18}$ is

a. ${}^{18}C_{14}\times{}^{14}C_8$ b. ${}^{18}C_{10}\times{}^{10}C_6$
c. ${}^{18}C_6\times{}^{12}C_8$ d. All of these

41. The greatest value of the term independent of x in expansion of $(x\sin\alpha+x^{-1}\cos\alpha)^{10}$, $\alpha\in R$, is

a. 2^5 b. $\frac{10!}{(5!)^2}$
c. $\frac{10!}{2^5\times(5!)^2}$ d. None of these

42. If the fourth term in expansion of $\left\{\sqrt{x\left(\frac{1}{\log x+1}\right)}+x^{1/12}\right\}^6$ is equal to 200 and $x>1$, then $x=$

a. $10^{\sqrt{2}}$ b. 10
c. 10^4 d. one of these

43. Let $(1+x)^n=\sum_{r=0}^{n}C_rx^r$ and, $\frac{C_1}{C_0}+2\frac{C_2}{C_1}+3\frac{C_3}{C_2}+\ldots n\frac{C_n}{C_{n-1}}=\frac{1}{k}n(n+1)$, then the value of k is

a. $\frac{1}{2}$ b. 2
c. $\frac{1}{3}$ d. 3

44. Let $(1+x)^n=\sum_{r=0}^{n}C_rx^r$ and $\sum_{r=0}^{n}\frac{C_r}{r+1}=k$, then the value of k is

a. $\frac{2^{n+1}+1}{n+1}$ b. $\frac{2^{n+1}-1}{n+1}$
c. $\frac{2^n+1}{n+1}$ d. $\frac{2^n-1}{n+1}$

45. The coefficient of x^{50} in expression $(1+x)^{1000}+2x(1+x)^{999}+3x^2(1+x)^{998}+\ldots\ldots+1001x^{1000}$ is

a. ${}^{1000}C_{50}$ b. ${}^{1001}C_{50}$
c ${}^{1002}C_{50}$ d. ${}^{1000}C_{51}$

46. The coefficient of x^{53} in expansion $\sum_{m=0}^{100}{}^{100}C_m(x-3)^{100-m}.2^m$ is

a. ${}^{100}C_{47}$ b. ${}^{100}C_{53}$
c. $-{}^{100}C_{53}$ b. $-{}^{100}C_{100}$

47. The number of rational terms in expansion of $\left(\sqrt[3]{4}+\frac{1}{\sqrt[4]{6}}\right)^{20}$, is

a. 3 b. 18
c. 4 d. 16

48. The sum ${}^rC_r+{}^{r+1}C_r+{}^{r+2}C_r+\ldots..+{}^nC_r\ (n\ge r)$ equals

a. ${}^nC_{r+1}$ b. ${}^{n+1}C_{r+1}$
c. ${}^{n+1}C_{r-1}$ d. ${}^{n+1}C_{2r}$

49. The unit digit of $17^{1983}+11^{1983}-71983$ is

a. 1 b. 2
c. 3 d. 0

50. If $(1+2x+3x^2)^{10}=a_1+a_1x+a_2x^2+\ldots\ldots a_{20}x^{20}$, then the value of a_1 is

a. 10 b. 20
c. 210 d. 420

Answer

1. a	**2.** a	**3.** c	**4.** a	**5.** a
6. c	**7.** d	**8.** d	**9.** a	**10.** a
11. c	**12.** c	**13.** b	**14.** b, c, d	**15.** a
16. b	**17.** b	**18.** b	**19.** c	**20.** a
21. b	**22.** d	**23.** d	**24.** c	**25.** d
26. c	**27.** d	**28.** c	**29.** d	**30.** a, b, d
31. b	**32.** b	**33.** c	**34.** c	**35.** c
36. c	**37.** c	**38.** b	**39.** a	**40.** d
41. c	**42.** b	**43.** b	**44.** b	**45.** c
46. c	**47.** a	**48.** b	**49.** a	**50.** b

Level – III For IIT-JEE Engg Entance Exams Only

1. Let $(1+x+x^2)^n = \sum_{r=0}^{2n} a_r x^r$, then prove that, $a_0+a_3+a_6+.........$ $= a_1+a_4+a_7+............ = a_2+a_5+a_8+.................. = 3^{n-1}$

2. Let $(1+x+x^2)^n = \sum_{r=0}^{2n} a_r x^r$, then prove that $a_0+a_1+a_2+...............+a_{n-1} = \frac{1}{2}(3^n - a_n)$

3. Let $(1+x+x^2)^n = \sum_{r=0}^{2n} a_r x^r$, then prove that $a_0\, a_1 - a_1 a_2 + a_2 a_3 - a_3 a_4 + ... = 0$

4. Find the co-efficient of x^{50} in the expansion of $(1+x)^{1000} + x(1+x)^{999} + x^2(1+x)^{998} + ... + x^{1000}$

5. Let $(1+x^2)^2(1+x)^n = \sum_{k=0}^{n+4} a_k x^k$. If a_1, a_2, a_3 are in A.P, then find n.

6. Find the co-efficient of x^{18} in the expansion of $(x+4)^{20} - C_1(x+4)^{19}.3 + C_2(x+4)^{18}.3^2 - .... + C_n 3^{20}$

7. In the expansion of $(1+x)(1+x+x^2).....(1+x+x^2+x^3+....+x^{2n})$, prove that the sum of the co-efficients is $(2n+1)!$

8. Prove that the value of ${}^nC_0 + {}^{n+1}C_1 + {}^{n+2}C_2 + ... + {}^{n+k}C_k = {}^{n+k+1}C_k = {}^{n+k+1}C_{n+1}$.

9. If $(1+x+2x^2)^{20} = a_0 + a_1 x + a_2 x^2 + ... + a_{40} x^{40}$, then prove that, $a_1 + a_3 + a_5 + a_7 + ... + a_{37} = 2^{19}(2^{20} - 21)$.

10. Prove that co-efficient of x^n in expansion of $\left(1+\frac{x}{1\,!}+\frac{x^2}{2\,!}+\frac{x^3}{3\,!}+ .... +\frac{x^n}{n!}\right)^n$ is $\frac{2^n}{n!}$.

11. If $(1+x)^n = C_0 + C_1 x + C_1 x^2 + ... + C_n x^n$, then prove that $\sum_{0\le i<j\le n}\sum (C_i - C_j)^2 = (n+1)^{2n}C_n - 2^{2n}$.

12. If $(1+x)^n = C_0 + C_1 x + C_2 x^2 + ... + C_n x^n$, then prove that $\sum_{0\le i<j\le n}\sum (i+j)C_i C_j = n\left(2^{n+1} - \frac{1}{2}\,{}^{2n}C_n\right)$.

13. If $(1+x)^n = C_0 + C_1 x + C_2 x^2 + ... + C_n x^n$, then prove that $\sum_{i=0}\sum_{j=1} ({}^nC_j . {}^jC_i),\ i \le j = 3^n - 1$.

14. If $\sum_{r=0}^{2n} a_r (x-2)^r = \sum_{b=0}^{2n} b_r (x-3)^r$ and $a_k = 1$ for all $k \ge n$, then prove that $b_n = {}^{2n+1}C_{n+1}$.

15. Prove that the sum $\sum_{i=0}^{m}\binom{10}{i}\binom{20}{m-i}$, where $\binom{p}{q} = 0$, if $p < q$, is maximum when $m = 15$.

16. If ${}^{n-1}C_r = (k^2-3)\,{}^nC_{r+1}$, then find k.

17. For $r =$ 0,1,2,.....,10, let A_r, B_r, C_r denote respectively, the co-efficient of x^r in expansion of $(1+x)^{10}$, $(1+x)^{20}$ and $(1+x)^{30}$, then prove that $\sum_{r=1}^{10} A_r(B_{10}B_r - C_{10}A_r) = C_{10} - B_{10}$.

18. Find the remainder, when $32^{32^{32}}$ is divided by 7.

19. Find the co-efficient of x^{49} in the prolynomial

$$\left(x-\frac{C_1}{C_0}\right)\left(x-2^2\frac{C_2}{C_1}\right)\left(x-3^2\frac{C_3}{C_2}\right)......\left(x-50^2\frac{C_{50}}{C_{49}}\right)$$

20. If the co-efficient of x^n in the expansion of $\left(1+\sum_{k=0}^{n} k.x^k\right)^2$ is 310, then find n.

21. If $\sum_{r=0}^{n}\left(r^2+r+1\right)r! = 2000.2000!$, then find the value of n.

22. If the last digit of the number 9^{9^9} is m and the last digit of $2^{m^{100}}$ is n, then find the value of $n - m + 2006$.

23. Find the sum of $\sum_{r=0}^{n}\left(\frac{n-3r+1}{n-r+1}\right)\frac{{}^nC_r}{2^r}$

24. If $\left(\sum_{r=0}^{2} x^r\right)^{2} = \sum_{r=0}^{2n} a_r x^r$, then prove that $\sum_{r=0}^{2n}\left(\frac{r}{a_r}\right) = n\sum_{r=0}^{2n}\left(\frac{1}{a_r}\right)$

25. Let $(1+x+x^2)^n = \sum_{r=0}^{2n} a_r x^r$, then prove that $a_0+a_3+a_6+.........=$ $a_1+a_4+a_7+.........= a_2+a_5+a_8+.........=3^{n-1}$

26. Let $(1+x+x^2)^n = \sum_{r=0}^{2n} a_r x^r$, then prove that $a_0+a_1+a_2+.......$ $.........+a_{n-1} = \frac{1}{2}(3^n - a_n)$

27. Let $(1+x+x^2)^n = \sum_{r=0}^{2n} a_r x^r$, then prove that $a_0a_1 - a_1a_2 + a_2a_3 - a_3a_4 + ...= 0$

28. In the expansion of $(1+x)(1+x+x^2).........(1+x+x^2+x^3+ ....x^{2n})$, prove that the sum of the co-efficients is $(2n+1)!$

29 Prove that the value of ${}^nC_0 + {}^{n+1}C_1 + {}^{n+2}C_2 + ... + {}^{n+k}C_k = {}^{n+k+1}C_k = {}^{n+k+1}C_{n+1}$

30. If $(1+x+2x^2)^{20} = a_0 + a_1x + a_2x^2 + ...+ a_{40}x^{40}$, then prove that, $a_1 + a_3 + a_5 + a_7 + ...a_{37} = 2^{19}(2^{20} - 21)$.

Answer

4. $1001C_{50}$	**5.** $n = 3,4$	**6.** $n = 190$	**18.** 4	**19.** 924
20. 12	**21.** 1999	**22.** 2013	**23.** $\frac{1}{2^n}$	

Linked Comprehension Type

Passage – 1

If n is a positive integer and if $(1+4x+4x^2)^n = \sum_{r=0}^{2n} a_r x^r$, where a_i's are $I = 0, 1, 2, 3, ...2n$ real numbers .

On basis of above information, answer the following questions:

1. The value of $2\sum_{r=0}^{n} a_{2r}$ is

a. $9^n - 1$ b. $9^n + 1$
c. $9^n - 2$ d. $9^n - 2$

2. The value of $2\sum_{r=0}^{n} a_{2r-1}$ is

a. $9^n - 1$ b. $9^n + 1$
c. $9^n - 2$ d. $9^n + 2$

3. The value of a_{2n-1} is

a. 2^{2n} b. $(n-1).2^{2n}$
c. $n.2^{2n}$ d. $(n+1).2^{2n}$

4. The value of a_2 is

a. $8n$ b. $8n^2 - 4$
c. $8n^2 - 4n$ d. $8n - 4$.

5. The correct statement is

a. $a_r = a_{n-r}, 0 \le r \le r \le n$ b. $a_{n+r} = a_{n-r}, 0 \le r \le n$
c. $a_r = a_{2n-r}, 0 \le r \le 2n$ d. None.

Passage – 2

Let us consider $(1+x+x^2)^{2n} = \sum_{r=0}^{4n} a_r x^r$, where $a_0, a_1, a_2, ..., a_{4n}$ are real numbers and $n \in I^+$

On the basis of the above information, answer the following questions.

1. The value of $\sum_{r=0}^{n-1} a_{2r}$ is

a. $\frac{9^n - 2a_{2n} - 1}{4}$ b. $\frac{9^n + 2a_{2n} + 1}{4}$
c. $\frac{9^n - 2a_{2n} + 1}{4}$ d. $\frac{9^n + 2a_{2n} - 1}{4}$

2. The value of $\sum_{r=1}^{n} a_{2r-1}$ is

a. $\left(\frac{9^n - 1}{2}\right)$ b. $\left(\frac{3^{2n} - 1}{4}\right)$
c. $\left(\frac{3^{2n} + 1}{4}\right)$ d. $\left(\frac{9^n + 1}{2}\right)$

3. The value of a_2 is

a. ${}^{4n+1}C_2$ b. ${}^{3n+1}C_2$
c. ${}^{2n+1}C_2$ d. ${}^{n+1}C_2$

4. The value of a_{4n-1} is

a. $2n$ b. $2n^2 + 4n$
c. $2n + 3$ d, $2n^2 + 3n$.

5. The correct statement is

a. $a_r = a_{n-r}, 0 \le r \le n$
b. $a_{n+r} = a_{n-r}, 0 \le r \le n$
c. $a_r = a_{2n-r}, 0 \le r \le 2n$
d. $a_r = a_{4n-r}, 0 \le r \le 4n$

Passage – 3

If m,n,r are positive integers and if $r < m, r < n$, then ${}^mC_r + {}^mC_{r-1}.{}^nC_1 + {}^mC_{r-2}.{}^nC_2 + {}^mC_{r-3}.{}^nC_3 + ...+ {}^nC_r$

= co-efficient of x^r in $(1+x)^m \times (1+x)^n$
= co-efficient of x^r in $(1+x)^{m+n}$
= ${}^{m+n}C_r$.

1. The value of ${}^nC_0.{}^nC_n + {}^nC_1.{}^nC_{n-1} + ...+ {}^nC_n.{}^nC_0$ is

a. ${}^{2n}C_{n-1}$ b. ${}^{2n}C_n$
c. ${}^{2n}C_{n+1}$ d. ${}^{2n}C_2$

2. The value of r for which ${}^{30}C_r.{}^{20}C_0 + {}^{30}C_{r-1}.{}^{20}C_1 + ...+ {}^{30}C_0.{}^{20}C_r$ is maximum, is

a. 10 b. 15
c. 20 d. 25.

3. The value of $r\ (0 \le r \le 30)$ ${}^{20}C_r.{}^{10}C_0 + {}^{20}C_{r-1}.{}^{10}C_1 + ...+ {}^{20}C_0.{}^{10}C_r$ is minimum , is

a. 0 b. 1
c. 5 d. 15.

4. If $S_n = {}^nC_0.{}^nC_1 + {}^nC_1.{}^nC_2 + {}^nC_2.{}^nC_3 + ... + {}^nC_{n-1}.{}^nC_n$ and if $\frac{S_{n+1}}{S_n} = \frac{15}{4}$, then n is
a. 2, 4 b. 4, 6
c. 6, 8 d. 8, 10.

5. If $(1+x)^n = C_0 + C_1x + C_2x^2 + ... + C_nx^n$ and n is odd, then the value of $C_0^2 - C_1^2 + C_2^2 - C_3^2 + ... + (-1)^n C_n^2$ is
a. 0 b. ${}^{2n}C_n$
c. $(-1)^n \times {}^{2n}C_{n-1}$ d. ${}^{2n}C_{n-2}$

PASSAGE – 4

If a,b are prime numbers and n is a natural number, then free from radical terms or rational terms in the expansion of $(a^{1/p} + b^{1/q})^n$ are the terms in which indices of a and b are integers.

On the basis of above information, answer the following questions:

1. In the expansion of $(7^{1/3} + 11^{1/9})^{6561}$, the number of terms free from radicals, is
a. 715 b. 725
c. 730 d. 745.

2. In the expansion of $(2^{1/2} + 3^{1/11})^{110}$, the number of irrational terms is
a. 85 b. 95
c. 105 d. 115.

3. In the expansion of $(2^{1/5} + 3^{1/2})^{20}$, the sum of rational terms, is
a. 21 b. 84
c. 97 d. None.

4. The number of integral terms in expansion of $(3^{1/2} + 5^{1/8})^{250}$ is
a. 32 b. 33
c. 34 d. 35.

5. The number of terms with integral co-efficients in the expansion of $(9^{1/4} + 8^{1/6})^{500}$ is
a. 501 b. 250
c. 253 d. 251.

PASSAGE – 5

If n is a positive integer and $a_1, a_2, a_3, ..., a_m \in C$, then

$$(a_1 + a_2 + a_3 + ... + a_m)^n = \sum \frac{n!}{n_1!n_2!n_3!....n_m!}.a_1^{n_1} a_2^{n_2} .....a_m^{n_m}$$

Where $n_1, n_2, n_3, ..., n_m$ are all non negative integers, subject to the condition $n_1 + n_2 + ... + n_m = n$.

On the basis of above information, answer the following questions:

1. The number of distinct terms in the expansion of $(x_1 + x_2 + x_3 + ...x_n)^4$ is
a. ${}^{n+1}C_4$ b. ${}^{n+2}C_4$
c. ${}^{n+3}C_4$ d. ${}^{n+4}C_4$

2. The co-efficient of x^3y^4z in the expansion of $(1 + x - y + z)^9$ is
a. 2320 b. 2420
c. 2520 d. 2620.

3. The co-efficient of $a^3b^4c^5$ in expansion of $(ab + bc + ca)^6$ is
a. 40 b. 60
c. 80 d. 100.

4. The co-efficient of x^{39} in the expansion of $(1 + x + 2x^2)^{20}$ is
a. 5.2^{19} b. 5.2^{20}
c. 5.2^{21} d. 5.2^{23}

5. If the co-efficients of x^{20} in $(1 - x + x^2)^{20}$ and in $(1 + x - x^2)^{20}$ are respectively a and b, then
a. $a = b$ b. $a > b$
c. $a < b$ d. $a + b = 0$

PASSAGE – 6

Suppose m divided by n, then quotient q and the remainder is r or, we can say that $m = nq + r$, for every $m,n,q,r \in I$ and $n \neq 0$.

On the basis of the above information, answer the following questions:

1. 5^{97} is divided by 52, then the remainder is
a. 3 b. 4
c. 5 d. 0

2. $13^{99} - 19^{92}$ is divided by 162, then the remainder is
a. 3 b. 4
c. 5 d. 0

3. $27^{10} + 7^{51}$ is divided by 10, then the remainder is
a. 0 b. 2
c. 4 d. 5

4. $(106)^{85} - (85)^{106}$ is divided 7, then the remainder is
a. 0 b. 1
c. 2 d. 3

5. $53^{53} - 33^3$ is divided by 10, then the remainder is
a. 0 b. 2
c. 4 d. 6.

ANSWERS

PASSEGE 1
1. b 2. a 3. c 4. c 5. d

PASSEGE 2
1. c 2. b 3. c 4. a 5. d

PASSEGE 3
1. b 2. d 3. a 4. a 5. a

PASSEGE 4
1. c 2. c 3. d 4. b 5. d

PASSEGE 5
1. c 2. c 3. b 4. c 5. b

PASSEGE 6
1. c 2. d 3. b 4. a 5. d

MATCH MATRIX

1. Observe the following columns:

I	II	
A. If λ be the number of terms in the expansion of $(5^{1/6}+7^{1/9})^{1824}$, which are integers, then λ is Divisible by	P Q	2 3
B. If λ be the number of terms in the expansion of $(5^{1/6}+2^{1/8})^{100}$, which are rational, then λ is Divisible by	R S	7 13
C. If λ be the number of terms in the expansion of $(3^{1/4}+4^{1/3})^{99}$, which are irrational, then λ is Divisible by	T	17

2. Observe the following columns:

I	II	
A. If the last digit of the number 9^{9^9} is λ and the last digit of $2^{\lambda^{100}}$ is μ, then	P	$\lambda+\mu=9$
	Q	$\lambda+\mu=11$
B. If the last digit of the number 2^{999} is λ and the last digit of $3^{\lambda\lambda\lambda}$ is μ, then	R	$\lambda+\mu=7$
	S	$\lambda+\mu=4$
C. Let $a=\frac{72!}{(36)!}-1$ is divisible by $10\lambda+\mu$	T	$\lambda^{\mu}+\mu^{\lambda}=9$

ANSWER

1. A → (P,Q,T); B → (P); C → (RS)

2. A → (Q,R); B → (P,R,T); C → (S)

Assertion and Reason

Codes

A. Both A and R are individually true and R is the correct explanation of A

B. Both A and R are individually true but R is not the correct explanation of A

C. A is true but R is false.

D. A is false but R is true.

1. Assertion A : Greatest co-efficient in the expansion of $(1+5x)^8$ is ${}^8C_4.5^4$

   Reason R : Greatest co-efficient in the expansion of $(1+x)^{2n}$ is the middle term

   a. A b. B c. C d. * D

2. Assertion A : Number of dis-similar terms in the sum of expansion $(x+a)^{102}+(x-a)^{102}$ is 206.

   Reason R : Number of terms in expansion of $(x+b)^n$ is $n+1$.

   a. A b. B c. C d. * D

3. Assertion A : The term independent of x in expansion of

   $$\left(x+\frac{1}{x}+2\right)^{21} \text{ is } {}^{42}C_{21}$$

   Reason R : In a binomial expansion, middle term is an independent of x.

   a. A b. B c. * C d. D

4. Assertion A : The number of terms in the expansion of

   $$\left(x+\frac{1}{x}+1\right)^n \text{ is } 2n+1.$$

   Reason R : The number of terms in the expansion of $(a_1+a_2+.........a_m)^n$ is ${}^{n+m-1}C_{m-1}$.

   a. A b. * B c. C d. D

5. Assertion A : No, three consecutive binomial co-efficents can be in G.P and H.P

   Reason R : Three consecutive binomial coefficients are in A.P

   a. A b. * B c. C d. D

6. Assertion A : The co-efficent of $x^{3\lambda+2}$ in the expansion of $(a+x)^{\lambda}(b+x)^{\lambda+1}(c+x)^{\lambda+2}, \forall\lambda\in N$ is $\lambda(a+b+c)$

   Reason R : The co-efficient of x^m in the expansion of $(a+x)^n$ is ${}^nC_m\, a^{n-m}$

   a. A b. B c. C d. * D

7. Assertion A : $\left(\sqrt{2}-1\right)^n$ can be expressed as $\sqrt{N}-\sqrt{N+1}$ for all $N>1$ and n is a +ve integer.

   Reason R : $\left(\sqrt{2}-1\right)^n$ can be expressed as $A+B\sqrt{2}$, where A and B are integers and n is A positive integer.

   a. A b. * B c. C d. D

8. Assertion A : If $\sum_{r=1}^{n} r^3\left(\frac{{}^nC_r}{{}^nC_{r-1}}\right)^2=196$, then the sum of the co-efficients of power x in the expansion of $(x-3x^2+x^3)^n$ is -1.

   Reason R : $\frac{{}^nC_r}{{}^nC_{r-1}}=\left(\frac{n-r+1}{r}\right) \forall n\in N$ and $r\in W$

   a. A b. B c. C d. * D

Questions asked in Roorkee Exams

1. If n is any positive integer, prove that ${}^nC_0^2+{}^nC_1^2+{}^nC_2^2+......+{}^nC_n^2=\frac{(2n)!}{(n)!\times(n)!}$ [Roorkee – 1983]

2. In the binomial expansion of $(1+y)^n$, where n is a natural number, the co-efficients of the fifth, sixth and seventh terms are in arithmetic progression. Find the value of n. [Roorkee – 1984]

3. Find out the term of expansion of $\left(\frac{1}{2}x^{1/8}+x^{-1/8}\right)^8$ which does not contain x? [Roorkee – 1985]

4. Find the co-efficient of x^n in series $1+\frac{(a+bx)}{1!}+\frac{(a+bx)^2}{2!}+\frac{(a+bx)^3}{3!}+...............$ [Roorkee – 1985]

5. If A be the sum of the odd terms and B the sum of even terms in the expansion of $(x+a)^n$, then prove that $A^2-B^2=(x^2-a^2)^n$ [Roorkee –1986]

6. Find the sum of the co-efficients in the expansions of the binomial $(5p-4q)^n$, where n is a positive integer.

7. Find the sum of $3.{}^nC_0-8{}^nC_1+13\,{}^nC_2-18{}^nC_3+.......$upto $(n+1)$ terms [Roorkee – 1988]

8. No questions in 1989.

9. Find the co-efficient of x^{50} in the expression $(1+x)^{1000}+2x(1+x)^{999}+3x^2(1+x)^{998}+...........+1001x^{1000}$ [Roorkee – 1990]

10. If n is a positive integer and $C_k={}^nC_k$, find the value of $\sum_{k=1}^{n}k^3\left(\frac{C_k}{C_{k-1}}\right)^2$ [Roorkee –1991]

11. Determine the value of x in the expansion $\left(x+x^{\log_{10}x}\right)^x$, if the third term is the equation is 10, 000. [Roorkee – 1992]

12. Find the value of the expression ${}^{47}C_4+\sum_{j=1}^{5}{}^{47-j}C_3$ [Roorkee – 1993]

13. Find the value of x for which the sixth term $\left(\sqrt{2^{\log(10-3^x)}}+\sqrt[5]{2^{(x-2)\log 3}}\right)^m$ is equal to 21 and co-efficients of 2nd, 3rd and 4th terms are the 1st, 3rd and 5th terms of an A.P. [Roorkee – 1993]

14. Given that the 4th term in the expansion of $\left(2+\frac{3}{8}x\right)^{10}$ has the maximum numerical values, find the range of values of x for which this will be true. [Roorkee – 1994]

15. No questions in 1995.

16. Let $(1+x^2)^2(1+x)^n=\sum_{k=0}^{n+4}a_nx^k$. If a_1, a_2 and a_3 are in A.P. then find the value of n. [Roorkee -1996]

17. In the expansion of the expression $(x+a)^{15}$, if the 11 th term is the G.M of the 8th and 12th terms, which term in the expansion is greatest. [Roorkee – 1997]

18. No questions in **1998, 1999.**

19. Find the largest co-efficient in the expansion of $(1+x)^n$, given that the sum of the co-efficients of the terms in its expansion is 4096. [Roorkee – 2000]

20. Find the co-efficient of x^{49} in the polynomial $\left(x-\frac{C_1}{C_0}\right)\left(x-2^2\frac{C_2}{C_1}\right)\left(x-3^2\frac{C_3}{C_2}\right).....\left(x-50^2\frac{C_{50}}{C_{49}}\right)$, where $C_r={}^{50}C_r$. [Roorkee – 2001]

ANSWERS

2. $n=7, 14$ **4.** $e^a\times\frac{b^n}{n!}$—[Roorkee – 1985] **6.** 1 **7.** 0 **8.** ${}^{1002}C_{50}$

10. $\frac{n}{12}\times(n+1)^2\times(n+2)$ **11.** $x=10, 10^{-5/2}$ **12.** ${}^{32}C_4$ **13.** $x=0.2.$ **14.** $x\geq\frac{16}{7}$

15. $n=2, 3, 4$ **17.** 8th term **19.** 924.—[Roorkee – 2000] **20.** 1665626

Questions asked in IIT-JEE Exams

1. Prove that $({}^{2n}C_0)^2-({}^{2n}C_1)^2+({}^{2n}C_2)^2-.....+({}^{2n}C_n)^2=(-1)^n\,{}^{2n}C_n$ [IIT-JEE – 1978]

2. Prove that $C_1^2-2.C_1^2+3.C_3^2-...........-2n.C_{2n}^2=(-1)^{n-1}n.C_n$ [IIT-JEE – 1979]

3. Given positive integers $r>1$, $n>2$ and the co-efficient of $(3r)$th and $(r+2)$th terms in the binomial expansion of $(1+x)^{2n}$ are equal, then [IIT-JEE – 1980]

   a. * $n=2r$ b. $n=2r+1$
   c. $n=3r$ d. None.

4. The value of $^{47}C_4 + \sum_{j=1}^{5} {}^{52-j}C_3$ is equal to [IIT-JEE – 1980]

a. $47C_5$ b. $52C_5$

c. * $52C_4$ d. None.

5. Let $u_1=1$, $u_2=1$, $u_{n+2} = u_{n+1} + u_n$, $n>1$. Use mathematical induction to show that $u_n = \frac{1}{\sqrt{5}}\left[\left(\frac{1+\sqrt{5}}{2}\right)^n - \left(\frac{1-\sqrt{5}}{2}\right)^n\right]$ for all $n > 1$ [IIT-JEE – 1981]

6. Prove that $7^{2n}+(2^{3n-3})(3^{n-1})$ is divisible by 25 for any natural number n. [IIT-JEE – 1982]

7. The sum of the co-efficients of polynomial $(1+x-3x^2)^{2163}$ is .... [IIT-JEE – 1982]

8. The co-efficient of x^{99} in the polynomial $(x-1)(x-2)(x-3)$ ....$(x-100)$ is .... [IIT-JEE – 1982]

9. The larger of $99^{50} + 100^{50}$ and 101^{50} is ....[IIT-JEE – 1982]

10. If $(1+ax)^n = 1 + 8x + 24x^2 + ...$, then a =......., n = ... where $(1+ax)^n = 1 + n(ax) + \frac{n(n-1)}{2}(ax)^2 + ...$

[IIT-JEE – 1983]

11. The co-efficient of x^4 in $\left(\frac{x}{2}-\frac{3}{x^2}\right)^{10}$ is [IIT-JEE – 1983]

a. *405/256 b. 504/259

c. 450/263 d. None.

12. If $(1+x)^n = C_0 + C_1x + C_2x^2 + C_3x^3 + ...+ C_nx^n$, then show that the sum of the products of the C_i′ is taken two at a time is represented by $\sum\sum_{0\le i<j\le n} C_i C_j = 2^{2n-1}$ [IIT-JEE–1983]

13. Use mathematical induction to prove : If n is any odd positive integer, then $n(n^2-1)$ is divisible by 24. [IIT-JEE – 1983]

14. Given $S_n = 1 + q + q^2 + q^3 + ...+ q^n$ and, $\delta_n = 1 + \left(\frac{q+1}{2}\right) + \left(\frac{q+1}{2}\right)^2 + \left(\frac{q+1}{2}\right)^3 + ...+ \left(\frac{q+1}{2}\right)$, $q \neq 1$ then prove that

$^{n+1}C_1 + {}^{n+1}C_2.S_1 + {}^{n+1}C_3.S_2 + ...+ {}^{n+1}C_{n+1}.S_n = 2^n\,\delta_n$

[IIT-JEE – 1984]

15. If p be a natural number, then prove that $p^{n+1}+(p+1)^{2n-1}$ is divisible by p^2+p+1 for every positive integer n.

[IIT-JEE – 1984]

16. Use method of mathematical induction to prove that $2.7^n + 3.5^n - 5$ is divisible by 24 for all $n > 0$ [IIT-JEE – 1985]

17. Find the sum of the series $\sum_{r=0}^{n}(-1)^r\,{}^nC_r\left[\frac{1}{2^r}+\frac{3^r}{2^{2r}}+\frac{7^r}{2^{3r}}\frac{7^r}{2^{3r}}+\frac{15^r}{2^{4r}}+ ..\text{upto } m \text{ terms}\right]$ [IIT-JEE -1985]

18. If C_r stands for ^nC_r, then sum of series $\frac{2\left(\frac{n}{2}\right)!\left(\frac{n}{2}\right)!}{n!} \times [C_0^2 + C_1^2 + C_2^2 + ...+(-1)^n(n+1)C_n^2]$, where n is an even positive integer, is equal to [IIT-JEE – 1986]

a. 0 b. $(-1)^{\frac{1}{2}}(n+1)$

c. $(-1)^n(n+2)$ d. * None.

19. Use mathematical induction or otherwise prove that $\sum_{k=0}^{n} k^2\,{}^nC_k = n(n+1)2^{n-2}$ for $n > 1$ [IIT-JEE – 1986]

20. Prove by mathematical induction that $\frac{(2n)!}{(2n)!\times(n)^2} \le \frac{1}{\sqrt{(3n+1)}}$ for every positive integer n.

[IIT-JEE – 1987]

21. Let $R = \left(5\sqrt{5}+11\right)^{2n+1}$ and $f = R - [R]$, where [,] denotes the greatest integer function. Prove that $Rf = 4^{2n+4}$ [IIT-JEE–1988]

22. Using mathematical induction, prove that $^mC_0.{}^nC_k + {}^mC_1.{}^nC_{k-1} + {}^mC_2.{}^nC_{k-2} + ...+ {}^mC_k.{}^nC_0 = {}^{m+n}C_k$ where m, n, k are positive integers, and $^pC_q = 0$ for $p < q$. [IIT-JEE – 1989]

23. Prove that $C_0 - 2^2C_1 + 3^2.C_2 - .... + (-1)^n(n+1)^2.C_n = 0$ $n > 1$ where $C_r = {}^nC_r$ [IIT-JEE–1989]

24. Prove that $\frac{n^7}{7}+\frac{n^5}{5}+\frac{2n^3}{3}-\frac{n}{105}$ is an integer for every positive integer n. [IIT-JEE – 1990]

25. The product of n positive numbers is unity. Then their sum is

a. a positive integer b. divisible by n

c. equal to $n+\frac{1}{n}$ d. * never less than n.

[IIT-JEE – 1991]

26. Using mathematical induction or otherwise, prove that for any non negative integers $m.n,r$ and k,

$$\sum_{m=0}^{k}(n-m)\frac{(r+m)!}{m!} = \frac{(r+k+1)!}{k!}\left[\frac{n}{r+1}-\frac{k}{r+2}\right]$$

[IIT-JEE – 1991]

27. If $\sum_{r=0}^{2n} a_r(x-2)^r = \sum_{r=0}^{2n} b_r(x-3)^r$ and $a_k = 1$ for all $k \ge n$, then show that $b_n = {}^{2n+1}C_{n+1}$ [IIT-JEE –1992]

28. Let $p \ge 3$ be an integer and α, β be the roots of $x^2 - (p+1)x + 1 = 0$. Using mathematical induction, show that $\alpha^n + \beta^n$

i. is an integer and ii. is not divisible by p.

[IIT-JEE – 1992]

29. Find the natural number 'a' for which $\sum_{k=1}^{n}(a+k) = 16(2^n-1)$,

where the function 'f' satisfies the relation $f(x+y)=f(x)f(y)$ for all natural numbers x, y and further $f(1)=2$.

[IIT-JEE – 1992]

30. Prove that, $\sum_{r=1}^{k}(-3)^{r-1}\ {}^{3n}C_{2r-1}=0$, where $k=\frac{3n}{2}$ and n is an even positive integer. [IIT-JEE – 1993]

31. Let n be a positive integer and $(1+x+x^2)=a_0+a_1x+a_2x^2+.......+a_{2n}x^{2n}$, then show that $a_0^{\ 2}-a_0^{\ 2}+.........+a_0^{\ 2}=a_n$

[IIT-JEE – 1994]

32. Let n be a positive integer. If the co-efficients of 2nd, 3rd and 4th terms in the expansion of $(1+x)^n$ are in A.P, then $n=$........... [IIT-JEE – 1994]

33. Prove that $\frac{3!}{2(n+3)}=\sum_{r=0}^{n}(-1)^r\left(\frac{C_r}{r+{}^3C_r}\right)$ [IIT-JEE – 1997]

34. The sum of the rational terms in expansion of $\left(2^{\frac{1}{2}}+3^{\frac{1}{5}}\right)^{10}$ is

.... [IIT-JEE – 1997]

35. If $a_n=a_n=\sum_{r=0}^{n}\frac{1}{{}^nC_r}$ then $\sum_{r=0}^{n}\frac{r}{{}^nC_r}=$ [IIT-JEE – 1998]

a. $(n-1)a_n$ b. $n\,a_n$

c. $\frac{n}{2}\times a_n$ d. None.

36. If in the expression of $(1+x)^m(1-x)^n$, the co-efficient of x and x^2 are 3 and -6 respectively, then m is

a. 6 b. 9

c. 12 d. 24. [IIT-JEE – 1999]

37. For a positive integer n. Let $a(n)=1+\frac{1}{2}+\frac{1}{3}+....+\frac{1}{2n-1}$, then

[IIT-JEE – 1999]

a. $a(100)\le 100$ b. $a(100)>100$

c. $a(200)\le 100$ d. $a(200)>100$

38. Let n be any positive integer. Prove that $\sum_{k=0}^{m}\left(\frac{\binom{2n-k}{k}}{\binom{2k-k}{k}}\right)$

$$\left(\frac{2n-4k+1}{2n-2k+1}\right)2^{n-2k}=\frac{\binom{n}{m}}{\binom{2n-2m}{n-m}}2^{n-2m}$$

For each non- negative integer $m\le n$. $\left(Here\binom{p}{q}={}^pC_q\right)$

[IIT-JEE – 1999]

39. For $2\le r\le n$, $\binom{n}{r}+2\binom{n}{r-1}+\binom{n}{r-2}=$

a. $\binom{n+1}{r-1}$ b. $2\binom{n+1}{r+1}$

c. $\binom{n+2}{r}$ d. $2\binom{n+1}{2}$ [IIT-JEE – 2000]

40. For any positive integer m,n (with $n\ge m$). Let $\binom{n}{m}=nC_m$.

Prove that $\binom{n}{m}+\binom{n-1}{m}+\binom{n-2}{m}+........+\binom{m}{m}=\binom{n+1}{m+1}$

Hence or otherwise, prove that, $\binom{n}{m}+2\binom{n-1}{m}+3\binom{n-2}{m}+$ ....$(n-m+1)\binom{n}{m}=\binom{n+2}{m+2}$ [IIT-JEE – 2000]

41. In the binomial expansion of $(a-b)^n$, $n\ge 5$, the sum of the 5th and 6th terms is zero, then $\frac{a}{b}$ is

a. $\frac{n-5}{6}$ b. $\frac{n-4}{5}$

c. $\frac{5}{n-4}$ d. $\frac{6}{n-5}$ [IIT-JEE – 2001]

42. The sum $\sum_{i=0}^{m}\binom{10}{i}\binom{p}{m-i}$, where $\binom{p}{q}=0$, if $p>q$, is maximum, when m is

a. 5 b. 10

c. 15 d. 20 [IIT-JEE – 2002]

43. Co-efficient of t^{24} in $(1+t^2)^{12}(1+t^{12})(1+t^{24})$ is

a. ${}^{12}C_6+3$ b. ${}^{12}C_6+1$

c. ${}^{12}C_6$ d. ${}^{12}C_6+2$ [IIT-JEE – 2003]

44. Prove that $2^k\binom{n}{0}\binom{n}{k}-2^{k-1}\binom{n}{1}\binom{n-1}{k-1}-2^{k-2}\binom{n}{2}\binom{n-2}{k-2}$ $+..............-(-1)^k\binom{n}{k}\binom{n-k}{0}=\binom{n}{k}$ [IIT-JEE – 2003]

45. If ${}^{n+1}C_r=(k^2-3)\,{}^nC_{r+1}$, then k lies in

a. $(-\infty,2]$ b. $(2,\infty]$

c. $\left[-\sqrt{3},\sqrt{3}\right]$ d. $\left(\sqrt{3},2\right]$ [IIT-JEE – 2004]

46. $\binom{30}{0}\binom{30}{10}-\binom{30}{1}\binom{30}{11}+\binom{30}{2}\binom{30}{12}+..........-\binom{30}{20}\binom{30}{30}=$

a. ${}^{65}C_{35}$ b. ${}^{30}C_{10}$

c. ${}^{60}C_{10}$ d. ${}^{30}C_{11}$ [IIT-JEE – 2005]

ANSWERS

8. 5050.—[IIT-JEE – 1982] **17.** $\frac{2^{mn}-1}{2^{mn}\left(2^n-1\right)}$—[IIT-JEE -1985] **29.** $a=3$—[IIT-JEE – 1992] **32.** 7 **34.** 41

CHAPTER 5 THE PERMUTATION AND COMBINATION

CONCEPT BOOSTER

5.1 Factorial Notation

The continued product of first n natural number is called a factorial of n. It is denoted by n ! and is defined as

$(n)! = n\times(n-1)! = n(n-1)\times(n-2)! = n(n-1)(n-2)\times(n-3)!$

and so on

(i) $0! = 1$

(ii) $(-n)!$ is not defined.

NOTE

1. $(1)! = 1$ 2. $(2)! = 2$ 3. $(3)! = 6$
4. $(4)! = 6$ 5. $(5)! = 120$ 6. $(6)! = 720$
7. $(2n)! = 2n \times (n)! \times \{1, 3, 5 \ldots\ldots\ldots (2n-1)\}$

5.2 Exponent of a prime p in n!.

Exponent of a prime p in n! is denoted by $E_p(n!)$ and is defined

as, $E_p(n\ !) = \left[\frac{n}{p}\right]+\left[\frac{n}{p^2}\right]+\left[\frac{n}{p^3}\right]+\ldots\ldots\ldots\ldots\ldots\ldots$ where [,] = G.I.F.

Ex-1 Find the exponent of 3 in 10!.

$$E_3(10!) = \left[\frac{10}{3}\right]+\left[\frac{10}{3^2}\right]+\left[\frac{10}{3^3}\right] = 3+1+0 = 4.$$

Ex-2 Prove that 33! Is divisible by 2^{19}.

Let 33! $= 2^a.3^b.5^c.7^d \ldots\ldots$

$$E_2(33\ !) = \left[\frac{33}{2}\right]+\left[\frac{33}{2^2}\right]+\left[\frac{33}{2^3}\right]+\left[\frac{33}{2^4}\right]+\left[\frac{33}{2^5}\right]+\left[\frac{33}{2^6}\right]$$

$$= 16+8+4+2+1+0 = 31$$

Hence, the exponent of 2 in (33 !) is 3.

So it is divisible by. Thus it is divisible by.

Ex-3 Find the number of zeroes at the end of (100 !).

We have $(100\ !) = 2^a.3^b.5^c.7^d \ldots\ldots$

$$E_2(100!) = \left[\frac{100}{2}\right]+\left[\frac{100}{2^2}\right]+\left[\frac{100}{2^3}\right]+\left[\frac{100}{2^4}\right]+\left[\frac{100}{2^5}\right]+\left[\frac{100}{2^6}\right]+\left[\frac{100}{2^7}\right]$$

$$= 50+25+12+6+3+1+0 = 97.$$

$$E_5(100!) = \left[\frac{100}{5}\right]+\left[\frac{100}{5^2}\right]+\left[\frac{100}{5^3}\right] = 20+4+0 = 24$$

Therefore, $(100!) = 2^{97}\times3^b\times5^{24}\times7^d\times\ldots\ldots\ldots$

$= 2^{73}\times3^b\times(2\times5)^{24}\times7^d\times\ldots\ldots\ldots$

Thus, the number of zeroes at the end of (100 !) is 24.

PERMUTATION

5.3 Fundamental Principle of Counting

(i) **Multiplication Principle:** If an operation can be performed in m-different ways, following which a second operation can be performed in n-different ways, then the whole operation can be performed in $m \times n$ ways.

NOTE

This can be extended in any finite number of operations.

Q.1 There are 5 doors in a room. In how many ways a student can enter the room and leave by a different door?

Sol. The number of possible ways = = 20.

Q.2 In a class there are 15 boys and 10 girls. In how many ways can the teacher form a team of one boy and one girl amongst the students of the class to represent the institute in a quiz competition?

Sol. The number of possible ways = 15 × 10 = 150.

(ii) **Addition Principle:** If one operation can be performed in m ways and another operation can be performed in n-ways. Then either of two operations can be performed in (m + n) ways.

Q.1 There are 4 students for physics, 6 students for chemistry and 8 students for Math's Gold Medal. In how many ways one of these gold medals be awarded?

Sol. The number of possible ways = (4 + 6 + 8) = 18.

Q.2 A college offers 5 courses in the morning and 4 in the evening. Find the number of ways a student can select exactly one course, either in the morning or in the evening.

Sol. The number of possible ways = (5 + 4) = 9.

5.4 Permutations

The different arrangements which can be made by taking some or all of them at a time is called Permutation.

The number of permutations of n different things taken r at a time is denoted by ^nP_r or P(n, r) and is defined as $^nP_r = \frac{n!}{(n-r)!}$. Where $r \leq n$.

Now, no. of permutations of n different things taken r at a time = No. of ways of filling up r vacant places with n different things.

No. of Places:	1st	2nd	3rd	....	r^{th}
No. of Choices:	n	n – 1	n – 2		n – (r – 1)

Thus, $^nP_r = n(n-1)(n-2)(n-3)\ldots\ldots(n-(r-1))$

$$= \frac{n(n-1)(n-2)\ldots\ldots(n-r+1)(n-r)\ldots\ldots3.2.1}{(n-r)\ldots\ldots6.5.4.3.2.1}$$

$$= \frac{n!}{(n-r)!}$$

Ex-1: Suppose 8 people enter an event in a swim meet. In how many ways could the gold, silver, and bronze prizes be awarded ?

Sol. The required number of possible ways

$$= {}^8P_3 = \frac{8!}{5!} = 8.7.6 = 336.$$

Ex-2: How many integers between 100 and 999 inclusive consists of distinct odd digits?

Sol. The odd digits are 1, 3, 5, 7, 9

The numbers between 100 and 999 are 3-digits numbers.

Hence, the total possible number ways

$$= {}^5P_3 = \frac{5!}{2!} = 5.4.3 = 60$$

Ex-3: How many numbers of 3-digits even number can be formed by using the digits 1, 2, 3, 4, 5 ?

Sol. The digits are 1, 2, 3, 4, 5.

A number will be even, if last digit is even.

The total number of even numbers

$$= 2 \times {}^4P_2 = \frac{2.4.3.2}{2} = 24.$$

Ex-4: Find the number of ways 6 flags of different colors are to be used to form a signal of 4 flags.

Ans. The total number of ways 6 flags of different colors = $^6P_4$

$$= \frac{6!}{4!} = 6.5 = 30.$$

Ex-5: A flag containing 4 strips of different colors to be designed. If 6 colors can be used, then find the number of possible flags.

Sol. The total number of possible flags = $^6P_4 = \frac{6!}{4!} = 6.5 = 30$.

Ex-6: In an experiment on social interaction, 6 people can sit in 6 seats in a row. In how many ways can this be done ?

Sol. The total number of possible ways = $^6P_6 = 6! = 720$

Ex-7: In how many ways can 3 men can stay in a hotel room, if there are 8 rooms are available?

Sol. The total number of possible ways 3 men can stay in a hotel = $^8P_3 = \frac{8!}{5!} = 8.7.6 = 336$.

Ex-8: In a club with 15 members , how many ways can a state of 3 officers consisting of president, vice-president and treasurer be chosen?

Sol. The total number of possible ways

$$= {}^{15}P_3 = \frac{15!}{12!} = 15.14.13 = 2730$$

Ex-9: Find the number of permutation of the letters of the word 'TABLE'.

Sol. The total number of arrangement of the letter of the word 'TABLE' = $^5P_5 = 5! = 120$.

Ex-10: If 'a' be the permutation of the letter of the word 'MAIN' and 'b' be the permutation of the Letter of the word 'EXAM' and 'c' be the permutation of the letter of the word 'LOVE', then find the value of a + b + c + 10.

Sol. We have a = $^4P_4 = 4! = 24$.

Similarly, b = $^4P_4 = 4! = 24$ and c = $^4P_4 = 4! = 24$

Thus, a + b + c + 10 = 24 + 24 + 24 + 10 = 82.

RULE

Sum of Numbers

(i) For given n different digits $a_1, a_2, a_3, \ldots\ldots, a_n$, the sum of the digits in the unit places of all numbers formed (where numbers are not repeated)

$$= (a_1 + a_2 + a_3 + \ldots\ldots + a_n) \times (n-1)!$$

$$= (\text{sumofthedigits}) \times (n-1)!$$

(ii) Sum of the total numbers which can be formed with given n - different digits $a_1, a_2, a_3, \ldots\ldots, a_n$

$$= (a_1 + a_2 + a_3 + \ldots\ldots + a_n) \times (n-1)! \times (1 + 10 + 100 + \ldots\ldots + n - \text{times})$$

$$= (n-1)! \times (a_1 + a_2 + a_3 + \ldots\ldots + a_n) \times \left(\frac{10^n - 1}{9}\right)$$

5.5 The number of permutation of n different things taken r at a time, when each thing can be repeated any number of times is.

Number of permutations of n different things taken r at a time, when repetition is allowed = No. of ways in which r blank places can be filled by n different things when repetition is allowed.

No. of Places:	1st	2nd	3rd	....	r^{th}
No. of Choices:	n	n	n		n

= n. n. n. .... r-times = n^r.

Ex-1: How many different outcomes are there in an experiment consisting of n tosses of a coin?

Sol. The total possible ways

$$= 2 \times 2 \times 2 \times 2 \times \ldots\ldots 2 \times 2(n - \text{times}) = 2^n.$$

Ex-2: In how many ways 4 delegates can be put in 5 hotels of a city, if there is no restriction?

Sol. The total number of possible ways = $5\times5\times5\times5=5^4$.

Ex-3: In how many ways 3 friends can be put up in a 5 hotel of a town if

(i) There is no restriction?

(ii) No two friends can stay together?

Sol. (i) The total possible number of ways 4 friends can stay in a 5 hotel = $5\times5\times5=5^3$

(iii) The total number of possible ways, when no two friends stay together = 5 × 4 × 3 = 60.

Ex-4: In how many ways 5 rings can be worn on the four fingers of one hand ?

Sol. The total number of possible ways 5 rings can be worn in 4 fingers = 6 × 6 × 6 × 6 = 1296.

Ex-5: If m is the number of ways, a child put 3 marbles in his 4 pockets and 'n' is the number of ways 3 digits distinct numbers can be made from the digits 1, 2, 3, 4, 5 , then find the value of m + n + 10.

Sol. Here, m = the number of ways a child put 3 marbles in his 4 pockets = 4 × 4 × 4 = 64

And n = the total number of 3 digits distinct number = 5 × 4 × 3 = 60

Thus, m + n + 10 = 64 + 60 +10 = 134.

5.6 Permutations of *n* things not all are different

The number of permutation of n-things taken all at a time, p are alike of one kind, q are alike of 2nd kind and r are alike of 3rd kind and the rest all are different is $\frac{n!}{p!\times q!\times r!}$.

Let x be the number of required permutation.

P things can be arranged in $(P)!$, q things can be arranged in $(q)!$ ways and r things can arranged $(r)!$ in.

Then by the fundamental principle of counting, we get, $x\times(p)!\times(q)!\times(r)!=(n)!$

$$\Rightarrow x=\frac{(n)!}{(p)!\times(q)!\times(r)!}$$

Ex-1: Find the number of permutation of the letter of the word 'IIT'

Sol. The number of different arrangement of letter of the word 'IIT' = $\frac{(3)!}{(2)!}=\frac{6}{2}=3$

Ex-2: In how many ways can you permute the letter of the word 'AIEEE' ?

Sol. The different arrangement of the letter of the word 'AIEEE' $=\frac{(5)!}{(3)!}=\frac{120}{6}=20$.

Ex-3: If 'm' be the permutation of the letter of the word 'JEE-MAIN' and 'n' be the permutation o f the letter of the word 'IIT', then find the value of m + n + 10.

Sol. We have, $m=\frac{7!}{2!}=\frac{5040}{2}=2520$ and $n=\frac{3!}{2!}=\frac{6}{2}=3$

Then $m+n+10=2520+3+10=2533$.

5.7 Restricted Permutations

String Method

(i) **Togetherness:** The number of permutations of n different things, taken all at a time, when m specified things always come together is $m!\times(n-m+1)!$.

(ii) **Non-Togetherness:** The number of permutations of n different things, taken all at a time when m - specified things never come together is $n!-m!\times(n-m+1)!$.

i.e. Never Together = Total - Together.

Ex-1: How many different words can be formed with the letters of the word 'UNIVERSITY', so that all the vowels are together.

Sol. Given word is 'UNIVERSITY' where the vowels are U, I, E, I and the rest are N, V, R, S , T, Y.

When 4 vowels are together , consider the 4 vowels as one unit. So, we have 6 + 1 = 7 letters

Can be arranged in 7! ways.

4 vowels can be arranged in $\frac{4!}{2!}=12$ ways.

Hence the total number of ways = 7! × 12.

Ex-2: In how many ways can 10 examination papers be arranged so that the best and the worst papers never come together?

Sol. As we know that, never come together = Total - together.

$=(10)!-2!\times9!=8\times9!$.

Ex-3: The number of arrangements which can be made using all the letters of the word 'LAUGH', if vowels occur together.

Sol. Given word is LAUGH where 2 are vowels and 3 are rest.

Number of arrangements = 4! × 2! = 48

Ex-4: Find the rank of the word ' TOUGH'

Sol. The alphabetical order of the word 'TOUGH' is GH, O, T, U

The number of words beginning with G is 4! = 24

The number of words beginning with H is 4! = 24

The number of words beginning with O is 4! = 24

The number of words beginning with TG is 3! = 6

The number of words beginning with TH is 3! = 6

The number of words beginning with TOG is 2

The number of words beginning with TOH is 2

The number of words beginning with TOU is TOUGH

Hence the rank of the word is = 24 + 24 + 24 + 12+ 2+2+1=89.

Ex-5: Find the rank of the word 'IIT'.

The alphabetical order of IIT is I, I, T.

So, the rank of the word 'IIT' is 1.

Ex-6: Find the rank of the word 'AIEEE'

Sol. The alphabetical order of the word 'AIEEE' is AEEEI

The number of words beginning with AE is $\frac{3!}{2!}=3$

The number of words beginning with AI is 1

Hence, the rank of the word AIEEE is = 3 + 1 = 4.

Ex-7: Find the rank of the word 'ANNA'

Sol. The alphabetical order of the word 'ANNA' is AANN.

The number of words beginning with AA is 1

The number of words beginning with AN is 1

The number of words beginning with ANNA is 1

Hence, the rank of the word 'ANNA' is = 1 + 1+ 1 = 3.

Ex-8: Find the rank of the word 'SURITI'

Sol. The alphabetical order of the word 'SURITI' is I, I, R, S, T, U

The number of words beginning with I is 5! = 120

The number of words beginning with R is $\frac{5!}{2!}=60$

The number of words beginning with SI is 4! = 24

The number of words beginning with SR is $\frac{4!}{2!}=12$

The number of words beginning with ST is $\frac{4!}{2!}=12$

The number of words beginning with SUI is 3! = 6

The number of words beginning with SURI is 1

The number of words beginning with SURITI is 1

Hence, the rank of the word 'SURITI' is = 120 + 60 + 48 +8 = 236.

5.8 When no two of a certain given things occur together

Gap Method: The number of permutations of n different things, taken all at a time when m - specified things, no two of which are to occur together is n+1 $P^m \times n!$

If we place n different things in a row, so we will get (n+1) gap.

m things can be filled in (n+1) gap is $^{n+1}P_m$ and n things can be arranged in ways

Thus, the total number of ways, it can be happened = $^{n+1}P_m \times n!$.

Ex-1: How many different words can be formed with five given letters of which three are vowels

And 2 are consonants, no two vowels being together in any word?

Sol. If we place 2 consonants in a row, then we will get 3 gap.

So 3 gaps can be filled by three vowels in 3 ways.

Hence, the total number of possible ways = $^3P_3 \times 2!$ $= 6 \times 2 = 12$.

Ex-2: In how many ways 5 girls and 6 boys in a class can be seated in a row so that all the girls will not seat together?

Sol. If we arrange the seating plan of 6 boys in a row, so we can get 7 gaps in between of them.

These 7 gaps is filled by the 5 girls in $^7P_5$ and 6 boys can be arranged themselves in 6! ways

Hence, the total number of possible ways = $^7P_5 \times 5!$

Ex-3: In how many ways 5 girls and 5 boys in a class can be seated in a row, so that they are alternate?

Sol. Case - I : when a boy sits at the first place

Then the number of possible ways = 5! × 5!.

Case-II : When a girl sits at the first place

Then the number of possible ways = 5! × 5!.

Thus, the required number of possible ways

= 5! × 5! + 5! × 5! = 2 ×5! × 5!.

Ex-4: Find the number of ways in which the letters of the word "SOCIETY" be arranged so that no two vowels are together.

Sol. Given word is 'SOCIETY' in which 3 are vowels, namely, O, I, E and 4 are consonants, namely, S, C T, Y.

If we place all the vowels in a row, then we can get 5 gaps.

We shall place the 3 vowels in $^5P_3$.

Hence, the total number of possible ways = $^5P_3 \times 3!$.

Ex-5: How many different nine digit numbers can be formed from the number 223355888 by rearranging its digits so that the odd digits occupy even positions?

Ans. 60

Sol. Odd digits are 3, 3, 5, 5 and even digits are 2, 2, 8, 8, 8.

Even positions are 4 and also odd positions are 5.

Hence the total number of possible ways

$$= \frac{4!}{2! \times 2!} \times \frac{5!}{2! \times 3!} = 6 \times 10 = 60.$$

5.9 Circular Permutations

We have discussed earlier so far, permutations of objects (or things) in a row. Such type of permutations are called linear permutations or linear arrangements. If n different things can be arranged in a row, then the number of linear arrangements = n!, every linear arrangement have a beginning and an end, but in circular permutations, there is neither a beginning nor an end.

5.9.1 Arrangement around a circular loop

Consider five objects on the circumference of a circular loop in order which has no head now.

Shifting one position in anti-clockwise direction, we will get arrangement as follows:

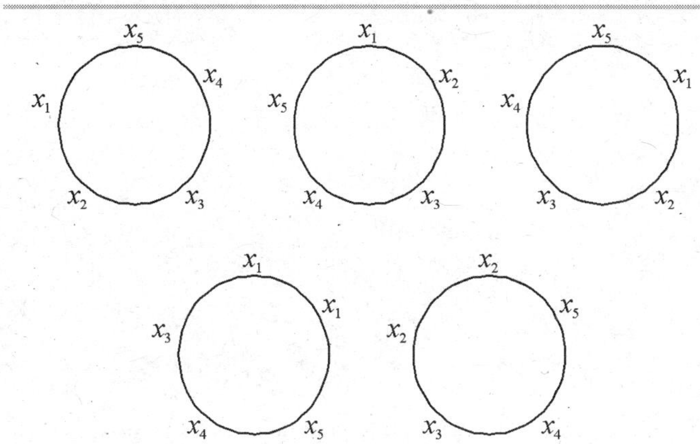

We see that arrangements in all figures are different.

If there be x circular permutations, then we have 5x linear permutations.

Now five different objects can be linearly arranged themselves in 5! ways.

Thus, $5x = 5! \Rightarrow x = \frac{5!}{5} = 4! = (5-1)!$.

If clockwise and anticlockwise orders are taken as different.

Thus, the number of circular permutations of n different things taken all a time is $(n-1)!$,

But if the clockwise and anti-clockwise permutations are not distinguishable.

i.e. arrangements of beads in a necklace, arrangements of flowers in a garland etc.

In this case, the number of permutations of n different things $= \frac{1}{2}(n-1)!$.

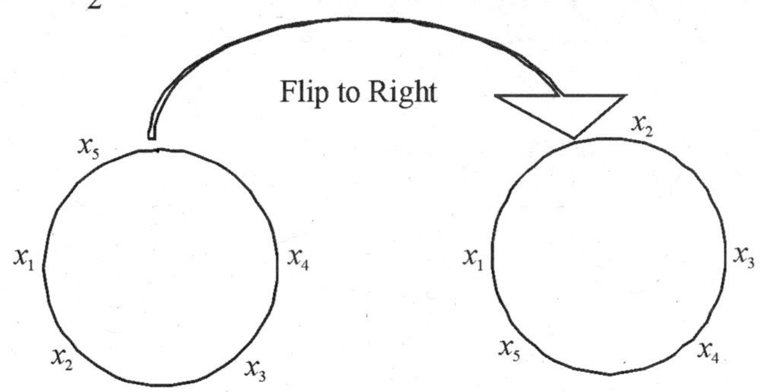

Ex-1: In how many ways 6 Indians and 5 Englishmen can be seated at a round table if

(i) there is no restriction ?

(ii) all the 5 Englishmen sit together?

(iii) all the 5 Englishmen do not sit together.

(iv) no two Englishmen sit together?

Sol. (i) Total number of persons = 6 + 5 = 11.

Thus, these 11 persons can be seated in a round table in (10)! ways.

(ii) Consider 5 Englishmen as one person.

Total number of persons = 6 + 1 = 7

Hence, the total number of possible ways they can be seated in a round table = 7! × 5!

(iii) Hence, the total number of arrangements when all the 5 Englishmen do not sit together = 10! – 7! × 5!.

(iv) 6 Indians can be seated in a round table in 5! ways.

If no two Englishmen do not sit together, then we can fill them in between 6 Indians in ${}^6P_5$ ways.

Hence, the total number of possible ways = ${}^6P_5 \times 5!$.

Ex-2: In how many ways can 50 different pearls be arranged to form a necklace ?

Sol. As we know that, to form a necklace , clock-wise and and anti-clockwise arrangements are same.

Hence the required number of arrangement

$$= \frac{1}{2} \times (50-1)! = \frac{49!}{2}$$

Ex-3: In how many ways can we arrange 6 different flowers in a circle ?

Sol. The number of circular arrangements of 6 different flowers = (6 – 1)! = 5! = 120.

Ex-4: In how many ways 3 ladies and 5 gentlemen arrange themselves about a round table so that every gentlemen may have at-least one lady ?

Sol. 5 gentlemen can arrange themselves in a round table in 4! ways.

If every gentlemen is to have at-least one lady by his side, then two ladies must be in two of the adjacent gaps and the third lady must occupy only one gap for every choice.

Thus, for every arrangement of gentlemen, ladies can be arranged in 5 × 3! ways.

Two adjacent gaps may be chosen in 5 ways and 3 ladies can be arranged themselves in 3! ways.

Hence, the required number of arrangements = 4 × 5 × 3!
= 720.

Ex-5. In how many ways can 20 persons sit around a round table in such a way that, there is exactly one person between A and B.

Sol. If two persons are A and B, then the remaining 18 persons are $P_1, P_2, \ldots\ldots, P_{18}$.

Take one of 18 persons, say P_1 and make him sit between A and B. i.e A, P_1, B.

In a similar way, we can place $P_2, P_3, \ldots\ldots, P_{18}$ in between A and B.

Thus, there are 18 ways of choosing one person between A and B.

Hence, the required number of possible ways = 18 × 17! × 2!.

5.10 Restricted Circular Permutations

Case - I: If clockwise and anticlockwise arrangements are taken as different, then the number of circular permutations of n different things taken r at a time $= \frac{{}^{n}P_r}{r}$

Case-II: If clockwise and anticlockwise arrangements are taken as not different, then the number of circular permutations of n different things taken r at a time $= \frac{{}^{n}P_r}{2r}$.

Ex-1: How many necklace of 20 beads, each can be made from 30 beads of various colors ?

Sol. In case of necklace, there is no distinction between clock-wise and anti-clockwise arrangements, then the total number of necklace $= \frac{1}{2} \times \left(\frac{{}^{30}P_{20}}{20}\right)$.

Ex-2: Find the number of ways of 20 different pearls of two colors can be set alternately on a necklace, there being 10 pearls of each color.

Sol. In case of necklace, there is no distinction between clock-wise and anti-clockwise arrangements, then the total number of possible ways

$$\frac{1}{2}\times(10)!\times(9)! = \frac{10}{2}\times(9)!\times(9)! = 5\times(9!)^2$$

Ex-3: In how many ways 20 persons be seated around a round table if there are 10 seats are available there ?

Sol. In case of a circular table, the clock-wise and the anti-clock-wise orders are different , then the total number of possible ways, they can be seated $= \frac{{}^{20}P_{10}}{20}$.

5.11 Combination

The different groups or selections of a number of things taken some or all of them at a time are called Combinations.

The number of combinations of n different things taken r at a time is denoted by ${}^{n}C_r$ and is defined as ${}^{n}C_r = \frac{n!}{r!\times(n-r)!}$, where $r \le n, r \in W, n \in N$.

Ex-1: In how many ways 7 different books be given to 2 students, if one gets 4 books and other gets 3 books.

Sol. The number of possible ways it can be distributed between two students

$$= {}^{7}C_4 \times {}^{4}C_3 = \frac{7!}{4!\times 3!}\times\frac{4!}{3!\times 1!} = \frac{7.6.5.4}{6} = 140$$

Ex-2: On a new year day, every student of a class sends a card to every other student. The postman delivers 600 cards . How many students are there in the class ?

Sol. Let n be the number of students.

Numbers of pairs of students $= {}^{n}C_2$

For ${}^{n}C_2$ pairs, number of cards sent = 2.

Thus, $2.{}^{n}C_2 = 600$

$\Rightarrow {}^{n}C_2 = 300$

$\Rightarrow \frac{n(n-1)}{2} = 300$

$\Rightarrow n(n-1) = 600$

$\Rightarrow n^2 - n - 600 = 0$

$\Rightarrow (n-24)(n+25) = 0$

$\Rightarrow n = 24$

Hence, the number of students = 24.

Ex-3: A man has 10 children to take them in a circus. He takes four of them at a time to the circus as often as he can without taking the same 4 children together more than once. How many times will he has to go to circus ?

Sol. Hence the required number of times he has to go to the circus with his children

$$= {}^{8}C_3 = \frac{8!}{3!\times 5!} = \frac{8.7.6}{6} = 56.$$

Ex-4: At an election, three wards of a town are canvassed by 4, 5 and 8 men respectively. If there are 20 volunteers, in how many ways can they be allotted to different wards ?

Sol. The total number of possible ways they can be allotted to different words $= {}^{20}C_4 \times {}^{16}C_5 \times {}^{11}C_8$.

5.12 Important results to remember

Let ${}^{n}C_0, {}^{n}C_1, {}^{n}C_2, \ldots\ldots, {}^{n}C_{n-1}, {}^{n}C_n$ are the binomial co-efficients in the expansion of $(1+x)^n$

(i) ${}^{n}C_0 + {}^{n}C_1 + {}^{n}C_2 + \ldots\ldots + {}^{n}C_{n-1} + {}^{n}C_n = 2^n$

(ii) ${}^{n}C_1 + {}^{n}C_2 + {}^{n}C_3 + \ldots\ldots + {}^{n}C_{n-1} = 2^n - 2$

(iii) ${}_{2} + {}^{n}C_4 + {}^{n}C_6 + \ldots\ldots =$
${}^{n}C_0 + {}^{n}C\,{}^{n}C_1 + {}^{n}C_3 + {}^{n}C_5 + {}^{n}C_7 + \ldots\ldots = 2^{n-1}$

(iv) ${}^{n}C_r = {}^{n}C_{n-r}$

(v) ${}^{n}C_r = \frac{n}{r}\times{}^{n-1}C_{r-1} = \frac{n(n-1)}{r(r-1)}\times{}^{n-2}C_{r-2}$ and so on.

(vi) ${}^{n}C_x = {}^{n}C_y \Rightarrow x = y \text{ or } x + y = n$

(vii) $\frac{{}^{n}C_r}{{}^{n}C_{r-1}} = \frac{n-r+1}{r}$

(viii) ${}^{n}C_r + {}^{n}C_{r-1} = {}^{n+1}C_r$

(ix) ${}^{n}C_0 - {}^{n}C_1 + {}^{n}C_2 - {}^{n}C_3 + \ldots\ldots + (-1)^n\,{}^{n}C_n = 0$

(x) ${}^{n}C_1 - 2.{}^{n}C_2 + 3.{}^{n}C_3 - 4.{}^{n}C_4 + \ldots\ldots + (-1)^{n-1} n.{}^{n}C_n = 0$

Ex-1: If ${}^{15}C_{3r} = {}^{15}C_{r+3}$, then find r .

Sol. We have ${}^{15}C_{3r} = {}^{15}C_{r+3}$, $\Rightarrow$ 3r + r + 3 = 15

$\Rightarrow$ 3r + r = 15 - 3 = 12

$\Rightarrow$ 4r = 12

$\Rightarrow$ r = 3

Ex-2: Find the value of $^{47}C_4 + \sum_{j=1}^{5} {}^{52-j}C_3$.

Sol. We have $^{47}C_4 + \sum_{j=1}^{5} {}^{52-j}C_3$

$= {}^{47}C_4 + {}^{51}C_3 + {}^{50}C_3 + {}^{49}C_3 + {}^{48}C_3 + {}^{47}C_3$

$= \left({}^{47}C_4 + {}^{47}C_3\right) + {}^{51}C_3 + {}^{50}C_3 + {}^{49}C_3 + {}^{48}C_3$

$= \left({}^{48}C_4 + {}^{48}C_3\right) + {}^{51}C_3 + {}^{50}C_3 + {}^{49}C_3$

$= \left({}^{49}C_4 + {}^{49}C_3\right) + {}^{51}C_3 + {}^{50}C_3$

$= \left({}^{50}C_4 + {}^{50}C_3\right) + {}^{51}C_3$

$= \left({}^{51}C_4 + {}^{51}C_3\right)$

$= {}^{52}C_4$

Ex-3: Solve for x : $^{x+3}P_2 = {}^{x+2}C_3 + 20$

Sol. We have $^{x+3}P_2 = {}^{x+2}C_3 + 20$

$\Rightarrow \quad \frac{(x+3)\ !}{(x+3-2)\ !} = \frac{(x+2)\ !}{(x+2-3)\ ! \times 3\ !} + 20$

$\Rightarrow \quad (x+3)(x+2) = \frac{x(x+2)(x+1)}{6} + 20$

$\Rightarrow \quad 6(x+3)(x+2) = x(x+2)(x+1) + 120$

$\Rightarrow \quad 6\left(x^2+5x+2\right) = x\left(x^2+3x+2\right) + 120$

$\Rightarrow \quad x^3 - 3x^2 - 28x + 84 = 0$

$\Rightarrow \quad (x-3)\left(x^2-28\right) = 0$

$\Rightarrow \quad x = 3 \text{ and } x = \pm 2\sqrt{7}$

$\Rightarrow \quad x = 3$ (since x is a whole number).

5.13 Restricted Combinations

(i) The number of selections of r objects out of n different objects when

(a) K particular things are always included $= {}^{n-k}C_{r-k}$

(b) K particular things are never included $= {}^{n-k}C_r$.

(ii) The number of combinations of r things out of n different things such that k particular things are not included in any selection $= {}^nC_r - {}^{n-k}C_{r-k}$

(iii) The number of selections of r consecutive things out of n things in a row = n - r + 1.

(iv) The number of selections of r consecutive things out of n things along a circle

$= \begin{cases} n, & \text{when } r < n \\ 1, & \text{when } r = n \end{cases}$

(v) The number of combinations of n objects, of which k are identical, taken r at a time

$= \begin{cases} {}^{n-k}C_r + {}^{n-k}C_{r-1} + {}^{n-k}C_{r-2} + \ldots\ldots\ldots + {}^{n-k}C_0, & \text{if } r \le k \\ {}^{n-k}C_r + {}^{n-k}C_{r-1} + {}^{n-k}C_{r-2} + \ldots\ldots\ldots + {}^{n-k}C_{r-k}, & \text{if } r \ge k \end{cases}$

(vi) The number of combinations of n different objects taking r at a time when p particular objects are always included and q particular things are always excluded

$= {}^{n-p-q}C_{r-p}$

Ex-1: In how many ways can we select the best 20 students for JEE - Advanced exam from a batch of 100 students if

(i) Two particular students are always chosen?

(ii) Five particular students are never chosen?

Sol. (i) Since two particular students are always chosen, the selection is needed for another 18 students from 98 students.

Hence, the required number of selection is $= {}^{98}C_{18}$.

(ii) Since five particular students are never chosen, then the selection is needed for 20 students from 95 students.

Hence the required number of selection is $= {}^{95}C_{20}$.

Ex-2: A group of students consists of 4 boys and 5 girls. Find the number of ways of selecting a team of at-least 3 boys and 4 girls.

Sol. Hence the required number of possible selection is

$= {}^4C_3 \times {}^5C_4 + {}^4C_4 \times {}^5C_4 + {}^4C_3 \times {}^5C_5 + {}^4C_4 \times {}^5C_5$

$= 4\times 5 + 1\times 5 + 4\times 1 + 1\times 1 = 20+5+4+1 = 30$

Ex-3: How many ways are there of choosing a hand of 6 cards containing an ace and a king of the same suit from a pack of 52 cards?

Sol. As a we know that, a pack of cards consists of 52 cards.

Out of 52 cards, 4 are aces & 4 are kings.

Hence, the required number of possible selection is $= {}^4C_1 \times {}^4C_1 \times {}^{44}C_4$.

Ex-4: Ten cards are taken out from an well shuffled pack of 52 cards. In how many ways of there of choosing a hand of 10 cards consists of at-least one ace ?

Sol. Out of 52 cards, 4 are aces.

Hence, the required number of possible selection is $= {}^4C_1 \times {}^{48}C_9 + {}^4C_2 \times {}^{48}C_8 + {}^4C_3 \times {}^{48}C_7 + {}^4C_4 \times {}^{48}C_6$

Ex-5: A bag contains 5 black and 6 red balls, all balls being different. Find the number of ways in which 2 black and 3 red balls can be selected.

Sol. Hence the required number of possible selection is

$= {}^5C_2 \times {}^6C_3$.

Ex-6: Out of 6 gentlemen and 4 ladies a committee of 5 is to be formed. In how many ways can this be done so as to include at-least one lady in each committee?

Sol. Total number of persons = 6 + 4 = 10.

Hence, the total number of required selection is $= {}^{10}C_5 - {}^6C_5$

$= \frac{(10)\ !}{5\ ! \times 5\ !} - 6 = \frac{10.9.8.7.6}{120} - 6$

$= 36\times 7 - 6 = 252 - 6 = 246.$

5.14 Selection of one or more objects

5.14.1 Combinations from distinct objects

(i) The number of selections of zero or more things out of n different things

$= {}^nC_0 + {}^nC_1 + {}^nC_2 + ...+ {}^nC_n = 2^n$

(ii) The number of selections of one or more things out of n different things

$= {}^nC_1 + {}^nC_2 + ...+ {}^nC_n = 2^n - 1$.

Ex-1: Master Amit has 8 friends 8. In how many ways he can invite one or more of them in his birthday?

Sol. The number of possible ways Master Amit can invite to his friends is

$= {}^8C_1 + {}^8C_2 + {}^8C_3 + {}^8C_4 + {}^8C_5 + {}^8C_6 + {}^8C_7 + {}^8C_8$

$= 2^8 - 1 = 255.$

Ex-2: In how many ways Master Roshan can give answer of at least one question out of 10 questions in his class test?

Sol. The number of possible ways Master Roshan can give the answer is

$= {}^{10}C_1 + {}^{10}C_2 + {}^{10}C_3 + {}^{10}C_4 + ...+ {}^{10}C_{10}$

$= 2^{10} - 1 = 1023.$

Ex-3: In an examination a student will pass if he/she passes all 5 subjects in his class. In how many ways he can fail the exam?

Sol. The student will fail if he fails in one or more subjects. Hence total number of possible ways he/she can fail the exam

$= {}^5C_1 + {}^5C_2 + {}^5C_3 + {}^5C_4 + {}^5C_5 = 2^5 - 1 = 31$.

Ex-4: A question paper consists of two sections having respectively 3 and 5 questions. One question from each section is compulsory. In how many ways can a student select the questions?

Sol. Hence, the total number of possible ways the student can select the questions

$= \left({}^3C_1 + {}^3C_2 + {}^3C_3\right) \times \left({}^5C_1 + {}^5C_2 + {}^5C_3 + {}^5C_4 + {}^5C_5\right)$

$= \left(2^3 - 1\right) \times \left(2^5 - 1\right)$

$= 7 \times 31 = 217$

Ex-5. A class has n students. we have to form a team of the students including at-least two students and also excluding two students. Find the number of ways of forming the team.

Sol. Hence the required number of ways

$= {}^nC_2 + {}^nC_3 + {}^nC_4 + {}^nC_5 + ...+ {}^nC_{n-2}$

$= \left({}^nC_0 + {}^nC_1 + {}^nC_2 + {}^nC_3 + {}^nC_4 + ...+ {}^nC_{n-2} + {}^nC_{n-1} + {}^nC_n\right)$

$- \left({}^nC_0 + {}^nC_1 + {}^nC_{n-1} + {}^nC_{n-2}\right)$

$= 2^n - (1 + n + n + 1)$

$= 2^n - 2(n + 1)$

Ex-6. A student is allowed to select at-most n books from a collection of (2n + 1) books. If the total number of ways in which he can select at-least one book is 63. Find the value of n.

Sol. Hence, the total number of possible selection is

$= {}^{2n+1}C_1 + {}^{2n+1}C_2 + {}^{2n+1}C_3 + ...+ {}^{2n+1}C_n$

Given, ${}^{2n+1}C_1 + {}^{2n+1}C_2 + {}^{2n+1}C_3 + ...+ {}^{2n+1}C_n = 63$ .....(i)

$\Rightarrow {}^{2n+1}C_{2n} + {}^{2n+1}C_{2n-1} + {}^{2n+1}C_{2n-2} + ...+ {}^{2n+1}C_{n+1} = 63$ ....(ii)

Adding (i) and (ii), we get

$\Rightarrow {}^{2n+1}C_1 + {}^{2n+1}C_2 + {}^{2n+1}C_3 + ...+ {}^{2n+1}C_n$

$+ {}^{2n+1}C_{n+1} + ...+ {}^{2n+1}C_{2n} = 63 + 63 = 126$

$\Rightarrow 2^{2n+1} - \left({}^{2n+1}C_0 + {}^{2n+1}C_{2n+1}\right) = 126$

$\Rightarrow 2^{2n+1} - 2 = 126$

$\Rightarrow 2^{2n+1} = 126 + 2 = 128$

$\Rightarrow 2^{2n+1} = 128 = 2^7$

$\Rightarrow 2n + 1 = 7$

$\Rightarrow n = 6$

5.14.2 Combinations from identical objects:

(i) The number of selections of r objects out of n identical objects = 1.

(ii) The number of selections of zero or more objects from n identical objects = n + 1

(iii) The total number of selections of at least one out of $(a_1 + a_2 + a_3 + ... + a_n)$, where a_1 are alike of one kind, a_2 are alike of 2nd kind, ..., a_n are alike of nth kind

$= \left[(a_1 + 1)(a_2 + 1)(a_3 + 1)..........(a_n + 1)\right] - 1$

Ex-1: In how many ways Master Himel can select 10 Red balls out of 20 Red balls?

Sol. Here all balls are in red colors. So the objects are identical. Hence, the total number of selections is = 1.

Ex-2: In how many ways Master Kalicharan can select 0 or more balls from 12 green balls?

Sol. Here all balls are in green colors. So the objects are identical.

As we know that, the number of selections of zero or more objects from n identical objects is n + 1. Thus the total number of possible selections is = 12 + 1 = 13.

Ex-3. In how many ways Master Bheem can select at least 1 ball out of 10 Red balls , 15 Green balls, 12 Blue balls and 5 Black balls ?

Sol. Hence, total number of possible selections

$= (10+1)(15+1)(12+1)(5+1)-1$

$= 11\times 16\times 13\times 6-1$

$= 176\times 78-1$

$= 13728-1$

$= 13727.$

5.14.3 Combination when both identical and distinct objects are present

The number of selections of one or more objects out of $(a_1+a_2+a_3+..............+a_n)$ objects, where a_1 are alike of one kind, a_2 are alike of 2nd kind ,.........., a_n are alike of nth kind and k are distinct

$$= [(a_1+1)(a_2+1)(a_3+1)..............(a_n+1)]$$
$$({}^kC_0+{}^kC_1+{}^kC_2+..........+{}^kC_k)-1$$
$$= [(a_1+1)(a_2+1)(a_3+1)..............(a_n+1)]\ 2^k\ -1$$

Proof: Since number of ways of selecting r things out of n identical things is 1, where $r\le n$..

Hence the number of ways of selecting zero thing out of a_1 identical things = 1, the number of ways of selecting one things out of a_1 identical things = 1, the number of ways of selecting two things out of a_1 identical things = 1,

....

....

The number of ways of selecting a_1 things out of a_1 identical things = 1

Thus, the number of ways of selecting zero or more things out of a_1 identical things = a_1+1

Similarly, the number of ways of selecting zero or more things out of a_2 identical things = a_2+1 the number of ways of selecting zero or more things out of a_3 identical things = a_1+1,

Also number of ways of selecting zero or more things out of k identical things

$= 2\times 2\times 2\times..............\times 2\ \ (k-\text{times}) = 2^k$

Thus, the number of ways of selecting zero or more things out of given things

$= (a_1+1)(a_2+1)(a_3+1)..............(a_n+1)2^k$

Also, the number of ways of selecting zero thing out of given things = 1.

Therefore, the total number of ways of selecting one or more things out of given things

$= (a_1+1)(a_2+1)(a_3+1)..............(a_n+1)2^k-1$

Ex-1: There are 4 oranges, 5 apples and 6 mangoes in a fruit basket. In how many ways can a person make a selection of fruits from among the fruits in the basket?

Sol. Hence, the total number of ways of selecting one or more fruits out of given fruits

$= (4+1)(5+1)(6+1)-1$

$= 210\ -1 = 209.$

Ex-2. Find the number of ways in which one or more letter be selected from the letters of the word 'ABRACADABRA'.

Sol. Given word is 'ABRACADABRA', in which 5 A's, 2 B's, 2 R's, 1 C, 1 D.

Hence, the total number of possible selection is

$= (5+1)(2+1)(2+1)2^2-1$

$= 54\times 4-1 = 216-1 = 215$

Ex-3. Find the number of selection that can be formed with 10 apples, 5 mangoes and 7 bananas when *(i)* at-least one fruit is taken *(ii)* at-least one fruit of each kind is taken.

Sol. (i) The required number of selection is

$= (10+1)(5+1)(7+1)-1$

$= 11\times 6\times 7-1 = 462-1 = 461$

(iii) The required number of possible selection is

5.15 Divisors of A Given Natural Number

Let $\alpha\in N$ and where $\alpha = p_1^{\alpha_1}p_2^{\alpha_2}p_3^{\alpha 3}..............p_k^{\alpha_k}$, I = 1, 2, 3, ..., k are different prime numbers and α_i, I = 1, 2, 3,.............., $k\in N$. Then

(i) the total number of divisors of α including 1 and α

$= (\alpha_1+1)(\alpha_2+1)(\alpha_3+1)............(\alpha_k+1)$

(ii) the total number of divisors of α excluding 1 and α

$= (\alpha_1+1)(\alpha_2+1)(\alpha_3+1)............(\alpha_k+1)-2$

(iii) the total number of divisors of α excluding either 1 or α

$= (\alpha_1+1)(\alpha_2+1)(\alpha_3+1)............(\alpha_k+1)-1$

(iv) Sum of the divisors

$$(p_1^0+p_1^1+p_1^2+....+p_1^{\alpha_1})(p_1^0+p_1^1+p_1^2+....+p_1^{\alpha_2})$$
$$........(p_1^0+p_1^1+p_1^2+....+p_1^{\alpha_k})$$
$$= \left(\frac{1-p_1^{\alpha_1+1}}{1-p_1}\right)\left(\frac{1-p_1^{\alpha_2+1}}{1-p_2}\right)........\left(\frac{1-p_1^{\alpha_k+1}}{1-p_k}\right)$$

(v) the number of ways in which can be resolved as a product of two factors

$$= \begin{cases} \frac{1}{2}\prod_{r=1}^{k}(a_k+1) & \text{,if a is not a perfect square} \\ \frac{1}{2}\left[\frac{1}{2}\prod_{r=1}^{k}(a_k+1)+1\right] & \text{, if a is a perfect square} \end{cases}$$

(vi) the number of ways in which composite number α can be resolved into two factors which are relatively prime (or co-prime) to each other is equal to 2^{k-1}, where k is the number of different factors (or different primes) in α.

Let $\alpha = p_1^{\alpha_1}p_2^{\alpha_2}p_3^{\alpha 3}..............p_k^{\alpha_k}$

Out of the two factors one must contain $p_1^{a_1}$, otherwise there should be some power of P_1 in the other factor and thus the two factors would not be prime to each other.

Similarly, $p_2^{\alpha_2}$ must occur one of the factors only and so on. Hence, the required number is equal to the number of ways in which the product $\alpha_1.\alpha_2.\alpha_3$.......... can be resolved into two factors is

$$=\frac{1}{2}(1+1)(1+1)(1+1)............(k-\text{times})$$

$$=\frac{1}{2}\times 2^k$$

$$=2^{k-1}$$

(vii) The number of ordered pairs (x, y) such that the L.C.M of x and y is a composite number of α is

$(2p_1+1)(2p_2+1)(2p_3+1)$........ .

Here, $\alpha = p_1^{\alpha_1} p_2^{\alpha_2} p_3^{\alpha 3}$ .... $p_k^{\alpha_k}$

Out of the two numbers x and y, one must contain $p_1^{\alpha_1}$

Otherwise the L.C.M would have smaller power of P_1

If x contain $p_1^{\alpha_1}$ then y can have one of the factors of

$1, p_1, p_1^2, p_1^2, ..., p_1^{a_1}$

And if y contain $p_1^{\alpha_1}$ then y can have one of the factors of

$1, p_1, p_1^2, ..., p_1^{a_1-1}$

Hence, the number of ways to distribute powers of a to x and y to ensure that the L.C.M contains $p_1^{a_1}$ is $(2\alpha_1+1)$.

Hence, the total number of ways is

$(2\alpha_1+1)(2\alpha_2+1)(2\alpha_3+1)$............

Ex-1: If α = 10800, then find the

(a) total number of divisors of — Ans. 60

(b) the number of even divisors. — Ans. 48

(c) the number of divisors of the form 4 m + 2 — Ans. 12

(d) the number of divisors which are multiple of 15. — Ans. 30

Sol. We have $\alpha = 10800 = 2^4\times 3^3\times 5^2$

(i) Hence, the total number of divisors

$= (4+1)(3+1)(2+1) = 60$

(ii) Hence, the number of even divisors

$4(3+1)(2+1) = 48$

(iii) Hence, the number of divisors of the form 4m + 2 is

= the number is of the form 6, 10

$= (3 + 1)(2 + 1)$ (since the number can be written as $(2 \times 3)^3$ or $(2 \times 5)^2$)

= 12.

(iv) Hence, the number of divisors of multiple of 15 is

$= (2 + 1)(4 + 1)(1 + 1)$ (since $10800 = 2^4 \times 3^3 \times 5^2$

$= (3 \times 5)^2 \times 2^4 \times 3^1$)

= 30

Ex-2. In how many ways the number 18900 can be split into two factors which are Relatively prime (or co-prime) Ans. 8

Ans. We have $18900 = 2^2 \times 3^3 \times 5^2 \times 7$.

Hence, the required number of possible ways $= 2^{4-1} = 2^3 = 8$.

Ex-3. Find the number of ordered pairs (p, q) such that the L.C.M of p and q is 2120.

Sol. We have $2520 = 2^3 \times 3^2 \times 5 \times 7$.

Hence, the total number of possible ordered pairs (p, q) is

$= (2.3 + 1)(2.2 + 1)(2.1 + 1)(2.1 + 1)$

$= 7 \times 5 \times 3 \times 3$

= 315.

Ex-4. Find the sum of all divisors of 2520.

Sol. We have $2520 = 2^3 \times 3^2 \times 5 \times 7$

Hence, the sum of the divisors of 2520

$= (1 + 2 + 2^2 + 2^3)(1 + 3 + 3^2)(1+ 5)(1 + 7)$

$= 15 \times 13 \times 6 \times 8$

= 9360.

Ex-5. Find the sum of all the odd divisors of 360.

Sol. We have $360 = 2^3 \times 3^2 \times 5$

Hence, the sum of the odd divisors of 360

$= (1 + 3 + 3^2)(1 + 5)$

$= 13 \times 6$

= 78.

Ex-6. Find the sum of all the even divisors of 38808

Sol. We have $= 38808 = 2^3 \times 3^2 \times 7^2 \times 11$.

Hence, the sum of the even divisors $= (1+2+2^2+2^3) = 15$.

5.16 Distribution Into Groups

5.16.1 Distribution into group of unequal size among sets (groups) and persons

(i) The number of ways in which (m + n + p) different things can be divided into unequal groups which contain m, n and p things respectively.

$$= {}^{m+n+p}C_m \cdot {}^{n+p}C_n \cdot {}^{p}C_p = \frac{(m+n+p)!}{m!\times n!\times p!}$$

(ii) The number of ways to distribute (m + n + p) things among three persons in the groups containing m, n and p things

= (Number of ways of divide) × (Number of Groups)

$$= \frac{(m+n+p)!}{m!\times n!\times p!}\times 3!$$

5.16.2 Distribution into groups of equal size among sets (groups) and persons

(i) The number of ways in which mn different things can be divided equally in n groups

$$= \left(\frac{(mn)!}{(m!)^n}\right)\times\frac{1}{n!}$$

(ii) The number of ways in which mn different things can be distributed equally among n different groups

$$= \left(\frac{(mn)!}{(m!)^n}\right)$$

Illustrations:

1. Dividing 4 different things P, Q, R, S into 2 sets one having 1 thing and second set having 3 things.

Set I	Set II	No. of ways
P	Q, R, S	
Q	P, R, S	${}^4C_1 \times {}^3C_3 = 4$
R	P, Q, S	
S	P, Q, R	

2. Distribution of 4 different things among 2 persons such that one person gets 3 things and other gets one thing

Person I	Person II	No. of ways
P	Q, R, S	
Q	P, R, S	
R	P, Q, S	
S	P, Q, R	
Q, R, S	P	${}^4C_3 \times {}^1C_1 \times 2! = 8$
P, R, S	Q	
P, Q, S	R	
P, Q, R	S	

3. Dividing 4 different things P, Q, R, S in two sets each having 2 things

Set I	Set II	No. of ways
(i) P, Q	R, S	
(ii) P, R	Q, S	
(iii) P, S	Q, R	$({}^4C_2 \times {}^2C_2)/2! = 3$
(iv) Q, R	P, S	
(v) Q, S	P, R	
(vi) R, S	P, Q	

Here, sets in (i) and (vi) are same; sets in (ii) and (v) are same; sets in (iii) and (iv) are same.

4. Distribution of 4 different things among 2 persons such that each gets 2 things.

Person I	Person II	No. of ways
P, Q	R, S	
P, R	Q, S	
P, S	Q, R	${}^4C_2 \times {}^2C_2 = 6$
Q, R	P, S	
Q, S	P, R	
R, S	P, Q	

5.17 Arrangement into Groups

5.17.1

The number of ways in which n different things can be arranged in r different groups is ${}^{n+r-1}P_n$ or ${}^{n-1}C_{r-1} \times n!$ according as blank groups are or are not permitted.

Ist part:

Consider the n-things are identical .

Let $1^{st}, 2^{nd}\, 3^{rd}, \dots\dots\dots, r^{th}$ groups be allotted $x_1, x_2, \dots\dots, x_r$ things respectively.

The number of solutions of $x_1 + x_2 + \dots\dots + x_r = n$ in non-negative integers is ${}^{n+r-1}C_{r-1}$.

Now n things can be arranged themselves in n! ways, considering them to be different among the r group.

Hence, the number of ways $= {}^{n+r-1}C_{r-1} \times n! = {}^{n+r-1}P_n$.

2nd Part:

Consider the n-things are identical

Let $1^{st}, 2^{nd}\, 3^{rd}, \dots\dots\dots, r^{th}$ groups be allotted $x_1, x_2, \dots\dots, x_r$ things respectively.

The number of solutions of $x_1 + x_2 + \dots\dots + x_r = n$ in positive integers is ${}^{n-1}C_{r-1}$.

Now n things can be arranged themselves in n! ways, considering them to be different among the r group.

Hence, the number of ways $= {}^{n-1}C_{r-1} \times n!$

Illustration :

1. In how many different ways 5 different balls can be arranged into 3 different boxes so that no box remains empty?

Sol:

Box	No. of balls	No. of ways		Box	No. of balls	No. of ways
I	1			I	1	
II	1	$5! \times \frac{3!}{2!}$	OR	II	2	$5! \times \frac{3!}{2!}$
III	3			III	2	

Thus the total number of ways $= 5! \times \frac{3!}{2!} + 5! \times \frac{3!}{2!}$

$= 120 \times 3 + 120 \times 3 = 720.$

5.17.2

The number of ways in which n different things can be distributed into r different groups is

$$= r^n - {}^rC_1(r-1)^n + {}^rC_2(r-2)^n - \dots\dots\dots + (-1)^{r-1}.{}^rC_{r-1}$$

Or coefficient of x^n in $(e^x - 1)^r \times n!$.

Here, blank groups are permitted.

NOTE

Co-efficient of x^n in e^{ax} is $\frac{a^n}{n!}$.

Illustration:

1. In how many ways 5 different balls can be distributed into 3 boxes so that no box remains empty?

Box	No. of balls	No. of ways		Box	No. of balls	No. of ways
I	1			I	1	
II	1	${}^5C_1 \times {}^4C_1 \times {}^3C_3 \times \frac{3!}{2!}$	Or	II	2	${}^5C_1 \times {}^4C_2 \times {}^2C_2 \times \frac{3!}{2!}$
III	3			III	2	

Hence the total number of ways = 60 + 190 = 250.

5.17.3

The number of ways in which n identical things can be distributed into r different groups is = ${}^{n+r-1}C_r$ or ${}^{n-1}C_{r-1}$ according as blank groups are or are not permitted.

1st Part

The number of ways in which n identical things can be distributed into r - different groups, when blank are permitted, is

= Co-efficient of x^n in $(1+x+x^2+x^3+\dots\dots\dots+x^n)^r$

= Co-efficient of x^n in $\left(\frac{1-x^{n+1}}{1-x}\right)^r$

= Co-efficient of x^n in $(1-x^{n+1})^r \times (1-x)^{-r}$

= Co-efficient of x^n in $(1-x)^{-r}$

= Co-efficient of x^n in ${}^{n+r-1}C_r$.

2nd Part

The number of in which n identical things can be distributed into r different groups, when blank groups are not permitted

= co-efficient of x^n in $(x+x^2+x^3+\dots\dots\dots+x^n)^r$

= co-efficient of x^{n-r} in $(1+x+x^2+\dots\dots\dots+x^{n-1})^r$

= co-efficient of x^{n-r} in $\left(\frac{1-x^{n+1}}{1-x}\right)^r$

= co-efficient of x^{n-r} in $(1-x^{n+1})^r \times (1-x)^{-r}$.

= co-efficient of x^{n-r} in ${}^{n-1}C_{r-1}$.

Illustrations:

1. Distribution of 4 identical things among two persons when each person gets at least one thing.

	Person I	Person II	No. of ways
No. of things	1	3	$1\times1=1$
	2	2	$1\times1=1$
	3	1	$1\times1=1$

Thus the total no. of ways = 3.

2. In how many ways 5 identical balls can be distributed into 3 different boxes, so that no box remains empty?

Box	No. of balls	No. of ways		Box	No. of balls	No. of ways
I	1			I	1	
II	1	$1\times\frac{3!}{2!}$	Or	II	2	$1\times\frac{3!}{2!}$
III	3			III	2	

Thus the total number of ways $= 1\times\frac{3!}{2!}+1\times\frac{3!}{2!} = 3+3=6.$

5.17.4

If a group has n things in which r are identical, then the number of ways of selecting k things from a group is

$$=\begin{cases}\sum_{k=0}^{k} {}^{n-r}C_k, & \text{when } k\le r\\ \sum_{k=k-r}^{k} {}^{n-r}C_k, & \text{when } k>r\end{cases}$$

Ex-1. A box contains 25 balls in which 10 are identical. Then find the number of ways of selecting 12 balls from the box.

Sol. Hence, the required number of possible selection is

$$=\sum_{k=0}^{12} {}^{25-10}C_k$$

$$= {}^{15}C_0+{}^{15}C_1+{}^{15}C_2+\dots\dots+{}^{15}C_{12}$$

$$=\left({}^{15}C_0+{}^{15}C_1+{}^{15}C_2+\dots\dots+{}^{15}C_{12}+\dots\dots+{}^{15}C_{15}\right) - \left({}^{15}C_{13}+{}^{15}C_{14}+{}^{15}C_{15}\right)$$

$$=2^{15}-(105+15+1)$$

$$=2^{15}-121$$

Ex-2. A bag contains 15 balls of which 6 are identical. Find the number of ways of selecting

(i) 8 balls Ans. 501

(ii) 4 balls. Abs. 256.

Sol. (i) Hence, the required number of possible selections is

$$=\sum_{k=8-4}^{8} {}^{9}C_k$$

$$= {}^9C_4+{}^9C_5+{}^9C_6+{}^9C_7+{}^9C_8$$

$$= 126+126+84+36+9$$

$$= 481.$$

(ii) Hence, the required number of possible selections is

$$=\sum_{k=0}^{4} {}^{9}C_k$$

$$= {}^9C_0+{}^9C_1+{}^9C_2+{}^9C_3+{}^9C_4$$

$$= 1+9+36+84+126$$

$$=256.$$

5.18 Derangements

5.18.1

Assume $x_1, x_2, x_3, x_4, \dots\dots\dots, x_n$ be n distinct objects such that their positions are fixed in a row. If we now re-arrange $x_1, x_2, x_3, x_4, \dots\dots\dots, x_n$ in such a way that no one occupy its original position, then such an arrangement is called derangement.

A derangement of $x_1, x_2, x_3, x_4, \dots\dots\dots, x_n$ is a bijection.

$$f:(x_1, x_2, x_3, x_4, \dots\dots\dots, x_n)\to(x_1, x_2, x_3, x_4, \dots\dots\dots, x_n)$$

is bijective function such that, $f(x_i)\ne x_i$, I = 1, 2, 3, ……, n.

If n things are arranged in a row, the number of ways in which they can be derangement in such a way that, no one of them occupied its original positions is denoted by D(n) and is defined as

$$D(n) = n!\times\left(1-\frac{1}{1!}+\frac{1}{2!}-\frac{1}{3!}+\frac{1}{4!}-\dots\dots\dots+(-1)^n\frac{1}{n!}\right).$$

When r things goes to wrong place out of n things, then (n-r) things goes to its original place.

Then $D_n = {}^{n-r}C_r \times D_r$, where D_n be the number of group, if all n things goes to the wrong place and D_n be the number of ways if r things goes to the wrong place.

Ex-1. Four different letters are written and the corresponding addresses are correctly written on four envelopes. One letter can be placed in one envelope. In how many ways can be letters be placed in the envelopes so that

(i) all the letters are in the wrong envelopes.

(ii) at least one of them be in the wrong envelope.

Ans. 23

(iv) at-least two of them in the wrong envelope.

Sol. (i) The number of ways to put 4 letters in 4 addressed envelopes, so that all are in wrong envelopes

$$= 4!\left(1-\frac{1}{1!}+\frac{1}{2!}-\frac{1}{3!}+\frac{1}{4!}\right)$$

$$= 24\times\left(\frac{1}{2}-\frac{1}{6}+\frac{1}{24}\right)$$

$$= 24\times\left(\frac{12-4+1}{24}\right)$$

$$= 9.$$

(ii) The number of ways to put 4 letters in 4 addressed envelopes, so that at-least one of them in the wrong envelope

$$= \sum_{r=1}^{4} {}^4C_{4-r}\times D_r$$

$$= {}^4C_3\times D_1 + {}^4C_2\times D_2 + {}^4C_1\times D_3 + D_4$$

$$= 4D_1 + 6D_2 + 4D_3 + D_4$$

$$= 4.1!\left(1-\frac{1}{1!}\right)+6.2!\left(1-\frac{1}{1!}+\frac{1}{2!}\right)+4.3!\left(1-\frac{1}{1!}+\frac{1}{2!}-\frac{1}{3!}\right) + 4!\left(1-\frac{1}{1!}+\frac{1}{2!}-\frac{1}{3!}+\frac{1}{4!}\right)$$

$$= 6+4+9$$

$$= 19$$

(ii) The number of ways to put 4 letters in 4 addressed envelopes, so that at-least two of them in the wrong envelope

$$= \sum_{r=1}^{4} {}^4C_{4-r}\times D_r$$

$$= {}^4C_2\times D_2 + {}^4C_1\times D_3 + {}^4C_0\times D_4$$

$$= 12.D_2 + 4.D_3 + D_4$$

$$= 12+4+9$$

$$= 25.$$

5.19 Multinomial Theorem

5.19.1 Combinations with Repetitions

(i) The number of combinations of r things out of n things of which p - alike of one kind, q alike of 2nd kind, s alike of 3rd kind and rest (n – p – q – s) things are all different.

= Co-efficient of x^r in

$$= \left(1+x+x^2+..+x^p\right)\left(1+x+x^2+..+x^q\right)\left(1+x+x^2+...+x^r\right)$$
$$\left(1+x\right)\left(1+x\right)...\text{to } (n-p-q-s)\text{times}$$

= Co-efficient of x^r in

$$\left(\frac{1-x^{p+1}}{1-x}\right)\left(\frac{1-x^{q+1}}{1-x}\right)\left(\frac{1-x^{s+1}}{1-x}\right)(1+x)^{n-p-q-s}$$

(ii) The number of selections of r things out of n things of which p alike things to one kind, q alike things of 2nd kind, s alike things of 3rd kind, when each things is taken at least once.

= Co-efficient of x^r in

$$(x+x^2+x^3+......+x^p)(x+x^2+x^3+.......+x^q)$$
$$(x+x^2+x^3+.......+x^s)$$

$$= \text{Co-efficient of in}\left(\frac{1-x^p}{1-x}\right)\left(\frac{1-x^q}{1-x}\right)\left(\frac{1-x^s}{1-x}\right).$$

5.19.1 Permutations with Repetitions

The number of permutations of r things out of n things in which p alike things of one kind, q alike things of 2nd kind, s alike things of 3rd kind and so on

= Co-efficient of x^r in

$$\left\{r!\times\left(1+\frac{x}{1!}+\frac{x^2}{2!}+......+\frac{x^p}{p!}\right)\left(1+\frac{x}{1!}+\frac{x^2}{2!}+......+\frac{x^q}{q!}\right)\right.$$
$$\left.\left(1+\frac{x}{1!}+\frac{x^2}{2!}+......+\frac{x^s}{s!}\right).....\right\}$$

Ex-1. Find the number of combinations and permutations of 4 letters taken from the word E N G I N E E R I N G

Ans. 43, 476.

Sol. Total number of letters = 11, in which E & N occurs 3 times, G & I occurs 2 times, R occurs one time.

The number of combinations

= Co-efficient of x^4 in $(1+x+x^2+x^3)^2\times(1+x+x^2)^2\times(1+x)$

$$= \text{Co-efficient of } x^4 \text{ in}\left(\frac{1-x^4}{1-x}\right)^2\times\left(\frac{1-x^3}{1-x}\right)^2\times(1+x)$$

$$= \text{Co-efficient of } x^4 \text{ in } (1-x^4)^2\times(1-x^3)^2\times(1+x)\times(1-x)^{-4}$$

$$= \text{Co-efficient of } x^4 \text{ in } (1-2x^4)\times(1-2x^3)\times(1+x)\times(1-x)^{-4}$$

$$= \text{Co-efficient of } x^4 \text{ in } (1+x-2x^3-4x^4)\times(1-x)^{-4}$$

= Co-efficient of x^4 in

$$\left(1+x-2x^3-4x^4\right)\times\left(1+{}^4C_1x+{}^5C_2x^2+{}^6C_3x^3+{}^7C_4x^4+......\right)$$

$$= ({}^7C_4+{}^6C_3-4-4.{}^2C_1)$$

$$= (35+20-4-8)$$

$$= 43.$$

The number of permutation of 4 alphabets is

= Co-efficient of x^4 in

$$4!\left(1+\frac{x}{1!}+\frac{x^2}{2!}+\frac{x^3}{3!}\right)^2\times\left(1+\frac{x}{1!}+\frac{x^2}{2!}\right)^2\times(1+x)$$

$= \text{Co-efficient of in}$

$4!\left(1+2x+2x^2+\frac{4}{3}x^3+\frac{7}{12}x^4\right)\times\left(1+3x+4x^2+3x^3+\frac{5}{4}x^4\right)$

$= 4!\times\left(\left(\frac{7}{12}+\frac{5}{4}\right)+(6+4)+8\right)$

$= 24\times\frac{22}{12}+24\times 18$

$= 44+432$

$= 476.$

Ex-2. Find the total number of ways of selecting 5 letters of the word "I N D E P E N D EN T". (72)

Sol. The total number of letters = 11 in which E & N occurs 3 times, D occurs 2 times, I, P T each occur is one time.

The total number of selection is

$= \text{Co-efficient of } x^5 \text{ in } (1+x+x^2+x^3)^2\times(1+x+x^2)\times(1+x)^3$

$= \text{Co-efficient of } x^5 \text{ in } \left(\frac{1-x^4}{1-x}\right)^2\times\left(\frac{1-x^3}{1-x}\right)\times(1+x)^3$

$= \text{Co-efficient of } x^5 \text{ in } (1-x^4)^2\times(1-x^3)\times(1-x)^{-3}\times(1+x)^3$

$= \text{Co-efficient of } x^5 \text{ in}$

$(1-2x^4)\times(1-x^3)\times(1-x)^{-3}\times(1+3x+3x^2+x^3)$

$= \text{Co-efficient of } x^5 \text{ in}$

$(1-x^3-2x^4)\times(1+3x+3x^2+x^3)\times(1-x)^{-3}$

$= \text{Co-efficient of } x^5 \text{ in } \left(1+3x+3x^2-5x^4-9x^5\right)\times$

$\left(1+{}^3C_1x+{}^4C_2x^2+{}^5C_3x^3+{}^6C_4x^4+{}^7C_5x^5+\ldots\ldots\right)$

$= \left({}^7C_5-9\right)+\left(3.\,{}^6C_4-15\right)+\left(3.\,{}^5C_3\right)$

$= (21-9)+(45-15)+(30)$

$= 12+30+30$

$= 72.$

5.19.3

The number of ways in which n identical things can be distributed into r groups so that no groups contains less than m things and more than k things (m < k).

$\text{Coefficient of } x^n \text{ in } \left(x^m+x^{m+1}+x^{m+2}+\ldots\ldots\ldots\ldots+x^k\right)^r$

$= \text{Co-efficient of } x^n \text{ in } x^{mr}\left(1+x+x^2+x^3+\ldots\ldots\ldots+x^{k-m}\right)^r$

$= \text{Co-efficient of } x^n \text{ in } x^{n-mr} \text{ in } \left(1-x^{k-m+1}\right)^r\times(1-x)^{-r}.$

Ex-1. In how many ways can three persons, each throwing a single dice once, make a sum of 15?

Sol. Hence, the number of possible ways

$= \text{co-efficient of } x^{15} \text{ in } \left(x+x^2+x^3+x^4+x^5+x^6\right)^3$

$= \text{co-efficient of } x^{12} \text{ in } \left(1+x+x^2+x^3+x^4+x^5\right)^3$

$= \text{co-efficient of } x^{12} \text{ in } \left(\frac{1-x^6}{1-x}\right)^3$

$= \text{co-efficient of } x^{12} \text{ in } (1-x^6)^3\times(1-x)^{-3}$

$= \text{co-efficient of } x^{12} \text{ in } \left(1-3x^6+3.x^{12}\right)\times$

$\left(1+{}^3C_1x+{}^4C_2x^2+\ldots\ldots+{}^8C_6x^6+\ldots\ldots\ldots+{}^{14}C_{12}x^{12}\right)$

$= \left({}^{14}C_{12}-3.\,{}^8C_6+3\right)$

$= 91-84+3$

$= 10.$

Aliter :

The number of possible triplets to get 15 are (5, 5, 5), (5, 6, 4) and (6, 6, 4)

Thus the number of arrangements are

$= \frac{3!}{3!}+3!+\frac{3!}{2!}$

$= 1+6+3$

$= 10.$

Q.2 In how many ways 16 identical things can be distributed among 4 persons if each person gets at least 3 things?

Ans. 35

Sol. Hence, the number of possible ways

$= \text{co-efficient of } x^{16} \text{ in } (x^3+x^4+x^5+x^6+x^7)^4$

$= \text{co-efficient of } x^4 \text{ in } (1+x+x^2+x^3+x^4)^4$

$= \text{co-efficient of } x^4 \text{ in } \left(\frac{1-x^5}{1-x}\right)^4$

$= \text{co-efficient of } x^4 \text{ in } (1-x^5)^4\times(1-x)^{-4}$

$= \text{co-efficient of } x^4 \text{ in}$

$\left(1+{}^4C_1x+{}^5C_2x^2+{}^6C_3x^3+{}^7C_4x^4+\ldots\ldots\right)$

$= {}^7C_4$

$= 35.$

Aliter :

The number of possible quadruplets to get sum 16 are (3, 3, 3, 7), (3, 3, 5, 5), (3, 3, 4, 6), (3, 4, 4, 5), (4, 4, 4, 4)

Hence the number of possible ways to distribute 16 things among 4 persons is

$= \frac{4!}{3!}+\frac{4!}{2!2!}+\frac{4!}{2!}+\frac{4!}{2!}+\frac{4!}{4!}$

$= 4+6+12+12+1$

$= 35.$

5.20 Solutions of the Equation with the Help of Multinomial Theorem

5.20.1

Find the number of solutions of the equation $x_1+x_2+x_3+\ldots\ldots+x_m=n$

(i) for positive integers.

(ii) for non - negative integers.

(iii) for integers such that $x_1 \geq c_1, x_2 \geq c_2, x_3 \geq c_2, \ldots\ldots\ldots, x_n \geq c_n$.

Solutions :

(i) The required number of solutions

$= \text{Coefficient of } x^n \text{ in } (x + x^2 + x^3 + \ldots\ldots + x^n)^m$

$= \text{Coefficient of } x^n \text{ in } x^m (1 + x + x^2 + x^3 + \ldots\ldots + x^{n-1})^m$

$= \text{Coefficient of } x^{n-m} \text{ in } (1 + x + x^2 + x^3 + \ldots\ldots + x^{n-1})^m$

$= \text{Coefficient of } x^{n-m} \text{ in } \left(\frac{1-x^n}{1-x}\right)^m$

$= \text{Coefficient of } x^{n-m} \text{ in } (1 - x^n)^m \times (1 - x)^{-m}$

$= \text{Coefficient of } x^{n-m} \text{ in } (1 - mx - \ldots\ldots)(1 - x)^{-m}$

$= {}^{m+n-m-1}C_{n-m}$

$= {}^{n-1}C_{m-1}$

(ii) The required number of solutions

$= \text{Co-efficient of } x^n \text{ in } (1 + x + x^2 + x^3 + \ldots\ldots + x^n)^m$

$= \text{Co-efficient of } x^n \text{ in } (1 + x^{n+1})^m (1 - x)^{-m}$

$= \text{Co-efficient of } x^n \text{ in } (1 + mx^{n+1} + \ldots\ldots)(1 - x)^{-m}$

$= {}^{m+n-1}C_n$

$= {}^{m+n-1}C_{m-1}$

(iii) Let $y_1 = x_1 - c_1, y_2 = x_2 - c_2, \ldots\ldots, y_m = x_m - c_m$

Then the given equation can be written as,

$y_1 + y_2 + y_3 + \ldots\ldots + y_m = n - (c_1 + c_2 + c_3 + \ldots\ldots + c_m)$

where $y_1 \geq 0$, i = 1, 2,........, m

Hence the required number of solution is

= the number of solutions for non negative integers

$= \left(n - \sum_{i=1}^{m} c_i\right) + {}^{m-1}C_{m-1}$

5.20.2

Find the number of solutions of the equation such that

(i) zero is included

(ii) zero is excluded.

Sol. (i) If zero is included , then the number of solutions

$= \text{Co-efficient of } x^n \text{ in}$

$(x^0 + x^1 + x^2 + \ldots\ldots)(x^0 + x^2 + x^4 + \ldots\ldots)(x^0 + x^3 + x^6 + \ldots\ldots)\ldots\ldots(x^0 + x^m + x^{2m} + \ldots)$

$= \text{Co-efficient of } x^n \text{ in}$

$(1-x)^{-1}(1-x^2)^{-1}(1-x^3)^{-1}\ldots\ldots(1-x^m)^{-1}.$

(ii) If zero is excluded , then the number of solutions

$= \text{Co-efficient of } x^n \text{ in}$

$(x + x^2 + x^3 + \ldots\ldots)(x^2 + x^4 + x^6 + \ldots\ldots)(x^3 + x^6 + x^9 + \ldots\ldots)\ldots(x^m + x^{2m} + \ldots\ldots)$

= Co-efficient of

$x^{n-(1+2+3+\ldots\ldots+m)}$ in

$(1 + x + x^2 + \ldots)(1 + x^2 + x^4 + \ldots)(1 + x^3 + x^6 + \ldots)\ldots(1 + x^m + x^{2m} + \ldots)$

= Co-efficient of

$x^{n - \frac{m(m+1)}{2}} \text{ in } (1-x)^{-1}(1-x^2)^{-1}(1-x^3)^{-1}\ldots\ldots(1-x^m)^{-1}.$

Ex-1. Find the number of positive solutions of x + y + z + w = 20 such that

(i) zero values are included.

(ii) zero values are excluded.

Sol. (i) Hence the total number of positive solutions

$= {}^{20+4-1}C_{4-1}$

$= {}^{23}C_3$

$= \frac{23 \times 22 \times 21}{6}$

= 1771.

(ii) Here $x \geq 1, y \geq 1, z \geq 1, w \geq 1$.

$\Rightarrow x - 1 \geq 0, y - 1 \geq 0, z - 1 \geq 0, w - 1 \geq 0$

Let p = x – 1, q = y – 1, r = z – 1, w = s + 1

$\Rightarrow x = p + 1, y = q + 1, z = r + 1, w = s + 1.$

We have, x + y + z + w = 20.

⇒ p + 1 + q + 1 + r + 1 + s + 1 = 20

⇒ p + q + r + s = 20 – 4 = 16

Hence, the number of positive solutions

$= {}^{16+4-1}C_{4-1}$

$= {}^{19}C_3$

$= \frac{19.18.17}{6}$

= 969.

Ex-2. Find the number of non - negative integral solutions of 3x + y + z = 24.

Sol. Given 3x + y + z = 24, $x \geq 0, y \geq 0, z \geq 0$.

Let x = k.

Thus, y + z = 24 – 3 k.

$\Rightarrow 0 \leq 24 - 3k \leq 24$

$\Rightarrow 0 \leq k \leq 8$

Thus, the total number of integral solutions is

$= {}^{24-3k+2-1}C_{2-1} = {}^{25-3k}C_1 = 25 - 3k.$

Hence, the total number of +ve integral solutions

$= \sum_{k=0}^{8} (25 - 3k)$

$= 25 \sum_{k=0}^{8} 1 - 3.\sum_{k=0}^{8} k$

$= 25 \times 9 - 3.\frac{8.9}{2} = 225 - 108 = 117.$

Ex-3. Find the number of non negative integral solutions of 2x + 2y + z = 10.

Sol. We have 2x + 2y + z = 10

$\Rightarrow \quad x + y = \frac{10 - z}{2}$

$\Rightarrow \quad 0 \leq x + y \leq 10$

Let $x + y + t = 10$, where $x \geq 0, y \geq 0, t \geq 0$

Hence, the number of non-negative solution $= {}^{10+3-1}C_{3-1}$
$= {}^{12}C_2 = 66$.

Ex-4. Find the number of non-negative solutions of the equation $x + y + z + t = 29$, where $x \geq 1, y \geq 2, z \geq 3, t \geq 4$

Sol. Here, $x - 1 \geq 0, y - 2 \geq 0, z - 3 \geq 0, t - 4 \geq 0$

Let $p = x - 1, q = y - 2, r = z - 3, s = t - 4$

Then $x = p + 1, y = q + 2, z = r + 3, t = s + 4$.

Now $x + y + z + t = 29$

$\Rightarrow \quad p + 1 + q + 2 + r + 3 + s + 4 = 29$

$\Rightarrow \quad p + q + r + s = 29 - 10 = 19$

Hence, the number of non-negative solutions
$= {}^{19+4-1}C_{4-1}$
$= {}^{22}C_3$
$= 1540$.

Ex-5. Find the number of non-negative integral solutions to the system of equations

$x + y + z + u + t = 20$ and $x + y + z = 5$.

Sol. Given system of equations are $x + y + z + u + t = 20, x + y + z = 5$.

$\Rightarrow \quad x + y + z = 5 \quad \text{.....(i)}$

and $\quad u + t = 15 \quad \text{.....(ii)}$

Now, number of non-negative integral solutions of (i) is
$= {}^{5+3-1}C_{3-1} = {}^7C_2 = 21$

Also, number of non-negative integral solutions of (ii) is
$= {}^{2+15-1}C_{2-1} = {}^{16}C_1 = 16$

Thus, the total number of non-negative solutions
$= 21 \times 16 = 336$.

Ex-6. Find the number of ordered triplets of positive integers which satisfy the inequality $20 \leq x + y + z \leq 50$.

Sol. Hence, The total number triplets
$= {}^{50}C_3 - {}^{19}C_3$.

Ex-7. Find the number of points (x, y, z) in space, whose each co-ordinate is a negative integer

Such that $x + y + z + 12 = 0$.

Sol. Let $x = -p, y = -q$ and $z = -r$, where $p, q, r > 0$

Then, $\quad -p - q - r + 12 = 0$

$\Rightarrow \quad p + q + r = 12$.

Hence, the required number of points in space is
$= {}^{12-1}C_{3-1}$
$= {}^{11}C_2$
$= 55$.

Ex-8. Find the number of positive integral solutions of $x_1 x_2 x_3 = 30$.

Sol. We have, $x_1 x_2 x_3 = 30\ 2 \times 3 \times 5$.

Hence, the number of positive integral solutions
$= {}^{3+1+1}C_1 \times {}^{3+1-1}C_1 \times {}^{3+1-1}C_1$
$= 3.\ 3.\ 3$
$= 27$

Ex-9. Find the number of positive integral solution of $x_1 x_2 x_3 x_4 = 210$

Sol. We have, $x_1 x_2 x_3 x_4 = 210 = 2 \times 3 \times 5 \times 7$

Thus, the total number of integral solutions

$= \left({}^{4+1-1}C_1 \times {}^{4+1-1}C_1 \times {}^{4+1-1}C_1 \times {}^{4+1-1}C_1\right) \times \left(1 + {}^4C_2 + {}^4C_4\right)$

(since, all are positive or any two are Negative or all four are negative)

$= 4^4\ (1 + 6 + 1)$
$= 4_4 \times 8$
$= 2048$.

Ex-10. In how many ways can a die be thrown thrice by a person to make a sum of 12?

Sol. This problem is equivalent to finding the number of integral solutions of $x_1 + x_2 + x_3 = 12$, where $1 \leq x_1, x_2, x_3 \leq 6$.

Hence, the required number of possible ways

$=$ Co-efficient of x^{12} in $(x + x^2 + x^3 + x^4 + x^5 + x^6)^3$

$=$ Co-efficient of x^9 in $(1 + x + x^2 + x^3 + x^4 + x^5)^3$

$=$ Co-efficient of x^9 in $\left(\dfrac{1 - x^6}{1 - x}\right)^3$

$=$ Co-efficient of x^9 in $(1 - x^6)^3 \times (1 - x)^{-3}$

$=$ Co-efficient of x^9 in

$(1 - 3x^6 + 3x^{12}) \times (1 + {}^3C_1 x + {}^4C_2 x^2 + {}^5C_3 x^3 + \ldots + {}^{11}C_9 x^9 + \ldots)$

$= {}^{11}C_9 - 3 \times {}^5C_2$
$= 55 - 30$
$= 15$.

5.21 Geometrical Problem

(i) If there are n points in a plane of which m (< n) are collinear, then the total number of straight lines obtain by joining these n points is $= {}^nC_2 - {}^mC_2 + 1$.

(ii) If there are n points in a plane of which m (< n) are collinear, then the total number of different triangles formed by joining these n points is $= {}^nC_3 - {}^mC_3$.

(iii) Number of diagonals in polygon of n sides is $= {}^nC_2 - n$

(iv) n straight lines are drawn in a plane such that no two lines are parallel and no three lines are concurrent. Then the number of parts into which these lines divides the plane is $= 1 + \sum n$

(v) If m parallel lines in a plane are intersected by a family of other n parallel lines. Then the total number of parallelograms so formed

$$= {}^mC_2 \times {}^nC_2 = \frac{mn(m-1)(n-1)}{4}$$

(vi) **Number of Squares :** The number of squares of any size that can be formed

$= np + (n-1)(p-1) + (n-2)(p-2) + ... + (n-(n-1))(p-(n-1))$

$$= \begin{cases} \sum_{r=1}^{n} (n-r+1)(p-r+1) & , \ n < p \\ \sum_{r=1}^{n} r^2 & , \ n = p \end{cases}$$

(vii) **Number of Rectangles :** The number of rectangles of any size that can be formed

$= {}^{n+1}C_2 \times {}^{p+1}C_2$

$$= \begin{cases} \dfrac{np(n+1)(p+1)}{4} & , \ n < p \\ \left(\dfrac{n(n+1)}{2}\right)^2 & ; \ n = p \end{cases}$$

(viii) If there are n rows, first row has n1 squares, 2nd row has n_2 squares, 3rd row has n_3 squares and so on. If we have to filled up the squares with β crosses such that each row has at least one cross, then the number of ways

= Co-efficient of xn in

$$\left({}^{n1}C_1x + {}^{n1}C_2x^2 + {}^{n1}C_3x^3 + ... + {}^{n1}C_nx^n\right) \times \left({}^{n2}C_1x + {}^{n2}C_2x^2 + {}^{n2}C_3x^3 + ... + {}^{n2}C_nx^n\right) \times \left({}^{n3}C_1x + {}^{n3}C_2x^2 + {}^{n3}C_3x^3 + ... + {}^{n3}C_nx^n\right) \times ....$$

Ex-1: There are 12 points in a plane. Out of these 12 points, 5 points are in a straight line and with the exception of these four points no other three points are in the same straight line.

Find (i) the number of straight lines formed.
(ii) the number of triangles formed.
(iii) the number of quadrilaterals formed by joining these ten points.

Sol. (i) Hence, the required number of straight lines is formed

$= {}^{12}C_2 - {}^{5}C_2 + 1$

$= 66 - 10 + 1$

$= 57.$

(ii) Hence, the required number of triangles is formed

$= 220 - 10$

$= 210$

(iii) Hence, the number of quadrilaterals is formed

$= {}^{5}C_0 \times {}^{7}C_4 + {}^{5}C_1 \times {}^{7}C_3 + {}^{5}C_2 \times {}^{7}C_2$

$= 35 + 175 + 210$

$= 420.$

Ex-2. Find the number of diagonals of a polygon of n - sides.

Sol. The number of diagonals of a polygon of n - sides

$= {}^{n}C_2 - n$

$= \dfrac{n(n-1)}{2} - n$

$= \dfrac{n(n-3)}{2}$

Ex-3. The number of diagonals of a polygon is 35. Then find the number of sides of the polygon.

Sol. Let the number of sides of the polygon = n

Given $\dfrac{n(n-3)}{2} = 35$

$\Rightarrow n^2 - 3n - 70 = 0$

$\Rightarrow (n-10)(n+7) = 0$

$\Rightarrow n = 10$

Hence, the number of sides of the polygon = 10.

Ex-4. Find the number of triangles whose vertices are at the vertices of an octagon but none of whose sides happen to come from octagon.

Sol. Hence, the required number of triangles

= Total number of triangles – number of triangles having two sides common – number of triangles having one side common.

$= {}^{8}C_3 - 8 - 8 \times 4$

$= 56 - 8 - 32$

$= 56 - 40$

$= 16.$

Ex-5. 10 parallel lines in a plane are intersected by a family of 8 parallel lines . Find the number of parallelogram so formed.

Sol. Hence, the required number of parallelogram

$= {}^{10}C_2 \times {}^{8}C_2$

$= 45 \times 40$

$= 1260$

Ex-6. Let T_n denote the number of triangles which can be formed using the vertices of a regular polygon of n sides. If $T_{n+1} - T_n = 21$, then find n.

Sol. Given, $T_{n+1} - T_n = 21$

$\Rightarrow {}^{n}C_3 - {}^{n+1}C_3 = 21$

$\Rightarrow \dfrac{1}{6}((n+1)(n-1) - n(n-1)(n-2)) = 21$

$\Rightarrow \dfrac{n}{6}((n+1)(n-1) - n(n-1)(n-2)) = 21$

$\Rightarrow \dfrac{n}{6}(n^2 - 1 - n^2 + 3n - 2) = 21$

$\Rightarrow \dfrac{n}{6}(3n-3) = 21$

$\Rightarrow \dfrac{n}{2}(n-1) = 21$

Ex-7. Find the number of rectangles of size 7×4.

Sol. Hence, the required number of rectangles

$= {}^{7+1}C_2 \times {}^{4+1}C_2$

$= 28 \times 6$

$= 168.$

Ex-8. Find the number of rectangles excluding squares from a rectangle of size 9×6.

Sol. Hence, the required number of rectangles

$= {}^{9+1}C_2 \times {}^{6+1}C_2 - (6\times9+5\times8+4\times7+3\times6+2\times5+1\times4)$

$= 45 \times 21 - (54 + 40 + 28 + 18 + 10 + 4)$

$= 945 - 154$

$= 791.$

Ex-9. Find the number of points of intersection of 5 circles.

Sol. Hence, the number of point of intersections of 5 circles

$= 2 \times {}^5C_2$

$= 20$

Ex-10. Find the number of points of intersection of 8 lines and 4 circles.

Sol. Hence, the number of points of intersection of 8 lines and 4 circles

$= {}^8C_2 + 2 \times {}^4C_2 + 2 \times {}^8C_1 \times {}^4C_1$

$= 28 + 12 + 64$

$= 104.$

Level—I QUESTIONS BASED ON FUNDAMENTALS

Exponent of a prime p in n!

1. Find the prime factor of (10!).
2. Find the exponent of 2 in X = 20 × 19 × 18 × .... × 11
3. If (250!) is divisible by q^P, then find the maximum value of P.
4. Find the number of zeroes at the end of (75!)
5. Find the number of divisors of $n = 2^7, 3^5, 5^3$, which are of the form 4m + 1,
   Where $m \in N$.
6. Exponent of 12 in 50!

FUNDAMENTAL PRINCIPLE OF COUNTING

7. How many three words (with or without meaning) of three distinct letters of the English alphabet are there ?
8. How many numbers are there between 100 and 1000 in which all the digits are distinct?
9. How many numbers are there between 100 and 1000 such that 7 is in the unit's place.
10. How many numbers are there between 100 and 1000 such that every digit is either 2 or 9?
11. In how many ways can the following prizes be given away to a class of 30 students, first and second in Mathematics, first and second in Physics, first in Chemistry and first in English?
12. From among the 36 teachers in a College, one Principal, One Vice-Principal and the teacher in charge are to be appointed. In how many ways can this be done?
13. Twelve students compete in a race. In how many ways first three prizes be given?
14. How many 9 digits number of different digits can be formed?
15. If three six faced die each marked with numbers 1 to 6 on six faces are thrown. Find the total number of possible outcomes.
16. A customers forgets a four digit code for an ATM in a bank. However, he remembered that this code consists of digits 3, 5, 6 and 9. Find the largest possible number of trials necessary to obtain the correct code.

PERMUTATIONS

17. If ${}^nP_5 = 20.\,{}^nP_3$, then find the value of n.
18. Find the value of r, if ${}^{10}P_{r+1} : {}^{11}P_r = 30 : 11$.
19. Find the positive terms are there in the sequence $< x_n >$,
    if $x_n = \dfrac{195}{4P_n} - \dfrac{{}^{n+3}P_3}{P_{n+1}}, n \in N$
20. Find the negative terms are there in the sequence $< x_n >$,
    if $x_n = -\dfrac{143}{4P_n} + \dfrac{{}^{n+4}P_4}{P_{n+2}}, n \in N$
21. If $\dfrac{{}^nP_{r-1}}{a} = \dfrac{{}^nP_r}{b} = \dfrac{{}^nP_{r+1}}{c}$, then prove that $b^2 = ab + ac$.
22. If P_m stands for ${}^mP_m$, then prove that $1 + 1.P_1 + 2.P_2 + 3.P_3 + \ldots\ldots\ldots + n.P_n = (n+1)!$
23. How many different signals can be made by 5 flags from 8 flags of different colors?
24. Find the number of permutation of the letter of the word "SIMPLETON" taken all at a time.
25. Find the number of different permutation of the letter of the word "TOUGH".
26. Find the number of different permutations of the letter of the word "SUNDAY TIMES".

PROBLEMS BASED ON FORMATION OF NUMBERS

27. How many number of four digits can be formed with the digits 1, 2, 3, 4 and 5 ? (If repetitions of digits is not allowed)
28. How many numbers between 400 and 1000 can be made with the digits 2, 3, 4, 5, 6 and 0 ?
29. Find the total number of nine digits numbers which have all different digits.
30. Find the number of numbers between 300 and 3000 that can be formed with the digits 0, 1, 2, 3, 4, and 5 , no digit being repeated in any number.
31. How many even numbers of four digits can be formed with the digits 0, 1, 2, 3, 4, 5 and 6 where no digit being used more than once ?
32. How many positive numbers can be formed by using any number of the digits 0, 1, 2, 3, and 4 , no digit being repeated in any number?
33. How many number of four digits can be formed with the digits 1, 2, 3 and 4 . Find the sum of those numbers.
34. Find the sum of all the four digit numbers that can be formed with the digits 0, 1, 2 and 3.
35. Find the sum of all the four digits numbers that can be formed with the digits 1, 2, 2 and 3.
36. Find the sum of 5 digits numbers which can be formed with the digits 3, 4, 5, 6, 7 using each digit only once in each arrangement.

THE NUMBER OF PERMUTATION OF n DIFFERENT THINGS TAKEN r AT A TIME, WHEN EACH THING CAN BE REPEATED ANY NUMBER OF TIMES IS n^r.

37. In how many ways 3 prizes can be given away to 7 boys when each boy is eligible for any of the prizes.
38. A gentleman has 6 friends to invite. In how many ways can he send invitation cards to them if he has three servants to carry the cards?
39. In how many ways Mohan can dispatch 5 letters in 10 different boxes to his friend?
40. A child has four pockets and three marbles. In how many ways can the child put the marble in his pockets?
41. In how many ways a student can give answer of 10 multiple choice questions, where each having 4 choices?
42. In how many ways 3 friends can stay in 2 hotels?
43. A telegraph has 5 arms and each arm is capable of 4 distinct positions, including the position of rest. What is the total number of signals that can be made.
44. In how many ways n things be given to p persons, when each person can get any number of things $(n > p)$
45. There are m men and n monkey $(m < n)$. If a man may have any number of monkeys, in how many ways may every monkey have a master?
46. In how many ways 6 rings of different type can be had in 4 fingers?

PERMUTATIONS OF n THINGS NOT ALL ARE DIFFERENT

47. Find the number of permutation of the word "M A T H E M A T I C S".
48. How many different permutation can be made out of the letter of the word "A S S A S S I N A T I O N".
49. Find the number of arrangement of the letter of the word "V I C E - C H A N C E L O R".
50. Find the number of arrangement of the letter of the word "A I E E E".
51. Find the number of permutation of "A M I T A B H B A C H C H A N".
52. If a denotes the number of permutation x + 2 things taken all at a time, b the number of permutations of x things taken 11 at a time and c the number of permutations of x – 11 thingstaken all at a time such that a = 182bc, then find the value of x.
53. Find the number of ways in which four particular persons A, B, C, D and six more persons can stand in a queue so that A always stands before B, B before C and C before D.
54. Find the number of permutations of the letters a, b, c, d such that b does not follow a, c does not follow b and d does not follow c.

RESTRICTED PERMUTATIONS (TOGETHERNESS AND NON-TOGETHERNESS)

55. In how many ways 6 persons can be seated in a row so that two persons can sit always together?
56. In how many ways can 8 Indians, 4 Americans and 4 Englishmen be seated in a row so that all persons of the same nationality sit together?
57. There are two books each of three volumes and two books each of two volumes. In how many ways can the ten books be arranged on a table so that the volumes of the same book are not separated?
58. There are 20 books of which 4 are single volume and the other are books of 8, 5 and 3 volumes respectively. In how many ways can all these books be arranged on a shelf so that volumes of the same books are not separated?
59. In how many ways can 10 examination papers be arranged so that the best and the worst papers never come together.
60. There are 5 boys and 3 girls . In how many ways can they be seated in a row so that all the three girls do not sit together.
61. Find the number of different words that can be formed from the letters of the word "TRIANGLE" so that no vowels are together.
62. Find the number of arrangement that can be made out of the letter of the word "SUCCESS" so that all S's do not come together.
63. Find the number of arrangement of the letters of the word "BANANA" in which the two N's do not appear adjacently.
64. In how many ways can 6 boys and 4 girls sit in a row so that no boy is between two girls?
65. What is position of the word "MOTHER" in a dictionary if words are printed in the same order as that of an ordinary dictionary?
66. Find the rank of the word
    (i) T O U G H (ii) S U R I T I
    (iii) S A C H I N (iv) R A N D O M
67. Prove that the number of ways in which n books may be arranged on a shelf so that two particular books shall not be together is $(n-2).(n-1)$.
68. In all the permutations of the letters of the word "A G A I N" are arranged as in dictionary, thên find the 50th word.
69. The letter of the word "N U M B E R" are written in all possible orders and these words are written out as in a dictionary. What is the rank of the word N U M B E R?
70. Find the number of permutations of the letters of the word "I N D E P E N D E N C E". Find also the number of re-arrangements?
71. Find the number of the words that appear before the word 'C O C H I N'

WHEN NO TWO OF A CERTAIN GIVEN THINGS OCCUR TOGETHER. (GAP METHOD)

72. In a class of students there are 4 girls and 6 boys. In how many ways can they be seated in a row so that all the four girls are not together?
73. Six papers are set in an examination, 2 of them in mathematics. In how many different orders can the papers be given if two mathematics papers are not successive?
74. In how many ways can 16 rupees and 12 paise coins be arranged in a line so that no two paise coins may occupy consecutive positions?

75. m men and n women are to be seated in a row so that no two women sit together. If m > n, then show that the number of ways in which they can be seated is $\frac{m!\times(m+1)!}{(m-n+1)!}$.

76. In how many ways 4 boys and 3 girls can be seated in a row so that they are alternate?

77. In how many ways 4 boys and 4 girls can be seated in row so that boys and girls are alternate?

78. Find the number of ways in which the letters of the word " FRACTION" be arranged so that no two vowels are together.

79. How many different nine digit numbers can be formed from the number 223355888 by rearranging its digits so that the odd digits occupy even positions?

80. There are 10 candidates for an examination out of which 4 are appearing in Mathematics and remaining 6 are appearing in different subjects . In how many ways can they be seated in a row so that no two mathematics candidates are together?

81. In how many ways can 7 plus (+) signs and 5 minus (-) signs be arranged in a row so that no two minus (-) signs are together?

82. How many words can be formed with the letters of the word " P A T A L I P U T R A " without changing the relative order of the vowels and consonants?

Problems Based on Word Formation

83. Find the number of words which can be made from the letters of the word 'INTERMEDIATE '

Under the following conditions:

(i) without any restriction
(ii) the word should start with I and end with E.
(iii) the word in which , vowels occur at even places.
(iv) vowels and consonants occupy at their original positions.
(v) vowels and consonants occur alternately.
(vi) no two vowels occur together.
(vii) all the vowels together.
(viii) all the E's should occur together.
(ix) no two E's should occur together
(x) two E's occur together.

84. In how many words can be formed using the letter of the word "TRIANGLE" so that

(i) A and N are always together?
(ii) T, R, I are always together?
(iii) relative order of vowels and consonants are not changed?

85. How many different words can be formed with the letter of the word

(i) M A T H E M A T I C S
(ii) U N I V E R S I T Y
(iii) V I C E C H A N C E L O R so that all the vowels are together.

86. Find the number of words formed by taking the letters of the word "P E N C I L" such that

(i) each words begin with P and end with L.
(ii) vowels occupy odd places.

87. In how many ways can the letters of the word "DIRECTOR" be arranged so that the three vowels are never together?

88. How many different words can be formed with five given letters of which three are vowels and two are consonants, no two vowels being together in any word?

89. How many words can be formed by using the letters of the word 'B H A R A T' ? How many of these words will not contain B and H together. How many of these start with B and end with T?

90. Find the number of arrangements of the letters of the word "D E L H I" if e always comes before i.

91. How many numbers of seven digits can be formed with the digits 1, 2, 3, 4, 3, 2, 1, so that the odd digits always occupy the odd places?

92. How many signals can be made by hoisting 2 blue, 2 red and 5 yellow flags on a pole at the same time?

Circular Permutations

93. In how many ways 5 Indians and 4 Englishmen can be seated in a round table if

(i) there is no restriction ?
(ii) all the four Englishmen sit together:
(iii) all the four Englishmen do not sit together ?
(iv) no two Englishmen sit together?

94. Find the number of ways in which 15 different beads can be arranged to form a necklace.

95. In how many ways can a garland be formed from 4 similar marigolds and 5 roses all of different colors?

96. In how many ways can 15 persons out of 25 persons be seated around a table.

97. How many necklace of 10 beads each can be made from 15 beads of various colors?

98. A round table conference is to be held between 20 delegates. How many seating arrangements are possible if two particular delegates are

(i) always to sit together ?
(ii) never to sit together?
(iii) Always separated by exactly one person?

99. In how many ways can 3 ladies and 5 gentlemen arrange themselves about a round table so that every gentleman may have at least one lady by his side?

Combination

100. If ${}^{15}C_3 = {}^{15}C_{r+3}$, then find r.

101. If ${}^{n}C_{r-1} = 36, {}^{n}C_r = 84$ and ${}^{n}C_{r+1} = 126$, then find r.

102. If ${}^{n}C_{n-r} + 3.{}^{n}C_{n-r+1} + 3.{}^{n}C_{n-r+2} + {}^{n}C_{n-r+3} = {}^{x}C_r$, then find the value of x.

103. Evaluate : ${}^{47}C_4 + \sum_{j=1}^{5} {}^{52-j}C_3$

104. Evaluate : ${}^{47}C_4 + \sum_{j=0}^{3} {}^{50-j}C_3 + \sum_{k=0}^{5} {}^{56-k}C_{53-k}$

105. If ${}^{n-1}C_3 + {}^{n-r}C_4 > {}^{n}C_3$, then prove that $n > 7$

106. Find the value of ${}^{18}C_2 + {}^{17}C_2 + {}^{16}C_2 + ... + {}^{14}C_2 + {}^{14}C_3$.

Restricted Combinations

107. In how many ways can a cricket eleven be chosen out of the batch of 15 players if
   (i) there is no restriction on the selection.
   (ii) a particular player is always chosen
   (iii) a particular player is never chosen?

108. From a class 25 students, 10 are to be chosen for an excursion party. There are 3 students who decide either all of them will join or none of them will join. In how many ways can they be chosen?

109. In how many ways can a cricket team be selected from a group of 25 players containing 10 batsman, 8 bowlers, 5 all rounder's and 2 wicket keepers? Assume that the team of 11 players requires 5 batsman, 3 all rounder's, 2 bowlers and 1 wicket keeper.

110. A committee of twelve is to be formed from 9 women and 8 men. In how many ways can this be done if at least five women have to be included in the committee?
   In how many of these committees
   (i) the women are in a majority?
   (ii) the men are in a majority?

111. A committee of 7 has to be formed from 9 boys and 4 girls . In how many ways can this be done when the committee consists of
   (i) Exactly 3 girls?
   (ii) At least 3 girls?
   (iii) At most 3 girls?

112. Out of 6 gentlemen and 4 ladies, a committee of 5 is to be formed. In how many ways can this be done so as to include at least one lady in each committee?

113. There are 7 men and 3 ladies contesting for two vacancies, an elector can vote for any number of candidates not exceeding the number of vacancies. In how many ways can he vote?

114. Find the number of ways in which three numbers in A.P. can be selected from 1,2,3,4,5,…,n.

115. Find the number of ways in which a mixed double game of tennis can be arranged among 9 teams of married couples such that no husband and wife play in the same game.

116. There are 20 railway stations between from A to B , find the number of different tickets required to be printed in order that it may be possible to travel from any station to any other station.

117. In a football championship, there were played 153 Matches. Every two teams played one match with each other . Find the number of teams participating in the championship.

Selection of One or More Objects

118. In how many ways Master Satyam can invite to his 10 friends in his birthday?

119. In how many ways Master Roshan can give answer of at least one question out of 8 questions?

120. A question paper consists of two sections having respectively 3 and 5 questions. One question from each section is compulsory. In how many ways can a student select the questions?

121. A student is allowed to select at most n books from a collection of $(2n + 1)$ books. If the total number of ways in which he can select a books is 63. Find the value of n.

122. John has x children by his first wife. Mary has (x+1) children by his first husband. They marry and have children their own. The whole family has 24 children. Assuming that two children of the same parents do not fight. Prove that the maximum number of fights that can be take place is 191.

123. In an examination a candidate has to pass in each of the papers. If the total number of different ways in which the candidate can fail is 63, then find the number of papers in the examination.

Combinations from Identical Objects

124. In how many ways Master Himel can select 10 Red balls out of 25 Red balls?

125. In how many ways Master Krishna can select 0 or more balls from 10 green balls?

126. In how many ways Master Kalia can select at least 1 ball out of 10 Red balls , 15 Green balls, 12 Blue balls and 5 Black balls?

Combination when Both Identical and Distinct Objects are Present

127. There are 4 oranges, 5 apples and 6 mangoes in a fruit basket. In how many ways can a person make a selection of fruits from among the fruits in the basket?

128. Given 5 different green dyes, 4 different blue dyes and 3 different red dyes. How many combinations of dyes can be chosen taking at least one green and one blue dyes?

129. There are 4 Mangoes, 3 apples and 2 oranges in a bag, fruits of the same variety being identical. In how many different ways can a selection of fruits be made if
   (i) there is no restriction.
   (ii) at least one mango is to be selected.
   (iii) at least one of each kind is to be selected?

Divisors of a Given Natural Number

130. If $\alpha = 10800$, then find the
   (a) total number of divisors of α
   (b) the number of even divisors.
   (c) the number of divisors of the form $4m + 2$
   (d) the number of divisors which are multiple of 15.

131. In how many ways the number 18900 can be split into factors which are
   Relatively prime (or co-prime)

132. Find the number of zeroes at the end of (100)!

133. Find the number of divisors of 428652000 excluding the number and unity. Also find the sum of the divisors.

134. A number is said to be a nice number if it has exactly 4 factors (including 1 and the number itself). Find the number of divisors of 2520 which are nice numbers.

Distribution into Groups

135. In how many ways can a pack of 52 cards be
   (i) distributed equally among four players in order?
   (ii) divided into four groups of 13 cards each?
   (iii) divided into four sets, three of them having 15 cards each and fourth having 7 cards?

136. In how many ways 12 different things can be divided equally among 3 persons?

137. In how many ways can these 12 things be divided in three sets each having 4 things?

Arrangement Into Groups

138. In how many ways 7 different balls can be arranged into 4 different boxes so that no box remains empty?

139. In how many ways 7 different balls can be distributed into 4 boxes so that no box remains empty?

140. In how many ways 7 identical balls can be distributed into 4 boxes so that no box remains empty?

141. A box contains 25 balls in which 10 are identical. Then find the number of ways of selecting 12 balls from the box.

142. A bag contains 15 balls of which 6 are identical. Find the number of ways of selecting
   (i) 8 balls
   (ii) 4 balls.

Derangements

143. Four different letters are written and the corresponding addresses are correctly written on four envelopes. One letter can be placed in one envelope. In how many ways can be letters be placed in the envelopes so that
   (i) at least one of them be in the wrong envelope.
   (ii) all the letters are in the wrong envelopes.

144. Find the number of ways in which 5 different letters can be put in their five addressed envelopes so that all the letters are in the wrong envelopes.

Multinomial Theorem

145. Find the number of combinations and permutations of 4 letters taken from the word E N G I N E E R I N G

146. Find the total number of ways of selecting 5 letters of the word "I N D E P E N D EN T"

147. Find the numbers of words that can be formed by taking 4 letters at a time out of the letters of the word "M A T H E M A T I C S"

148. Find the number of words that can be made by 4 letters of the word "P R O P O R T I O N" can be made.

149. 4 letters are to be formed out of the letters of the word "P A S S P O R T". Find their number.

150. Find the number of ways in which we can select 5 letters of the word "I N T E R N A T I O N A L".

The number of ways in which n identical things can be distributed into r groups so that no groups contains less than m things and more than k things (m < k).

151. In how many ways can three persons, each throwing a single dice once, make a sum of 15?

152. In how many ways 16 identical things can be distributed among 4 persons if each person gets at least 3 things?

153. If three dice are thrown together, then the number of ways in which the sum of the numbers appearing on the dice is n, $9 \le n \le 14$.

154. In how many ways 30 marks can be allotted to 8 questions if each question carries at least 2 marks.

155. Show that a selections of 10 balls Can be made from an unlimited number of red, white, blue and green balls in 286 different ways and that 84 of those contain balls of all four colors.

Solutions of the Equation with the Help of Multinomial Theorem

156. Find the positive number of solutions of $x + y + z + w = 20$ such that
   (i) zero values are included.
   (ii) zero values are excluded.

157. Find the number of non - negative integral solutions of $3x + y + z = 24$.

158. Find the number of non negative integral solutions of $2x + 2y + z = 10$.

159. Find the number of positive integral solutions to the system of in equations $3x + y + z \le 30$.

160. Find the number of integral solutions of the equation $x + y + z + t = 29, x \ge 1, y \ge 2, z \ge 3$ and $t \ge 0$.

161. Find the number of non-negative integral solutions to the system of equations $x + y + z + u + t = 20$ and $x + y + z = 5$.

162. In an examination, the maximum marks for each of the three papers are 50 each. Maximum marks for the fourth paper are 100. Find the number of ways in which the candidate can score 60% marks in the aggregate.

163. Find the total number of positive integral solutions of the equation $xyz = 140$.

164. Find the number of positive integral solutions of $xyz = 105$.

165. If $a, b, c \in N$, then find the number of points having position vectors $a\hat{i} + b\hat{j} + c\hat{k}$ such that $6 \le a + b + c \le 10$.

Geometrical Problems

166. There are 10 points in a plane. Of these ten points four points are in a straight line and with the exception of these four points, no other three points are in the same straight line.
   (i) Find the number triangles formed.
   (ii) the number of straight lines formed.
   (iii) the number of quadrilaterals formed, by joining these ten points.

167. There are 15 points in a plane , no three of which are in the same straight line with the exception of 6, which are all in the same straight line. Find the number of
    (i) straight lines formed.
    (ii) triangles formed by joining these points.
168. Which regular polygon has the same number of diagonals as side?
169. Find the maximum number of points of intersection of 8 circles.
170. Find the number of rectangles excluding squares from a rectangle of size 7 × 4.
171. Find the number of rectangles excluding squares form of rectangles of size 11 × 8.
172. There is a polygon of n sides ($n > 5$). Triangles are formed by joining the vertices of the polygon. How many triangles are there ?
    Also prove that the number of these triangles which have no side common with any of the sides of the polygon $= \frac{1}{6} \times n(n-4)(n-5)$.
173. Find the maximum number of points into which 4 circles and 4 straight lines.
174. There are 10 points in a plane of which no three points are collinear but 4 points are concyclic. Find the number of different circles that can be drawn through at least 3 points of these points.
175. ABCD is a convex quadrilateral 3, 4, 5 and 6 points are marked on the sides AB, BC, CD and DA respectively. Find the number of triangles with vertices on different sides.
176. (i) n different things are arranged around a circle. In how many ways can 3 object be selected when no two of the selected objects are consecutive.
    (ii) There is convex polygon of n sides (n > 0). Find the number of quadrilaterals having vertices at the vertices of the polygon and at-least one side common with the sides of the polygon.
177. There are n straight lines in a plane, no two of which are parallel and no three passes through the same point. Their point of intersection is joined. Show that the number of fresh lines thus introduced is $\frac{1}{8} \times n(n-1)(n-2)(n-3)$.
178. 14 X's have to placed in squares of Following figure such that each row contains at least one X. In how many ways can this be done?

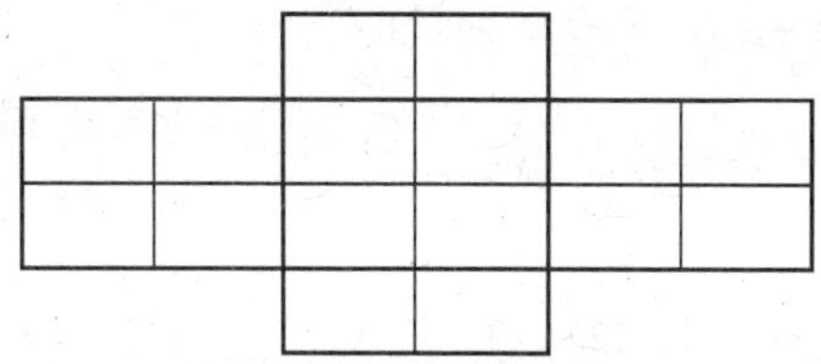

179. In how many ways the letters of the word "P E R S O N" cab be placed in the square of the following figure so that no row remains empty?

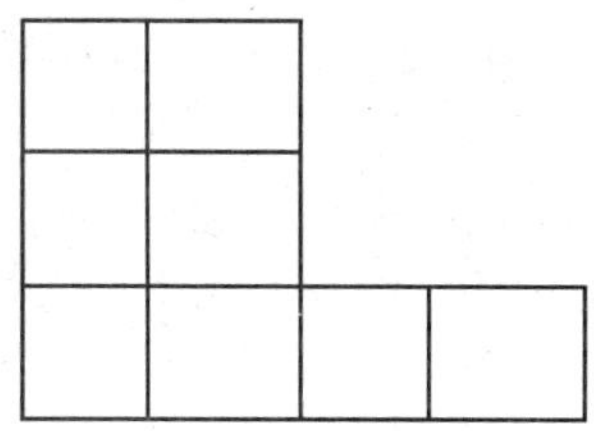

180. Let A_i , I = 1, 2, 3, ..., 21 be the vertices of a 21 - sided regular polygon inscribed in a circle with centre origin. Triangles are formed by joining the vertices of 21 sided polygon. How many of them are
    (i) Equilateral triangles
    (ii) Isosceles triangles.
181. Find the number of triangles which can be formed by joining vertices of a regular polygon of (n > 3) sides .
182. Find the number of isosceles or equilateral triangles none of whose sides exceeds 2n.

ANSWERS KEY

1. *	2. 10	3. *	4. 18	5. 24	6. 22
7. 15600	8. 648	9. 90	10. 8	11. 68121×10^8	12. 42840
13. 1320	14. 9 × 9!	15. 216	16. 24	17. *	18. *
19. 4	20. – 63/4, –23/8	23. $^8P_5$	24. 9!	25. 5!	26. (11)!
27. 120	28. 60	29. 9 × 9!	30. 180	31. 420	32. 260
33. 66660	34. 38664	35. 2664	36. 6666600	37. 343	38. 729
39. 10^5	40. 64	41. 4^{10}	42. 2^3	43. $4^5 - 1$	44. p^n
45. m^n	46. 4^6	52. 12	53. 151200	54. 11	55. 240
56. 3! × 8! × 4! × 4!	57. 96 × 4! × 3!	58. 7! × 8! × 3! × 3!	59. 8 × 9!	60. 50 × 6!	61. 14400
62. 360	63. 40	64. 120960	65. 309th	66. (i) 309th (ii) 236th (iii) 601st (iv) 614th	
68. NAAIG	69. 469	70. 1663200, 1663199	71. 96	72. $^7P_4 \times 6!$	73. $^5P_2 \times 4!$
74. *	76. 144	77. 1152	78. 14400	79. 60	80. 60480
81. 56	82. 3600				

83. (i) 19958400 (ii) 907200 (iii) 21600 (iv) 21600 (v) 43200 (vi) 151200 (vii) 151200 (viii) 90720 (ix) 10886400 (x) 9072000

84. (i) 100800 (ii) 4320 (iii) 720	85. *	86. *	87. *	88. 12

89. 360; 240; 12   90. 60   91. 18   92. 756   93. (i) 8! (ii) 5! 4! (iii) 8! - 5! 4! (iv) 4! 5!

94. $\frac{1}{2}\times(14)!$ 95. 840   96. $\frac{25!}{15\times10!}$ 97. $\frac{15!}{20\times5!}$ 98. (i) 2 × 18! (ii) 17 × 18! (iii) 2 × 18!

99. 720   100. r = 9   101. r = 3   102. x = n + 3   103. ${}^{52}C_4$ 104. ${}^{57}C_4$

106. ${}^{19}C_3$ 107. (i) 1365 (ii) 1001 (iii) 364   108. ${}^{22}C_7$, 817190   109. 141120

110. 6062, (i) 2702 (ii) 1008   111. (i) 504 (ii) 588 (iii) 1632   112. 246   113. 55

114. $\begin{cases}\frac{n(n-2)}{4}: \text{whenniseven}\\ \frac{1}{4}(n-1)^2: \text{whennisodd}\end{cases}$ 115. 1512   116. 462   117. 18   118. 1023

119. 255   120. 217   121. 3   122. *   123. 6   124. 1

125. 11   126. 42   127. 209   128. 3720   129. (i) 59 (ii) 48 (iii) 27

130. (a) 60 (b) 48 (c) 12 (d) 30   131. 8   132. 12   133. 574, 1408790879.   134. 7

135. (i) $\frac{(52)!}{(13!)^4}$ (ii) $\frac{(52)!}{(13!)^4\times4}$ (iii) $\frac{(52)!}{(15!)^2\times3!\times7!}$ 136. $\frac{(52)!}{(4!)^3}$ 137. $\frac{(12)!}{(4!)^3\times3!}$ 138. 100800

139. 20688   140. 20   141. ${}^{16}C_2+2({}^{16}C_4+{}^{16}C_6)$ 142. (i) 501 (ii) 256   143. (i) 23 (ii) 9

144. 44   145. 43, 476   146. 72   147. 2454   148. 10   149. 606

150. 256   151. 10   152. 35   153. $-n^2+21n-83$ 154. 116280   156 (i) 1771 (ii) 969

157. 117   158. 66   159. 1215   160. 2600   161. 336   162. 110566

163. 54   164. 27   165. 110   166. (i) 116 (ii) 40 (iii) 185   167. (i) 91 (ii) 435

168. 5   169. 56   170. 220   171. 2064   172. ${}^{n}C_3$ 173. 50

174. 117   175. 342   176. (i) $\frac{1}{6}n(n-4)(n-5)$ (ii) $\frac{1}{2}n(n-3)(n-4)$ 178. 118

179. 18720   180. (i) 7 (ii) 196   181. ${}^{n-4}C_4+{}^{n-3}C_3$ 182. $3.n^2$

Level—II FOR JEE-MAIN AND ADVANCED EXAMS ONLY

1. The exponent of 2 in x 20 × 19 × .... × 11 is
(a) 8   (b) 10
(c) 12   (d) 14

2. If 250! is divisible by q^p, then the maximum value of p is
(a) 61   (b) 62
(c) 63   (d) 64

3. The number of zeroes at the end of (60)! is
(a) 14   (b) 15
(c) 16   (d) 20

4. The value of the expression $\frac{(2n)!}{\{1.3.5..........(2n-1)\}\times n!}$ is
(a) 2^{n-1} (b) 2^n
(c) 2^{n+1} (d) 2^{n-2}

5. If a set A has 4 elements and another set B has 5 elements, then the number of one-one functions from A to B is
(a) 12   (b) 108
(c) 120   (d) 625

6. If a set A has 3 elements and another set B has 2 elements, then the number of functions from A to B is
(a) 9   (b) 8
(c) 27   (d) 0

7. If a set A has 4 elements and another set B has 5 elements, then the number of relations from A to B is
(a) 2^9 (b) 2^{10}
(c) 2^{20} (d) 2^{30}

8. The number of ways 4 friends can stay in 10 hotels such that all the friends don't stay in a same hotel is
(a) $4^{10}-4$ (b) 10^4-10
(c) 10^4-4 (d) ${}^{10}P_4-4$

9. Let the number of elements in a set A is m and the number of elements of another set B is n if the number of one one functions from the set A to the set B is 240, then m – n is
(a) 4   (b) 6
(c) 8   (d) – 3

10. The rank of the word 'TACKLE' according to the English dictionary is
(a) 602   (b) 603
(c) 604   (d) 605

11. The number of ways in which 8 distinct toys can be distributed among 5 children is
(a) 5^8 (b) 8^5
(c) ${}^8P_5$ (d) 40

12. The number of ways in which one can post 5 letters in 7 letter boxes is
(a) 35   (b) ${}^7P_5$
(c) 7^5 (d) 5^7

13. Three dice are rolled. The number of possible outcomes in which at-least one die shows 5 is

(a) 215 (b) 36
(c) 125 (d) 91

14. If all the permutations of the letters of the word 'AGAIN' are arranged as in dictionary, then fiftieth word is

(a) NAAGI (b) NAGAI
(c) NAAIG (d) NAIAG

15. The value of ${}^nC_0{}^2 + {}^nC_1{}^2 + {}^nC_2{}^2 + \ldots\ldots\ldots\ldots + {}^nC_n{}^2$ is

(a) ${}^{2n}C_n$ (b) ${}^{2n}C_{n+1}$
(c) ${}^{2n}C_{n-1}$ (d) ${}^{2n}C_{n+2}$

16. The total number of selections of at most n things from (2n+1) different things is 63. Then the value of n is

(a) 6 (b) 3
(c) 4 (d) 5

17. The number of arrangements which can be made using all the letters of the word 'LAUGH', if vowels occur together is

(a) 96 (b) 72
(c) 48 (d) 24

18. The rank of the word 'IIT' according to English dictionary is

(a) 2 (b) 1
(c) 3 (d) 4

19. In how many ways can the letters of the word 'ARRANGE' be arranged so that two R's are never together is

(a) 800 (b) 600
(c) 900 (d) 700

20. The number of ways in which 10 candidates $A_1, A_2, A_3, \ldots\ldots\ldots\ldots, A_{10}$ can be ranked so that A_1 always above A_2 is

(a) 10 ! (b) $\frac{10!}{2}$
(c) 9! (d) $\frac{9!}{2}$

21. There are 4 letters and 4 directed envelopes. The number of ways in which all the letters can be put in the wrong envelope is

(a) 8 (b) 9
(c) 16 (d) 20

22. 6-boys and 6-girls sit along a line alternately in x ways and along a circle in y ways , then

(a) x = y (b) y = 12 x
(c) x = 10 y (d) x = 12 y

23. The number of ways, in which 7 persons can be arranged at a round table if two particular Persons may not sit together is

(a) 480 (b) 120
(c) 80 (d) 100

24. A round table conference is to be held between 20 delegates and 20 countries. The number of ways can they be seated if two particular delegates sit together, is

(a) 2 × (17)! (b) 2 × (19)!
(c) 2 × (18)! (d) 2 × (20)!

25. The number of positive integral solutions of x y z = 30 is

(a) 9 (b) 27
(c) 81 (d) 243

26. The number of positive integral solutions of x + y + z = 10 is

(a) 33 (b) 55
(c) 66 (d) 44

27. The number of positive integral solutions of 2 x + 2 y + z = 10 is

(a) 33 (b) 55
(c) 66 (d) 44

28. The number of points of intersection of 5 circles is

(a) 30 (b) 20
(c) 66 (d) 40

29. The number of points of intersection of 10 lines and 5 circles is

(a) 155 (b) 165
(c) 175 (d) 185

30. The number of rectangles of size 6 × 4 is

(a) 110 (b) 160
(c) 210 (d) 160

31. The number of rectangles of any size in a chess board is

(a) 216 (b) 1296
(c) 64 (d) 1024

32. The number of squares of any size in a rectangle of size 8 × 5 is

(a) 150 (b) 130
(c) 100 (d) 160

33. The number of zeroes at the end of (2013)! is

(a) 400 (b) 500
(c) 250 (d) 247

34. The number of ways of 52 cards can be equally divided among 4 persons is

(a) $\frac{52!}{(13!)^4 \times 4}$ (b) $\frac{52!}{(13!)^4}$
(c) $\frac{52!}{(13!)^4 \times 4!}$ (d) $\frac{52!}{(13!)^4 \times 2!}$

35. The number of ways 12 balls can be divided between 2 boys, one receiving 5 and the other gets 7 is

(a) 1584 (b) 1284
(c) 1384 (d) 1484

36. The number of non-negative integral solutions of $3x + y + z = 24$ is

(a) 115 (b) 117
(c) 119 (d) 121

37. The number of solutions of the equation $x + y + z = 6$, where x, y, z ∈ W, is

(a) 180 (b) 280
(c) 380 (d) 480

38. The number of ways 5 different balls can be arranged into 3 different boxes, so that no box is remain empty, is

(a) 420 (b) 620
(c) 720 (d) 520

39. The number of ways 5 identical balls can be distributed into 3 different boxes, so that no box remains empty, is

(a) 5 (b) 6
(c) 10 (d) 15

40. The number of ways 16 identical balls can be distributed among 4 persons, if each person get at-least 3 things is

(a) 55 (b) 25
(c) 35 (d) 45

41. The sum of all odd divisors of 360 is

(a) 75 (b) 76
(c) 78 (d) 88

42. The number of ways the number 18900 can be resolved as a product of two factors, is

(a) 25 (b) 30
(c) 35 (d) 40

43. The number of ways the number 18900 can be split into two factors, which are relatively prime , is

(a) 8 (b) 10
(c) 12 (d) 6

44. The number of ways to put 5 letters in 5 addressed envelopes so that all are in wrong envelopes is

(a) 22 (b) 33
(c) 44 (d) 55

45. The number of ways to put 6 letters in 6 addressed envelopes so that all are in wrong envelopes is

(a) 262 (b) 363
(c) 265 (d) 565

46. The number of permutations of the letters a, b, c, d such that b does not follow a, c does not follow b and d does not follow c, is

(a) 12 (b) 11
(c) 14 (d) 13

47. The number of functions f from the set {1, 2, 3} into the set {1, 2, 3, 4, 5} such that $f(i) \geq f(j)$, whenever $I < j$ is

(a) 30 (b) 35
(c) 50 (d) 60

48. The number of ways of distributing 12 identical oranges among 4 children so that every child gets at-least one and no child gets more than 4 is

(a) 31 (b) 32
(c) 35 (d) 42

49. The number of ways, in which one or more balls can be selected out of 10 white, 9 green and 7 blue balls is

(a) 892 (b) 881
(c) 891 (d) 879

50. The number of ways, in which 12 identical balls can be put into 5 different boxes so that no boxes remains empty is

(a) 660 (b) 110
(c) 165 (d) 330

Level—III FOR JEE ADVANCED EXAMS ONLY

1. Find the number of signals that can be made by five flags of different colors when any number of them may be used.

2. According to the English dictionary if the rank of the word TOUGH is 'm' and the rank of the rank of IIT is 'n' , then find the value of m + n +10. **(Ans. 100)**

3. There is a polygon of n sides (n > 5). Triangles are formed by joining the vertices of the polygon. Find the number of triangles which have no side common with any of the sides of the polygon.

4. There are 12 intermediate stations between two places A and B . In how many ways can a train be made to stop at 4 of these 12 intermediate stations no two of which are consecutive.

5. A straight is a five card hand containing consecutive values. How many different straight there ?

6. If each of m points on one straight line be joined to each of m points on the other straight line terminated by the points, then excluding the points on the given two lines. Find the number of points of intersection of these lines is.

7. John has x children by his first wife . Mary has (x+1) children by her first husband. They marry and have children of their own. The whole family has 24 children. Assuming that two children of the same parents do not fight. Prove that the maximum number of flights that can take place is 191.

8. Five balls of different colors are to be placed in three boxes of different sizes. Each box can hold all five balls. In how many different ways can we place the balls so that no box is remain empty.

9. In how many ways 16 identical balls can be distributed among 4 persons if each person gets at-least 3 things?

10. In how many ways 30 marks can be allotted to 8 questions if each question carries at-least 2 marks?

11. In an examination the maximum marks for each of the three papers are 50 each. Maximum marks for the fourth paper are 100. Find the number of ways in which the candidate can score 60 % marks in the aggregate.

12. Find the number of positive unequal integral solutions of a + b + c + d = 20.

13. Find the number of selections of n letters together out of 3n letters of which n are 'a' and n are 'b' and the rest unlike.

14. Find the total number of ways of selecting five letters from the letters of the word ' INDEPENDENT'.

15. Find the number of permutations of the letters of the word 'PARALLEL' taken four at a time.

16. How many three digit numbers are of the form xyz with $x < y > z$ and $x \neq 0$.

17. In how many ways can 7 plus (+) signs and 5 minus (-) signs be arranged in a row so that no two minus (-) signs are together ?

18. Find the number of positive integral solutions of $x + 2y + 3z = 100$.

19. India and Pakistan play one day international series until one team wins 4 matches. No match ends in a draw. In how many ways series can be win ?

20. Find the number of quintuples (x, y, z, u, v) of positive integers satisfying both.

ANSWERS KEY

1. 325	**2.** 100	**3.** $\frac{1}{6}n(n-4)(n-5)$	**4.** 126	**5.** 9216
8. 150	**9.** 35	**10.** 116280	**11.** 110556	**12.** 552
13. $(n+2)2^{n-1}$	**14.** 72	**15.** 286	**16.** 240	**17.** 56
18. 780	**19.** 70	**20.** 2600		

LINKED COMPREHENSION TYPE

PASSAGE - I

Let p be a prime number and n be a positive integer, then exponent of p is n! is denoted by $E_p(n!)$ and is given by

$$E_p(n!) = \left[\frac{n}{p}\right] + \left[\frac{n}{p^2}\right] + \left[\frac{n}{p^3}\right] + \dots\dots\dots + \left[\frac{n}{p^k}\right], \text{ where}$$

$P^k < n < P^{k+1}$ and [,] = G.I.F.

If we isolate the power of each prime contained in any number N, then N can be written as $N = 2^{\alpha 1}.3^{\alpha 2}.5^{\alpha 3}.7^{\alpha 4}$. Where α_1 are whole numbers.

On the basis of above information, answers the following questions.

1. The exponent of 7 in ${}^{100}C_{50}$ is

(a) 0 (b) 1
(c) 2 (d) 3

2. The number of zeroes at the end of 108 ! is

(a) 10 (b) 13
(c) 25 (d) 26

3. The last non zero digit in 20! must be equal to

(a) 2 (b) 4
(c) 6 (d) 8

4. The exponent of 12 in 100! is

(a) 32 (b) 48
(c) 97 (d) None

5. The number of prime numbers among the numbers

$105!+2, 105!+3, 105!+4, \dots\dots\dots, 105!+104$ and $105!+105$ is

(a) 31 (b) 32
(c) 33 (d) None

PASSAGE - II

Suppose a lot of n objects contains n_1 objects of one kind, n_2 objects of second kind, n_3 objects of third kind, ..., n_k objects of kth kind, such that $n_1 + n_2 + n_3 + \dots\dots + n_k = r$.

Then the number of possible arrangements /permutations of r objects out of this lot is the co-efficient of x^r in the expansion of

$$r! \times \prod\left(\sum_{\lambda=0}^{n_1}\left(\frac{x^\lambda}{\lambda\ !}\right)\right).$$

On the basis of above information, answer the following questions:

1. The number of permutations of the letters of the word INDIA taken three at a time must be

(a) 27 (b) 30
(c) 33 (d) 57

2. If $n_1 = n_2 = n_3 = \dots\dots\dots = n_k = 1$, then the number of permutations of r objects must be

(a) ${}^nP_r$ (b) ${}^nC_r$
(c) ${}^kP_r$ (d) ${}^kC_r$

3. The number of permutations of the letters of the word 'INEFFECTIVE' taken four at a time must be

(a) 2214 (b) 1422
(c) 5424 (d) 2454

4. If $n_1 + n_2 + n_3 + \dots\dots\dots + n_k = r$, then the number of permutations must be

(a) ${}^nC_r$ (b) ${}^nP_r$
(c) $(k+r)!$ (d) $\frac{r!}{n_1! \times n_2! \times \dots\dots\dots \times n_k!}$

5. Five letter words are to be formed out of the letters of the word 'INFINITESIMAL', then the number of permutations must be

(a) 16995 (b) 5665
(c) 11330 (d) 22660

PASSAGE - III

Different words are being formed by arranging the letters of the word 'SUCCESS'.

All the words obtained by written in the form of a dictionary.

On the basis of above information, answer the following questions:

1. The number of words in which the two C are together but no two S are together is

(a) 120 (b) 96
(c) 24 (d) 420

2. The number of words in which no two C and no two S are together is

(a) 120 (b) 96
(c) 24 (d) 420.

3. The number of words in which the consonants appear in alphabetic order is

(a) 42 (b) 40
(c) 420 (d) 280

4. The rank of the word ' SUCCESS' in the dictionary is

(a) 328 (b) 329
(c) 330 (d) 331

5. The number of words in which the relative positions of vowel and consonant unaltered is

(a) 20 (b) 60
(c) 180 (d) 540

PASSAGE - IV

Different words are being formed by arranging the letters of the word ' ARRANGE'.

All the words obtained are written in the form of a dictionary.

On the basis of the above information , answer the following questions:

1. The number of words in which the two R are not together

(a) 1260 (b) 660
(c) 900 (d) 240

2. The number of words in which neither two R nor two A come together is

(a) 1260 (b) 660
(c) 900 (d) 240

3. The number of words in which the consonants appear in alphabetical order is

(a) 100 (b) 105
(c) 360 (d) 240

4. The rank of the word 'ARRANGE' in the dictionary is

(a) 340 (b) 341
(c) 342 (d) 343

5. The number of words in which at least one vowel is in between two consonants is

(a) 18 (b) 36
(c) 624 (d) 836

ANSWERS

PASSEGE 1

1. a **2.** c **3.** b **4.** b **5.** d

PASSEGE 2

1. c **2.** a **3.** b **4.** d **5.** d

PASSEGE 3

1. c **2.** b **3.** a **4.** d **5.** a

PASSEGE 4

1. c **2.** b **3.** b **4.** c **5.** b

MATCH MATRIX

1. Observe the following columns :

Column- I	Column-II
(A) The number of +ve integral solutions of the equation $x_1x_2x_3x_4x_5 = 1050$ is λ, then λ is divisible by	(P) 3
(B) Let y be the element of the set $A = \{1,2,3,5,6,10,15,30\}$	(Q) 4
And be integers x_1, x_2, x_3 such that $x_1.x_2.x_3 = y$, If λ be	(R) 5
The number of integral solutions of $x_1.x_2.x_3 = y$, then λ Is divisible by	(S) 8
(C) Let a be a factor of 120. If λ be the number of +ve integral solutions of $x_1.x_2.x_3 = a$, then λ is divisible by	(T) 16

2. Observe the following columns :

Column- I	Column-II
(A) If λ be the number of ways in which 6 boys and 5 girls can be arranged in a line so that they are alternate, then λ is divisible by	(P) 5 !
	(Q) 6 !
(B) If λ be the number of ways in which 6 boys and 5 girls can be seated in a row such that two girls are never together, then is divisible by	(R) 7 !
(C) If λ be the number of ways in which 6 boys and 5 girls can be seated around a round table if all the five girls do not sit together, then λ is divisible by	(S) 5!×6!
	(T) 5!×6!

3. Observe the following columns :

Column- I	Column-II
(A) If n be the number of ways in which 12 different books can be distributed equally among 3 persons, then $\frac{(4!)}{12!} \times n \rightarrow$ is divisible by	(P) 4
	(Q) 6
(B) If n be the number of ways in which 12 different things can be distributed in 3 groups, then $\frac{(4!)^3 \times (3!)^2}{12!} \times n$ is divisible by	(R) 12
	(S) 24
(C) If n be the number of ways in which 12 different things can be distributed in 5 sets of 2, 2, 2, 3, 3 things. Then $\frac{(3!)^3 \times (2!)^4 \times 5!}{12!} \times n$ is divisible by	(T) 30

4. Observe the following columns:

Column- I	Column-II
(A) If λ_1 be the number of positive integral solutions of $x + y + z + w = 10$, then λ_1 is divisible by	(P) 3
(B) If λ_2 be the non-negative integral solutions of x + y + z = 6, then λ_2 is divisible by	(Q) 4
	(R) 5
(C) If λ_3 be the number of solutions of x + y + z = 15 Such that $x \geq 1, y \geq 2 \text{ and } z \geq 3$, then λ_3 is divisible by	(S) 7
	(T) 11

ANSWER

1. $A \rightarrow (P,R); B \rightarrow (Q,S,T); C \rightarrow (Q,R,S,T)$

2. $A \rightarrow (P,Q,S); B \rightarrow (P,Q,R,S,T); C \rightarrow (P,Q,S)$

3. $A \rightarrow (P,Q,R,S); B \rightarrow (Q); C \rightarrow (P,Q,R,S,T)$

4. $A \rightarrow (P,Q,S); B \rightarrow (Q,S); C \rightarrow (R,T)$

Assertion and Reason

Codes :

(A) **Both A and R are individually** true and R is the correct explanation of A.

(B) **Both A and R are individually** true but R is not the correct explanation of A.

(C) **A is true but R is false.**

(D) **A is false but R is not true.**

1. **Assertion (A) :** If a polygon has 45 diagonals, then its number of its sides is 10.

Reason (R) : Number of ways of selecting 2 points from n non-collinear points is $^nC_2$.

(a) A (b) B
(c) C (d) D

2. **Assertion (A) :** Number of rectangles in a Chess Board is $^nC_2 \times {}^nC_2$.

Reason (R) : To form a rectangle we have to select any two of the horizontal line and any two of the vertical line.

(a) A (b) B
(c) C (d) D

3. **Assertion (A) :** A bag has contain 23 balls in which 7 are identical, then the number of ways of selecting 12 balls from bag is $^{18}C_6 + {}^{15}C_8$.

Reason (R) : If a group has n things in which p are identical, then the number of ways os selecting R things from a group is $\sum_{r=0}^{r} {}^{n-p}C_r$.

(a) A (b) B
(c) C (d) D

4. **Assertion (A) :** The expression $n! \times (20 - n)!$ is minimum, where n = 10

Reason (R) : $^{2p}C_r$ is maximum when r = p.

(a) A (b) B
(c) C (d) D

5. **Assertion (A) :** The number of non-negative integral solutions of $(x_1 + x_2 + x_3 + ... + x_n) = r$ is $^{n+r-1}C_r$.

Reason (R) : The number of ways in which n identical things can be distributed into r different groups is $^{n+r-1}C_r$.

(a) A (b) B
(c) C (d) D

6. **Assertion (A) :** From a group of 8 men and 4 women at team of 5, including at-least one woman can be formed in 736 ways.

Reason (R) : The number of ways of selecting at-least one woman from m men and n women is $^{n+m}C_n - {}^mC_n$.

(a) A (b) B
(c) C (d) D

7. **Assertion (A) :** If N be the number of +ve integral solution of $x_1 x_2 x_3 x_4 = 770$, then N is divisible by 4 Distinct primes.

Reason (R) : Prime numbers are 2, 3, 5, 7, 11, 13,.........

(a) A (b) B
(c) C (d) D

8. **Assertion (A) :** $E = \left[\frac{1}{3} + \frac{1}{50}\right] + \left[\frac{1}{3} + \frac{2}{50}\right] + ...$ upto 50 terms, then E is divisible by exactly two primes

Reason (R) : $[x + n] = [x] + n, n \in I$ and $[x + y] = [x] + [y]$, if $x, y \in I$

(a) A (b) B
(c) C (d) D

9. **Assertion (A) :** Number of terms in the expansion of $(x_1 + x_2 + x_3 + ... + x_n)^6 = {}^{16}C_6$.

Reason (R) : Number of ways of distributing n identical things among persons when each person get 0 or more things $= {}^{n+r-1}C_n$.

(a) A (b) B
(c) C (d) D

10. **Assertion (A) :** If a, b, c are +ve integers such that $a + b + c \geq 8$, then the number of possible values of the ordered triplets (a, b, c) is 56.

Reason (R) : The number of ways in which n identical things can be distributed into r different groups is $^{n-1}C_{r-1}$

(a) A (b) B
(c) C (d) D

Questions asked in Roorkee Exams

1. If $^{56}P_{r+6} : {}^{54}P_{r+2} = 30800 : 1$, then find r. **[Roorkee - 1983]**

2. There are 10 points in a plane. Of these ten points, four points are in a straight line and with the exception of these four points, no other three points in a straight line. Find
(i) the number of straight lines
(ii) the number of triangles that can be formed by joining these points. **[Roorkee - 1984]**

3. From 4 officers and 8 jawans, in how many ways can 6 be chosen
(i) to include exactly one officer?
(ii) to include at least one officer? **[Roorkee - 1985]**

4. No questions asked in between 1986 to 1996.

5. Find the total number of ways of selecting five letters from the letters of the word 'INDEPENDENT' **[Roorkee - 1997]**

6. No questions asked in between 1998 to 2001.

ANSWER

1. $r = 4$ 2. (i) 40, (ii) 116. 3. (i) 224, (ii) 896. 5. 72.

Questions asked in IIT-JEE Exams

1. A man has 7 relatives, 4 of them are ladies and 3 gentlemen; his wife has also 7 relatives, 3 of them are ladies and 4 are gentlemen. In how many ways can they invite a dinner party of 3 ladies and 3 gentlemen so that there are 3 of man's relative and 3 of wife's relatives? **(IIT - 1985)**
2. A box contains 2 white balls, 3 black balls and 4 red balls. In how many ways can 3 balls be drawn from the box if at least one ball is included in the draw ? **(IIT - 1986)**
3. A student is allowed to select atmost n books from a collection of (2n + 1) books. If the total number of ways in which he can select at least one book is 63. Find the value of n. **(IIT - 1987)**
4. Find the total number of ways in which 6 '+' and 4 '-' signs can be arranged in a line such that no 2 '-' signs occur together. **(IIT - 1988)**
5. A 5 digit number divisible by 3 is to be formed using the numbers 0, 1, 2, 3, 4 and 5 without repetition. Find the total number of ways this can be done. **(IIT - 1989)**
6. 18 guests have to be seated, half on each side of a long table. 4 particular guests desire to sit on one particular side and three others on the other side. Determine the number of ways in which the sitting arrangement can be made. **(IIT - 1991)**
7. There are four balls of different colors and four boxes of colors, same as those of the balls. Find the number of ways in which the balls, one each in a box, could be placed such that a ball does not go to a box of its own color. **(IIT - 1992)**
8. A committee of 12 is to be formed from 9 women and 8 men. In how many ways this can be done if at least 5 women have to be included in a committee? In how many of these committees;

   (i) the women are in majority?

   (ii) the men are in majority ? **(IIT - 1994)**
9. Find the number of ways of selecting 5 letters from the letters of the word 'I N D E P E N D E N T" **(IIT - 1997)**
10. Find the number of divisors of the form 4 n + 2 (≥ 0) of the integer 240. **(IIT - 1998)**
11. How many different nine digit numbers can be formed from the number 223355888 by re-arranging its digits so that the odd digits occupy even positions? **(IIT - 2000)**
12. For $2 \leq r \leq n$, prove that **(IIT - 2000)**
13. Let T_n denote the number of triangles which can be formed using the vertices of a regular polygon of n sides. If $T_{n+1} - T_n$ = 21, then find the value of n **(IIT - 2001)**
14. Find the arrangement of the letters of the word BANANA in which the two N's do not appear adjacently. **(IIT- 2002)**
15. If ${}^{n-1}C_r = (k^2 - 3) \times {}^nC_{r+1}$, then find the value of k **(IIT - 2004)**
16. A rectangle with sides (2n - 1) and (2m - 1) is divided into squares of unit length . Find the number of rectangles which can be formed with sides of odd length. **(IIT - 2005)**
17. If the L.C.M of p, q is $r^2\, t^4\, s^2$ where r, s, t are prime numbers and p, q are the positive integers, then find the number of ordered pairs (p, q). **(IIT - 2006)**
18. The letters of the word COCHIN are permuted and all the permutations are arranged in an alphabetical order as in an English dictionary. Find the number of words that appear before the word COCHIN. **(IIT - 2007)**
19. Consider all possible permutations of the letters of the word 'E N D E A N O E L '. Match the statements expressions in Column I with the statements / expressions in Column II

	Column- I	Column-II
(A)	The number of permutations containing the word ENDEA is	(P) 5 !
(B)	The number of permutations in which the letter E occurs in the first and the last position is	(Q) 5!×2
(C)	The number of permutations in which none of the N occurs in the first five position is	(R) 5!×7
(D)	The number of permutations in which the letters A, E, O Occur only in odd positions is	(S) 5!×21

(IIT - 2008)

20. Find the number of seven digit integers with sum of the digits equal to 10 and formed by using the digits 1, 2 and 3 only. **(IIT - 2009)**
21. Let S = {1, 2, 3, 4}. The total number of unordered pairs of disjoint subsets of S is equal to

    (a) 25 (b) 34

    (c) 42 (d) 41

    [IIT-2010]
22. No questions asked in 2011.
23. The total number of ways of 5 balls of different colors can be distributed among 3 persons So that each person get at-least one ball is

    (a) 75 (b) 150

    (c) 210 (d) 243

    [IIT-2012]

ANSWERS

1. 485
2. 6, if the balls of the same color are alike and 64, if the balls of the same color are different.

3. 3 **4.** 35 **5.** 216 **7.** 9 **8.** 6062, (i) 2702 (ii) 1008 **9.** 72 **10.** 4 **11.** 60

13. 7 **14.** 40. **15.** 16. **17.** 225 **18.** 96 **20.** 77.

Self Assesment Test

TIME : 1 HOURS. CHAPTER : THE PERMUTATION AND COMBINATION MAX MARKS: 50

NOTE: Give answers of the following questions by yourself only

1. Ten persons , amongst whom are A, B and C , are to speak at a function . If n is the number of ways in which it can be done if A wants to speak before B, and B wants to speak before C. Find n/ 800.
2. Find the number of rectangles that you can find on a chessboard.
3. Find the number of positive integral solutions of .
4. Find the number of ways in which we can choose 5 letters from the word 'INTERNATIONAL.'
5. The number of ways in which we can arrange 4 letters of the word ' MATHEMATICS' is given by
   (a) 136 (b) 2454 (c) 1680 (d) 192.
6. The number of ways in which we can get a score of 11 by throwing three dice is
   (a) 18 (b) 27 (c) 45 (d) 56.
7. The number of squares which can form on a chessboard is
   (a) 64 (b) 160 (c) 224 (d) 204
8. Find the number of three digit numbers of the form x y z with x < y, z < y, $x \neq 0$.
9. Find the number of ways in which 15 identical balls can be distributed among 6 people.
10. Let $m = 2^{20} - 1$, $n = 2^{110} - 1$, then $h.c.f(m, n)$ is
    (a) 41 (b) 205 (c) 1025 (d) 1023.

ANSWERS

1. 756 **2.** 1296 **3.** 1875 **4.** 242 **5.**(b) **6.** (b) **7.** (d) **8.** 240 **9.** 15504 **10.** (d)

CHAPTER 6

MATRICES AND DETERMINANTS

6.1 Matrix

A set of mn numbers (real or complex) arranged in the form of a rectangular array having *m* rows and n columns is called an $m \times n$ matrix . We read as m by n matrix .

An $m \times n$ matrix is usually written as

$$\begin{bmatrix} a_{11} & a_{12} & \cdots & a_{1n} \\ a_{21} & a_{22} & \cdots & a_{2n} \\ \cdots & \cdots & \cdots & \cdots \\ a_{m1} & a_{m2} & \cdots & a_{mn} \end{bmatrix}$$

It is also denoted as $[a_{ij}]_{m \times n}$.

NOTE

A matrix is not a number. It just an ordered collection of numbers arranged in the form of a rectangular array.

6.1.1. Order: If a matrix has m rows and n columns , then the order of the matrix is m by n or $m \times n$.

(i) The order of the matrx $[1 \quad 2 \quad 3]$ is 1×3

(ii) The order of the matrix $\begin{bmatrix} 1 & 2 & 3 \\ 4 & 3 & 2 \\ 5 & 6 & 4 \end{bmatrix}$ is 3×3.

(iii) The order of the matrix $\begin{bmatrix} 1 & 4 & 8 \\ 2 & 3 & 5 \end{bmatrix}$ is 2×3.

6.2 Types of Matrices

(i) **Row Matrix** : A matrix having only one row is called a row matrix.

Let $A = [1 \quad 2 \quad 3]$

(ii) **Colmn Matrix** :A matrix having only one column is called a column matrix .

Let $B = \begin{bmatrix} 1 \\ 2 \\ 5 \\ 9 \end{bmatrix}$.

(iii) **Rectangular Matrix** : A matrix in which number of rows and number of columns are not equal is called a rectangular matrix.

Let $C = \begin{bmatrix} 1 & 4 & 8 \\ 2 & 3 & 5 \end{bmatrix}$.

Let $A = \begin{bmatrix} 1 & 0 \\ 0 & 5 \end{bmatrix}$, $B = \begin{bmatrix} 2 & 0 & 0 \\ 0 & 4 & 0 \\ 0 & 0 & 7 \end{bmatrix}$ etc..

(xi) **Scaler Matrix** : In a square matrix , if all the diagonal elements are same and rest of the lements are zero , then it is called a scaler matrix.

Let $A = \begin{bmatrix} 4 & 0 \\ 0 & 4 \end{bmatrix}$, $B = \begin{bmatrix} 2 & 0 & 0 \\ 0 & 2 & 0 \\ 0 & 0 & 2 \end{bmatrix}$

(xii) **Identity Matrix :** In a scaler matrix if all the diagonal elements are 1, then it is called an identity matrix .

Let $I_2 = \begin{bmatrix} 1 & 0 \\ 0 & 1 \end{bmatrix}$, $I_3 = \begin{bmatrix} 1 & 0 & 0 \\ 0 & 1 & 0 \\ 0 & 0 & 1 \end{bmatrix}$

(xii) **Comparable Matrices :** Two matrices are said to be comparable matrices , if their orders are same.

Let $A = \begin{bmatrix} 1 & 2 \\ 3 & 4 \end{bmatrix}$ and

$B = \begin{bmatrix} a & b \\ c & d \end{bmatrix}$ are two comparable matrices.

(xiii) **Equality of two matrices :** Two comparable matrices are said to be equal if their corresponding elements are same.

If $\begin{bmatrix} 2 & 3 \\ 4 & 6 \end{bmatrix} = \begin{bmatrix} a & b \\ c & d \end{bmatrix}$ then a = 2 , b = 3 , c = 4 and d = 6.

(xiv) **Sub-matrix :** Any matrix is obtained by eleminating some rows and some columns from a given matrix A, then it is called a sub-matrix of A.

Let $A = \begin{bmatrix} 1 & 3 & 4 & 6 \\ 7 & 0 & 5 & 2 \\ 2 & 5 & 9 & 0 \end{bmatrix}$ and $B = \begin{bmatrix} 1 & 3 & 4 \\ 7 & 0 & 5 \end{bmatrix}$, then B is a sub-matrix of A.

6.3 Addition of Matrices

We can find the addition of two or more matrices if they are comparable matrices. Otherwise addition is not defined.

Let $A=\begin{bmatrix}1 & 3\\ 6 & 5\end{bmatrix}$ and $B=\begin{bmatrix}2 & 3\\ 4 & 1\end{bmatrix}$,

then $A+B=\begin{bmatrix}3 & 6\\ 10 & 6\end{bmatrix}$

6.3.1 PROPERTIES OF ADDITION OF MATRICES :

(i) Matrix addition is commutative
(ii) Matrix addtion is associative.
(iii) Additive identity of a matrix is exist.
(iv) Additive inverse of a matrix is exist.

6.3.2. SCALER MULTIPLICATION :

If $A=\begin{bmatrix}2 & 4\\ 6 & 7\end{bmatrix}$, then $kA=\begin{bmatrix}2k & 4k\\ 6k & 7k\end{bmatrix}$,

where k is the scaler multiple of A.

6.3.3. NEGATIVE OF MATRIX :

If $A=\begin{bmatrix}2 & 4\\ 6 & 7\end{bmatrix}$, then $-A=\begin{bmatrix}-2 & -4\\ -5 & -7\end{bmatrix}$

6.5 Multiplication of Matrices

If the number of columns of a first matrix is equal to the number of rows of a second matrix, then we can find out the product. Otherwise product is not defined.

If $A=[a_{ij}]_{m\times n}$ and $B=[b_{ji}]_{n\times p}$, then $AB=[c_{ij}]_{m\times p}$

Thus, if $A=\begin{bmatrix}a_{11} & a_{12}\\ a_{21} & a_{22}\end{bmatrix}$ and $B=\begin{bmatrix}b_{11} & b_{12}\\ b_{21} & b_{22}\end{bmatrix}$, then

$$AB=\begin{bmatrix}a_{11}b_{11}+a_{12}b_{21} & a_{11}b_{12}+a_{12}b_{22}\\ a_{21}b_{11}+a_{22}b_{21} & a_{21}b_{12}+a_{22}b_{22}\end{bmatrix}.$$

Properties of matrix multiplication :

(i) In genral, matrix multiplication is not commutative.
(ii) Matrix multiplication is associative.
(iii) Matrix multiplication is distributive over addition.
(iv) Multiplicative identity of a matrix is exist.

5. Transpose of a matrix

Transpose of a matrix is obtained by interchanging rows into columns and columns into rows.

If A be any matrix, then its transpose is denoted by A^T or A'.

Let $A=\begin{bmatrix}1 & 2 & 3\\ 4 & 5 & 6\\ 7 & 8 & 9\end{bmatrix}$, then $A^T=\begin{bmatrix}1 & 4 & 7\\ 2 & 5 & 8\\ 3 & 6 & 9\end{bmatrix}$

Properties of matrices :

(i) $(A+B)^T = A^T + B^T$
(ii) $(A^T)^T = A$
(iii) $(kA)^T = k(A)^T$ $(kA)^T = k(A)^T$
(iv) $(AB)^T = B^T A^T$.

6.5.1 SYMMETRIC MATRIX

A square matrix A is said to be symmtric if $A^T = A$.

Let $A=\begin{bmatrix}1 & 2\\ 2 & 6\end{bmatrix}$, $B=\begin{bmatrix}2 & 5\\ 5 & 7\end{bmatrix}$, $C=\begin{bmatrix}1 & 2 & 3\\ 2 & 4 & 5\\ 3 & 5 & 7\end{bmatrix}$ and

$D=\begin{bmatrix}a & h & g\\ h & b & f\\ g & f & c\end{bmatrix}$ etc are symmtric matrices.

6.5.2 SKEW SYMMTRIC MATRIX

A square matrix is said to be skew symmetric if $A^T = -A$

Let $A=\begin{bmatrix}0 & 3\\ -3 & 0\end{bmatrix}$ and $B=\begin{bmatrix}0 & 2 & 3\\ -2 & 0 & 5\\ -3 & -5 & 0\end{bmatrix}$

are skew symmetric matrices..

Properties of Symmetric and skew-symmetric matrices :

(i) In skew symmetric matrix all the diagonal elements are zero.
(ii) For any square matrix A, $A+A^T$ is symmetric and $A-A^T$ is skew - symmetric.
(iii) Any square matrix can be expressed uniquely as a sum of of a symmetric and a skew symmetric matrices.
(iv) The sum of skew symmtric matrices is also a skew symmetric matrix.
(v) The square of a skew symmetric matrix is not a skew symmetric.
(vi) The cube of a skew syemmetric matrices is also skew syemmetric matrix.
(vii) If A is syemmetric matrix, then kA is also syemmetric.
(viii) If A is skew syemmetric matrix, then kA is also skew syemmetric matrix.
(ix) If A is syemmetric, then AA^T and A^TA are syemmetric matrices.
(xii) If A is syemmetric (skew syemmetric) matrix, then B^TAB is syemmetric (skew syemmetric) matrix.

6.6 Determinant

For every square matrix of order n, there is associated a number (real or complex) is called a determinant of the same order.

A determinant is a polynomial of the elements of a square matrix. It is scaler. It has some finite values. Determinants are defined only for square matrices.

Determinants of a non square matrices is not defined. Determinant of a square matrix A is denoted by det A or |A|

6.6.1 MINOR OF AN ELEMENT OF A MATRIX

Minor of an element of a matrix is obtained after deleting the corresponding rows and corresponding columns.

Let $A=\begin{bmatrix}1 & 3\\5 & 8\end{bmatrix}$. Then the minor of 1 = 8, minor of 3

= 5, minor of 5 = 3 etc.

Also, let $B=\begin{bmatrix}1 & 2 & 3\\4 & 5 & 6\\7 & 8 & 9\end{bmatrix}$. Then the minor of 1

$=\begin{vmatrix}5 & 6\\8 & 9\end{vmatrix}$, minor of 2 $=\begin{vmatrix}4 & 6\\7 & 9\end{vmatrix}$ etc.

6.6.2 Cofactor of an Element of a Matrix

Cofactor of an element of a matrix is obtained after deleting the corresponding rows and correponding columns with a proper sign.

sign scheme can be used for 2nd order matrix $\begin{pmatrix}+ & -\\- & +\end{pmatrix}$ and for 3-rd order matrix $\begin{pmatrix}+ & - & +\\- & + & -\\+ & - & +\end{pmatrix}$.

Let $A=\begin{pmatrix}2 & 3\\4 & 5\end{pmatrix}$. Then the co-factor of 2 = 5, co-factor of 3

= –4, cofactor of 4 = – 3.

Also, if $B=\begin{pmatrix}1 & 0 & -2\\4 & -5 & 6\\-7 & -3 & 6\end{pmatrix}$, then the co-factor of 1 =

$\begin{vmatrix}-5 & 6\\-3 & 6\end{vmatrix}=-30+18=-12.$

co-factor of 0 $=\begin{vmatrix}4 & 6\\-7 & 6\end{vmatrix}=24+42=66.$ and so on.

6.6.3 Expansion of a Determinant

Expansion of a determinant is the sum of the product of the elements of any one row or column with their corresponding co-factors.

Let $A=\begin{pmatrix}a & b\\c & d\end{pmatrix}$,

then $|A| = a.\ d\ +\ b.\ (-c) = ad-bc$

Also, if $B=\begin{pmatrix}a & h & g\\h & b & f\\g & f & c\end{pmatrix}$,

then $|B| = a\begin{vmatrix}b & f\\f & c\end{vmatrix} - h\begin{vmatrix}h & f\\g & c\end{vmatrix} + g\begin{vmatrix}h & b\\g & f\end{vmatrix}$

$= a(bc-f^2)-h(ch-gf)+g(fh-bg)$

$= abc-af^2-ch^2+fgh+fgh-bg^2$

$= abc+2fgh-af^2-bg^2-ch^2$..

6.6.4 Properties of Determinants :

1. The value of a determinan is remained unchanged, if the rows and columns are interchanged.

If A is any square matrix, then $|A|=|A^T|$.

2. If any two rows or columns of a determinant are interchanged, then the value of determinant is remain same but in opposite sign.

Let $D_1=\begin{vmatrix}a_1 & b_1 & c_1\\a_2 & b_2 & c_2\\a_3 & b_3 & c_3\end{vmatrix}$ and $D_2=\begin{vmatrix}a_2 & b_2 & c_2\\a_1 & b_1 & c_1\\a_3 & b_3 & c_3\end{vmatrix}$.

Then $D_1=-D_2$.

3. If every element of a row or coulmn of a determinant is zero, then the value of a determinant is zero.

Let $D_1=\begin{vmatrix}0 & 0\\0 & 0\end{vmatrix}=0$

4. If any two rows (or columns) of a determinant are identical, then the value of determinant is zero.

Let $D_1=\begin{vmatrix}a_1 & b_1 & c_1\\a_1 & b_1 & c_1\\a_2 & b_2 & c_2\end{vmatrix}$, then $D_1=0$.

5. If any two rows or columns of a determinant are proportional, then the value of a determinant is 0.

Let $D_1=\begin{vmatrix}1 & 2 & 3\\2 & 4 & 6\\4 & 5 & 7\end{vmatrix}$, then $D_1=0$.

6. If every elements of any one row or column is multiplied by a non zero constant , then the value of a determinant is multiplied by that number.

Let $D_1=\begin{vmatrix}a_1 & b_1 & c_1\\a_2 & b_2 & c_2\\a_3 & b_3 & c_3\end{vmatrix}$ and $D_2=\begin{vmatrix}ka_1 & kb_1 & kc_1\\a_2 & b_2 & c_2\\a_3 & b_3 & c_3\end{vmatrix}$, then

$D_1=k\ D_2$

7. If every element of a row or column as a sum of two or more terms , then the given determinant is equal to sum of two or more determinants .

For example,

$$\begin{vmatrix}a_1+x & b_1+y & c_1+z\\a_2 & b_2 & c_2\\a_3 & b_3 & c_3\end{vmatrix}=\begin{vmatrix}a_1 & b_1 & c_1\\a_2 & b_2 & c_2\\a_3 & b_3 & c_3\end{vmatrix}+\begin{vmatrix}x & y & z\\a_2 & b_2 & c_2\\a_3 & b_3 & c_3\end{vmatrix}.$$

8. The value of a determinant is not changed by adding to the elements of any row or column with the same multiples of the corresponding elements of any other row or column.

Let $D_1 = \begin{vmatrix} a & b \\ c & d \end{vmatrix}$ and $D_2 = \begin{vmatrix} a+cm & b+dm \\ c & d \end{vmatrix}$,

then $D_1 = D_2$.

6.5 Special determinants

(i) Symmetric determinant

$$\begin{vmatrix} a & h & g \\ h & b & f \\ g & f & c \end{vmatrix} = abc + 2\ fgh\text{-}af^2 - bg^2 - ch^2$$

(ii) Skew symmteric determinant of odd order

$$\begin{vmatrix} 0 & b & c \\ -b & 0 & a \\ -c & -1 & 0 \end{vmatrix} = 0$$

(iii) Circulant

$$\begin{vmatrix} a & b & c \\ b & c & a \\ c & a & b \end{vmatrix} = -\left(a^3 + b^3 + c^3 - 3abc\right)$$

(iv) Some imprtant determinants to remember

1. $\begin{vmatrix} 1 & a & b+c \\ 1 & b & c+a \\ 1 & c & a+b \end{vmatrix} = 0$

2. $\begin{vmatrix} 1 & a & a^2 \\ 1 & b & b^2 \\ 1 & c & c^2 \end{vmatrix} = (a-b)(b-c)(c-a) = \begin{vmatrix} 1 & a & bc \\ 1 & b & ca \\ 1 & c & ab \end{vmatrix}$

3. $\begin{vmatrix} 1 & a & a^3 \\ 1 & b & b^3 \\ 1 & c & c^3 \end{vmatrix} = (a-b)(b-c)(c-a)(a+b+c)$

4. $\begin{vmatrix} 1 & a^2 & a^3 \\ 1 & b^2 & b^3 \\ 1 & c^2 & c^3 \end{vmatrix} = (a-b)(b-c)(c-a)(ab+bc+ca)$

5. $\begin{vmatrix} 1 & \omega & \omega^2 \\ \omega & 1 & \omega^2 \\ \omega & \omega^2 & 1 \end{vmatrix} = 0$

6. $\begin{vmatrix} 1 & bc & ca+ab \\ 1 & ca & ab+bc \\ 1 & ab & bc+ca \end{vmatrix} = 0$

7. $\begin{vmatrix} a-b & b-c & c-a \\ p-q & q-r & r-p \\ x-y & y-z & z-x \end{vmatrix} = 0$

8. $\begin{vmatrix} \sin A & \cos A & \sin(A+\ ) \\ \sin B & \cos B & \sin(B+\ ) \\ \sin C & \cos C & \sin(C+\ ) \end{vmatrix} = 0$

6.6 Cramers Rule

Statement : The solutions of the system of equations $a_1x + b_1y + c_1z = d_1, a_2x + b_2y + c_2z = d_2, a_3x + b_3y + c_3z = d_3$

are given by $x = \frac{D_1}{D}$, $y = \frac{D_2}{D}$, $z = \frac{D_3}{D}$, where

$$D = \begin{vmatrix} a_1 & b_1 & c_1 \\ a_2 & b_2 & c_2 \\ a_3 & b_3 & c_3 \end{vmatrix}, D_1 = \begin{vmatrix} d_1 & b_1 & c_1 \\ d_2 & b_2 & c_2 \\ d_3 & b_3 & c_3 \end{vmatrix},$$

$$D_2 = \begin{vmatrix} a_1 & d_1 & c_1 \\ a_2 & d_2 & c_2 \\ a_3 & d_3 & c_3 \end{vmatrix} \text{ and } D_3 = \begin{vmatrix} a_1 & b_1 & d_1 \\ a_2 & b_2 & d_2 \\ a_3 & b_3 & d_3 \end{vmatrix}$$

Nature of solutions of the system of equations by Camers Rule :

(i) If $D \neq 0$, then the system of equations has a unique solution and is said to be consistent.

(ii) If D = 0 as well as $D_1 = 0 = D_2 = D_3$, then the syatem of equations have infinitely many solutions and is said to be consistent.

(iii) If $D = 0$ and atleast one of D_1, D_2, D_3 is non zero , then the system of equations have no solution and is said to be in-consistent.

6.7 Homogeneous system of equations

The given homogenous system of equations are $a_1x + b_1y + c_1z = 0, a_2x + b_2y + c_2z = 0, a_3x + b_3y + c_3z = 0$

Let $D = \begin{vmatrix} a_1 & b_1 & c_1 \\ a_2 & b_2 & c_2 \\ a_3 & b_3 & c_3 \end{vmatrix}$, $D_1 = \begin{vmatrix} 0 & b_1 & c_1 \\ 0 & b_2 & c_2 \\ 0 & b_3 & c_3 \end{vmatrix}$,

$$D_2 = \begin{vmatrix} a_1 & 0 & c_1 \\ a_2 & 0 & c_2 \\ a_3 & 0 & c_3 \end{vmatrix} \text{ and } D_3 = \begin{vmatrix} a_1 & b_1 & 0 \\ a_2 & b_2 & 0 \\ a_3 & b_3 & 0 \end{vmatrix}$$

Nature of solutions by homogeneous system of equations :

(i) If $D \neq 0$, then the system of equations has only trivial solution , say , x = 0 = y = z and the system of equations is said to be consistent.

(ii) If D = 0 , then the system of equations has non trivial solution.*ie.* infinite solutions and the system of equations is said to be also consistent.

6.8 Multiplication of two determinants

Two determinants can be multiplied by a variety of ways. Row - by - Column , Row - by - row, column - by - column and column - by - row multiplication rule.

Let $A=\begin{vmatrix} a_1 & b_1 \\ a_2 & b_2 \end{vmatrix}$ and $B=\begin{vmatrix} m_1 & n_1 \\ m_2 & n_2 \end{vmatrix}$

Then

$$AB=\begin{vmatrix} a_1 & b_1 \\ a_2 & b_2 \end{vmatrix}\times\begin{vmatrix} m_1 & n_1 \\ m_2 & n_2 \end{vmatrix}=\begin{vmatrix} a_1m_1+b_1n_1 & a_1m_2+b_1n_2 \\ a_2m_1+b_2n_1 & a_2m_2+b_2n_2 \end{vmatrix}.$$

Ex-1: Prove that

$$\begin{vmatrix} a & 0 & c \\ a & b & 0 \\ 0 & b & c \end{vmatrix}^2=\begin{vmatrix} c^2+a^2 & a^2 & c^2 \\ a^2 & a^2+b^2 & b^2 \\ c^2 & b^2 & b^2+c^2 \end{vmatrix}$$

Sol. We have, $\begin{vmatrix} a & 0 & c \\ a & b & 0 \\ 0 & b & c \end{vmatrix}^2=\begin{vmatrix} a & 0 & c \\ a & b & 0 \\ 0 & b & c \end{vmatrix}\times\begin{vmatrix} a & 0 & c \\ a & b & 0 \\ 0 & b & c \end{vmatrix}$

$$=\begin{vmatrix} a.a+0.0+c.c & a.a+0.0+0.0 & a.0+0.b+c.c \\ a.a+b.0+0.c & a.a+b.b+0.0 & a.0+b.b+0.c \\ 0.a+b.0+c.c & 0.a+b.b+c.0 & 0.0+b.b+c.c \end{vmatrix}$$

$$=\begin{vmatrix} c^2+a^2 & a^2 & c^2 \\ a^2 & a^2+b^2 & b^2 \\ c^2 & b^2 & b^2+c^2 \end{vmatrix}.$$

6.9 Differentiation of determinant

Let $F(x)=\begin{vmatrix} f(x) & g(x) & h(x) \\ p(x) & q(x) & r(x) \\ u(x) & v(x) & w(x) \end{vmatrix}$

Then

$$F'(x)=\begin{vmatrix} f'(x) & g'(x) & h'(x) \\ p(x) & q(x) & r(x) \\ u(x) & v(x) & w(x) \end{vmatrix}+\begin{vmatrix} f(x) & g(x) & h(x) \\ p'(x) & q'(x) & r'(x) \\ u(x) & v(x) & w(x) \end{vmatrix}+\begin{vmatrix} f(x) & g(x) & h(x) \\ p(x) & q(x) & r(x) \\ u'(x) & v'(x) & w'(x) \end{vmatrix}$$

or

$$F'(x)=\begin{vmatrix} f'(x) & g(x) & h(x) \\ p'(x) & q(x) & r(x) \\ u'(x) & v(x) & w(x) \end{vmatrix}+\begin{vmatrix} f(x) & g'(x) & h(x) \\ p(x) & q'(x) & r(x) \\ u(x) & v'(x) & w(x) \end{vmatrix}+\begin{vmatrix} f(x) & g(x) & h'(x) \\ p(x) & q(x) & r'(x) \\ u(x) & v(x) & w'(x) \end{vmatrix}.$$

Ex-1 If $F(x)=\begin{vmatrix} 1 & a & a^2 \\ x & x^2 & x^3 \\ e^{x-a} & e^{x^2-a^2} & e^{x^3-a^3} \end{vmatrix}$, then find the value of $F'(a)$.

Sol. We have,

$$F'(x)=\begin{vmatrix} 0 & 0 & 0 \\ x & x^2 & x^3 \\ e^{x-a} & e^{x^2-a^2} & e^{x^3-a^3} \end{vmatrix}+\begin{vmatrix} 1 & a & a^2 \\ 1 & 2x & 3x^2 \\ e^{x-a} & e^{x^2-a^2} & e^{x^3-a^3} \end{vmatrix}+\begin{vmatrix} 1 & a & a^2 \\ x & x^2 & x^3 \\ e^{x-a} & 2x\times e^{x^2-a^2} & 3x^2\times e^{x^3-a^3} \end{vmatrix}$$

$$=\begin{vmatrix} 1 & a & a^2 \\ 1 & 2x & 3x^2 \\ e^{x-a} & e^{x^2-a^2} & e^{x^3-a^3} \end{vmatrix}+\begin{vmatrix} 1 & a & a^2 \\ x & x^2 & x^3 \\ e^{x-a} & 2x\times e^{x^2-a^2} & 3x^2\times e^{x^3-a^3} \end{vmatrix}$$

$$\Rightarrow F'(a)=\begin{vmatrix} 1 & a & a^2 \\ 1 & 2a & 3a^2 \\ 1 & 1 & 1 \end{vmatrix}+\begin{vmatrix} 1 & a & a^2 \\ a & a^2 & a^3 \\ 1 & 2a & 3a^2 \end{vmatrix}$$

$$\Rightarrow F'(a)=\begin{vmatrix} 1 & a & a^2 \\ 1 & 2a & 3a^2 \\ 1 & 1 & 1 \end{vmatrix}+a\begin{vmatrix} 1 & a & a^2 \\ 1 & a & a^2 \\ 1 & 2a & 3a^2 \end{vmatrix}=\begin{vmatrix} 1 & a & a^2 \\ 1 & 2a & 3a^2 \\ 1 & 1 & 1 \end{vmatrix}$$

$= 2a - 3a^2 - a + 3a^3 + a^2 - 2a^3$

$= a - 2a^2 + a^3.$

14. Integration of determinant

If $F(x)=\begin{vmatrix} f(x) & g(x) & h(x) \\ a & b & c \\ l & m & n \end{vmatrix}$,

then

$$\int_a^b F(x)\,dx=\begin{vmatrix} \int_a^b f(x)\,dx & \int_a^b g(x)\,dx & \int_a^b h(x)\,dx \\ a & b & c \\ l & m & n \end{vmatrix}$$

Ex-1. If $f(x)=\begin{vmatrix} \sin^2x & \log(\sin x) & \frac{\sqrt{\sin x}}{\sqrt{\sin x}+\sqrt{\cos x}} \\ n & \sum_{k=1}^{n}(k) & \prod_{k=1}^{n}(k) \\ \frac{8}{15} & \frac{}{2}\log\left(\frac{1}{2}\right) & \frac{}{4} \end{vmatrix}$,

then find the value of $\int_0^{/2} f(x)\,dx$

Sol. $\int_0^{/2} f(x)\,dx$

$$=\begin{vmatrix} \int_0^{/2}\sin^2x\,dx & \int_0^{/2}\log(\sin x)\,dx & \int_0^{/2}\left(\frac{\sqrt{\sin x}}{\sqrt{\sin x}+\sqrt{\cos x}}\right)dx \\ n & \sum_{k=1}^{n}(k) & \prod_{k=1}^{n}(k) \\ \frac{8}{15} & \frac{}{2}\log\left(\frac{1}{2}\right) & \frac{}{4} \end{vmatrix}$$

$$=\begin{vmatrix} \frac{8}{15} & \frac{}{2}\log\left(\frac{1}{2}\right) & \frac{}{4} \\ n & \sum_{k=1}^{n}(k) & \prod_{k=1}^{n}(k) \\ \frac{8}{15} & \frac{}{2}\log\left(\frac{1}{2}\right) & \frac{}{4} \end{vmatrix}=0$$

6.11 Adjoint of a matrix

The adjoint of a matrix is the transpose of the cofactors of the corresponding elements of a given matrix . If A be any square matrix, then Adj A= $\left(C_{ij}\right)^T$.

Let $A=\begin{pmatrix}2 & 3\\ 4 & 5\end{pmatrix}$, then $Adj\ (A)=\begin{pmatrix}5 & -3\\ -4 & 2\end{pmatrix}$.

Theorem : If A is any square matrix, then $A.(adj(A))=|A|.\ I_n=(adj(A)).A$.

Properties of adjoint of matrix or matrices :

(i) If A is any square matrix of order n, then $|adj(A)|=|A|^{n-1}$

(ii) If $|A|=0$, then $|adj(A)|=0$

(iii) $adj(kA)=k^{n-1}\ (adj(A))$

(iv) $adj(A^T)=(adj\ A)^T$

(v) $adj(AB)=(adj\ B)(adj\ A)$

(vi) If A is a non singular matrix, then adj (adj(A)) = $|A|^{n-2}.A$.

(vii) $|adj(adj(A))|=|A|^{(n-1)2}$

(viii) If A be a square matrix of order n and B be its adjoint, then $\det(AB+k\,I_n)=(\det A+k)^n$.

6.12 Singular and non - singular matrices

Singular Matrix : If the determinant of a matrix is zero, then it is called singular matrix.

Let $A=\begin{pmatrix}1 & 2\\ 2 & 4\end{pmatrix}$, then $|A|=4-4=0$. Thus A is singular matrix.

Non-singular matrix : If the determinant of a matrix is non zero , then it is called non singular matrix.

Let $A=\begin{pmatrix}1 & 2\\ 3 & 4\end{pmatrix}$, then $|A|=\begin{vmatrix}1 & 2\\ 3 & 4\end{vmatrix}=4-6=-2\neq 0$

Thus A is non singular.

6.13 Inverse of a matrix

For every non - singular square matrix of order n, there exist another square matrix of the same order n such that $AB=I_n$, then B is called the inverse of A.

As we know that, $A.(adj(A))=|A|.I_n$

$$\Rightarrow\ A.\left(\frac{(adj\ (A))}{|A|}\right)=I_n$$

$$\Rightarrow\ A^{-1}=\left(\frac{(adj\ (A))}{|A|}\right).$$

Let $A=\begin{pmatrix}1 & 2\\ 3 & 4\end{pmatrix}$: $|A|=\begin{vmatrix}1 & 2\\ 3 & 4\end{vmatrix}=4-6=-2\neq 0$.

Thus, its inverse is exist.

Now, $adj(A)=\begin{pmatrix}4 & -2\\ -3 & 1\end{pmatrix}$.

Hence, $A^{-1}=\frac{1}{-2}\begin{pmatrix}4 & -2\\ -3 & 1\end{pmatrix}$.

Properties of inverse of a matrix or matrices :

(i) $(A^{-1})^{-1}=A$

(ii) $|A^{-1}|=\frac{1}{|A|}$

(iii) $(A^T)^{-1}=(A^{-1})^T$

(iv) If k is non zero and A is non singular, then $(kA)^{-1}=\frac{1}{k}(A^{-1})$

(v) $(I^{-1})=I$

(vi) $(adj\ A^{-1})=(adj\ A)^{-1}=\frac{A}{|A|}$.

(vii) If A, B be two non singular matrices, then $(AB)^{-1}=(B^{-1}A^{-1})$.

6.14 Soltions of the system of equations by matrix (inverse) method

Consider the system of equations are

$a_1x+b_1y+c_1z=d_1,\ a_2x+b_2y+c_2z=d_2,\ a_3x+b_3y+c_3z=d_3$

The given system of equations can be written in matrix form is

$$\begin{pmatrix}a_1 & b_1 & c_1\\ a_2 & b_2 & c_2\\ a_3 & b_3 & c_3\end{pmatrix}\begin{pmatrix}x\\ y\\ z\end{pmatrix}=\begin{pmatrix}d_1\\ d_2\\ d_3\end{pmatrix}$$

$\Rightarrow\ AX=B,$

where $A=\begin{pmatrix}a_1 & b_1 & c_1\\ a_2 & b_2 & c_2\\ a_3 & b_3 & c_3\end{pmatrix},\ X=\begin{pmatrix}x\\ y\\ z\end{pmatrix};\ B=\begin{pmatrix}d_1\\ d_2\\ d_3\end{pmatrix}$

6.14.1 Nature of solutions by the matrix method :

(i) If $|A|\neq 0$, then the system of equations has a unique solution and the system of equation is said to be consistent.

(ii) If $|A|=0$ and $(adj\ A).B=O$, then the system of equations has infinily many solutions and the system of equations is said to be consistent.

(iii) If $|A|=0$ and $(adj\ A).B\neq O$, then the system of equations have no solution and the system of equations is said to be inconsistent.

6.15 Elementary transformations of a Matrix

There are six operations (transformations) on a matrix , three of which are due to rows and three of columns, which are known as elementary transformations.

(i) The interchange of any two rows (or columns).

Symbolically, $R_i\leftrightarrow R_j$ or $C_i\leftrightarrow C_j$

(ii) The multiplications of the elements of any one row (or column) by a non zero constant, say, k, i.e. symbolically:

$R_i\to k\ R_j$ or $C_i\to k\ C_j$

(iii) The addition to the elements of any one row (or column) with the corresponding elements of any other row (or column) muliplied by a non zero number. i.e. symbolically,

$R_i\to R_i+k\ R_j$ or $C_i\to C_i+k\ C_j$

Equivalent matrices : Two matrices are said to be equivalent, if one is obtained from other by elementary transformations. We genrally write it, A ~ B.

Ex-1. By using elementary row operation , find the inverse of $A=\begin{pmatrix}1&2\\3&4\end{pmatrix}$.

Sol. We have, A = I.A

$$\Rightarrow \begin{pmatrix}1&2\\3&4\end{pmatrix}=\begin{pmatrix}1&0\\0&1\end{pmatrix}.A$$

$$\Rightarrow \begin{pmatrix}1&2\\0&-2\end{pmatrix}=\begin{pmatrix}1&0\\-3&1\end{pmatrix}.A \quad (R_2\to R_2-2R_1)$$

$$\Rightarrow \begin{pmatrix}1&0\\0&-2\end{pmatrix}=\begin{pmatrix}-2&1\\-3&1\end{pmatrix}.A \quad (R_1\to R_1+R_2)$$

$$\Rightarrow \begin{pmatrix}1&0\\0&1\end{pmatrix}=\begin{pmatrix}-2&1\\3/2&-1/2\end{pmatrix}.A \quad \left(R_2\to\left(\frac{-1}{2}\right)\times R_2\right)$$

Thus. $A^{-1}=\begin{pmatrix}-2&1\\3/2&-1/2\end{pmatrix}$.

LEVEL - I QUESTIONS BASED ON FUNDAMENTALS

Construction of Matices :

1. Construct a 2×2, 2×3 and 3×3 matrices whose elements a_{ij} are given by

(i) $\frac{(i+j)^2}{2}$ (ii) $\frac{(i-2j)^2}{2}$

(iii) $\frac{(2i-j)^2}{2}$ (iv) $2i+\frac{i}{j}$

(v) $\frac{i-j}{i+j}$ (vi) $\left|\frac{2i-3j}{2}\right|$

(vii) $\left|\frac{-3i+j}{2}\right|$ (viii) $i^2+\frac{1}{i^2}$

Equality of Matices :

2. Find x,y and z such that $\begin{bmatrix}x-y&2z+w\\2x-y&2x+w\end{bmatrix}=\begin{bmatrix}5&3\\12&15\end{bmatrix}$

3. If $\begin{bmatrix}x-y&z\\2x-y&w\end{bmatrix}=\begin{bmatrix}3&2\\4&7\end{bmatrix}$, then find x, y and z.

4. Find the values of x and y if $\begin{bmatrix}x+10&y^2+2y\\0&-4\end{bmatrix}=\begin{bmatrix}3x+4&3\\0&y^2-5y\end{bmatrix}$

Addition of Matices :

5. Let $A=\begin{bmatrix}-1&0&2\\3&1&4\end{bmatrix}$ and $B=\begin{bmatrix}0&-2&5\\1&-3&1\end{bmatrix}$ and $C=\begin{bmatrix}1&-5&2\\6&0&-4\end{bmatrix}$

Compute 2A-3B+4C.

6. Find Matrices X and Y, if $X+Y=\begin{bmatrix}5&2\\0&9\end{bmatrix}$ and $X-Y=\begin{bmatrix}3&6\\0&1\end{bmatrix}$

7. Find X, if $Y=\begin{bmatrix}3&2\\1&4\end{bmatrix}$ and $2X+Y=\begin{bmatrix}1&0\\-3&2\end{bmatrix}$

8. If $A=\begin{bmatrix}1&-3&2\\2&0&2\end{bmatrix}$, $B=\begin{bmatrix}2&-1&1\\1&0&-1\end{bmatrix}$, find a matrix C such that A+B+C is a zero matrix.

9. Find a matrix X such that 2A+B+X=O, where $A=\begin{bmatrix}-1&2\\3&4\end{bmatrix}$, $B=\begin{bmatrix}-3&-2\\1&5\end{bmatrix}$

Multiplication of Matrices :

10. Compute the products AB and BA whichever exists in each of the following cases :

(i) $A=\begin{bmatrix}-3&-2\\1&5\end{bmatrix}$ and $B=\begin{bmatrix}1&2&3\\2&3&1\end{bmatrix}$

(ii) $A=\begin{bmatrix}3&2\\-1&0\\-1&1\end{bmatrix}$ and $B=\begin{bmatrix}4&5&6\\0&1&2\end{bmatrix}$

(iii) $A=[1\ \ -1\ \ 2\ \ 3]$ and $B=\begin{bmatrix}0\\1\\3\\2\end{bmatrix}$

(iv) $[a,b]\begin{bmatrix}c\\d\end{bmatrix}+\begin{bmatrix}a&b&c&d\end{bmatrix}\begin{bmatrix}a\\b\\c\\d\end{bmatrix}$

(v) $A=\begin{bmatrix}1&-3&-1\\2&-1&-1\\3&0&-1\end{bmatrix}$ and $B=\begin{bmatrix}-2&3&-1\\-1&2&-1\\-6&9&-4\end{bmatrix}$

11. If $\begin{bmatrix}1&1&x\end{bmatrix}\begin{bmatrix}1&0&2\\0&2&1\\2&1&0\end{bmatrix}\begin{bmatrix}1\\1\\1\end{bmatrix}=0$, then find x

12. If $\begin{bmatrix}x&4&1\end{bmatrix}\begin{bmatrix}1&2&3\\4&5&7\\3&4&2\end{bmatrix}\begin{bmatrix}2\\1\\1\end{bmatrix}=0$, then find x.

13. If $A=\begin{bmatrix}3&1\\-1&2\end{bmatrix}$, show that $A^2-5A+7I_2=O$

14. Prove that product of two non-zero matrices can be a zero matrix.

Symmetric and Skew-symmteric Matrices :

15. Prove that the elements on the main diagonal of a skew-symmetric matrix are all zero.

16. Prove that every square matrix can be expressed as a sum of a symmteric and skew-symmteric matrices.

17. Expres the matrix $A = \begin{bmatrix} 1 & 2 \\ 3 & 4 \end{bmatrix}$ as the sum of a symmetric and skew-symmteric matrices.

18. Express the matrix $A = \begin{bmatrix} 3 & 2 & 3 \\ 4 & 5 & 3 \\ 2 & 4 & 5 \end{bmatrix}$ as the sum of a symmetric and skew-symmterics matrix.

Determinants :

19. Evaluate the following determinants :

(i) $\begin{vmatrix} x-1 & 1 \\ x^3 & x^2+x+1 \end{vmatrix}$

(ii) $\begin{vmatrix} 1 & \log_b a \\ \log_a b & 1 \end{vmatrix}$

(iii) $\begin{vmatrix} 3x & 7 \\ 2 & 4 \end{vmatrix}$

(iv) $\begin{vmatrix} 1 & \omega & {}^2 \\ \omega & {}^2 & 1 \\ \omega^2 & 1 & \end{vmatrix}$

(v) $\begin{vmatrix} 1 & a & b+c \\ 1 & b & c+a \\ 1 & c & a+b \end{vmatrix}$

(vi) $\begin{vmatrix} 1 & bc & a(b+c) \\ 1 & ca & b(c+a) \\ 1 & ab & c(a+b) \end{vmatrix}$

(vii) $\begin{vmatrix} x+y & y+z & z+x \\ z & x & y \\ 1 & 1 & 1 \end{vmatrix}$

(viii) $\begin{vmatrix} b^2c^2 & bc & b+c \\ c^2a^2 & ca & c+a \\ a^2b^2 & ab & a+b \end{vmatrix}$

20. Evaluate the following determinants :

(i) $\begin{vmatrix} 1 & a & a^2 \\ 1 & b & b^2 \\ 1 & c & c^2 \end{vmatrix}$ (ii) $\begin{vmatrix} 1 & a & a^3 \\ 1 & b & b^3 \\ 1 & c & c^3 \end{vmatrix}$ (iii) $\begin{vmatrix} x & y & z \\ x^2 & y^2 & z^2 \\ x^3 & y^3 & z^3 \end{vmatrix}$

21. Prove that $\begin{vmatrix} \alpha & \beta & \gamma \\ \alpha^2 & \beta^2 & \gamma^2 \\ \alpha^3 & \beta^3 & \gamma^3 \end{vmatrix} = (\alpha - \beta)(\beta - \gamma)(\gamma - \alpha)\alpha\beta\gamma$.

22. Prove that $\begin{vmatrix} 1+a & 1 & 1 \\ 1 & 1+b & 1 \\ 1 & 1 & 1+c \end{vmatrix} = abc\left(1+\frac{1}{a}+\frac{1}{b}+\frac{1}{c}\right)$

$= abc + bc + ca + ab.$

23. Prove that $\begin{vmatrix} b+c & c+a & a+b \\ q+r & r+p & p+q \\ y+z & z+x & x+y \end{vmatrix} = 2\begin{vmatrix} a & b & c \\ p & q & r \\ x & y & z \end{vmatrix}$

24. Prove that $\begin{vmatrix} a & a+b & a+b+c \\ 2a & 3a+2b & 4a+3b+2c \\ 3a & 6a+3b & 10a+6b+3c \end{vmatrix} = a^3$

25. Prove that $\begin{vmatrix} 1 & 1+p & 1+p+q \\ 2 & 3+2p & 1+3p+2q \\ 3 & 6+3p & 10+6p+3q \end{vmatrix} = 10$

26. Prove that $\begin{vmatrix} a+b+2c & a & b \\ c & b+c+2a & b \\ c & a & c+a+2b \end{vmatrix} = 2\,(a+b+c)^3$

27. Prove that $\begin{vmatrix} a-b-c & 2a & 2a \\ 2b & b-c-a & 2b \\ 2c & 2c & c-a-b \end{vmatrix} = (a+b+c)^3$.

28. Prove that $\begin{vmatrix} 1 & a & a^2 \\ a^2 & 1 & a \\ a & a^2 & 1 \end{vmatrix} = (a^3-1)^2$

29. Prove that $\begin{vmatrix} (a+1)(a+2) & a+2 & 1 \\ (a+2)(a+3) & a+3 & 1 \\ (a+3)(a+4) & a+4 & 1 \end{vmatrix} = -2$

30. Prove that $\begin{vmatrix} b+c & a & a \\ b & c+a & b \\ c & c & a+b \end{vmatrix} = 4abc$.

31. Prove that $\begin{vmatrix} b^2+c^2 & ab & ac \\ ba & c^2+a^2 & bc \\ ca & cb & a^2+b^2 \end{vmatrix} = 4a^2b^2c^2$.

32. Prove that $\begin{vmatrix} 1+a^2-b^2 & 2ab & -2b \\ 2ab & 1-a^2+b^2 & 2a \\ 2b & -2a & 1-a^2-b^2 \end{vmatrix}$

$= (1+a^2+b^2)^3$.

33. If $x \neq y \neq z$ & $\begin{vmatrix} x & x^2 & 1+x^3 \\ y & y^2 & 1+y^3 \\ z & z^2 & 1+z^3 \end{vmatrix} = 0$,

then prove that $xyz = -1$.

34. If a, b, c are real numbers, prove that

$\begin{vmatrix} a & b & c \\ b & c & a \\ c & a & b \end{vmatrix} = -(a+b+c)(a+b\omega+c\omega^2)(a+b\omega^2+c\omega)$.

35. (i) Prove that $\begin{vmatrix} a & a+b & a+2b \\ a+2b & a & a+b \\ a+b & a+2b & a \end{vmatrix} = 9(a+b)b^2$

(ii) If the derminant $\begin{vmatrix} a & b & a\alpha+b \\ b & c & b\alpha+c \\ a\alpha+b & b\alpha+c & 0 \end{vmatrix} = 0$, then prove that a, b, c are in G.P.

(iii) If ω is a cube root of unity, then prove that

$$\begin{vmatrix} 1 & 1 & 1 \\ 1 & -1-\omega^2 & \omega^2 \\ 1 & \omega^2 & \omega^4 \end{vmatrix} = 3\omega(\omega-1)$$

36. If a, b, c are all +ve and are pth, qth and rth terms of a G.P., then prove that

$$\begin{vmatrix} \log a & p & 1 \\ \log b & q & 1 \\ \log c & r & 1 \end{vmatrix} = 0$$

37. If α, β, γ are the roots of the equation $x^2(px+q) = r(x+1)$, prove that

$$\begin{vmatrix} 1+\alpha & 1 & 1 \\ 1 & 1+\beta & 1 \\ 1 & 1 & 1+\gamma \end{vmatrix} = 0$$

38. Let $\Delta_r = \begin{vmatrix} r & x & \frac{n(n+1)}{2} \\ 2r-1 & y & n^2 \\ 3r-2 & z & \frac{n(3n-1)}{2} \end{vmatrix}$,

then prove that $\sum_{r=1}^{n} \Delta_r = 0$.

39. If $\Delta_r = \begin{vmatrix} 2^{r-1} & 2.3^{r-1} & 4.5^{r-1} \\ x & y & z \\ 2^n-1 & 3^n-1 & 5^n-1 \end{vmatrix}$,

then prove that $\sum_{r=1}^{n} \Delta_r =$ constant.

40. Prove that $\begin{vmatrix} a^2+1 & ab & ac \\ ab & b^2+1 & bc \\ ac & bc & c^2+1 \end{vmatrix} = \left(1+a^2+b^2+c^2\right)$

41. Prove that $\begin{vmatrix} {}^xC_1 & {}^xC_2 & {}^xC_3 \\ {}^yC_1 & {}^yC_2 & {}^yC_3 \\ {}^zC_1 & {}^zC_2 & {}^zC_3 \end{vmatrix} = \frac{xyz}{12} \times (x-y)(y-z)(z-x)$

42. Prove that $\begin{vmatrix} 1 & \log_x y & \log_x z \\ \log_y x & 1 & \log_y z \\ \log_z x & \log_z y & 1 \end{vmatrix} = 0.$

43. If $a_1, a_2, \ldots\ldots\ldots a_n, \ldots\ldots\ldots\ldots$ are in G.P., then find the value of

$$\begin{vmatrix} \log a_n & \log a_{n+1} & \log a_{n+2} \\ \log a_{n+3} & \log a_{n+4} & \log a_{n+5} \\ \log a_{n+6} & \log a_{n+7} & \log a_{n+8} \end{vmatrix}$$

44. Let the three digit numbers A28, 3B9 and 62C, where A, B, C are integers between 0 and 9, be divisible by a fixed integer k, then show that the determinant $\begin{vmatrix} A & 3 & 6 \\ 8 & 9 & C \\ 2 & B & 2 \end{vmatrix}$ is also divisible by the same integer k.

Applications of Determinants to the Co-ordinate Geometry :

45. Show that the points (a, b+c), (b, c+a) and (c, a+b) are collinear.

46. If $A(x_1, y_1)$, $B(x_2, y_2)$ and $C(x_3, y_3)$ are the verices of an equilateral triangle whose each side is equal to a, then prove

that $\begin{vmatrix} x_1 & y_1 & 2 \\ x_2 & y_2 & 2 \\ x_3 & y_3 & 2 \end{vmatrix}^2 = 3a^4.$

47. If the points (2, -3), (λ, -1) and (0,4) are collinear, find the value of λ.

48. If the points (a,0), (0,b) and (1,1) are collinear, then prove that $\frac{1}{a}+\frac{1}{b}=1.$

Cramer's Rule :

49. Solve the following system of equations by Cramer's Rule :

(i) $2x-y=17$, $3x+5y=6$ (ii) $2x+y=3$, $4x+2y=5$ (iii) $x+2y=3$, $4x+8y=5$

50. Solve the following system of equations by Cramers Rule :

(i) $5x-7y+z=11$
$6x-8y-z=15$
$3x+2y-6z=7$

(ii) $x+y+z=1$
$ax+by+cz=k$
$a^2x+b^2y+c^2z=k^2$

(iii) $x+y=1$
$x+z=-1$
$x-y-2z=-3=3$

(iv) $x+y=5$
$y+z=3$
$z+x=4$

(v) $\frac{2}{x}+\frac{3}{y}+\frac{10}{z}=4$, $\frac{4}{x}-\frac{6}{y}+\frac{5}{z}=1$, $\frac{6}{x}+\frac{9}{y}-\frac{20}{z}=2$.

(vi) $x+y+z=3$
$2x-y+z=2$
$3x+6y+5z=20$

(vii) $3x-y+2z=3$
$2x+y+3z=5$
$x-2y-z=1$

(viii) $2x+y-2z=4$
$x-2y+z=-2$
$5x-5y+z=-2$

(ix) $x+y-z=0$
$x-2y+z=0$
$3x+6y-5z=0$

Homogeneous system of Linear Equations:

51. Solve the following system of homogeneous equations :

$3x-4y+5z=0$
$x+y-2z=0$
$2x+3y+z=0$

52. Solve the following system of homogeneous equations :

$x+y-z=0$
$x-2y+z=0$
$3x+6y-5z=0$

53. If the system of equations $\begin{matrix} x=cy+bz \\ y=az+bx \\ z=bx+ay \end{matrix}$ has a non trivial solution, then prove that $a^2+b^2+c^2+2\,abc=1$

54. If x, y, z are not all zero such that $\begin{matrix} ax+y+z=0 \\ x+by+z=0 \\ x+y+cz=0 \end{matrix}$

then prove that $\frac{1}{1-a}+\frac{1}{1-b}+\frac{1}{1-c}=1.$

Adjoint of a Matrix:

55. (i) If $A=\begin{pmatrix} a & b \\ c & d \end{pmatrix}$, then find Adj A.

(ii) If $A=\begin{pmatrix} -3 & 5 \\ 2 & 4 \end{pmatrix}$, then find Adj A.

(iii) Find Adj A, if $A=\begin{pmatrix} 1 & 2 & 2 \\ 2 & 1 & 2 \\ 2 & 2 & 1 \end{pmatrix}$.

(iv) Find Adj A, if $A=\begin{pmatrix} 1 & 2 & 5 \\ 2 & 3 & 1 \\ -1 & 1 & 1 \end{pmatrix}$

56. If $A=\begin{pmatrix} -4 & -3 & -3 \\ 1 & 0 & 1 \\ 4 & 4 & 3 \end{pmatrix}$, then prove that Adj A = A.

Inverse of a matrix:

57. Find the inverse of each of the following matrices :

(i) $A=\begin{pmatrix} 0 & 1 \\ 1 & 0 \end{pmatrix}$

(ii) $B=\begin{pmatrix} 2 & 5 \\ -3 & 1 \end{pmatrix}$

(iii) $C=\begin{pmatrix} 1 & 2 & 3 \\ 2 & 3 & 1 \\ 3 & 1 & 2 \end{pmatrix}$

(iv) $D=\begin{pmatrix} 1 & 2 & 5 \\ 1 & -1 & -1 \\ 2 & 3 & -1 \end{pmatrix}$

58. (i) If $A=\begin{pmatrix} 2 & 3 \\ 5 & -2 \end{pmatrix}$, prove that $A^{-1}=\frac{1}{19}A$.

(ii) If $A=\begin{pmatrix} 1 & 3 & 3 \\ 1 & 4 & 3 \\ 1 & 3 & 4 \end{pmatrix}$, prove that $A^{-1}A=I_3$

(iii) Prove that $A=\begin{pmatrix} -8 & 5 \\ 2 & 4 \end{pmatrix}$ satisfies the equation $A^2+4A-42I_2=O$. Hence, find A^{-1}.

(iv) Show that $A=\begin{pmatrix} 5 & 3 \\ -1 & 2 \end{pmatrix}$ satisfies the equation $x^2-3x-7=0$. Thus, find A^{-1}.

59. (i) Find the matrix X such that $\begin{pmatrix} 3 & 2 \\ 7 & 5 \end{pmatrix} X \begin{pmatrix} -1 & 1 \\ -2 & 1 \end{pmatrix} = \begin{pmatrix} 2 & -1 \\ 0 & 4 \end{pmatrix}$

(ii) Find the matrix X, if $\begin{pmatrix} 5 & 4 \\ 1 & 1 \end{pmatrix} X=\begin{pmatrix} 1 & -2 \\ 1 & 3 \end{pmatrix}$ where $X=(a_{ij})_{2\times 2}$

(iii) For the matrix $A=\begin{pmatrix} 3 & 1 \\ 7 & 5 \end{pmatrix}$, find x and y so that $A^2+xI_2=yA$. Hence, find A^{-1}.

Solutions of Simultaneous Linear Equations :

60. Use matrix method to solve the following system of equations:

(i) $5x-7y=2$, $7x-5y=3$

(ii) $x-2y=4$, $3x-5y=7$

(iii) $4x-2y=3$, $6x-3y=5$

(iv) $2x+3y=5$, $6x+9y=15$

61. Solve the following system of equations by matrix method :

(i) $x+y-z=3$
$2x+3y+z=10$
$3x-y-7z=1$

(ii) $x+y+z=3$
$2x-y+z=2$
$x-2y+3z=2$

(iii) $x+y=0$
$y+z=1$
$x+z=3$

(iv) $x-y+z=2$
$2x-y=0$
$2y-z=1$

(v) $x-y+z=3$
$2x+y-z=2$
$-x-2y+2z=1$

$$x+y+z=6$$
(vi) $x+2y+3z=14$
$$x+4y+7z=30$$

$$3x-y-2z=2$$
(vii) $2y-z=-1$
$$3x-5y=3$$

62. If $A=\begin{pmatrix}1 & -1 & 0\\ 2 & 3 & 4\\ 0 & 1 & 2\end{pmatrix}$ and $B=\begin{pmatrix}2 & 2 & -4\\ -4 & 2 & -4\\ 2 & -1 & 5\end{pmatrix}$ are two square matrices, find AB and hence solve the system of linear equations $x-y=3,\ 2x+3y+4z=17,\ y+2z=7$.

63. Find A^{-1}, if $A\begin{pmatrix}1 & 2 & 5\\ 1 & -1 & -1\\ 2 & 3 & -1\end{pmatrix}$. Hence solve the following system of linear equations $x+2y+5z=10,\ x-y-z=-2,\ 2x+3y-z=-11$.

Inverse of a Matrix by Elementary Row Transformations :

64. Find the inverse of each of the following matrices by E.R.T.

(i) $\begin{bmatrix}1 & 2\\ 3 & 4\end{bmatrix}$ (ii) $\begin{bmatrix}3 & 5\\ 7 & 2\end{bmatrix}$

(iii) $\begin{bmatrix}-4 & 3\\ 9 & 11\end{bmatrix}$

(iv) $\begin{bmatrix}1 & 3 & 2\\ 3 & 2 & 4\\ 2 & 5 & 1\end{bmatrix}$

(ii) $\begin{bmatrix}1 & 2 & 3\\ 4 & 5 & 7\\ 3 & 4 & 2\end{bmatrix}$.

Multiplication of Two determinants of the same order :

65. Prove that = 0

$$\begin{vmatrix}2 & \alpha+\beta+\gamma+\delta & \alpha\beta+\gamma\delta\\ \alpha+\beta+\gamma+\delta & (\alpha+\beta)(\gamma+\delta) & \alpha\beta(\gamma+\delta)+\gamma\delta(\alpha+\beta)\\ \alpha\beta+\gamma\delta & \alpha\beta(\gamma+\delta)+\gamma\delta(\alpha+\beta) & 2\alpha\beta\gamma\delta\end{vmatrix}$$

66. Prove that $\begin{vmatrix}\cos(A-P) & \cos(A-Q) & \cos(A-R)\\ \cos(B-P) & \cos(B-Q) & \cos(B-R)\\ \cos(C-P) & \cos(C-Q) & \cos(C-R)\end{vmatrix}=0$

67. Prove that $\begin{vmatrix}1 & \cos(\beta-\alpha) & \cos(\gamma-\alpha)\\ \cos(\alpha-\beta) & 1 & \cos(\gamma-\beta)\\ \cos(\alpha-\gamma) & \cos(\beta-\gamma) & 1\end{vmatrix}=0$

Differentiation of a determinanat:

68. Find the co-efficient of x in the determinant

$$\begin{vmatrix}(1+x)^{a_1b_1} & (1+x)^{a_1b_2} & (1+x)^{a_1b_3}\\ (1+x)^{a_2b_1} & (1+x)^{a_2b_2} & (1+x)^{a_2b_3}\\ (1+x)^{a_3b_1} & (1+x)^{a_3b_2} & (1+x)^{a_3b_3}\end{vmatrix}$$

69. If $y=\frac{u}{v}$, where u and v are functions of x, show that

$$v^3\frac{d^2y}{dx^2}=\begin{vmatrix}u & v & 0\\ u' & v' & v\\ u'' & v'' & 2v'\end{vmatrix}$$

70. Let $f(x)=\begin{vmatrix}\cos x & \sin x & \cos x\\ \cos 2x & \sin 2x & 2\cos 2x\\ \cos 3x & \sin 3x & 3\cos 3x\end{vmatrix}$

Then find the value of $f'\left(\frac{\pi}{2}\right)=$ ....

Integration of a Determinant:

71. If $f(x)=\begin{vmatrix}\sin^5 x & \log\sin x & \frac{\sqrt{\sin x}}{\sqrt{\sin x}+\sqrt{\cos x}}\\ n & \sum_{k=1}^{n}k & \prod_{k=1}^{n}k\\ \frac{8}{15} & \frac{\pi}{2}\log\left(\frac{1}{2}\right) & \frac{\pi}{4}\end{vmatrix}$,

then find the value of $\int_0^{\frac{\pi}{2}} f(x)\ dx$

72. Let $f(x)=\begin{vmatrix}\sec x & \cos x & \sec^2 x+\cot x\operatorname{cosec} x\\ \cos^2 x & \cos^2 x & \operatorname{cosec}^2 x\\ 1 & \cos^2 x & \cos^2 x\end{vmatrix}$, then find the value $\int_0^{\frac{\pi}{2}} f(x)\ dx$.

ANSWER KEY

11. $x=-1$

12. $x=-\frac{100}{7}$

19. *(i)* – 1, *(ii)* 0, *(iii)* –2, *(iv)* 0, *(vi)* 0, *(vii)* 0, *(viii)* 0

20. *(i)* $(a-b)(b-c)(c-a)$ *(ii)* $(a-b)(b-c)(c-a)(a+b+c)$ *(iii)* $xyz(x-y)(y-z)(z-a)$

43. 0

50. (i) $x=1, y=-1=z$

(ii) $x=\frac{(c-k)(k-b)}{(c-a)(a-b)}$, $y=\frac{(k-c)(a-k)}{(b-c)(a-b)}$, $z=\frac{(b-k)(k-a)}{(b-c)(c-a)}$

(iii) $x=-2, y=3, z=1$

(iv) $x=3, y=2, z=1$

(v) $x=2, y=3, z=5$

(vi) in consistent

(vii) in consistent

(viii) $x=\frac{6+3k}{5}, y=\frac{8+4k}{5}$,

(ix) $x=k, y=2k, z=3k$

51. $x=0=y=z$

52. $x=\frac{k}{3}, y=\frac{2k}{3}, z=k$

61. (i) $x=3, y=1, z=1$

(ii) $x=1, y=1, z \neq 1$

(iii) $x=1, y=-1, z=2$

(iv) $x=1, y=2, z=3$

(v) $x=\frac{5}{3}, y=-\frac{4}{3}+4, z=k$

(vi) $x=k-2, y=8-2k, z=k$

68. zero

70. 4

71. 0

72. $-\left(\frac{8}{15}+\frac{\pi}{4}\right)$

6.16 Advance Types of Matrices

6.16.1 Idempotent Matrix

A square matrix A is said to be an idempotent matrix if $A^2 = A$.

For Example :, $A=\begin{bmatrix} 2 & -2 & 4 \\ -1 & 3 & 4 \\ 1 & -2 & -3 \end{bmatrix}$ is an idempotent matrix.

Ex-1. Prove that the matrix $A=\begin{bmatrix} 2 & -3 & -5 \\ -1 & 4 & 5 \\ 1 & -3 & -4 \end{bmatrix}$ is idempotent

Sol. We have $A^2 = A.A = \begin{bmatrix} 2 & -3 & -5 \\ -1 & 4 & 5 \\ 1 & -3 & -4 \end{bmatrix}\begin{bmatrix} 2 & -3 & -5 \\ -1 & 4 & 5 \\ 1 & -3 & -4 \end{bmatrix}$

$$=\begin{bmatrix} 4+3-5 & -6-12+15 & -10-15+20 \\ -2-4+5 & 3+16-15 & 5+20-20 \\ 2+3-4 & -3-12+12 & -5-15+16 \end{bmatrix}$$

$$=\begin{bmatrix} 2 & -3 & -5 \\ -1 & 4 & 5 \\ 1 & -3 & -4 \end{bmatrix}=A$$

Thus, A is idempotent.

6.16.2 Periodic Matrix

A square matrix A is said to periodic with period k (where k is a least positive integer such that $A^{k+1} = A$.that, is, if $A^3 = A, A^5 = A, A^7 = A$, then it is a periodic matrix and $A^{2+1} = A$, so its period = 2.

Ex-1. Prove that the matrix $A=\begin{bmatrix} 2 & -2 & -4 \\ -1 & 3 & 4 \\ 1 & -2 & -1 \end{bmatrix}$ is periodic.

Sol. We have $A^2 = A.A$

$$=\begin{bmatrix} 2 & -2 & -4 \\ -1 & 3 & 4 \\ 1 & -2 & -1 \end{bmatrix}\times\begin{bmatrix} 2 & -2 & -4 \\ -1 & 3 & 4 \\ 1 & -2 & -1 \end{bmatrix}=\begin{bmatrix} 2 & -2 & -4 \\ -1 & 3 & 4 \\ 1 & -2 & -1 \end{bmatrix}$$

$= A$.

Hence, A is periodic.

6.16.3. Nilpotent Matrix

A square matrix A is called a nilpotent matrix if there exist $k \in N$ suct that $A^k = 0$, where k is called the index of the nilpotent of matrix A..

For example, $A=\begin{bmatrix} 0 & 0 \\ 0 & 2 \end{bmatrix}$ is a nilpotent Matrix.

Ex- 1. Show that $\begin{bmatrix} 1 & 1 & 3 \\ 5 & 2 & 6 \\ -2 & -1 & -3 \end{bmatrix}$ is nilpotent matrix of order 3.

Sol : Let $A=\begin{bmatrix} 1 & 1 & 3 \\ 5 & 2 & 6 \\ -2 & -1 & -3 \end{bmatrix}$

$$\Rightarrow \quad A^2 = A.A = \begin{bmatrix} 1 & 1 & 3 \\ 5 & 2 & 6 \\ -2 & -1 & -3 \end{bmatrix}\begin{bmatrix} 1 & 1 & 3 \\ 5 & 2 & 6 \\ -2 & -1 & -3 \end{bmatrix}$$

$$=\begin{bmatrix} 0 & 0 & 0 \\ 3 & 3 & 9 \\ -1 & -1 & -3 \end{bmatrix}$$

Now, $A^3 = A^2.A = \begin{bmatrix} 0 & 0 & 0 \\ 3 & 3 & 9 \\ -1 & -1 & -3 \end{bmatrix}\begin{bmatrix} 1 & 1 & 3 \\ 5 & 2 & 6 \\ -2 & -1 & -3 \end{bmatrix}$

$$=\begin{bmatrix} 0 & 0 & 0 \\ 0 & 0 & 0 \\ 0 & 0 & 0 \end{bmatrix}=O$$

Hence **A** is nilpotent of order 3.

6.16.4. Involutory Matrix

A square matrix A is called an involutory matrix if $A^2 = I$ i.e. $A^{-1} = A$.

For example $A=\begin{bmatrix} 1 & 0 & 0 \\ 0 & 1 & 0 \\ 0 & 0 & 1 \end{bmatrix}$ is an involutory matrix.

Ex- 1: Show that the matrix $A=\begin{bmatrix} -5 & -8 & 0 \\ 3 & 5 & 0 \\ 1 & 2 & -1 \end{bmatrix}$ is involuntory.

Sol : Let $A = \begin{bmatrix} -5 & -8 & 0 \\ 3 & 5 & 0 \\ 1 & 2 & -1 \end{bmatrix}$

$$\Rightarrow A^2 = A.A = \begin{bmatrix} -5 & -8 & 0 \\ 3 & 5 & 0 \\ 1 & 2 & -1 \end{bmatrix}\begin{bmatrix} -5 & -8 & 0 \\ 3 & 5 & 0 \\ 1 & 2 & -1 \end{bmatrix}$$

$$= \begin{bmatrix} 1 & 0 & 0 \\ 0 & 1 & 0 \\ 0 & 0 & 1 \end{bmatrix} = I$$

Hence **A** is involuntory.

6.16.5. Orthogonal Matrix

A square matrix A is said to be orthogonal matrix iff $AA^T = I$, where A^T is the transpose of matrix A and I is an identity matrix.

For example, $A = \frac{1}{3}\begin{bmatrix} 1 & -2 & 2 \\ -2 & 1 & 2 \\ -2 & -2 & -1 \end{bmatrix}$ is an orthogonal matrix.

Ex- 1: Prove that the matrix $A = \frac{1}{3}\begin{bmatrix} 1 & 2 & 2 \\ 2 & 1 & -2 \\ -2 & 2 & -1 \end{bmatrix}$ is orthogonal matrix.

Sol. $\because A = \frac{1}{3}\begin{bmatrix} 1 & 2 & 2 \\ 2 & 1 & -2 \\ -2 & 2 & -1 \end{bmatrix}$.

For orthogonal matrix $\mathbf{AA^T = A^TA = I}$

$$\therefore \mathbf{AA^T} = \frac{1}{9}\begin{bmatrix} 1 & 2 & 2 \\ 2 & 1 & -2 \\ -2 & 2 & -1 \end{bmatrix}\begin{bmatrix} 1 & 2 & -2 \\ 2 & 1 & 2 \\ 2 & -2 & -1 \end{bmatrix} = \begin{bmatrix} 1 & 0 & 0 \\ 0 & 1 & 0 \\ 0 & 0 & 1 \end{bmatrix} = I$$

Hence **A** is an orthogonal matrix

NOTE :

(i) If $AA^T = I$, then $A^{-1} = A^T$.
(ii) very orthogonal matrix is non-singular.
(iii) I is an orthogonal matrix
(iv) If A and B are orthogonal then AB is also orthogonal v
> If A is orthogonal then A^{-1} and A^T are also orthogonal.

6.16.6. Conjugate of a Matrix

Lct A bc any matrix containing complcx number as its elements, then a matrix is obtained from A on replacing its elements by the corresponding conjugate complex numbers, is called the conjugate of the matrix A and it is denoted by $\overline{A}$.

For example "If $A = \begin{bmatrix} 1+2i & 2+3i \\ 1-i & 3+4i \end{bmatrix}$, then $\overline{A} = \begin{bmatrix} 1-3i & 2-3i \\ 1+i & 3-4i \end{bmatrix}$.

6.16.7. Complex Conjugate Transpose of a Matrix

The conjugate of the transpose of the matrix A is called the conjugate transpose of A and is denoted by A^{Θ}.

If $A = \begin{pmatrix} 2+4i & 3 \\ 4 & +i \end{pmatrix}$, then $A = \begin{pmatrix} 2-4i & 3 \\ 4 & -i \end{pmatrix}$.

6.16.8. Hermitian Matrix

A square matrix A is called a hermitian matrix if $A^{\theta} = A$.

For example, Let $A = \begin{pmatrix} 2 & \alpha+i\beta \\ \alpha-i\beta & 3 \end{pmatrix}$.

Ex- 1 Prove that $A = \begin{bmatrix} 3 & 3-4i & 5+2i \\ 3+4i & 5 & -2+i \\ 5-2i & -2-i & 2 \end{bmatrix}$ is an Hermitian Matrix.

Sol. We have, $A^T = \begin{bmatrix} 3 & 3+4i & 5-2i \\ 3-4i & 5 & -2-i \\ 5+2i & -2+i & 2 \end{bmatrix}$

$$\Rightarrow \left(\overline{A^T}\right) = \begin{bmatrix} 3 & 3-4i & 5+2i \\ 3+4i & 5 & -2+i \\ 5-2i & -2-i & 2 \end{bmatrix} = A$$

Thus, A is am Hermitian Matrix.

6.16.9. Skew Hermitian Matrix

A square matrix A is called a skew Hermitian Matrix if $A^{\theta} = -A$

For example, Let $A = \begin{pmatrix} 2i & -\alpha-i\beta \\ \alpha+i\beta & -i \end{pmatrix}$.

Ex- 1. Prove that $A = \begin{bmatrix} 2i & -2-3i & 2+i \\ 2-3i & -i & 3i \\ 2+i & 3i & 0 \end{bmatrix}$ is an skew-Hermitian matrix..

Sol. We have $A^T = \begin{bmatrix} 2i & -2-3i & 2+i \\ -2-3i & -i & 3i \\ 2+i & 3i & 0 \end{bmatrix}$

$$\Rightarrow \left(\overline{A^T}\right) = \begin{bmatrix} -2i & 2+3i & 2-i \\ -2+3i & -i & -3i \\ -2-i & -3i & 0 \end{bmatrix}$$

$$\Rightarrow \left(\overline{A^T}\right) = -\begin{bmatrix} 2i & -2-3i & -2+i \\ 2-3i & -i & 3i \\ 2+i & 3i & 0 \end{bmatrix} = -A$$

Hence A is an skew hermitian matrix.

6.16.10. Unitary Matrix

A square matrix A is called unitary if $AA^{\theta} = I$.

For example, let $A = \frac{1}{\sqrt{3}}\begin{pmatrix} 1 & 1+i \\ 1-i & -1 \end{pmatrix}$

NOTE :

1. If A and B are unitary, then AB is also a unitary.

Ex- 1. Prove that the matrix $\frac{1}{\sqrt{3}}\begin{bmatrix}1 & 1+i\\ 1-i & -1\end{bmatrix}$ is unitary.

Sol : Let $\mathbf{A}=\frac{1}{\sqrt{3}}\begin{bmatrix}1 & 1+i\\ 1-i & -1\end{bmatrix}$, $\mathbf{A}^{\theta}=\frac{1}{\sqrt{3}}\begin{bmatrix}1 & 1+i\\ 1-i & -1\end{bmatrix}$

$$\mathbf{AA}^{\theta}=\frac{1}{\sqrt{3}}\begin{bmatrix}1 & 1+i\\ 1-i & -1\end{bmatrix}\frac{1}{\sqrt{3}}\begin{bmatrix}1 & 1+i\\ 1-i & -1\end{bmatrix}=\begin{bmatrix}1 & 0\\ 0 & 1\end{bmatrix}=I$$

Hence **A** is unitary matrix.

6.16.11. Equivalent Matrices

Let A and B are two matrices . If B is obtained from A by elementary transformation , then A and B are called equivalent Matrices.

6.16.12. Rank of a Matrix

Rank of a matrix is represents the non zero rows of an equivalent matrix .

Rule to find out the rank of a matrix

Let A be any type of matrix

Case - I : When A is a null matrix

Then the rank of a matrix is zero.

Case - II : When A is a square matrix.

Then we shall first find determinant of A

(i) If A is non-singular (i.e. $|A| \neq 0$) , then Rank of the matrix = Order of the matrix

(ii) If A is singular (i.e. $|A| = 0$) , then we shall find the minor along rows

(a) If atleast one minor is zero and rest are non zero , then Rank of the matrix = Order of the matrix - 1.

(b) If all minor is non - zero , then Rank of the matrix = 0.

Case - III : When A is a Rectangular matrix of order $m \times n$

Then we shall find an equivalent matrix of A

(i) If any one row is zero, then Rank of the matrix = Min of { m-1, n-1 }

(ii) If any two row is zero, then Rank of the matrix = Min of { m-2, n-2 }

(iii) If all rows are non zero, then Rank of the matrix = Min of {m, n}.

Ex-1. Find the Rank of $A=\begin{pmatrix}1 & 2 & 3\\ 2 & 4 & 7\\ 3 & 6 & 10\end{pmatrix}$

Sol. We have $|A| = \begin{vmatrix}1 & 2 & 3\\ 2 & 4 & 7\\ 3 & 6 & 10\end{vmatrix}$

$= 1(40-42)-2(20-21)+3(12-12)$

$=-2+2+0=0$

Since the determinant of A is zero , so the rank of the given matrix is 2

Ex-2. Find the rank of $A=\begin{pmatrix}2 & 4 & 3\\ 1 & 2 & -1\\ -1 & -2 & 6\end{pmatrix}$

Sol. We have $|A|=\begin{vmatrix}2 & 4 & 3\\ 1 & 2 & -1\\ -1 & -2 & 6\end{vmatrix}$

$= 2(12-2)-4(6-1)+3(-2+2)$

$= 20-20+0$

$=0$

Since the determinant of A is zero , so the rank of the given matrix is 2.

Ex-3. Find the rank of $\begin{pmatrix}1 & 2 & 3\\ 2 & 3 & 4\\ 4 & 5 & 6\end{pmatrix}$.

Sol. We have $|A|=\begin{vmatrix}1 & 2 & 3\\ 2 & 3 & 4\\ 4 & 5 & 6\end{vmatrix}$

$= 1(18-20)-2(12-12)+3(10-12) = -2-6=-8$

Since the determinant of A is non zero , so the rank of the given matrix is 3.

(iii) $A=\begin{pmatrix}5 & 3 & 14 & 4\\ 0 & 1 & 2 & 1\\ 1 & -1 & 2 & 0\end{pmatrix}$

(iv) $A=\begin{pmatrix}1 & 2 & 3 & 0\\ 2 & 4 & 3 & 2\\ 3 & 2 & 1 & 3\\ 6 & 8 & 7 & 5\end{pmatrix}$

Ex-4. Find the rank of $A=\begin{pmatrix}1 & -2 & 1 & -1\\ 1 & 1 & -2 & 3\\ 4 & 1 & -5 & 6\end{pmatrix}$

Sol. We have $A=\begin{pmatrix}1 & -2 & 1 & -1\\ 1 & 1 & -2 & 3\\ 4 & 1 & -5 & 6\end{pmatrix}$

$\Leftrightarrow \begin{pmatrix}1 & -2 & 1 & -1\\ 0 & 3 & -3 & 4\\ 0 & 9 & -9 & 12\end{pmatrix}$

$(\because R_2 \rightarrow R_2-R_1.\ R_3 \rightarrow R_3-4R_1)$

$\Leftrightarrow \begin{pmatrix}1 & -2 & 1 & -1\\ 0 & 1 & -1 & 4/3\\ 0 & 0 & 0 & 0\end{pmatrix}$ $(\because R_3 \rightarrow R_3-9R_2)$

Since the number of non-zero rows is 2 , so the rank of the given matrix is 2.

LEVEL — II FOR JEE – MAIN AND ADVANCED EXAMS ONLY

1. If a, b and c are non-zero real numbers, then

$$\Delta = \begin{vmatrix} b^2c^2 & bc & b+c \\ c^2a^2 & ca & c+a \\ a^2b^2 & ab & a+b \end{vmatrix} =$$

(a) abc (b) $a^2b^2c^2$
(c) ab + bc + ca (d) none of these

2. The value of the determinant $\begin{vmatrix} 1/a & a^2 & bc \\ 1/b & b^2 & ca \\ 1/c & c^2 & ab \end{vmatrix}$ is

(a) abc (b) 1/abc
(c) ab + bc + ca (d) 0

3. The value of the determinant

$$\begin{vmatrix} b^2+c^2 & a^2 & a^2 \\ b^2 & c^2+a^2 & b^2 \\ c^2 & c^2 & a^2+b^2 \end{vmatrix} =$$

(a) abc (b) 4abc
(c) $4a^2b^2c^2$ (d) $a^2b^2c^2$

4. The value of the determinant

$$\begin{vmatrix} a-b-c & 2a & 2a \\ 2b & b-c-a & 2b \\ 2c & 2c & c-a-b \end{vmatrix} =$$

(a) $(a+b+c)^2$ (b) $(a+b+c)^3$
(c) $(a+b+c)(ab+bc+ca)$ (d) None of these

5. The value of the determinant $\begin{vmatrix} a-b & b-c & c-a \\ x-y & y-z & z-x \\ p-q & q-r & r-p \end{vmatrix} =$

(a) $a(x+y+z)+b(p+q+r)+c$ (b) 0
(c) $abc+xyz+qr$ (d) None of these

6. The value of the determinant $\begin{vmatrix} a & b & c \\ b & c & a \\ c & a & b \end{vmatrix} =$

(a) $3abc+a^3+b^3+c^3$ (b) $3abc-a^3-b^3-c^3$
(c) $abc-a^3+b^3+c^3$ (d) $abc+a^3-b^3-c^3$

7. For non-zero a, b, c if $\Delta = \begin{vmatrix} 1+a & 1 & 1 \\ 1 & 1+b & 1 \\ 1 & 1 & 1+c \end{vmatrix} = 0$ then the vaue of $\frac{1}{a}+\frac{1}{b}+\frac{1}{c} =$

(a) abc (b) $\frac{1}{abc}$
(c) $-(a+b+c)$ (d) none of these

8. The value of the determinant $\begin{vmatrix} a_1 & la_1+mb_1 & b_1 \\ a_2 & la_2+mb_2 & b_2 \\ a_3 & la_3+mb_3 & b_3 \end{vmatrix}$ is.

(a) 0 (b) l
(c) m (d) lm

9. If T_p, T_q, T_r are pth, qth and rth terms of an A.P., then $\begin{vmatrix} T_p & T_q & T_r \\ p & q & r \\ 1 & 1 & 1 \end{vmatrix}$ is equal to

(a) 1 (b) – 1
(c) 0 (d) p + q + r

10. The value of the determinant

$$\begin{vmatrix} 2ac-b^2 & a^2 & c^2 \\ a^2 & 2ab-c^2 & b^2 \\ c^2 & b^2 & 2bc-a^2 \end{vmatrix} =$$

(a) 4abc (b) – 4abc
(c) 0 (d) $(a^3+b^3+c^3-3abc)^2$

11. If $a \neq b \neq c$ and $\begin{vmatrix} 1 & 1 & 1 \\ a & b & c \\ a^3 & b^3 & c^3 \end{vmatrix} = 0$

then the value of (a + b + c) is

(a) 1 (b) 0
(c) 2 (d) – a

12. Let $\Delta = \begin{vmatrix} 1 & \sin\alpha & 1 \\ -\sin\alpha & 1 & \sin\alpha \\ -1 & -\sin\alpha & 1 \end{vmatrix}$ then the value of Δ lies in the interval

(a) [2, 3] (b) [3, 4]
(c) [1, 4] (d) [2, 4]

13. If A, B, C are the angles of triangle, then the value of

$$\Delta = \begin{vmatrix} -1 & \cos C & \cos B \\ \cos C & -1 & \cos A \\ \cos B & \cos A & -1 \end{vmatrix}$$ is

(a) cosA cosB cosC (b) sinAsinBsinC
(c) 0 (d) none of these

14. If a, b, c are in A.P., then the value of $\begin{vmatrix} x+2 & x+3 & x+a \\ x+4 & x+5 & x+b \\ x+6 & x+7 & x+c \end{vmatrix}$ is

(a) $x-(a+b+c)$ (b) $9x^2+a+b+c$
(c) a + b + c (d) 0

15. The value of the determinant

$$\begin{vmatrix} a & a+b & a+2b \\ a+2b & a & a+b \\ a+b & a+2b & a \end{vmatrix} =$$

(a) $9a^2(a+b)$ (b) $9b^2(a+b)$
(c) $a^2(a+b)$ (d) $b^2(a+b)$

16. The value of the determinant

$$\begin{vmatrix}(a^x+a^{-x})^2 & (a^x-a^{-x})^2 & 1\\(b^x+b^{-x})^2 & (b^x-b^{-x})^2 & 1\\(c^x+c^{-x})^2 & (c^x-c^{-x})^2 & 1\end{vmatrix}=$$

(a) 0 (b) 2abc
(c) $a^2b^2c^2$ (d) none of these

17. If $\begin{vmatrix}a & b & c\\b & c & a\\c & a & b\end{vmatrix}=k(a+b+c)(a^2+b^2+c^2-bc-ca-ab)$, then the value of k is

(a) 1 (b) 2
(c) -1 (d) -2

18. If the determinant $\begin{vmatrix}a & a+d & a+2d\\a^2 & (a+d)^2 & (a+2d)^2\\2a+3d & 2(a+d) & 2a+d\end{vmatrix}=0$ then

(a) $d=0$ (b) $a+d=0$
(c) $d=0$ or $a+d=0$ (d) none of these

19. The value of the determinant $\begin{vmatrix}a+b & a+2b & a+3b\\a+2b & a+3b & a+4b\\a+4b & a+5b & a+6b\end{vmatrix}=$

(a) $a^2+b^2+c^2-3abc$ (b) 3ab
(c) $3a+5b$ (d) 0

20. If $0<\theta<\frac{\pi}{2}$ and $\begin{vmatrix}1+\sin^2\theta & \cos^2\theta & 4\sin 4\theta\\\sin^2\theta & 1+\cos^2\theta & 4\sin 4\theta\\\sin^2\theta & \cos^2\theta & 1+4\sin 4\theta\end{vmatrix}=0$

than q is equal to

(a) $\frac{\pi}{24},\frac{5\pi}{24}$ (b) $\frac{5\pi}{24},\frac{7\pi}{24}$
(c) $\frac{7\pi}{24},\frac{11\pi}{24}$ (d) none of these

21. The value ofthe determinant

$$\begin{vmatrix}1 & \cos(\alpha-\beta) & \cos(\alpha-\gamma)\\\cos(\alpha-\beta) & 1 & \cos(\beta-\gamma)\\\cos(\alpha-\gamma) & \cos(\beta-\gamma) & 1\end{vmatrix}$$ is

(a) $\begin{vmatrix}\cos\alpha & \sin\alpha & 1\\\cos\beta & \sin\beta & 1\\\cos\gamma & \sin\gamma & 1\end{vmatrix}^2$ (b) $\begin{vmatrix}\sin\alpha & \cos\alpha & 0\\\sin\beta & \cos\beta & 0\\\sin\gamma & \cos\gamma & 0\end{vmatrix}^2$

(c) $\begin{vmatrix}\cos\alpha & \sin\alpha & 0\\\sin\beta & 0 & \cos\beta\\0 & \cos\gamma & \sin\gamma\end{vmatrix}^2$ (d) none of these

22. In a Δ ABC, if $\begin{vmatrix}1 & a & b\\1 & c & a\\1 & b & c\end{vmatrix}=0$ then $\sin^2A+\sin^2B+\sin^2C=$

(a) $\frac{9}{4}$ (b) $\frac{4}{9}$
(c) 1 (d) $3\sqrt{3}$

23. $a\neq p, b\neq q, c\neq r$ and $\begin{vmatrix}p & b & c\\p+a & q+b & 2c\\a & b & r\end{vmatrix}=0$,

then $\frac{p}{p-a}+\frac{q}{q-b}+\frac{r}{r-c}=$

(a) 3 (b) 2
(c) 1 (d) 0

24. The value of the determinant $\begin{vmatrix}bc & ca & ab\\p & q & r\\1 & 1 & 1\end{vmatrix}$ where a, b, c are the pth, q^{th}, r^{th} terms of an H.P. is

(a) $ap+bq+cr$ (b) $(a+b+c)(p+q+r)$
(c) 0 (d) none of these

25. If $\sqrt{-1}=i$ and ω is non real cube root of unity, then the value of $\begin{vmatrix}1 & \omega^2 & 1+i+\omega^2\\-i & -1 & -1-i+\omega\\1-i & \omega^2-1 & -1\end{vmatrix}=$

(a) 1 (b) i
(c) ω (d) 0

26. Let $f(n)=\begin{vmatrix}n & n+1 & n+2\\{}^nP_n & {}^{n+1}P_{n+1} & {}^{n+2}P_{n+2}\\{}^nC_n & n+1C_{n+1} & {}^{n+2}C_{n+2}\end{vmatrix}$ where the symbols have their usual meanings.

Then f(n) is divisible by

(a) n^2+n+1 (b) $(n+1)!$
(c) n ! (d) none of these

27. If $a+b+c=0$, then one root of $\begin{vmatrix}a-x & c & b\\c & b-x & a\\b & a & c-x\end{vmatrix}=0$ is

(a) $x=1$ (b) $x=2$
(c) $x=a^2+b^2+c^2$ (d) $x=0$

28. $\begin{vmatrix}x+1 & \omega & \omega^2\\x+\omega & \omega^2 & 1\\x+\omega^2 & 1 & \omega\end{vmatrix}=3$ is an equation of x, where ω , ω^2 are the complex cube roots of unity, then the value of x is

(a) 0 (b) 1
(c) -1 (d) 2

29. If $ab+bc+ca=0$ and $\begin{vmatrix}a-x & c & b\\c & b-x & a\\b & a & c-x\end{vmatrix}=0$ then one of the value of x is

(a) $\left(a^2+b^2+c^2\right)^{\frac{1}{2}}$ (b) $\left[\frac{3}{2}(a^2+b^2+c^2)\right]^{\frac{1}{2}}$

(c) $\left[\frac{1}{2}(a^2+b^2+c^2)\right]^{\frac{1}{2}}$ (d) none of these

30. Let $\begin{vmatrix} 1+x & x & x^2 \\ x & 1+x & x^2 \\ x^2 & x & 1+x \end{vmatrix} = ax^5+bx^4+cx^3+dx^2+lx+m$ be an identity in x, where a, b, c, d, l, m are independent of x. Then the value of x is

(a) 3 (b) 2
(c) 4 (d) none of these

31. If the entries in a 3 × 3 determinat are either 0 or 1, then the greatest value of this determinant is

(a) 1 (b) 2
(c) 3 (d) 9

32. If $\Delta = \begin{vmatrix} a & c & b \\ b & b & a \\ c & a & c \end{vmatrix}$ and $\Delta' = \begin{vmatrix} a^2 & c^2 & b^2 \\ b^2 & b^2 & a^2 \\ c^2 & a^2 & c^2 \end{vmatrix}$, then

(a) $\Delta = a^2b^2c^2\Delta'$ (b) $\Delta' = a^2b^2c^2\Delta$

(c) $\Delta = abc\Delta'$ (d) None of these

33. If $\Delta = \begin{vmatrix} x & y & z \\ p & q & r \\ a & b & c \end{vmatrix}$, then $\begin{vmatrix} 2x+4p & p+6a & a \\ 2y+4q & q+6b & b \\ 2z+4r & r+6c & c \end{vmatrix} =$

(a) 2Δ (b) 4Δ

(c) 6Δ (d) Δ

34. If $\Delta_1 = \begin{vmatrix} 1 & 0 \\ a & b \end{vmatrix}$ and $\Delta_2 = \begin{vmatrix} 1 & 0 \\ c & d \end{vmatrix}$, then $\Delta_2\Delta_1 =$

(a) ac (b) bd
(c) (b – a)(d – c) (d) none of these

35. If $D_r = \begin{vmatrix} 1 & n & n \\ 2r & n^2+n+1 & n^2+n \\ 2r-1 & n^2 & n^2+n+1 \end{vmatrix}$ and $\sum_{r=1}^{n} D_r = 56$, then the value of n is

(a) 4 (b) 6
(c) 7 (d) 8

36. If $f(x) = \begin{vmatrix} \cos x & 1 & 0 \\ 1 & \cos x & 1 \\ 0 & 1 & \cos x \end{vmatrix}$, then $f'(\pi/3)$ equals

(a) $\frac{11\sqrt{3}}{8}$ (b) $\frac{5\sqrt{3}}{8}$

(c) $\frac{-5\sqrt{3}}{8}$ (d) none of these

37. If $f(x) = \begin{vmatrix} \sec x & \cos & \sec^2 x+\cot x \; \operatorname{cosec}^2 x \\ \cos^2 x & \cos^2 x & \operatorname{cosec}^2 x \\ 1 & \cos^2 x & \operatorname{cosec}^2 x \end{vmatrix}$, then $\int_0^{\pi/2} f(x)dx =$

(a) $\frac{\pi}{4}+\frac{8}{15}$ (b) $\left(-\frac{\pi}{4}+\frac{8}{15}\right)$

(c) $-\left(\frac{\pi}{4}+\frac{8}{15}\right)$ (d) none of these

38. Equations x + y = 2, 2x + 2y = 3 will have

(a) Only one solution (b) Infinite many solutions
(c) No solution (d) None of these

39. The system of equations x + y + z = 2, 3x – y + 2z = 6 and 3x + y + z = –18 has

(a) A unique solution
(b) No solution
(c) An infinite number of solutions
(d) Zero solution as the only solution

40. x + y + z = 6, x – y + z = 2 and 2x + y – z = 1 then x, y, z are respectively

(a) 3, 2, 1 (b) 1, 2, 3
(c) 2, 1, 3 (d) none of these

41. The value of k for which the set of equations 3x + ky – 2z = 0, x + ky + 3z = 0 and 2x + 3y – 4z = 0 has a non-trivial solution is

(a) 15 (b) 16
(c) 31/2 (d) 33/2

42. If the system of equations 3x – y + 4z – 3 = 0, x + 2y – 3z + 2 = 0, 6x + 5y + lz + 3 = 0 has infinite number of solutions, then l =

(a) 7 (b) –7
(c) 5 (d) –5

43. If the system of following equations 2x + 3y + 5 = 0, x + ky + 5 = 0, kx – 12y – 14 = 0 be constant, then k =

(a) $2, \frac{12}{5}$ (b) $-1, \frac{1}{5}$

(c) $-6, \frac{17}{5}$ (d) $6, -\frac{12}{5}$

44. If $A = \begin{bmatrix} i & 0 \\ 0 & i \end{bmatrix}, n \in N$, then A^{4n} equals

(a) $\begin{bmatrix} 0 & i \\ i & 0 \end{bmatrix}$ (b) $\begin{bmatrix} 0 & 0 \\ 0 & 0 \end{bmatrix}$

(c) $\begin{bmatrix} 1 & 0 \\ 0 & 1 \end{bmatrix}$ (d) $\begin{bmatrix} 0 & i \\ i & 0 \end{bmatrix}$

45. Let $A=\begin{bmatrix} a & 0 & 0 \\ 0 & a & 0 \\ 0 & 0 & a \end{bmatrix}$ then A^n is equal to

(a) $\begin{bmatrix} a^n & 0 & 0 \\ 0 & a^n & 0 \\ 0 & 0 & a \end{bmatrix}$ (b) $\begin{bmatrix} a^n & 0 & 0 \\ 0 & a & 0 \\ 0 & 0 & a \end{bmatrix}$

(c) $\begin{bmatrix} a^n & 0 & 0 \\ 0 & a^n & 0 \\ 0 & 0 & a^n \end{bmatrix}$ (d) $\begin{bmatrix} na & 0 & 0 \\ 0 & na & 0 \\ 0 & 0 & na \end{bmatrix}$

46. If $A=\begin{bmatrix} 1 & -1 \\ 2 & -1 \end{bmatrix}, B=\begin{bmatrix} a & 1 \\ b & -1 \end{bmatrix}$ and $(A+B)^2=A^2+B^2$, values of a and b are

(a) $a=4, b=1$ (b) $a=1, b=4$
(c) $a=0, b=4$ (d) $a=2, b=4$

47. The matrix $A=\frac{1}{3}\begin{bmatrix} 1 & 2 & 2 \\ 2 & 1 & -2 \\ -2 & 2 & -1 \end{bmatrix}$ is

(a) orthogonal (b) involutory
(c) idempotent (d) nilpotent

48. If $A=\begin{bmatrix} 2 & 2 \\ -3 & 2 \end{bmatrix}, B=\begin{bmatrix} 0 & -1 \\ 1 & 0 \end{bmatrix}$, then $(B^{-1}A^{-1})^{-1}=$

(a) $\begin{bmatrix} 2 & -2 \\ 2 & 3 \end{bmatrix}$ (b) $\begin{bmatrix} 3 & -2 \\ 2 & 2 \end{bmatrix}$

(c) $\frac{1}{10}\begin{bmatrix} 2 & 2 \\ -2 & 3 \end{bmatrix}$ (d) $\frac{1}{10}\begin{bmatrix} 3 & 2 \\ -2 & 2 \end{bmatrix}$

49. If A is a non-singular matrix of order 3, then adj (adj A) is equal to

(a) $|A|A$ (b) $|A|^2A$
(c) $|A|^{-1}A$ (d) None of these

50. Let the matrix $A=\begin{bmatrix} i & 1-2i \\ -1-2i & 0 \end{bmatrix}$, then A matrix is

(a) symmetric (b) skew-symmetric
(c) hermitian (d) skew-hermitian

51. If $E(\theta)=\begin{bmatrix} \cos^2\theta & \cos\theta\sin\theta \\ \cos\theta\sin\theta & \sin^2\theta \end{bmatrix}$ and q and f differ by an odd multiple of $\frac{\pi}{2}$, then E (q) E (f) is a

(a) null matrix (b) unit matrix
(c) diagonal matrix (d) none of these

52. The inverse of a symmetric matrix is

(a) symmetric (b) skew-symmmwtric
(c) diagonal matrix (d) none of these

53. The inverse of a diagonal matrix is

(a) a symmetric matrix (b) a skew-symmetric matrix
(c) a diagonal matrix (d) none of these

54. If A is a symmetric matrix and $n \in N$, the A^n is

(a) symmetric (b) skew-symmetric
(c) a diagonal matrix (d) none of these

55. If A is a skew-symmetric matrix and n is a positive integer, then A^n is

(a) a symmetric matrix (b) a skew-symmetric matrix
(c) a diagonal matrix (d) none of these

56. if A is a skew-symmetric matrix and n is odd positive integer, then A^n is

(a) a symmetric matrix (b) a skew-symmetric matrix
(c) a diagonal matrix (d) none of these

57. If A is a square matrix of order $n \times n$ and k is a scalar, then adj (kA) is equal to

(a) k adj A (b) k^nadj A
(c) k^{n-1}adj A (d) k^{n+1}adj A

58. If A and B are square matrices of order 3 such that $|A|=-1$, $|B|=3$, then $|3AB|$ equals

(a) -9 (b) -81
(c) -27 (d) 81

59. The number of all possible matrices of order 3×3 with each entry with 1 or 0 is

(a) 27 (b) 18
(c) 81 (d) 512.

60. If A is a square matrix such that $A^2=A$, then $(I+A)^3-7A$ is

(a) A (b) I-A
(c) I (d) 3A.

61. If A be a square matrix of order 3 such that $|A|=2$, then $|adj\ A^{-1}|$ is

(a) 11 (b) 13
(c) 17 (d) 19.

62. If $A=\begin{pmatrix} 1 & 2 & x \\ 0 & 1 & 0 \\ 0 & 0 & 1 \end{pmatrix}$ and $B=\begin{pmatrix} 1 & -2 & y \\ 0 & 1 & 0 \\ 0 & 0 & 1 \end{pmatrix}$ and $AB=I_3$, then x + y is

(a) 0 (b) -1
(c) 2 (d) 5

63. If the value of $D=\begin{vmatrix} {}^{10}C_4 & {}^{10}C_5 & {}^{11}C_m \\ {}^{11}C_6 & {}^{11}C_7 & {}^{12}C_{m+2} \\ {}^{12}C_8 & {}^{12}C_9 & {}^{13}C_{m+4} \end{vmatrix}$ is zero, then m is

(a) 6 (b) 4
(c) 5 (d) 10

64. If $\begin{vmatrix} x & 2 & x \\ x^2 & x & 6 \\ x & x & 6 \end{vmatrix} = Ax^4 + Bx^3 + Cx^2 + Dx + E$, then the value of $5A + 4B + 3C + 2D + E$ is

(a) 0 (b) -16

(c) 16 (d) None

65. The number of values of 't' for which the system of equations $(a-t)x + by + cz = 0$; $b\ \ x + (c-t)y + az = 0$; $c\ \ x + a\ \ y + (b-t)z = 0$ has non trivial solution is

(a) 3 (b) 4

(c) 5 (d) 6

ANSWERS KEY

1. (d)	**2.** (d)	**3.** (c)	**4.** (b)	**5.** (b)	**6.** (b)	**7.** (d)
8. (a)	**9.** (c)	**10.** (d)	**11.** (b)	**12.** (d)	**13.** (c)	**14.** (d)
15. (b)	**16.** (a)	**17.** (c)	**18.** (c)	**19.** (d)	**20.** (c)	**21.** (b)
22. (a)	**23.** (b)	**24.** (c)	**25.** (d)	**26.** (c)	**27.** (d)	**28.** (b)
29. (a)	**30.** (a)	**31.** (b)	**32.** (d)	**33.** (a)	**34.** (b)	**35.** (c)
36. (b)	**37.** (d)	**38.** (c)	**39. a)**	**40.** (b)	**41.** (d)	**42.** (d)
43. (c)	**44.** (c)	**45.** (c)	**46.** (b)	**47.** (a)	**48.** (a)	**49.** (a)
50. (d)	**51.** (a)	**52.** (a)	**53.** (c)	**54.** (a)	**55.** (d)	**56.** (b)
57. (c)	**58.** (a)	**59.** (d)	**60.** (c)	**61.** (d)	**62.** (a)	**63.** (c)
64. (d)	**65.** (a)					

Level–III FOR JEE ADVANCED EXAM ONLY

1. Prove that

$$\begin{vmatrix} 1 & \cos x - \sin x & \cos x + \sin x \\ 1 & \cos y - \sin y & \cos y + \sin y \\ 1 & \cos z - \sin z & \cos z + \sin z \end{vmatrix} = 2\begin{vmatrix} 1 & \cos x & \sin x \\ 1 & \cos y & \sin y \\ 1 & \cos z & \sin z \end{vmatrix}$$

2. Prove that

$$\begin{vmatrix} 2 & \alpha+\beta+\gamma+\delta & \alpha\beta+\gamma\delta \\ \alpha+\beta+\gamma+\delta & 2(\alpha+\beta)(\gamma+\delta) & \alpha\beta(\gamma+\delta)+\gamma\delta(\alpha+\beta) \\ \alpha\beta+\gamma\delta & \alpha\beta(\gamma+\delta)+\gamma\delta(\alpha+\beta) & 2\alpha\beta\gamma\delta \end{vmatrix} = 0$$

3. Prove that $\begin{vmatrix} \cos(A-P) & \cos(A-Q) & \cos(A-R) \\ \cos(B-P) & \cos(B-Q) & \cos(B-Q) \\ \cos(C-P) & \cos(C-Q) & \cos(C-R) \end{vmatrix} = 0$

4. If $S_r = \alpha^r + \beta^r + \gamma^r$, then prove that

$$\begin{vmatrix} 1 & 1 & 1 \\ \alpha & \beta & \gamma \\ \alpha^3 & \beta^3 & \gamma^3 \end{vmatrix} \times \begin{vmatrix} 1 & 1 & 1 \\ \alpha & \beta & \gamma \\ \alpha^2 & \beta^2 & \gamma^2 \end{vmatrix} = \begin{vmatrix} S_0 & S_1 & S_2 \\ S_1 & S_2 & S_3 \\ S_3 & S_4 & S_5 \end{vmatrix}$$

5. Solve the system of equations ;

$x + 2y + 3z = 1$; $2x + 3y + 2z = 2$; $3x + 3y + 4z = 1$

6. Solve the system of equations ;

$2x + 3y - 3z = 0$; $3x - 3y + z = 0$; $3x - 2y - 3z = 0$

7. Let $A = \begin{pmatrix} a & b \\ 0 & 1 \end{pmatrix}$, where $a \neq 0$. Show that for $n \geq 0$,

$$A^n = \begin{pmatrix} a^n & \dfrac{b(a^n-1)}{a-1} \\ 0 & 1 \end{pmatrix}$$

8. If A, B, C are three matrices such that $A = [x\ y\ z]$, $B = \begin{bmatrix} a & h & g \\ h & b & f \\ g & f & c \end{bmatrix}$, $C = \begin{bmatrix} x \\ y \\ z \end{bmatrix}$, then find the value of ABC.

9. Find the value of the determinant

$$\begin{vmatrix} 1 & a & a^2 \\ \cos(p-dx) & \cos\ px & \cos(p+d)x \\ \sin(p-d)x & \sin px & \sin(p+d)x \end{vmatrix}$$

10. Without expanding the determinant at any stage, show that

$$\begin{vmatrix} x^2+x & x+1 & x-2 \\ 2x^2+3x+1 & 3x & 3x-3 \\ x^2+2x+3 & 2x-1 & 2x-1 \end{vmatrix} = xA + B$$, where A and B are determinants of order 3 not involving x

11. Let the three digit numbers A28, 3B9 and 62C where A, B, and C are integers between 0 and 9 be divisible by a fixed integer

k. Show that the determinant $\begin{vmatrix} A & 3 & 6 \\ 8 & 9 & C \\ 2 & B & 2 \end{vmatrix}$ is divisible by k.

12. If $a \neq p, \quad b \neq q, \quad c \neq r$

and $\begin{vmatrix} p & b & c \\ a & q & c \\ a & b & r \end{vmatrix}$, then find the value of $\frac{p}{p\text{-}a}+\frac{q}{q-b}+\frac{r}{r-c}$.

13. Prove that for all values of θ,

$$\begin{vmatrix} \sin & \cos & \sin 2 \\ \sin\left(\;+\frac{2}{3}\right) & \cos\left(\;+\frac{2}{3}\right) & \sin\left(2 \;+\frac{4}{3}\right) \\ \sin\left(\;-\frac{2}{3}\right) & \cos\left(\;-\frac{2}{3}\right) & \sin\left(2 \;-\frac{4}{3}\right) \end{vmatrix} = 0$$

14. Let a, b, c be real numbers with $a^2+b^2+c^2=1$, then show that $\begin{vmatrix} ax-by-c & bx+ay & cx+a \\ bx+ay & -ax+by-c & cy+b \\ cx+a & cy+b & -ax-by+c \end{vmatrix}$ represents a striaght line.

ANSWERS

5. x = -3/7, y = 8/7, z = -2/7 **6.** x = 0, y = 0, z = 0. **9.** p **12.** 2

LINKED COMPREHENSION TYPE

PASSAGE - I

Let $A = \begin{bmatrix} 1 & 0 & 0 \\ 2 & 1 & 0 \\ 3 & 2 & 1 \end{bmatrix}$ and U_1, U_2 and U_3 are columns of a 3×3 matrix U. If columns matrices U_1, U_2 & U_3 satisfying $AU_1 = \begin{bmatrix} 1 \\ 0 \\ 0 \end{bmatrix}$, $AU_2 = \begin{bmatrix} 2 \\ 3 \\ 0 \end{bmatrix}$, $AU_3 = \begin{bmatrix} 2 \\ 3 \\ 1 \end{bmatrix}$ evaluated as directed in the following questions.

1. The value of $|U|$ is

(a) 3 (b) -3
(c) 3/2 (d) 2

2. The sum of the elements of the matrix U^{-1} is

(a) -1 (b) 0
(c) 1 (d) 3

3. The value of $\begin{bmatrix} 3 & 2 & 0 \end{bmatrix} \; U \; \begin{bmatrix} 3 \\ 2 \\ 0 \end{bmatrix}$ is

(a) 5 (b) 5/2
(c) 4 (d) 3/2

PASSAGE - II

Let A be the set of all 3×3 symmetric matrices all of whose entries are either 0 or 1. Five of these entries are 1 and four of them are zeroes

1. The number of matrices in A is

(a) 12 (b) 6
(c) 9 (d) 3

2. The number of matrices A to A for which the system of linear $A\begin{bmatrix} x \\ y \\ x \end{bmatrix} = \begin{bmatrix} 1 \\ 0 \\ 0 \end{bmatrix}$ equations A has a unique solution, is

(a) less than 4 (b) at-least 4 but less than 7
(c) at-least 7 but less than 10 (d) at-least 10

3. The number of matrices A in A for which the system of linear equation $A\begin{bmatrix} x \\ y \\ x \end{bmatrix} = \begin{bmatrix} 1 \\ 0 \\ 0 \end{bmatrix}$ is inconsistent is

(a) 0 (b) more than 2
(c) 2 (d) 1

PASSAGE - III

If $D = \begin{vmatrix} x^2+x+2 & 2x^2+3x+1 & 3x^2+5x+3 \\ 20x^2+20x+59 & 40x^2+60x+20 & 60x^2+100x+70 \\ 2x^2+2x+6 & 4x^2+6x+2 & 6x^2+10x+7 \end{vmatrix} = ax^2+bx+c$,

then

1. The value of a is

(a) $\begin{vmatrix} 1 & 2 & 3 \\ 1 & 0 & 1 \\ 2 & 1 & 1 \end{vmatrix}$ (b) $\begin{vmatrix} 1 & 2 & 3 \\ 1 & 1 & 1 \\ 2 & 0 & 1 \end{vmatrix}$

(c) $\begin{vmatrix} 1 & 2 & 3 \\ 1 & 0 & 1 \\ 2 & 0 & 1 \end{vmatrix}$ (d) $\begin{vmatrix} 1 & 2 & 3 \\ 1 & 0 & 1 \\ 0 & 2 & 1 \end{vmatrix}$

2. The value of b is

(a) $\begin{vmatrix} 1 & 3 & 5 \\ 1 & 0 & 1 \\ 2 & 0 & 1 \end{vmatrix}$ (b) $\begin{vmatrix} 1 & 3 & 5 \\ 1 & 0 & 1 \\ 2 & 1 & 1 \end{vmatrix}$

(c) $\begin{vmatrix} 1 & 3 & 5 \\ 2 & 0 & 1 \\ 1 & 1 & 1 \end{vmatrix}$ (d) $\begin{vmatrix} 1 & 3 & 5 \\ 1 & 1 & 1 \\ 2 & 0 & 1 \end{vmatrix}$

3. The value of c is

(a) $\begin{vmatrix} 2 & 1 & 3 \\ 1 & 0 & 1 \\ 2 & 1 & 1 \end{vmatrix}$ (b) $\begin{vmatrix} 2 & 1 & 3 \\ 1 & 0 & 1 \\ 2 & 0 & 1 \end{vmatrix}$

(c) $\begin{vmatrix} 2 & 1 & 1 \\ 3 & 2 & 0 \\ 1 & 1 & 1 \end{vmatrix}$ (d) $\begin{vmatrix} 2 & 1 & 3 \\ 1 & 0 & 1 \\ 2 & 1 & 0 \end{vmatrix}$

PASSAGE - IV

Let p ba an odd prime number and let T_p be the following set of 2×2 matrices :

$$T_p = \left\{ A = \begin{pmatrix} a & b \\ c & d \end{pmatrix} : a, b, c \in \{0, 1, 2, \ldots\ldots, (p-1)\} \right\}$$

1. The number of A in T_p such that A is either symmetric or skew symmetric or both , and det (A) is divisible by p, is

(a) $(p-1)^2$ (b) $2(p-1)$

(c) $(p-1)^2 + 1$ (d) $2p-1$

2. The number of A in T_p such that the trace of A is not divisible by p but det (A) is divisible by p, is

(a) $(p-1)(p^2-p+1)$ (b) $p^3-(p-1)^2$

(c) $(p-1)^2$ (d) $(p+1)(p-1)^2$

3. The number of A in T_p such that det (A) is not divisible by p, is

(a) $2p^2$ (b) $p^3-5\,p$

(c) $p^3-3\,p$ (d) $p^3-\,p^2$

ANSWERS

PASSEGE 1

1. (d) 2. (b) 3. (a)

PASSEGE 2

1. (a) **2.** (b) **3.** (b)

PASSEGE 3

1. (c) 2. (a) 3. (b)

PASSEGE 4

1. (d) **2.** (c) **3.** (d)

MATCH MATRIX

1. Match the following columns.

Column-I **Column-II**

(A) The value of $\begin{vmatrix} 1 & a & b+c \\ 1 & b & c+a \\ 1 & c & a+b \end{vmatrix}$ is (P) 1

(B) The value of $\begin{vmatrix} 1 & ab & bc+ca \\ 1 & bc & ca+ab \\ 1 & ca & ab+bc \end{vmatrix}$ is (Q) (a–b) (b–c) (c–a)

(C) The value of $\begin{vmatrix} 1 & a & bc \\ 1 & b & ca \\ 1 & c & ab \end{vmatrix}$ is (R) -1

(D) The value of $\begin{vmatrix} a & b & c \\ b & c & a \\ c & a & b \end{vmatrix}$ is (S) $-(a^3+b^3+c^3-3abc)$

(T) 0

2. Match the following columns.

Column-I **Column-II**

(A) Rank of the matrix $\begin{pmatrix} 1 & 2 & 3 \\ 4 & 5 & 6 \\ 7 & 8 & 9 \end{pmatrix}$ (P) 3

(B) Rank of the matrix $\begin{pmatrix} 1 & 2 & 3 \\ 2 & 4 & 6 \\ 3 & 6 & 9 \end{pmatrix}$ (Q) 2

(C) Rank of the matrix $\begin{pmatrix} 1 & 0 & 0 \\ 0 & 1 & 0 \\ 0 & 0 & 1 \end{pmatrix}$ (R) 1

(D) Rank of the matrix $\begin{pmatrix} 1 & 2 & 3 \\ 0 & 1 & 4 \\ 0 & 0 & 1 \end{pmatrix}$ (S) 0

3. Match the following columns :

Column-I **Column-II**

(A) The value of

$\begin{vmatrix} b+c & a & a \\ b & c+a & b \\ c & c & a+b \end{vmatrix}$ is (P) P

(B) The value of

$\begin{vmatrix} ab+ac & ab & ac \\ ab & bc+ab & bc \\ ac & bc & ac+bc \end{vmatrix}$ is (Q) 2 abc

(C) The value of

$\begin{vmatrix} \cos(A-P) & \cos(A-Q) & \cos(A-R) \\ \cos(B-P) & \cos(B-Q) & \cos(B-Q) \\ \cos(C-P) & \cos(C-Q) & \cos(C-R) \end{vmatrix}$ is (R) $4a^2b^2c^2$

(D) The value of

$$\begin{vmatrix} 1 & a & a^2 \\ \cos(P-D)x & \cos Px & \cos(P+D)x \\ \sin(P-D)x & \sin Px & \sin(P+D)x \end{vmatrix}$$ is (S) 0

4. Match the following columns. Let

$$\begin{vmatrix} x^2 & 3x & x+4 \\ x+4 & x^2 & 3x \\ 3x & x+4 & x \end{vmatrix} = ax^5 + bx^4 + cx^3 + dx^2 + ex + f.$$

Then

Column-I	Column-II
(A) the value of f is	(P) -6
(B) the value of e is	(Q) 48
(C) the value of b + d is	(R) 64
(D) the value of a + c is	(S) 2

ANSWER

1. (A)$\to$(T); (B)$\to$(T); (C)$\to$(Q); (D)$\to$(S)
2. (A)$\to$(Q); (B)$\to$(R); (C)$\to$(P); (D)$\to$(P)
3. (A)$\to$(Q); (B)$\to$(R); (C)$\to$(S); (D)$\to$(P)
4. (A)$\to$(R); (B)$\to$(Q); (C)$\to$(P); (D)$\to$(S)

Assertion and Reason

Codes:

(A) Both A and R are tru and R is the correct explanation of A
(B) Both A and R are true and R is not the correct explanantion of A
(C) A is true but R is False
(D) A is false but R is true.

1. Assertion : If $A = \begin{pmatrix} 3 & -3 & 4 \\ 2 & -3 & 4 \\ 0 & -1 & 1 \end{pmatrix}$, then $\text{Adj}(\text{Adj} A) = A$

Reson : $|\text{Adj}(\text{Adj} A)| = |A|^{(n-1)^2}$, where A be n -rowed non singular matrix.

(a) A (b) B
(c) C (d) D

2. Assertion : If $A = \begin{pmatrix} a & 0 & 0 \\ 0 & b & 0 \\ 0 & 0 & c \end{pmatrix}$, then $A^{-1} = \begin{pmatrix} 1/a & 0 & 0 \\ 0 & 1/b & 0 \\ 0 & 0 & 1/c \end{pmatrix}$

Reason: The inverse of a diagonal matrix is also a diagonal matrix

(a) A (b) B
(c) C (d) D

3. Assertion : The inverse of the matrix $A = \begin{pmatrix} 1 & 1 & 1 \\ 1 & 2 & 3 \\ 1 & 4 & 7 \end{pmatrix}$ does not exist

Reason : The matrix A is singular

(a) A (b) B
(c) C (d) D

4. Assertion : The inverse of the matrix $A = \begin{pmatrix} 1 & 2 & 4 \\ 1 & 2 & 3 \\ 1 & 4 & 7 \end{pmatrix}$ does not exist

Reason : The matrix A is non-singular

(a) A (b) B
(c) C (d) D

5. Assertion : The value of a determinant $\begin{vmatrix} 1 & a & b+c \\ 1 & b & c+a \\ 1 & c & a+b \end{vmatrix}$ is non zero

Reason : If any two columns of a determinant are identical, then the value of a determinant is zero.

(a) A (b) B
(c) C (d) D

6. Assertion : The rank of a matrix $A = \begin{pmatrix} 1 & 2 & 4 \\ 6 & 3 & 2 \\ 3 & 4 & 5 \end{pmatrix}$ is 2

Reason : If the determinant of a matrix of order 3 is non zero, then the rank of the matrix is 3

(a) A (b) B
(c) C (d) D

7. Assertion : Let $A = \begin{pmatrix} 0 & 2 & 4 \\ -2 & 0 & 5 \\ -4 & -5 & 0 \end{pmatrix}$. Then A is skew symmetric matrix

Reason: The diagonal of every skew symmetric matrix is zero.

(a) A (b) B
(c) C (d) D

8. Assertion : Let $A = \begin{bmatrix} 2 & -3 & -5 \\ -1 & 4 & 5 \\ 1 & -3 & -4 \end{bmatrix}$. Then A is idempotent

Reason : A matrix A is idempotent if $A^2 = A$

(a) A (b) B
(c) C (d) D

Questions asked in Roorkee Exams

1. Evaluate $\begin{vmatrix} {}^xC_1 & {}^xC_2 & {}^xC_3 \\ {}^yC_1 & {}^yC_2 & {}^yC_3 \\ {}^zC_1 & {}^zC_2 & {}^zC_3 \end{vmatrix}$ **[Roorkee - 1990]**

2. If f, g, h are differentiable function of x and

$$\Delta = \begin{vmatrix} f & g & h \\ (xf)' & (xg)' & (xh)' \\ (x^2f)'' & (x^2g)'' & (x^2h)'' \end{vmatrix}$$ then prove that

$$\Delta' = \begin{vmatrix} f & g & h \\ f' & g' & h' \\ (x^2f'')' & (x^2g'')' & (x^2h'')' \end{vmatrix}$$ **[Roorkee - 1991]**

3. Find the value of $\begin{vmatrix} \sqrt{13}+\sqrt{3} & 2\sqrt{5} & \sqrt{5} \\ \sqrt{15}+\sqrt{26} & 5 & \sqrt{10} \\ 3+\sqrt{65} & \sqrt{15} & 5 \end{vmatrix}$

[Roorkee-1992]

4. No questions asked in 1993.

5. Using determinants , solve the following equations : $x+2y+3z=6\ ;\ 2x+4y+z=17\ ;\ 3x+2y+9z=2$

[Roorkee - 1994]

6. For what values of p and q , the system of equations $2x+py+6z=8\ ;\ x+2y+qz=5\ ;\ x+y+3z=4$ has
   (i) no solution (ii) a unique solution
   (iii) infinitely many solutions ?

[Roorkey - 1995]

7. Find those values of c for which the equations $2x+3y=3\ ;\ (c+2)x+(c+4)y=c+6\ ;$ $(c+2)^2x+(c+4)^2y=(c+6)^2$ are consistent.
   Also solve above equations for those values of c .

[Roorkee - 1996]

8. For what real values of k, the system of equations $x+2y+z=1\ ;\ x+3y+4z=k\ ;\ x+5y+10z=k^2$ has solution. Find the solution in each case.
   Ans. $k=1,\ x=1+5t, y=-3t; k=2, x=-1+5t, y=1-3t$, where $t\in R$ **[Roorkee - 1997]**

9. Using matrix method , find the values of λ and μ so that the system of equations $2x-3y+5z=12\ ;\ 3x+y+\lambda z=\mu\ ;$ $x-7y+8z=17$ has
   (i) a unique solution (ii) infinite solution
   (iii) no solution

[Roorkee - 1998]

10. For all values of λ, find the rank of the matrix
$$\begin{pmatrix} 1 & 4 & 5 \\ \lambda & 8 & 8\lambda-5 \\ 1+\lambda^2 & 8\lambda+4 & 2\lambda+21 \end{pmatrix}$$

[Roorkee - 1999]

11. Find the real values of r for which the following system of linear equations has a non trivial solution. Also find the non trivial solutions of $2rx-2y+3z=0;\ x+ry+2z=0;\ 2x+rz=0$

[Roorkee - 2000]

12. Solve for x; $\begin{vmatrix} a^2 & a & 1 \\ \sin(n+1)x & \sin nx & \sin(n-1)x \\ \cos(n+1)x & \cos nx & \cos(n-1)x \end{vmatrix}=0$

[Roorkee - 2001]

ANSWER

1. $\frac{xyz}{12}(x-y)(y-z)(z-x)$

3. $5\sqrt{3}\left(\sqrt{6}-5\right)$

5. $x=1, y=4, z=-1$

6. (i) $p=2, q=3$, (ii) $p=2,\ q\neq 3$, (iii) $p\neq 2,\ q=3$

7. $c=-10, x=-1/2, y=1/3$

8. $k=1,\ x=1+5t, y=-3t; k=2, x=-1+5t, y=1-3t$, where $t\in R$

9. (i) $\lambda\neq 2$ (ii) $\lambda=2\ \&\ \mu=7$ (iii) $\lambda=2\ \&\ \mu\neq 7$

10. $\lambda\neq 2, -1$, Rank = 3; $\lambda=2$, Rank = 1; $\lambda=-1$, Rank = 2

11. $r=2\ ;\ \left(p,\ \frac{p}{2},\ -p\right),\ p\in R-\{0\}$

12. $x=\cos^{-1}\left(\frac{a^2+1}{2a}\right)\pm 2n\pi$

Questions asked in IIT-JEE Exams

1. If the system of equations $x-ky-z=0$; $kx-y-z=0$; $x+y-z=0$ has a non zero solution, then the possible values of k are

(a) -1, 2 (b) 1, 2
(c) 0, 1 (d) -1, 1

[IIT-JEE - 2000]

2. The number of distinct real roots of $\begin{vmatrix} \sin x & \cos x & \cos x \\ \cos x & \sin x & \cos x \\ \cos x & \cos x & \sin x \end{vmatrix} = 0$ in $\left[-\frac{\pi}{4}, \frac{\pi}{4}\right]$, is

(a) 0 (b) 2
(c) 1 (d) 3

[IIT-JEE - 2001]

3. Let a, b, c be real number with $a^2+b^2+c^2=1$, then show that

$$\begin{vmatrix} ax-by-c & bx+ay & cx+a \\ bx+ay & -ax+by-c & cy+b \\ cx+a & cy+b & -ax-by+c \end{vmatrix}$$

represents a straight line

[IIT-JEE - 2001]

4. Let $\quad = -\frac{1}{2}+i\frac{\sqrt{3}}{2}$. Then the value of the determinant

$$\begin{vmatrix} 1 & 1 & 1 \\ 1 & -1-\omega^2 & \omega^2 \\ 1 & \omega^2 & \omega^4 \end{vmatrix}$$ is

(a) $3w$ (b) $3w(w-1)$
(c) $3w^2$ (d) $3w(1-w)$

[IIT-JEE - 2002]

5. The number of values of k for which the system of equations $(k+1)x+8y=4k$; $kx+(k+3)y=3k-1$ has infinitely many solutions is

(a) 0 (b) 1
(c) 2 (d) infinite

[IIT-JEE - 2002]

6. If $A=\begin{pmatrix} a & 0 \\ 1 & 1 \end{pmatrix}$ and $B=\begin{pmatrix} 1 & 0 \\ 5 & 1 \end{pmatrix}$, then the value of a for which $A^2=B$ is

(a) 1 (b) -1
(c) 4 (d) No real values

[IIT-JEE - 2003]

6. If the system of equations $x+ay=0$, $ax+z=0$, $az+y=0$ has infinite solutions, then the value of a is

(a) - 1 (b) 1
(c) 0 (d) no real values.

[IIT-JEE - 2003]

7. If $A=\begin{pmatrix} a & b & c \\ b & c & a \\ c & a & b \end{pmatrix}$ where a, b, c are real positive numbers. $abc=1$ and $A^T=I$, then find the value of $a^2+b^2+c^2$

[IIT-JEE - 2003]

8. Given $2x-y+2z=2$, $x-2y+z=-4$, $x+y+\lambda z=4$, then the value of λ such that the given system of equation has no solution is

(a) 3 (b) 1
(c) 0 (d) -3

[IIT-JEE - 2004]

9. If $A=\begin{pmatrix} \alpha & 2 \\ 2 & \alpha \end{pmatrix}$ and $|A^3|=125$, then the value of α is

(a) ±1 (b) ±2
(c) ±3 (d) ±5

[IIT-JEE - 2004]

10. If $A=\begin{pmatrix} a & 0 & 1 \\ 1 & c & b \\ 1 & d & b \end{pmatrix}$, $B=\begin{pmatrix} a & 1 & 1 \\ 0 & d & c \\ 1 & d & b \end{pmatrix}$, $U=\begin{pmatrix} f \\ g \\ h \end{pmatrix}$, $V=\begin{pmatrix} a^2 \\ 0 \\ 0 \end{pmatrix}$, $X=\begin{pmatrix} x \\ y \\ z \end{pmatrix}$ and $AX=U$ hasinfinite solutions, prove that $BX=V$ can have a unique solution. If at d ¹ 0, then prove that $BX=V$ has no solution

[IIT-JEE - 2004]

11. If $A=\begin{pmatrix} 1 & 0 & 0 \\ 0 & 1 & 1 \\ 0 & -2 & 4 \end{pmatrix}$ and $I=\begin{pmatrix} 1 & 0 & 0 \\ 0 & 1 & 0 \\ 0 & 0 & 1 \end{pmatrix}$

and $A^{-1}=\left[\frac{1}{6}\left(A^2+c\ \ A+d\ \ I\right)\right]$, then the value of c and d are

(a) (-6, -1) (b) (6, 11)
(c) (-6, 11) (d) (6, -11)

[IIT-JEE - 2005]

12. If $P=\begin{pmatrix} \frac{\sqrt{3}}{2} & \frac{1}{2} \\ -\frac{1}{2} & \frac{\sqrt{3}}{2} \end{pmatrix}$ and $A=\begin{pmatrix} 1 & 1 \\ 1 & 0 \end{pmatrix}$ and $Q=PAP^T$ and

$x=P^TQ^{2005}P$, then x is equal to

(a) $\begin{pmatrix} 1 & 2005 \\ 0 & 1 \end{pmatrix}$ (b) $\begin{pmatrix} 4+2005\sqrt{3} & 6015 \\ 2005 & 4-2005\sqrt{3} \end{pmatrix}$

(c) $\frac{1}{4}\begin{pmatrix} 2+\sqrt{3} & 1 \\ -1 & 2-\sqrt{3} \end{pmatrix}$ (d) $\frac{1}{4}\begin{pmatrix} 2005 & 2-\sqrt{3} \\ 2+\sqrt{3} & 2005 \end{pmatrix}$

[IIT-JEE - 2005]

13. Let $A=\begin{bmatrix}1&0&0\\2&1&0\\3&2&1\end{bmatrix}$ and U_1, U_2 and U_3 are columns of a 3×3 matrix U. If columns matrices U_1, U_2 & U_3 satisfying

$AU_1=\begin{bmatrix}1\\0\\0\end{bmatrix}$, $AU_2=\begin{bmatrix}2\\3\\0\end{bmatrix}$, $AU_3=\begin{bmatrix}2\\3\\1\end{bmatrix}$ evaluated as directed in the following questions.

(i) The value of $|U|$ is

(a) 3 (b) -3

(c) 3/2 (d) 2

(ii) The sum of the elements of the matrix U^{-1} is

(a) -1 (b) 0

(c) 1 (d) 3

(iii) The value of $\begin{bmatrix}3&2&0\end{bmatrix}U\begin{bmatrix}3\\2\\0\end{bmatrix}$ IS

(a) 5 (b) 5/2

(c) 4 (d) 3/2

[IIT-JEE - 2006]

14. No questions asked in IIT-JEE - 2007.

15. Consider the system of equations

$x-2y+3z=-1, -x+y-2z=k, x-3y+4z=1$

Assertion : The system of equation has no soiution for k ¹ 3

Reason : The determinant $\begin{vmatrix}1&3&-1\\-1&-2&k\\1&4&1\end{vmatrix}\neq 0$ for k ¹ 3.

[IIT-JEE - 2008]

16. Let A be the set of all 3×3 symmetric matrices all of whose entries are either 0 or 1. Five of these entries are 1 and four of them are zeroes

(i) The number of matrices in A is

(a) 12 (b) 6

(c) 9 (d) 3

(ii) The number of matrices A to A for which the system of linear $A\begin{bmatrix}x\\y\\x\end{bmatrix}=\begin{bmatrix}1\\0\\0\end{bmatrix}$ equations A has a unique solution, is

(a) less than 4 (b) at-least 4 but less than 7

(c) at-least 7 but less than 10 (d) at-least 10

(iii) The number of matrices A in A for which the system of linear equation $A\begin{bmatrix}x\\y\\x\end{bmatrix}=\begin{bmatrix}1\\0\\0\end{bmatrix}$ is inconsistent is

(a) 0 (b) more than 2

(c) 2 (d) 1

[IIT-JEE - 2009]

17. Let k be a positive real number and let

$A=\begin{pmatrix}2k-1&2\sqrt{k}&2\sqrt{k}\\2\sqrt{k}&1&-2k\\-2\sqrt{k}&2k&-1\end{pmatrix}$ and

$B=\begin{pmatrix}0&2k-1&\sqrt{k}\\1-2k&0&2\sqrt{k}\\-\sqrt{k}&-2\sqrt{k}&0\end{pmatrix}$.

If det(Adj A) + det(Adj B) = 10^6, then $[k]$ is

[IIT-JEE - 2009]

18. The number of 3×3 matrices A whose entries are either 0 or 1 and for which the system A

$\begin{bmatrix}x\\y\\z\end{bmatrix}=\begin{bmatrix}1\\0\\0\end{bmatrix}$ has exactly two solutions, is

(a) 0 (b) 2^9-1

(c) 168 (d) 12

[IIT-JEE - 2010]

19. Let p ba an odd prime number and let T_p be the following set of 2×2 matrices:

$$T_p=\left\{A=\begin{pmatrix}a&b\\c&d\end{pmatrix} : a, b, c \in \{0, 1, 2, \ldots\ldots, (p-1)\}\right\}$$

(i) The number of A in T_p such that A is either symmetric or skew symmetric or both, and det (A) is divisible by p, is

(a) $(p-1)^2$ (b) $2(p-1)$

(c) $(p-1)^2$ (d) $2p-1$

(ii) The number of A in T_p such that the trace of A is not divisible by p but det (A) is divisible by p, is

(a) $(p-1)(p^2-p+1)$ (b) $p^3-(p-1)^2$

(c) $(p-1)^2$ (d) $(p+1)(p-1)^2$

(iii) The number of A in T_p such that det (A) is not divisible by p, is

(a) $2p^2$ (b) p^3-5p

(c) p^3-3p (d) p^3-p^2

[IIT-JEE - 2010]

20. Let M and N be two 3×3 non singular skew symmetric matrices such that MN = NM. If p^T denotes the transpose of P, then $M^2N^2(M^TN)^{-1}(MN^{-1})^T$ is

(a) M^2 (b) $-N^2$

(c) $-M^2$ (d) MN

[IIT-JEE - 2011]

21. Let M be a square matrix of order 3 such that

$M\begin{pmatrix}0\\1\\0\end{pmatrix}=\begin{pmatrix}-1\\2\\3\end{pmatrix}$, $M\begin{pmatrix}1\\-1\\0\end{pmatrix}=\begin{pmatrix}1\\1\\-1\end{pmatrix}$ & $M\begin{pmatrix}1\\1\\1\end{pmatrix}=\begin{pmatrix}0\\0\\12\end{pmatrix}$

Then sum of the diagonal entries of M is

[IIT-JEE - 2011]

22. If P is a matrix of order 3 such that $P^T = 2P + I$, where P^T is the transpose of P and I is the identity matrix of order 3, then there exist a column matrix X such that $X = \begin{pmatrix} x \\ y \\ z \end{pmatrix} \neq \begin{pmatrix} 0 \\ 0 \\ 0 \end{pmatrix}$

(a) $PX = \begin{pmatrix} 0 \\ 0 \\ 0 \end{pmatrix}$ (b) $PX = X$

(c) $PX = 2X$

(d) $PX = -X$

[IIT-JEE - 2012]

23. If the adjoint of a matrix P of order 3 is $\begin{pmatrix} 1 & 4 & 1 \\ 2 & 1 & 7 \\ 1 & 1 & 3 \end{pmatrix}$, then the possible values of the determinant of P is (are)

(a) -2 (b) -1

(c) 1 (d) 2

[IIT-JEE - 2012]

ANSWER

7. 4 **15.** (A) **17.** 4 **21.** 9

Self Assesment Test

TIME : 2 HOURS. CHAPTER : MATRICES AND DETERMINANT MAX MARKS: 50

Note : Give answers the following questions

1. If $\begin{vmatrix} (b+c)^2 & a^2 & a^2 \\ b^2 & (c+a)^2 & b^2 \\ c^2 & c^2 & (a+b)^2 \end{vmatrix} = k \ abc \ (a+b+c)^2$, then the value of k is

(a) 1 (b) 2

(c) 3 (d) 4

2. Let $f(x) = \begin{vmatrix} x^3 & \sin x & \cos x \\ 6 & -1 & 0 \\ p & p^2 & p^3 \end{vmatrix}$, where p is a constant, then

$\frac{d^3}{dx^3}(f(x))$ at $x=0$

(a) p (b) $p+p^2$

(c) $p+p^2$ (d) None.

3. If $\begin{vmatrix} e^x & \sin x & 1 \\ \cos x & \log_e(1+x^2) & 1 \\ x & x^2 & 1 \end{vmatrix} = a + bx + cx^2$, then the value of b is

(a) 0 (b) –1

(c) 2 (d) 3

4. If F (x), G (x) and H (x) are three polynomials of degree 2, then $(x) = \begin{vmatrix} F(x) & G(x) & H(x) \\ F'(x) & G'(x) & H'(x) \\ F''(x) & G''(x) & H''(x) \end{vmatrix}$ is a polynomial of degree

(a) 0 (b) 1

(c) 2 (d) 3

5. If one root of $\begin{vmatrix} 7 & 6 & x \\ 2 & x & 2 \\ x & 3 & 7 \end{vmatrix} = 0$ is - 9, then the other two roots are

(a) 2, 6 (b) 3, 6

(c) 2, 7 (d) 3, 7

6. If a, b, c are all different and $D = \begin{vmatrix} a & a^2 & 1+a^3 \\ b & b^2 & 1+b^3 \\ c & c^2 & 1+c^3 \end{vmatrix} = 0$, then

(a) $abc = -1$ (b) $a+b+c=1$

(c) $a^2+b^2+c^2=2$ (d) $\frac{1}{a}+\frac{1}{b}+\frac{1}{c}=-1$

7. For all values of θ, the value of

$$D = \begin{vmatrix} \sin\theta & \cos\theta & \sin 2\theta \\ \sin\left(\theta+\frac{2\pi}{3}\right) & \cos\left(\theta+\frac{2\pi}{3}\right) & \sin\left(2\theta+\frac{4\pi}{3}\right) \\ \sin\left(\theta-\frac{2\pi}{3}\right) & \cos\left(\theta-\frac{2\pi}{3}\right) & \sin\left(2\theta-\frac{4\pi}{3}\right) \end{vmatrix}$$ is

(a) 0 (b) $\sin\theta$

(c) $\cos\theta$ (d) 1

8. If $A = \begin{pmatrix} a & b \\ c & d \end{pmatrix}$ satisfies the equation $x^2 - (a+d)x + k = 0$, then A^{-1} exists if

(a) $k = bc$ (b) $k = ad$

(c) $k = a^2+b^2+c^2+d^2$ (d) None

9. If $A = \begin{pmatrix} 1 & a \\ 0 & 1 \end{pmatrix}$, then A^n, where $n \in N$, is

(a) $\begin{pmatrix} 1 & na \\ 0 & 1 \end{pmatrix}$ (b) $\begin{pmatrix} 1 & n^2a \\ 0 & 1 \end{pmatrix}$

(c) $\begin{pmatrix} 1 & na \\ 0 & 0 \end{pmatrix}$ (d) $\begin{pmatrix} n & na \\ 0 & n \end{pmatrix}$

10. If $A = \begin{pmatrix} 1 & 2 & x \\ 0 & 1 & 0 \\ 0 & 0 & 1 \end{pmatrix}$ and $B = \begin{pmatrix} 1 & -2 & y \\ 0 & 1 & 0 \\ 0 & 0 & 1 \end{pmatrix}$ and $AB = I_3$, then $x + y$ is

(a) 2 (b) –1

(c) 3 (d) 0

CHAPTER 7

THE PROBABILITY

CONCEPT BOOSTER

7.1. Introduction

The probability theory is originated from the game of chance, related to gambling, namely, tossing a coin, throwing a die, drawing a card from a pack of well-shuffle 52 cards, etc., in which the outcome of a trial is uncertain.Actual appearence of one of these result is not predicted.

The word 'Probability' or (Chance) is very commonly used in day-to-day conversation and also generally people have a rough idea about its meaning.

For example, the statements, "Probably it will rain today", "It is likely that Principal Sir may not come for taking his class today", "The chance of passing of Nidhi in the examination is good", It is possible that Captain of Indian Cricket team will be replaced next year", etc.

All these terms - Probably, Likely, Chance, Probable, etc. convey in the same sense of uncertainty. So, the objective of the probability theory is to make such statements precise by giving them numerical measures.

7.2 Importance of the Concept of the Probability:

Now-a-days, the applications of probability theory for beyond games of chance. It has contributed to the solutions of problems in Biology, Physics, Chemistry, in other natural sciences as well. Business, industry and Government are finding each year solutions to some of their problems through the use of probability theory. Life Insurance Companies have long made use of the principles of probabilty to help themselves to remain solvent.

7.3. Sample Space:

The set of all possible outcomes of a Random Experiment is called a sample space or a probability space. It is denoted by S.
Each element of a sample space is called a sample point.
It is denoted by the symbol ω (Omega).

For example

i. On tossing a coin the sample space is S = {H, T}, where H and T are sample points.
ii. On throwing a die , the sample space is S = { 1, 2, 3, 4, 5, 6 }, where 1, 2, 3, 4, 5 and 6 are sample points.

Note

i. If the number of sample points is finite , then the sample space is called Discrete Sample Space, Otherwise Continuous Sample Space..

7.4 Event Space

Any subset of a sample space is called an event or simply an event . It is generally denoted by Capital letters of English aplhabet, say A , B, C etc.

An event having only one element is called a simple event. For example, on throwing a die, the sample space is
$S=\{1,2,........,6\}$
Then $A=\{1\}$ is a simple event.
An event having more than one element is called a compound event or a mixed event or a composite event.On throwing a die , the sample space is
$S=\{1,2,............,6\}$. Then $B=\{1,3,5\}$ is a mixed event.
An event whose occurrence is inevitable when a certain random experiment is performed is called a sure event (or certain) event. On throwing of a die, the occurence of the numbers 1 to 6 is a sure event.

Probability theory is used to estimate whether a missile hit its target or not , to determine premium of insurance policies and to make important business decision such as where to locate a super market and how many clerks to employ so that customers will not be kept waiting in line too long. Various sampling techniques , which are used in opinion polls and in the quality control of mass produced items are based on the the theory of probability.

Infact , it has become indispensable tool for all types of formal studies that involve uncertainty . It should be noted that the concept of probabilty is employed not only for various type of investigations but also for many problems in everydays life.

Now we shall define some terms which are essential for the study of the concept of the theory of the probabilty.

7.5 Some basic definitions

1.Experiment

An operation which can produce some well defined outcomes, is known as an experiment.

Ingeneral, when we perform an experiment in the study of science under identical conditions, we get almost the same result in every time. But here, under identical conditions, we do not get the same outcome in every time. For example, if we throw a die, we can get any one of the numbers from 1 to 6.

2.Random Experiment

In an experiment if all the possible outcomes are known in

advance and none of them can be predicted with certainty, is known as **Random Experiment.**

For example, throwing a die, tossing of a fair coin, drawing a card from a pack of 52 cards, etc.

In the study of probabilty, we shall quiet often use the words like coin, die, cards etc.

Let us try to give some brief descriptions about said words.

1. *Coin* : It is a piece of stamped metal, used as money and has two faces known as H (head) or T (tail). On tossing a coin, we can get either H or T.
2. *Die* : It is a solid cube , used for playing ludo and has six faces marked with 1, 2, 3, 4, 5, 6. On throwing a die, we can get any of the numbers from 1 to 6. The plural of die is dice.
3. *Cards* : A pack of cards has 52 cards in two colors and divided equally in four suits.They are Spades, Clubbs (are black cards) and Hearts and Diamonds (are red cards). Each suits consists of 13 cards, namely, 1 is an ace, i is a king, 1 is a queen, 1 is a jack and 9 are number cards from 2 to 10.
   i. *Face Cards* : The kings , the queens and the jacks are called face cards. Obviously they are 12 in numbers.
   ii. *Court Cards* : The Aces, The kings, the queens and the jacks are called Court cards. Obvioulу they are 12 in numbers.
   iii. *Honours Cards* : The aces, the kings and the queens are called Honours cards. Obviously they are 12 in numbers.
   iv. *Game of Bridge* : It is played by 4 players. They will play individually and each player will get 13 cards.
   v. *Game of Whist* : It is also played by 4 players. But they will play it into two groups. Group members will sit opposite to each other and also each player will get 13 cards.

An event which can never occur when a certain random experiment is performed is called an impossible event. It is denoted by ϕ or { }. On throwing of a die, the occurence of 7 is an impossible event.

An event which may or may not occur while performing a certain random experiment is called a random event. On throwing of a die , occurence of 1 or 2 or 3 or 4 or 5 or 6 is a random event.

Equally Likely events

Two or more events are said to be equally likely if the chance of their happening is equal. Head and Tail are equally likely events , on tossing of a fair coin. 1, 2, 3, 4, 5 and 6 are equally likely events on throwing of an unbaised die.

Exhaustive Events :

The total number of possible outcomes of a random experiment is known as exhaustive events.

On tossing of a fair coin , exhaustive events is 2 on throwing of a die , exhaustive events is 6.

On drawing a card from a pack of 52 cards, exhaustive events is 52.

Mutually Exclusive Events :

Two or more events are said to be mutually exclusive if they cannot occur simultaneouly in a single trial. All simple events are mutually exclusive.

If a sample space consists of E_1 E_2, E_3, ..., E_n events, then $E_1 \cap E_2 \cap E_3 \cap ....E_{n-1} \cap E_n = \phi$

Mutually Exclusive and Exhaustive Events :

A set of events E_1, E_2, ..., E_n of a sample space S are said to be mutually exclusive and exhaustive events if

i. $E_1 \cap E_2 \cap E_3 \cap ....E_{n-1} \cap E_n = \phi$

ii. $E_1 \cup E_2 \cup E_3 \cup ....E_{n-1} \cup E_n = S$.

For examples :

1. If we throw an unbiased die, then $S = \{1, 2, ..., 6\}$ in which $E_1 = \{2, 4, 6\}$ and $E_2 = \{1, 3, 5\}$. Clearly $E_1 \cup E_2 = S$ and $E_1 \cap E_2 = \phi$. Thus E_1 and E_2 are mutually exclusive and exhaustive events.
2. Let a die is thrown. Then the sample is $S = \{1, 2, 3, 4, 5, 6\}$ Let $A = \{2, 4, 6\}$ and $B = \{1, 2, 3, 5\}$ Then A and B are not mutually exclusive . i.e. $A \cap B \quad \phi$

   But $A \cup B = \{1, 2, 3, 4, 5, 6\} = S$. Thus A and B are exhaustive events.

   From the above explanation we can conclude that, mutually exclusive events can be a exhaustive events and also conversly.

Independents Events :

Two or more evnts are said to be independent event when the occurence of one does not affect the other.

For example , if we toss a coin twice, the occurence of the second toss will in no way be affected by the outcome of the first toss.

But if we throw a die, the sample space is $S = \{1, 2, ..., 6\}$. Let E be the event of getting even number and F be the event of getting odd number, then $E = \{2, 4, 6\}$ and $F = \{1, 3, 5\}$clearly $E_1 \cap E_2 = \phi$.

Thus E and F are mutually exclusive events . But these events are not independent.

Event of getting a tail on the first coin and the event of getting a tail on the second coin in a simultaneous throw of two coins are independent.

7.6 Probability of occurrence of an event :

Let S be a sample space and A be any event.

Then $P(A) = \dfrac{n(A)}{n(S)}$

$= \dfrac{\text{No. of cases favourable to event A}}{\text{total number of cases}}$

7.7 If A is any event and A' be the complement event of A on a sample S , then

$P(A) + P(A') = 1$

Proof: Here A and A` are mutually exclusive and exhaustive event of a sample sapce S.

Thus $A \cap A' = \phi$ and $A \cup A' = S$

Now, $P(A \cup A') = P(S) = 1$

$\Rightarrow \quad P(A) + P(A') = 1.$

$\Rightarrow \quad P(A) = 1 - P(A').$

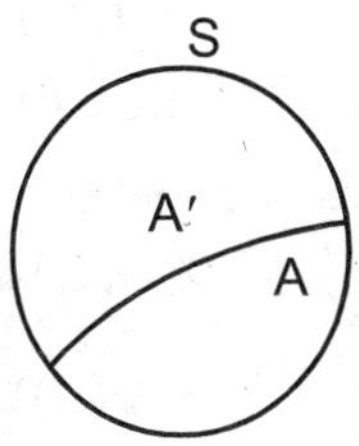

7.8 Odds in favour and against of an event

Let S be a sample space and A be an event .

Let A` be the complement of an event A . then

i. Odds in favour of an event A

$= \frac{\text{no.of cases favourable to event A}}{\text{no.of cases against to the event A}}$

$= \frac{n(A)}{n(A')} = \frac{n(A)/n(S)}{n(A')/n(S)} = \frac{P(A)}{P(A')}.$

ii. Odds against of an event A

$= \frac{\text{no.of cases against the event A}}{\text{no.of cases favourable to the event A}} = \frac{n(A')}{n(A)} = \frac{P(A')}{P(A)}.$

For examples :

i. If Odds in favour of $A = \frac{3}{8}$, then

the odds against of $A = \frac{8}{3}$ and $P(A) = \frac{3}{11}$.

ii. If Odds in against of $A = \frac{3}{11}$, then

the Odds in favour of $A = \frac{11}{3}$ and $P(A) = \frac{11}{14}$.

iii. If $P(A) = \frac{2}{7}$, then Odds in favour of $A = \frac{2}{5}$ and

Odds against of $A = \frac{5}{2}$.

7.9 Axioms of Probability

Let A be any event of a sample space S. Then

Axioms - 1 : $0 \le P(A) \le 1$

Axioms - 2 : P(S) = 1.

Axioms - 3 : $P\left(\bigcup_{i=1}^{\infty} A_i\right) = \sum_{i=1}^{\infty} P(A_i)$..

7.10 Some solved examples

Ex.1 : A coin is tossed twice. Find the probability of getting
(i) 2 heads (ii) exactly one head (iii) exactly two tails

Sol. Here , $S = \{HH, HT, TH, TT\}$

Then, (i) the probability of 2 heads $= \frac{1}{4}$

(ii) the probability of exactly one head.

i.e. $\{HT, TH\}$ is $= \frac{2}{4} = \frac{1}{2}$.

(iii) the probability of exactly two tails is

i.e. {TT} is $= \frac{1}{4}$.

Ex.2 : A coin is tossed three times. Find the probability of getting
(i) exactly 2 heads (ii) at-least 2 heads (iii) exactly 1 head.

Sol. Here,

$S = \{HHH, HHT, HTH, THH, TTT, TTH, THT, HTT\}$

Then (i) the probability of exactly two heads .

i.e. {HHT,HTH, THH} is $\frac{3}{8}$

(ii) the probability of at-least two heads i.e. {HHT, HTH, THH, HHH} is $\frac{4}{8} = \frac{1}{2}$

(iii) the probability of eaxctly one head

.ie. { TTH, THT, HTT} is $\frac{3}{8}$.

Ex.3: A die is thrown twice. Find the probability of getting

(i) a sum of 10

(ii) a sum of at-least 9.

(iii) a sum of even numbers

(iv) a sum of odd numbers.

(v) a sum of perfect numbers.

(vi) both the dice shows prime numbers.

Sol. Here, $S = \{(1,1),\ (1,2),\ (1,3), \ldots\ldots\ldots\ldots\ldots\ldots\ldots, (6,6)\}$

(i) Let A be the event, which shows the outcome, a sum of $10 = \{(4,\ 6),\ (6,\ 4),\ (5,\ 5)\}$

Then the probability of A is = $P(A) = \frac{3}{36} = \frac{1}{12}$

(ii) Let B, be the event , which shows the outcome, a sum of at-least 9 ={ a sum of 9 , 10 , 11 and 12}
= {(3, 6), (6, 3), (4, 5), (5, 4), (4, 6), (6, 4), (5, 5), (5, 6), (6, 5), (6, 6)}

Then the probability of B is = $P(B) = \frac{10}{36} = \frac{5}{18}$

(iii) Let C be the event which shows the outcome a sum of even numbers = {a sum of 2, 4, 6, 8, 10, 12}
= {(1,1), (1,3), (3,1), (2,2), (1,5), (5,1), (2,4), (4,2), (3,3), (2,6), (6,2), (3,5), (5,3), (4,4), (4,6), (6,4), (5,5), (6,6)}.

Then the probability of C is = $P(C) = \frac{18}{36} = \frac{1}{2}$.

(iv) Let D be the event shows the outcome a som of odd numbers = { a sum of 3, 5, 7, 9, 11 }
= {(1, 2), (2, 1), (1, 4), (4, 1), (2, 3), (3, 2), (1, 6), (6, 1), (2, 5), (5, 2), (3, 4), (4, 3), (3, 6), (6, 3), (4, 5), (5, 4), (5, 6), (6, 5)}

Then the probability of D is = $P(D) = \frac{18}{36} = \frac{1}{2}$

(v) Let E be the event, a sum of perfect numbers = {a sum of 6} (since only two perfect number exist from 1 to 100 natural numbers, say, 6 and 28}

$= \{(1,5),(5,1),(2,4),(4,2),(3,3)\}$

Then the probability of E is = $P(E) = \frac{5}{36}$.

(vi) Let F be the event, both the dice are shows prime numbers $= \{2,3,5\}$

$= \{(2,3),(2,5),(5,2),(3,2),(3,5),(5,3)\}$

Then the probability of F is = $P(F) = \frac{6}{36} = \frac{1}{6}$.

Ex.4: A die is thrown 3 times. Find the probability of getting

(i) a sum of 3

(ii) a sum of 4.

(iii) a sum of 5.

(iv) a sum of 6.

(v) a sum of 7.

(vi) a sum of at-least 15

(vii) a sum of at-most 16

Sol. Here, $S = \{(1,1,1),(1,1,2),(1,1,3),.........,(6,6,6)\}$

(i) Let A be the event of getting a sum of 3 = $\{(1,1,1,)\}$

Then the probability of A is = $P(A) = \frac{1}{216}$.

(ii) Let B be the event of getting a sum of 4 $\rightarrow (1,1,2)$

These three numbers can be arranged themselves in

$\frac{(3)!}{(2)!}$ ways = 3 ways

Hence, the probability of B is = $\frac{3}{216} = \frac{1}{72}$

(iii) Let C be the event of getting a sum of 5 $\rightarrow (1,1,3),(1,2,2)$

Hence, the probability of C is = $\frac{3+3}{216} = \frac{6}{216} = \frac{1}{36}$

(iv) Let D be the event of getting a sum of 6

$\rightarrow (1,2,3),(1,1,4),(2,2,2)$

Hence, the probability of D is

$= P(D) = \frac{3+6+3}{216} = \frac{12}{216} = \frac{1}{18}$

(v) Let E be the event of getting a sum of 7

$\rightarrow (1,1,5),(1,2,4),(1,3,3),(2,2,3)$

Hence, the probability of E is

$= P(E) = \frac{3+6+3+3}{216} = \frac{15}{216} = \frac{5}{72}]$.

(vi) Let F be the event of getting a sum of at-least 15

= a sum of { 15, 16, 17, 18}

$15 \rightarrow (3,6,6),(4,5,6),(5,5,5)$,

$16 \rightarrow (4,6,6),(5,5,6)$, $17 \rightarrow (5,6,6)$ and

$18 \rightarrow (6,6,6)$

Hence, the required probability

$= P(F) = \frac{10+6+3+1}{216} = \frac{20}{216} = \frac{5}{54}$.

(vii) Let G be the event of getting a sum of at - least 16 $= \{16,17,18\}$

$16 \rightarrow (4,6,6),(5,5,6)$, $17 \rightarrow (5,6,6)$

and $18 \rightarrow (6,6,6)$

Hence, the required probability

$= P(G) = \frac{6+3+1}{216} = \frac{10}{216} = \frac{5}{108}$

Ex.5: A card is drawn from a pack of 52 cards. Find the probability of getting

(i) a red card

(ii) a black card

(iii) a king card

(iv) a king of a red color.

(v) a queen of spade.

(vi) A face card.

Sol. (i) Required probability of a red card = $\frac{26}{52} = \frac{1}{2}$

(ii) Required probability of a black card = $\frac{26}{52} = \frac{1}{2}$

(iii) Required probability of a king card $\frac{4}{52} = \frac{1}{13}$

(iv) Required probability of a king of a red color = $\frac{2}{52} = \frac{1}{26}$

(v) Required probability of a queen of a spade = $\frac{1}{52}$

(vi) Required probability of a face card = $\frac{12}{52} = \frac{3}{13}$.

Ex.6: Two cards are drawn at random from a well shuffled pack of 52 cards. Find the probability of getting

(i) both are red cards.

(ii) both are kings.

(iii) one is face card and another one is a king of a red color.

(iv) one is court card and another one is an ace card

(v) both are of the same suit.

(vi) both are of the different suit.

Sol. (i) Required probability of getting both are red cards

$= \frac{^{26}C_2}{^{52}C_2} = \frac{26 \times 25}{52 \times 51} = \frac{25}{102}$

(ii) Required probability of getting both are king cards

$= \frac{^{4}C_2}{^{52}C_2} = \frac{4 \times 3}{52 \times 51} = \frac{1}{13 \times 17} = \frac{1}{221}$

(iii) Required probability of getting one is face card and another one is a king of a red color.

$= \frac{^{12}C_1 \times {^2C_1}}{^{52}C_2} = \frac{12 \times 2 \times 2}{52 \times 51} = \frac{12}{13 \times 51} = \frac{12}{663}$

(iv) Required probability of getting one is court card and another one is an ace card

$$= \frac{{}^{16}C_1 \times {}^4C_1}{{}^{52}C_2} = \frac{16 \times 4 \times 2}{52 \times 51} = \frac{32}{13 \times 51} = \frac{32}{663}$$

(v) Required probability of getting both are of the same suit.

$$= \frac{{}^{13}C_2 + {}^{13}C_2 + {}^{13}C_2 + {}^{13}C_2}{{}^{52}C_2} = \frac{4 \times {}^{13}C_2}{{}^{52}C_2} = \frac{4 \times 13 \times 12}{52 \times 51} = \frac{4}{13}$$

(vi) Required probability of getting both are of the different suit.

$$= \frac{{}^{13}C_1 \times {}^{13}C_1 + {}^{13}C_1 \times {}^{13}C_1 + {}^{13}C_1 \times {}^{13}C_1 + {}^{13}C_1 \times {}^{13}C_1 + {}^{13}C_1 \times {}^{13}C_1 + {}^{13}C_1 \times {}^{13}C_1 + {}^{13}C_1 \times {}^{13}C_1}{{}^{52}C_2}$$

$$= \frac{169}{{}^{52}C_2} = \frac{169 \times 2}{52 \times 51} = \frac{13}{102}.$$

Ex.7. Four cards are drawn at random from a pack of 52 cards. Find the probability of getting

(i) 2 red cards and 2 kings of black color.
(ii) all are of different suit.
(iii) all are of same suit.
(iv) all are honours cards
(v) all are face cards.
(vi) 3 are court cards.
(vii) 2 are aces0
(viii) 2 slave cards.
(ix) all are number cards.
(x) all are same numbers cards.

Sol. (i) Required probability of getting 2 red cards and 2 kings of black color. $= \frac{{}^{26}C_2 \times {}^2C_2}{{}^{52}C_4}$.

(ii) Required probability of getting all have come from different suit. $= \frac{{}^{13}C_1 \times {}^{13}C_1 \times {}^{13}C_1 \times {}^{13}C_1}{{}^{52}C_4}$

(iii) Required probability of getting the cards all have coming from same suit

$$= \frac{{}^{13}C_4 + {}^{13}C_4 + {}^{13}C_4 + {}^{13}C_4}{{}^{52}C_4} = \frac{4 \times {}^{13}C_4}{{}^{52}C_4}$$

(iv) Required probability of getting all the cards are honours cards $= \frac{{}^{12}C_4}{{}^{52}C_4}$.

(v) Required probability of getting all are face cards $= \frac{{}^{12}C_4}{{}^{52}C_4}$.

(vi) Required probability of getting 3 are court cards

$$= \frac{{}^{16}C_3 \times {}^{36}C_1}{{}^{52}C_4}$$

(vii) Required probability of getting 2 are aces $= \frac{{}^4C_2 \times {}^{48}C_2}{{}^{52}C_4}$

(viii) Required probability of getting 2 slave cards

$$= \frac{{}^{12}C_2 \times {}^{40}C_2}{{}^{52}C_4}$$

(ix) Required probability of getting all are numbers cards

$$= \frac{{}^{36}C_4}{{}^{52}C_4}$$

(x) Required probability of getting all are same number cards

$$= \frac{{}^4C_4 \times 9}{{}^{52}C_4}$$

Ex.8: A natural number x is choen at random from first 100 natural number. Find the probability of getting

(i) an even number.
(ii) an odd number.
(iii) a prime number.
(iv) a perfect number.
(v) a number which have only three factors.
(vi) a number which have only four factors.
(vii) a perfact square.
(viii) a perfect cube.
(ix) a perfect fourth power.
(x) a perfect sixth prower.

Sol. (i) Required probability of getting an even number

$$= \frac{50}{100} = \frac{1}{2}$$

(ii) Required probability of getting an odd number

$$= \frac{50}{100} = \frac{1}{2}$$

(iii) Required probability of getting a prime number

$$= \frac{24}{100} = \frac{6}{25}$$

(iv) Required probability of getting a perfect number

$$= \frac{2}{100} = \frac{1}{50}$$

(v) Required probability of getting a number which have three factors only. $= \frac{4}{100} = \frac{1}{25}$

(vi) Required probability of getting a number which have only 4-factors $= \frac{30}{100} = \frac{3}{10}$

(those numbers are 6, 8, 10, 14, 15, 21, 22, 26, 27, 33, 34, 35, 38, 46, 51, 55, 57, 58, 65, 69, 74, 78, 82, 85, 86, 87, 89, 91, 94, 95}

(vii) Required probability of getting a perfect square is

$$= \frac{10}{100} = \frac{1}{10}$$

(viii) Required probability of getting a perfect cube is $= \frac{3}{100}$

(ix) Required probability of getting a perfect fourth power

$$= \frac{2}{100} = \frac{1}{50}$$

(x) Required probability of getting a perfect sixth power

$$= \frac{2}{100} = \frac{1}{50}$$

Ex.9: Two natural numbers are drawn at random from 100 natural numbers. Find the probability that

(i) both are divisible by 2 and 3

(ii) both are divisible by 3 and 4.

(iii) both are divisible by 3 and 7.

(iv) both are divisible by 3 and 5

(v) one is divisible by 2 and another one is divisible by 5.

(vi) their sum is 10.

(vii) their product is 10.

(viii) both are perfect numbers.

(ix) both the numbers are less than 11 and having difference 2.

(x) sum of the squares of both the numbers is a square of another number.

Sol. Here, $S=\{1,2,..,100\}$

(i) Let A be the event which is divisible by both 2 and 3.

$=\{6,12,18,....................................,96\}$

Then the probability of A is

$$=P(A)=\frac{n(A)}{n(S)}=\frac{^{16}C_2}{^{100}C_2}=\frac{16\times15}{100\times99}=\frac{1}{5\times33}=\frac{1}{165}.$$

(ii) Let B be the event which is divisible by both 3 and 4.

$=\{12,24,...............................,96\}$

Then the probability of B is

$$=P(B)=\frac{n(A)}{n(S)}=\frac{^{8}C_2}{^{100}C_2}=\frac{8\times7}{100\times99}=\frac{7}{2475}$$

(iii) Let C be the event which is divisible by 3 and 7 $=\{21,42,63,84\}$

Then the probability of C is

$$P(C)=\frac{n(A)}{n(S)}=\frac{^{4}C_2}{^{100}C_2}=\frac{4\times3}{100\times99}=\frac{1}{25\times33}=\frac{1}{825}$$

(iv) Let D be the event which ios divisible by both 3 and 5.

$=\{15,30,..............................,90\}$

Then the probability of D is

$$P(D)=\frac{n(A)}{n(S)}=\frac{^{6}C_2}{^{100}C_2}=\frac{6\times5}{100\times99}=\frac{1}{330}.$$

(v) Let E be the event , whose first outcome is divsible by 2 and 2nd outcome is div by 5.

Then the probability of E is

$$=P(E)=\frac{^{50}C_1\times{}^{10}C_1}{^{100}C_2}=\frac{50\times10\times2}{100\times99}=\frac{10}{99}$$

(vi) Let F be the event , whose sum is 10

$=\{(1,9),(2,8),(3,7),(4,6),(5,5),(6,4),(7,3),(8,2),(9,1)\}$

Then the probability of F is

$$P(F)=\frac{^{9}C_2}{^{100}C_2}=\frac{9\times8}{100\times99}=\frac{2}{275}$$

(vii) Let G be the event , whose product of the integer is 10.

$=\{(1,10),(2,5),(5,2),(10,1)\}$.

Then the probability of G is

$$=P(G)=\frac{^{4}C_2}{^{100}C_2}=\frac{4\times3}{100\times99}=\frac{1}{825}$$

(viii) Let H be the event , where both integers are perfect numbers.

$=\{6,28\}$

Then the probability of H is

$$=P(H)=\frac{^{2}C_2}{^{100}C_2}=\frac{1\times2}{100\times99}=\frac{1}{4950}$$

(ix) Let I be the event , where both integers are less than 11 and their differenece is 2.

$=\{(1,3,),(3,1),(2,4),(4,2),(3,5),(5,3),(4,6),(6,4),(5,7),(7,5),(7,9),(9,7),(8,10),(10,8)\}$

Then the probability of I is

$$=P(I)=\frac{^{12}C_2}{^{100}C_2}=\frac{12\times11}{100\times99}=\frac{3}{25\times9}=\frac{1}{75}.$$

(x) Let J be the event , where sum of the squares of both the numbers is a square of another number

$=\{(3,4,5),(6,8,10)\}$

Then the probability of J is

$$=P(J)=\frac{2}{^{100}C_2}=\frac{2\times2}{100\times99}=\frac{1}{25\times99}=\frac{1}{2475}.$$

Ex.10: Two balls are drawn at random from a bag containing 4 red and 6 black balls.. Find the probability that

(i) both are red

(ii) both are black.

(iii) one is red and another one is black.

(iv) either both are red or both are black.

Sol. (i) Required probability $=\frac{^{4}C_2}{^{10}C_2}=\frac{4\times3}{10\times9}=\frac{2}{15}$

(ii) Required probability $=\frac{^{6}C_2}{^{10}C_2}=\frac{6\times5}{10\times9}=\frac{1}{3}$

(iii) Required probability

$$=\frac{^{4}C_1\times{}^{6}C_1}{^{10}C_2}=\frac{4\times6\times2}{10\times9}=\frac{2\times2\times2}{5\times3}=\frac{8}{15}$$

(iv) Required probability

$$=\frac{^{4}C_2+{}^{6}C_2}{^{10}C_2}=\frac{4\times3+6\times5}{10\times9}=\frac{12+30}{90}=\frac{42}{90}=\frac{7}{15}$$

Ex.11: A natural no. x is selected at random from first 100 natural numbers . Find the probability that x satisfies the equation (s)

(i) $x^2-3x\le 30$

(ii) $\frac{(x-40)(x-60)}{(x-20)}<0$

(iii) $x^2-16\ge 0$ and $x^2-81\le 0$.

Sol. (i) Given in-equation is $x^2-3x\le 10$

$\Rightarrow \quad x^2-3x-10\le 0$

$\Rightarrow \quad (x-5)(x+2)\le 0$

$\Rightarrow \quad -2\le x\le 5$

$\Rightarrow \quad x=1,2,3,4,5$

Hence, the required probability is $=\dfrac{5}{100}=\dfrac{1}{20}$

(ii) Given in-equation is $\dfrac{(x-40)(x-60)}{(x-20)}<0$

$\Rightarrow \dfrac{(x-40)(x-60)}{(x-20)}<0 \Rightarrow x\in(1,20)\cup(40,60)$

Hence, the required probability is $=\dfrac{37}{100}$

(iii) Given in - equations are $x^2-16\,^3\,0$ and $x^2-81\le 0$.

$\Rightarrow (x+4)(x-4)\ge 0$ and $(x+9)(x-9)\le 0$

$\Rightarrow \quad x\in[1,4]\cup[1,9]$

Hence, the required probability is $=\dfrac{13}{100}$.

Ex.12: In a hand of bridge, what is the chance that the 4 kings are held by a specified player?

Sol. Hence the required probability is $=\dfrac{{}^4C_4\times{}^{48}C_9}{{}^{52}C_{13}}=\dfrac{{}^{48}C_9}{{}^{52}C_{13}}$.

Ex.13: What is the chance of getting a total of less than 12 on throwing a die two times?

Sol. Hence, the required probability is $=1-\dfrac{1}{36}=\dfrac{35}{36}$.

Ex.14: If 12 persons are seated at a round table . What is the chance that two perticular person sit together?

Sol. Hence the required probability is $=\dfrac{(11)!\times(2)!}{(12)!}=\dfrac{1}{6}$

Ex.15: 6 boys and 6 girls sit in a row randomly, find the probability that all 6 girls sit together.

Sol. Hence, the required probability is $=\dfrac{(7)!\times(6)!}{(12)!}$

Ex-16. There are 5 envelopes corresponding to 5 letters . If the letters are placed in the envelope at random , what is the probability that all the letters are not placed in the right envelopes?

Sol. Hence the required probability is $=1-\dfrac{1}{(5)!}=\dfrac{119}{120}$

Ex.17: The letters of the word 'IIT' are palced at random. Find the probability that '2' vowels come together.

Sol. Hence, the required probability is

$$=\dfrac{(2)!\times\dfrac{(2)!}{(2)!}}{\dfrac{(3)!}{(2)!}}=\dfrac{4}{6}=\dfrac{2}{3}$$

Ex.18: In a random arrangement of the letters of the word 'AIEEE', what is the chance that 3 E's come together.

Sol. Hence, the required probability is

$$=\dfrac{(3)!\times\dfrac{(3)!}{(3)!}}{\dfrac{(5)!}{(3)!}}=\dfrac{36}{120}=\dfrac{3}{10}$$

Ex.19: There are 6 persons are seated at a row. Find the probability that '2' persons always sit together.

Sol. Hence, the required probability is

$$=\dfrac{(5)!\times(2)!}{(6)!}=\dfrac{2}{6}=\dfrac{1}{3}$$

Ex.20: In a science conference hall, there are 5 Indians Scientist, 10 American Scientists and 8 Latian American Scientists are seated in a row. What is the chance that all persons of the same naticnality will sit together ?

Sol. Hence, the required probability is

$$=\dfrac{(5)!\times(10)!\times(8)!\times(3)!}{(23)!}$$

Ex.21: In a class there are 6 boys and 4 girls are seated in a row. Find the probability that no boy is between two girls.

Sol. Hence, the required probability is $=\dfrac{(7)!\times(4)!}{(10)!}$

Ex.22: In a differrent arrangement of the letters of the word 'BANANA' , what is the chance that two N's do not appear adjacently?

Sol. Hence, the required probability is

$$=\dfrac{\dfrac{(6)!}{(2)!\times(3)!}-\dfrac{(5)!}{(3)!}}{\dfrac{(6)!}{(2)!\times(3)!}}=\dfrac{60-20}{50}=\dfrac{40}{60}=\dfrac{2}{3}.$$

Ex.23: In a random arrangement of the letters of the word 'SUCCESS', find the probabbility that all S's do not come together.

Sol. Hence, the required probability is

$$=\dfrac{\dfrac{(7)!}{(2)!\times(3)!}-\dfrac{(5)!}{(2)!}\times\dfrac{(3)!}{(3)!}}{\dfrac{(7)!}{(2)!\times(3)!}}=\dfrac{7\times60-60}{7\times60}=\dfrac{6\times60}{7\times60}=\dfrac{6}{7}$$

Ex.24: In a class there are 4 girls and 6 boys. Find the probability that they will be seated in a row so that all the four girls are not together.

Sol. Hence, the required probability is $=\dfrac{(6)!\times{}^7P_4}{(10)!}$.

Ex.25: In a class there 10 boys and 9 girls. Find the probability that they will be seated in a row so that they are alternate.

Sol. Hence, the required probability is $=\dfrac{(10)!\times(9)!}{(19)!}$

Ex.26: In a class 5 boys and 5 girls. Find the probability that they will be seated in a row so that boys and girls are alternate.

Sol. Hence, the required probability is $= \dfrac{(5)!\times(5)!\times 2}{(10)!}$

7.11 Addition theorem on Probability

Theorem : If A and B be any two events of a sample space S, then

$$P(A\cup B)=P(A)+P(B)-P(A\cap B)$$

Proof : We have, n(A È B) = n(A) + n(B) – n(A Ç B)

$$\Rightarrow \quad \frac{n(A\cup B)}{n(S)}=\frac{n(A)}{n(S)}+\frac{n(B)}{n(S)}-\frac{n(A\cap B)}{n(S)}$$

$$\Rightarrow \quad P(A\cup B)=P(A)+P(B)-P(A\cap B).$$

NOTE :

(i) If A and B are mutually exclusive events, then $P(A\cup B) = P(A)+P(B)$.

(ii) If A, B and C are any three events, then $P(A\cup B\cup C)= P(A)+P(B)+P(C)-P(A\cap B)-P(A\cap C)-P(B\cap C)+ P(A\cap B\cap C)$

(iii) If A, B and C are three mutually exclusive events, then $P(A\cup B\cup C)=P(A)+P(B)+P(C)$.

(iv) Probability of an event altleast one of A and B is $P(A\cup B)$.

(v) $P(A-B)=P(A)-P(A\cap B)$

Ex.1: A natural number is chosen at random from first 100 natural numbers. Find the probability that it is divisible by 2 or 3.

Sol. Here, $S=\{1,2,3,\ldots\ldots,100\}$

Let A be the event, where the natural numbers is divisible by $2=\{2,4,6,\ldots\ldots,100\}$ and B be the event, where the natural numbers is divisible by both 3.

$=\{3,6,9,\ldots\ldots,99\}$. and

$A\cap B$ is the evnt, which is divisible by both 2 and 3.

$=\{6,12,18,\ldots\ldots,96\}$

Hence, the required probability

= P(A or B) = P(A È B) = P(A) + P(B) – P($A\cap B$)

$$=\frac{50}{100}+\frac{33}{100}-\frac{16}{100}=\frac{67}{100}.$$

Ex.2: A natural number is chosen at random from first 200 natural numbers. Find the probability that it is divisible by 3 or 4 or 5.

Sol. Here, $S=\{1,2,3,\ldots\ldots,200\}$

Let A be the event, where the natural numbers is divisible by 3.

$=\{3,6,\ldots\ldots198\}$,

B be the event, where the natural number is divisible by $4=\{4,8,12,\ldots\ldots,200\}$ and C be the event, where the natural number is divisible by 5.

$=\{5,10,15,\ldots\ldots,200\}$

Hence, the required probability = P(A or B or C)

$= P(A\cup B\cup C) = P(A) + P(B) + P(C) - P(A\cap B) - P(B\cap C)-P(C\cap A)+P(A\cap B\cap C)$

$$=\frac{66}{200}+\frac{50}{200}+\frac{40}{200}-\frac{16}{200}-\frac{13}{200}-\frac{10}{200}+\frac{3}{200}$$

$$=\frac{120}{200}=\frac{3}{5}$$

Ex.3. A card is drawn at random from a pack of 52 cards. Find the probability that it is a court card or a face card.

Sol. Hence, the required probability

$=P(C \text{ or } F)=P(C\cup F)$

$=P(C)+P(F)-P(C\cup F)$

$$=\frac{{}^{16}C_1}{{}^{52}C_1}+\frac{{}^{12}C_1}{{}^{52}C_1}-\frac{{}^{12}C_1}{{}^{52}C_1}=\frac{16}{52}=\frac{4}{13}$$

Ex.4: A card is drawn from a pack of 52 cards . Find the probability that , the card drawn is a King or a Heart card or a Red Card.

Sol. Required Probability $=P(K\cup H\cup R)$

$=P(K)+P(H)+P(R)-P(K\cap H)-P(K\cap R)-P(H\cap R)+P(K\cap H\cap R)$

$$=\frac{4}{52}+\frac{13}{52}+\frac{26}{52}-\frac{1}{52}-\frac{2}{52}-\frac{13}{52}+\frac{1}{52}$$

$$=\frac{28}{52}=\frac{7}{13}.$$

Ex.5. A die is thrown twice. Find the probability that the sum of the numbers of the two faces is divisible by 4 or 5.

Sol. Here, $S=\{(1,1),(1,2),(1,3),\ldots\ldots,(6,6)\}$

Let A be the event where the sum of the numbers of two faces is divisible by 4

$=\{(1,3),(3,1),(2,2),(2,6),(6,2),(3,5),(5,3),(4,4),(6,6)\}$, B be the event, where the sum of the numbers of two faces is divisible by 5.

$=\{(1,4),(4,1),(2,3),(3,2),(4,6),(6,4),(5,5)\}$

Clearly A and B are mutuall exclusive events. Thus, the required probability

$$=P(A\cup B)=P(A)+P(B)=\frac{9}{36}+\frac{7}{36}=\frac{16}{36}=\frac{4}{9}$$

Ex.6: A die is thrown two times. Find the probability that atleast one of them shows the number 3.

Sol. Here, $S=\{1,1),(1,2),(1,3),\ldots\ldots,(6,6)\}$

Let A be the event , where the first die always shows 3

$=\{(3,1),(3,2),\ldots\ldots,(3,6)\}$

B be the event where the second die always shows 3

$=\{(1,3),(2,3),\ldots\ldots,(6,3)\}$ and A Ç B be the event where both the die always shows 3.

$=\{(3,3)\}$

Hence, the required probability $=P(A\cup B)=P(A)+P(B)-P(A\cap B)$

$$=\frac{6}{36}+\frac{6}{36}-\frac{1}{36}=\frac{11}{36}.$$

Ex.7: A dis is thrown two times. Find the probability of getting an odd number on the first die or a total of 7 .

Sol. Here, $S=\{\{1,1),(1,2),(1,3), \ldots\ldots\ldots\ldots\ldots, (6,6)\}$

Let A be the event , where the first die always shows odd numbers.

$=\{(1,1),(1,2),\ldots\ldots,(1,6),(3,1),\ldots\ldots,(5,1),\ldots\ldots(5,6),\}$

B be the event , where the sum of two outcome is 7.

$=\{(1,6),(6,1),(2,5),(5,2),(3,4),(4,3)\}$ and $A\cap B$ be the event, where first die is an odd number and sum of the outcome is a 7.

$=\{(1,6),(3,4),(5,2)\}$

Hence, the required probability

$$=P(A\cup B)=P(A)+P(B)-P(A\cup B)$$

$$=\frac{18}{36}+\frac{6}{36}-\frac{3}{36}=\frac{21}{36}=\frac{7}{12}$$

Ex.8: If two dice are thrown simultaneously, find the probability of the sum of the numbers coming up is greater than 9.

Sol. Here, $S=\{1,1),(1,2),(1,3), \ldots\ldots\ldots\ldots\ldots, (6,6)\}$

Let A be the event , where the sum of the numbers is coming up more that 9.

$=\{(4,6),(6,4),(5,5),(5,6),(6,5),(6,6)\}$

Hence, the require probability $=\frac{6}{36}=\frac{1}{6}$

Ex.9: The probability of a student selected in IIT is 1/3 and in AIEEE is 1/2. Find the probability that he/she will get chance either of them.

Sol. Hence the required probability

$=P(I\cup A)=P(I)+P(A)-P(I\cap A)$

$=\frac{1}{3}+\frac{1}{2}-\frac{1}{6}=\frac{4}{6}=\frac{2}{3}.$

Ex.10: Four cards are drawn from a pack of 52 cards . Find the probability that , the drawn cards are of the same suit.

Sol. Required Probability $=P(S\cup C\cup H\cup D)$

$=P(S)+P(C)+P(H)+P(D)$

$$=\frac{{}^{13}C_4}{{}^{52}C_4}+\frac{{}^{13}C_4}{{}^{52}C_4}+\frac{{}^{13}C_4}{{}^{52}C_4}+\frac{{}^{13}C_4}{{}^{52}C_4}$$

$$=\frac{4\times {}^{13}C_4}{{}^{52}C_4}.$$

Ex.11: The pobability of a student passing in Maths is 1/3 and Physics is 1/4 and the probability of passing both in physics and maths is 1/5 . Find the probability that the student will pass at-least one of the subject and none of the subject.

Sol. Hence, the required probability.

$=P(M\cup P)$

$=P(M)+P(P)-P(P\cap M)$

$$=\frac{1}{3}+\frac{1}{4}-\frac{1}{5}=\frac{20+15-12}{60}=\frac{23}{60}$$

7.12 Inequalities in Probability :

Let S be a sample space and A and B be two events associated with the same sample space.

1. If A is a proper subset of B i.e $A\subset B$, then $P(A)\le P(B)$
2. $P(AB)\le P(A)\le P(A\cup B)\le P(A)+P(B)$
3. $\max\{P(A),P(B)\}\le P(A\cup B)\le \min\{1,(P(A)+P(B))\}$
4. **Bon-ferroni's Inequality**
   (i) $P(A)+P(B)-1\le P(AB)\le \min\{P(A),P(B)\}$
   (ii) $\max\{0,(1-P(\bar{A})-P(\bar{B}))\}\le P(AB)$
5. **Boole's Inequality :**
   For a finite set of events $A_1, A_2, \ldots\ldots\ldots\ldots\ldots\ldots, A_n$
   $P(A_1\cup A_2\cup \ldots\ldots\ldots\ldots\cup A_n)\le P(A_1)+P(A_2)+\ldots\ldots\ldots+P(A_n)$

Ex.1: If $P(A)=\frac{3}{5}$ and $P(B)=\frac{2}{3}$, then prove that

(i) $P(A\cup B)\ge\frac{2}{3}$

(ii) $\frac{4}{15}\le P(A\cap B)\le\frac{3}{5}$

Sol. (i) From the definition of in-equalities of probability, we can write $P(A\cup B)\ge P(B)$

$\Rightarrow\quad P(A\cup B)\ge\frac{2}{3}$

(ii) From the definition of in-equalities of probability, we can write $P(A\cap B)\le P(A)$

$\Rightarrow\quad P(A\cap B)\le\frac{3}{5}$

Also, $P(A\cap B)=P(A)+P(B)-P(A\cap B)\ge P(A)+P(B)-1$

$\Rightarrow\quad P(A\cap B)\ge\frac{3}{5}+\frac{2}{3}-1=\frac{9+10-15}{15}=\frac{4}{15}$

Hence from the above two relation,

we get, $\frac{4}{15}\le P(A\cap B)\le\frac{3}{5}.$

Ex.2: If $P(A)=\frac{3}{4}$ and $P(B)=\frac{3}{8}$, then prove that

(i) $P(A\cup B)\ge\frac{1}{8}$

(ii) $\frac{1}{8}\le P(A\cap B)\le\frac{3}{4}$

Sol. (i) From the definition of in-equalities of probability, we can write,

$$P(A\cup B)\ge P(A)+P(B)-1=\frac{3}{4}+\frac{3}{8}-1=\frac{6+3-8}{8}=\frac{1}{8}.$$

(ii) From the definition of in-equalities of probability, we can write, $P(A)+P(B)-1\le P(A\cap B)\le P(A)$

$\Rightarrow\ \frac{1}{8}\le P(A\cap B)\le\frac{3}{4}.$

7.13 Conditional Probability

Let A and B be two events associated with the same sample space S . The conditional probability of an event A under B , where B is already occurred, is denoted as $P\left(\frac{A}{B}\right)$ and is defined as

$$P\left(\frac{A}{B}\right)=\frac{P(A\cap B)}{P(B)},\ P(B)\neq 0$$

that means we shall find out the probability of $(A\cap B)$ in B.

7.13.1 Properties of Conditional Probability

Prop-I: If A be any non empty event of a sample space S, then $P(S/A)=1$

Proof: From the definition of conditional probability, we have,

$$P(S/A)=\frac{P(S\cap A)}{P(A)}=\frac{P(A)}{P(A)}=1$$

Prop-II: If A and B be any two events of sample space S such that $P(A)\neq 0$\

then $P\left(\frac{(A\cup B)}{A}\right)=P\left(\frac{A}{A}\right)+P\left(\frac{B}{A}\right)-P\left(\frac{(A\cap B)}{A}\right)$

Proof: We have, $P\left(\frac{(A\cup B)}{A}\right)=\frac{P((A\cup B)\cap A)}{P(A)}$

$$=\frac{P((A\cap A)\cup(A\cap B))}{P(A)}$$

$$=\frac{P(A\cap A)+P(A\cap B)-P(A\cap B\cap A)}{P(A)}$$

$$=\frac{P(A\cap A)}{P(A)}+\frac{P(A\cap B)}{P(A)}-\frac{P((A\cap B)\cap A)}{P(A)}$$

$$=P\left(\frac{A}{A}\right)+P\left(\frac{B}{A}\right)-P\left(\frac{(A\cap B)}{A}\right)$$

Hence, the result.

Prop-III: If A and B be any two events of a sample space S such that $P(A)\neq 0$

then, $P\left(\frac{B'}{A}\right)=1-P\left(\frac{B}{A}\right)$

Proof: As we know that, $P\left(\frac{S}{A}\right)=1$

$\Rightarrow\ P\left(\frac{B\cup B'}{A}\right)=1$

$\Rightarrow\ P\left(\frac{B}{A}\right)+P\left(\frac{B'}{A}\right)=1$, since B and B are mutually exclusive events.

$\Rightarrow\ P\left(\frac{B'}{A}\right)=1-P\left(\frac{B}{A}\right)$

Hence, the result.

Ex.1: A die is rolled. If the outcome is an odd number, find the probability that, it is a prime.

Sol. Let $S=\{1,2,3,4,5,6\}$ and $B=\{1,3,5\}$ & $A=\{2,3,5\}$

Required Probability $=P\left(\frac{A}{B}\right)=\frac{P(A\cap B)}{P(B)}=\frac{2}{3}$.

Ex.2: A pair of dice is thrown. Find the probability of getting 7 as the sum, if it is known that the second die always exhibits a prime number.

Sol. Let $S=\{(1,1),(1,2),.........................,(6,6)\}$

$B=\{(1,2),..........(6,2),(1,3),........,(6,3),(1,5),...........,(6,5)\}$

and $A=\{(2,6),(6,2),(3,5),(5,3),(4,4)\}$.

Required Probability $=\frac{P(A\cap B)}{P(B)}=\frac{3}{5}$.

Ex.3: Two dice are thrown. Find the probability that sum of the numbers coming up on them is 9, if it is known that the mumber 5 always occurs on the first die.

Sol. Here, $S=\{(1,1),(1,2),...............(6,6)\}$

Let A be the event, the sum of the numbers coming up is 9 $=\{(3,6),(6,3),(5,4),(4,5)\}$ and

B be the event, where first will shows5 $=\{(5,1),(5,1),(5,3),...........(5,6)\}$

$A\cap B$ be the event, where sum of two outcomes is 9 and first die shows 5. $=\{(5,4)\}$

Hence, the required probability $=P\left(\frac{A}{B}\right)=\frac{P(A\cap B)}{P(B)}=\frac{1}{6}$.

Ex.4: Two coins are tossed. What is the chance of coming up of two heads, if it is known that at least one heads comes up ?

Sol. Here, $S=\{(1,1),(1,2),...............(6,6)\}$

Let A be the event of coming up two heads $=\{(H,H)\}$ and B be the event of coming up atleast one head $=\{(H,H),(H,T),(T,H)\}$

Hence, the required probability

$$=P\left(\frac{A}{B}\right)=\frac{P(A\cap B)}{P(B)}=\frac{1}{3}$$

Ex.5: A card is drawn at random from a pack of 52 cards. What is the chance that it is a king if it is known that red card is drawn?

Sol. Let A be the event of drawing a King card and B be the event of drawing a red card.

Hence, the required probability

$$=P\left(\frac{A}{B}\right)=\frac{P(A\cap B)}{P(B)}=\frac{{}^{2}C_1}{{}^{26}C_1}=\frac{2}{26}=\frac{1}{13}$$

7.14 Independent Events

Two events are said to be independent if the ocurrence (non occurrence) of one does not affect the other one.

A coin is tossed two times. The outcome of first head does not affect the outcome of second head.

So the outcome of the first head and second head are independent events.

Theorem : If A and B are two independent events , then

$$P(A\cap B)=P(A).P(B).$$

Proof: As we know that , if A and B any events of same sample space S, then

$$P\left(\frac{A}{B}\right)=\frac{P(A\cap B)}{P(B)}.$$

If A and B are independent events , then

$$P\left(\frac{A}{B}\right)=P(A)$$

Thus , $P(A\cap B)=P(A).P(B)$.

Deduction -1: If A and B are independent events , then A and B` are independent events

i.e. $P(A\cap B')=P(A).P(B')$

Proof : We have,

$$P(A\cap B')=P(A)-P(A\cap B)=P(A)-P(A)P(B)$$
$$=P(A)(1-P(B))=P(A)P(B')$$

Deduction-2: If A and B are two independent events , then A` and B are independent events .

i.e. $P(A'\cap B)=P(A')P(B)$

Proof : We have ,

$$P(A'\cap B)=P(B)-P(A\cap B)=P(B)-P(A).P(B)$$
$$=P(B).(1-P(A))=P(B).P(A')$$

Deduction - 3: If A and B are two independent events , then A `and B`are independent events .

i.e. $P(A'\cap B')=P(A').P(B')$

Proof : We have, $P(A'\cap B')=P((A\cup B)')=1-P(A\cup B)$

$$=1-[P(A)+P(B)-P(A)P(B)]$$
$$=1-P(A)-P(B)+P(A).P(B)$$
$$=(1-P(A))-P(B)(1-P(A))$$
$$=(1-P(A))(1-P(B))$$
$$=P(A').P(B').$$

Deduction - 4: If Aand B are independent events such that

$$P(B)\neq\phi\text{ ,then } P\left(\frac{A}{B}\right)+P\left(\frac{A'}{B}\right)=1.$$

Proof : We have , $P\left(\frac{A}{B}\right)+P\left(\frac{A'}{B}\right)$

$$=\frac{P(A\cap B)}{P(B)}+\frac{P(A'\cap B)}{P(B)}$$
$$=\frac{P(A\cap B)+P(A'\cap B)}{P(B)}$$
$$=\frac{P(B)}{P(B)}\ (\because (A\cap B)\cup(A'\cap B)=B\ )$$
$$=1.$$

Ex.1: A bag contains 3 white and 2 black balls and another bag contains 3 white and 5 black balls . If one ball is drawn from each bag , find the probability that

(i) both are white

(ii) both are black

(iii) one is white and one is black.

Sol. We have, Bag1 $\rightarrow$ (4 W, 2B)

and Bag 2 $\rightarrow$ (3 W, 5B)

Here, $W_1 \& W_2$ and $B_1 \& B_2$ are independents.

(i) $P(W_1\cap W_2)=P(W_1).P(W_2)=\frac{4}{6}\times\frac{3}{8}=\frac{1}{4}$

(ii) $P(B_1\cap B_2)=P(B_1).P(B_2)=\frac{1}{3}\times\frac{5}{8}=\frac{5}{24}$

(iii) $P((W_1\cap B_2)\cup(W_2\cap B_1))=P(W_1\cap B_2)+P(W_2\cap B_1)$

$$=P(W_1).P(B_2)+P(W_2).P(B_1)$$
$$=\frac{2}{3}\times\frac{5}{8}+\frac{1}{3}\times\frac{3}{8}=\frac{5}{12}+\frac{1}{8}=\frac{13}{24}$$

Ex.2: A problem in mathematics is given to 3 students whose chances of solving it are 1/2, 1/3 ,1/4 . What is the probability that the problem is solved ?

Sol. Let three students are A, B, C.

Consider the problem is not solved by any one of them.

Thus $P(\bar{A}\cap\bar{B}\cap\bar{C})$

$$=P(\bar{A}).P(\bar{B}).P(\bar{C})=\left(1-\frac{1}{2}\right).\left(1-\frac{1}{3}\right).\left(1-\frac{1}{4}\right)$$
$$=\frac{1}{2}.\frac{2}{3}.\frac{3}{4}=\frac{1}{4}$$

Hence , the required probability is $=1-\frac{1}{4}=\frac{3}{4}$:

Ex.3: A speak truth in 75% cases and B in 80% of the cases . In what percentage of the cases are they likely to contradict each other in stating the same fact ?

Sol. Hence, the required probability

$$=P(A\cap\bar{B}\text{ or }\bar{A}\cap B)=P(A\cap\bar{B})+P(\bar{A}\cap B)$$
$$=P(A)\,P(\bar{B})+P(\bar{A})\,P(B)$$
$$=\frac{75}{100}\times\frac{20}{100}+\frac{25}{100}\times\frac{80}{100}$$
$$=\frac{15}{100}+\frac{20}{100}=\frac{7}{20}$$

Ex.4: Three students appear at an examination of JEE - Advanced . The probabilities of their success are $\frac{1}{3},\frac{1}{4},\frac{1}{5}$ respectively. Find the probability of success of at-least two.

Sol. Let three students are A, B, C respectively.

Hence, the required probability

$$= P(A\cap B\cap \bar{C})+P(A\cap \bar{B}\cap C)$$
$$+P(\bar{A}\cap B\cap C)+P(A\cap B\cap C)$$
$$= P(A).P(B).P(\bar{C})+P(A).P(B).P(\bar{C})$$
$$+P(A)P(\bar{B})P(C)$$
$$+P(\bar{A})P(B).P(C)+P(A)P(B)P(C)$$
$$=\frac{1}{3}.\frac{1}{4}\left(1-\frac{1}{5}\right)+\frac{1}{3}\left(1-\frac{1}{4}\right).\frac{1}{5}+\left(1-\frac{1}{3}\right).\frac{1}{4}.\frac{1}{5}+\frac{1}{3}.\frac{1}{4}.\frac{1}{5}$$
$$=\frac{4}{60}+\frac{2}{60}+\frac{3}{60}+\frac{1}{60}=\frac{10}{60}=\frac{1}{6}$$

Ex.5: A person is known to hit a target 3 out of 4 times and another person hit the target 2 out of 3 times. Find the probability that the target will be hit when they both try.

Sol. Let two persons be A and B respectively.

Consider none of them hit the target.

Now, $P(\bar{A}\cap \bar{B})=P(\bar{A})\times P(\bar{B})$

$$=\left(1-\frac{3}{4}\right)\times\left(1-\frac{2}{3}\right)=\frac{1}{12}$$

Hence, the required probability

$$=1-\frac{1}{12}=\frac{11}{12}.$$

Ex.6: A and B throw alternately with a pair of dice. A wins if he throws 6 before B throws 7 and B wins if he throws 7 before A throws 6. Find the chance of winning if A makes the first throw.

Sol. Let E_1 be the of throwing 6 with a pair of dice and E_2 be the event of throwing 7 with a pair of dice

Thus, $E_1=\{(1,5),(5,1),(2,4),(4,2),(3,3)\}$

and $E_2=\{(1,6),(6,1),(2,5),(5,2),(3,4),(4,3)\}$

The probability of A can win =

$$P(A)=P(E_1 \text{ or } \overline{E_1}.\overline{E_2}.E_1 \text{ or } \overline{E_1}.\overline{E_2}.\overline{E_1}.\overline{E_2}.E_1 \text{ or}.........)$$

$$=\frac{5}{36}+\frac{31}{36}.\frac{5}{6}.\frac{5}{36}+\left(\frac{31}{36}\right)^2\left(\frac{5}{6}\right)^2\left(\frac{5}{36}\right)+...............\text{to } \infty$$

$$=\frac{5}{36}+\left(\frac{155}{216}\right).\frac{5}{36}+\left(\frac{155}{216}\right)^2\left(\frac{5}{36}\right)+...............\text{to } \infty$$

$$=\frac{\frac{5}{36}}{1-\frac{155}{216}}=\frac{30}{61}$$

The probability that B can win $=1-\frac{30}{61}=\frac{31}{61}$

7.15 Total Probability

Theorem : Let $E_1, E_2, E_3......E_n$ are n mutually exclusive and exhaustive events associated with the same sample space S. If A is any event, which occurs either of $E_1 \text{ or } E_2 \text{ or } E_3 \text{ or} .... \text{or } E_n$, then

$$P(A)=P(E_1)P(A/E_1)+P(E_2)P(A/E_2)+....+P(E_n)P(A/E_n)$$

Proof:

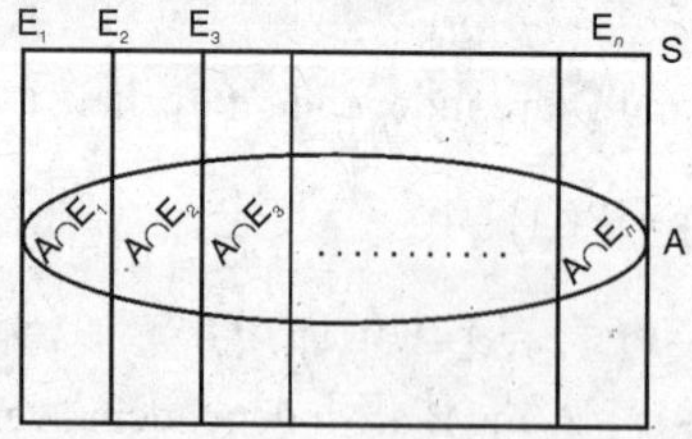

Since $E_1, E_2, E_3, ..., E_n$ are n mutually exclusive and exhaustive events,

then $E_i\cap E_j=\phi$ and $E_1\cup E_2\cup E_3\cup ....\cup E_n=S$

Now, $A=A\cap S=A\cap(E_1\cup E_2\cup E_3\cup ....\cup E_n)$

$=(A\cap E_1)\cup(A\cap E_2)\cup ....\cup(A\cap E_n)$

Thus, $P(A)=P((A\cap E_1)\cup(A\cap E_2)\cup ....\cup(A\cap E_n))$

$=P(A\cap E_1)+P(A\cap E_2)+..............+P(A\cap E_n)$

$=P(E_1)P(A/E_1)+P(E_2)P(A/E_2)+$

$...........+P(E_n)P(A/E_n).$

Hence, the result.

Ex.1: A bag contains 4 red and 3 black balls. A second bag contains 2 red and 4 black balls. One bag is selected at random. From the selected bag, one ball is drawn. Find the probability that the ball drawn red.

Sol. Let A be the event that a randomly selected ball is a red. E_1 and E_2 be denote two bags resp.

Then $P(A)=P(E_1)P(A/E_1)+P(E_2)P(A/E_2)$

$$=\frac{1}{2}\times\frac{4}{7}+\frac{1}{2}\times\frac{2}{6}=\frac{2}{7}+\frac{1}{6}=\frac{19}{42}.$$

Ex.2: One bag contains 4 white and 5 black balls. Another bag contains 6 white and 7 black balls. A ball is transferred form the first bag to the second bag and then a ball is drawn from the second bag. Find the probability that the ball drawn is white.

Sol. **Case - I:** When a white ball is transferred from the first bag to a second bag .

Then $P(W)=\frac{4}{9}\times\frac{7}{14}=\frac{2}{9}$

Case - II: When a black ball is transferred from the first bag to a 2nd bag.

Then $P(W)=\frac{4}{9}\times\frac{6}{14}=\frac{2}{3}\times\frac{2}{7}=\frac{4}{21}$

Hence, the reuired probability $=\frac{2}{9}+\frac{4}{21}=\frac{14+12}{63}=\frac{26}{63}.$

Ex.3: A lot contains 20 articles . The probability that the lot contains exactly two defective articles is 0.4 and the probability that the lot contains exactly 3 defective articles is 0.6 . Articles are drawn from the lot at random one by one , without replacement and are tested till all the defective articles are found . What is the probability that the testing procedure ends at the 12th testing ?

Sol. Let E_1, E_2 and A denote the events , the lot contains 2 defective , 3 defective and all the defective articles are found by 12th test.

i.e the event A means that all but one defective article must be found in the first eleven testings.

Now, $P(E_1)=0.4$, $P(E_2)=0.6$

$$P(A/E_1)=\frac{{}^2C_1\times{}^{18}C_{10}}{{}^{20}C_{11}}\times\frac{1}{9}=\frac{11}{190}$$

and $$P(A/E_2)=\frac{{}^3C_2\times{}^{17}C_9}{{}^{20}C_{11}}\times\frac{1}{9}=\frac{11}{228}.$$

Hence the required probability

$$=P(A)=P(E_1)P(A/E_1)+P(E_2)P(A/E_2)$$

$$=(0.4)\left(\frac{11}{190}\right)+(0.6)\left(\frac{11}{228}\right)=\frac{99}{1900}.$$

Ex.4: An urn contains 2 white and 2 black balls . A ball is drawn at random. If it is white , it is not replaced into the urn. Otherwise it is replaced along with another ball of the same color. The process is repeated. Find the probability that the third ball drawn is black.

Sol. Let E_{xy} denote the event that the first ball drawn has color x and second ball drawn has color y and A be the event that the third ball drawn is black.

$$P(E_{ww})=\frac{2}{4}\times\frac{1}{3}=\frac{1}{6},\ P(E_{wb})=\frac{2}{4}\times\frac{2}{3}=\frac{1}{3},$$

$$P(E_{bw})=\frac{2}{4}\times\frac{2}{5}=\frac{1}{5},\ P(E_{bb})=\frac{2}{4}\times\frac{3}{5}=\frac{3}{10}$$

Also, $P(A/E_{ww})=\frac{2}{2}=1$, $P(A/E_{wb})=\frac{3}{4}$,

$$P(A/E_{bw})=\frac{3}{4},\ P(A/E_{bb})=\frac{4}{6}=\frac{2}{3}$$

Hence the required probability $= P(A)$

$$=P(E_{ww}).P(A/E_{ww})+P(E_{wb}).P(A/E_{wb})+$$
$$P(E_{bw}).P(A/E_{bw})+P(E_{bb}).P(A/E_{bb})$$

$$=\frac{1}{6}\times1+\frac{1}{3}\times\frac{3}{4}+\frac{1}{5}\times\frac{3}{4}+\frac{3}{10}\times\frac{2}{3}=\frac{23}{30}.$$

Ex.5: An unbiased coin is tossed . If the result is head , a pair of unbaised dice is rolled and the number obtained by adding the number on the two faces is noted . If the result is a tail , a card from well shuffle pack of eleven cards numbered 2, 3, ..., 12 is picked and the number on the card is noted. What is the probability that the noted number is either 7 or 8 ?

Sol. Let E_1, E_2 denote the events that the coin shows a head, tail and A be the event that the noted number is either 7 or 8.

We have $P(E_1)=\frac{1}{2}$ and $P(E_2)=\frac{1}{2}$

Now, $7\rightarrow\{(1,6),(6,1),(2,5),(5,2),(3,4),(4,3)\}$

and $8\rightarrow\{(2,6),(6,2),(3,5),(5,3),(4,4)\}$

Thus, $P(A/E_1)=\frac{11}{36}$, $P(A/E_2)=\frac{2}{11}$

Hence, the required probability

$$=P(A)=P(E_1)P(A/E_1)+P(E_2)P(A/E_2)$$

$$=\left(\frac{1}{2}\right)\left(\frac{11}{36}\right)+\left(\frac{1}{2}\right)\left(\frac{2}{11}\right)=\frac{193}{792}.$$

Ex.6: An urn contains m white and n black balls. A ball is drawn at random and is put into the urn along with k additional balls of the same color as that of the ball drawn. A ball is again drawn at random. What is the probability that the ball drawn now is white ?

Sol. Let W be the event that a white ball is drawn at the first draw B be the event that a black ball is drawn at the first draw and A be the event that a white ball is drawn at the second draw.

We have, $P(W)=\frac{m}{m+n}$, $P(B)=\frac{n}{m+n}$

and $P(A/W)=\frac{m+k}{m+n+k}$, $P(A/B)=\frac{m}{m+n+k}$

Hence the required probability

$$=P(A)=P(W).P(A/W)+P(B).P(A/B)$$

$$=\frac{m}{m+n}.\frac{m+k}{m+n+k}+\frac{n}{m+n}.\frac{m}{m+n+k}$$

$$=\frac{m}{m+n}.$$

7.16 Bayes Theorem

Statement : Let $E_1, E_2, E_3, ..., E_n$ are n mutually exclusive and exhaustive events associated with the same sample space S. If A is any event, which occurs either of E_1 or E_2 or E_3 or............... or E_n and the probabilities $P(A/E_i)$, i = 1, 2,,........,n , are known ,

then $$P(E_i/A)=\frac{P(E_i)P(A/E_i)}{\sum_{i=1}^{n}P(E_i)P(A/E_i)}.$$

Proof : Here , we shall find out the probability of $(A\cap E_i)$ in the event A , i = 1, 2, 3, ...,n

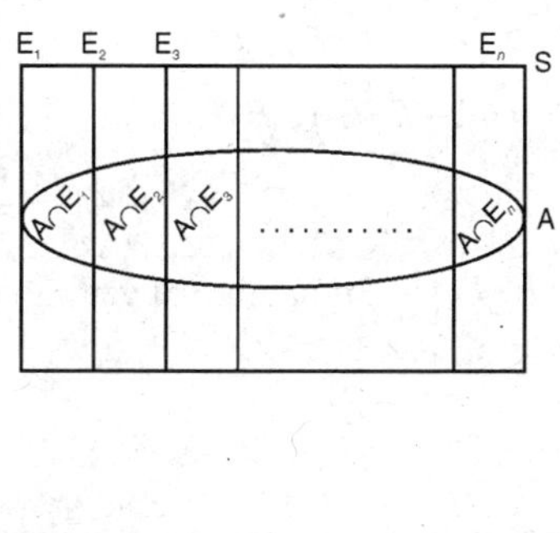

Thus , $P(E_i/A)=\dfrac{P(A\cap E_i)}{P(A)}=\dfrac{P(E_i)\,P(A/E_i)}{\sum\limits_{i=1}^{n} P(E_i)\,P(A/E_i)}$.

Ex.1: A bag contains 3 red and 4 black balls and 2nd bag contains 5 red and 6 black balls . One ball is drawn at random from one of the bags and is found to be red. Find the probability that it was drawn from 2nd bag .

Sol. Hence the required probability

$$=P(E_2/B)=\frac{P(E_2)\,P(A/E_2)}{P(E_1)\,P(A/E_1)+P(E_2)\,P(A/E_2)}$$

$$=\frac{\frac{1}{2}\times\frac{5}{11}}{\frac{1}{2}\times\frac{3}{7}+\frac{1}{2}\times\frac{5}{11}}=\frac{35}{68}.$$

Ex.2: A man is known to speak truth 3 times out of 5 times . He throws a die and reports that it is a six . Find the probability that it is actually six.

Sol. Let A be the event that the man reports that six occurrs on throwing a die.
E_1 is the event that six occurx and E_2 is the event that six does not occur.

$P(E_1)=\frac{1}{6}$ and $P(E_2)=\frac{5}{6}$

$P(A/E_1)=\frac{3}{5}$ and $P(A/E_2)=\frac{2}{5}$

Hence the required probability $=P(E_1/A)$

$$=\frac{P(E_1)P(A/E_1)}{P(E_1)P(A/E_1)+P(E_2)P(A/E_2)}$$

$$=\frac{\frac{1}{6}\times\frac{3}{5}}{\frac{1}{6}\times\frac{3}{5}+\frac{5}{6}\times\frac{2}{5}}=\frac{3}{3+10}=\frac{3}{13}.$$

Ex.3: In a test an examinee either guess or copies or knows the answer to a multiple choice questions with four choices . The probability that he makes a guess is 1/3 and the probability that he copies the answer is 1/6 . The probability that his answer is correct , given that he copied it is 1/8 . Find the probability that he knew the answer to the question , given that he correctly answered it.

Sol. Let E_1, E_2 and E_3 be the events that the answer is guessed , copied and knows the answer and E be the event that the examinee answers correctly.

Given $P(E_1)=\frac{1}{3}$, $P(E_2)=\frac{1}{6}$

Here, E_1, E_2 and E_3 are exhaustive events .

Thus $P(E_1)+P(E_2)+P(E_3)=1$

$\Rightarrow\quad P(E_3)=1-P(E_1)-P(E_2)$

$$=1-\frac{1}{3}-\frac{1}{6}=\frac{6-2-1}{6}=\frac{3}{6}=\frac{1}{2}$$

Now, $P(E/E_1)$ = Probability of getting correct answer by guessing = 1/4

$P(E/E_2)$ = Probability of getting correct answer by copying = 1/8.

$P(E/E_3)$ = Probability of getting correct answer by knowing = 1.

Hence, the required probability $=P(E_3/E)=$

$$\frac{P(E_3).P(E/E_3)}{P(E_1).P(E/E_1)+P(E_2).P(E/E_2)+P(E_3).P(E/E_3)}$$

$$=\frac{\frac{1}{2}\times 1}{\frac{1}{3}\times\frac{1}{4}+\frac{1}{6}\times\frac{1}{8}+\frac{1}{2}\times 1}=\frac{24}{29}\ldots$$

Ex.4: A pack of playing cards was found to contain only 51 cards. If the first 13 cards which are examined are all red. What is the probability that the missing card is a black card.

Sol. Let E_1, E_2 be donote the events that the black and red card are lost. and A denote the event that the ocurrence of 13 cards which are examined and found all are red.

Obviously , $P(E_1)=\frac{1}{2}=P(E_2)$.

Also $P(A/E_1)=\frac{^{26}C_{13}}{^{51}C_{13}}$ and $P(A/E_2)=\frac{^{25}C_{13}}{^{51}C_{13}}$

Hence, the required probability is

$$=P(E_1/A)=\frac{P(E_1)P(A/E_1)}{P(E_1)P(A/E_1)+P(E_2)P(A/E_2)}$$

$$=\frac{\frac{1}{2}\cdot\frac{^{26}C_{13}}{^{51}C_{13}}}{\frac{1}{2}\cdot\frac{^{26}C_{13}}{^{51}C_{13}}+\frac{1}{2}\cdot\frac{^{25}C_{13}}{^{51}C_{13}}}$$

$$=\frac{^{26}C_{13}}{^{26}C_{13}+{^{25}C_{13}}}=\frac{2}{2+1}=\frac{2}{3}.$$

Ex.5: An employer sends a letter to his employee but he does not receive the reply (It is certain that employee would have replied it if he did receive the letter.) It is known that one out of n letters does not reach it destination . Find the probability that employee does not receive the letter...

Sol. Let E be the event that employee receive the letter and A be the event that employer received the reply..

$P(E)=\frac{n-1}{n}$ and $P(\overline{E})=\frac{1}{n}$

$P(A/E)=\frac{n-1}{n}$ and $P(A/\overline{E})=0$

Now, $P(A)=P(E\cap A)+P(\overline{E}\cap A)$

$$=P(E).P(A/E)+P(\overline{E}).P(A/\overline{E})$$

$$=\left(\frac{n-1}{n}\right)\cdot\left(\frac{n-1}{n}\right)+\frac{1}{n}.0=\left(\frac{n-1}{n}\right)^2$$

Thus, $P(\bar{A})=\frac{2n-1}{n^2}$.

Hence, the required probability

$$= P(E/\bar{A})=\frac{P(E\cap\bar{A})}{P(\bar{A})}=\frac{P(E)-P(E\cap A)}{P(\bar{A})}$$

$$=\frac{P(E)-P(E).P(A/E)}{P(\bar{A})}$$

$$=\frac{\left(\frac{n-1}{n}\right)-\left(\frac{n-1}{n}\right).\left(\frac{n-1}{n}\right)}{\frac{2n-1}{n^2}}$$

$$=\frac{n-1}{2n-1}.$$

Ex.6: In a combat between A, B and C , A tries to hit B and C and B and C try to hit A . Probability of A, B and C hitting the tagrets are 2/3, 1/2 and 1/3 respectively . If A is hit , find the probability that B hits and A and C does not.

Sol. We have to find the probability of A being hit by B but not by C.

Thus, P(BC′/A) =

$$\frac{P(BC').P(A/BC')}{P(BC').P(A/BC')+P(B'C).P(A/B'C)+P(BC).P(A/BC)+P(B'C').P(A/B'C')}$$

$$=\frac{1.\frac{1}{2}.\frac{2}{3}}{1.\frac{1}{2}.\frac{2}{3}+1.\frac{1}{2}.\frac{1}{3}+1.\frac{1}{2}.\frac{1}{3}+0.\frac{1}{2}.\frac{2}{3}}$$

$$=\frac{\frac{1}{3}}{\frac{1}{3}+\frac{1}{6}+\frac{1}{6}}=\frac{1}{2}.$$

Ex.7: A box contains N coins , m of which are fair and the rest are biased . The probability of getting a head when a fair coin is tossed is 1/2 , while it is 2/3 when a biased coin is tossed . A coin is drawn from the box at random and is tossed twice. The first time it shows head and the second time it shows tail. What is the probability that the coin drawn is fair ?

Sol. Let E_1 be the event that the coin drawn is fair and E_2 be the event that the coin drawn is biased.

$$P(E_1)=\frac{m}{N} \text{ and } P(E_2)=\frac{N-m}{N}$$

Let A is the event that on tossing a coin the head appears first and then appears tail.

Now, $P(A)=P(E_1\cap A)+P(E_2\cap A)$

$$= P(E_1).P(A/E_1)+P(E_2).P(A/E_2)$$

$$=\frac{m}{N}\left(\frac{1}{2}\right)^2+\left(\frac{N-m}{N}\right)\left(\frac{2}{3}\right)\left(\frac{1}{3}\right)$$

Hence the required probability

$$= P\left(\frac{E_1}{A}\right)=\frac{P(E_1\cap A)}{P(A)}=\frac{P(E_1).P(A/E_1)}{P(A)}$$

$$=\frac{\frac{m}{N}\left(\frac{1}{2}\right)^2}{\frac{m}{N}\left(\frac{1}{2}\right)^2+\frac{N-m}{N}\left(\frac{2}{3}\right)\left(\frac{1}{3}\right)}$$

$$=\frac{9m}{m+8N}.$$

Ex.8: A bag contains 6 white and 12 red balls . Six balls are drawn at random without replacement . If at least four of these are white , find the probability that in the next two draws exactly one white ball is drawn.

Sol. Let E_i denote the event that exactly i white balls are drawn.

We have $P(E_i)=\frac{{}^6C_i\times{}^{12}C_{6-i}}{{}^{18}C_6}$

Let E denote the event that at least 4 white balls are drawn, then $E=E_4\cup E_5\cup E_6$

Let A denote the event that exactly one of the two balls drawn next is white.

Now, $P(A/E_4)=\frac{{}^2C_1\times{}^{11}C_1}{{}^{12}C_2}=\frac{20}{66}$,

$P(A/E_5)=\frac{{}^1C_1\times{}^{11}C_1}{{}^{12}C_2}=\frac{1}{66}$, $P(A/E_6)=0$

Thus, the required probability $= P(A/E)=\frac{P(A\cap E)}{P(E)}$

$$=\frac{P(A\cap E_4)+P(A\cap E_5)+P(A\cap E_6)}{P(E)}$$

$$=\frac{P(E_4)P(A/E_4)+P(E_5)P(A/E_5)+P(E_6)P(A/E_6)}{P(E_4)+P(E_4)+P(E_4)}$$

$$=\frac{20\times{}^6C_4\times{}^{12}C_4+11\times{}^6C_5\times{}^{12}C_1}{66\left[{}^6C_4\times{}^{12}C_2+{}^6C_5\times{}^{12}C_1+1\right]}.$$

Ex.9: A person goes to the office either by a car or by a scooter or by bus or by train . The probabilities of his using car , scooter, bus and train are resp. 1/2, 2/7, 3/7 and 1/7 . The probabilities of his reaching late in the office by using these modes of transport are 2/9 , 4/9 , 1/9 and 1/9 resp. If the person reaches the office in time , then find the probability that he used car to reach the office.

Sol. Let C, S, B and T denote the events that the person goes to the office by car, scooter , bus and train resp. and let L denote the event that he reaches late in the office.

We have, $P(C)=\frac{1}{7}$, $P(S)=\frac{2}{7}$, $P(B)=\frac{3}{7}$, $P(T)=\frac{1}{7}$

$P(L/C)=\frac{2}{9},\ P(L/S)=\frac{4}{9},\ P(L/B)=\frac{1}{9}, P(L/T)=\frac{1}{9}$

Thus,

$P(L'/C)=\frac{7}{9}, P(L'/S)=\frac{5}{9},\ P(L'/B)=\frac{8}{9}, P(L'/T)=\frac{8}{9}$

Hence the required probability,= P(C/L')

$$=\frac{P(C)P(L'/C)}{P(C)P(L'/C)+P(S)P(L'/S)+P(B)P(L'/B)+P(T)P(L'/T)}$$

$$=\frac{\frac{1}{7}\cdot\frac{2}{9}}{\frac{1}{7}\cdot\frac{7}{9}+\frac{2}{7}\cdot\frac{5}{9}+\frac{3}{7}\cdot\frac{8}{9}+\frac{1}{7}\cdot\frac{8}{9}}$$

$$=\frac{1}{7}..$$

Ex.10: A card from a pack of 52 cards is lost. From the remaining cards of the pack two cards are drawn at random and are found to be spade. Find the probability that the missing card to be a spade.

Sol. Let E_1, E_2, E_3, E_4 be the events of lossing a card from spades, hearts, diamonds and clubs and E be the event of drawing 2 spades from the remaining cards.

Hence the required probability $= P(E_1/E)$

$$=\frac{P(E_1)P(E/E_1)}{P(E_1)P(E/E_1)+P(E_2)P(E/E_2)+P(E_3)P(E/E_3)+P(E_4)P(E/E_4)}$$

$$=\frac{\frac{^{13}C_1}{^{52}C_1}\times\frac{^{12}C_2}{^{51}C_2}}{\frac{^{13}C_1}{^{52}C_1}\times\frac{^{12}C_2}{^{51}C_2}+\frac{^{13}C_1}{^{52}C_1}\times\frac{^{13}C_2}{^{51}C_2}+\frac{^{13}C_1}{^{52}C_1}\times\frac{^{13}C_2}{^{51}C_2}+\frac{^{13}C_1}{^{52}C_1}\times\frac{^{13}C_2}{^{51}C_2}}$$

$$=\frac{\frac{1}{4}\times\frac{66}{1275}}{\frac{1}{4}\times\frac{66}{1275}+\frac{1}{4}\times\frac{78}{1275}+\frac{1}{4}\times\frac{78}{1275}+\frac{1}{4}\times\frac{78}{1275}}$$

$$=\frac{66}{66+78+78+78}$$

$$=\frac{66}{300}=\frac{11}{50}$$

Ex.11: A speaks truth 3 times out of 5 while b 7 times out of 10. A ball is drawn at random from a bag conatiining one black ball and 5 other balls of different colors. Both A and B report that a black ball has been drawn from the bag. Find the probability of their assertion being true.

Sol. Let T and L be the events that both A and B speak truth and lies and B the event that a ball is drawn from the bag.

Claearly $P(B)=\frac{1}{6}$ and $P(\overline{B})=\frac{5}{6}$

$P(T/B)=\frac{3}{5}\times\frac{7}{10},\ P(L/\overline{B})=\frac{2}{5}\times\frac{3}{10}.$

Hence, the required probability

$$=\frac{\frac{1}{6}\times\frac{3}{5}\times\frac{7}{10}}{\frac{1}{6}\times\frac{3}{5}\times\frac{7}{10}+\frac{1}{6}\times\frac{2}{5}\times\frac{3}{10}}$$

$$=\frac{21}{21+6}=\frac{21}{27}=\frac{7}{9}$$

Ex.12: A letter is know to have come from CALCUTTA or TATANAGAR. On the envelope, just two consecutive letters TA are visible. Find the probability that the letter came from CALCUTTA.

Sol. Let E_1, E_2 be the event that the letter came from CALCUTTA and TATANAGAR.

and A be the event that two consecutive alphabets visible on the envelope are TA.

Clearly, $P(E_1)=\frac{1}{2}=P(E_2)$

and $P(A/E_1)=\frac{2}{8}=\frac{1}{4},\ P(A/E_2)=\frac{1}{7}.$

Hence, the required probability $= P(E_2/A)$

$$=\frac{P(E_2)P(A/E_2)}{P(E_1)P(A/E_1)+P(E_2)P(A/E_2)}$$

$$=\frac{\frac{1}{2}\cdot\frac{1}{7}}{\frac{1}{2}\cdot\frac{1}{4}+\frac{1}{2}\cdot\frac{1}{7}}=\frac{4}{11}.$$

Ex.13: A and B are two independent witnesses (i.e there is no collusion between them) The probability that A and B will speak truth s are x and y resp. A and B are agree in a certain statement. Prove that the probability that the statement is true is $\frac{xy}{1-x-y+xy}$.

Sol. Let E_1 be the event that both A and B speak truth, E_2 be the event that both A and B tell a lie, E be the event that A and B agree in a certain statement, C be the event that A speaks the truth and D be the event that B speaks truth.

Thus, $E_1 = C\cap D,\ E_2 = C'\cap D'$

Therefore, $P(E_1)=P(C\cap D)=P(C)P(D)=xy$ and $P(E_2)=P(C'\cap D')=P(C')P(D')$

$$=(1-x)(1-y)=1-x-y+xy.$$

Now, $P\left(\frac{E}{E_1}\right)$ = Probability that A and B will agree when both of them speak the truth = 1 and $P\left(\frac{E}{E_2}\right)$ = Probability that A and B will agree when both of them tell a lie = 1.

Hence, the required probability

$$=P\left(\frac{E_1}{E}\right)$$

$$= \frac{P(E_1).P\left(\frac{E}{E_1}\right)}{P(E_1).P\left(\frac{E}{E_1}\right)+P(E_2).P\left(\frac{E}{E_2}\right)}$$

$$= \frac{xy.1}{xy.1+(1-x-y+xy).1}$$

$$= \frac{xy}{1-x-y+2xy}$$

7.17 Probability Distribution.

Before discussing Probability distribution, we must define some important terms.

Random Variable : Random variable is a function form a sample space to a real number .

Let X be a random variable .

Then $X : S \to R$ is a function from a sample space S to a real number R. There are two types of random variable. Discrete Random Variable and Continuous Random Variable.

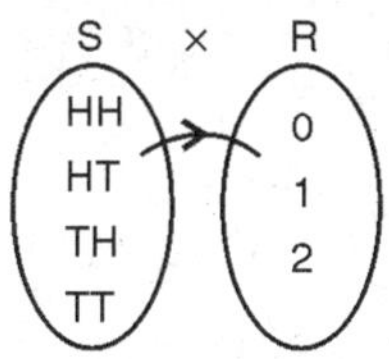

(i) Consider , tossing a coin two times, we shall count only head.

Thus range of X is $\{0,1,2\}$ If the range of X is finite , then it is Discrete Random Variavle

(ii) Consider a coin is tossed till a head occurs.

Thus range of X is $\{1,2,3,4,..........\}$

If the range of X is infinite , then it is also Discrete Random Variable.

Thus , a random variable which can take only finite and countably infinite number of values is called a **Discrete Random Variable.**

A random variable which can take any value between two given limits is called a **Continuous Random Variable.**

Now we shall discuss about probability distribution :

Consider a coin is tossed two times , we shall count only tail.

Then, $S = \{HH, TH, HT, TT\}$ and $R_X = \{0,1,2\}$

$P(X=0)=\frac{1}{4}$, $P(X=1)=\frac{2}{4}$, $P(X=2)=\frac{1}{4}$.

Thus,

X:	0	1	2
P(X):	1/4	2/4	1/4

A tabular representation of a Random varible with their corresponding probabilities is called a Probability Distribution.

Mean and Variance of a Probability Distribution:

Mean of a P.D. $= \sum_{i=1}^{n} p_i x_i$

Variance of a P.D. $= \sum_{i=1}^{n} p_i x_i^2 - (\text{Mean})^2$.

7.18 Binomial Distribution :

Let the number of trials of a random experiment is n , where p is the probability of the occurence of an event and q is the probability of non occurence of an event such that p + q = 1.

Let X be the number of successes.

Then the probability of occurence of event exactly r times in n trials is denoted by $P(X=r)$ and is defined as

$$P(X=r) = {}^nC_r.p^r.q^{n-r}.$$

Mean and Variance of a Binomial Distribution :

(i) Mean $= \sum_{r=0}^{n} r P(r)$

$$= \sum_{r=0}^{n} r P(X=r)$$

$$= \sum_{r=0}^{n} r.\ {}^nC_r.p^r.q^{n-r}$$

$$= \sum_{r=0}^{n} r.\frac{n}{r}.\ {}^{n-1}C_{r-1}.p^r.q^{n-r}$$

$$= n\sum_{r=0}^{n} {}^{n-1}C_{r-1}.p^r.q^{n-r}$$

$$= n\left({}^{n-1}C_1.p.q^{n-1} + {}^{n-1}C_2.p^2.q^{n-2} + ... + {}^{n-1}C_n.p^{n-1}\right)$$

$$= np\left({}^{n-1}C_1.q^{n-1} + {}^{n-1}C_2.p.q^{n-2} + ... + {}^{n-1}C_n.p^{n-1}\right)$$

$$= np(q+p)^{n-1} = np.1 = np$$

(ii) **Variance** $= \sum_{r=0}^{n} r^2 P(r) - (np)^2$

$$= \sum_{r=0}^{n} r^2 P(X=r) - (np)^2$$

$$= \sum_{r=0}^{n} r(r-1).{}^nC_r.p^r.q^{n-r} + \sum_{r=0}^{n} r.{}^nC_r.p^r.q^{n-r} - (np)^2$$

$$= n(n-1)p^2\sum_{r=0}^{n} {}^{n-2}C_{r-2}.p^{r-2}.q^{(n-2)-(r-2)} + np - (np)^2$$

$$= n(n-1)p^2(q+p)^{n-2} - (np)^2$$

$$= n^2p^2 - np^2 + np - n^2p^2$$

$$= np(1-p)$$

$$= npq.$$

(iii) **Mode of Binomial distribution.:**

Mode of binomial distribution is the value of r for which $P(X=r)$ is maximum.

$$\frac{P(X=r)}{P(X=r-1)} = \frac{{}^nC_r\,p^r q^{n-r}}{{}^nC_{r-1}\,p^{r-1} q^{n-r+1}} = \left(\frac{n-r+1}{r}\right)\frac{p}{q}$$

Replacing r by r +1 , we get ,

$$\frac{P(X=r+1)}{P(X=r)}=\frac{{}^{n}C_{r+1}\,p^{r+1}q^{n-r-1}}{{}^{n}C_{r}\,p^{r}q^{n-r}}=\left(\frac{n-r}{r+1}\right)\frac{p}{q}$$

For P(X=r) to be maximum ,

$$\frac{P(X=r)}{P(X=r-1)}\ge 1\Rightarrow\left(\frac{n-r+1}{r}\right)\frac{p}{q}\ge 1\Rightarrow r\le(n+1)p$$

Also for P(X=r) to be maximum ,

$$\frac{P(X=r+1)}{P(X=r)}\le 1\Rightarrow\left(\frac{n-r}{r+1}\right)\frac{p}{q}\le 1\Rightarrow r\ge(n+1)p-1$$

Hence, $(n+1)p-1\le r\le(n+1)p$, where r is a +ve integer.

7.19 Some solved examples:

Ex.1: A die is thrown 6 times. If getting a number six is a success, then find the probability that

(i) atleast 5 successes
(ii) atmost 5 successes
(iii) exactly 5 successes
(iv) no success.

Sol. Here $n=6,\ p=\frac{1}{6},\ q=1-\frac{1}{6}=\frac{5}{6}$

(i) $P(X\ge 5)=P(X=5)+P(X=6)$

$={}^{6}C_5\,p^5\,q^1+{}^{6}C_6\,p^6\,q^0$

$=6p^5q+p^6=p^5(6p+q)=\left(\frac{1}{6}\right)^5\times\left(\frac{11}{6}\right)$

(ii) $P(X\le 5)=1-P(X>5)=1-P(X=6)$

$=1-{}^{6}C_6p^6q^0=1-\left(\frac{1}{6}\right)^5$

(iii) $P(X=5)={}^{6}C_5p^5q^1=6\times\left(\frac{1}{6}\right)^5\times\left(\frac{5}{6}\right)$

(iv) $P(X=0)={}^{6}C_0p^0q^6=6\times\left(\frac{5}{6}\right)^6$

Ex.2: Two fair dice are thrown simultaneously. If the operation is repeated 5 times , then find the probability that the sum will be 7 exactly 4 times.

Sol. Here $S=\{(1,1),(1,2),\ldots\ldots\ldots,(6,6)\}$

and $n=5$.

Now, $7\rightarrow\{(1,6),(6,1),(2,5),(5,2),(3,4),(4,3)\}$

Thus, $p=\frac{6}{36}=\frac{1}{6},\ q=1-\frac{1}{6}=\frac{5}{6}$

Hence, the required probability

$=P(X=4)={}^{7}C_4\,p^4\,q^3=35\times\left(\frac{1}{6}\right)^4\times\left(\frac{5}{6}\right)^3$

Ex.3: The probability that Pakistan wins a cricket match against India is 1/5 . If India and Pakistan play 5 test matches , then what is the probability that India will win 4 test matches .?

Sol. Here, $n=5,\ p=\frac{1}{5},\ q=1-\frac{1}{5}=\frac{4}{5}$.

Hence, the required probability

$=P(X=4)={}^{5}C_4\,p^4\,q^1=5\times\left(\frac{1}{5}\right)^4\times\left(\frac{4}{5}\right)=\frac{4}{625}$

Ex.4: A pair of fair dice is thrown 4 times . Find the probability of getting a doublet at-least 2 times.

Sol. Here, n = 4. The possible outcome of doublet is $\{(1,1),(2,2),(3,3),(4,4),(5,5),(6,6)\}$

Thus, $p=\frac{6}{36}=\frac{1}{6},\ q=1-\frac{1}{6}=\frac{5}{6}$

Hence, the required probability

$=P(X\ge 2)=1-P(X<2)=1-\{P(X=1)+P(X=0)\}$

$=1-\left({}^{4}C_1\,p^1q^3+C_0\,p^0q^4\right)=1-\left(4pq^3+q^4\right)$

$=1-q^3(4p+q)=1-\frac{3}{2}\left(\frac{5}{6}\right)^3=1-\frac{125}{144}=\frac{19}{144}$

$1-\left({}^{4}C_1\,p^1q^3+C_0\,p^0q^4\right)=1-\left(4pq^3+q^4\right)$

$=1-q^3(4p+q)=1-\frac{3}{2}\left(\frac{5}{6}\right)^3=1-\frac{125}{144}=\frac{19}{144}$

Ex.5: If a coin is tossed n times Find the rpobability that the head will appear an odd number of times.

Sol. Here, $p=\frac{1}{2},\ q=1-\frac{1}{2}=\frac{1}{2}$

Hence, the required probability

$=P(X=1)+P(X=3)+P(X=5)$

$+P(X=7)+\ldots\ldots\ldots$ to ∞

$={}^{n}C_1\,p^1\,q^{n-1}+{}^{n}C_3\,p^3\,q^{n-3}+{}^{n}C_5\,p^5\,q^{n-5}+\ldots\ldots$

$={}^{n}C_1\left(\frac{1}{2}\right)^1\left(\frac{1}{2}\right)^{n-1}+{}^{n}C_3\left(\frac{1}{2}\right)^3\left(\frac{1}{2}\right)^{n-3}$

$+{}^{n}C_1\left(\frac{1}{2}\right)^5\left(\frac{1}{2}\right)^{n-5}+{}^{n}C_1\left(\frac{1}{2}\right)^7\left(\frac{1}{2}\right)^{n-7}+\ldots\ldots$

$=\left(\frac{1}{2}\right)^n\left({}^{n}C_1+{}^{n}C_3+{}^{n}C_5+{}^{n}C_7+\ldots\ldots\ldots\text{to }\infty\right)$

$=\left(\frac{1}{2}\right)^n\times 2^{n-1}=\frac{1}{2}$

Ex.6: The probability that a student is not a cricketer is 1/10 . Then find the probability that out of 10 students , 7 are cricketer .

Sol. Here, $n=10,\ p=1-\frac{1}{10}=\frac{9}{10},\ q=\frac{1}{10}$

Hence, the required probability

$=P(X=7)={}^{10}C_7p^7q^3={}^{10}C_7\times\left(\frac{9}{10}\right)^7\times\left(\frac{1}{7}\right)^3$

Ex.7: The probability that a student can get in IIT is 3/4. He tries 5 times to get a chance. Find the prob ability that he tries to get a chance in IIT atleast 3 times.

Sol. Here, $n=5,\ p=\frac{3}{4},\ q=1-\frac{3}{4}=\frac{1}{4}$.

Hence, the required probability

$$=P(X\ge 3)=P(X=3)+P(X=4)+P(X=5)$$

$$={}^5C_3p^3q^2+{}^5C_4p^4q+{}^5C_5p^5q^0$$

$$=10p^3q^2+5p^4q+p^5q^0$$

$$=p^3\left(10q^2+5pq+p^2\right)$$

$$=\frac{27}{64}\left(\frac{10}{16}+\frac{15}{16}+\frac{3}{16}\right)=\frac{27}{64}\times\frac{28}{64}=\frac{27}{64}\times\frac{7}{16}=\frac{189}{1024}$$

Ex.8: The probability of guessing correctly straight objective type multiple choice questions in IIT is 2/7. Find the probability that a student can give right answer atleast 8 questions out of 10 questions.

Sol. Here, $n=10,\ p=\frac{2}{7},\ q=1-\frac{2}{7}=\frac{5}{7}$

Hence, the required probability =

$$P(X\ge 8)=P(X=8)+P(X=9)+P(X=10)$$

$$={}^{10}C_8\,p^8q^2+{}^{10}C_9\,p^9q^1+{}^{10}C_{10}\,p^{10}q^0$$

$$=p^8\left(45q^2+10pq+p^2\right)$$

$$=\left(\frac{2}{7}\right)^9\times\left(\frac{45\times 25}{49}+\frac{100}{49}+\frac{4}{49}\right)=\left(\frac{2}{7}\right)^9\times\left(\frac{1129}{49}\right)$$

Ex.9: A family has 5 children. Assuming that the probability of a male child and a female child is equal.

Find the probability that the family has atleat 2 male child.

Sol. Here, $n=5,\ p=\frac{1}{2},\ q=1-\frac{1}{2}=\frac{1}{2}$

Hence, the required probability =

$$P(X\ge 2)=1-P(X<2)=1-\{P(X=1)+P(X=0)\}$$

$$=1-\left\{\left({}^5C_1p^1q^4+{}^5C_0\,p^0q^5\right)\right\}$$

$$=1-\left(\frac{5}{32}+\frac{1}{32}\right)=1-\frac{6}{32}=\frac{26}{32}=\frac{13}{32}$$

Ex.10: If n chocolates are distributed among m students in MIIT-JEE Instt. Find the probability that a particular student will get r (< n) chocolates.

Sol. Hence, the required probability

$$=P(X=r)={}^nC_r\,p^r\,q^{n-r}$$

$$={}^nC_r\times\left(\frac{1}{m}\right)^r\times\left(\frac{m-1}{m}\right)^{n-r}={}^nC_r\times\frac{(m-1)^{n-r}}{m^n}.$$

7.20 Geometrical Probability:

If we are interested in finding the probability that a point is selected at random in a given region will lie in a specified part of it. The classical definition of probability is modified and extended to what is called geometrical probability or probability in continuum. In this case the general expression for probability p

= Measure of specified part of the region / measure of the whole region.

When 'measures' refers to the length, area and the volume of the region if we are dealing with one, two and three dimensional space respectively.

Ex.1: A telephone subscriber has ordered a call. He may get it at any time in the next hour. What is the probability of the call taking place in the last 20 minutes of the hour ?

Sol. Let A be the event is the call taking place in the last 20 minutes of the hour.

Let us represent the sample space as a line segment of length 20.

Hence, the required probability

$$=\frac{\text{Measure of specified part of the region}}{\text{Measure of the whole region}}=\frac{20}{60}=\frac{1}{3}$$

Ex.2: Two points are selected in a line AB of length 'a' so as to lie in opposite sides of its middle point C. Find the probability that the distance between them is less than a/3.

Sol. Consider two points P and Q on the segments CB and CA respectively.

Let CP = x and CQ = y so that $0\le x\le a/2,\ 0\le y\le a/2$

We are interested in the event $x+y<a/3$

Here, first we make a square of side length a/2 and its sub region triangle with base a/3 and height is also a/3

Hence, the required probability $=\dfrac{\frac{1}{2}\left(\frac{a}{3}\right)\left(\frac{a}{3}\right)}{\left(\frac{a}{2}\right)\left(\frac{a}{2}\right)}=\frac{2}{9}$

Ex.3: Two points are chosen independently at random from the interval [0,1]. What is the chance that the two numbers differ by more than 1/2 ?

Sol. Let the two numbers be x and y such that $0\le x,\ y\le 1$.

To find the probability of $P\left(|x-y|>\frac{1}{2}\right)$

Hence the required probability

$$=\frac{\frac{1}{2}\times\frac{1}{2}\times\frac{1}{2}+\frac{1}{2}\times\frac{1}{2}\times\frac{1}{2}}{1\times 1}=\frac{1}{4}$$

Ex.4: Two numbers are selected independently at random from the interval [0,1]. If the smaller one is less than 1/3, then find the probability that the larger one is greater than 3/4 is 3/10.

Sol. Let us consider two numbers be x and y where $0 \le x,\ y \le 1$, so that the geometric configuration is a square.

$$= P\left(xy \ge \frac{3}{4}\times(12)^2\right) = P(xy \ge 108) = P(x(24-x)\ge 108)$$

$$= P((x-18)(x-6)\le 0) = P(6\le x\le 18)$$

$$= \frac{12}{24} = \frac{1}{2}.$$

Let $M = \text{Max}\{x, y\}$ and $m = \min\{x, y\}$

Hence the reuired probability

$$= P\left(\frac{M\ge 3/4}{m\le 1/3}\right) = \frac{P(M\ge 3/4,\ m\le 1/3)}{P(m\le 1/3)}$$

$$= \frac{2.\frac{1}{3}.\frac{1}{4}}{\frac{1}{3}+\frac{1}{3}-\frac{1}{9}} = \frac{\frac{1}{6}}{\frac{5}{9}} = \frac{3}{10}.$$

Ex.5: A line is divided at random into three parts . What is the chance that they form the sides of a possible triangle ?

Sol. Let AB be the straight line divided at P and Q such that $AB = a$.

Let AP = x and BQ = y

Now in favourable cases , we must have , x < a/2 , y < a/2 and x + y > a/2

Hence , the required probability $= \frac{\frac{1}{2}.\frac{a}{2}.\frac{a}{2}}{\frac{1}{2}.a.a} = \frac{1}{4}$.

Ex.6: Let the sum of two +ve numbers be 24 . Find the probability that the product of two numbers is not less than 3/4 times of their greatest product.

Sol. Let two numbers be x and y such that x + y = 24. For extremum , it is clear that , the greatest value of xy is $(12)^2$.

Hence, the requied probability

Ex. 7: A circular target is divided into three zones bounded by concentric circles of radii 1/3, 1/2 and 1 respectively . If three shots are fixed at random at the target , what is the probability that exactly one shot lands in each zone ?

Sol. Let the probability of a shot falling in the region A of radius 1/3 is $p_1 = \frac{\pi.(1/3)^2}{\pi.(1)^2} = \frac{1}{9}$

the probability of a shot falling in the region B of radius 1/2 is $p_2 = \frac{\pi.(1/2)^2 - \pi(1/3)^2}{\pi.(1)^2} = \frac{5}{36}$

and the probability of a shot failling in the region C of radius 1 is $p_3 = \frac{\pi.(1)^2 - \pi(1/2)^2}{\pi.(1)^2} = \frac{3}{4}$

Hence the required probability is

$$= P(p_1.p_2.p_3\times 3!) = \frac{6\times 5}{432} = \frac{5}{72}.$$

Ex.8: If p is chosen at random in [0,5], what is the probability of the equation $x^2 + px + \frac{p+2}{4} = 0$ to have real roots ?

Sol. Let A be the event that the length of the interval in which the given equation has real roots and S be the sample space .i.e the length of the interval [0,5].

Since roots are real, $D\ge 0 \Rightarrow p^2 - 4.1.\frac{(p+2)}{4}\ge 0$

$$\Rightarrow p^2 - p - 2\ge 0 \Rightarrow (p-2)(p+1)\ge 0$$

$$\Rightarrow p\le -1,\ p\ge 2$$

Thus , $A = [2,\ 5]$, since $p\in[0,\ 5]$.

Hence the required probability, $= \frac{n(A)}{n(S)} = \frac{3}{5}$.

Ex.9: Two real numbers x and y are selected at random , given that $0\le x\le 1,\ 0\le y\le 1$. Find the probability that $y^2\le x$.

Sol. Consider a point with co-ordinates (x, y) correponds to the pair of numbers x and y.

The sample space is a square whose sides are unit segments to the co-ordinate axes.

The region , whose set of points corresponds to the outcome favourable to the event $y^2\le x$ is bounded by the graphs of the function y = 0 , x = 1 and $y^2 = x$

Hence, the required probability

$$= \int_0^1 \sqrt{x}\,dx = \left(\frac{2}{3}\left(x^{3/2}\right)\right)_0^1 = \frac{2}{3}.$$

Ex.10: Two persons Aand B agree to meet at a place between 11 to 12 noon . The first one to arrive waits for 20 mins and then leave. If the time of their arrival be independent and at random , what is the probability that A and B meet ?

Sol. Let A and B arrive at the place of their meeting x and y mins after 11 A.M

As per the condition , their meeting is possible only when $|x-y|\le 20$

Hence, the required probability

$$= \frac{60\times 60 - \frac{1}{2}\times 40\times 40 - \frac{1}{2}\times 40\times 40}{60\times 60} = \frac{2000}{3600} = \frac{5}{9}.$$

Level – I UESTIONS BASED ON FUNDAMENTALS

Questions based on Sample Space :

1. In a simultaneous toss of two coins, find the probability of getting
   (i) 2 heads (ii) exactly one head
   (iii) exactly 2 tails (iv) exactly one tail
   (v) no tails
2. Three coins are tossed once. Find the probability of getting
   (i) all heads (ii) at least two heads \
   (iii) at most two heads (iv) no heads
   (v) exactly one tail (vi) exactly 2 tails
3. (a) Two dice are thrown simultaneously. Find the probability of getting :
   (i) an even number as the sum
   (ii) the sum as a prime number
   (iii) a total of at least 10
   (iv) a doublet of even number
   (v) a multiple of 2 on one dice and a multiple of 3 on the other dice
   (vi) same number of both dice
   (vii) a multiple of 3 as the sum
   (b) Three dice are thrown together. Find the probability of getting a total of at least 6.
   (c) Three dice are thrown together. Find the probability of getting a total of atleast 15.
4. A coin is tossed. If head comes up, a die is thrown but if tail comes up, the coin is tossed again.
   Find the probability of obtaining
   (i) two tails
   (ii) head and number 6
   (iii) head and an even number
5. (a) One card is drawn from a pack of 52 cards, each of the 52 cards being equally likely to be drawn. Find the probability that the card drawn is :
   (i) an ace
   (ii) red
   (iii) either a red or a king
   (iv) a red and a king
   (v) a red and an honours card.
   (b) Four cards are drawn at random from a pack of 52 playing cards. Find the probability of getting
   (i) all the four cards of the same suit
   (ii) all the four cards of the same number
   (iii) one card from each suit
   (iv) two red cards and two black cards
   (v) all cards of the same colour
   (vi) all face cards
6. Find the probability that when a hand of 7 cards is dealt from a well-shuffled deck of 52 cards, it contains
   (i) all 4 kings
   (ii) exactly 3 kings
   (ii) at least 3 kings
7. The face cards are removed from a full pack. Out of the remaining 40 cards, 4 are drawn at random.
   What is the probabily that they belong to different suits ?
8. In a hand of whist, what is the probability that four kings are held by a specified player ?
9. An urn contains 9 red, 7 white and 4 black balls. If two balls are drawn at random, find the probability that :
   (i) both the balls are red,
   (ii) one ball is white
   (iii) the balls are of the same colour
   (iv) one is white and other red
10. Two unbiased dice are thrown. Find the probability that :
    (i) neither a doublet nor a total of 8 will appear
    (ii) the sum of the numbers obtained on the two dice is neither a multiple of 2 nor a multiple of 3.
11. A bag contains 8 red, 3 white and 9 blue balls. If three balls are drawn at random, determine the probability that
    (i) all the three balls are blue balls
    (ii) all the balls are of different colours.
12. In a lottery of 50 tickets numbered 1 to 50, two tickets are drawn simultaneously. Find the probability that :
    (i) both the tickets drawn have prime numbers
    (ii) none of the tickets drawn has prime number
    (iii) one ticket has prime number
13. A bag contains 50 tickets numbered 1, 2, 3,......, 50 of which five are drawn at random and arranged in ascending order of magnitude ($x_1 < x_2 < x_3 < x_4 < x_5$). Find the probability that $x_3 = 30$.
14. A bag contains tickets numbered from 1 to 20. Two tickets are drawn. Find the probability that
    (i) both the tickets have prime numbers on them
    (ii) on one there is a prime number and on the other there is a multiple of 4.
15. The letters of the word 'SOCIETY' are placed at random in a row. What is the probability that three vowels are come together ?
16. Find the probability that in a random arrangement of the letters of the word 'UNIVERSITY', so that two I's come together.
17. Find the probability that the birth days of six different persons will fall in exactly two calender months.
18. What is the probability that in a group of n persons, at least two of them will have the same birth-day?
19. The odds in favour of an event are 3:5. Find the probability of occurrence of this event.
20. A card is drawn from an ordinary pack of 52 cards and a gambler bets that, it is a spade or an ace. What are the odds against his winning this bet ?

Questons Based on Addition Theorem :

21. One number is chosen from numbers 1 to 200. Find the probability that it is divisible by 4 or 6 ?
22. Find the probability of getting on even number on the first die or a total of 8 in a single throw of two dice.

23. A die is thrown twice. What is the probability that at least one of the two throws comes up with the number 4 ?
24. Two dice are thrown together. What is the probability that the sum of the numbers on the two faces is divisible by 3 or 4 ?
25. Four cards are drawn at a time from a pack of 52 playing cards. Find the probability of getting all the four cards of the same suit.
26. Two cards are drawn from a pack of 52 cards. What is the probability that either both are red or both are kings ?
27. The probability that a person will get an electric contract is 2/5 and the probability that he will not get plumbing contract is 4/7. If the probability of getting at least one contract is 2/3, what is the probability that he will get both ?
28. Probability that Hameed passes in mathematics is 2/3 and the probability that he passes in English is 4/9. If the probability of passing both courses is 1/4, what is the probability that Hameed will pass in at least one of these subjects ?
29. The probability that a person will travel by plane is 3/5 and that he will travel by train is 1/4. What is the probability that he (she) will travel by plane or train ?
30. (i) A card is drawn from a deck of 52 cards. Find the probability of getting a king or a heart or a red card.
    (ii) Two cards are drawn at random from a deck of 52 cards. Find the probability of getting that they will both are Spade, Heart or Club
31. (i) In integer is chosen at random from the numbers ranging from 1 to 50. What is the probability that the integer chosen is a multiple of 2 or 3 or 10 ?
    (ii) What is the chance of getting 4 or 7 or 12 in a throw of two dice ?.
32. Let A, B, C be three events. If the probability of occuring exactly one event out of A and B is $1 - x$, out of B and C is $1 - 2x$, out of C and A is $1 - x$, and that of occuring three events simultaneously is x^2, then prove the probability that atleast one out of A, B, C will occur is greater than 1/2.

Questions based on Conditional Probability :

33. A die is rolled. If the outcome is an odd number, what is the probability that it is prime ?
34. A pair of dice is thrown. Find the probability of getting the sum 8 or more, if 4 appears on the first die.
35. A pair of dice is thrown. Find the probability of getting 7 as the sum of it is known that the second die always exhibits a prime number.
36. A pair of dice is thrown. Find the probability of getting 7 as the sum, if it is known that the second die always exhibits an odd number.
37. Two dice are thrown. Find the probability that the numbers appeared has the sum 8, if it is known that the second die always exhibits 4.
38. A dice is thrown twice and the sum of the numbers appearing is observed to be 6. What is the conditional probability that the number 4 has appeared at least once ?
39. To test the quality of electric bulbs produced in a factory, two bulbs are randomly selected from a large sample without replacement. If either bulb is defective, the entire lot is rejected. Suppose a sample of 200 bulbs contains 5 defective bulbs. Find the probability that the sample will be rejected.
40. A bag contains 10 white and 15 black balls. Two balls are drawn in succession without replacement. What is the probability that first is white and second is black ?
41. Find the probability of drawing a diamond card in each of the two consecutive draws from a well shuffled pack of cards, if the card drawn is not replaced after the first draw.
42. A bag contains 5 white, 7 red and 8 black balls. If four balls are drawn one by one without replacement, find the probability of getting all white balls.
43. Two integers are selected at random from integers 1 through 11. If the sum is even, find the probability that both the numbers are odd.
44. A couple has 2 children. Find the probability that both are boys, if it is known that
    (i) one of the children is a boy
    (ii) the older child is a boy
45. Two coins are tossed. What is the probability of coming up two heads if it is known that at least one head comes up.?

Questions based on Independent Events :

46. A problem in mathematics is given to 3 students whose chances of solving it are 1/2, 1/3 ,1/4 . What is the probability that the problem is solved ?
47. A can solve 90% of the problems given in a book and B can solve 70%. What is the probability that at least one of them will solve the problem, selected at random from the book ?
48. Probabilities of solving a specific problem independently by A and B are 1/2 and 1/3 respectively. If both try to solve the problem independently, find the probability that
    (i) the problem is solved
    (ii) exactly one of them solves the problem
49. Given the probability that A can solve a problem is 2/3 and the probability that B can solve the same problem is 3/5 . Find the probability that none of the two will be able to solve the problem.
50. Three cards are drawn with replacement from a well shuffled pack of cards. Find the probability that the cards drawn are king, queen and jack.
51. The probability that A hits a target is 1/3 and the probability that B hits it, is 2/5. What is the probability that the target will be hit, if each one of A and B shoots at the target ?
52. A bag contains 5 white, 7 red and 4 black balls. If four balls are drawn one by one with replacement, what is the probability that none is white ?
53. A bag contains 5 white, 7 red and 8 black balls. Four balls are drawn one by one with replacement, what is the probability that at least one is white ?
54. A can hit a target 4 times in 5 shots, B 3 times in 4 shots, and C 2 times in 3 shots. Calculate the probability that
    (i) A, B, C all may hit
    (ii) B, C may hit and A may lose.
55. A box contains 3 red and 5 blue balls. Two balls are down one by one at a time at random without replacement. Find the probability of getting 1 red and 1 blue ball.

56. Two cards are drawn from a well shuffled pack of 52 cards without replacement, What is the probability that one is a red queen and the other is a king of black colour ?

57. Two cards are drawn without replacement from a well shuffled pack of 52 cards. Find the probability that one is a spade and other is a queen of red colour.

58. Cards are numbered 1 to 25. Two cards are drawn one after the other. Find the probability that the number on one card is multiple of 7 on the other it is a multiple of 11.

59. The probability of A, B, C solving a problem are $1/3$, $2/7$ and $3/8$ respectively. If all the three try to solve the problem simultaneously, find the probability that exactly one of them can solve it.

60. A speaks truth in 60% of the cases and B in 90% of the cases. In what percentage of cases are they likely to contradict each other in stating the same fact ?

61. The probability of student A passing an examination is $3/7$ and of student B passing is $5/7$. Assuming the two events "A passes", "B passes", as independent, find the probability:

(i) Only A passing the examination

(ii) Only one of them passing the examination

62. Two persons A and B throw a die alternately till onw of them gets a 'three' and wins the game. Find their respectively probabilities of winning, if A begins.

63. A and B throw alternately a pair of dice. A wins if he throws 6 before B throws 7 and B wins if he throws 7 before A throws 6. Find their respective change of winning, if A begins.

64. Three persons A, B, C throw a die in succession till one gets a 'six' and wins the game. Find their respectively probabilities of winning, if A begins.

Questions Based on the Law of Total Probability :

65. A bag contains 4 red and 3 black balls. A second bag contains 2 red and 4 black balls. One bag is selected at random. From the selected bag, one ball is drawn. Find the probability that the ball drawn red.

66. In a bolt factory, machines A, B and C manufacture respectively 25%, 35% and 40% of the total bolts. Of their output 5, 4 and 2 percent are respectively defective bolts. A bolt is drawn at random from the product. What is the probability that the bolt drawn is defective ?

67. Two thirds of the students in a class are boys and the rest girls. It is known that the probability of a girl getting a first class is 0.25 and that of a boy getting a first class is 0.28. Find the probability that a student chosen at random will get first marks in the subject.

68. One bag contains 4 white and 5 black balls. Another bag contains 6 white and 7 black balls. A ball is transferred form first bag to the second bag and then a ball is drawn from the second bag. Find the probability that the ball drawn is white.

69. A bag contains 6 red and 5 blue balls and another bag contains 5 red and 8 blue balls. A ball is drawn from the first bag and without noticing its colour is put in the second bag. A ball is then drawn from the second bag. Find the probability that the ball drawn is blue in colour.

70. One bag contains 4 yellow and 5 red balls. Another bag contains 6 yellow and 3 red balls. A ball is transferred from the first bag to the second bag and then a ball is drawn from the first bag to the second bag and then a ball is drawn from the second bag. Find the probability that ball drawn is yellow.

Questions based on the Baye's Theorem :

71. In a bolt factory, machines A, B and C manifacture respectively 25%, 35%, and 40% of the total bolts. Of their output 5, 4 and 2 percent are respectively defective bolts. A bolt is drawn at random from the product. If the bolt drawn is found to be defective, what is the probability that it is manufactured by the machine B ?

72. A company has two plants to manufacture scooters. Plant I manufactures 70% of the scooters and Plant II manufactures 30%. At Plant 1, 80% of the scooters are rated as of standard quality and at Plant II, 90% of the scooters are rated as of standard quality. A scooter is chosen at random and is found to be of standard quality. What is the probability that it has come from Plant 11 ?

73. An insurance company insured 2000 scooter drivers, 4000 car drivers and 6000 truck drivers. The probability of an accident involving a scooter driver, car driver and truck is 0.01, 0.03 and 0.15 respectively. One of the insured person meets with an accident. What is the probability that he is a scooter driver ?

74. A man is known to speak truth 3 out of 4 times. He throws a die and reports that it is a six. Find the probability that it is actually a six.

75. A speaks the truth 3 out of 4 times , and B 5 out of 6 times . What is the probability that they will contradict each other in stating the same fact ?

76. A speaks the truth 2 out of 3 times and B 4 times out of 5 . They agree in the assertion that from a bag containing 6 balls of different colors a red ball has been drawn. Find the probability that the statement is true.

77. In a test, an examinee either guesses or copies or knows the answer to a multiple choice question with four choices. The probability that he makes a guess is $1/3$ and the probability that he copies the answer is $1/6$. The probability that his answer is correct, given that he copied it, is $1/8$. Find the probability that he knew that answer to the question, given that he correctly answered it.

78. A company has two plants to manufacture bicycles. The first plant manufactures 60% of the bicycles and the second plant 40%. Out of that 80% of the bicycles are rated of standard quality at the first plant and 90% of standard quality at the second plant. A bicycle is picked up at random and found to be standard quality. Find the probability that it comes from the second plant.

79. A factory has three machines A, B and C, which produce 100, 200 and 300 items of a particular type daily. The machines produce 2%, 3% and 5% defective items respectively. One day when the production was over, an item was picket up randomly and it was found to be defective. Find the probability that it was produced by machine A.

80. Three urns A, B and C contain 6 red and 4 white; 2 red and 6 white; and 1 red and 5 white balls respectively. An urn is chosen at random and a ball is drawn. If the ball drawn is found to be red, find the probability that the ball was drawn from urn A.

81: A letter is known to have come from either MAHARASTRA or MADRAS . On the post mark only consecutive letters RA can be read clearly . What is the chance that the letter came from MAHARASTRA ?

82: A can hit a target 4 times in 5 shots , B can hit 3 times in 4 shots and C twice in 3 shots . They fire once each. If two of them hit . What is the chance that C has missed it ?

83: A man has three coins A, B, C . The coin A is unbiased. The probability that a head will show when B is tossed is 2/3 while it is 1/3 for the coin C . A coin is chosen at random and tossed 3 times giving 2 heads and 1 tail . Find the probability that the coin was chosen.

84: An urn contains two balls each of which is either white or black . A white ball is added to the urn. What is the probability of drawing a white ball from the urn now ?

85. There are two bags, one of which contains 3 B and 4 W balls and the other contains 4 B and 3 W white balls. A die is thrown . If the face 1 or 3 turns up, a ball is taken out from the first bag , But if any other face turns up , a ball is taken from the second bag. Find the probability of getting a black ball.

86. A and B are two independent witnesses (i.e there is no collusion between them) The probability that A and B will speak truth s are x and y resp. A and B are agree in a certain statement. Prove that the probability that the statement is true is $\frac{xy}{1-x-y+xy}$.

Questions based on the Probability Distribution :

87. Find the probability distribution of X, the number of heads in two tosses of a coin (or a simultaneous toss of two coins).

88. An urn contains 4 white and 6 red balls. Four balls are drawn at random from the urn. Find the probability distribution of the number of white balls.

89. An unbiased die is thrown twice. Find the probability distribution of the number is sixes.

90. Two cards are drawn successively with replacement from a well-shuffled pack of 52 cards. Find the probability distribution of the number of kings.

91. Three cards are drawn from a pack of 52 playing cards. Find the probability distribution of the number of aces.

92. From a lot of 30 bulbs which includes 6 defectives, a sample of 4 bulbs is drawn at random with replacement . Find the probability distribution of the number of defective bulbs.

93.. A random variable X takes the values –3, –2, 0, 1, 2 and 3 such that :

$P(X=0)=P(X>0)=P(X<0);$

$P(X=-3)=P(X-2)=P(X=-1);$

$P(X=1)=P(X=2)=P(X=3);$

Obtain the probability distribution of X.

94. Let X be a random variable which assumes values x_1, x_2, x_3, x_4 such that $2P(X=x_1)=3P(X=x_2)=P(X=x_3)=5P(X=x_4)$. Find the probability distribution of X.

Questions based on Mean and Variance of a Probability Distributions :

95. Find the mean and varialce of the numberof heads in the two tosses of a coin.

96. Find the mean, variance and standard deviation of the number of heads in a simultaneous toss of three coins.

97. A die is tossed twice. A "success" is "getting an odd number" on a random toss. Find the variance of the number of successes.

98. Two cards are drawn successively with replacement from a well-shuffled deck of 52 cards. Find the mean and standard deviation of the number of aces.

99. Two cards are drawn successively without replacement from a well-shuffled deck of 52 cards. Compute the variance of the number of aces.

100. Find the variance of the number obtained on a throw of an unbiased die.

101. A and B throw with one die for a stake of Rs. 11 , which is to be won by the player who first throws 6. If A has the first throw , what are their respective expectations?

Questions based on Binomial Distributions :

102. A die is thrown 6 times. If "getting an odd number" is a "success", what is the probability of
   (i) 5 successes?
   (ii) at least 5 successes.?
   (iii) at most 5 successes?
   (iv) at least one success?
   (v) no success?

103. A pair of dice is thrown 7 times. If getting a total of 7 as a success, what is the probability of
   (i) no success ?
   (ii) 6 successes ?
   (iii) at least 6 successes?
   (iv) at most 6 successes ?

104. An urn contains 5 white, 7 red and 8 black balls. If four balls are drawn one by one with replacement, what is the probability that
   (i) all are white ? (ii) only 3 are white ?
   (iii) none is white ? (iv) at least three are white ?

105. A man takes a step forward with probability 0.4 and backwards with probability 0.6. Find the probability that at the end of eleven steps he is just one step away from the starting point.

106. An urn contains 25 balls of which 10 balls bear a mark 'A' and the remaining 15 balls bear a mark 'B'. A ball is drawn at random from the urn, its mark is noted down and it is replaced. If 6 balls in this way, find the probability that
   (i) all will bear 'A' mark
   (ii) not more than 2 will bear 'B' mark
   (iii) the number of balls with 'A' mark and 'B' mark will be equal
   (iv) at least one ball will bear 'B' mark

107. The probability of a man hitting a target is 1/4 . How many times must he fire so that the probability of his hitting the target at least once is greater than 2/3?

108. How many dice must be thrown so that there is a better than even chance of obtaining a six ?

109. If m things are distributed among 'a' men and 'b' women, show that the probability that the number of things received by men is odd is $\frac{1}{2}\times\left\{\frac{(b+a)^m-(b-a)^m}{(b+a)^m}\right\}$.

110. Suppose the probability for A to win a game against B is 0.4. If A has an option of playing a " best of 3 games" or a " best of 5 games " match against B, which option should A choose so that the probability of his winning the match is higher ? (No game ends in a draw).

111. Find the max number of tosses of a pair of dice so that the probability of getting the sum of the digits on the dice equal to 7 on atleast one toss is greater than 0.95.

112. A die is thrown (2n+1) times . Prove that the probability of getting 1 , 3 or 4 atmost n times is 1/2.

113. In a hurdle race, a player has to cross 10 hurdles . The probability that he will clear each hurdle is 5/6 . Find the probability that he will knock down fewer than hurdles.

Questions based on Mean and Variance of a Binomial Distribution:

114 Find the mean ,variance and standard deviation of the binomial distribution with parameters 4 and 1/3.

115. The mean and variance of a binomial distribution are 4 and 4/3 respectively, find $P(X\geq 1)$.

116. If the sum of the mean and variance of binomial distribution for 5 trails is 1.8, find the distribution.

117. The mean and variance of a binomial variable X are 2 and 1 resp. Find the probability that X takes values greater than 1.

118. If a die is thrown ten times , find the probability that a one will occur exactly twice and a three exactly three times.

119. A die is thrown 12 times. What is the probability that each number will come up twice ?

120. If an ordinary die is thrown 20 times. What is the expected number of times that a six will turn up ?

Questions based on Geometrical probability:

121. Two real numbers x and y are chosen at random and are such that $|x|\leq 3$, $|y|\leq 5$. What is the probability that the fraction $\frac{x}{y}$ being positive ?

122. Two real numbers are selected at random from $[-1, 2]$. What is the probability that their sum is greater than unity and their product is less than unity? .

123. Three points P, Q, R are selected at random from the circumference of a circle. Find the probability that the points lie on a semi circle.

124. The sides of a rectangle are chosen at random , each less than a given length 'a' all such lengths being equally likely. Show that the probability that the diagonal is less than a is $\pi/4$.

125. On a straight line of length 'a' ., two points are taken at random. Find the probability that the distance between them is grater than b.

126. Two +ve numbers x and y are chosen at random for which , each of which does not exceed 2 . Find the probability that $xy\leq 1,\ \frac{y}{x}\leq 2$ ...

127. Two friends decide to meet at a spot between 2 P.M and 3 P.M . Whosoever arrives first agrees to wait for 15 minutes or the other . What is the probability that they meet ?

ANSWER

3. (b) $\frac{103}{108}$	**7.** $\frac{1000}{9139}$	**8.** $\frac{11}{4165}$	**13.** $\frac{551}{15134}$	**15.** . $\frac{1}{7}$
16. $\frac{1}{5}$	**17.** $\frac{341}{12^5}$	**18.** $1-\frac{365!}{(365-n)!(365)^n}$	**19.** $\frac{3}{8}$	**20.** $\frac{9}{4}$
21. $\frac{5}{9}$	**22.** $\frac{67}{200}$	**23.** $\frac{11}{36}$	**24.** $\frac{44}{4165}$	**25.** $\frac{4}{9}$
26. $\frac{55}{221}$	**27.** $\frac{17}{105}$	**28.** $\frac{31}{36}$	**29.** $\frac{17}{20}$	**30.** $\frac{7}{13}$
31. $\frac{33}{50}$	**32.**	**33.** $\frac{2}{3}$	**34.** $\frac{1}{2}$	**35.** $\frac{1}{6}$
36. $\frac{1}{6}$	**37.** $\frac{1}{6}$	**38.** $\frac{2}{5}$	**39.** $\frac{197}{3980}$	**40.** $\frac{1}{4}$
41. $\frac{1}{17}$	**42.** $\frac{1}{969}$	**43.** $\frac{3}{5}$	**44.** (i) $\frac{1}{3}$ (ii) $\frac{1}{2}$	**45.** $\frac{1}{3}$
46. $\frac{3}{4}$	**47.** $\frac{97}{100}$	**48.** (i) $\frac{2}{3}$ (ii) $\frac{1}{2}$	**49.** $\frac{2}{15}$	**50.** $\frac{6}{2197}$
51. $\frac{3}{5}$	**52.** $\left(\frac{11}{16}\right)^4$	**53.** $1-\left(\frac{3}{4}\right)$	**54.** (i) $\frac{2}{5}$ (ii) $\frac{1}{10}$	**55.** $\frac{15}{28}$

56. $\frac{8}{663}$ **57.** $\frac{1}{51}$ **58.** $\frac{1}{50}$ **59.** $\frac{25}{56}$ **60.** $\frac{21}{50}$

61. (i) $\frac{6}{49}$ (ii) $\frac{26}{49}$ **62.** $\frac{6}{11}, \frac{5}{11}$ **64.** $\frac{30}{61}, \frac{31}{61}$ **65.** $\frac{19}{42}$ **66.** 0.0345

67. 0.27 **68.** $\frac{29}{63}$ **69.** $\frac{93}{154}$ **70.** $\frac{29}{45}$ **71.** $\frac{28}{69}$

72. $\frac{27}{83}$ **73.** $\frac{1}{52}$ **74.** $\frac{3}{8}$ **75.** 1/3 **76.** 40/41

77. $\frac{24}{29}$ **78.** $\frac{3}{7}$ **79.** $\frac{2}{23}$ **80.** $\frac{36}{61}$ **81.** 10/19

82. 6/13 **83.** 84 2/3 85 11/21 **87.**

87.

X:	0	1	2
P(X):	$\frac{1}{4}$	$\frac{2}{4}$	$\frac{1}{4}$

88.

X:	0	1	2	3	4
P(X):	$\frac{^6C_4}{^{10}C_4}$	$\frac{^4C_1 \times {}^6C_3}{^{10}C_4}$	$\frac{^4C_2 \times {}^6C_2}{^{10}C_4}$	$\frac{^4C_3 \times {}^6C_1}{^{10}C_4}$	$\frac{^4C_4}{^{10}C_4}$

89.

X:	0	1	2
P(X):	$\frac{25}{36}$	$\frac{10}{36}$	$\frac{1}{36}$

90.

X:	0	1	2
P(X):	$\frac{144}{169}$	$\frac{24}{169}$	$\frac{1}{169}$

91.

X:	0	1	2
P(X):	$\frac{144}{169}$	$\frac{24}{169}$	$\frac{1}{169}$

92.

X:	0	1	2	3
P(X):	$\frac{^{48}C_3}{^{52}C_3}$	$\frac{^4C_1 \times {}^{48}C_3}{^{52}C_3}$	$\frac{^4C_2 \times {}^{48}C_2}{^{52}C_3}$	$\frac{^4C_3}{^{52}C_3}$

93.

X:	0	1	2	3	4
P(X):	$\left(\frac{4}{5}\right)^4$	$\frac{4^3}{5^4}$	$\frac{4^2}{5^4}$	$\frac{4}{5^4}$	$\frac{1}{5^4}$

95.

X:	1	2	3	4
P(X):	$\frac{15}{61}$	$\frac{10}{61}$	$\frac{30}{61}$	$\frac{6}{61}$

100. 35/12

101. (Ans. Expectations of A and B are Rs. 6 and Rs. 5.)

102 (i) $6 \times \left(\frac{1}{2}\right)^6$ (ii) $7 \times \left(\frac{1}{2}\right)^6$ (iii) $1-\left(\frac{1}{2}\right)^6$ (iv) $1-\left(\frac{1}{2}\right)^6$ (v) $\left(\frac{1}{2}\right)^6$

103. (i) $\left(\frac{5}{6}\right)^7$ (ii) $35 \times \left(\frac{1}{6}\right)^7$ (iii) $36 \times \left(\frac{1}{6}\right)^7$ (iv) $1-\left(\frac{1}{6}\right)^7$

104. (i) $\left(\frac{1}{4}\right)^4$ (ii) $\frac{12}{4^4}$ (iii) $\left(\frac{3}{4}\right)^4$ (iv) $\frac{13}{4^4}$

105. $^{11}C_5 \times \left(\frac{6}{25}\right)^5$

106. (i) $\left(\frac{2}{5}\right)^6$ (ii) $\frac{23040}{5^6}$ (iii) $\frac{12960}{5^6}$ (iv) $1-\left(\frac{2}{5}\right)^6$.

107. n = 4 **108.** 1/7 **110.** 0.352 **111.** 17 **113.** 3/10

117. 11/16 **118.** 43/1000 **119.** 34/1000 **120.** 10/3 **121.** 1 / 2

122. $\frac{2}{9}\ln 2 + \frac{1}{12} = 0.237$ **123.** 3 / 4 **125.** $\left(\frac{a-b}{a}\right)^2$ **126.** $\left(\frac{3\ln 2+1}{8}\right)$

127. 7/16.

Level – II FOR JEE-MAIN AND ADVANCED EXAMS ONLY

1.Find the probability that

(i) a leap year selected randomly have 53 sundays ? Ans.(2/7)

(ii) a non leap year selected randomly will have 53 sundays. ? Ans.(1/7)

(iii) in a year of 22nd Century chosen at random , there will be 53 sundays.? Ans.(5/28)

2.. A natural number x is chosen at random from first 100 natural numbers such that

$\frac{(x-10)(x-20)}{(x-30)}<0$. Then find the probability of x.

3. A natural number x is chosen at random from the first 100 natural numbers . Then find theprobability of

(i) $\frac{1}{x-2}-1\geq 0$.

(ii) $\frac{1}{x}-1\geq 0$

(iii) $x^2-10x+16\leq 0$

(iv) x, where x is the the least value of

$f(x)=x^{2012}+\frac{4}{x^{500}}+\frac{6}{x^2}$.

(v) $\left(x-\omega^2\right)+2010+2011\omega+2012\omega^2=0$, where w is the non real cube roots of unity.

4. A natural number x is chosen at random from first 50 natural numbers . Find the probabilty of

(i) x, where x satisfies the range of the function

$f(x)=x^{40}+\frac{40}{x}$

(ii) x, where x satisfies the range of the function

$f(x)=\frac{4}{\cos^2 x}+\frac{9}{\cos ec^2 x}$.

(iii) the number of solutions of x in the equations $3^x+4^x+5^x=6^x$.

(iv) x , where x is the number of solutions of $|Z|=6$ and $|Z-3-4i|=5$, where $z\in C$.

(v) x satisfies the in-equation $\frac{1}{|x|-3}<\frac{1}{2}$

(vi) $\log_2\left(\frac{x-3}{x+2}\right)<0$.

(vi) the exponent of 2 in $x=20\times19\times18\times\ldots\ldots\ldots\ldots\times11$.

(vii) x, where x is the number of solution of

$\left[\frac{x}{2}\right]+\left[\frac{x}{3}\right]+\left[\frac{x}{5}\right]=\frac{31}{30}x$, where [,] = G.I.F

5. A natural number is selected at random from the first 100 natural numbers .

Find the probability that the number

(i) is a perfect square.

(ii) is a perfect cube .

(iii) is a perfect fourth power.

(iv) is a perfect fifth power.

(v) is a perfect sixth power.

(vi) is a perfect number.

(vii) has only two factors.

(viii) has only three factors.

(ix) has only four factors.

(x) has only five factors.

6. A natural number. x is chosen at random from $\{1,2,\ldots\ldots\ldots\ldots\ldots,10\}$ such that $x^3-6x^2+11x-6=0$

Then find the probability of x.

7. Two natural numbers are chosen at random from the first 30 natural numbers .

Find the probability of getting

(i) the sum is even.

(ii) the sum is odd.

(iii) both are prime numbers.

(iv) both are twin primes.

(v) both are co-primes.

(vi) both are perfect numbers.

(vii) both the numbers have only two factors.

(viii) both the numbers have only thre factors.

(ix) their product always lies in the set.

(x) their product is 20

(xi) Difference of two numbers is 2.

(xii) Difference of two numbers is 3.

8. Two distict natural numbers are chosen at random from the first 100 natural numbers . Find the probability that

(i) first one is divisible by 2 and the 2nd one is divisible by 3.

(ii) both are divisible by 2 or 3.

(iii) both are divisible by 2 and 3.

(iv) both are neither divisible by 2 nor 3.

(v) the two numbers x and y satisfies the equation 3x - 4 y = 0.

9. Two distict natural numbers are chosen at random from the first 50 natural numbers . Find the probability that

(i) if 2nd one is the square of the fist one.

(ii) their product has only three factors.

(iii) one is an odd number and the other is a perfect number.

(iv) both are composite numbers.

(v) if 2nd one is the cube of the first one..

10. A die is thrown thrice . Find the probabilty of getting

(i) a sum.of 3

(ii) a sum of 4..

(iii) a sum of 5..

(iv) a sum of at-least 5..

(v) a sum of 7

(vi) a sum of 8.

(vii) a sum of 10

(viii) a sum of 15.

(ix) a sum of at-least 15.

(x) a sum of at-least 16.

11. If two of the 64 squares are chosen at random on a chess board. Find the probabilty that they have a side in common. Ans. (1/18)
12. In throwing 3 dice, find the probabilty that atleast 2 of the three numbers obtained are same.
13. A committee of 5 is to be chosen from a group of 9 people . Find the probability that a certain married couple will either serve together or not at all.
14. A natural number x is chosen at random from the first 1000 natural numbers . Find the probability that x has 3-factors.
15. A coin is tossed and a die is thrown . Find the rpobability that the outcome will be a head or a number greater than 4 .
16. Thirteen persons take their place at a round table . Find the odds against two particular persons sitting together.
17. A bag contains 5 white, 7 black and 4 red balls . Find the probability that three balls drawn at random are all white.
18. Two red balls , 3 green balls and 4 blue balls are placed in a row in random order . Find the probability that no two blue ball are adjacent.
19. Of all the mapping that can be defined from the set A = $\{1,2,3,4\}$ to the set B = $\{5,6,7,8,9\}$, a mapping is a selected at random . Find the probability that the selected mapping is strictly monotonic.
20. In a singlle throw of three dice. Find the probability of getting a total of 5 . Ans (1/36)
21. In a single throw of three dice . Find the probability of getting a total of atleast 5. Ans. (5/108)
22. An unbiased cubic die marked with 1, 2, 2, 3, 3, 3 is rolled 3 times . Find the probability of getting a total score of 4 or 6.
23. In a single throw of three dice , find the probability of getting a total of atleast 15.
24. A determinant is chosen at random from the set of all determinants of order 2 with elements 0 or 1 only. Find the probability that that determinant chosen has the value non - ve . Ans. (13/16)
25. A gambler draws a card from a pack of 52 cards, replace it and shuffles the pack. He continues during this till he draws a spade. Find the probability that he will fail exactly the first two time.
26. Three dice are thrown . Find the probabilty of getting a sum, which is a perfect square.
27. Three distict numbers are selected at random from the set A = $\{1,2,..........,10\}$. Find the probability that the product of two of the number is equal to the third.
28. (i) Two numbers a and b are chosen at random from the set A = $\{1,2,..........,10\}$. Then find the probability that $a^2 + b^2$ is divisible by 5.

    (ii) Three naturan number a, b and c are chosen at random from the set A = $\{1,2,..........,10\}$.

    Then find the probability that $a^2 + b^2 + c^2$ is divisible by 5.

    (iii) Two natural numbers are chosen at random from the set A = $\{1,2,..........,10\}$. Then find the probability that $a^3 + b^3$ is divisible by 2.
29. Find the probability out of 10 persons (all born in 1st April) atleast two of them have same birthday.
30. Three natural numbers are chosen at random without replacement from the set $A = \{x : 1 \le x \le 10,\ x \in N\}$. Find the probability that min of the chosen number is 3 and the maximum is 7.
31. A and B draw two cards each , one after another , from a pack of 52 cards. Find the probability that all the four cards drawn are of the same suit.
32.. There are 7 seats in a row. three persons take seats at random. Find the probability that the middle seat is always occupied and no two persons are consecutive. Ans. (4/35)
33.. A word is selected at random from the word MIRACLE. Find the probability of all those words , where vowel occupied odd places. Ans. (4/35).
34. From a group of 10 persons consisting of 5 Lawers , 3 Doctors and 2 Engineers . Four persons are selected at random . Find the probability that the selection contains atleast one of each category.
35. A coin is tossed repeatedly. A and B call alternately for winning a prize of Rs 30 one who call correctly first wins the prize. A strts call. The find the expectation of A and B.
36. The interrior angles of a regular polygon are 150° each. Find the probability of getting of the number of diagonals of the given regular polygon.
37. Three distict numbers are selected random from the first 100 natural numbers . Find the probability that all the three natural numbers are divisible by 2 and 3.
38.. A function is selected at random from all the functions defined over a given set A consisting of 3-distict elements. Find the probability that the mapping selected is one-one.
39. In a convex haxagon , two diagonals are drawn at random . Find the probability that the diagonals intersect at an interrior point of the hexagon.
40. If all the letters of the word' SOCIETY' are arranged , then find the probability that all vowels come together.
41. If all the letters of the word 'RANDOM' are arranged , then find the probability that two vowels never come together.
42.. If all the letters of the word 'SUNDAYTIMES' are arranged, then find the probability that no two vowels occur together.
43. If all the letters of the word 'INDEPENDENT' are arranged , then find the probability that no two E's are adjacent.
43.. Three letters are to be sent to different persons and addresses on the three envelopes are also be written without

looking at the address . Find the probability that the letters go into the right envelope.

44. Four letters are to be written to four different persons and addresses on the 4 envelopes are also written. Without looking at the addresses , the letters are kept in those envelopes. Find the probability that all the letters are not placed into their right envelopes.

45. Four letters are to be written to four different persons and addresses on the 4 envelopes are also written. Without looking at the addresses , the letters are kept in those envelopes. Find the probability that atleast one letter into right envelope.

46 Four letters are to be written to four different persons and addresses on the 4 envelopes are also written. Without looking at the addresses , the letters are kept in those envelopes. Find the probability that 2 letters are in right envelope.

47. Three identical dice are rolled . Find the probability that same number will appear on each of them.

48. In a throw of a die . Find the probability of getting one in even number of throw.

49. Consider the system of equations ax+by = 0 , cx+dy = 0 , where a, b, c, d $\in \{0,1\}$. Find the probability that the system of equations has a unique solutions. Ans.(1/8)

50. Let ω be a complex cube root of unity with $\omega \neq 1$. A fair die is thrown 3 times. If r_1, r_2, r_3 are the number obtained on the die. then find the probability that $\omega^{r_1} + \omega^{r_2} + \omega^{r_3} = 0$.

51. If four vertices of a regular Octagon are chosen at random , then find the probability that the quadrilateral formed by them is a rectangle.

52. 6 girls and 6 boys sit together randomly in a row. Then find the probability that no two boys sit together.

53. Three of the six vertices of a regular hexagon are chosen at random . Find the probability that the triangle formed by these vertices is an equilateral.

54. A mapping is selected at random from the set of all mapping of the set $A = \{1, 2, ..., n\}$. Find the probability that the mapping selected is bijective.

55. A mapping is selected at random from $f : \{x_1, x_2, x_3, x_4, x_5\} \rightarrow \{y_1, y_2, y_3, y_4, y_5\}$ such that $f(x_i) \neq y_i$, i = 1, 2, 3, 4, 5 . Find the probability that the selected mapping is one-one.

56. Two lovers decide to meet at a spot between 2 P.M and 3 P.M . Whomsoever arrives first agrees to wait for 15 minutes for the other . What is the probability that they meet?

57. A pair of dice is rolled together till a sum of either 5 or 7 is obtained . Find the probability that 5 comes before 7.

58. The probability of India winning a test match against West-indies is ½. Assuming independence from match to match, find the probability that in a 5 match series India's second win occurs at the third test.

59. A and B each throw a die. Find the probability that A's throw is not greater than B's throw.

60. You are given a box with 20 cards in it. 10 of these cards have the letter I printed on them. The other ten have the letter T printed on them. If you pick up 3 cards at random and keep them in the same order , find the probability of making the word 'IIT'.

61. If three distinct numbers are chosen randomly from the first 100 natural numbers . Find the probability that all three of them are divisible by both 2 and 3.

62. Let set A has 7 elements and set B has 5 elements . If one function is selected from all possible defined functions from A to B , then find the probability that it is onto.

63. A die is rolled three times. Find the probability of getting a larger number than the previous number.

64. Four small squares on a chess board are selected at random. Find the probability that they form a square of the size 2 × 2.

ANSWER

2. 9/50

3. (i) 1/100, (ii) 1/100, (iii) 7/100, (iv) 11/100, (v) 1/100

4. (i) 1/5, (ii) 13/25, (iii) 1/50, (iv) 0, (v) 47/50, (vi) 1, (vii) 1/5, (viii) 3/5

5. (i) 1/10, (ii) 1/25, (iii) 3/100, (iv) 1/50, (v) 1/50, (vi) 1/50, (vii) 6/25

6. 3/10

7. (iii) 3/29, (vi) 1/15, (vii) 1/3, (ix) 1/3, (x) 1/5

8. (i) 1/25, (ii) 67/100, (iii) 1/25, (iv) 21/25, (v) 1/2

9. (i) 9/50, (ii) 1/5, (iii) 1, (v) 3/50,

10. (i) 1/216, (ii) 1/72, (iii) 1/36, (iv) 207/216, (v) 5/72, (vi) 7/72, (vii) 1/9, (viii) 1/54, (ix) 13/216, (x) 5/108

11. (1/18) **12.** (1/2) **13.** (4/9) **14.** 11/1000 **15.** 2/3

16. 5 : 1 **17.** 1/56 **18.** 5/42 **19.** 2/125 **20.** 1/36

21. 5/108 **22.** 13/216 **23.** 5/108 **24.** 13/16 **25.** 9/64

26. 17/108 **27.** 1/40**28.** (i) 1/15 **29.** $\left(1 - \frac{{}^{30}C_{10}}{(30)^{10}}\right)$. **30.** 1/40

31. $\left(\frac{44}{85 \times 49}\right)$ **32.** 4/35 **33.** 4/35 **34.** 1/2 **35.** A-**Rs.**20, B-Rs 10

36. 9/11 **37.** 4/1155 **38.** 2/9 **39.** 5/12 **40.** 1/7

41. 2/3 **42.** 7/33 **43.** 28/55 **43.** 1/6 **44.** 9/24
45. 23/24 **46.** 5/24 **47.** 1/36 **48.** 5/11 **49.** 1/8
50. 2/9 **51.** 1/8 **52.** 1/22 **53.** 1/10 **54.** $\left(\frac{n^n}{n!}\right)$
55. 11/30 **56.** 7/16 **57.** 2/5 **58.** 1/4 **59.** 7/12
60. 9/80 **61.** 4/1155 **62.** $\left(\frac{7!\times 2}{3\times 5^6}\right)$ **63.** 5/54 **64.** 7/90768

OBJECTIVE TYPE QUESTIONS (FOR JEE-MAIN AND ADVANCED EXAMS ONLY)

1. A person draws a card from a pack of playing cards, replaces it and shuffles the pack. He continues doing this until he shows a spade. The chance that he will fail the first two times is
(a) $\frac{9}{64}$ (b) $\frac{1}{64}$
(c) $\frac{1}{16}$ (d) $\frac{9}{16}$

2. Three letter are written to diffrent persons, and addresses on three envelopes are also written. Without looking at the adresses, one letter is put in each envelope the probability that the letters go into right envelope is
(a) $\frac{1}{27}$ (b) $\frac{1}{6}$
(c) $\frac{1}{9}$ (d) $\frac{1}{15}$

3. Three identical dice are rolled . The probability that the same number will appear on each of them is
(a) $\frac{1}{6}$ (b) $\frac{1}{36}$
(c) $\frac{1}{18}$ (d) $\frac{1}{28}$

4. The probability that a leap year have 52 tuesday is
(a) $\frac{1}{7}$ (b) $\frac{3}{7}$
(c) $\frac{2}{7}$ (d) $\frac{5}{7}$

5. The probability that at-least one of the events A and B occurs is 0.6 . If A and B occur simulta neously with probability 0.2 , then $P(\overline{A})+P(\overline{B})$ is
(a) 0.4 (b) 0.8
(c) 1.2 (d) 1.4

6. A and B are two independent events . The probability that both A and B occur is $\frac{1}{6}$ and the probability that neither of them is $\frac{1}{3}$. Then the probability of the two events are respectively, is
(a) $\frac{1}{2}\&\frac{1}{3}$ (b) $\frac{1}{5}\&\frac{1}{6}$
(c) $\frac{1}{2}\&\frac{1}{6}$ (d) $\frac{2}{3}\&\frac{1}{4}$

7. The probability that a person will hit a target is 0.3 . If he shoots 10 times , then the probability that the target is hit is
(a) 1 (b) $1-(0.7)^{10}$
(c) $(0.7)^{10}$ (d) $(0.3)^{10}$

8. The probability that a man lives after 10 years is 1/4 and the probability of his wife is alive after 10 years is 1/3. The probability that neither of them alive after 10 years is
(a) 1/2 (b) 1/12
(c) 7/12 (d) 3/4

9. A coin is tossed twice. If the second throw result in a tail, a die is thrown . The number of points in the sample space is
(a) 5 (b) 9
(c) 10 (d) 14.

10. The probability that three persons have same birthday is
(a) $\frac{1}{(365)^2}$ (b) $\frac{1}{(365)^3}$
(c) $\frac{364}{(365)^2}$ (d) $1-\frac{364\times 363}{(365)^2}$

11. A sample space has only 3 points $\omega_1,\omega_2,\omega_3$. If ω_1 is twice as likely to occur as ω_2 and ω_2 is twice as likely as ω_3, then the probability of ω_3 is
(a) 1/7 (b) 2/7
(c) 3/7 (d) 4/7

12. Three coins are tossed simultaneously . The head may appear in one, two , all the three or in none.
The probabilities assigned to these events are respectively
(a) $\frac{1}{4},\frac{1}{4},\frac{1}{4},\frac{1}{4}$ (b) $\frac{3}{8},\frac{2}{8},\frac{3}{8},0$
(c) $\frac{1}{8},\frac{2}{8},\frac{3}{8},\frac{2}{8}$ (d) $\frac{3}{8},\frac{3}{8},\frac{1}{8},\frac{1}{8}$

13. P and Q stand in a line with 10 other people. The probability that there will be three persons between P and Q is
(a) 4/33 (b) 1/66
(c) 2/99 (d) 5/132

14. If p, q, r be the probability of three independent events of the given alternatives, which one is true ?
(a) $p+q+r=1$ (b) $p+q+r \leq 3$
(c) $p+q+r<3$ (d) $p+q+r<4$

15. There are three children in a family, then the probability that there is one girl child in the family is
(a) 2/3 (b) 1/3
(c) 3/28 (d) 3/8.

16. A fair die is thrown and a number greater than 4 appears. The probability that an even number of tosses is needed is
(a) 1/2 (b) 2/5
(c) 1/5 (d) 2/3

17. A coin is tossed 3 times. Let E be the event that the second toss results is a tail. Then P(E) is
(a) 1/2 (b) 3/8
(c) 5/8 (d) 1/4

18. Let $P(E)=x$, $P(F)=y$ and $P(E \cap F)=z$, then $P\left(\left(E \cap \bar{F}\right) \cup \left(\bar{E} \cap F\right)\right)$ is
(a) $x+y+z$ (b) $x+y-z$
(c) $x+y-2z$ (d) $2x+y-2z$.

19. A coin is tossed and a die is rolled. The probability that the coin shows the head and die shows 6 is
(a) 1/2 (b) 1/6
(c) 1/12 (d) 1/24

20. Two natural numbers are randomly chosen from first 40 natural numbers. The probability that the sum of two numbers is odd is
(a) 14/29 (b) 20/39
(c) 1/2 (d) 1/3

21. Given that a throw of three fair dice shows different faces, the probability that at least one face shows 6 is
(a) 5/6 (b) 5/18
(c) 1/2 (d) 13/18

22. A single letter is selected at random from the word 'PROBABILITY'. The probability that it is a vowel is
(a) 3/11 (b) 4/11
(c) 2/11 (d) 5/11

23. From each of three married couples, one of the partners is selected at random. The probability of their being of same sex is
(a) 1/8 (b) 1/9
(c) 1/4 (d) 1/2

24. Three natural numbers are chosen at random from first 10 natural numbers. The probability that the minimum of the chosen number is 3 and the maximum is 7, is
(a) 29/40 (b) 11/40
(c) 1/4 (d) 31/40

25. A die is thrown n times. For the probability of a six appearing at-least once to be more than 1/2 is
(a) $n=6$ (b) $n>3$
(c) $n<4$ (d) $n=2$

26. Four digit numbers are formed using the digits 1, 2, 3, ..., 8 only once. One number is chosen at random. The probability that the selected number contains unity is
(a) 1/8 (b) 1/4
(c) 1/2 (d) 1/3

27. Six fair dice are thrown. The probability that different numbers will turn up is equal to
(a) 5/36 (b) 5/324
(c) 1/108 (d) 1/324

28. A fair coin is tossed repeatedly. If tail appears on first four tosses, then the probability of head appearing on fifth toss is
(a) 1/2 (b) 1/32
(c) 31/32 (d) 1/5

29. If from each of the three boxes containing 3 white and 1 black, 2 white and 2 black, 1 white and 3 black balls, one ball is drawn at random, then the probability that 2 white and 1 black ball will be drawn is
(a) 13/32 (b) 1/4
(c) 1/32 (d) 3/16.

30. Three dice are thrown together. The probability of getting the same digit on each of them will be
(a) 1/6 (b) 1/36
(c) 1/18 (d) 3/28

31. Three dice are rolled. The probability of getting different faces is
(a) 1/3 (b) 1/4
(c) 5/9 (d) 4/9

32. Three distinct natural numbers are chosen at random from first 100 natural numbers. The probability that all the three numbers are divisible by 2 and 3 is
(a) 4/25 (b) 4/35
(c) 4/55 (d) 4/1155

33. A six faced fair dice is thrown until 1 comes, then the probability that 1 comes in even number of trials is
(a) 5/11 (b) 5/6
(c) 6/11 (d) 1/6

34. If x is a positive integer, then the probability that 3^x has 3 at unit place is
(a) 1/4 (b) 1/5
(c) 3/10 (d) 1/8

35. A natural number x is chosen at random from first 30 natural numbers. The probability of $x^2-10x+21<0$ is
(a) 1/6 (b) 1/10
(c) 1/12 (d) 1/15.

36. A matrix of order 2 is formed from the set of $\{-1, 1\}$. The probability that the matrix is singular is
(a) 1/2 (b) 1/3
(c) 1/4 (d) 1/5

37. A determinant of order 2 is formed from the set of $\{0, 1\}$. The probability that the value of the determinant is non-ve is

(a) 13/16 (b) 3/8
(c) 1/16 (d) 5/16

38. In a class there are 5 boys and 4 girls are seated in a row. The probabilty that they will seat in alternate is
(a) $\frac{(5)!\times(4)!}{(9)!}$ (b) $\frac{(6)!\times(4)!}{(9)!}$
(c) $\frac{(3)!\times(4)!}{(9)!}$ (d) $\frac{2\times(5)!\times(4)!}{(9)!}$

39. In a class there are 6 boys and 6 girls are seated in a row. The probability that they will seat in alternate is
(a) $\frac{2\times(6)!\times(5)!}{(12)!}$ (b) $\frac{2\times(6)!\times(6)!}{(12)!}$
(c) $\frac{(6)!\times(6)!}{(12)!}$ (d) $\frac{(5)!\times(6)!}{(12)!}$

40. Two events A and B have probabilities 0.25 and 0.50 respectively , the probability that both A and B occur simultaneously is 0.14 , then the probability that neither A nor B occurs is
(a) 0.39 (b) 0.25
(c) 0.11 (d) None.

41. The probability that an event A happens in one trial or an experiment is 0.4. Three independent trials of these experiments are performed. The probability that the event A happens at least once is
(a) 0.936 (b) 0.784
(c) 0.904 (d) None

42. If A and B are two independent events such that P(A) > 0 and P(B) $\neq$ 1 , then $P\left(\frac{\overline{A}}{\overline{B}}\right)$ is equal to
(a) $1-P(A/B)$ (b) $1-P(A/\overline{B})$
(c) $\frac{1-P(A\cup B)}{P(B)}$ (d) $\frac{P(\overline{A})}{P(\overline{B})}$

43. The probability that at least one of the events A and B occurs is 0.6 . If A and B occur simultaneously with probability 0.2 , then $P(\overline{A})+P(\overline{B})$ is
(a) 0.4 (b) 0.8
(c) 1.2 (d) 1.4

44. India plays two matches each with west Indies and Australia. In any match the probabilities of India getting points 0, 1 and 2 are 0.45 , 0.05 and 0.50 respectively. Assuming that the outcomes are independent , the probability of india getting at least 7 points is
(a) 0.8750 (b) 0.0875
(c) 0.0625 (d) 0.0250

45. An unbiased die with faces marked 1, 2, 3, 4, 5 and 6 is rolled four times. Out of four face values obtained, the probability that the minimum face value is not less than 2 and the maximum face value is not greater than 5 is then
(a) 16/81 (c) 1/81
(c) 80/81 (d) 65/81

46. The probability of India winning a test match against West Indies is ½ . Assuming independence from match to match the probability that in a 5 match series India's second win occurs at third test is
(a) 1/8 (b) 1/4
(c) 1/2 (d) 2/3

47. Let $0<P(A)<1, 0<P(B)<1$ and $P(A\cup B)=P(A)+P(B)-P(A)P(B)$, then
(a) $P(B/A)=P(B)-P(A)$
(b) $p(A'-B')=P(A')-P(B')$
(c) $P(A\cup B)'=P(A')\,P(B')$
(d) $P(A/B)=P(A)$.

48. Three of the six vertices of a regular hexagon are chosen at random . The probability that the triangle with three vertices is equilateral , equals
(a) 1/2 (b) 1/5
(c) 1/10 (d) 1/20.

49. For the three events A, B, C , P(Exactly one of A or B occurs) = P(Exactly one of B or C occurs) = P (Exactly one of C or A occurs) = p and P(all the three events occurs simultaneously) $=p^2$, where $0<p<1/2$, then the probability that at-least one of A, B, C occurring is
(a) $\frac{3p+2p^2}{2}$ (b) $\frac{p+3p^2}{4}$
(c) $\frac{p+3p^2}{2}$ (d) $\frac{3p+2p^2}{4}$

50. Three numbers are chosen at random without replacement from {1, 2,..........., 10 }. The probability that the minimum of the chosen numbers is 3 , or their maximum is 7, is ....
(a) 13/60. (b) 17/60
(c) 19/60 (d) 23/60

51. Seven white balls and three black balls are randomly placed in a row. The probability that no two black balls are placed adjacently equals ,
(a) 1/2 (b) 7/15
(c) 2/15 (d) 1/3

52. If from each of the three boxes containing 3 white and 1 black , 2 white and 2 black , 1 white and 3 black balls , one ball is drawn at random , then the probability that 2 white and 1 black ball will be drawn is
(a) 13/32 (b) 1/4
(c) 1/32 (d) 3/16

53. If the integers m and n are chosen at random b/w 1 and 100, then the probability that a number of the form is divisible by 5 equals
(a) 1/4 (b) 1/7
(c) 1/8 (d) 1/49.

54. Two numbers are selected randomly from the set S = { 1, 2, 3, 4, 5, 6} without replacement one by one. The probability that minimum of the two numbers is less than 4 is

(a) 1/15 (b) 14/15
(c) 1/5 (d) 4/5.

55. If $P(B)=\frac{3}{4}$, $P(A\cap B\cap \bar{C})=\frac{1}{3}$ and $P(\bar{A}\cap B\cap \bar{C})=\frac{1}{3}$, then $P(B\cap C)$ is
(a) 1/12 (b) 1/8
(c) 1/15 (d) 1/9

56. A fair die is rolled. The probability that the first time 1 occurs at the even number of trials is
(a) 6/11 (b) 1/6
(c) 5/36 (d) 5/11

57. Let ω be a complex cube root of unity with $\omega \neq 1$. A fair die is thrown three times. If r_1, r_2 & r_3 are the numbers obtained on the die, then the probability that $\omega^{r_1}+\omega^{r_2}+\omega^{r_3}=0$ is
(a) 1/18 (b) 1/9
(c) 2/9 (d) 1/36

58. A signal which can be green or red with probability 4/5 and 1/5 respectively, is received by station A and then transmitted to station B. The probability of each station receiving the signal correctly is 3/4. If the signal received at station B is green, then the probability that the original signal was green is
(a) 3/5 (b) 6/7
(c) 20/21 (d) 9/20

ANSWER

1. (a)	2. (b)	3. (b)	4. (d)	5. (c)	6. (a)	7. (b)	8. (a)	9. (d)	10. (d)
11. (a)	12. (d)	13. (a)	14. (a)	15. (d)	16. (b)	17. (a)	18. (c)	19. (c)	20. (b)
21. (d)	22. (b)	23. (c)	24. (b)	25. (a)	26. (c)	27. (b)	28. (a)	29. (a)	30. (b)
31. (c)	32. (d)	33. (a)	34. (a)	35. (b)	36. (b)	37. (b)	38. (a)	39. (a)	40. (a)
41. (c)	42. (b)	43. (c)	44. (b)	45. (c)	46. (b)	47. (c)	48. (c)	49. (a)	50. (a)
51. (b)	52. (a)	53. (a)	54. (d)	55. (a)	56. (b)	57. (a)	58. (a)		

Level – III FOR JEE ADVANCED EXAM ONLY

1. The probability that a person will hit a target in a shooting practice is 0.3. If he shoots 10 times, then find the probability
2. A ten digits number is formed using the digits from 0 to 9, every digit being used exactly once. Find the probability that the number is divisible by four.
3. The probability that a man lives after 10 years is 1/4. The probability that his wife is alive after 10 years is 1/3. Find the probability that neither of them is alive after 10 years.
4. Three persons A, B, C in order cut a pack of cards, replacing them after each cut, on the condition that the first who cuts a card of spade shall win a prize. Find their respective probabilities.
5. Find the probability that three persons have same date and month of the birthday.
6. Find the minimum number of tosses of a pair of dice, so that probability of getting the sum of the dice equal to 7 on atleast one toss is greater than 0.95 [Given, $\log_{10} 2 = 0.3010$ and $\log_{10} 3 = 0.4771$]
7. Two numbers are selected at random from 1, 2, 3, ..., 100 and are multiplied. Find the probability correct to two places of decimals that the product thus obtained, is divisible by 3.
8. Three groups A, B and C are competing for positions on the Board of Directors of a company. The probabilities of their winning are 0.5, 0.3, 0.2 respectively. If the group A wins the probability of introducing a new product is 0.7 and the corresponding probabilities for group B and C are 0.6 and 0.5 respectively. Find the probability that the new product will be introduced.
9. A factory A produces 10% defective valves and another factory B produces 20% defective. A bag contains 4 valves of factory A and 5 valves of factory B. If two valves are drawn at random from the bag. Then find the probability that at least one valve is defective. Give your answer upto two places of decimals.
10. From each of three married couples one of the partners is selected at random. Find the probability of their being of same sex.
11. A die is thrown n times. Find the probability of a six appearing at least once to be more than 1/2.
12. There is 30% chance that it rains on any particular day. What is the probability that there is at-least one rainy day within a period of 7-days? Given that there is at least one rainy day. What is the probability that there are at least two rainy days?
13. Each co-efficient in the equation $ax^2+bx+c=0$ is determined by throwing an ordinary die. Find the probability that the equation will have equal roots.
14. Four cards are drawn from a pack of 52 playing cards. Find the probability (correct upto two places of decimals) of drawing exactly one pair.
15. A and B are two independent events. The probability that both occur simultaneously is 1/6, and the probability that neither occurs is 1/3. Find the probabilities of occurrence of the events A and B separately.

16. Two cards are drawn at random from a pack of 52 playing cards. Find the probability that one card is a heart and the other is an ace.
17. A pair of four dice is rolled together till a sum of either 5 or 7 is obtained. Then the probability that 5 comes before 7 is ....
18. A is a set containing n elements . A subset P of A is chosen at random . The set A constructed by replacing the elements of P. A subset Q of A is again chosen at random. Find the probability that P and Q have no common elements.
19. Let A and B between such that P(A) = 0.3 and $P(A \cup B) =$ 0.8 . If A and B are independent events , then P(B) is ....
20. In a test an examination either guesses or copies or knows the answer to a multiple choice question with four choices. The probability that he make a guess is 1/3 and the probability that he copies the answer is 1/6 . The probability that his answer is correct given that he copied it is 1/8 . Find the probability that he knew the answer to the question given that he correctly answered it.
21. Numbers are selected at random, one at a time , from the two digit numbers 00, 01, 02, 03,...........,99 with replacement. An event E occurs if and only if the product of the two digits of a selected number is 18. If four numbers are selected, find the probability that the event E occurs at least 3 times.
22. Three faces of a fair die are yellow, two faces red and one blue. The die is tossed three times. The probability that the colors , yellow, red, and blue appear in the first, second and the third tosses respectively is ....
23. There are four balls of different colors and four boxes of colors , same as those of the balls. The number of ways in which the balls , one each in a box, could be placed such that a ball does not go to a box of its own color is ....
24. An unbiased coin is tossed . If the result is a head a pair of unbiased dice is rolled and the number obtained by adding the numbers on the two faces is noted. If the result is a tail , a card from a well shuffled pack of eleven cards numbered 2, 3, 4, ..., 12 is picked and the number is noted. What is the probability that the noted number is 7 or 8.
25. In how many ways three girls and nine boys can be seated in two vans , each having numbered seats, 3 in the front and 4 at the back ? How many seating arrangement are possible if 3 girls should sit together in a back row on adjacent seats ? Now if all the seating arrangements are equally likely, what is the probability of 3 girls sitting together in a back row on adjacent seats ?
26. If p and q are chosen randomly from the set { 1, 2, 3, 4, 5, 6, 7, 8, 9, 10} with replacement, determine the probability that the roots of the equation $x^2 + px + q = 0$ are real.
27. Sixteen players $S_1, S_2, ..., S_{16}$ play in a tournament. They are divided into eight pairs at random. From each pair a winner is decided on the basis of a game played between the two players are of equal strength.

    (a) Find the probability that the player S_1 is among the eight winners.

    (b) Find the probability that exactly one of the two players S_1 and S_2 is among the eight winners.
28. The probabilities that a student passes in Mathematics , Physics and Chemistry are m, p and c resp. of these subjects, the student has a 75% change of passing in at least one , a 50% change of passing in at-least two , and a 40% change of passing in exactly two. Which of the following relations are true.

    (a) p+m+c=19/20 (b) p+m+c=27/20

    (c) pmc=1/10 (d) pmc=¼.
29. Eight players play a knock-out tournament . It is known that whenever the players and play, the player will win if. Assuming that the player are paired at random in each round, what is the probability that the player reaches the final ?
30. A coin has probability of showing head when tossed. It is tossed n times , let denote the probability that no two (or more) consecutive heads occur. Prove that

    $P_1 = 1,\ P_2 = 1 - P^2$ and

    $P_n = (1-P)P_{n-1} + P(1-P)P_{n-2}$ for all $n \geq 3$.
31. An urn contains m white and n black balls . A ball is drawn at random and is put back into the urn along with k additional balls of the same color as that of the ball drawn. A ball is again drawn at random . What is the probability that the ball drawn now is white ?
32. An unbiased die, with faces numbered 1, 2, 3, 4, 5, 6 is thrown n-times and the list of numbers showing up is noted. What is the probability that among the number 1, 2, 3, 4, 5, 6 only three numbers appear in this list?
33. A box contains N coins , m of which are fair and the rest are biased . The probability of getting a head when a fair coin is tossed is 1/2, while it is 2/3 when a biased coin is tossed. A coin is drawn from the box at random and is tossed twice. The first time it shows head and the second time it shows tail . What is the probability that the coin drawn is fair.
34. A is targeting to B , B and C are targeting to A . Probability of hitting the target by A, B and C are 2/3, 1/2 and 1/3 respectively . If A is hit then find the probability that hits the target and C does not.
35. For a student to qualify , he must pass at least two out of three exams . The probability that he will pass the 1st exam is p. If he fails in one of exams then the probability of his passing in the next exam is p/2 , otherwise it remains the same. Find the probability that he will qualify ?
36. Rohan goes to office either by car , scooter , bus or train , probability of which being 1/7 , 3/ 7 , 2/7 and 1/7 respectively and probability that he is reaching office late if he takes car, scooter , bus or train is 2/9 , 1/9 , 1/7 and 1/9 respectively. Find the probability that he has travelled by car, if he reaches office in time.
37. A box contains 12 red and 6 white balls. Balls are drawn from the bag one at a time without replacement . If in 6 draws there are at least 4 white balls , find the probability that exactly one white is drawn in the next two draws (binomial co-efficients can be left as such).

ANSWER

1. $(0.3)^{10}$.
2. 0.26.
3. 1/2
4. P(A)= 16/37 ; P(B) = 12/37 ; P(C) = 9/37.
5. $1-\frac{364\times363}{(365)^2}$
6. n = 17.
7. 33/50.\
8. 0.63.
9. 0.98.
10. ¼.
11. n > 3
12. $1-{}^7C_0\left(\frac{7}{10}\right)^7$, 0.73.
13. 5/216.
14. 0.3204.
15. P(A) = ½, P(B) = 1/3.
16. 191/2652.
17. 2/5.
18. $\frac{1}{2^r}$.
19. 5/7.
20. 24/29.
21. 2.4832×10^{-4}
22. 1/36.
23. 9.
24. 193/792.
25. 1/91.
26. 0.62.
27. (a) 1/2, (b) 8/15.
28. (b), (c)
29. 4/35.
31. $\frac{m}{m+n}$.
32. $\frac{{}^6C_3\times\left[3^n-3.2^n+3\right]}{6^n}$
33. $\frac{9m}{m+8N}$.
34. 1/2
35. $2p^2-p^3$.
36. 1/7.
37. $\frac{{}^{10}C_1\times{}^2C_1}{{}^{12}C_2}\cdot\frac{{}^{12}C_2\times{}^6C_4}{{}^{18}C_6}+\frac{{}^{11}C_1\times{}^1C_1}{{}^{12}C_2}\cdot\frac{{}^{12}C_1\times{}^6C_5}{{}^{18}C_6}$.

LINKED COMPREHENSION TYPE

PASSAGE-1

There are four boxes A1, A2, A3 and A4 . Box A1 has i cards and on each card a number is printed, the numbers are from 0 to i . A box is selected randomly , the probability of selecetion of box Ai is 1/10 and then a card is drawn . Let Ei denote the event that a card with number 'i' is drawn.

(i) P(Ei) is equal to

(a) 1/5 (b) 1/10 (c) 2/5 (d) 1/4.

(ii) P(A3/E2) is equal to

(a) 1/4 (b) 1/3 (c) 1/2 (d) 2/3

(iii) Expectation of the number on the card is

(a) 2 (b) 2.5 (c) 3 (d) 3.5.

PASSAGE-2

A biased coin shows head with a probbility 3/4 and tails with a probability 1/4 . Let Pn denote the probability that no three or more heads appear consecutively in 'n' throws of the coins.

On the basis of the above information answer the following questions.

(i) If $P_n = P_{n-1} + P_{n-2} + P_{n-3}$, then the value of 64(+ +) is

(a) 37 (b) 23 (c) 121 (d) 119.

(ii) The value of P4 is

(a) 121/256 (b) 23/64 (c) 37/64 (d) 119/256

(iii) If the coin is tossed 4-times and let 'A' be the event that three or more head occurs in four tosses and 'B' is the event that three heads do not occur in first three tosses , then P(A/B) is

(a) 27/148 (b) 4/37 (c) 81/148 (d) 5/49.

PASSAGE-3

Let U_1 and U_2 be two urns and U_1 contains 3 white and 2 red balls and U_2 contains only 1 white ball . A fair coin is tossed . If head appears then 1 ball is drawn at random from U_1 and put into U_2.

However, if tail appears then 2 balls are drawn at random from U_1 and put into U_2 . Now 1 ball is drawn at random from U_2.

(i) The probability of the drawn ball from U_2 being white is

(a) 13/30 (b) 23/30 (c) 19/30 (d) 11/30

(ii) Given that the drawn ball from U_2 is white , the probability that head appeared on the coin is

(a) 17/23 (b) 11/23 (c) 15/23 (d) 12/23.

PASSAGE-4

A fair die is tossed repeated untill a six is obtained . Let X denote the number of tosses required.

(i) The probability that X = 3 equals

(a) 25/216 (b) 25/36 (c) 5/36 (d) 125/216.

(ii) The probability that $X\geq3$ equals

(a) 125/216 (b) 25/36 (c) 5/36 (d) 25/216.

(iii) The conditional probability that $X\geq6$ is given X > 3 equals

(a) 125/216 (b) 25/36 (c) 5/36 (d) 25/216.

PASSAGE-5

There are n urns each containing n +1 balls such that ith urn contains I white balls and (n+1-i) red balls. Let be the event of selecting ith urn , i=1, 2, 3,................,n and w denotes the event of getting a white ball.

(i). If $P(u_i)$=i , where i=1,2, 3,..........., n , then $\lim_{n\to\infty} P(w)$ is equal to

(a) 1 (b) 2/3 (c) 3/4 (d) 1/4

(ii) If $P(u_i)$ = c , where c is a constant, then, then $P(u_n/w)$ is equal to

(a) $\frac{2}{n+1}$ (b) $\frac{1}{n+1}$ (c) $\frac{n}{n+1}$ (d) $\frac{1}{2}$.

(iii) If n is even and E denotes the event of choosing even numbered urn $\left(P(u_i)=\frac{1}{n}\right)$, then the value of $P(w/E)$ is

(a) $\frac{n+2}{2n+1}$ (b) $\frac{n+2}{2(n+1)}$

(c) $\frac{n}{n+1}$ (d) $\frac{1}{n+1}$.

ANSWERS

PASSEGE I

(i) (c) (ii) (b) (iii) (a)

PASSEGE II

(ii) (a) (iii) (c)

PASSEGE III

(ii) (d)

PASSEGE IV

(i) (a) (ii) (b)

PASSEGE V

(i). (b) (ii) (a) (iii) (b)

MATCH MATRIX

1. Match the following columns.

A natural number x is chosen at random from first 100 natural numbers.

Column-I	Column-II
(A) If x is the number of solutions of the equation $1^x+6^x+8^x=9^x$, then the probability of x is	(P) 1/50
(B) If x is the number of solution of $3^{\frac{x}{2}}+2^x=5^{\frac{x}{2}}$ then the probability of x is	(Q) 3/50
(C) If x is the number of solutions of $2^x=x^2+1$, then the probability of x is	(R) 1/100
(D) If x is the number of solutions of $\sin(\pi x)=\left|\log_e|x|\right|$ then the probability of x is	(S) 1/25
	(T) 1/5

2. Match the following columns.

A natural number x is chosen at random from first 200 natural numbers .

Column-I	Column-II
(A) If x is the number of solutions of the equation $3^{\lvert x\rvert}\left|2-\lvert x\rvert\right|=1$, then the probability of x is	(P) 3/100
(B) If x is the number of solution of $\left[\frac{x}{2}\right]+\left[\frac{x}{3}\right]+\left[\frac{x}{5}\right]=\frac{31}{30}x$ where [,] = G.I.F , then the probability of x is	(Q) 1/50
(C) If x is the number of solutions of $\left(\frac{3}{5}\right)^x+\frac{x}{5}=2^x$, then the probability of x is	(R) 0
(D) If x is the number of solutions of $5^x+5^{-x}=\log_{10}25$ then the probability of x is	(S) 1/200

3. Match the following columns .

Three distinct natural numbers are chosen at random from first 100 natural numbers . Then the probability of all three of them .

Column-I	Column-II
(A) are divisible by 2 and 3 is	(P) ${}^{8}C_3/{}^{100}C_3$
(B) are divisible by 3 and 4 is	(Q) $1/{}^{100}C_3$
(C) are divisible by 5 and 6 is	(R) $10/{}^{100}C_3$
(D) are divisible by 3 and 7 is	(S) ${}^{16}C_3/{}^{100}C_3$
	(T) $4/{}^{100}C_3$

4. Match the following columns .

Two distinct natural numbers are chosen at random from first 10 natural numbers . Then the probability that .

Column-I	Column-II
(A) Minimum of two numbers is less than 4, is	(P) 1/3
(B) Minimum of two numbers is more than 4, is	(Q) 1/15
(C) Maximum of two numbers is less than 8, is	(R) 2/15
(D) Maximum of two numbers is more than 6, is	(S) 7/15
	(T) 4/15.

5. Match the following columns .

A natural number is chosen at random from first 100 natural numbers . Then the probability that

Column-I	Column-II
(A) the number is a perfect number, is	(P) 1/25
(B) the number is a perfect cube, is	(Q) 3/100

(C) the number has only three factors, is (R) 1/50

(D) the number is a perfect 4th power, is (S) 1/20

(T) 1/10.

6. Match the following columns.

A fair die is rolled. Then the probability that

Column-I	Column-II
(A) the first time 6 occurs at the odd throw, is	(P) 5/11
(B) the first time 3 occurs at the even throw, is	(Q) 3/11
(C) the first time 1 occurs at the odd throw, is	(R) 1/11
(D) the first time 5 occurs at the even throw, is	(S) 5/11

7. Match the following columns :

Five identical pieces of paper have the digits 1 to 5 written on them. The experiment consists in choosing at random three pieces and arranging them in a row from left to right in the order of arrival.

Column-I	Column-II
(A) If A = { the number 123 will appear } then P(A) =	(P) 1/20
(B) If B = { a number will appear that contains 3 }, then P(B) =	(Q) 9/10
(C) If C = { a number will appear that consists of consecutive digits}, P(C) =	(R) 1/60
(D) If D={ an even number will appear } then P(D) =	(S) 1/5
	(T) 2/5.

8. Match the following columns :

An elevator starts with 7 passengers and stops at 10 floors.

Column-I	Column-II
(A) If A = {no two passengers leave at the same floor} then P(A) =	(P) $(10)^{-7}$
(B) If B= {all the passengers are discharged on the 5th floor }, then P(B) =	(Q) $(10)^{-6}$
(C) If C= {all of the passengers are discharged on the same unspecified floor}, then P(C) =	(R) $\dfrac{(10)!}{6\times(10)^7}$
(D) If D = { exactly three of them are discharged on the 2nd floor }, then P(D) =	(S) ${}^7C_3(7)^3/(10)^7$
	(T) ${}^7C_3(7)^4/(10)^7$.

9. Match the following columns :

Over some time interval an amoeba may perish with probability 1/4, survive with probability 1/4 or divide into two with probability 1/2. Over the next time interval of the same duration, whatever its "origin" may be, every emoeba has the same things happen to it. At then end of the second interval match the number of amoeba with the probabilities;

Column-I	Column-II
(A) There may exist 1 amoeba with probability	(P) 1/8
(B) There may exist 2 amoeba with probability	(Q) 5/32
(C) There may exist 3 amoeba with probability	(R) 7/32
(D) There may exist 4 amoeba with probability	(S) 9/32
	(T) 11/32.

10. Match the following columns.

If a fair coin is tossed 10 times, then the probability of

Column-I	Column-II
(A) Exactly six heads is	(P) 53/64
(B) Atleast six heads is	(Q) 105/512
(C) Atmost six heads is	(R) 193/512
(D) No head is	(S) 121/512
	(T) 1/1024

ANSWER

1. (A)→(R); (B)→(R); (C)→(P); (D)→(Q).
2. (A)→(Q); (B)→(R); (C)→(S); (D)→(R).
3. (A)→(S); (B)→(P); (C)→(Q); (D)→(T).
4. (A)→(Q); (B)→(P); (C)→(S); (D)→(R).
5. (A)→(R); (B)→(P); (C)→(P); (D)→(Q).
6. (A)→(S); (B)→(P); (C)→(S); (D)→(P).
7. (A)→(R); (B)→(T); (C)→(P); (D)→(T).
8. (A)→(R); (B)→(P); (C)→(Q); (D)→(T).
9. (A)→(P); (B)→(S); (C)→(P); (D)→(P).
10. (A)→(Q); (B)→(R); (C)→(P); (D)→(T).

Questions asked in Roorkee Exams

1. Three of 6 faced dice are tossed together. Find out the probability of obtaining a sum of 15 of all the three numbers on the dice. **[Roorkee – 1983]**
2. Two cards are drawn one after another from a pack of 52 ordinary cards. Find the probability that the first card drawn is an ace and the second card is an honours card. The first card is not replaced while drawing the 2nd card.
3. No questions asked in **1984.**
4. Three groups of children contain respectively 3 girls and 1 boy, 2 girls and 2 boys, 8 girls and 3 boys. One child is selected at random from each group. What is the probability that three children selected consistsof 1 girl and two boys. **[Roorkee – 1985]**
5. No questions asked in **1986.**
6. In the manufacturer of light bulbs, filaments, glass casings and bases are manufactured separately and then assembled

into final product. From past records we know that 2% of all the filaments are defective , 3 % of all the glass casings are defective, 1 % of all the bases are defective . what is the probability that a bulb randomly selected is defective? **[Roorkee – 1987]**

7. Out of 21 tickets marked with numbers from 1 to 21 , three tickets are drawn at random. Find the probability that the three numbers on them are in A.P. **[Roorkee - 1988]**
8. A five digit number is formed by the digits 1, 2, 3, 4, 5 without repetition . Find the probability that the number formed is divisible by 4. **[Roorkee – 1989]**
9. Five persons entered the lift cabin on the ground floor of an 8 – floor house. Suppose that each of them, independently and with equal probability , can leave the cabin at any floor beginning with the first. Find out the probability of all five persons leaving at different floor. **[Roorkee – 1990]**
10. The probability that a person will hit a target in a shooting practice is 0.3. If he shoots 10 times, then find the probability. **[Roorkee – 1991]**
11. A ten digits number is formed using the digits from 0 to 9 , every digit being used exactly once. Find the probability that the number is divisible by four. **[Roorkee – 1991]**
12. The probability that a man lives after 10 years is 1/4 . The probability that his wife is alive after 10 years is 1/ 3. Find the probability that neither of them is alive after 10 years. **[Roorkee – 1992]**
13. Three persons A, B, C in order cut a pack of cards , replacing them after each cut , on the condition that the first who cuts a card of spade shall win a prize. Find their respective probabilities. **[Roorkee – 1992]**
14. Find the probability that three persons have same date and month of the birthday. **[Roorkee – 1993]**
15. Find the minimum number of tosses of a pair of dice , so that probability of getting the sum of the dice equal to 7 on atleast one toss is greater than 0.95 [Given, $\log_{10} 2 = 0.3010$ and $\log_{10} 3 = 0.4771$] **[Roorkee – 1993]**
16. Two numbers are selected at random from 1, 2, 3 , ..., 100 and are multiplied. Find the probability correct to two places of decimals that the product thus obtained, is divisible by 3. **[Roorkee – 1993]**
17. Three groups A, B and C are competing for positions on the Board of Directors of a company. The probabilities of their winning are 0.5, 0.3, 0.2 respectively . If the group A wins the probability of introducing a new product is 0.7 and the corresponding probabilities for group B and C are 0.6 and 0.5 respectively. Find the probability that the new product will be introduced. **[Roorkee – 1994]**
18. A factory A produces 10% defective valves and another factory B produces 20% defective. A bag contains 4 valves of factory A and 5 valves of factory B . If two valves are drawn at random from the bag. Then find the probability that at least one valve is defective. Give your answer upto two places of decimals. **[Roorkee – 1995]**
19. The probabilities of three events A, B and C are P(A) = 0.6 , P(B) = 0.4 and P(C) = 0.5 .If $P(A \cup B) = 0.8$, $P(A \cap C) = 0.3$, $P(A \cap B \cap C) = 0.2$ and $P(A \cup B \cup C) \geq 0$, then find $P(B \cup C)$. **[Roorkee – 1996]**
20. From each of three married couples one of the partners is selected at random. Find the probability of their being of same sex. **[Roorkee – 1997]**
21. A die is thrown n times. Find the probability of a six appearing at least once to be more than 1/2. **[Roorkee – 1997]**
22. There is 30% chance that it rains on any particular day . What is the probability that there is at-least one rainy day within a period of 7-days? Given that there is at least one rainy day. What is the probability that there are at least two rainy days? **[Roorkee – 1997]**
23. Each co-efficient in the equation $ax^2 + bx + c = 0$ is determined by throwing an ordinary die . Find the probability that the equation will have equal roots. **[Roorkee – 1998]**
24. Four cards are drawn from a pack of 52 playing cards. Find the probability (correct upto two places of decimals) of drawing exactly one pair. **[Roorkee – 1999]**
25. A and B are two independent events. The probability that both occur simultaneously is 1/6, and the probability that neither occurs is 1/3 . Find the probabilities of occurrence of the events A and B separately. **[Roorkee – 2000]**
26. Two cards are drawn at random from a pack of 52 playing cards. Find the probability that one card is a heart and the other is an ace. **[Roorkee – 2001]**

ANSWER

1. 5/108 **2.** 4/221 **4.** 13/32. **6.** 3/5 **7.** 10/133.
8. 1/20. **9.** ${}^7P_5 / 7^5$ **10.** $(0.3)^{10}$. **11.** 0.26. **12.** 1/2
13. P(A)= 16/37 ; P(B) = 12/37 ; P(C) = 9/37. **14.** $1 - \frac{364 \times 363}{(365)^2}$ **15.** n = 17. **16.** 33/50.
17. 0.63. **18.** 0.98. **19.** $P(B \cup C) \leq 0.35$. **20.** ¼. **21.** n > 3
22. $1 - {}^7C_0 \left(\frac{7}{10}\right)^7$, 0.73. **23.** 5/216. **24.** 0.3204. **25.** P(A) = ½, P(B) = 1/3.
26. 191/2652.

Questions asked in IIT-JEE Exams

1. Six boys and six girls are sited in a row at random. Find the probability that
   (i) The six girls sit together
   (ii) The boys and girls sit alternately. **[IIT-JEE – 1978]**
2. A box contains 2 black, 4 white and 3 red balls. One ball is drawn at random from the box and kept aside. From the remaining balls in the box, another ball is drawn at random and kept beside the first. This process is repeated till all the balls drawn are in the sequence of 2 black, 4 white and 3 red. **[IIT-JEE – 1979]**
3. Two events A and B have probabilities 0.25 and 0.50 respectively, the probability that both A and B occur simultaneously is 0.14, then the probability that neither A nor B occurs is
   (a) 0.39 (b) 0.25 (c) 0.11 (d) None. **[IIT-JEE- 1980]**
4. The probability that an event A happens in one trial or an experiment is 0.4. Three independent trials of these experiments are performed. The probability that the event A happens at least once is
   (a) 0.936 (b) 0.784 (c) 0.904 (d) None **[IIT-JEE–1980]**
5. If A and B are two independent events such that P(A) > 0 and P(B) $\neq$ 1, then $P\left(\frac{\overline{A}}{\overline{B}}\right)$ is equal to
   (a) $1-P(A/B)$ (b) $1-P(A/\overline{B})$
   (d) $\frac{1-P(A\cup B)}{P(B)}$ (d) $\frac{P(\overline{A})}{P(\overline{B})}$
   [IIT-JEE – 1980]
6. An anti-craft gun can take a maximum of four shots at an enemy plane moving away from it. The probabilities of hitting the plane at the 1st, 2nd, 3rd and 4th shots are 0.4, 0.3, 0.2 and 0.1 respectively. What is the probability that the gun hits the plane? **[IIT-JEE – 1981]**
7. For a biased die the probabilities for different faces to turn up are given below:

Face	1	2	3	4	5	6
Probability	0.1	0.32	0.21	0.15	0.05	0.17

   This die is tossed and you are told that either face 1 or face 2 has turned up. Then the probability that it is face 1 is ……………… **[IIT-JEE – 1981]**
8. A and B are two candidates seeking admission in IIT. The probability that A is selected is 0.5 and the probability that both A and B are selected is almost 0.3. Is it possible that the probability of B getting selected is 0.9? **[IIT-JEE – 1982]**
9. Fifteen coupons are numbered 1,2,3,…………,15 resp. Seven coupons are selected at random one at a time with replacement. The probability that the largest number appearing on a selected coupon is 9 is
   (a) $\left(\frac{9}{15}\right)^7$ (b) $\left(\frac{8}{15}\right)^7$ (c) $\left(\frac{3}{5}\right)^7$ (d) None. **[IIT-JEE – 1983]**
10. Cards are drawn one by one at random from a well shuffled full pack of 52 playing cards until 2 aces are obtained for the first time. If N is the number of cards required to be drawn, then show that $P(N=n)=\frac{(n-1)(n-52)(n-51)}{50\times49\times17\times13}$. **[IIT-JEE – 1983]**
11. If A, B, C are events such that P(A) = 0.3, P(B) = 0.4, P(C) = 0.8, P(AB) = 0.08, P(AC) = 0.28, P(ABC) = 0.09 and $P(A\cup B\cup C)\geq 0.75$, then show that P(BC) lies in the interval $0.23\leq x\leq 0.48$. **[IIT-JEE – 1983]**
12. If the letters of word "ASSASSIN" are written down at random in a row. The probability that no two's occur together is 1/35. **[IIT-JEE – 1983]**
13. Three identical dice are rolled. The probability that the same number will appear on each of them is
   (a) $\frac{1}{6}$ (b)* $\frac{1}{36}$ (c) $\frac{1}{18}$ (d) $\frac{3}{28}$ **[IIT-JEE – 1984]**
14. A box contain 24 identical balls of which 12 are white and 12 are black. The balls are drawn at random from the box one at a time with replacement. The probability that a white ball is drawn for the 4th time on the 7th draw is
   (a) 5/64 (b) 27/32 (c) 5/32 (d) ½. **[IIT-JEE – 1984]**
15. If M and N are two events, the probability that exactly one of them occurs is
   (a) $P(M)+P(N)-2P(M\cap N)$
   (b) $P(M)+P(N)-P(\overline{M\cup N})$
   (c) $P(\overline{M})+P(\overline{N})-2P(\overline{M}\cap\overline{N})$
   (d) $P(M\cap\overline{N})-P(\overline{M}\cap N)$
   [IIT-JEE – 1984]
16. A and B are two independent events. The probability that both A and B occur is 1/6 and the probability that neither of them occur is 1/3. Find the probability of the occurrence of A. **[IIT-JEE – 1984]**
17. In a certain city only two newspaper A and B are published. It is known that 25% of the city population reads A and 20% reads B. While 8% reads both A and B. It is also known that 30% of those who read A but not B look into advertisement while 50% of those who read A and B look into advertisements. What is the percentage of the population reads an advertisements. **[IIT-JEE – 1984]**
18. In a multiple choice question, there are four alternative answers of which one or more are correct. A candidate will get marks in the question only if he ticks the correct answers. The candidate decide to tick the answers at random. If he is allowed upto three chances to answer the questions, find

the probability that he will get marks in the question. **[IIT-JEE – 1985]**

19. If $P(A \cup B) = P(A \cap B)$ if and only if the relation between P(A) and P(B) is................ **[IIT-JEE – 1985]**

20. A box contains 100 tickets numbered 1, 2, ..., 100 . Two tickets are chosen at random . It is given that the maximum number on the two chosen tickets is not more than 10 . The minimum is 5 with probability....................... **[IIT-JEE – 1985]**

21. A lot contains 20 articles. The probability that the lot contains exactly 2 defective articles is 0.4 and the probability that the lot contains exactly 3 defective articles is 0.6 . Articles are drawn from the lot at random one by one without replacement and are tested till all defective articles are found. What is the probability that the testing procedure ends at the 12th testing. **[IIT-JEE – 1986]**

22. A student appear for tests I, II and III. The student is successful if he passes either in tests I and II or test I and II. The probabilities of the student passing in tests I, II and III are p, q and ½ respectively. If the probability that the student is successful is ½, then
(a) $p = q = 1$ (b) $p = q = ½$
(c) $p = 1, q = 0$ (d) None **[IIT-JEE – 1986]**

23. If $\frac{1+3p}{p}, \frac{1-p}{4}$ and $\frac{1-2p}{2}$ are the probabilities of three mutually exclusive events , then the set of all values of p is........................ **[IIT-JEE – 1986]**

24. The probability that at least one of the events A and B occurs is 0.6 . If A and B occur simultaneously with probability 0.2 , then $P(\overline{A}) + P(\overline{B})$ is
(a) 0.4 (b) 0.8 (c) 1.2 (d) 1.4 **[IIT-JEE – 1987]**

25. A man takes a step forward with probability 0.4 and backwards with probability 0.6 . Find the probability that at the end of eleven steps he is one step away from the starting point. **[IIT-JEE – 1987]**

26. An urn contains 2 white and 2 black balls . A ball is drawn at random. If it is white , it is not replaced into the urn. Otherwise, it is replaced along with another ball of the same color. The process is repeated . Find the probability that the third ball drawn is black. **[IIT-JEE – 1987]**

27. One hundred identical coins, each with probability p of showing up heads are tossed once. If 0 < p < 1 and the probability of heads showing on 50 coins is equal to that of heads showing on 51, coins , then the value of p is
(a) 1/2 (b) 49/101 (c) 50/101 (d) 51/101 **[IIT-JEE – 1988]**

28. For two events A and B, $P(A \cap B)$
(a) not less than P(A) + P(B) – 1
(b) not greater than P(A) + P(B)
(c) equal to $P(A) + P(B) - P(A \cup B)$
(d) equal to $P(A) + P(B) + P(A \cup B)$. **[IIT-JEE – 1988]**

29. A box contains 2 fifty paise coins, 5 twenty five paise coins and a certain fixed number N (≥ 2) of ten and five paise coins . Five coins are taken out of the box at random. Find the probability that the total vaue of these 5 coins is less than one rupee and fifty paise. **[IIT-JEE- 1988]**

30. Urn A contains 6 red , 4 black balls and urn B contains 4 red and 6 balls . One ball is drawn at random from urn A and placed in urn B . Then one ball is drawn at random from urn B and placed in urn A . If one ball is now drawn at random from urn A , the probability that it is found to be red is... .... **[IIT-JEE – 1988]**

31. If E and F are independent events such that 0 < P(E) , P(F) < 1 , then
(a) E and F are mutually exclusive
(b) E and F are independent
(c) E^c and F^c are independent
(d) $P(E/F) + P(E^c/F) = 1$ **[IIT-JEE – 1989]**

32. Suppose the probability for A to win a game against B is 0.4. If A has an option of playing either test of 3 games or a best of 5 games match against B , which option should be chosen so that the probability of his winning the match is higher ? **[IIT-JEE – 1989]**

33. If the probability for A to fail in an examination is 0.2 and that for B is 0.3 , then the probability that either A or B fails is 0.5. Is it true or False ? **[IIT-JEE – 1989]**

34. A pair of four dice is rolled together till a sum of either 5 or 7 is obtained. Then the probability that 5 comes before 7 is .... **[IIT-JEE – 1989]**

35. A is a set containing n elements . A subset P of A is chosen at random . The set A constructed by replacing the elements of P. A subset Q of A is again chosen at random. Find the probability that P and Q have no common elements. **[IIT-JEE – 1990]**

36. Let A and B between such that P(A) = 0.3 and $P(A \cup B) =$ 0.8 . If A and B are independent events , then P(B) is .... **[IIT-JEE – 1990]**

37. For any two events A and B in a sample space
(a) $P(A/B) \geq \frac{P(A) + P(B) - 1}{P(B)}$, $P(B) \neq 0$ is always true
(b) $P(A \cap \overline{B}) = P(A) - P(A \cap B)$ does not hold.
(c) $P(A \cup B) = 1 - P(\overline{A})P(\overline{B})$, if A and B are independent.
(d) $P(A \cup B) = 1 - P(\overline{A})P(\overline{B})$, if A and B are disjoint. **[IIT-JEE – 1991]**

38. In a test an examination either guesses or copies or knows the answer to a multiple choice question with four choices . The probability that he make a guess is 1/3 and the probability that he copies the answer is 1/6 . The probability that his answer is correct given that he copied it is 1/8 . Find the probability that he knew the answer to the question given that he correctly answered it. **[IIT-JEE – 1991]**

39. If the mean and the variance of a binomial variate X are 2 and 1 respectively , then the probability that X takes a value

greater than one is equal to ....

[IIT-JEE – 1991]

40. India plays two matches each with west Indies and Australia. In any match the probabilities of India getting points 0, 1 and 2 are 0.45 , 0.05 and 0.50 respectively. Assuming that the outcomes are independent , the probability of india getting at least 7 points is

(a) 0.8750 (b) 0.0875 (c) 0.0625 (d) 0.0250

[IIT-JEE – 1992]

41. A lot contains 50 defective and 50 non-defective bulbs. Two bubs are drawn at random , one at a time with replacement. The events A, B, C are defined as A = {The first bulb is defective } , B = {the second bulb is non-defective} C = {the two bulbs are both defective or both non-defective } . Determine whether

(i) A, B, C are pair wise independent

(ii) A, B, C are independent. [IIT-JEE – 1992]

42. An unbiased die with faces marked 1, 2, 3, 4, 5 and 6 is rolled four times. Out of four face values obtained, the probability that the minimum face value is not less than 2 and the maximum face value is not greater than 5 is then

(a) 16/81 (c) 1/81 (c) 80/81 (d) 65/81

[IIT-JEE – 1993]

43. E and F are two independent events. The probability that both E and F happens is 1/12 and the probability that neither E nor F happens is 1/2, then

(a) P(E) = 1/3, P(F) = 1/4 (b) P(E) = 1/2 , P(F) = 1/6

(c) P(E) = 1/6 , P(F) = 1/2 (d) P(E) = 1/4 , P(F) = 1/3

[IIT-JEE – 1993]

44. Numbers are selected at random, one at a time , from the two digit numbers 00, 01, 02, 03,..........,99 with replacement. An event E occurs if and only if the product of the two digits of a selected number is 18. If four numbers are selected, find the probability that the event E occurs at least 3 times.

[IIT-JEE – 1993]

45. Three faces of a fair die are yellow , two faces red and one blue . The die is tossed three times. The probability that the colors , yellow, red, and blue appear in the first , second and the third tosses respectively is ....

[IIT-JEE – 1992]

46. There are four balls of different colors and four boxes of colors , same as those of the balls. The number of ways in which the balls , one each in a box, could be placed such that a ball does not go to a box of its own color is ....

[IIT-JEE – 1992]

47. Let A, B, C be three mutually independent events. Consider the two statements S_1 and S_2 .

S_1: A and B ∪ C are independent.

S_2 : A and B ∩ C are independent. Then

(a) Both S_1 and S_2 are two

(b) only S_1 is true

(c) only S_2 is true

(d) neither S_1 nor S_2 is true. [IIT-JEE – 1994]

48. An unbiased coin is tossed . If the result is a head a pair of unbiased dice is rolled and the number obtained by adding the numbers on the two faces is noted. If the result is a tail, a card from a well shuffled pack of eleven cards numbered 2, 3, 4, ..., 12 is picked and the number is noted. What is the probability that the noted number is 7 or 8.

[IIT-JEE – 1994]

49. If two events A and B are such that $P(A^c) = 0.3$, $P(B) = 0.4$ and $P(A \cap B^c) = 0.5$, then $P(B/B \cap B^c) =$.................... [IIT-JEE – 1994]

50. The probability of India winning a test match against West Indies is ½ . Assuming independence from match to match the probability that in a 5 match series India's second win occurs at third test is

(a) 1/8 (b) 1/4 (c) 1/2 (d) 2/3

[IIT-JEE – 1995]

51. Let $0 < P(A) < 1$, $0 < P(B) < 1$ and $P(A \cup B) = P(A) + P(B) - P(A)P(B)$, then

(a) $P(B/A) = P(B) - P(A)$

(b) $p(A' - B') = P(A') - P(B')$

(c) $P(A \cup B)' = P(A')\, P(B')$

(d) $P(A/B) = P(A)$. [IIT-JEE – 1995]

52. Three of the six vertices of a regular hexagon are chosen at random. The probability that the triangle with three vertices is equilateral, equals

(a) 1/2 (b) 1/5 (c) 1/10 (d) 1/20.

[IIT-JEE – 1995]

53. For the three events A, B, C , P(Exactly one of A or B occurs) = P(Exactly one of B or C occurs) = P (Exactly one of C or A occurs) = p and P(all the three events occurs simultaneously) = p^2, where $0 < p < 1/2$, then the probability that at-least one of A, B, C occurring is

(a) $\dfrac{3p+2p^2}{2}$ (b) $\dfrac{p+3p^2}{4}$

(c) $\dfrac{p+3p^2}{2}$ (d) $\dfrac{3p+2p^2}{4}$

[IIT-JEE-1996]

54. In how many ways three girls and nine boys can be seated in two vans , each having numbered seats, 3 in the front and 4 at the back ? How many seating arrangement are possible if 3 girls should sit together in a back row on adjacent seats? Now if all the seating arrangements are equally likely, what is the probability of 3 girls sitting together in a back row on adjacent seats ? [IIT-JEE – 1996]

Ans. 1/91.

55. If p and q are chosen randomly from the set { 1, 2, 3, 4, 5, 6, 7, 8, 9, 10 } with replacement, determine the probability that the roots of the equation $x^2 + px + q = 0$ are real.

[IIT-JEE – 1997]

56. Sixteen players S_1, S_2............, S_{16} play in a tournament . They are divided into eight pairs at random. From each pair a winner is decided on the basis of a game played between the two players are of equal strength.

(a) Find the probability that the player S_1 is among the eight winners.

(b) Find the probability that exactly one of the two players S_1 and S_2 is among the eight winners.

[IIT-JEE – 1997]

57. Three numbers are chosen at random without replacement from {1, 2,..........., 10 }. The probability that the minimum of the chosen numbers is 3 , or their maximum is 7, is .... [IIT-JEE – 1997]

58. Seven white balls and three black balls are randomly placed in a row. The probability that no two black balls are placed adjacently equals,

(a) 1/2 (b) 7/15 (c) 2/15 (d) 1/3

[IIT-JEE – 1998]

59. If from each of the three boxes containing 3 white and 1 black, 2 white and 2 black, 1 white and 3 black balls, one ball is drawn at random, then the probability that 2 white and 1 black ball will be drawn is

(a) 13/32 (b) 1/4 (c) 1/32 (d) 3/16

[IIT-JEE – 1998]

60. If $\overline{E}$ and $\overline{F}$ are the complementary events of events E and F respectively and 0 < P(E) < 1, then

(a) $P(E/F)+P(\overline{E}/F)=1$

(b) $P(E/F)+P(E/\overline{F})=1$

(c) $P(\overline{E}/F)+P(E/\overline{F})=1$

(d) $P(E/\overline{F})+P(\overline{E}/F)=1$ [IIT-JEE – 1998]

61. If E and F are events with $P(E)\le P(F)$ and $P(E\cap F)>0$, then

(a) Occurrence of E $\Rightarrow$ Occurrence of F

(b) Occurrence of F Occurrence of E

(c) Non-occurrence of E Non-occurrence of F

(d) None. [IIT-JEE-1998]

62. A fair coin is tossed repeatedly . If the tail appears on first four tosses , then the probability of the head appearing on the fifth toss equals

(a) 1/2 (b) 1/32 (c) 31/32 (d) 1/5

[IIT-JEE-1998]

63. There are four machines and it is known that exactly two of them are faulty. They are tested, one by one , in a random order till both the faulty machines are identified. Then the probability that only two tests are needed , is

(a) 1/3 (b) 1/6 (c) 1/2 (d) 1/4

[IIT-JEE- 1998]

64. Three players A, B and C toss a coin cyclically in that order (that is A, B, C, A, B, C, A, B,.........) till a head shows . Let p be the probability that the coin shows a head. Let and be respectively, the probabilities that A, B and C gets the first head. Prove that. Determine in terms of p.

[IIT-JEE – 1998]

65. If the integers m and n are chosen at random b/w 1 and 100, then the probability that a number of the form is divisible by 5 equals

(a) 1/4 (b) 1/7 (c) 1/8 (d) 1/49.

[IIT-JEE – 1999]

66. The probabilities that a student passes in Mathematics , Physics and Chemistry are m, p and c resp. of these subjects, the student has a 75% change of passing in at least one , a 50% change of passing in at-least two , and a 40% change of passing in exactly two. Which of the following relations are true.

(a) p+m+c=19/20 (b) p+m+c=27/20

(c) pmc=1/10 (d) pmc=¼.

[IIT-JEE – 1999]

67. Eight players play a knock-out tournament . It is known that whenever the players and play, the player will win if. Assuming that the player are paired at random in each round, what is the probability that the player reaches the final ?

[IIT-JEE – 1999]

68. A coin has probability of showing head when tossed. It is tossed n times , let denote the probability that no two (or more) consecutive heads occur. Prove that $P_1=1,\ P_2=1-P^2$ and $P_n=(1-P)P_{n-1}+P(1-P)P_{n-2}$ for all $n\ge 3$.

[IIT-JEE – 2000]

69. An urn contains m white and n black balls . A ball is drawn at random and is put back into the urn along with k additional balls of the same color as that of the ball drawn. A ball is again drawn at random . What is the probability that the ball drawn now is white ? [IIT-JEE – 2001]

70. An unbiased die, with faces numbered 1, 2, 3, 4, 5, 6 is thrown n-times and the list of numbers showing up is noted. What is the probability that among the number 1, 2, 3, 4, 5, 6 only three numbers appear in this list . ?

[IIT-JEE – 2001]

71. A box contains N coins , m of which are fair and the rest are biased . The probability of getting a head when a fair coin is tossed is 1/2 , while it is 2/3 when a biased coin is tossed. A coin is drawn from the box at random and is tossed twice. The first time it shows head and the second time it shows tail . What is the probability that the coin drawn is fair.

[IIT-JEE – 2002]

72. Two numbers are selected randomly from the set S = { 1, 2, 3, 4, 5, 6} without replacement one by one. The probability that minimum of the two numbers is less than 4 is

(a) 1/15 (b) 14/15 (c) 1/5 (d) 4/5.

[IIT-JEE- 2003]

73. If $P(B)=\frac{3}{4}$, $P(A\cap B\cap\overline{C})=\frac{1}{3}$ and $P(\overline{A}\cap B\cap\overline{C})=\frac{1}{3}$, then $P(B\cap C)$ is

(a) 1/12 (b) 1/8 (c) 1/15 (d) 1/9

[IIT-JEE – 2003]

74. A is targeting to B , B and C are targeting to A . Probability of hitting the target by A, B and C are 2/3, 1/2 and 1/3 respectively . If A is hit then find the probability that hits the target and C does not.

[IIT-JEE – 2003]

75. For a student to qualify, he must pass at least two out of three exams. The probability that he will pass the 1st exam is p. If he fails in one of exams then the probability of his passing in the next exam is p/2, otherwise it remains the same. Find the probability that he will qualify?

[IIT-JEE – 2003]

76. If three distinct numbers are chosen randomly from the first 100 natural numbers, then the probability that all three of them are divisible by both 2 and 3 is

(a) 4/25 (b) 4/35 (c) 4/33 (d) 4/1155.

[IIT-JEE-2004]

77. A box contains 12 red and 6 white balls. Balls are drawn from the bag one at a time without replacement. If in 6 draws there are at least 4 white balls, find the probability that exactly one white is drawn in the next two draws (binomial co-efficients can be left as such).

[IIT-JEE – 2004]

78. If A and B are two independent events, prove that $P(A \cup B).P(A' \cap B') \le P(C)$, where C is an event defined that exactly one of A and B occurs. **[IIT-JEE – 2004]**

79. A fair die is rolled. The probability that the first time 1 occurs at the even number of trials is

(a) 6/11 (b) 1/6 (c) 5/36 (d) 5/11

[IIT-JEE- 2005]

80. Rohan goes to office either by car, scooter, bus or train, probability of which being 1/7, 3/7, 2/7 and 1/7 respectively and probability that he is reaching office late if he takes car, scooter, bus or train is 2/9, 1/9, 1/7 and 1/9 respectively. Find the probability that he has travelled by car, if he reaches office in time. **[IIT-JEE – 2005]**

Comprehensive Link

Paragraph (81 to 83) : There are n urns each containing n +1 balls such that ith urn contains I white balls and (n+1-i) red balls. Let be the event of selecting ith urn, i=1, 2, 3,................,n and w denotes the event of getting a white ball.

[IIT-JEE – 2006]

81. If $P(u_i)$=i, where i=1,2, 3,..........., n, then $\lim_{n \to \infty} P(w)$ is equal to

(a) 1 (b) 2/3 (c) 3/4 (d) 1/4.

82. If $P(u_i) = c$, where c is a constant, then, then $P(u_n / w)$ is equal to

(a) $\frac{2}{n+1}$ (b) $\frac{1}{n+1}$ (c) $\frac{n}{n+1}$ (d) $\frac{1}{2}$.

83. If *n* is even and E denotes the event of choosing even numbered urn $\left(P(u_i) = \frac{1}{n}\right)$, then the value of $P(w/E)$ is

(a) $\frac{n+2}{2n+1}$ (b) $\frac{n+2}{2(n+1)}$

(c) $\frac{n}{n+1}$ (d) $\frac{1}{n+1}$.

84. One Indian and four American men and their wives are to be seated randomly around a circular table. Then the conditional probability that the Indian man is seated adjacent to his wife given that each American man is seated adjacent to his wife is

(a) 1/2 (b) 1/3 (c) 2/5 (d) 1/5

[IIT-JEE – 2007]

85. Let E^c denote the complement of an event E. Let E, F, G be pair-wise independent events with P(G) > 0 and $P(E \cap F \cap G) = 0$. Then $P(E^c \cap F^c / G)$ equals

(a) $P(E^c) + P(F^c)$ (b) $P(E^c) - P(F^c)$

(c) $P(E^c) - P(F)$ (d) $P(E) - P(F^c)$.

[IIT-JEE- 2007]

86. An experiment has 10 equally likely outcomes. Let A and B be two non empty events of the same experiment. If A consists of 4 outcomes, the number of outcomes that B must have so that A and B are independent, is

(a) 2, 4 or 8 (b) 3 6 or 9 (c) 4 or 8 (d) 5 or 10.

[IIT-JEE - 2008]

87. Consider the system of equations a x + b y = 0, c x + d y = 0, where $0 \le a, b, c, d \le 1$

Statement - I: The probability that the system of equation has a unique solution.

Statement - II: The probability that the ystem of equation has a solution is 1. **[IIT-JEE-2008]**

Comprehensive Link Passage

88. A fair die is tossed repeated untill a six is obtained. Let X denote the number of tosses required.

(i) The probability that X = 3 equals **[IIT-JEE-2009]**

(a) 25/216 (b) 25/36 (c) 5/36 (d) 125/216.

(ii) The probability that $X \ge 3$ equals

(a) 125/216 (b) 25/36 (c) 5/36 (d) 25/216.

(iii) The conditional probability that $X \ge 6$ is given X > 3 equals

(a) 125/216 (b) 25/36 (c) 5/36 (d) 25/216.

89. Let ω be a complex cube root of unity with $\omega \ne 1$. A fair die is thrown three times. If r_1, r_2 & r_3 are the numbers obtained on the die, then the probability that $\omega^{r_1} + \omega^{r_2} + \omega^{r_3} = 0$ is

(a) 1/18 (b) 1/9 (c) 2/9 (d) 1/36

[IIT-JEE-2010]

90. A signal which can be green or red with probability 4/5 and 1/5 respectively, is received by station A and then transmitted to station B. The probability of each station receiving the signal correctly is 3/4. If the signal received at station B is green, then the probability that the original signal was green is

(a) 3/5 (b) 6/7 (c) 20/21 (d) 9/20

[IIT-JEE-2010]

91. Let E and F be two independent events. The probability that exactly one of them occurs is 11/25 and the probability that none of them occurs is 2/25. If P(T) denotes the

probability of occurrence of the event T, then

(a) P(E)=4/5, P(F)=3/5 (b) P(E)=2/5, P(F)=2/5
(c) P(E)=2/5, P(F)=1/5 (d) P(E)=3/5, P(F)=4/5

[IIT-JEE-2011]

COMPREHENSIVE LINK PASSAGE

Let U_1 and U_2 be two urns and U_1 contains 3 white and 2 red balls and U_2 contains only 1 white ball. A fair coin is tossed. If head appears then 1 ball is drawn at random from U_1 and put into U_2. However, if tail appears then 2 balls are drawn at random from U_1 and put into U_2. Now 1 ball is drawn at random from U_2.

[IIT-JEE-2011]

(i) The probability of the drawn ball from U_2 being white is
(a) 13/30 (b) 23/30 (c) 19/30 (d) 11/30

(ii) Given that the drawn ball from U_2 is white, the probability that head appeared on the coin is
(a) 17/23 (b) 11/23 (c) 15/23 (d) 12/23.

93. A ship is fitted with three engines E_1, E_2 and E_3. The engines function independently of each other with respective probabilities 1/2, 1/4 and 1/4. For the ship to be operational at least two of its engines must function. Let X denote the event that the ship is operational and let X_1, X_2 and X_3 denote respectively the events that the engines E_1, E_2 and E_3 are functioning. Which of the following is(are) true ?

(a) $P[X_1^c / X] = 3/16$
(b) $P[X / X_2] = 5/16$
(c) $P[X / X_1] = 7/16$
(d) P [Exactly two engines of the ship are functioning $|X] = 7/8$.

[IIT-JEE-2012]

94. Four fair dice D_1, D_2, D_3 and D_4, each having six faces numbered 1, 2, 3, 4, 5, and 6, are rolled simultaneously. The probability that D_4 shows a number appearing on one of D_1, D_2 and D_3 is
(a) 91/216 (b) 108/216 (c) 125/216 (d) 127/216

[IIT-JEE-2012]

95. Let X and Y be two events such that P(X/Y)=1/2, P(Y/X)=1/3, $P(X \cap Y) = 1/6$, which of the following is (are) correct ?.

(a) $P(X \cup Y) = \frac{2}{3}$
(b) X and Y are independent.
(c) X and Y are not independent.
(d) $P(X^C \cap Y) = \frac{2}{3}$

[IIT-JEE-2012]

ANSWER

1. (i) 1/132, (ii) 1/462	**2.** 1/1260	**3.** (a)	**4.** (d)	**5.** (b)
6. 0.6976.	**7.** 5/21.	**8.** No.	**9.** (d)	**12.** False
13. (b)	**14.** (c)	**15.** (a), (c)	**16.** 1/2 or 1/3	**17.** 13.9%
18. 1/5.	**19.** P(A)=P(B)	**20.** 1/9.	**21.** 11/190	**22.** (d)
23. $\frac{1}{3} \le p \le \frac{1}{2}$.	**24.** (d)	**25.** $462 \times (0.24)^5$	**26.** 23/30.	**27.** (d)
28. (a), (b), (c)	**29.** $\frac{1-10(N+2)}{N+{}^7C_5}$.	**30.** 32/55.	**31.** (b)	**32.** Best of three games
33. False.	**34.** 2/5.	**35.** $\frac{1}{2^r}$.	**36.** 5/7.	**37.** (c)
38. 24/29.	**39.** 11/16.	**40.** (b)		
41. A, B, C are pair-wise independent but dependent.			**42.** (a)	**43.** 2.4832×10^{-4}
45. 1/36.	**46.** 9.	**47.** (a)	**48.** 193/792.	**49.** 1/4.
50. (d)	**51.** (c)	**52.** (c)	**53.** (a)	**54.** 1/91.
55. 0.62.	**56.** (a) 1/2, (b) 8/15	**57.** 13/60.	**58.** (b)	**59.** (a)
60. (a)	**61.** (d)	**62.** (a)	**63.** (c)	**64.** (a)
65. (a)	**66.** (b), (c)	**67.** 4/35.	**68.** (a)	**69.** $\frac{m}{m+n}$.
70. $\frac{{}^6C_3 \times [3^n - 3.2^n + 3]}{6^n}$	**71.** $\frac{9m}{m+8N}$.	**72.** (d)	**73.** (a)	**74.** 1/2
75. $2p^2 - p^3$.	**76.** (d)	**77.** $\frac{{}^{10}C_1 \times {}^2C_1}{{}^{12}C_2} \cdot \frac{{}^{12}C_2 \times {}^6C_4}{{}^{18}C_6} + \frac{{}^{11}C_1 \times {}^1C_1}{{}^{12}C_2} \cdot \frac{{}^{12}C_1 \times {}^6C_5}{{}^{18}C_6}$.		**79.** (b)
80. 1/7.	**81.** (b)	**84.** (c)	**85.** (c)	**86.** (d)
88. (a)	**89. (iii)** (b)	**94.** (a)		

Self Assesment Test

TIME : 2 HOURS.	CHAPTER : THE COMPLEX NUMBER — TEST MATHEMATICS	MAX MARKS: 100

SELF ASSESMENT TEST

Give answers the following questions:

1. Two natural numbers are chosen at random from first 30 natural numbers. The probability that they are perfect numbers, is

   (a) 2/225 (b) 1/225 (c) 3/225 (d) 4/225.

2. Three natural numbers are chosen at random from first 40 natural numbers. The probability that ths sum of the squares of two is equal to the square of the third, is

   (a) 1/1614 (b) 1/161400 (c) 7/161400 (d) 11/161400

3. Two natural numbers a and b are chosen at random from 50 natural numbers such that a is satishfying the equation $a^2-4a-12<0$ and b is the number of solution of the equation $2^x = x^2+1$. Then the probability of a and b is

   (a) 1/150 (b) 1/125 (c) 1/175 (d) 1/200.

4. Three numbers are chosen at random without replacement from $\{1, 2, 3, ..., 8\}$. The probability that their minimum is 3 and their maximum is 6, is

   (a) 1/4 (b) 2/5 (c) 3/8 (d) 1/5.

5. A five digit number is formed by the digits 1, 2, 3, 4, 5 without repitition. The probability that the is divisible by 4 is

   (a) 1/4 (b) 2/5 (c) 3/8 (d) 1/5.

6. 15 persons among whom are A and B, sit down at random at a round table. The probability that there are 4 persons between A and B is

   (a) 1/7 (b) 2/7
   (c) 3/11 (d) 1/5.

7. Four tickets marked 00, 01, 02, ..., 11 respectively, are placed in a bag. A ticket is drawn at random 5-times, being replaced each time. The probability that the sum of the numbers on the ticket is 15, is

   (a) 3/1024 (b) 5/1024 (c) 3/512 (d) 1/2048.

8. A man can take a step forward, backward, left or right with equal probability. The probability that after 9-steps he will be just one step away from his initial position, is

   (a) $\frac{3969}{4^9}$ (b) $\frac{3969}{4^7}$
   (c) $\frac{9569}{4^7}$ (d) $\frac{9369}{4^7}$.

9. In a class 30 % students fail in Mathematics, 20 % students fail in Physics and 10 % students fail in Mathematics and Physics both. A student is chosen at random, then the probability that he / she will fail in Mathematics if he has failed in Physics, is

   (a) 1/2 (b) 1/3 (c) 1/4 (d) 2/5.

10. One ticket is drawn at random from 50 tickets numbered $\{00, 01, 02, ..., 49\}$ Then the probability that the sum of the digits on the selected ticket is 8, given that the product of these digits is zero, is

    (a) 1/7 (b) 5/14 (c) 1/50 (d) 1/14.

ANSWER

1.(a)	2.(b)	3.(c)	4.(d)	5.(d)
6.(a)	7.(b)	8.(b)	9.(a)	10.(d)